PRAISE FOR

A Machine That Would Go of Itself

"Packed with fascinating discoveries and little-known information, Kammen's book challenges some of our most cherished views of American constitutionalism and illuminates the amazingly diverse ways in which Americans have interpreted, celebrated, condemned and ignored their Constitution. . . . *A Machine That Would Go of Itself* is Michael Kammen's most original and impressive book."
            —DAVID BRION DAVIS, Yale University

"A lucid and engaging history of American constitutionalism . . . It puts the Constitution into its historical and cultural context, asks the important questions, and introduces the themes around which a national discussion can be fruitfully structured. . . . Kammen's important contribution is to show how well the Constitution has served the U.S. for more than two centuries."
            —JAMES H. ANDREWS, *Christian Science Monitor*

"A delightful book . . . brimming with fresh and profound insights about both the Constitution and American culture."
            —FORREST MCDONALD, University of Alabama

"A powerful, fascinating history of the episodic and ambiguous relationship of the American people to their Constitution. It is replete with Kammen's special gifts of intellectual feistiness, lucidity of style, and historical insight. The book is an instructive delight, and bids fair to be one of the major scholarly adornments of the Bicentennial."
            —MORTON KELLER, Brandeis University

"Superb . . . a sweeping history . . . packed to the rafters with spectacular archival quotes."
            —CARLIN ROMANO, *Philadelphia Inquirer*

ALSO BY MICHAEL KAMMEN

SPHERES OF LIBERTY:
Changing Perceptions of Liberty in American Culture (1986)

A SEASON OF YOUTH:
The American Revolution and the Historical Imagination (1978)

COLONIAL NEW YORK: *A History* (1975)

PEOPLE OF PARADOX: *An Inquiry Concerning
the Origins of American Civilization* (1972)

EMPIRE AND INTEREST: *The American Colonies
and the Politics of Mercantilism* (1970)

DEPUTYES & LIBERTYES: *The Origins of
Representative Government in Colonial America* (1969)

A ROPE OF SAND: *The Colonial Agents, British Politics,
and the American Revolution* (1968)

(EDITOR)

THE PAST BEFORE US:
Contemporary Historical Writing in the United States (1980)

"WHAT IS THE GOOD OF HISTORY?"
Selected Letters of Carl L. Becker, 1900-1945 (1973)

THE HISTORY OF THE PROVINCE OF NEW-YORK,
by William Smith, Jr. (1972)

THE CONTRAPUNTAL CIVILIZATION: *Essays Toward
a New Understanding of the American Experience* (1971)

POLITICS AND SOCIETY IN COLONIAL AMERICA:
Democracy or Deference? (1967)

(CO-AUTHOR)

SOCIETY, FREEDOM, AND CONSCIENCE: *The American
Revolution in Virginia, Massachusetts, and New York* (1976)

A MACHINE THAT WOULD GO OF ITSELF

WASHINGTON GIVING THE LAWS TO AMERICA, ENGRAVING BY
J. P. ELVEN (CA. 1800). (*Courtesy of the Prints Division, The New York
Public Library, Astor, Lenox and Tilden Foundations*)

A MACHINE THAT WOULD GO OF ITSELF

The Constitution in American Culture

Michael Kammen

92-1098

VINTAGE BOOKS
A DIVISION OF RANDOM HOUSE
NEW YORK

For Carol
once again

To celebrate the gift and joys
of twenty-five years together

First Vintage Books Edition, September 1987

Library of Congress Cataloging-in-Publication Data
Kammen, Michael G.
A machine that would go of itself.
Bibliography: p.
Includes index.
1. United States—Constitutional history.
2. Public opinion—United States—History.
3. United States—Civilization.   I. Title.
[JK31.K34 1987]   342.73′029   87-40115
ISBN 0-394-75600-2 (pbk.)   347.30229

Grateful acknowledgment is made to the following for permission to reprint previously published material:

Doubleday & Company, Inc.: excerpt from *Memoirs of Earl Warren* by Earl Warren. Copyright © 1977 by Nina E. Warren as Executrix of the Estate of Earl Warren. Reprinted by permission of Doubleday & Company, Inc. *Harvard Law School:* excerpt from the letter of Thomas Reed Powell to Charles A. Beard dated February 3, 1944. Thomas Reed Powell Papers, Harvard Law School Library. Reprinted with permission. *Reader's Digest:* "A Constitution for the New Deal" by H. L. Mencken, condensed from the American Mercury. Reprinted with permission from the July 1937 *Reader's Digest.*

Manufactured in the United States of America
10 9 8 7 6 5 4 3 2 1

Contents

List of Illustrations   ix
Forethoughts   xi
Acknowledgments   xxi

1   The Problem of Constitutionalism in American Culture   3

PART ONE
The Most Wonderful Instrument Ever
Drawn by the Hand of Man

2   To Make the Constitution a Practical System   43
3   All That Gives Us a National Character   68
4   The Constitution Threatens to Be a
    Subject of Infinite Sects   95

PART TWO
A Machine That Would Go of Itself

5   On This Day, One Hundred Years Ago   127
6   The American and the British Constitution
    Are Two Entirely Different Things   156
7   The Crisis in Constitutionalism   185

Contents

PART THREE

America Is Always Talking About
Its Constitution

8   *God Knows How Dearly We Need a
    Constitutional Revival*   219
9   *Decisions Are Politics When Constitutional
    Questions Are Up for Decision*   255
10 *My God! Making a Racket out of
    the Constitution*   282

PART FOUR

The Pendulum of Public Opinion

11 *Illegal Defiance of Constitutional Authority*   315
12 *Our Bill of Rights Is Under
    Subtle and Pervasive Attack*   336
13 *The Public Got Strange and Distorted
    Views of the Court and Its Rulings*   357
14 *It's What Holds Us All Together*   381

Appendix A A Note on the Sources   403
Appendix B A Supplementary Note on Iconography   405
Appendix C "A Constitution for the New Deal," by
    H. L. Mencken   407
Appendix D The Constitution   411
Abbreviations   429
Notes   431
Index   527

Illustrations

Frontispiece *Washington Giving the Laws to America,* engraving by J. P. Elven (ca. 1800).

Following page 262

1. Wooden fire bucket painted ochre with a dark green banner and yellow lettering highlighted in red (dated 1802 on the bottom).
2. *James Madison,* by Charles Willson Peale (Philadelphia, ca. 1792).
3. *Mr. and Mrs. Oliver Ellsworth of Connecticut,* by Ralph Earl (1792).
4. *Andrew Jackson,* by David Rent Etter (ca. 1832–33).
5. *Born to Command. King Andrew the First,* anonymous lithograph (ca. 1832).
6. Oval silver tray commemorating the seventy-fifth anniversary of the signing of the Constitution (made by S. H. Black of Black, Star and Gorham, ca. 1862).
7. Plate commemorating the death of Elijah Lovejoy, killed by an anti-abolitionist mob in Alton, Illinois (made in England, ca. 1837).
8. *Interior view of Independence Hall, Philadelphia,* a chromolithograph drawn by Max Rosenthal and printed by L. N. Rosenthal (ca. 1856).
9. *Washington Addressing the Constitutional Convention,* by Junius Brutus Stearns (1856); also entitled *Adoption of the Constitution.*
10. *Signing of the Constitution of the United States,* by Thomas P. Rossiter (ca. 1860–70).

11. *Union,* engraved by H. S. Sadd after a painting by T. S. Matteson (ca. 1861).

12. *Constitution & Laws,* from the *Ithaca Democrat* (July 4, 1882).

13. Official invitation to the Constitution Centennial Celebration, September 15–17, 1887, in Philadelphia.

14. A float in the Civic and Industrial Pageant, Constitution Centennial Celebration (September 15, 1887).

15. *Chief Justice John Marshall,* by William Wetmore Story (1884).

16. *The Constitutional Convention—Philadelphia in 1787—The Creation of a Strong and True Union,* by Violet Oakley (1917).

17. President and Mrs. Calvin Coolidge, Speaker of the House Frederick H. Gillett, Librarian of Congress Herbert Putnam, and others at the dedication of the Shrine of the Constitution and the Declaration of Independence (Library of Congress, February 28, 1924).

18. Cass Gilbert in 1931, architect of the U.S. Supreme Court Building, Washington, D.C.

19. Congressman Sol Bloom, Director General of the United States Constitution Sesquicentennial Commission (1935–39).

20. Replica of the Shrine of the Constitution and the Declaration of Independence (1937).

21. Sales desk at the Library of Congress exhibition for the Sesquicentennial of the Constitution (1937).

22. Window display at the Hecht Company department store, Washington, D.C. (1937).

23. The first of five display rooms at the Sesquicentennial loan exhibition of portraits of the signers and delegates to the Convention of 1787 (held at the Corcoran Gallery of Art, Washington, D.C., November 1937–March 1938).

24. Mrs. Ralph E. Doherty, a Girl Scout official, and Irma Beverly Siebel of Troop 114 (touring the Sesquicentennial loan exhibition at the Corcoran Gallery on December 18, 1937).

25. *We, the People,* by Howard Chandler Christy (1937).

26. The official Sesquicentennial medallion, designed by Howard Chandler Christy (1937).

27. "Our Overworked Supreme Court," by J. Keppler (*Puck,* December 9, 1885).

Forethoughts

THIS BOOK EXAMINES THE CULTURAL IMPACT of the United States Constitution. Although a vast literature exists in the traditional field of constitutional history—including works on the Supreme Court, biographies of justices, so-called biographies of the Constitution, and pertinent aspects of American legal history—no one has attempted to describe the place of the Constitution in the public consciousness and symbolic life of the American people. Consequently I consider this a study in popular constitutionalism, by which I mean the perceptions and misperceptions, uses and abuses, knowledge and ignorance of ordinary Americans. "Ordinary" does not refer to their social status or degree of education, but rather to the fact that they are nonprofessionals: not lawyers, nor judges, nor professors of constitutional law.

Even though our libraries are filled with books and journals telling us what the specialists think, we do not have a single study that traces what the Constitution has meant to the rest of the populace. Pieces of the story have appeared here and there; but no one has brought them together or established a framework for exploring their cultural significance. Moreover, the most revealing clusters of pertinent source material have been ignored entirely. I have in mind, for example, the papers of the Constitution Centennial Commission of 1886–87 (2,200 items in the Historical Society of Pennsylvania); the records of the Constitution Sesquicentennial Commission of 1935–39 (sixteen cartons in the National Archives); the extraordinary correspondence of Cass Gilbert, architect of the Supreme Court building in Washington, D.C. (9,000 items in the Library of Congress's Manuscript Division); and all the public opinion polls taken since their genesis in 1936 that pertain to the Constitution, Supreme Court, and civil liberties (in the archive of the Roper Center at the University of Connecticut).

The sources I have utilized most extensively suggest the sort of book this is. More attention is given to an essay by Senator Albert J. Beveridge in *The Saturday Evening Post,* for example, or to an interview with Chief Justice Warren Burger in *The Reader's Digest* (which has more than 18 million subscribers), than to original and exhaustively researched articles that have appeared in law reviews with limited circulation. I am more interested in the content and impact of best-sellers like *The Nine Old Men* (1936) by Drew Pearson and Robert S. Allen, or *The Brethren: Inside the Supreme Court* (1979) by Bob Woodward and Scott Armstrong, than I am in weighty tomes that reach a highly select circle of readers. Sidney George Fisher's *The Trial of the Constitution* (1862), for example, is a thoughtful work concerning the most serious crisis of American constitutionalism, and was favorably reviewed. Nevertheless, it sold only 650 copies (out of 1,000 that were printed) during the first two years after publication.

I have devoted more space to the rise and demise of Constitution Day following 1919 than to the emergence or decline of Supreme Court doctrines. Opinions rendered by the Court have been exceedingly important, but they are read by relatively few individuals; and some of the most famous opinions were ignored by the press and the public when they first appeared. In any case, the literature concerning significant Court decisions is already massive. Similarly, although books about the intellectual antecedents and formation of the Constitution fill many shelves, we know amazingly little about the Constitution in American education, or the constitutional knowledge required of those millions of immigrants who have been applicants for naturalization and U.S. citizenship, or the content of cartoons and editorials in the press, or oratorical statements uttered on celebratory occasions.

In examining this range of sources, I have come across a recurrent complaint that the Constitution is a "dry" document. Curiously enough, that lament has usually been uttered by its most ardent devotees. As James M. Beck, then Solicitor General of the United States, observed in 1924 (with a wistful blend of pride and realism): "the Constitution, in which there is not a wasted word, is as cold and dry a document as a problem in mathematics or a manual of parliamentary law."[1] When Frank Gannett, the conservative newspaper magnate, took a prominent role in organizing national opposition to Franklin D. Roosevelt's 1937 "Court-packing" plan, he told Senator William E. Borah that they faced tough going because the Constitution was a dry subject in which most people were not interested. Congressman Sol Bloom of New York, who organized the Sesquicentennial celebration of 1937–39, echoed Gannett's concern.[2]

Borah replied to Gannett, however, that whenever he discussed the Constitution, people seemed to be *quite* interested. That response was neither hyperbolic nor boastful, for there is another theme that laces the sources and was forcefully expressed in 1918 by Senator Beveridge when he finished his massive, four-volume biography of Chief Justice John Marshall. "The more I study history," he remarked to Edward S. Corwin, "the clearer it becomes to me that too little account is taken by historians of the human conditions under which men do things." Max Farrand, editor of the multivolume *Records of the Federal Convention of 1787* (1911), made the same point a few years later. After referring to "the dry-as-dust work I had been engaged in for ten year [sic] editing the Records of the Federal Convention," Farrand explained that he gradually achieved "an appreciation, through the study of those records, of the necessity of understanding the human aspects which lay behind the formal actions."[3]

Having devoted the past seven years to exploring the cultural impact of the Constitution, I can heartily concur, and would like to demonstrate the point with two illustrations that also exemplify the comparative dimension of this book.

On July 11, 1908, Turkish newspapers printed a curt imperial communiqué: His Majesty, the Sultan, intended to restore the constitution of 1876. Groups of educated men and women gathered privately to discuss the implications of this announcement. As one of them recalled two decades later, "the subject seemed alien and hard to discuss. The word 'constitution,' after its exile from the dictionary, was now suddenly used again in an imperial communiqué."

The omnipotent sultan, Abdul Hamid, had ruled repressively for more than thirty years. In 1906, however, a group of revolutionaries based in Saloniki, the central city of Macedonia, began to plot a revolution. Covert contacts attracted new members. Sympathetic groups formed in other Macedonian towns; the movement spread; and the "young Turks," as they were known, assassinated or kidnapped high-ranking deputies of the sultan who opposed their plans.

A major turning point occurred when regiments from Smyrna sided with the rebels. On July 10, 1908, three of the leaders announced their goal of returning to constitutional government. They telegraphed Abdul

Hamid to demand official restoration of the constitution, and threatened that if he refused they would march on Istanbul with the Third Army Corps. The sultan responded immediately with his grudging communiqué. During the next few days Turkish cities erupted, wild with excitement. Among the organizers of this movement, the most popular public speaker was Dr. Riza Tewfik. He travelled among the crowds on horseback, calming them with explanations of the meaning of an upheaval that had been created in the name of constitutionalism. One witness described a typical scene where Dr. Tewfik faced a crowd of Kurdish porters in Istanbul.

"Tell us what constitution means," the porters shouted.

"Constitution is such a great thing that those who do not know it are donkeys," Tewfik responded.

"We are donkeys," brayed the porters.

"Your fathers also did not know it. Say that you are the sons of donkeys," Tewfik harangued.

"We are the sons of donkeys," the porters chanted.

For more than a generation, the concept of constitutionalism had been unmentionable in Turkey. Suddenly an ecstatic society could speak of little else.[4] To Americans, whether in 1908 or today, this whole episode must appear both fascinating and bizarre—but ultimately alien. Before as well as after 1908, according to Edward S. Corwin, a "cult of the Constitution" existed in the United States.[5] We have had a rich tradition of constitutionalism, a tradition that is fundamental to our political culture. Right? Well not quite. Perhaps a second episode may help to reveal why.

During the spring of 1923, transport workers who belonged to the IWW (International Workers of the World) went on strike in San Pedro Harbor, California, and received repressive treatment by the police, who had strong encouragement from the Los Angeles Merchants' and Manufacturers' Association. Upton Sinclair, the well-known novelist and muckraker, went to San Pedro on May 15. He planned to speak before a large gathering of strikers and their families, and carefully arranged that the event should take place on private property with the owner's written permission.[6]

Because six or seven hundred dockworkers had already been "packed into a jail under especially shocking conditions," Sinclair began the rally by attempting to read aloud the Bill of Rights of the U.S. Constitution. The police waited while he recited three sentences, those guaranteeing "freedom of speech and of the press, and the right of the people peaceably to assemble, and to petition the government for the redress of their grievances." Before Sinclair could complete his recitation of the First Amendment, the police not only arrested him but, according to most accounts, "kidnapped" him. They drove Sinclair around Los Angeles for hours, taking him from one station house to another without actually lodging charges against him. The Los Angeles police chief intended to bring Sinclair into a court just before it closed at five o'clock, ask the judge to appoint defense attorneys, place Sinclair in jail without bail, and then conceal his whereabouts.

As it happened, however, a subordinate of the police chief secretly telephoned an associate of Sinclair's so that his lawyers could be ready with a writ when Sinclair was brought into court. All in all, he had been held "incommunicado" for twenty-two hours. The complaint issued against him, and the basis for his arrest, charged Upton Sinclair with "discussing, arguing, orating and debating certain thoughts and theories, which . . . were detrimental and in opposition to the orderly conduct of affairs of business, affecting the rights of private property. . . ."[7]

Two days after being seized, and less than a day following his release, Sinclair wrote a public letter to Louis D. Oaks, the chief of police—a letter that Sinclair reprinted in his autobiography. Some of the most pertinent passages follow.

Pasadena, California, May 17, 1923

Louis D. Oaks,
Chief of Police, Los Angeles

Having escaped from your clutches yesterday afternoon, owing to the fact that one of your men betrayed your plot to my wife, I am now in position to answer your formal statement to the public, that I am "more dangerous than 4,000 I.W.W." I thank you for this compliment, for to be dangerous to lawbreakers in office such as yourself is the highest duty that a citizen of this community can perform.

In the presence of seven witnesses I obtained from Mayor Cryer on Tuesday afternoon the promise that the police would respect my constitutional rights at San Pedro, and that I would not be molested unless I incited to violence. But when I came to you, I learned that you had taken over the mayor's office at the Harbor. Now, from your signed statement to the press, I learn that you have taken over the district attorney's office also; for you tell the public: "I will prosecute Sinclair with all the vigor at my command, and upon his conviction I will demand a jail sentence with hard labor." And you then sent your men to swear to a complaint charging me with "discussing, arguing, orating, and debating certain thoughts and theories, which thoughts and theories were contemptuous of the constitution of the State of California, calculated to cause hatred and contempt of the government of the United States of America, and which thoughts and theories were detrimental and in opposition to the orderly conduct of affairs of business, affecting the rights of private property and personal liberty, and which thoughts and theories were calculated to cause any citizen then and there present and hearing the same to quarrel and fight and use force and violence." And this although I told you at least a dozen times in your office that my only purpose was to stand on private property with the written permission of the owner, and there to read the Constitution of the United States; and you perfectly well know that I did this, and only this, and that three sentences from the Bill of Rights of the Constitution was every word that I was permitted to utter—the words being those which guarantee "freedom of speech and of the press, and the right of the people peaceably to assemble, and to petition the government for the redress of grievances."

But you told me that "this Constitution stuff" does not go at the Harbor. You have established martial law, and you told me that if I tried to read the Constitution, even on private property, I would be thrown into jail, and there would be no bail for me—and this even though I read you the provision of the State constitution guaranteeing me the right to bail. When you arrested me and my friends, you spirited us away and held us "incomunicado," denying us what is our clear legal right, to communicate with our lawyers. . . .

You did all you could to keep me from contact with the strikers in jail; nevertheless I learned of one horror that was perpetrated only yesterday—fifty men crowded into one small space, and because they committed some slight breach of regulations, singing their songs, they were shut in this hole for two hours without a breath of air, and almost suffocated. Also I saw the food that these men are getting twice a day, and you would not feed it to your dog. And now the city council has voted for money to build a "bull-pen" for strikers, and day by day the public is told that the strike is broken, and the men, denied every civil right, have no place to meet to discuss their policies, and no one to protect them or to protest for them. That is what you want—those are the orders you have got from the Merchants' and Manufacturers' Association; the men are to go back as slaves, and the Constitution of the United States is to cease to exist so far as concerns workingmen.[8]

Sinclair went free, and along with his associates hired a large hall in Los Angeles on a weekly basis. They held crowded meetings every afternoon and evening, and promptly established the Southern California branch of the American Civil Liberties Union. Within a month, police chief Oaks was dismissed by the "city fathers." He had been found parked in his car at night with a woman and a jug of whiskey.[9]

Taken all alone, *l'affaire* Sinclair demonstrates nothing conclusively. What happened during that warm week in May 1923 was neither a unique episode in American history nor part of a flagrant pattern. Although similar episodes have occurred, they have not been the norm. What took place in Los Angeles does suggest, however, that cynicism about constitutions and civil liberties is not to be found exclusively among authorities in other nations. It also serves as a reminder that ignorance of the Constitution—not to mention ignoring the Constitution—has also been commonplace in our past. And finally, an editorial response that appeared in the Hartford, Connecticut, *Times* urged readers not to take for granted a document that so often had received perfunctory praise while simultaneously being slighted: "There is nothing to indicate that the Constitution and the preamble thereof are to be read only at Fourth of July meetings, convocations of the Ku Klux Klan . . . and teas for Women Patriots. There is nothing in that preamble to indicate that the blessings of liberty were suspended during dock strikes or that they do not apply to socialist novelists."[10]

The lesson of *l'affaire* Sinclair is that constitutional conflict in various forms has been an integral though episodic part of American cultural history. Nevertheless, most of us have rather blithely managed to take that lesson for granted, perhaps because the role of constitutionalism in American culture has been more complicated than one might expect. Whatever the reasons, that role is part of a fascinating story that has never been told. The purpose of this book is to tell it, and to do so with particular attention to the *problématique* of constitutionalism in the United States.

At this point some readers may want a working definition of constitutionalism. I will oblige them, though briefly, because the concept has a complicated history that ranges from Aristotle's *Politics* and Polybius' *Histories* to *The Republic*, written by Charles A. Beard more than two millennia later. The most pertinent definition that I have encountered was prepared by Walton H. Hamilton in 1931. Although superb in several respects, it is also aphoristic, even sardonic, and presumes considerable knowledge of the Constitution's place in American political culture. It impressed me far more after I had completed the research for this book than when I began.[11]

According to Hamilton, constitutionalism "is the name given to the trust which men repose in the power of words engrossed on parchment to keep a government in order." He declared (with sarcasm rather than chauvinism) that "the constitutionalism of the United States is richest in incident and meaning"; and after a succinct historical discussion, asserted that "the rising constitutionalism, which was to outlast the [nineteenth] century, left a varied expression. There was worship at the shrine of liberty and of law. The document was the most perfect instrument of government ever contrived. . . ." Hamilton then elaborated several additional points, all of them germane, and the final one a slightly opaque anticipation of my central theme in this inquiry:

- "The magic of infallibility was extended from the constitution to its official exposition and even to the president's appointment of justices."

- "In the decorous course of time a simple text is elaborated into a complicated code."

- "If there is to be appraisal, the constitutionalism of the people must be distinguished from that of the bench. . . . The object of worship is an ideal of law; the act of faith is almost untainted with knowledge. . . ."

Walton Hamilton implied, quite validly, that a glaring discrepancy exists in the history of American constitutionalism between the recurrent declarations of reverence for "our Ark of Covenant" (Congressman Caleb Cushing called the Constitution that in 1834, and Chief Justice Taft did so again in 1922)[12] and the ongoing reality that most of us do not adequately understand the Constitution; that most of us fail to appreciate how frequently means have been found to circumvent the Constitution and to flout or even attack the Supreme Court; or that the Golden Jubilee of 1837, the Centennial of 1887, and the Sesquicentennial celebration of 1937 failed to generate very much genuine enthusiasm. What is widely assumed to have been a great success story—not the functional adequacy of our Constitution but the public's relationship to it—turns out to have been a failure.

Why? This book attempts to answer that question. The most important explanations will be found in the character of our public culture, in our educational system and self-perceptions; but a few words should be said here about the subdiscipline of constitutional history. For a generation following the 1880s it made a strong start. For more than three decades after that, however, denigration of the discipline was heard, even from some who had been pioneers in the field. As Max Farrand wrote to a colleague: "In order to understand the development of America it is necessary to study something more than the political and constitutional history." Subsequently, others called for constitutional history to marry social history, with the latter as dominant partner. Eventually, in 1950, an able historian urged us to regard constitutional history "as an aspect of intellectual history—that is, constitutional ideas and ideals and those institutions and procedures which have been intended to embody them."[13]

Each of these objectives sounded perfectly sensible at the time, and each one seems unexceptionable in retrospect. Yet the appeals went largely unanswered and the field somehow failed to progress. As Henry Steele Commager wrote to Andrew C. McLaughlin upon the latter's retirement from the University of Chicago in 1935: "I am inclined to doubt that you will have a successor, because it seems to me that constitutional history has been shelved. I think you will agree with me that one consequence of the neglect of constitutional history in favor of social etc. history, is a discouraging tendency to loose and fuzzy thinking."[14]

If the field has not exactly been shelved, neither has it flourished over the past half century. It was never even betrothed to social history, and has managed only an occasional flirtation with intellectual history. There is still no scholarly organization of constitutional historians, and no journal exclusively devoted to constitutional history (unless one counts *The Supreme Court Review,* an annual founded in 1961 that is equally concerned with legal history, public policy, and constitutional law).

In 1968, G. R. Elton's inaugural lecture as Professor of English Constitutional History in the University of Cambridge included a statement of his perception of the purpose of the field: "to study government, the manner in which men, having formed themselves into societies, then arranged for the orderly existence, through time, and in space, of those societies." That part would have been familiar and acceptable, I believe, to anyone from John Locke to F. W. Maitland. Elton then talked about constitutional history as "a form of social history, a form of the history of society." Very well. That part sounds like our avant-garde scholars of the 1920s and '30s. But eventually, in step three of his statement, Elton moved toward our own perspective: "What does the society think its government is, how does it treat it, what does it do to amend it?"[15]

Over the years, Americans have applied various images to their Constitution. In his first inaugural address, in 1809, James Madison called it "the cement of the Union."[16] Others have referred to it as "the great code," as "a frame of government," and as "that fundamental law." My concern throughout this book, if I may paraphrase Elton, hinges upon this query: How has the society felt about its frame of government? (When it has felt or thought about it at all.) Another British observer recently made an acute comment upon "our age's preference, in intellectual history, for the subversive and rancorous over the official and self-congratulatory."[17] This exercise in cultural history will be much concerned, though by no means exclusively, with the official and self-congratulatory.

One other matter must be mentioned: my disqualifications and my intended audience. Davy Crockett boasted in his autobiography (1831) that he "had never read a page in a law book in all my life." I could say the same, at least until rather recently, though I am not so proud of my parochialism as Crockett seems to have been. Aware of my limitations, I have tried to maintain some distance from technical aspects of legal and constitutional history. I cannot say whether this book represents a marriage between cultural and constitutional history or merely a flirtation. Perhaps the answer lies somewhere in between: a sustained affair in which the cultural side is dominant. I do sympathize with a sentence written by Theodore Roosevelt in 1901: "I am not a lawyer, but I have never believed that a layman who thought soberly was incompetent to express a judgement upon the constitution."[18]

Above all, I have attempted to prepare a substantial, original, serious yet engaging work for nonspecialists. A few years ago, Charles E. Wyzanski, senior federal judge of the U.S. District Court in Boston, offered this observation: "There is always the risk . . . that persons start with the totally false assumption that the Constitution is the province of the lawyers. . . . Moreover, I think it is quite clear that there is a grave danger that if we think of the Constitution exclusively in terms of constitutional law, we shall lose some of its most important symbolic, as well as practical, values to our society."[19] If my major contention proves to be correct—that Americans have taken too much pride and proportionately too little interest in their frame of government—then this book will have helped by calling attention to that disparity, by explaining how it evolved over time, by indicating the undesirable consequences, and by suggesting some ways in which the gap between ideal and reality might be reduced.

Acknowledgments

ALTHOUGH I CANNOT ADEQUATELY THANK ALL of the people who have helped me with this project over the past seven years, it is a pleasure at least to acknowledge their generous co-operation. In addition to numerous librarians and archivists at many institutions, particularly those cited in Appendix A, I am especially obliged to three research assistants, all Cornell undergraduates, whose diligence and good cheer were indispensable: Laura Dick, Robert P. Frankel, and Lorri Staal.

Funds for travel and research expenses were made available by the Colonel Return Jonathan Meigs Fund at Cornell. The Philadelphia Center for Early American Studies provided a stipend to facilitate work in Philadelphia repositories during the summer of 1983. The National Endowment for the Humanities awarded me a Constitutional Fellowship during 1984–85, which allocated more than a calendar year for writing and revision. Corrinne Sheppard Eastman showed extraordinary patience and precision in typing, proofreading, and retyping the entire manuscript. Her promptness and reliability were essential and deeply appreciated. Ann Adelman provided her customary meticulous care in copyediting the manuscript; and Toula Polygalaktos facilitated production logistics at Alfred A. Knopf, Inc. Anne Eberle prepared the index with thorough professionalism and dispatch. I am fortunate to have had their help.

Various institutions, seminars, and conferences supplied opportunities to send up trial balloons. I am grateful for the hospitality and responses that I received at the Ecole des Hautes Etudes en Sciences Sociales in Paris, where I taught a seminar during 1980–81; to the Center for

American Studies in Rome, where I lectured for a week in April 1981; to the Institute for Anglo-American History at the University of Cologne in West Germany; to the University of Florida, where I served as Wentworth Scholar-in-Residence for a week in October 1982; to Union College; to the University of Dallas; to the Cornell Law School; and to a symposium co-sponsored by the Constitution Study Group of the National Archives and the American Bar Association's Commission on Public Understanding about the Law, held in Washington, D.C., on March 14, 1985. I profited very much from all of these opportunities to explore materials used in this book.

A number of colleagues and friends took the time and trouble to read chapters on which they have special expertise and give me critical suggestions. I wish to thank Harry S. Ashmore, Sherman Cochran, Linda Greenhouse, Maeva Marcus, Ian Mylchreest, Mary Beth Norton, Russell K. Osgood, William Peters, Richard Polenberg, Arthur M. Schlesinger, Jr., and Joel Silbey.

Three friends who read the entire manuscript deserve special mention as well as total absolution from errors of judgment and misinterpretation that remain: Jane N. Garrett, my editor at Knopf for more than fifteen years; Douglas S. Greenberg of Princeton University; and Paul L. Murphy of the University of Minnesota. I imposed a heavy burden upon them, and they responded with candor and critical acumen. I am deeply grateful.

Perhaps I may quote and even embellish Montesquieu's preface to *The Spirit of the Laws:* "If this work meets with success, I shall owe it chiefly to the grandeur and majesty of the subject." And a little help from my friends.

Above Cayuga's Waters
September 1985   M. K.

"The Federal Constitution by a fair construction is a good one prinsapaly, but I have no dout but that the Convention who made it intended to destroy our free governments by it, or they neaver would have spent 4 Months in making such an inexpliset thing. As one said at the time of its adoption, it is made like a Fiddle, with but few Strings, but so that the ruling Majority could play any tune upon it they please."

WILLIAM MANNING (1798)

"How easily men satisfy themselves that the Constitution is exactly what they wish it to be."

JUSTICE JOSEPH STORY (1845)

"It is . . . particularly true of constitutional government that its atmosphere is opinion. . . . It does not remain fixed in any unchanging form, but grows with the growth and is altered with the change of the nation's needs and purposes."

WOODROW WILSON (1908)

A MACHINE
THAT WOULD
GO OF ITSELF

CHAPTER 1

The Problem of Constitutionalism in American Culture

ALTHOUGH THE FOUNDERS DIFFERED OVER MANY important matters, they shared a belief that the constitutional system created between 1787 and 1791 (when the Bill of Rights received approval) should be fully comprehensible to the American people. At the close of his first inaugural address Thomas Jefferson called the Constitution "the text of civil instruction—the touchstone by which to try the services of those we trust." That is, those entrusted with responsibility for public affairs. More recently Associate Justice Owen J. Roberts, writing in 1930, observed that "the Constitution was written to be understood by the voters; its words and phrases were used in their normal and ordinary as distinguished from [their] technical meaning. . . ."[1]

The recurrence of such assertions obliges us to raise this candid question: To what extent has our constitutional system, in reality, served as a text of civil instruction? I contend that the Constitution occupies an anomalous role in American cultural history. For almost two centuries it has been swathed in pride yet obscured by indifference: a fulsome rhetoric of reverence more than offset by the reality of ignorance. One American woman, while travelling abroad in 1840, heaped lavish praise upon "our own glorious *Constitution* (whose every article should be held as sacred and unchangeable as were the laws of the Persian and the Mede)." Schoolbooks of that era often stated that the Constitution had been divinely inspired. Their authors could not refer to the Constitution without a choral vocabulary of "revered," "glorious," and "sacred."[2]

Those very same schoolbooks, however, also contained all sorts of inaccuracies about the Constitution. Nevertheless, sheer neglect may have been even more problematic than misinformation. In 1852 Edward Everett, recently the president of Harvard and soon to become Secretary of State, spoke at an exhibition in Cambridge. Referring to exercises held during the morning, he expressed regret "that want of time obliged you to omit the recitation on the Constitution of the United States. That, too, is a very important subject, and one on which none too much knowledge prevails, even in our own country." Such chidings occurred often during Everett's era, and have been echoed frequently ever since. In 1924, for example, a little primer aimed at the masses opened with this lament: "The average citizen has rather hazy ideas about the Constitution."[3]

Simultaneously, Solicitor General James M. Beck brought out a much larger book, with a foreword written by President Coolidge, directed to a more educated yet general audience. "The average American," Beck declared, takes "scant interest in the nature of the Constitution." He then specified that his accusation applied equally to all levels of society, and complained that "the Constitution is in graver danger than at any other time in the history of America. This is due, not to any conscious hostility to the spirit or letter, but to the indifference and apathy with which the masses regard the increasing assaults upon its basic principles." He went on to ask: "even among the educated classes, can one man in ten pass an intelligent examination as to its contents?" Beck's book reached a broad readership; and he received many favorable letters about it, including one from H. L. Mencken. In reply, Beck elaborated upon his intent: "I tried, from the beginning, to stress the fact that, after all, the success of the Constitution depended upon a people who would be politically receptive. . . . I wanted to raise the serious question whether, as a people, we still have that political receptivity."[4]

Forty-four years later, in an unusual television interview, Martin Agronsky asked Associate Justice Hugo Black whether he thought "that most Americans understand the Constitution?" Black responded without hesitation: "No, I think most of them do not."[5] If Black, Beck, Everett, and many others have been correct, then we need to explain the phenomenon and inquire about its implications. I will attempt to do so in five phases. First, why should the subject of constitutionalism in America be perplexing or confusing? Second, in the realm of attitudes, how have Americans *felt* about their Constitution? Third, in the realm of understanding, what have Americans *known* and not known? Fourth, in the realm of impact, what have been the consequences of our curious blend of reverence and ignorance? And finally, is cultural constitutionalism in the United States distinctive, or does it have parallels elsewhere?

This agenda of historical questions seems intrinsically significant and interesting. By pursuing them we also respond to a recent challenge of a more general nature, namely, that human ignorance ought to be studied as well as human knowledge.[6]

I

What have been the basic causes of misunderstanding? We must begin with the fact—occasionally recognized by politicians and diplomats during the Jeffersonian generation, by abolitionists and political theorists during the Civil War era, and by some twentieth-century jurists and scholars—that the Constitution itself contains a number of ambiguities. The most troublesome of all, perhaps, pertains to the very nature of the Union created in 1787. How much sovereignty did the states actually surrender to the central government? Did the Union in some sense originate with the Continental Congresses of 1774 and 1775 (thereby antedating the existence of states), as so many arch-nationalists have claimed from Daniel Webster's day to our own?[7] One's understanding (or misunderstanding) of federalism and the enduring issue of states' rights hangs in the balance.

James Madison, Alexander Hamilton, and others among the founders were unclear about the meaning of direct versus indirect taxation, and acknowledged that they had been. As Hamilton conceded: "What is the distinction between *direct* and *indirect* taxes? It is a matter of regret that terms so uncertain and vague in so important a point are to be found in the Constitution."[8] In 1807 (when the trial of Aaron Burr took place), and again during the years 1861–68, Americans learned that the treason clause of the Constitution could be construed in various ways. In 1868, and once again in 1974, Americans found that the proper constitutional grounds for impeaching a President are exceedingly murky. During the middle third of the nineteenth century fierce disputes occurred between northerners and southerners, as well as among abolitionist splinter groups, over the founders' intentions regarding several aspects of slavery. After examining the Constitution "with greater care and deeper interest than ever before," one abolitionist observed in 1869 "that every article of the Constitution usually quoted as intended to favor the assumptions of slaveholders admitted of an opposite interpretation." Ultimately he concluded that the Constitution "might be whichever the people pleased to make it."[9]

If that judgment is correct, it may help to explain yet another cause of our confusion: that so many prominent figures who have made major statements about the Constitution changed (or *appeared* to have changed) their positions during the course of their careers. James Madison, for instance, sounded like a nationalist in 1787–88, like an advocate of states' rights in 1798–99, and like a divided soul during the last dozen years of his life, 1825–36. Herbert Hoover spoke enthusiastically about states' rights; but as a nationalist and a Progressive devoted to efficiency, his actions moved the country toward increased centralization. Throughout the 1930s and '40s Charles Beard wrote much more positively about the Constitution and its authors than he had during the teens and twenties.

A related phenomenon has sometimes been a cause but at other times a consequence of the one just described: namely, that a number of leading "custodians" of constitutionalism in the United States have been men with mixed ideological convictions. I would describe most of them as conservative liberals; and their dualistic vision has additional importance if one tries to look at constitutional values in biographical terms, which has been a standard approach. Consider, for example, Thomas M. Cooley, the nineteenth-century author of influential constitutional treatises, whose impulses were simultaneously conservative and reformist, and whose reactions to the growing tensions between capital and labor during the 1870s and 1880s were highly ambivalent. I also have in mind Professor Zechariah Chafee, Jr. (1885–1957), Professor of Law at Harvard and perhaps the leading twentieth-century authority on civil liberties, whose career has been described as "a modern demonstration of how in America libertarian sympathies can often be yoked to strongly conservative convictions." Chafee's difficulty in accepting the dynamics of American society, according to a sympathetic analyst,

> appears less as an expression of ignorance or naïveté than as a function of dilemmas which have frequently emerged to trouble proponents of conservative liberalism in this country. He was committed to the notion that there were no really fundamental contradictions in American society, but at the same time forced to admit that Americans frequently turned upon themselves with a ferocity indicative of just such contradictions. He believed that the ultimate authority should be vested in the people, but could not help observing how the exercise of the popular will often destroyed freedom.[10]

Among Supreme Court justices one thinks of Louis D. Brandeis, a Progressive humanitarian who never shed his Wilsonian commitment to traditional federalism and therefore had grave doubts about many features of Franklin D. Roosevelt's nationalizing New Deal. Or Charles Evans Hughes, liberal on most matters involving civil liberties but more conservative on issues concerning political economy. Or Robert H. Jackson, whose constitutional position on the relative priority of property rights and human rights vacillated between 1941 when he joined the Court and his death in 1954.

Yet another cause of public misunderstanding has resulted from the Court's mystique, its reluctance to explain its procedures, and the press's related failure to cover the Court adequately during most of its history. For at least two generations following 1787 the Court did not encourage public attendance when cases were being heard. The Dred Scott case, one of the most notorious in American history, started in a Missouri court in 1846 and reached the Supreme Court on December 30, 1854, which finally rendered its decision on March 6, 1857. The American public knew nothing of the case throughout 1855, and had little sense of its explosive implications until the very end of 1856. The fact that such a case—so critical to the most tumultuous issue of the preceding twenty years—could remain hidden from view for so long was not at all unusual.[11]

Some of the most important transformations in our constitutional system occur so gradually that the general public only becomes aware of them, if at all, after they have occurred. One major example involves the alteration of the "due process of law" clause in the Fourteenth Amendment from a guarantee to accused persons of a certain mode of judicial procedure into a "bulwark of the *laissez-faire* conception of governmental function." Another involves the still more gradual process by which the Bill of Rights became applicable to the states as well as to the federal government—a process that began slowly in the mid-1920s, remained highly controversial among jurists and constitutional scholars during the 1940s, and was not completed until the later 1960s.[12]

How many Americans appreciate the extent to which the conservative Court of the period 1890–1937 was nonetheless the most activist (that is, interventionist) in our history? How many persons among the so-called educated public understand that the Court has reversed itself within a year (the Legal Tender cases of 1870–71), within a century (whether the federal judiciary can control common law at the state level: opinions in 1842 and 1938), but more commonly at intervals ranging between twenty and sixty years? As Robert G. McCloskey remarked of the Court:

One moment's resolution yields to another's self-doubt. A compulsory school flag salute is upheld against religious scruples in the name of democratic self-education and national unity; three years later the decision is overruled. An eight justice majority concurs in an opinion which apparently endows labor picketing with the status of a "preferred freedom"; subsequent qualifying holdings whittle that freedom down to a near-nullity. The right to counsel is required in state courts for some indigent defendants but not for others; a state may not affirmatively authorize arbitrary search and seizure, but it need not exclude evidence thus obtained from its courts. . . . Doctrinal indecisiveness appears at every hand. . . . Is federalism still a reigning value, or merely a practical inconvenience? Are there preferred freedoms or are there not? The Court can be found at one time or another on both sides of all these questions, and the incertitude seems to exist not only as between different wings of the Court but within the hearts of individual justices.[13]

If the Court and some of its members have been ambivalent about key constitutional issues, that tendency compounds yet another major source of misunderstanding. Felix Frankfurter declared in 1930, when he was still a professor of law, that "in good truth, the Supreme Court *is* the Constitution." The authors of a widely used textbook, *The Supreme Court in a Free Society* (1959), seem to have been so persuaded that they took Frankfurter's assertion as the title of their first chapter.[14] Some prominent politicians, such as John F. Kennedy, as well as many Americans at the grass roots level have clearly shared Frankfurter's view as Gospel truth. The mail that congressmen received from their constituents in 1937, when Franklin D. Roosevelt proposed his "Court-packing" plan, amply illustrates this.

- "We are depending on you to uphold the Constitution and to vote against any tampering with the Supreme Court."

- [Referring to the nine Supreme Court justices]: "Just as thay are thay have stood the test & give very good Satisfaction, so we the people should leave well enough alone [.] do all you can to keep our Constitution safe."

- [Congratulations on your stand] "in opposing proposed drastic changes in the Supreme Court and incidentally the constitution. This must remain a free people."

- "I pray that you will do all you can to defeat any legislation relative to changing the Constitution or its personnel."[15]

This propensity to conflate the Court and the Constitution is hardly limited to grass roots America. It seems to have been shared by a great many scholars because the constitutional history of the United States has primarily been written as the history of Supreme Court decisions, doctrines, procedures, and personalities. As Robert McCloskey put it on more than one occasion: "American constitutional history has been in large part a spasmodic running debate over the behavior of the Supreme Court."[16] I find that perspective needlessly narrow.

I have also found, however, a countervailing inclination among informed Americans, regardless of their ideological persuasion, to differentiate between the Constitution and the Court. Sometimes this inclination has been propelled by political expediency: that was true of Andrew Jackson's veto in 1832, when Congress and the Court upheld the constitutionality of the Bank of the United States; or of Lincoln in 1861, explaining his prospective policies; or of FDR in 1937, during the "Court-packing" controversy, when he declared in a fireside chat that we had "reached the point as a Nation where we must take action to save the Constitution from the Court and the Court from itself. . . . We want a Supreme Court which will do justice under the Constitution—not over it."[17]

For many others, though, their cultural values (in the broadest sense) have figured more significantly than political expediency as a reason for differentiating between the Constitution and the Court. The crisis of 1937 merely provides the most contested example, a time when the Kaufman and Hart musical *I'd Rather Be Right* has the Supreme Court declare the U.S. Constitution unconstitutional.[18] During the 1920s politicians as diverse as Republican Senator Edwin F. Ladd of North Dakota and Progressive Senator Robert M. LaFollette of Wisconsin could lament situations in which "the Constitution of the United States is not what its plain terms declare but what these nine men construe it to be." From the mid-1950s until quite recently, conservatives have complained relentlessly that the Court violates the Constitution. As the governor of Virginia put it, reacting to the school desegregation order, "I saw the Court ignore the Constitution."[19] The liberal line of the 1930s was now being voiced by the opposition. In 1936 Heywood Broun argued in his nationally syndicated column for the need "to keep the Supreme Court from kicking the Constitution around." Three decades later editorial writer David Lawrence, whose words reached millions, bemoaned "provisions of the Constitution that have been torn to shreds by the autocratic action of a judicial oligarchy."[20]

It is tempting to conclude that people who are content with the Court's orientation at any given time are likely to believe that the Court embodies the Constitution, whereas those unhappy with the Court (or more particularly, with its exercise of judicial review) will adhere to an opposite position. The historical record, however, is more complicated than that. First, intermittent attacks upon the Supreme Court have been an integral part of constitutionalism in American culture. The years 1819, 1833, 1857, 1895, 1912, 1924, 1937, 1957, and 1964 are only the most obvious. From 1955 until 1964, in fact, the Court remained an object of intense vilification.

Second, there have on occasion been more subtle formulations, such as 1972 when Eric Sevareid talked with Justice William O. Douglas for one hour during prime-time television on a commercial network—an event all too rare in our public life. "The Court is really the keeper of the conscience," Douglas remarked as the interview came to a close. "And the conscience is the Constitution."[21] That crisp maxim is meaningful as well as mystical; but most valid, obviously, when the Court is in top form.

A different formulation that depends less upon subjective or partisan considerations appeared in a sensible yet forgotten essay written more than thirty years ago by the late Mark Howe. His insight is both clever and clear. When the Supreme Court is in an activist phase, the Constitution and the Court most nearly coincide because the Court largely determines what the Constitution means in applied and practical terms. When the Court shows restraint, the Constitution is shaped by many other determinants, and then Court and Constitution coincide least of all.[22]

The academic tendency to describe our constitutional history as predominantly the Court's history is unfortunate because Supreme Court decisions (and the responses to them) constitute merely the most visible portion of a large and ever-moving iceberg. So many actions (and inactions) germane to an understanding of constitutionalism in American culture have remained obscure either because they fail (whereas most of the history that is written records success), or because the media neglect to cover them. Justice Robert H. Jackson put it very well in 1951: "Subtle shifts take place in the centers of real power that do not show on the face of the Constitution." Many Americans assume that the Supreme Court is not just the ultimate guardian of the Constitution, but the only one. Many do not realize that numerous bills introduced in Congress get nowhere because congressmen who are not their sponsors perceive them to be unconstitutional. In particular, bills that pertain to constitutional matters—such as attempts to strip the Supreme Court of its power of judicial review, or proposals for congressional review of Court decisions regarding controversial questions—have customarily been referred to the judiciary committee and never reported out.[23]

Three other sections of the submerged part of our iceberg should also be noted. During the first century of national government, more than 1,600 resolutions for amendments to the Constitution were introduced in Congress. By 1986, no fewer than 10,124 amendments had been proposed, of which only 16 were actually adopted. These aggregate figures conceal the periodicity of constitutionalism in American political culture, however. During many sessions of Congress not a single resolution has been introduced; but during the 39th Congress (1865–67), for example, nearly two hundred proposals arose. During the second session of the 62nd Congress (1911–12) and first session of the 63rd (1913), a time when the reform-minded Progressive movement was most active and when the judiciary became very controversial, eighty-five amendments were introduced. Slavery and issues arising from its abolition stimulated more than five hundred proposed amendments. Following the Supreme Court's restrictive decisions pertaining to school prayer, 1962–64, more than 170 amendment bills appeared. Considering all of these proposals, by now numbering well in excess of 2,000, some have been sensible; many have been interesting; and a lot fairly crackpot in character. Our knowledge of them, of their stimuli, and of the controversies they generated is woefully limited.[24]

Another section of the submerged iceberg may be found in constitutionalism at the state level, notably in the many revisions that have been made in our state constitutions; in the conventions held for that purpose; and, once again, in the chimerical influence of ideas that were discussed extensively yet never implemented. The nature of these discussions was frequently nationwide in scope, as one constitutional scholar explained to another in 1909.

> Some of the most interesting questions are those connected with proposals which were made but not adopted. For example, the proposal for an indirectly elected legislative council or senate appeared first in George Mason's draft of a constitution for Virginia; was shortly afterward adopted in Maryland upon the proposal of Charles Carroll of Carrollton . . . was later presented to the New York convention; and turned up in different forms in both the New Hampshire and Massa-

chusetts conventions. A study of the first state constitutions would necessarily take into consideration these rejected proposals.[25]

A different portion of the iceberg has not been entirely submerged; but neither has it been accessible to the lay public. Although the U.S. Constitution contains only about 6,000 words, millions of additional words have been issued by the courts, at several levels of the judicial system, in order to elucidate it. Harlan Fiske Stone summed up the implications in a private letter. "I could not say that one who seeks to apply the Constitution today can dispense with an extensive technical training. The gloss which has been placed on the Constitution by a century of decisions and interpretation certainly has produced a labyrinth through which the judge would find great difficulty in threading his path, and at the same time keep his balance, unless he had an extensive legal knowledge of the forestry and what lawyers think it all means."[26]

The varied ways in which jurists interpret and politicians construe the Constitution have, in a sense, become an extension of it. They thereby comprise an integral part of constitutionalism in the United States. That much is not news. What compounds the problem of public understanding, however, is that people seem to be incapable of consistency. Not only do jurists and politicians change their positions, but by doing so they become vulnerable to charges of hypocrisy or, even worse, having their words subsequently manipulated for partisan purposes. Sometimes these distortions are willful, and sometimes inadvertent. Either way the results range from legal uncertainty to outright confusion. John Marshall and James Madison have frequently been invoked, or else quoted out of context, to bolster arguments that would have appalled them. Southern misuses of Madison and Jefferson to support states' rights polemics, especially between the 1820s and the 1850s, were simply outrageous.[27] A similar pattern developed during the half century following 1875 among persons with divergent views about the original motivations behind and meaning of the Fourteenth, Fifteenth, and Eighteenth amendments. A Massachusetts congressman caught the essence of it in 1923.

I am very much afraid that it is possibly true that our public bodies, as well as our private citizens, are possessed of very little respect for the inherent obligation of obedience to law. They set aside those parts of the Constitution and those laws which they do not fancy, and then insist on passing constitutional amendments and laws to restrain by force even the social practices and private habits of which they do not approve. . . . Were I to make a list of our dangerous radicals I should name, first, the Congress of the United States which treats with contempt the plain mandates of the Constitution.[28]

Moreover, most Americans fail to appreciate the extent to which they have accepted a passel of constitutional fictions. Although these are not entirely false, neither are they historically sound. Most notable, perhaps, is the myth that the entire people of the United States established the Constitution. This notion became a recurrent theme in John Marshall's major decisions and a basic premise in Joseph Story's *Commentaries* (1833): "The constitution is the will, the deliberate will, of the people." James Bryce echoed this fiction in *The American Commonwealth,* an extremely influential work; and it became a staple in public rhetoric during the nineteenth and twentieth centuries.[29] The efforts of Oliver Wendell Holmes and the so-called legal realists of the 1920s and '30s to demystify the Constitution met with some success, but in limited circles. Attempts by scholars during the past half century to extend this trend—to "dispose of historical and legal myths," as one of them put it—have barely altered public perceptions.[30]

II

When Alexis de Tocqueville discussed the U.S. Constitution, he found it "frightening to see how much diverse knowledge and discernment it assumes on the part of the governed. The government of the Union rests almost entirely on legal fictions." Tocqueville became more sanguine, however, when he took into account the pragmatic character of the people he was observing. "Nothing has made me admire the good sense and practical intelligence of the Americans more than the way they avoid the innumerable difficulties deriving from their federal Constitution," he remarked.[31] Expedient might be a more accurate word than practical; but, be that as it may, Tocqueville's rumination reminds us that public opinion about constitutional matters, however ill-informed or well-informed in various situations, has not been negligible.

Although it has barely been chronicled, a fair number of American leaders have been quite aware of that fact ever since the 1790s. They have utilized interchangeably such phrases as "public sentiment," "public will," "public mind," and "public pulse."[32] To complicate matters, there has never been agreement about the role of public opinion—either as an ideal or in reality. Most members of the Supreme Court who have responded to the issue share the view expressed by Brandeis (and Justice David J. Brewer in 1908) that "constitutional questions are not settled by even a consensus of present public opinion." Chief Justice Burger takes an even stronger position by insisting that the very purpose of a written constitution is "to provide safeguards for certain rights that *cannot* yield to public opinion."[33]

Observers of the Court and of constitutional history, on the other hand, have tended to be more cynical, more apprehensive, or more programmatic. Christopher G. Tiedeman, a prominent analyst during the later nineteenth century, contended that "when public opinion . . . requires the written word to be ignored the court justly obeys the will of the popular mandate, at the same time keeping up a show of obedience to the written word by a skillful use of legal fictions." Note the reiteration of Tocqueville's emphasis upon the manipulation of legal fictions. James M. Beck insisted that the Constitution "depends upon public opinion"; and in 1931 a reform-minded critic urged "the radical revision of our Constitution to make our government at least as responsible, as flexible, as sensitive to public opinion as the parliamentary systems of Great Britain and the leading democracies of Europe."[34]

Given this diversity of opinion, is it any wonder that one constitutional scholar would throw up his hands in despair and confess that "I have never been able to reach a conclusion myself with regard to what is ordinarily termed public opinion on the Constitution."[35]

One reason the problem has seemed so knotty, perhaps, is because most American perceptions of the Constitution have not remained fixed. They have altered over time, in some instances quite markedly. Nevertheless, one of the most significant assumptions changed very little during the long stretch when it was widely held. Therefore we need next to indicate the character of this constant, and then to describe three other important variables where change has been both prominent and consequential.

The first schoolbook to discuss the Constitution appeared in 1796. Called *A Plain Political Catechism*, it assured American youngsters that the Constitution provided for the happiness and prosperity of their country. In 1922 a basic civics text stressed exactly the same point. During the intervening 126 years, no connection was more commonly made. Not until the Great Depression began in 1929 did it begin to wither. As James M. Beck, by then a member of Congress, bemoaned: "the Constitution of the United States is practically a dead thing so far as being a great instrument in the commerce of the United States."[36] The linkage lingered on for almost a decade, however, sometimes in the context of discussing whether New Deal programs to repair the economy were constitutional; sometimes in planning historical pageants and films for the Sesquicentennial; and finally from opponents of Roosevelt's "Court-packing" plan.[37] After 1937 the connective assumption virtually disappeared.

It emerged as early as 1788 and can be found in *The Federalist* as an argument in favor of ratification; or in the grand parade held at Philadelphia that year on July 4. The bakers' banner read: "May the federal government revive our trade." Their wish would be fulfilled, perhaps as much because of public confidence in the new nation as because of any particular get-rich-quick device in the Constitution itself. "Our government is going on with a firm & steady pace," Jefferson wrote in 1791. "Our credit both at home & abroad equal to our wishes. So that on the whole we are in as prosperous a way as a nation can well be. This shews the advantage of the changeableness of a constitution. Had our former one been unalterable . . . we must have gone to ruin with our eyes open."[38]

Within a few years people in public life insisted that it had happened by design rather than by serendipity. In 1794, Congressman Richard Bland Lee found "fields a few years ago waste and uncultivated [now] filled with inhabitants and covered with harvests, new habitations reared, contentment in every face, plenty on every board. To produce this effect," he concluded, "was the intention of the Constitution, and it has succeeded." When the Hartford Convention met in 1814, a time of great national divisiveness, such assertions were heard from partisans on all sides; and by the later 1820s they had become an indispensable ingredient in Fourth of July orations. One explanation, frequently voiced, was that the Constitution had vastly improved interstate commerce.[39] Yet another, issued increasingly during John Marshall's stewardship, insisted that the Supreme Court had made a special contribution to national economic growth. The Court's decision in *Gibbons* v. *Ogden* (1824) later came to be known as "the emancipation proclamation of American commerce"; and Chief Justice Taney's opinion in the famous Charles River Bridge case (1837) referred to "prosperity" often while mediating the conflict between monopolistic property rights and the potential for general economic growth in favor of the latter.[40]

During the middle decades of the nineteenth century, most American presidents (and former presidents) invoked this formulaic link: James Madison did so in his carefully considered will, written in 1835; and Millard Fillmore did so as part of a predictable argument against change in his third annual message to Congress: "Our Constitution, though not perfect, is doubtless the best that ever was formed. Therefore let every proposition to change it be well weighed and if found beneficial, cautiously adopted. Every patriot will rejoice to see its authority so exerted as to advance the prosperity and honor of the nation. . . ." By the 1880s, formula had given way to hackneyed cliché, whether the orator was Republican Rutherford B. Hayes in 1883 or Democrat Grover Cleveland at the Centennial celebration in 1887.[41]

Only a few more subtle minds saw beyond the formulaic. In an 1831 oration, for example, John Quincy Adams intoned the standard line; but eight years later, in his carefully prepared address for the Golden Jubilee of the Constitution, Adams acknowledged that the relationship between prosperity and the Constitution "may perhaps be differently estimated by speculative minds." A fragment written by Abraham Lincoln early in 1861 went farther: "Without the *Constitution* and the *Union,* we could not have attained the result; but even these, are not the primary cause of our great prosperity. There is something back of these, entwining itself more closely about the human heart. That something, is the principle of 'Liberty to all'—the principle that clears the *path* for all—gives *hope* to all—and, by consequence, *enterprize,* and *industry* to all."[42]

It is symptomatic that Lincoln never used this musing in a speech; it remains virtually unique. The customary linkage must have been more compelling in public discourse. It remained the conventional wisdom for two additional generations, invoked even by foreigners. At the World's Columbian Exposition held at Chicago in 1893, the apostolic delegate from the Vatican charged his audience to "Go forward, in one hand bearing the book of Christian truth and in the other the constitution of the United States. Christian truth and American liberty will make you free, happy and prosperous."[43] The papal delegate had grafted Lincoln's view to the traditional one by reductively equating the U.S. Constitution with liberty. Although variations on this theme continued to be heard until the late 1920s, they ceased to be the lyric of a national consensus. They served instead as a relentless monotone for those who feared threats against private property and its guardian, the Supreme Court.[44]

So much for a leitmotif that changed relatively little over a long period of time. In contrast we can look to language, to the metaphors and images that have been most popular. Although their periodization cannot be pinned down precisely, a perceptible phasing has occurred and reveals much about constitutionalism in the United States. The most common way of referring to the Constitution—the oldest as well as the most enduring—is simply as an "instrument," often preceded by such modifiers as "written," "practical," "sacred," and "wonderful." We are thereby reminded of an earlier constitution, Oliver Cromwell's famous Instrument of Government (1653). That document did not last, however, nor did the word-concept ever achieve the salience in British public discourse that it has had in America. Benjamin Franklin invoked it in 1787 as the Convention came to a close. John Marshall and many of his successors employed it constantly in their opinions. Daniel Webster often used it in speeches, as have presidents, publicists, and scholars.[45]

During the second half of the nineteenth century another metaphor came into vogue, more vivid than instrument but also more ephemeral: the analogy to an anchor. In Jefferson's first inaugural (1801), he pointed to "the preservation of the general government in its whole constitutional vigor, as the sheet anchor of our peace at home," a formulation so logical in the age of sail that anti-Jeffersonian Federalists promptly adopted it.[46] Not until 1860, however, when Andrew Johnson announced that he would "stand by it [the Constitution] as the sheet anchor of the Government," did the allusion become both more specific and more frequent. One reason may have been Lord Macaulay's well-publicized sally, made to an American in 1857, that "your Constitution is all sail and no anchor." By 1876 Chief Justice Morrison Waite had appropriated and converted the image. "The Court," he proclaimed, "is now looked upon as the sheet anchor."[47] It recurred from time to time during the next half century, but essentially was supplanted by two others that gained even wider currency.

The first of these, the notion of a constitution as some sort of machine or engine, had its origins in Newtonian science. Enlightened philosophers, such as David Hume, liked to contemplate the world with all of its components as a great machine.[48] Perhaps it was inevitable, as politics came to be regarded as a science during the 1770s and '80s, that leading revolutionaries in the colonies would utilize the metaphor to suit their purposes. In 1774 Jefferson's *Summary View* mentioned "the great machine of government"; and in 1775 John Adams, writing as "Novanglus," described the British imperial constitution as a vast but broken mechanism: "the great machine will not go any longer without a new wheel. She [Britannia] will make this herself. We think she is making it of such materials and workmanship as will tear the whole machine to pieces." During the Convention held at Philadelphia in 1787, however, delegates referred to the "admirable mechanism of the English Constitution." It is scarcely surprising, therefore, that during the debates over ratification in 1787–88, Federalists and Anti-Federalists occasionally discussed the newly drafted Constitution in these terms.[49]

Over the next one hundred years such imagery did not disappear. But neither did it notably increase; and hardly anyone expressed apprehension about the adverse implications of employing mechanistic metaphors.[50] Occasionally an observer or enthusiast might call the Constitution "the best national machine that is now in existence" (1794); or, at the Golden Jubilee in 1839, John Quincy Adams could comment that "fifty years have passed away since the first impulse was given to the wheels of this political machine."[51]

James Fenimore Cooper uttered one of the few expressions of concern couched in this language between 1787 and 1887. "The boldest violations of the Constitution are daily proposed by politicians in this country," he observed in 1848, "but they do not produce the fruits which might be expected, because the nation is so accustomed to work in the harness it has placed on itself, that nothing seems seriously to arrest the movement of the great national car." Although his metaphors are ridiculously muddled, the message is clear enough. Exactly forty years later James Russell Lowell articulated this same apprehension much more cogently in an address to the Reform Club of New York. The pertinent passage marks the apogee of the metaphor, and remains today as profound a warning as it was in 1888.

After our Constitution got fairly into working order it really seemed as if we had invented a machine that would go of itself, and this begot a faith in our luck which even the civil war itself but momentarily disturbed. Circumstances continued favorable, and our prosperity went on increasing. I admire the splendid complacency of my countrymen, and find something exhilarating and inspiring in it. We are a nation which has *struck ile* [sic], but we are also a nation that is sure the well will never run dry. And this confidence in our luck with the absorption in material interests, generated by unparalleled opportunity, has in some respects made us neglectful of our political duties.[52]

That statement epitomizes not merely the main historical theme of this book, but the homily that I hope to convey as well. Machine imagery lingered on for fifty years, casually used by legal scholars, journalists, civics textbooks, even great jurists like Holmes, and by Franklin D. Roosevelt in his first inaugural address.[53] On occasion, during the 1920s and '30s especially, conservatives would declare that the apparatus, being more than adequate, should not be tampered with, whereas reformers insisted that "the machinery of government under which we live is hopelessly antiquated" (a word they loved) and therefore "should be overhauled."[54]

In the quarter century that followed Lowell's 1888 lament, a cultural transition took place that leads us to the last of the major constitutional metaphors. We may exemplify it with brief extracts from three prominent justices: Holmes, who wrote in 1914 that "the provisions of the Constitution are not mathematical formulas ... they are organic living institutions"; Cardozo, who observed in 1925 that "a Constitution has an organic life"; and Frankfurter, who declared in 1951 that "the Constitution is an organism."[55]

Unlike the other analogies that have been discussed, which were not mutually exclusive, this shift was not merely deliberate but intellectually aggressive at times. The quarter century is punctuated by the declarations of two political scientists deeply involved in public affairs. At the close of the 1880s, A. Lawrence Lowell wrote that "a political system is not a mere machine which can be constructed on any desired plan. ... It is far more than this. It is an organism ... whose various parts act and react upon one another." In 1912, when Woodrow Wilson ran for the presidency, a key passage in his campaign statement, *The New Freedom,* elaborated upon Lowell's assertion. "The makers of our Federal Constitution," in Wilson's words, "constructed a government as they would have constructed an orrery,*—to display the laws of nature. Politics in their thought was a variety of mechanics. The Constitution was founded on the law of gravitation. The government was to exist and move by virtue of the efficacy of 'checks and balances.' "

Lowell and Wilson had obviously responded to the same current of cultural change; but they were not attempting to be intellectually trendy by explaining government in terms of evolutionary theory. The word-concept they both used in condemning a Newtonian notion of constitutionalism was "static." Wilson spelled out the implications: "Society is a living organism and must obey the laws of life, not of mechanics; it must develop. All that progressives ask or desire is permission—in an era when 'development,' 'evolution,' is the scientific word—to interpret the Constitution according to the Darwinian principle; all they ask is recognition of the fact that a nation is a living thing and not a machine."[56]

Between Lowell's formulation and Wilson's we find lesser lights illu-

*An apparatus for representing the motions and phases of the planets, satellites, etc., in the solar system; named after the Earl of Orrery (1676–1731), for whom it was first made.

minating the transition as well. In 1900, for example, a journalist and popularizer named Amos K. Fiske published a long essay in *The New York Times* entitled "The Constitution: An Organism Not a Mechanism." A few analysts casually mixed their metaphors, as when George Ticknor Curtis, writing early in the 1890s, mentioned the "necessity of organic laws to supply the machinery of the new government [after 1789]." Most writers were conditioned, however, to favor the metaphor that best matched their politics. Consequently conservatives who resisted change, like David Jayne Hill, accused Woodrow Wilson of being hostile to the Constitution as the founders envisioned it, whereas Progressives and advocates of constitutional flexibility tended to favor the Lowell-Wilson line of thought.[57]

Needless to say, Lowell did not introduce organicism to American constitutionalism *de novo*. The linkage did not even have to wait for Darwin's influence. Back in 1835 Tocqueville had called the U.S. Constitution "that body of organic laws," a label that appeared from time to time over the next half century. John C. Calhoun's *Disquisition on Government*, written late in the 1840s, used the word "organism" often but peculiarly. Occasionally Calhoun referred to government itself as an organism; but basically he had in mind the societal conditions that pre-existed the formation of a constitution.[58]

For half a century after 1889, when Lowell first published his revisionist assertion, "organic law" became a standard designation, though sometimes used interchangeably with "instrument."[59] It did not linger for so long on account of inertia, but because it served to rationalize particular psychological needs and partisan purposes. For strident nationalists, especially northerners and westerners, it helped to bolster the contention that the Union was older than the states, thereby repudiating doctrines of state sovereignty and secession. For advocates of American distinctiveness, it helped to validate the contention that "the absolutely unique feature of the political and legal institutions of the American Republic is its written Constitutions which are organic limitations." For those who feared a glut of constitutional amendments, and wished to maintain a sharp distinction between the fundamental law and legislative statutes, organic theory proved exceedingly useful.[60] During the 1930s, however, it became equally attractive to New Dealers who applied the evolutionary aspect of organic theory to reinforce their plea for adapting the Constitution in response to radically altered socio-economic conditions.[61]

. . .

My second example of a shift in American attitudes toward the Constitution exhibits a startling turnabout, which is uncommon in the history of political culture. Early in this century, J. Allen Smith, Charles A. Beard, and others offered the view that the Constitutional Convention of 1787, and its product, comprised nothing less than a conservative counterrevolution. They argued that republicanism had given way to oligarchy, a repudiation of the principles of 1776. With some modifications, that view has been widely shared or taken seriously ever since.[62] Throughout the nineteenth century, however, with the exception of a group of radical abolitionists, very different perceptions obtained and we find little precedent for the Progressives' insistence upon a counterrevolution in 1787.

Young Daniel Webster gave an oration on July 4, 1800, at Hanover, New Hampshire. Ratification and implementation of the Constitution, he declared, "shall stand on the catalogue of American anniversaries—second to none but the birthday of [our] Independence!" Throughout the century, in fact, Fourth of July orators were just as likely to discuss the Constitution as the Declaration of Independence; and the reverse was equally true. At the time of the Centennial celebration in September 1887, notables like James G. Blaine and the governor of Pennsylvania matter-of-factly mentioned that "next to the Declaration of Independence the ordaining of the Constitution is the great event to be celebrated for all time by the American people."[63]

Not everyone agreed. Henry Cabot Lodge considered the formation of the Constitution "the most momentous event in the history of the American people," and others concurred. Almost no one, however, perceived the political or ideological meaning of 1787 as being antithetical to that of 1776. John Quincy Adams epitomized the view that predominated from the 1790s until the first years of this century. The American Revolution "was a work of thirteen years," he explained, incomplete until 1787. "The Declaration of Independence and the Constitution of the United States, are parts of one consistent whole, founded upon one and the same theory of government." Some nineteenth-century observers went so far as to insist that the *real* revolution took place in the years 1787–89. It was not unusual for engravings and lithographs honoring the Fourth of July to feature such phrases as "CONSTITUTION & LAWS" in bold letters (see figure 12).[64] Whether the nineteenth-century view was historically correct is not at issue here. (Modern scholarship has demonstrated that the ideological relationship between 1776 and 1787 is extremely complex.) The point is simply that a striking change took place. For more than a century, the Constitution was regarded as a fulfillment of the Revolution rather than a repudiation or modification of its ideals.

My third illustration of flux and ambiguity in American feelings about the Constitution is unlike the first two. Many interested observers note that there has been a "cult of the Constitution" in the United States; yet there is little agreement on how it originated or when the phenomenon was most intensely felt. Looking back from the late nineteenth century, it appeared that Constitution worship had begun immediately in 1789. But compared with the years 1875 to 1900, when Constitution worship was very strong indeed, overt criticism of the Constitution seems more common between 1788 and 1860 than after that date. The few scholars who have discussed this tendency have been unable to achieve any agreement about its dynamics through time. Following an exchange of letters on the subject in 1937, Max Farrand altered his description of the pre–Civil War era to read: "there was at least an admiration growing into veneration." Farrand fudged his case.[65]

The post–Civil War era is equally perplexing. One historian, writing in 1940, believed that the "cult of the Constitution" began in 1887 with the Centennial celebration. In 1876, however, when Hermann E. von Holst published the first of his eight volumes on *The Constitutional and Political History of the United States,* he entitled chapter 2 "The Worship of the Constitution, and Its Real Character." He found that Americans had initially regarded their instrument of government as being best suited to their own needs, but then had gradually grown to regard it as "a masterpiece, applicable to every country." Von Holst also complained that blind veneration for the Constitution prevented Americans from achieving a realistic understanding of their government.[66]

In 1889, just when national chauvinism went soaring toward its peak, public criticism came from persons who were dispassionate neither because of foreign birth nor on account of radical politics. A. Lawrence Lowell of Harvard declared that

> For a long time the Constitution of the United States was the object of what has been called a fetish worship; that is, it was regarded as something peculiarly sacred, and received an unquestioned homage for reasons quite apart from any virtues of its own. The Constitution was to us what a king has often been to other nations. It was the symbol and pledge of our national existence, and the only object on

which the people could expend their new-born loyalty. Let us hope that such a feeling will never die out, for it is a purifying and enno-bling one; but to-day our national union is so fully accomplished, that we need no symbol or pledge to assure us of the fact.[67]

By 1914, Professor Evarts B. Greene of Columbia could observe that "the men of this generation are less in need than their fathers were of being cautioned against the worship of the Constitution." Six years later, following repeated waves of criticism by Charles Beard, J. Allen Smith, Gustavus Myers, and others, a leading authority proclaimed that "worship of the Constitution is at an end!" If we only read what liberals wrote, this sounds like a reasonable assessment. One Progressive reformer, looking back from 1925 to the first years of the twentieth century, explained that as a youth he had "cherished . . . the marvellous prevision of the makers of the Constitution." Practical experience as a state legislator, however, had disillusioned him. "Business men and bosses showed no respect for the Constitution that I had been taught to revere. It had no sanctity in their eyes." Consequently, he confessed, "my text-book government had to be discarded; my worship of the Constitution scrapped."[68]

Nevertheless, by the early 1920s Constitution worship not only re-turned, it became more pervasive than it had been in any of its earlier phases. As one skeptic wrote in 1924: the Constitution "has been sub-jected to every possible patriotic exaggeration and antic. . . . According to the lights of Constitution worship you are no less a Red if you seek change through the very channels which the Constitution itself provides."[69] By 1924 a higher morality had blossomed. Arch-nationalists borrowed a phrase from George Grote, the British historian, and "constitutional mo-rality" became popular buzz-words for more than a decade. The founding generation had that morality in abundance. Whether Americans still did was at issue.

III

A distinction between American perceptions of the Constitution and actual knowledge of it must not be insisted upon too categorically. In discussing attitudes, I have already alluded to some aspects of understanding and ig-norance. Others remain, however, and they are best reviewed under a sep-arate rubric. Three elements seem especially important: the Constitution's treatment in American education; the question of how information about the Constitution filters down to laymen; and finally the nexus between the Constitution, the Supreme Court, and the media. Confidentiality, accessibility, and public communication have been important problems in the cultural history of the U.S. Constitution and for its custodians on the Court. To my way of thinking, a case can be made that Americans have known the Constitution best when they have revered it least, and that idolatry has too often served as a convenient cover for ignorance. Realism rather than mindless reverence has been the strongest bulwark of constitutional liberty in the United States.

The Constitution is too often neglected or poorly taught in American schools. Textbooks have tended to be unclear, superficial, inconsistent, and inaccurate. Take as an example *The Child's History of the United States from the Earliest Time to the Present Day,* by one Charles Morris, Ll.D. (Philadelphia, 1900). The author devoted a little over four pages (out of 254) to the Constitutional Convention and system of government that it created. Looking only at sins of commission (because those of omission and emphasis might be considered unfair to a child's history), we find John Adams and Thomas Jefferson active at the Convention when, in fact, they were serving in 1787 as our ministers to Great Britain and France, respectively. We also learn that the famous rising sun, utilized by Benjamin Franklin on the Convention's final day as a symbol of the new nation, was painted on a wall rather than (in fact) above the splat on George Washington's Chippendale chair. And strangest of all, we get a picture of Carpenters' Hall, where, we are told, the Convention met. Most people have at least heard of Independence Hall, but not Mr. Morris. His editor and publisher didn't blink an eye, apparently. One wonders whether they read the text? One hopes that few American schoolchildren did.

It would be comforting to find that such petty (yet glaring) gaffes get cleared up when we cast our gaze above the level of history and civics books for kids; but that has not been the case. Much too often we read about "the happy constitution of 1789" (Edward Everett) or even the "Philadelphia Convention in 1789" (John A. Garraty).[70] When the portly Ben Perley Poore produced his massive edition of *The Federal and State Constitutions* in 1877, he explained in a covering letter to Senator Henry B. Anthony that "numerous editions of different compilations of 'The American Constitutions' have been published by private enterprise, many of them containing important errors. In two instances constitutions were published which had not been adopted by the States to which they were assigned, and there were often grave mistakes in copying."[71]

A decade later jurists and politicians were scandalized to discover that

Daniel Webster had once misquoted the Constitution in an important speech to the Senate. "It seems incredible," wrote a Boston judge, "that Webster could have made a mistake as to the provisions of the Constitution, incredible that he should have wilfully made a misquotation. . . ." To cite just one additional example, John Fiske's *The Critical Period of American History, 1783–1789* (1888) is probably the most widely read book ever published on the formation of the U.S. Constitution. Students at several levels read it for decades, and Fiske's argument that the Constitution resolved a grave national crisis remains viable despite numerous revisionist attacks upon it. In 1924, however, when James M. Beck was writing extensively about the Constitution, he reread Fiske's account of the Convention of 1787 and "was struck with the inaccuracies that it contained."[72] Given Fiske's fantastic impact as a popularizer, his sloppiness as a synthesizer seems especially unfortunate.

Even more regrettable has been the reluctance of many American leaders to serve the public as constitutional educators. The tradition begins with Washington and Jefferson. The same man who in 1801 spoke so eloquently about "the text of civil instruction" stonewalled in 1820 when a correspondent sought his opinion about a recent publication on the Constitution. Jefferson's response is significant for several reasons: he knew more than most Americans about the complexities of constitutional interpretation; his passionate commitment in the years following his presidency was public education; but above all, his response anticipated that of many public officials for generations to come. "You ask for my opinion of the work you send me," he wrote, "and to let it go out to the public."

> This I have ever made a point of declining, (one or two instances only excepted). Complimentary thanks to writers who have sent me their works, have betrayed me sometimes before the public, without my consent having been asked. But I am far from presuming to direct the reading of my fellow citizens, who are good enough judges themselves of what is worthy their reading. I am, also, too desirous of quiet to place myself in the way of contention. Against this I am admonished by bodily decay, which cannot be unaccompanied by corresponding wane of the mind. . . . I hope our political bark will ride through all its dangers; but I can in future be but an inert passenger.

Jefferson remains an enigma on constitutional matters. Late in 1824, for instance, he sent Madison an interesting proposal for a basic textbook to be used by the law faculty at the University of Virginia. The syllabus included the Declaration of Independence, *The Federalist Papers*, and the Report of Virginia's legislature on the Alien and Sedition Acts (1798–99). The syllabus omitted the U.S. Constitution![73]

Madison's periodic abdication of his responsibility as constitutional educator involves a more complicated story. Many of his letters explicating constitutional issues, written during the twenty years after he left the White House, 1817–36, were either marked "private," or worse, were never even sent. He had several reasons. First, like Jefferson, he did not find it seemly to sway (or attempt to sway) public opinion from retirement. Second, his political sympathies did not always coincide with what he knew to be historically correct. And third, as he explained in 1821 to a friend who begged him to publish his invaluable notes on the Convention of 1787: the appearance of those copious notes "should be delayed till the Constitution should be well settled by practice and till a knowledge of the controversial part of the proceedings of its framers could be turned to no improper account."[74]

A century later public officials found other sorts of excuses, some of them partially valid, to rationalize restraint in their exercise of constitutional exegesis. To a degree the dilemma depended upon circular reasoning. Those people best qualified by experience and position to explicate the Constitution could not do so without undermining the integrity of their office. Even James M. Beck, who seems to have been outspoken, complained about his situation in 1924 to H. L. Mencken. "I am a public official, and this has prevented me from expressing some strong views that I have with reference to the last four Amendments to the Constitution. When I cease to be Solicitor General, I may again expand my book, and I hope then to be—as you are—a 'free lance' to say, in my last years of public service, some of the things that, as a public official, I am not at liberty now to say." Twelve years later, in a variation on that theme, one New Deal administrator decried "the state of advanced fetishism" in public attitudes toward the Supreme Court. He explained that during the spring of 1936, "a group of us here in Washington sought to organize a National Committee to educate the public on the Supreme Court–Constitutional-Amendment question. The efforts have fallen through, largely because every public figure we approached with a view to heading the committee felt it necessary to decline in order not to embarrass the Administration in the election campaign."[75]

To complicate matters further, the one institution whose members have both professional clout and a natural pulpit—the U.S. Supreme

Court—is caught in an awkward position and has, for most of American history, abjured the role of public educator. Some people may know how a constitutional issue has *arisen;* and they can learn the Court's *resolution* of the issue, but not the process by which those nine men (until 1981) reached that resolution. The reasons for confidentiality, and its necessity, have been explained many times; yet they do not prevent those who are hostile to a particular Court, or those committed to open decisions openly arrived at, from complaining bitterly. Jefferson made the most cynical and partisan case: the justices "consider themselves secure for life; they skulk from responsibility to public opinion. . . . An opinion is huddled up in conclave, perhaps by a majority of one, delivered as if unanimous, and with the silent acquiescence of lazy or timid associates, by a crafty chief judge, who sophisticates the law to his mind, by the turn of his own reasoning."[76]

In 1819 John Marshall stated that opinions should be written to "be understood by the public." He sought simplicity and clarity. Even though decisions have become more technical since Marshall's era, his successors have essentially shared the view that opinions speak for themselves. Many Americans still accept the argument that all the exegesis the Brethren are obliged to supply is contained within their decisions. Perhaps; but after Marshall and his colleague Story, out-of-Court illumination of the Constitution by Supreme Court justices dimmed. During the decades 1865–85 and 1920–40 it dwindled almost to nil. The Centennial generated some informative speeches in 1887–89; Justice Samuel Miller gave a few lectures; and at the turn of the century Justice David Brewer could be positively breezy in public talks—to the embarrassment of his colleagues.[77]

By the 1920s and '30s a tradition of tight-lipped discretion had developed. The behavior of Justice Willis Van Devanter is illustrative. In May 1937, when he announced that he would retire after twenty-six years on the Court, NBC and CBS separately invited him "to make an address to the country . . . relative to your long and colorful career on the Supreme Bench." He refused. Two months later, asked to serve as the guest speaker in Syracuse, New York, at Sesquicentennial festivities, he declined and offered vague excuses for doing so. He concluded his letter, however, with the wish that the celebration "will serve to quicken the general interest in the Constitution." Fine. A few months later Edgar Lee Masters asked Van Devanter for an interview that could be published in *The Saturday Evening Post,* "suited to popular taste," and subsequently reprinted as part of a book. "With little taste for publicity," the justice replied, "and a disinclination to interviews for publication, I fear that I would not prove to you to be a fertile or helpful subject."[78] This sort of behavior, part of a pattern that lasted for more than a century, did not help to enhance Americans' understanding of their Constitution.

For the past thirty years or so, out-of-Court commentary has become somewhat more frequent, yet remains guarded. Candor is not common. Caution is. The cloud of constitutional mystery has lifted a bit; but the resulting impact upon public knowledge is not easy to gauge. Members of the Court often blame the press for this unfortunate impasse—and the media respond with resentment. Earl Warren insisted, in the principal message of his memoirs, that "the judicial process as it functions in the Supreme Court is more open than that of either the legislative or executive branches of the government." Anthony Lewis, on the other hand, has declared that "in the Executive and in Congress the process of decision is at least partly, often substantially, open to view. . . . I feel sure that the process of decision in the Supreme Court is just as instructive and interesting as in the other branches. . . . But alas, all this is out of view." Lawrence M. Friedman, a distinguished constitutional historian at Stanford University's Law School, put it tersely in 1984: "The Court is a secretive institution."[79]

Friedman may exaggerate a bit, but the basic reality cannot be denied. Whenever the Court wears an inscrutable mask, for whatever reasons and to whatever degree, American perception of constitutional development becomes more problematic. One direct consequence hasn't been adequately appreciated: that many of our so-called landmark cases were not viewed as such by contemporaries. The decision in *Ex parte Milligan,* for example, which denied the President authority to bring persons to trial before military tribunals in areas where the civil courts remained functional, was announced on April 3, 1866. It had important implications and seemed a great blow to the Radical Republicans. Initially the press paid scant attention, however, and the public knew little about it. Not until mid-December did controversy begin. Similarly the Slaughterhouse cases of 1873 attracted slight interest outside of legal circles even though the justices regarded this as the Court's most important decision since Dred Scott in 1857. Predictability is, well, unpredictable. The Civil Rights cases of 1883 elicited hundreds of newspaper editorials and pervasive public reaction. The notorious decision in *Plessy* v. *Ferguson* (1896), on the other hand, aroused the barest indifference.[80] Hence my insistence that American constitutional history be regarded and written as much more than the running record of so-called major cases decided by the Supreme Court.

If we are to do so, moreover, it is necessary to notice the historical impact of technology and new developments in journalism, especially since the 1920s. When former Senator Albert J. Beveridge published "Common Sense and the Constitution" in *The Saturday Evening Post* in 1923, he reached millions of readers. As Beveridge explained to a friend, "I tried to deal in simple and 'popular' fashion with the Courts and Constitution." That same year a conservative organization known as Sentinels of the Republic wanted to enlist Charles Warren, the foremost authority in the United States on Supreme Court history, to participate in a debate via "the columns of the Baltimore Evening Sun," a debate answering "the anarchists with regard to the Supreme Court's jurisdiction over the constitutionality of legislation." Reformers soon pursued similar techniques in order to persuade the widest possible audience that their programs were constitutional.[81]

By 1927, partisans had begun to utilize the radio to get their message across. Four years later, for example, the National Security League, an avidly anti-communist organization, boasted that it was broadcasting "on all patriotic days of the year" and "twenty-four radios covering the entire country and every two weeks one national hook-up (Columbia Broadcasting System) of from forty to seventy stations covering the United States." By 1937 Paramount News had made a film about the Supreme Court and its justices, a film that Paramount's newsreel editor considered "the outstanding historical film of this year."[82]

IV

It may be helpful at this point to ask what has been the legacy of those tendencies and issues described thus far? If our query is: What's been the impact and Where do we stand? The essential answer is that we have developed substantial ambiguities in our constitutional tradition.

I would describe the basic pattern of American constitutionalism as one of *conflict within consensus.* At first glance, perhaps, we are more likely to notice the consensus. Observers remind us how swiftly the Federalists and Anti-Federalists reached common ground. Although their disagreements about particular policy issues grew, within five years of ratification so many of those who had vigorously opposed the Constitution in 1788 warmly affirmed it. Similarly, in the crisis of 1860–61, southerners proclaimed their loyalty to the Constitution and imitated it closely (with a few key exceptions) in preparing the Confederate Constitution. Throughout the Civil War, Democrats and Republicans in the North disagreed about many matters but vied with one another in expressing reverence for the Constitution. The Democrats may have been stricter constructionists, and may have bludgeoned Lincoln with constitutional criticisms; but their positions, though politically expedient, were not cynical. They were consistent with stances they had taken prior to 1861. Republicans similarly respected the Constitution, felt bound by its constraints, and followed them carefully.[83]

In 1889, however, John Bach McMaster called attention to a countervailing reality: "before the Government was two years old the people were dividing into two great parties—the loose constructionists and the strict constructionists; the men who believed in implied powers and the men who believed in reserved powers; the supporters of a vigorous national government and the supporters of State rights." James Madison had explicitly acknowledged that reality, and so, repeatedly, did Theodore Roosevelt and many others in the Progressive era. During the New Deal controversies a broad range of commentators, from journalists like Drew Pearson to jurists like Henry M. Bates, discussed the great issues of the day in terms of Hamilton and Marshall versus Jefferson and Madison. As Bates, the dean of Michigan's Law School, explained: "While my own judgment has been for a strong national government, I must say that I believe that when the Constitution was adopted it was the prevailing belief that the Madison view was a sound view and the view intended to be translated into the Constitution. I think that Marshall, by the lucidity and persuasiveness of his argument and his powerful personality, put over views which were not generally accepted at the time." Inclinations in the opposite direction were expressed by an attorney from Patchogue, New York: "There has been and probably always will be a marked difference of opinion among the American people as to just what the Constitution should be. As for myself, I am strongly in favor of the Madisonian view and believe that the Federal government should be only for and to the extent of the convenience and safety of the quasi-sovreign [sic] powers (the States). . . ."[84]

The volume of evidence is overwhelming that our constitutional conflicts have been consequential, and considerably more revealing than the consensual framework within which they operate. When Americans have been aware of the dynamic of conflict within consensus, most often they have regarded it as a normative pattern for a pluralistic polity. In the recent past, however, a few pundits have offered more acerbic explanations. Thurman W. Arnold, a New Deal administrator and subsequently a judge, wrote this passage in 1935, partly spoof but also partly truth.

The Constitution is praised in general as the great bulwark, even though there could be no possible agreement in the group which was praising it as to how that Constitution should reconcile their conflicting interests. The Supreme Court hovers over the whole picture, and it is to it that prayers are addressed. However, they are fearful prayers, because the group knows that there is never any certainty as to what the next decision will be. Yet in times of confusion and fear, there is nothing that so comforts the heart of timid men as a combination of prayer and denunciation. For this purpose the Constitution becomes for most conservatives the symbol of security in which all conflicting hopes and fears are somehow resolved.[85]

Much of the fuss during the mid-1930s, and hence Arnold's sarcasm, resulted from the Court's exercise of judicial review—yet another major development about which there has been no consensus. Indeed, here is one of our most curious constitutional dualisms. The process of judicial review has often been puffed as the most distinctive American contribution to the entire history of constitutionalism. Foreign jurists and visitors have regarded the Court's capacity to scrutinize both state and federal laws as the most singular feature of the U.S. Constitution.[86]

Nevertheless, it is not widely appreciated that the procedure and its supporting doctrine developed gradually, was used sparingly for almost a century, and has never lacked critics who were both harsh and astute: Presidents Jefferson, Monroe, Jackson, and Van Buren, for example; or Francis Lieber, a prominent authority on constitutionalism during the Civil War era, who regarded judicial review as an "intolerable nuisance"; or Republicans, both conservative and radical, in the years of Reconstruction, some of whom proposed the abolition of judicial review by congressional action; or prominent Progressives as different as Senators LaFollette and Borah; or wise judges like Learned Hand; or constitutional scholars like Henry Steele Commager, who wrote in 1943 that "judicial review has been a drag upon democracy"; not to mention many members of Congress during the decade following 1956.[87]

From 1789 until 1869 the Court invalidated only six acts of Congress. Between 1870 and 1873 it swiftly held four acts to be unconstitutional; but after 1890 the procedure began to be utilized far more frequently. Thereafter critics of the Supreme Court made "usurpation of power" a veritable cliché in public discourse; and the phrase remains a standard weapon in the arsenal of those who would attack the Court.[88] Controversy over the Dred Scott decision in 1857 gave rise to a distinction between judicial review and judicial supremacy: that is, should the Court serve as the ultimate arbiter of *all* questions requiring constitutional interpretation? By the 1930s scholars and jurists were carrying on lengthy discussions about the differences between judicial review and judicial supremacy, between variant conceptions of judicial review, and between "that which is politically anti-constitutional and that which is juridically *un*constitutional" (James M. Beck). By 1936–37 strong words were being exchanged as to whether the Court had "overextended" judicial review and whether judicial review should be preserved at all in view of what many critics perceived as abuses of the process.[89]

The ongoing dispute—it remains vigorous in the 1980s[90]—derives from the fact that the Constitution does not explicitly provide for judicial review, and the founders' intentions seem to have varied. The concept of a governmental action being considered unconstitutional certainly antedates 1787 in American thought. On the other hand, the state constitutions written during the Revolutionary War, which previewed so much that emerged at Philadelphia, did not clearly anticipate judicial review as we know it.[91] Therefore it has been possible for well-intentioned persons to disagree ever since. In 1936 Heywood Broun announced to his nationwide audience that "three times the original Constitutional Convention went on record [whatever that may mean] against the right of the Supreme Court to invalidate the acts of the national legislature." Justice Harlan Fiske Stone assessed the matter more dispassionately in a letter (marked "PRIVATE AND CONFIDENTIAL!!") written in 1939 after reading Corwin's *Court Over Constitution: A Study of Judicial Review as an Instrument of Popular Government* (1938). Stone's statement is so thoughtful as to justify a lengthy extract.

> To tell the truth, I have never been able to get greatly excited over the much discussed (of late) question of judicial review. We know very little of what the framers and those who set the wheels of our government in motion really thought about the matter. But they were intelligent men, and when one stops to think that they adopted the Judiciary Article, giving to the federal court jurisdiction of "cases" arising under the Constitution, and the 25th section of the Judiciary Act authorizing appeal from state courts on writ of error to the Supreme Court of the United States, it is difficult for me to believe that they did not expect some form of judicial review in cases involving constitutional questions. At any rate, the proceedings in the ratifying conventions seem to indicate that the participants in a

number of them understood it that way. The matter seems to be settled by long usage, and without it I think we would have to look
about for some substitute so far as holding the balance between the
rival claims of powers of the state and national governments.

There are, however, two matters which greatly interest me, relating to judicial review. Both of them you touch on in the early
chapters of your book. One is the exact effect of judicial review, both
technically and also in its practical influence on the processes of government. The recent public debate over the Court and its doings has
displayed an extraordinary ignorance of the precise effect of a judgment of the Supreme Court declaring a law unconstitutional. There
is lack of discrimination between the case where statutes are declared
unconstitutional "on their face" and cases where a statute is declared
to be unconstitutional in its application.[92]

The proponents of judicial review, from John Marshall to Earl Warren, have articulated positions that really are epitomized by Stone's.[93]
What remains clear and most pertinent to our discussion is that the long-
standing conflict over judicial review has usually been politically motivated. Jeffersonians attacked the Marshall Court; Whigs and Republicans
attacked the Taney Court; labor advocates attacked the Fuller, White, and
Taft courts; and conservatives attacked the Warren Court. By the later
1950s, however, when the last-mentioned reviling was well under way, a
reversal had occurred in the traditional alignment of those who condemned
and those who defended review by the Court. Customarily some sort of
regulatory or property issue had been at stake, which resulted in conservatives rationalizing a strong role for the federal judiciary. Following 1954,
issues concerning equality and justice became much more common. Given
the sympathies and activist propensity of the Warren Court, it then became the liberals' time to justify a strong role by the Supreme Court.[94]

That, in turn, calls our attention to a third aspect of American
constitutionalism about which there has been no consensus: the issue of
continuity versus discontinuity. The national mood at the time of the
Centennial (1887–89), for example, presumed that there had been development and progress within a broad context of political and constitutional
continuity, the Civil War to the contrary notwithstanding. A similar outlook prevailed in British constitutionalism at that time, despite the landmark shifts caused by the Reform Acts of 1832 and 1867.[95] National
sentiment during the Sesquicentennial, despite the Constitution's obvious
longevity, emphasized socio-economic change, the inevitability of govern-

mental adjustments, and therefore discontinuity. Although broad agreement did not exist, increasing numbers of people believed that conditions unforeseen by the founders required an adaptable fundamental law. Even the advocates of states' rights, for example, and there were many during the 1930s, acknowledged that the meaning and implications of their cause were quite different from the meaning of state sovereignty in antebellum times.[96]

There is yet another closely linked aspect of American constitutionalism about which there has been no consensus: namely, whether our frame of government was meant to be fairly unchanging or flexible. Commentators are quick to quote Justice Holmes's "theory of our Constitution. It is an experiment, as all life is an experiment." Although much less familiar, and less eloquent, more Americans have probably shared this sentiment, written in 1936 by an uncommon common man, the chief clerk in the Vermont Department of Highways: "I regard the Constitution as of too much value to be experimented with."[97]

The assumption that our Constitution is lapidary has a lineage that runs, among the justices, from Marshall and Taney to David J. Brewer and George Sutherland. It has been the dominant assumption for most of our history, and provided the basis for Walter Bagehot, Lord Bryce, and others to regard the U.S. Constitution as "rigid" by comparison with the British. The idea that adaptability was desirable emerged gradually during the mid-nineteenth century, appeared in some manuals aimed at a popular audience by the 1880s, and achieved added respectability in 1906 when Justice Henry Billings Brown spoke at a dinner in his honor. The Constitution, he said, "should be liberally interpreted—interpreted as if it were intended as the foundation of a great nation, and not merely a temporary expedient for the united action of thirteen small States. . . . Like all written Constitutions, there is an underlying danger in its inflexibility." For about a generation that outlook slowly gained adherents, until the two contradictory views were essentially counterpoised in strength by the 1930s.[98]

Meanwhile, a third position appeared during the early decades of the twentieth century—one that might be considered a compromise because it blended facets of the other two. This moderately conservative, evolutionary position was expressed in 1903 by James Ford Rhodes, a nationalistic businessman-turned-historian. The Constitution, in his mind, "is rigid in those matters which should not be submitted to the decision of a legislature or to a popular vote without checks which secure reflection and a chance for the sober second thought, [yet] it has proved flexible in its adaptation to the growth of the country." Justice William H. Moody wrote an opinion in 1908 that asserted an enduring quality of the Constitution: "its unchanging provisions are adaptable to the infinite variety of the changing conditions of our National life."[99]

All three perspectives on flexibility still have strong sponsors, thereby revealing once more a pattern of conflict within consensus. Reaching out to a broad lay audience in 1955, Earl Warren praised the Constitution because it had "demonstrated again and again its capacity for adaptation to the most challenging new conditions." During Potter Stewart's confirmation hearings, however, one senator asked whether he was a "creative judge" or one who would adhere to precedents; and whether the Constitution meant in 1959 just what it had meant in 1787.[100] When the Court becomes a contested institution in American political culture, public questions about one's understanding of the Constitution can be awkward to answer with a modicum of intellectual integrity.

V

Throughout most of American history traditionalists have tended to believe that the Constitution should change as little as possible. In Great Britain, where the unwritten constitution is in key respects a different sort of phenomenon, the situation has been variable. Sir Matthew Hale, for example, a seventeenth-century royalist, remarked that the common law had changed and that even Magna Carta had altered and amended earlier law. By and large, British conservatives as well as innovators acknowledge that significant constitutional changes have occurred over time. Between 1828 and 1969, thirty-three of the original thirty-seven clauses in Magna Carta were actually repealed as part of a general movement to simplify and clarify British law. Nevertheless, Magna Carta continues to be cherished despite its inescapable history of discontinuity. In 1831, during a debate over the Reform Bill, one Member of Parliament pointed out that back in 1215 Magna Carta itself had been "a great innovation." He then went on to ask: "had our forefathers been guided by the much-extolled maxim of 'let things alone,' where would have been our boasted constitution?"[101]

Comparisons between the long-established veneration of Magna Carta in Britain and Constitution worship in the United States can be instructive on several counts. Our pattern of conflict within consensus has curiously meant that each "side" in any given situation commonly pays lip service to the Constitution without really knowing very much about it. In certain respects, circumstances in Britain have been just the reverse. Critical moments in British political history suggest the absence, or at least the precariousness, of any constitutional consensus: think of the 1630s and '40s, the Glorious Revolution of 1688–89, the crisis of 1831–32, and the development of divergent interpretations, between the seventeenth century and the late nineteenth, of England's "ancient constitution." Yet within that tradition of conflict there has been a consensus concerning the centrality of Magna Carta. Both sides in any dispute are likely to invoke it, though neither one can claim an exclusive identification with the tradition. During the seventeenth century, for instance, although Magna Carta was more vital to radical political theory, royalists used it too, albeit cautiously. By the Augustan age, however, between the 1720s and 1750s, Tories were most likely to invoke Magna Carta against usurpations of power by the Whig Parliament. The likes of Swift, Defoe, and Bolingbroke referred to that "sacred Covenant" and to the "radiant Volume" of Magna Carta. The pendulum swung back during the age of the American Revolution, however, and once again Magna Carta became a rallying cry for radicals and liberal Whigs.[102]

At that point, however, the contrast between cultural constitutionalism in Britain and in the United States becomes less striking than the similarities. By the late 1760s and '70s, when Magna Carta was widely used as a political shibboleth by the followers of John Wilkes, "the charter had become totally divorced from its historical setting and it is doubtful whether half of those who referred to it had any personal knowledge of its contents; they merely read back into it whatever political maxim or precedent they required." If that sounds distressingly familiar, just listen to an anonymous pamphleteer explaining in 1765 the danger of such behavior: "*Liberty, Constitution, Magna Charta*, the *Revolution* are Words which, if they were less frequently founded, would probably be more strongly felt, and more duly revered." In 1810, once again, a defender of Parliament against radical attack voiced the suspicion that "persons talk of Magna Charta who have never read it."[103]

A British observer recently attempted an assessment of the symbolic significance of the Constitution in American political culture. "Lacking—by definition—that popular prehistory of kinship and custom from which to fashion an effective 'national consciousness,' an inclusive US nationalism could look no further back than the Constitution, before which there was, mythically, nothing but a wilderness and a latter-day project of Creation. Thus the founding texts of the US polity and the themes that cluster around them were internalized, in a kind of para-nationalist constitutional fetishism, as one of the true *longues durées* of American culture."[104] My objection to this condescending analysis, although acute in several respects, is simply that we have not been alone or peculiar in our "paranationalist constitutional fetishism." One finds comparable tendencies in Renaissance Florence and in Great Britain, to cite just two examples; and neither of those societies lacked the "popular prehistory of kinship and custom" that Mr. Mulhern finds wanting in the United States.

We have seen that partisans of all persuasions in Britain have been inclined to invoke Magna Carta and the constitution, even if that meant doing so in blithe ignorance. What happened in Renaissance Florence is even more bizarre. The Florentine constitution, about which panegyrics were written, underwent ten major revisions between 1378 and 1512. The Medici treated all constitutional bodies with disdain. Cosimo I detested the Florentine tradition of drafting constitutions, and crassly manipulated constitutions of the nearby Tuscan communes. Even the Florentine constitution of 1527, intended to be definitive, lasted only two years. Pietro Leopoldo treated the constitution of 1532 with contempt. One result of these tendencies was debilitating instability that lasted for several centuries, a fate the United States has not suffered.[105]

There are also, to be sure, similarities between cultural constitutionalism in the Florentine city-state, Great Britain, and the United States. Cynicism is a proper point of comparison. We *have* had politicians who reportedly quipped: "What's the Constitution between friends?" We've also had ordinary citizens whose attitude has been epitomized by that query.[106] Nevertheless, we have had less cynicism than many other societies and it has not been as blatant. Perhaps that partially helps to explain why we have also had less constitutional instability than Renaissance Florence, or France, or Germany, or the Latin American republics, to cite just a few of the most obvious examples.[107]

Admittedly, our strict constructionists have on occasion stretched the Constitution, as Jefferson did in 1803 to acquire the vast Louisiana Territory. Lincoln, Wilson, and FDR each stood accused of ignoring constitutional restraints; yet each one could honestly respond that, within the framework of a Constitution intended to be flexible in an emergency, his goal had been to preserve the Union, to win a war fought for noble goals, or to overcome the worst and most prolonged economic disaster in American history. In each instance their constitutional critics spoke out clearly, a national debate took place, and clarification of our constitutional values occurred. Sometimes that clarification has come from the Supreme

Court; sometimes from a presidential election campaign; sometimes from a combination of the two; and sometimes by means of political compromise. Each mode of resolution is a necessary part of our democratic system. I am led to conclude that Americans have been more likely to read and understand their Constitution when it has been controversial, or when some group contended that it had been misused, than in those calmer moments when it has been widely venerated as an instrument for all time.

Progress in history is rarely easy, however, and veneration has often become most intense as part of the process whereby controversies are resolved and issues reconciled. To take merely one example, here is Thurman Arnold's sardonic description of the outlook shared by many Americans during the mid-1930s:

> The Constitution became for them a sort of abracadabra which would cure all disease. Copies of the Constitution, bound together with the Declaration of Independence and Lincoln's Gettysburg Address, were distributed in cigar stores; essays on the Constitution were written by high-school students; incomprehensible speeches on the Constitution were made from every public platform to reverent audiences which knew approximately as much about the history and dialectic of that document as the masses in the Middle Ages knew about the Bible—in those days when people were not permitted to read the Bible. The American Liberty League was dedicated to Constitution worship. Like the Bible, the Constitution became the altar whenever our best people met together for tearful solemn purposes, regardless of the kind of organization. Teachers in many states were compelled to swear to support the Constitution. No attempt was made to attach a particular meaning to this phrase, yet people thought that it had deep and mystical significance, and that the saying of the oath constituted a charm against evil spirits. The opponents of such oaths became equally excited, and equally theological about the great harm the ceremony might do.[108]

Arnold's is not an edifying condemnation, and only slightly exaggerated. It describes a process that we seem to undergo periodically, but from which we manage to emerge whole. Not necessarily wiser, nor destined never again to repeat the same silly performance; yet with our polity intact and our constitutional system more clearly defined than it had been prior to the crisis. That is a form of progress—the methodical but democratic progress of a tortoise rather than the bounding, hasty motion of a hare. When the tortoise gets upended, he flails, looks ridiculous, and must struggle to get foursquare back on his feet. After he does so, however, he is stable once again and moves ahead steadily, more determined to avoid, if at all possible, whatever caused that previous upheaval. The crises that cause upsets seem to be part of a slow learning process, and that too has been a perdurable quality of constitutionalism in American culture.

PART ONE

THE MOST WONDERFUL INSTRUMENT EVER DRAWN BY THE HAND OF MAN

"In travelling through various parts of the United States, I find fields a few years ago waste and uncultivated filled with inhabitants and covered with harvests, new habitations reared, contentment in every face, plenty on every board; confidence is restored and every man is safe under his own vine and fig tree, and there is none to make him afraid. To produce this effect was the intent of the Constitution, and it has succeeded."

CONGRESSMAN RICHARD BLAND LEE (1794)

"It is a lamentable fact, that the Constitution of the United States . . . has not yet had a general circulation. I hope it may be introduced into our schools, academies, and all our seminaries of learning, and studied to be understood."

SENATOR SIDNEY BREESE (1847)

CHAPTER 2

To Make the Constitution a Practical System

ON SEPTEMBER 18, 1787, THE DAY AFTER THE Convention adjourned, George Washington mailed to the Marquis de Lafayette one of the first five hundred printed copies of the Constitution. "It is now a Child of fortune," Washington wrote wistfully, "to be fostered by some and buffeted by others. what will be the General opinion on, or the reception of it, is not for me to decide, nor shall I say any thing for or against it: if it be good I suppose it will work its way good; if bad, it will recoil on the Framers."[1] His tone was understandably apprehensive yet resigned. An intense summer had been invested in preparing the instrument, and those who participated held strong feelings about inadequacies of the current government under the Articles of Confederation.

How did other Americans feel? Not surprisingly, no matter what level of society we examine, conflicting impulses seem to surface. After all, hadn't Aristotle, more than two thousand years earlier, observed that "there is quite as much trouble in the reformation of an old constitution as in the establishment of a new one, just as to unlearn is as hard as to learn"?[2]

John Adams expressed various reservations late in 1787, though fewer than Jefferson, who remarked from Paris that "all the good of this new constitution might have been couched in three or four new articles to be added to the good, old, and venerable fabrick. . . ." While Adams then went through a skeptical phase and viewed the new government as an experiment likely to fail, Jefferson hailed the new Constitution in 1789 as "unquestionably the wisest ever yet presented to men." By 1797 Adams also held a more exalted opinion of it; but in 1813, with both men retired from public life, each felt reconciled to a cordial acceptance of fallible government. As Jefferson put it, "a constitution has been acquired which, tho neither of us think perfect, yet both consider as competent to render our fellow-citizens the happiest and the securest on whom the sun has ever shone. If we do not think exactly alike as to it's imperfections, it matters little to our country. . . ."[3] From vacillation to admiration to serene acquiescence in twenty-five years.

When we shift to the level of less illustrious men, we still find an element of vacillation or outright reversal of anticipated positions—a tendency that alarmed contemporaries. Cyrus Griffin, president of the Continental Congress, wrote to a Pennsylvania delegate early in 1788 that "the proposed Constitution now stands upon a firm basis." Griffin listed the states he expected would ratify, mentioned men who "are relinquishing their opposition; but what to us is very extraordinary and unexpected, we are told that Mr. George Mason has declared himself so great an enemy to the constitution that he will heartily join Mr. [Patrick] Henry and others in promoting a Southern Confederacy—alas! how inconstant is the mind of man."[4]

Would the Constitution be approved? Which state would enjoy the prestige, and with it perhaps the influence, of being the ninth (and hence decisive) one to ratify? Many men wanted to support the Constitution but on account of their genuine integrity sought more information and a firmer basis for joining the Federalist side. Rumors of discontent, even conspiratorial plots, ran rampant. As Samuel Tenney, a physician and judge, explained convolutedly to Nicholas Gilman, member of the Convention from New Hampshire and later a congressman and senator:

> Some of our Patriots (I mean Antifederalists, for they possess all the patriotism there is left in the country) would have us believe that the current of opinions, not only in N. York but in Maryland, Virginia & the Carolinas, is much against the constitution; which those of us, who favor the *infernal plot*, laid by you & your confederates in the grand convention to subvert the liberties of the country, are very unwilling to believe. They also inform us that Pennsylvania is all in a ferment—& that this will terminate in a new state convention, which will undo the transactions of the first. If you can communicate any information which will tend to strengthen my faith in the success of

the Constitution, upon which I believe our political salvation entirely depends, you will oblige me by doing it.[5]

The elaborate "Federal Procession" that took place in Philadelphia on July 4, 1788, combined homage to the new government with a pro-Constitution public relations campaign. "The triumphal car was truly sublime," wrote Benjamin Rush. "The Constitution was carried by a great law-officer [Chief Justice Thomas McKean of Pennsylvania], to denote the elevation of the government and of law and justice above everything else in the United States. . . . I do not believe that the Constitution was the offspring of inspiration, but I am as perfectly satisfied that the Union of the States, in its *form* and *adoption,* is as much the work of a Divine Providence as any of the miracles recorded in the Old and New Testament were the effects of a divine power."[6]

A Quaker merchant from Bristol, Pennsylvania, happened to be in Philadelphia with members of his family on July 4. Their letters back to friends in Bristol catch much of the contemporary mood, a mixture of euphoria and anxiety. "I unite with thee," Thomasine Clifford commented, "in earnest desires that our new Constitution may be attended with happy effects but I fear the Heart will not be changed[.] if the smallest Dore is left open for Tyran'y and oppression we shall feel its weight." Anna Clifford told her sister-in-law that whether or not the new "union is to produce happiness or misery[,] the pageantry of the day will not soon be forgotten, it was altogether a most magnificent shew, superior several English gentlemen have said to any thing of the kind they ever saw in Europe." These Quakers took pride in the pomp and circumstance of the occasion.[7]

The Constitution became an object of intense popular concern at the very outset—in part because it had to be ratified by specially elected conventions, rather than by the existing state legislatures, and in part because debates aroused by the ratification controversy stimulated broad interest in constitutional issues. Both Hamilton and Madison insisted that the people themselves "spoke" by means of the ratification process. Madison featured this point emphatically in *Federalist* Number 39. Others among their contemporaries made the same assertion, including James Wilson of Pennsylvania, a major contributor and early commentator upon the Constitution, and John Marshall.

What remained ambiguous from the beginning, however, was whether the states individually (as states) or whether the entire people of the United States had affirmed the Constitution. So far as Madison was concerned, according to Garry Wills, sovereignty was divided on a state by state basis, and not simply retained in "the whole body of the people" in order to remedy grievances. Although Madison said various things at various times, the argument that the Constitution had been a grant from the people of the several states, and not from the people of the United States taken in the aggregate, gained ground among many northerners as well as southerners during the antebellum period. Henry Baldwin of Pennsylvania, appointed to the Supreme Court by Andrew Jackson, argued this position forcefully in 1837.[8]

There is an important line of interpretation that has been reiterated in each generation during the past century. Von Holst said it in 1876, Woodrow Wilson later on, and most recently Lance Banning: "The quick apotheosis of the American Constitution was a phenomenon without parallel in the western world. Nowhere has fundamental constitutional change been accepted with so much ease. Nowhere have so many fierce opponents of the constitutional revision been so quickly transformed into an opposition that claimed to be more loyal than the government itself." This argument is forcefully made, and is bolstered by strong evidence. "Whatever might have been the opinions entertained in forming the Constitution," Madison wrote in 1821, "it was the duty of all to support it in its true meaning as understood *by the Nation* at the time of its ratification."[9]

After examining diverse sources, however, my own conclusions are somewhat different. In the preceding chapter I suggested that the cult of the Constitution did not arise as early, nor so pervasively, as scholars have believed.[10] Similarly, I do not see a strong constitutional consensus emerging almost from the start. Instead I find complaints about disloyalty to the Constitution (in 1793, for example), and expressions of hostility verging upon denunciation. Here is a sample taken from a letter written by John Sergeant, a Federalist member of Pennsylvania's lower house.

> We have had a very interesting debate upon the resolution for altering [amending] the Constitution of the United States. . . . In the course of it there has been a great deal of zeal manifested on both sides and occasionally considerable heat. . . . I confess to you I felt alarmed and offended too when I heard the whole constitution denounced, and a decided hostility to it boldly avowed. [Democrat Michael] Leib called it an *affair* of compromise, the work of a secret

[?], produced amidst distractions and distresses artificially created for the purpose of introducing monarchy &c.[11]

In 1811, Senator William H. Crawford, a Democrat from Georgia, complained that too many people, including politicians and judges, regarded the Constitution as perfect. Three years later the Federalist Noah Webster lamented that it was a naïve and excessively democratic document. Two years after that Thomas Jefferson, still the symbolic leader of the Democratic Republicans, remarked disparagingly that "some men look at constitutions with sanctimonious reverence, and deem them like the ark of the covenant, too sacred to be touched."[12]

In 1823–24, when pro-slavery advocates in South Carolina felt that an opinion rendered by the U.S. Attorney General (who happened to be a southern nationalist and an authority on the Constitution) was invidious to their interests, the governor and state senators defied the Attorney General and declared that "the supreme and permanent law of nature" stood above any constitution. Within a generation William Lloyd Garrison and his disciples would offer similar reasons in order to justify quite the opposite point of view about the legitimacy of slavery. In sum, the most extreme exponents of Negro inferiority as well as the most fanatical wing of the antislavery movement were both quite ready to reject or minimize the Constitution when it failed to valorize their contradictory positions.[13] A true constitutional consensus simply could not exist so long as human bondage remained the great national sore, open and festering.

During the first decade of the nineteenth century, moreover, sharp disagreements over the federal judiciary provoked intense partisan differences. The introduction of Jeffersonian bills pertaining to the judiciary caused Federalists in 1802 and 1803 to declare that "the Constitution has received a wound it cannot long survive." According to another Federalist, the Constitution had become a "mere old woman's story . . . its evanescent authority will soon be forgotten." One Washington journalist reported that even numerous Republicans doubted whether the judiciary bill of 1802 was constitutional; and an opposition journalist screamed that "the men who govern in these evil times . . . were never the friends of the National Constitution. . . ."[14]

The basic issue was explained by a New Hampshire surgeon serving his state as a representative: "whether Congress have a constitutional right to repeal an act under which judges are appointed, who are by the Constitution, to hold their offices during good behaviour. The leaders of the democratic party in our house took a bold position, and asserted that the

Judiciary is not a coordinate & paramount branch of our constitution, but subordinate & dependent." Shrill accusations, caused by genuine differences, continued for several more years; and in 1805, for example, moderates in Pennsylvania organized the Society of Constitutional Republicans in order to defend the federal and state constitutions. A widely shared apprehension assumed that all existing systems of government were highly vulnerable.[15]

I

Although historians and political scientists may have strained the evidence in claiming that a constitutional consensus emerged soon after 1789, it is notable that notions of constitutional legitimacy were present from the beginning, more than a quarter of a century, even, before John Marshall's Supreme Court first exercised the power of judicial review in a negative manner. On this point, at least, we do find a consensual framework within which fierce conflicts took place. Back in 1774 Samuel Adams had declared to Joseph Warren: "You know there is a charm in the word 'constitutional.' " In 1790 Virginia's assembly denounced federal assumption of state debts as being repugnant to the Constitution. Alexander Hamilton replied that Virginia's stance was "the first symptom of a spirit which must either be killed or kill the constitution of the United States." Throughout the next decade, both Jeffersonians and Federalists explicitly used the word "unconstitutional" in referring pejoratively to both domestic and foreign policy proposals. By the early years of the nineteenth century, partisans maligned their antagonists by proclaiming that they must be hostile to the Constitution. Federalists frequently declared themselves "the friends of the Constitution"; and in 1802 one disenchanted Republican hoped to form "a party of Constitutionalists."[16] Such phrases had become commonplace whenever people wanted to indicate their ideological persuasion or political affiliation.

There has been a tendency to assume, however, that almost from the start the Supreme Court came to be acknowledged by all as the ultimate arbiter of issues involving the determination of what is or is not constitutional. Following his visit in 1831, Tocqueville asserted that the Court had been "given higher standing than any known tribunal." He even headed the pertinent section of his chapter on "The Federal Constitution" with these words: "No other nation ever constituted so powerful a judiciary as the Americans."[17] Perhaps; but historical evidence from the period 1793 until 1835 (the year John Marshall died and Tocqueville published his first volume) hardly suggests consistent acquiescence in, or deference to, major decisions made by the Court. In *Chisholm* v. *Georgia* (1793), for example, the justices determined that a state *could* be sued by a citizen of another state. This caused such a furor that Georgia declined to accept the Chisholm decision. The next day Congress met and the Eleventh Amendment was enthusiastically proposed, thereby reversing the Court. The state legislatures swiftly approved it. Similarly, in 1816 Judge Spencer Roane of Virginia simply refused to execute the Supreme Court's decree in *Martin* v. *Hunter's Lessee.* Roane insisted that the Court had no authority to review decisions made by state courts because they were not part of the federal judiciary.[18]

Between 1815 and 1835, attacks on the Supreme Court erupted frequently. The states feared an extension of federal power in general, but more particularly the encroachment of federal authority over commerce, transportation, internal improvements, and chattel slavery. The nationalistic decision in *McCulloch* v. *Maryland* (1819), disallowing a state's right to tax the Second Bank of the United States, brought an outburst of nasty criticism and personal attacks upon John Marshall. Democratic Republicans, the party of Jefferson, Madison, and Monroe, cried in anguish that states' rights were being trampled. As one Mississippi newspaper put it in May 1819: "our privileges as a people have been of late so frittered away that we may as well inter at once the form of a Constitution, of which the spirit has been murdered." Strident language? Yes, but strong feelings had been stimulated. In 1823 and once again in 1824 members of Congress introduced several resolutions that would have required the concurrence of seven Supreme Court justices in any case concerning the validity of state *or* federal legislation. Opposition to judicial review ran high in these years.[19]

During this same period, the first third of the nineteenth century, several American presidents held notions of judicial review very much at odds with those of John Marshall and the Court. Two of the most prominent presidents did not even conceal their hostility to the Court. Their ideas were shared by many members of the party they headed. Jefferson's aggressiveness toward the Court continued throughout both of his administrations, fueled by Federalist attempts to control the judiciary, by Jefferson's unsuccessful attempt in 1804 to impeach Justice Samuel Chase, and by the titanic struggle between Jefferson and Marshall over the trial of Aaron Burr in 1807. As Marshall achieved the apogee of his strength and influence, Jefferson repeatedly insisted that the judiciary did not enjoy an exclusive right to interpret the Constitution. Accepting such a view would make the Constitution "a mere thing of wax in the hands of the judiciary, which they may twist and shape into any form they please." In Jefferson's opinion each branch of government "is truly independent of the others, and has an equal right to decide for itself what is the meaning of the constitution in the cases submitted to its action." In 1824, when John Cartwright sent Jefferson his new book on the English constitution, the sage of Monticello could not suppress his enthusiasm: "I was glad to find in your book a formal contradiction, at length, of the judiciary usurpation of legislative powers."[20]

James Madison vacillated, and over a span of four decades tacked his course respecting the Court's right to declare an act of Congress unconstitutional. Although Andrew Jackson strongly upheld the Union during South Carolina's confrontation over Nullification (1829–33), he often took a states' rights and strict constructionist position (see figures 4–5). We may never know whether Jackson really exclaimed defiantly, "John Marshall has made his decision, now let him enforce it"; but we do know that *Worcester* v. *Georgia* (1832) has been the only case in which a President flatly refused to carry out a verdict rendered by the Supreme Court. On July 4, 1834, Asher Robbins (a Whig senator from Rhode Island) delivered an angry oration that epitomized the views of some disaffected Democrats as well as those becoming known as Whigs. "The man we have made our President has made himself our despot, and the Constitution now lies a heap of ruins at his feet." A few lines later Robbins bellowed a blast that was characteristic of King Andrew's critics: "When the way to his object lies through the Constitution, the Constitution has not the strength of a cobweb to restrain him from breaking through it."[21]

One cumulative result of Jefferson's criticisms, of Jackson's hostility and that of their followers, was a crisis of confidence that began to deepen early in the 1820s and lingered for more than a decade. Speaking in 1821, Justice Joseph Story conveyed his anxiety to a local Massachusetts bar association. "We have lived to see this constitution, the great bond and bulwark of the Union, subjected to a minute and verbal criticism. . . . Attempts have been made . . . to cripple its general powers, by denying the means, when the end is required; to interpret a form of government, necessarily dealing in general expressions . . . instead of interpreting it as a constitution to regulate great national concerns. . . . Even its enumerated powers have been strained into a forced and unnatural posture, and tied down upon the uneasy bed of Procrustes."[22]

Six years later John Marshall lapsed into gloomy forebodings, initially because of devious maneuvering by the presidential candidates in 1827–28. As he said to Story, "I begin to fear that our constitution is not doomed to be so long lived as its real friends have hoped." Then, as Marshall's capacity to make the justices speak with a single voice waned, as he feared increasingly that American politicians and journalists lacked a sufficient commitment to constitutionalism, and as his wife's last illness and death blackened his mood into a somber depression, he wrote to Story in 1832 that "slowly and reluctantly [I yield] to the conviction that our Constitution cannot last. . . . The Union has been preserved thus far by miracles. I fear they cannot continue."[23]

By 1837, a relentless sequence of attacks upon the Supreme Court caused Story to doubt whether the institution could maintain "that strong hold of the public confidence" so essential to its role as custodian of the Constitution. He commented poignantly to Chancellor Kent of New York that he had "no hopes for the future" and a desperate sense "that all, which for twenty five years I have aided in building up, in the doctrines of constitutional law, are to be directly or indirectly overturned. . . ." Similar sentiments also began to be expressed at the same time about state constitutions.[24] Four decades after 1787, therefore, American constitutionalism remained a fragile fabric. One cannot say that a consensus existed about serious matters of constitutional interpretation. Many people, moreover, were eager for constitutional changes, offered most often in the name of "Reform."[25]

II

No issue involving constitutional interpretation during these decades was more delicate or persistent than the nature of the federal Union in general and the problem of state sovereignty in particular.[26] The first great flare-up occurred in 1798–99 when Federalists passed the Alien and Sedition Acts, a tale that has been told many times before. Republicans considered them despotic and unconstitutional. The state legislatures of Kentucky and Virginia then promulgated resolutions which had been drafted by Jefferson and Madison, respectively. The Kentucky Resolutions insisted that when the national government exercised powers not *specifically* delegated to it, each individual state "has an equal right to judge for itself" both what had been transgressed, if anything, and "the mode and measure of redress."

The Virginia Resolutions said that in such situations the states collectively "have the right and are in duty bound to interpose for arresting the progress of the evil." After several northern states explicitly repudiated these doctrines, Kentucky's legislature responded by declaring that the states were entitled to determine infractions of the Constitution, and "that a nullification of those sovereignties, of all unauthorized acts done under color of that instrument, is the rightful remedy." When federal courts up-held and administered the Alien and Sedition Acts, Jeffersonians firmly believed that the Constitution had been breached. Moreover, the Virginia and Kentucky Resolutions called upon the citizens of other states to join in "the most scrupulous fidelity to that Constitution, which is the pledge of mutual friendship, and the instrument of mutual happiness."[27]

Anti-Federalists had long feared that "the Constitution is meant to swallow all the State Constitutions by degrees"; and in 1792 Attorney General Edmund Randolph warned George Washington of an inevitable confrontation—"so crude is our judiciary system, so jealous are State Judges of their authority, so ambiguous is the language of the Constitution. . . ." John Marshall tried to clarify these ambiguities in a series of major decisions. In *Fletcher* v. *Peck* (1810), for example, he ruled that a state is "a member of the American union; and that union has a constitution the supremacy of which all acknowledge, and which imposes limits to the legislatures of the several states. . . ." In *Martin* v. *Hunter's Lessee* (1816), Justice Story held that state legislatures are bound by the paramount authority of the national government.[28]

Despite these landmark cases—perhaps, to some degree, because of them—the strength of state sovereignty sentiment grew between 1798 and 1832. In New England the staunchest Federalists shifted from a pro-Union stance in 1798–99 to an interpositionist stance during the War of 1812 (i.e., a state may challenge the constitutionality of a national law or executive action). In 1803, meanwhile, St. George Tucker published a five-volume edition of *Blackstone's Commentaries,* adding as a gloss his book-length essay in support of state sovereignty. Twenty years later John Taylor of Caroline brought out what became the southern Bible during antebellum times: a tract demanding dual sovereignty and decentralized government, preferring a truly federal to a national government, and ex-pressing fear of a judicial aristocracy (meaning an all-powerful Supreme Court). No wonder Henry Adams looked back to this period from the perspective of 1890 and concluded that political polarization had "left un-settled the disputed principles of government. No one could say with con-fidence what theory of the Constitution had prevailed."[29]

The much-discussed Nullification Crisis took place amid these murky circumstances, with each side claiming to be more constitutional than the other. In December 1827, Governor John Taylor of South Carolina asked his citizens to *"venerate the instrument"* and "hold fast to it as the rock of our safety." Speaking in 1830, Senator Robert Y. Hayne declared that "the Union which I revere . . . is founded on the Constitution of my country. It is a constitutional Union." To John C. Calhoun, who by 1828 became the principal theorist of the Nullification movement, the Constitution had been put together by autonomous states. The government they created was their agent, and the federal Union was composed of states rather than an ensemble of people. In a speech given at Fort Hill on July 26, 1831, Calhoun explained that "the object of a constitution is to *restrain the government, as that of laws* is to restrain *individuals."* Later in the same address he had harsh words for judicial review in general and for John Marshall's aggrandizement of the Supreme Court in particular. Calhoun condemned "the novel, the hazardous, and . . . fatal project of giving to the General Government the sole and final right of interpreting the Constitution;—thereby reversing the whole system, making that instrument the creature of its will."[30]

The best known version of the nationalist rebuttal was articulated by Daniel Webster on several occasions. Most useful for our purposes, perhaps, is a speech he delivered in the Senate on February 16, 1833, in response to one by Calhoun. Wordy as ever, Webster gave close linguistic attention to the difference between "Constitution" as a noun and "constitutional" used as an adjective preceding Calhoun's beloved word "compact." Webster relied upon a rhetorical flourish to inquire what Calhoun meant by "the term *constitutional"*:

He cannot open the book, and look upon our written frame of government, without seeing that it is called a *constitution.* This may well be appalling to him. It threatens his whole doctrine of compact, and its darling derivatives, nullification and secession, with instant confutation. Because, if he admits our instrument of government to be a *constitution,* then, for that very reason, it is not a compact between sovereigns; a constitution of government and a compact between sovereign powers being things essentially unlike in their very natures, and incapable of ever being the same. Yet the word *constitution* is on the very front of the instrument. He cannot overlook it. He seeks, therefore, to compromise the matter, and to sink all the substantial sense of the word, while he retains a resemblance of its sound. He introduces a new word of his own, viz. *compact,* as importing the principal idea, and designed to play the principal part, and degrades *constitution* into an insignificant, idle epithet, attached to *compact*. The whole then stands as a *"constitutional compact"*! And in this way he hopes to pass off a plausible gloss, as satisfying the words of the instrument. But he will find himself disappointed. Sir, I must say to the honorable gentleman, that, in our American political grammar, CONSTITUTION is a noun substantive; it imports a distinct and clear idea of itself; and it is not to lose its importance and dignity, it is not to be turned into a poor, ambiguous, senseless, unmeaning adjective, for the purpose of accommodating any new set of political notions. . . . By the Constitution, we mean, not a "constitutional compact," but, simply and directly, the Constitution, the fundamental law; and if there be one word in the language which the people of the United States understand, this is that word.[31]

Subsequently, in this address that must have lasted for several hours, Webster maintained:

1. That the Constitution of the United States is not a league, confederacy, or compact between the people of the several States in their sovereign capacities; but a government proper, founded on the adoption of the people, and creating direct relations between itself and individuals.

2. That no State authority has power to dissolve these relations; that nothing can dissolve them but revolution; and that, consequently, there can be no such thing as secession without revolution.

Later, just in case anyone had missed the message, he asked outright: "What is a *constitution?* Certainly not a league, compact or confederacy, but *a fundamental law."* And in conclusion, mixing irony with a touch of arrogance, Webster declared that he would hold South Carolina to "her own [Unionist] claims and pretensions" of 1789 and 1816.[32]

Numerous northerners either echoed Webster or else offered variations on his theme. The substance of their remarks is well known. What matters in this context is that the nation listened for more than four years to a sustained discussion of the most fundamental constitutional issues. James Fenimore Cooper, an ardent Unionist, wrote from Paris in 1830 that, "in the Constitution itself, the mode is pointed out by which that *Constitution can be altered,* a sufficient proof that each State surrendered its *principle* of sovereignty. . . . It is important to remember that no state was bound to accept this constitution, though it was determined that when nine did, the present Government should commence." In an *Oration* delivered on July 4, 1831, John Quincy Adams mocked "this hallucination of State sovereignty, identified with unlimited power, which blasted the Confederation [pre-1789] from its birth." Adams maintained categorically that the Constitution was "the supreme law of the land," and dismissed the possibility of "a power to nullify any act of the United States in Congress assembled. The people of no State were competent to grant such a power. The pretence to grant it would itself have been null and void—a violation of the Constitution of the United States."[33]

Tocqueville, whose visit to America occurred midway through the Nullification Crisis, left no doubt about his own view when in 1835 he published his chapter on "The Federal Constitution." He believed that the document rested upon an entirely new theory. Whereas local sovereignty had been retained in all previous confederations, the instrument designed in 1787 mandated "not only that the federal government should dictate the laws but that it should itself see to their execution." He concluded by noting an anomaly, however—a serious one in which the language of constitutionalism had not kept pace with realities. "Clearly here we have not a federal government but an incomplete national government. Hence a form of government has been found which is neither precisely national nor federal; but things have halted there, and the new word to express this new thing does not yet exist."[34]

Thus far the story seems fairly familiar. The dimension that has *not* been explored, however, may enhance our understanding of why the origins of American constitutionalism were misjudged by the Jacksonian generation and have been partially obscured by a cloud of confusion ever since. The 1828 "Exposition" of South Carolina's legislature was written anonymously by Vice President John C. Calhoun. It formally presented the doctrine of Nullification and ascribed its intellectual legitimacy and genesis to James Madison. When Daniel Webster rebutted Calhoun, however, he too cited Madison at length. Here, by way of illustration, is just one brief extract that Webster plucked from the father of the Constitution.[35] "While these states retained the power of making regulations of trade, they had the power to cherish such institutions. By adopting the present Constitution, they have thrown the exercise of this power into other hands."[36]

To make matters even more perplexing, during the famous Senate debate between Webster and Hayne in 1830, both men appropriated Madison's views to support their contradictory arguments about the constitutionality of the protective tariff! While Webster cited Madison's analysis, published in the *National Intelligencer* after the presidential election of 1828, Hayne referred to Madison's state sovereignty doctrine in the Virginia Resolution of 1798 and *Virginia Report* of 1800. Each man mailed a copy of his speech to Madison at Montpelier, his Virginia home, seeking the framer's approbation. In addition, Senator Edward Livingston of Louisiana, a transplanted New Yorker, also sent his speech, which mediated between the extremes of Webster and Hayne. Madison preferred that intermediate position, and sent Hayne a 4,000-word rebuttal, explaining that Hayne's error had "arisen from a failure to distinguish between . . . the right of *the parties* to the Constitution, and of a single *party*." Madison dispatched a version of this letter to Edward Everett, then a congressman as well as editor of *The North American Review*, which Everett published in October 1830. Meanwhile, Madison also wrote to Webster in order to explicate his complex and subtle analysis of governmental authority in America. Madison did, after all, believe in a system of divided sovereignty. Although he strongly opposed Nullification, and conceded as early as 1827 that nothing in the founders' intentions precluded a protective tariff, it scarcely pleased Madison to find himself in the same constitutional camp as Webster.[37]

What complicated this strange situation even more, and made Madison so hypersensitive to being misquoted or having his views manipulated, is that the Webster-Hayne battle came as a virtual reprise of a comparable contretemps within Virginia state politics during the later 1820s. As early as 1825, in fact, Madison's 1798 position on state sovereignty had been misused by Virginia politicians, who then did the very same thing in 1827 to Jefferson. Basically, Madison's proposed remedy against *unconstitutional* actions in 1798 (the Alien and Sedition Acts) was later invoked against tariff laws which he grudgingly believed to be constitutional, and against another set of laws, involving roads and canals, which he found desirable. In 1829 Governor Giles of Virginia recklessly distorted a statement about federalism that Jefferson had made in 1825, and attacked Madison for publishing letters to State Senator Cabell upholding the tariff on manufactures as being constitutional. Giles declared that he didn't care what Madison thought at the age of seventy-nine; he preferred to cite what Madison had said at fifty in his 1800 *Virginia Report*. Like Calhoun, moreover, Giles carefully excised those passages by Madison that excluded the notion of Nullification.[38]

By 1834–35, Madison had become a much stronger nationalist than advocates of state sovereignty in the South. He feared the consequences of

Nullification even more than he did Jackson's "abuses" of executive power. As he explained to one correspondent, with grave apprehension: "Nullification has the effect of putting powder under the Constitution and Union, and a match in the hand of every party to blow them up at pleasure." Six weeks later, in October 1834, Madison wrote his now famous political testament, a passionate plea for the Union called "Advice to My Country." When it was published in 1850, southerners were once again misquoting Madison on matters involving state sovereignty. Many of them insisted that the document must surely be fraudulent. It was not; but there is yet another interesting contrast to be drawn in this drama. Whereas Madison's final word was, above all, to preserve the Union, John C. Calhoun's last public utterance called for protection of the Constitution—as he understood it.[39]

III

The larger lesson to be learned from these episodes is that many prominent American politicians have been inconsistent on constitutional matters, large and small. Not only have they been inconsistent from one to the next, but many of them (even the best) have been inconsistent as individuals. James Madison is not the most flagrant example, but he is one of the most important because of his prestige as father of the Constitution. His unsettling experience of being misquoted, of passages from his writings being misused, made him understandably cautious rather than forceful during the critical decade from 1826 until 1836, when the legitimacy of his historical perspective might have dampened some of the noisier and most outrageous constitutional claims. Instead he wrote letters marked "private," not knowing which would have their contents leaked and which would not. With all due respect to the difficulty of his situation—awkward for several reasons—he did not play the role of constitutional educator that he might have. South Carolina hotheads would surely have ignored him, as would Virginia's conservatives. But the larger national audience might have gained a better purchase on the great issues of the day and acted accordingly in a culture where everyone proclaimed the power of public opinion.

Part of the problem, to be sure, lay in knotty circumstances beyond the control of Madison or any other single person. But part of the problem also lay in Madison's own ambivalence about various constitutional issues, and the fact that he did make contradictory utterances on different occasions. From the very outset, in 1787–88, he regarded the nature of the new Union as a blend of "federal" and "national" principles. As he wrote much later, in 1831, "it ought to have occurred [to those seeking constitutional clarification] that the Govt. of the U.S. being a novelty & a compound, had no technical terms or phrases appropriate to it; and that old terms were to be used in new senses explained by the context."[40] Madison and Tocqueville struck the same chord at the same moment.

Speaking in the Constitutional Convention on June 26, 1787, Madison commented that "in framing a system which we wish to last for ages, we shd. not lose sight of the changes which ages will produce." Nevertheless, he did not want subsequent conventions to be held or new constitutions to be considered. Nor did he really want constitutional issues to be appealed to the people; and he considered popular scrutiny of the Constitution, as an ongoing process, very unwise. He believed that any such process might be unsettling to public confidence and destabilizing to the polity.[41]

Madison did, on occasion, write confidential letters elucidating constitutional problems by recalling what the framers' intentions had been in 1787. He discussed the compromise that prohibited Congress from interfering with the slave trade until 1808, for example. He also discussed the propriety of congressional control over the territories, admitting that the matter was open to dispute and referring to his own "habit of guarded construction of Constl. powers." Some of these letters were circulated and read by persons other than their designated recipients. A few were published in ephemeral form during Madison's lifetime, and are referred to allusively as much as a generation later, suggesting that their contents were a matter of common knowledge.[42] It is impossible to ascertain what impact they may have had in general, however, or what they contributed to American perceptions of constitutionalism in particular. Although James Madison richly deserves his sobriquet as father of the Constitution, the perceived impact of his paternity remains enigmatic.

If Madison is enigmatic, then the appropriate word for Jefferson must be quixotic. First of all, despite their close and enduring friendship, despite the tendency to regard them in tandem because of the Kentucky and Virginia Resolutions, their constitutional views were different in key respects. Madison's partiality toward state sovereignty was more restrained than Jefferson's. The latter had a stronger inclination toward dual sovereignty than Madison, a greater mistrust of the federal judiciary (though Madison also engaged John Marshall in sharp conflict, especially between 1819 and 1821), and much more flexibility in contemplating constitutional change. Several of these differences are epitomized by a letter that Jefferson wrote to Robert Garnett in 1824.

> The best general key for the solution of questions of power between our governments, is the fact that "every foreign and federal power is given to the federal government, and to the States every power purely domestic." I recollect but one instance of control vested in the federal, over the State authorities, in a matter purely domestic, which is that of metallic tenders. The federal is, in truth, our foreign government, which department alone is taken from the sovereignty of the separate States. The real friends of the Constitution in its federal form, if they wish it to be immortal, should be attentive, by amendments, to make it keep pace with the advance of the age in science and experience.[43]

In 1803, when Jefferson had a chance to purchase the Louisiana Territory, his behavior was quixotic, pragmatic, or hypocritical—depending upon the outlook and passion for consistency of the beholder. He knew perfectly well that, as a strict constructionist, he was vulnerable to harsh charges of hypocrisy, even if he acted in the national interest. So he swallowed hard and warned members of his cabinet: "I infer that the less we say about constitutional difficulties the better; and that what is necessary for surmounting them must be don [sic] *sub silentio.*" Republican friends tried to help Jefferson rationalize or legitimize the purchase. Although he politely acknowledged the "force" of their observations, he remained unpersuaded. Consequently he called for an option with which he always felt comfortable: formally changing the Constitution.

> When an instrument admits two constructions, the one safe, the other dangerous, the one precise, the other indefinite, I prefer that which is safe and precise. I had rather ask an enlargement of power from the nation, where it is found necessary, than to assume it by a construction which would make our powers boundless. Our peculiar security is in the possession of a written Constitution. Let us not make it a blank paper by construction. . . . Let us go on then perfecting it, by adding, by way of amendment to the Constitution, those powers which time and trial show are still wanting.

Ultimately, however, Jefferson had to act swiftly or risk losing a superb opportunity. Time did not permit an amendment to precede and validate the purchase. He therefore used the necessary casuistry and said that he would be guided by the wishes of his party, particularly his inner circle. As we well know, he blinked away his scruples and bought Louisiana: "I confess, then, I think it important, in the present case, to set an example against broad construction, by appealing for new power to the people. If, however, our friends shall think differently, certainly I shall acquiesce with satisfaction; confiding, that the good sense of our country will correct the evil of construction when it shall produce ill effects."[44]

A similar and equally significant situation, though much less familiar, developed between 1817 and 1822 when President Monroe faced constitutional ambiguities in deciding whether Congress could properly legislate internal improvements, such as the National Road (Turnpike), or whether a constitutional amendment would be necessary in order to legitimize a nationwide system of improvements. When Monroe consulted Madison about possible precedents, the latter conceded that Jefferson had not paid much attention to the constitutionality of such matters.

> The Cumberland road having been a measure taken during the administration of Mr. Jefferson . . . I can not assign the ground assumed for it by Congress, or which produced his sanction. I suspect that the question of Constitutionality was but slightly if at all examined by [Congress] and that the Executive assent [Jefferson's] was doubtingly or hastily given. Having once become a law, and being a measure of singular utility, additional appropriations took place of course under the same administration, and with the accumulated impulse thence derived, were continued under the succeeding one [Madison's] with less of critical investigation perhaps than was due to the case. . . . As to the case of post roads & military roads, instead of implying a general power to make roads, the constitutionality of them must be tested by the bona fide object of the particular roads. The post [mail] can not travel, nor troops march without a road. If the necessary roads can not be found, they must of course be provided.
>
> Serious danger seems to be threatened to the genuine sense of the Constitution, not only by an unwarrantable latitude of construction, but by the use made of precedents which can not be supposed to have had in the view of their authors the bearing contended for. . . . Another and perhaps a greater danger is to be apprehended from the influence which the usefulness & popularity of measures may have on questions of their Constitutionality. It is difficult to conceive that any

thing short of that influence cd. have overcome the constitutional and other objections to the Bill on roads & canals which passed the 2 houses at the last session.[45]

The constitutionality of congressional appropriations for internal improvements continued to be sharply contested during the next two decades. Andrew Jackson's controversial veto of the Maysville Road in Kentucky (1830) is simply the most notorious illustration in a protracted series that cut across American political culture. Some figures, like Jackson and Madison, became increasingly cautious "in considering the authority as limited to the enumerated objects in the Const. which require money for carrying them into execution." Others, however, especially the Whigs, shared a view that was clearly conveyed in a letter to Henry Clay in 1833: "If the system of internal improvements could go on for a few years with vigor . . . this Union would be bound by ties stronger than all the Constitutions that human wisdom could devise."[46] Obviously, public discourse in antebellum America accommodated alike both casual allegiance and literal-minded adherence to the Constitution.

It became customary for American presidents to allude to the Constitution in some laudatory though general fashion in their inaugural addresses and annual messages to Congress. When the references became at all specific, rather than merely rhetorical, the speaker ordinarily viewed the Constitution as a source of restraint—a convenient rationale for compromising conflict because the Constitution itself had resulted from compromises.

- James Madison's first inaugural (1809): He intended "to support the Constitution, which is the cement of the Union, as well in its limitations as in its authorities."

- Martin Van Buren's inaugural (1837): "The principle that will govern me in the high duty to which my country calls me is a strict adherence to the letter and spirit of the Constitution as it was designed by those who framed it. Looking back to it as a sacred instrument carefully and not easily framed; remembering that it was throughout a work of concession and compromise."

- Franklin Pierce's inaugural (1853): "The great scheme of our constitutional liberty rests upon a proper distribution of power between the State and Federal authorities. . . . If the Federal Government will confine itself to the exercise of powers clearly granted by the Constitution, it can hardly happen that its action upon any question should endanger the institutions of the States or interfere with their right to manage matters strictly domestic according to the will of their own people."[47]

For more than sixty years the task of defining an ideal distribution of power between state and national levels of authority had been the most challenging aspect of American constitutionalism. Those who proposed an exquisite balance were likely to use the language of Newtonian physics: "The operations of the government are in no small degree mechanical; and the adjustment and balance of its powers are as much mechanical as the adjustment of the principles and powers of a machine."[48] Many other advocates, however, tended to be partial to a preponderance of either national or state sovereignty. There had not been agreement in the beginning, and conflicting points of view only intensified as midcentury approached.[49]

The Constitution had always been bound up with the Union in American minds, both as concept and reality. The two were commonly linked in catch phrases of public rhetoric, as "a sacred inheritance," for example. One finds the linkage in Madison's political testament, in the speeches of a Whig like Webster and the essays of an abolitionist such as Owen Lovejoy. During the prelude to the American Civil War this pattern appeared to continue, and did not differentiate southerners from northerners. When Jefferson Davis spoke at Boston in 1858, he declared that "we became a nation by the Constitution; whatever is national springs from the Constitution; and national and constitutional are convertible terms." In the mid- and later 1850s, southern leaders continued to proclaim their loyalty to the Constitution, and some even conceded that the Union had been defined by and incorporated into the Constitution.[50]

During the fifteen years before civil strife ruptured the nation, however, symptomatic shifts in public discourse provided clear signs that a delicate equilibrium in American constitutionalism was disintegrating. Back in 1835, for example, when Horace Binney, a member of Congress, delivered a eulogy for John Marshall before the Select and Common Councils of Philadelphia, he responded to recent sectional tensions and "seized the occasion to point to the Union, established by the Constitution, as the only ark of safety. . . ." The eulogy was intended to be an expression of the federal ideal; and Binney's exposition was formulaic for the 1820s, '30s, and '40s.[51]

As the extension of slavery into new territories became increasingly controversial, the founders' intentions regarding federal control over the territories became a primary basis for constitutional dispute. As a consequence the standard formulations of a generation past, such as Binney's, gave way to a bewildering variety of idiosyncratic and aggressive statements—from northerners as well as southerners. A politician like William H. Seward of New York, with abolitionist sympathies, could declaim that "the Constitution devotes the domain to union, to justice, to defence, to welfare and to liberty. . . . But there is a higher law than the Constitution, which regulates our authority over the domain. . . ." Others explained that the Constitution was man-made, whereas the Union had been God-made. Therefore they elevated it above the Constitution. On January 7, 1861, the ultimate dissonance of disintegration was sounded. Senator Robert Toombs of Georgia called the customary link between the Union and the Constitution "nonsense," explaining that union under the Constitution of 1787 had not been an adequate bond.[52]

IV

As early as the 1820s and '30s, a few farsighted and deeply committed people, like Marshall and Story, had expressed gloomy forebodings about the stability of the Union and the future of the Constitution. By the 1840s and '50s a broader cross section of the populace began to share those apprehensions. Some found solace, however, in a comparative perspective. In May 1848, for example, the lead essay in *The United States Magazine, and Democratic Review,* entitled "The United States Constitution," observed that for more than twenty-five years glowing letters from America about successful government and economic prosperity had been "republicanizing" Europe. Nevertheless, despite experiments with constitutionalism in numerous countries, the only successful republic had been created in the United States. After describing the varied interests and conflicts in a heterogeneous society, this anonymous author explained that "the chief element of cohesion, which has kept the federation together in its vigorous and rapid growth, has been the scrupulous adhesion of all parties to the constitution, whose extreme elasticity enables it to comprehend within its limits so many interests, diversified by circumstances of settlement and climate." The author added that compromise had been required for the genesis and preservation of "the glorious constitution," acknowledged the political significance of state sovereignty, and concluded by expressing contempt for the cynical "mode of sustaining written constitutions" in nations like

Mexico and France. "In other countries the world has been afforded the frequent example of a violated constitution and political disorganization verging upon anarchy, to gratify the ambition of party leaders and dynamic despots."[53]

A burst of national pride—the natural ebullience of youth! Given the author's emphasis upon the stability of our governmental system, it is all too tempting to look ahead to 1861 and smugly say that premature republican pride precedeth an immature fall. But that is too easy, too obvious, and doesn't tell us anything we didn't already know about the heady chauvinism of Young America. The more striking lesson, at least in our context, is that by 1848 this author had *some* basis in fact for his boasting; and that basis suggests that Americans may not have been quite so parochial and oblivious to foreign affairs as historians have tended to assume.

Many had heard something about the Mexican constitution of 1824, modelled partly on the American, which organized a federal republic. They also knew that the regime of Santa Ana had simply abolished that constitution in 1836 and replaced it with a centralized one more to Santa Ana's liking. The states of the former federal republic were transformed into military departments governed by political bosses hand-picked by the president.[54] There were also Americans who knew that in 1837 the new ruler of Hanover (within what would become Germany a generation later) had cynically abrogated the constitution that his predecessor had given to their subjects. And the failure of liberal constitutionalism in Germany after 1848 resulted in a gradual abandonment there of constitutional ideals by the middle classes.[55] Unlike Hanover, the United States survived the Nullification Crisis. Some accused Andrew Jackson of tyranny, to be sure, but a strong majority felt grateful that the Union had been saved on constitutional grounds. And unlike the abortive German Revolution of 1848, the failure of the Confederacy did not cause southerners to lose faith in constitutionalism as an ideal.

In Italy, Duke Pietro Leopoldo, having read the new constitutions of Virginia and Pennsylvania, decided in 1779 that Florence should have a written constitution. He asked his resident intellectual, Francesco Gianni, to write one. Filled with admiration for the republican spirit radiating from America, Gianni produced a final version in 1782. In 1787, after years of indecision and skepticism, Pietro Leopoldo put Gianni's Americanized draft in a drawer, forgotten forever. King Ferdinand of Naples in 1820 capitulated to intense pressure and granted a constitution that he repeatedly pledged to maintain. He soon abolished it. In 1821 a revolution in Piedmont led to demands for a constitution; but hostility from the Holy

Alliance prevented it. Austria then supported Charles Felix in annulling the constitution at Turin and imprisoning or executing leaders of the liberal constitutionalist movement.[56]

It is difficult, if not dangerous, to generalize about American reactions to constitutional developments in western Europe and Latin America from, say, the 1780s until the mid-nineteenth century. On the one hand, for example, there is evidence that Americans were quite intrigued by the Society for Constitutional Information that became active in England during the 1780s and '90s. On the other hand, there seems to have been far more interest by the French in new American constitutions written between 1776 and 1787 than American curiosity about the French constitution of 1791 and its successors. French constitutionalism was considerably more influential in the newly independent states of Latin America (1816–30) than in the United States.[57]

American inconsistency in these matters was neither peculiar nor distinctive, however. The enlightened French *philosophes* had been great admirers of the British constitution until 1789, when they sharply reversed their course and sought, in the words of Joseph Antoine Cerutti, "the glory of building a Constitution which makes the English in their turn our disciples and imitators." To advocate English ideas in France after 1789 would mean pleading for evolutionary change in a revolutionary situation. What had been the pattern of almost a century in French constitutionalism was suddenly doomed to swift defeat.[58]

It was characteristic of the Enlightenment mentality, especially in France, to assume that the character of a culture depended heavily upon its governmental frame.[59] The most active participants in designing the U.S. Constitution certainly shared this perspective. But they had also read the *Histories* of Polybius, and knew the passage in Book VI where he commented upon "the regular cycle of constitutional revolutions, and the natural order in which constitutions change, are transformed, and return again to their original stage. If a man have a clear grasp of these principles he may perhaps make a mistake as to the dates at which this or that will happen to a particular constitution; but he will rarely be entirely mistaken as to the stage of growth or decay at which it has arrived, or as to the point at which it will undergo some revolutionary change." Polybius derived his notions from reading the record of constitutional history in ancient Greece.

The American framers absorbed this dualistic blend of cultural relativism combined with theoretical universalism; and it affected their assumptions in ways as interesting as they are instructive. During the first generation after 1787, despite an understandable tone of chauvinism that often shone through, the essence of their basic assertion was that our Constitution happens to be the one best suited to our particular values. As Jefferson wrote: "Such indeed are the different circumstances, prejudices, and habits of different nations, that the constitution of no one would be reconcilable to any other in every point."[60]

With the passage of time, however, two developments occurred. The American republic survived, even flourished, and that seemed a sign that its governmental system was well adapted to its needs. In addition, foreign visitors tended to be impressed and said so publicly. That sort of reinforcement had a powerful psychological impact. Frances Wright, a perceptive young Scotswoman who visited the United States in 1819, observed two years later in her widely read book that "the establishment of the federal Constitution was an era in the history of man. It was an experiment never before made." That much wasn't new. Many Americans had been saying the same for thirty years. She then went on to make two observations that were more likely to emanate from a visitor. First, that in Europe the very concept of a constitution was vague and ill-defined. It meant different things to different people. In the United States, by comparison, "the Constitution is in the hands of all the people: they give it to their representatives, and say, 'There is your guide.'" She also remarked upon "one peculiar excellence in the American Constitution—that while an able statesman has it in his power to promote the public good he must ever find it difficult to work public mischief."[61]

Compliments like these, combined with political survival and prosperity, tended to make the next generation of Americans more than cultural relativists. Their Constitution was not merely different but superior; and they said so aggressively. Members of the Convention in 1787 had found much to admire in the British constitution even where they chose not to emulate inappropriate particulars. Frances Wright, despite her favorable view, did not even find it fruitful to compare the two. They were dissimilar, the products of divergent historical circumstances.[62] How different the attitude expressed by James Fenimore Cooper in 1831:

> It is necessary to remember that the fictions which have so long enshrouded the English Constitution have been rudely torn aside of late years. . . . It is quite evident that while a King can *make use* of a parliament he is all the stronger for it, but after a time the Parliament got the power, set aside the King and made a new Constitution. . . .

Suffering drove the English people to dissect the fallacies of their Constitution. . . . There is a violation of natural right in the English constitution which is fatal to the system in a nation so far advanced in intelligence—It could not have existed so long, had not the empire been as artificial as the Constitution, and had it not required extraordinary means to keep it together.[63]

The British constitution compared unfavorably with the American because it appeared both contrived and excessively changeable, even manipulable in the hands of ambitious, unscrupulous men. Stability and continuity characterized our Constitution; hence it seemed so clearly preferable. That became the widely shared wisdom of Cooper's generation. Needless to say, the Americans had also shrouded their "instrument" with fictions. Even as Cooper wrote, "King Andrew" Jackson was accused by the opposition of being just as despotic as any English monarch. In 1831 he tried to run roughshod over the state of Georgia. The next year he thumbed his nose at John Marshall and the Supreme Court's controversial decision in *Worcester* v. *Georgia.* That happened in March 1832. On December 10, 1832, however, Jackson's "Proclamation to the People of South Carolina" concerning Nullification indicated considerably more respect for the Court than he had shown nine months earlier.[64]

My emphasis here is not upon Jackson's apparent inconsistency, which has been skillfully discussed by his biographers and historians of that era. My point is that Americans had already acquired the capacity to view their Constitution with a vision that was occasionally clouded and frequently bifocal: bifocal in the sense that the Constitution as a cultural symbol, rationalized in various ways, could be seen on a separate plane—or literally through a discrete lens—from the Constitution as a "practical system." The development of that discrepancy between the applied Constitution and the symbolic constitution deserves detailed attention.

CHAPTER 3

All That Gives Us a National Character

EDWARD S. CORWIN PUBLISHED AN ESSAY IN 1936 entitled "The Constitution as Instrument and as Symbol" that swiftly became a scholarly classic. Significant for having alerted students of government and history to the dual role that the Constitution has played in American political culture, it remains fascinating because it is so resonant to major public issues of the mid-1930s. Corwin attacked the "rise of constitutional negativism" in general, and a conservative organization called the Liberty League in particular for its tendency to perceive the Constitution only in terms of constraints, and for the League's "fetishism" and unwillingness to accept the inevitability of change.[1]

Corwin's treatment of the genesis and development of the constitution as a national symbol was necessarily sketchy. No one subsequently has enlarged upon his cursory schematization, however. It is both logical and essential to do so here. It may be correct to contend, as Corwin did, that the U.S. Constitution emerged as a national symbol between 1789 and 1860; but that assertion only becomes meaningful and valid if we add that the process occurred both haltingly and incompletely in antebellum America.

I

"Constitution" as a word-concept first appeared in English literature during the sixteenth century, but seems to have been used primarily in discussing the human body and its condition. During the seventeenth and early eighteenth centuries, "constitution" emerged in Anglo-American usage as an important term in political discourse. In January 1776, writing in *Common Sense,* Thomas Paine developed his persuasive and influential prospect of dethroning a king followed by the coronation of a new constitution for America. Instead of actually using the word "constitution," however, he substituted "charter." Later that same year, the newly independent states prepared their own charters in response to a recommendation from the Continental Congress that the colonies assume governmental authority within their respective areas of jurisdiction. We call those charters "constitutions" even though Congress did not actually use the word. The point, therefore, is that constitution as a word-concept was embryonic between 1776 and 1787. The concept per se had existed for millennia, of course; but its particular application in the American context was not yet fully defined in the years between Independence and the creation of a new national government.[2]

If one asks what influence promulgation of the Constitution in 1787 had upon the governance of American organizations (public and private), the answer has to be ambiguous because the historical evidence is. Congregation Shearith Israel, for example, had been incorporated in New York City on June 4, 1784, soon after the state legislature enacted a statute providing for the legal incorporation of religious associations. Within a few years following 1787, most likely in 1790, the congregation drafted and adopted a document known as the Constitution and Bylaws of Congregation Shearith Israel. The form of this constitution, as well as its comparative brevity combined with the length of the bylaws, suggest an immediate intellectual impact by the new U.S. Constitution.[3] On the other hand, many organizations founded during the first half of the nineteenth century, such as the Historical Society of Pennsylvania (1824), acquired bylaws but not a constitution. The expectation that an association should have a constitution instead of or in addition to bylaws did not become normative until the second half of the nineteenth century.[4]

Why the idea should have been slow to take hold is not at all clear. Sources do suggest, though, that during the decade following the later 1820s, the notion became popular that developing and having a constitution was a sign of maturity or, in a symptomatic phrase, "the test and proclamation of our manhood." As Edward Everett observed in an 1828 oration: "The framers of our constitution established every thing on the pure natural basis of a uniform equality of the elective franchise. . . . Thus was completed the great revolutionary movement; thus was perfected that mature organization of a free system. . . ."[5]

Very gradually over the half century from about 1835 until 1885 the meaning of maturity developed into a more complex yet thoroughly chauvinistic understanding of constitutional origins in colonial America. Everett's formulation by 1836 was already well developed though not yet typical: "Our institutions, political, civil, and social, are not of yesterday; they are substantially two hundred years old. . . . In all things there has been a measured progress, and a slow ripening towards maturity. The federal constitution, and the constitutions of the states, which have most attracted the notice of Europe, are indeed the work of the last generation; but the great principles on which they are founded are coeval with the country."[6] This evolutionary emphasis became immensely popular during the final decades of the century. It will be discussed in detail when we reach chapter 6.

Just as the Constitution began to flourish as a symbol of political maturity, it simultaneously reached full flower in public consciousness as both the cause and the symbol of national prosperity. We have already touched upon this theme in chapter 1, and little more is required here. Evidence indicating the notion's pervasiveness in antebellum America is overwhelming. Democrats and Whigs, northerners and southerners, members of the Revolutionary generation as well as their successors all subscribed to it. We find a rather mindless version, virtually an article of faith, in one typical oration, "The Principle of the American Constitutions," given on July 4, 1826: "The greatest engine of moral power known to human affairs, is an organized, prosperous state." Our particular constitutions, state as well as national, creating sound, well-organized governments and implemented by virtuous republican people, made prosperity inevitable. Even such a sophisticated man as James Madison, writing his will in 1835, could not resist incorporating this conventional formulation, referring to the Constitution's favorable "effects during a trial of so many years on the prosperity of the people living under it. . . ." Madison, like the rest of his countrymen, had accepted this nexus as a given.[7]

American presidents from Washington to Lincoln all helped to nourish the Constitution as a national symbol by invoking it explicitly to justify various attitudes and actions. George Washington chose to issue his famous Farewell Address on September 17, 1796, nearly six months in advance of his actual retirement, in order to provide a noteworthy observance for the ninth anniversary of the completion and signing of the

Constitution. In a pragmatic moment he reminded the American people that "experience is the surest standard by which to test the real tendency of the existing constitution of a country." In a more mystical mood he expressed the hope that "the Constitution may be sacredly maintained."[8]

James Madison's eighth annual message, delivered in December 1816, served as his formal farewell to the nation. Not surprisingly he included a passage elaborating upon Washington's link between applied republicanism and the priceless product of 1787. For forty years the American people "have had experience of their present Constitution, the offspring of their undisturbed deliberations and of their free choice. . . . I shall read in the character of the American people, in their devotion to true liberty and to the Constitution which is its palladium, sure presages that the destined career of my country will exhibit a Government pursuing the public good as its sole object, and regulating its means by the great principles consecrated in its charter and by those moral principles to which they are so well allied." Nine years later, in his first inaugural address, John Quincy Adams sustained this congratulatory tone in a tribute to the American "social compact": "It has promoted the lasting welfare of that country so dear to us all; it has to an extent far beyond the ordinary lot of humanity secured the freedom and happiness of this people. We now receive it as a precious inheritance. . . ."[9]

In 1841, when President William Henry Harrison expired prematurely just one month after taking office, a death notice prepared by Daniel Webster and four others declared that "the last utterance of his lips expressed a fervent desire for the perpetuity of the Constitution and the preservation of its true principles." When Harrison's successor, John Tyler, became angry with Congress for proceeding with a bill he opposed, he protested "in the name of that Constitution which is not only my own shield of protection and defense, but that of every American citizen." Political adversity and frustration caused Tyler to make the Constitution an incantation. He warned against "the utter destruction of the checks and balances of the Constitution and the accumulating in the hands of the House of Representatives, or a bare majority of Congress for the time being, an uncontrolled and despotic power."[10]

Zachary Taylor's first annual message to Congress (1849) emphasized the constitutional injunction that one branch of government should not encroach upon another. Seven years later Franklin Pierce found himself in a less adversarial situation; so his fourth annual message praised Congress in lavish terms.

> They have asserted the constitutional equality of each and all of the
> States of the Union as States; they have affirmed the constitutional
> equality of each and all of the citizens of the United States as citizens,
> whatever their religion, whatever their birth or their residence; they
> have maintained the inviolability of the constitutional rights of the
> different sections of the Union, and they have proclaimed their de-
> voted and unalterable attachment to the Union and to the Constitu-
> tion . . . as the safeguard of the rights of all, as the spirit and the
> essence of the liberty, peace, and Greatness of the Republic.[11]

By the mid-nineteenth century, the term "constitutional" used as an adjective had become a convenient camouflage for moral compromise and
political expediency. A symbolic modifier could be utilized as a spurious
legitimizer. America, the land where politicians kept "Constitution"
poised on their palates.

Yet not entirely; and to understand why puts us on the path toward appre-
ciating the fact that the Constitution only emerged as a national symbol
haltingly and incompletely in the antebellum era. Let's begin at the beginning, with the physical location, peregrinations, and century-long entomb-
ment of the actual Constitution. On September 18, 1787, the morning
after it had been signed, the document was placed on the 11:00 a.m. stage-
coach for delivery to the Congress in New York City. There all the papers
of the Convention were entrusted to Roger Alden, deputy secretary of the
Congress. On September 26, 1789, almost five months after George
Washington took office, the Constitution was casually passed along to
Thomas Jefferson with the understanding that the Secretary of State
should serve as permanent custodian of such documents. In June 1800 it
came from Philadelphia to Washington by coach along with many other
bundles of records; and they were placed in the Treasury, the only building sufficiently completed to accommodate them. Five months later the
Constitution was housed in a building at Pennsylvania Avenue and 20th
Street. In 1801 it moved again, this time to a large brick building at 17th
and G Streets, where it remained for thirteen years.[12] Out of sight, almost
out of mind. Few American citizens could have said where the Constitution was being kept. Not many government officials knew either. Or
cared.

On August 22, 1814, as British troops advanced upon Washington,
three State Department clerks began to stuff miscellaneous records and
documents, including the Constitution, into coarse linen sacks. When the

Battle of Bladensburg took place two days later, the sacks were loaded on carts and hauled to an unoccupied grist mill a few miles above Chain Bridge on the Virginia side of the Potomac River. When it became clear that the British were in an ugly mood, capable of behavior above and beyond the normal call of battle, these bags of documents were advanced to the village of Leesburg, thirty-five miles from Washington, locked in an unoccupied house, and the keys entrusted to a Reverend Mr. Littlejohn. In September, after the British fleet departed from Chesapeake waters, the bags were brought back to Washington and placed in a rented structure until the State Department, which had been demolished, could be rebuilt.

In 1820 the Constitution went to the North Wing of the Treasury, and remained there until 1866–75, when it was appropriately placed at the Washington Orphan Asylum. In 1875, after the State Department moved to the old War and State Building, authorities relegated the U.S. Constitution to cellar storage; and there it remained, except for a few ceremonial occasions, until 1921, when President Harding directed that custody of the Declaration of Independence and the Constitution be transferred from the State Department to the Library of Congress so that Americans could actually view them. The Bill of Rights and the other ten amendments, however—although they comprised an integral part of the Constitution—remained in cellar storage within an ordinary green cabinet that also contained six ancient Japanese swords and the sword of Dessalene, an erstwhile emperor of Haiti.[13] No special effort to protect them; no special effort to see them. Out of sight, and almost out of mind. It's not a very edifying story, especially considering the constant use of words like "wonderful," "sacred," and "reverenced" to precede any allusion to the Constitution throughout the nineteenth century.

There is a different sort of reason why the Constitution emerged so haltingly as a symbol: criticism of it—even rumors of conspiratorial plots against it—surfaced with sufficient frequency that it appeared to be too controversial to achieve the elevated and unambiguous status of a truly national symbol. New England Federalists, like the Reverend Dr. Manasseh Cutler, reported in 1801 that "conjecture is alive & some deep laid plans, in opposition to the spirit of the Constitution, are said to be concerted." In 1808, Benjamin Rush of Philadelphia wondered what might inspire genuine unity among the American people. Writing to John Adams, he asked with more than rhetorical flourish (but less than true hyperbole): "In case of a rupture with Britain or France, which shall we fight for? For our Constitution? I cannot meet with a man who loves it. It is considered as too weak by one half of our citizens and too strong by the other half." Such statements occurred less frequently with the passage of time. Nonetheless, one still encounters them on the eve of the Civil War.[14]

To complicate matters even more, public figures not only differed over substantive issues of constitutional interpretation, many recognized that they could not even agree about the proper nature of constitutional interpretation. Did one refer to the text of the document exclusively; or should one also utilize contemporary and ancillary works of exegesis, like *The Federalist Papers*?[15] How helpful would a historical approach be? Or an attempt to learn everything possible about the discussions that took place at Philadelphia and hence the underlying intentions of the framers? No consensus.

- Gouverneur Morris (1814): "But, my dear sir, what can a history of the Constitution avail towards interpreting its provisions? This must be done by comparing the plain import of the words with the general tenor and object of the instrument. That instrument was written by the fingers which write this letter. Having rejected redundant and equivocal terms, I believed it to be as clear as our language would permit; excepting, nevertheless, a part of what relates to the judiciary. On that subject, conflicting opinions had been maintained with so much professional astuteness that it became necessary to select phrases which, expressing my own notions, would not alarm others nor shock their self-love. . . . But, after all, what does it signify that men should have a written constitution containing unequivocal provisions and limitations? The legislative lion will not be entangled in the meshes of a logical net."[16]

- James Madison (1817): "I am not unaware that my beliefs, not to say knowledge of the views of those who proposed the Constitution, and, what is of more importance, my deep impression as to the views of those who bestowed on it the stamp of authority, may influence my interpretation of the Instrument. On the other hand, it is not impossible that those who consult the Instrument without a danger of that bias, may be exposed to an equal one in their anxiety to find in its text an authority for a particular measure of great apparent utility."[17]

- James Fenimore Cooper (1844): "The Constitution must be construed as it reads, and not through mental reservations. . . . The understanding of the people, whose acceptance alone gave validity to the instrument, is the essential point. . . . The meaning of a law is to be inferred from matter inherent in itself, from its language, from analogy, and not from the after thoughts, or convenient party [partisan] recollections of individuals."[18]

After more than half a century of operative existence, the Constitution was becoming a national symbol, but an ambiguous one. Perhaps that is why antebellum lawyers liked to cut through this whole problem of contextual interpretation by arguing that because America has written constitutions, "reason is the great authority upon constitutional questions, and the faculty of reasoning is the only instrument by which it can be exercised."[19] Perhaps, too, the emergence of diverse patterns of reasoning may explain why John Marshall, Joseph Story, and John Quincy Adams reflected with "gloomy anticipations" upon "the whole course of our history from the organization of the present Constitution."[20]

II

In April of 1788 George Washington wrote to Lafayette expressing his hope that the Constitution would be ratified. In his realistic way, Washington acknowledged the nasty partisanship that had been provoked; but he also had the prescience to anticipate a need for constitutional education. "Although it is not to be expected that every individual, in Society, will or can ever be brought to agree upon what is, exactly, the best form of government," he remarked, "yet, there are many things in the Constitution which only need to be explained, in order to prove equally satisfactory to all parties." Meanwhile, throughout the debate over ratification that raged during 1787–88, numerous Anti-Federalists insisted that a constitution should be sufficiently simple so that anyone could understand it. They objected vociferously that the Constitution written in Philadelphia was too complicated for the average American to comprehend.[21]

Between Washington's belief in the beneficial effects of sound civic instruction and the opposition's insistence that a constitution ought to be self-explanatory, a gap existed in 1788 that has not really narrowed with the passage of time. It may well be one of the oddest phenomena in American political culture; but the Constitution has not turned out to be readily comprehensible to ordinary citizens, nor has the story of constitutional education been a successful one through most of our past. As the Reverend Isaac Jones lamented in 1827, "it is a matter of astonishment that our Constitution has been so long, and so generally, neglected."[22] The nature of that neglect has changed significantly over time. The trans-

formation and its outcome will be treated in section III below. Here, however, we want to ask how Americans managed to learn what they did know
about the Constitution during the six or seven decades that followed its
promulgation.

The most obvious source involves controversy generated by Supreme
Court decisions. When potentially volatile opinions elicited public dissent,
and the press vetted criticisms, the populace usually took notice and got a
civics lesson. This was particularly true in years like 1803, 1819, 1821,
and 1830.[23] In each instance the issue was different. Unfortunately the
educational effect has not ordinarily been cumulative or enduring. Another
useful way to gauge public awareness of the Court's activity involves close
attention to the phasing or periodicity of attempts to control the Supreme
Court. Between 1802 and 1957, congressmen introduced 165 bills designed to "curb" the Court in one way or another. The rhythm of their
efforts has been irregular, however, and can be seen quite simply in the following table:[24]

HIGH FREQUENCY		LOW FREQUENCY	
Period	*No. of bills*	*Period*	*No. of bills*
1802–04	2	1789–1801	0
1823–31	12	1805–22	0
1858–69	22	1832–57	1
1893–97	9	1870–92	8
1922–24	11	1898–1921	6
1935–37	37	1925–34	2
1955–57	53	1939–54	2

Over the time span taken as a whole there has been a general trend away
from bills that would remove or circumscribe some broad area of the
Court's power, and instead toward bills that would constrain a more specific portion of the Court's jurisdiction.

Yet another form of applied constitutional education occurred, especially in the young republic, when Supreme Court justices visited their circuit courts and explicated charges to grand juries. People were able to
imbibe the principles of their new Constitution through that practice. As a
federal judiciary began to develop at the beginning of the nineteenth century, this process broadened out and filtered down. A Walpole, New
Hampshire, newspaper described it superbly in 1799: "Among the more
vigorous productions of the American pen, may be enumerated the various

charges delivered by the Judges of the United States at the opening of their respective Courts. In these useful addresses to the jury, we not only discern sound legal information conveyed in a style at once popular and condensed, but much political and constitutional knowledge."[25]

The deaths of great men who had been closely associated with the Constitution or its interpretation, such as John Marshall (1835) and James Madison (1836), elicited eulogies that tended more toward declaring how wonderful the fundamental law was than illuminating its character in any specific way.

For a full generation after 1789, few books or pamphlets about the Constitution appeared. The earliest ones of any consequence were first published between 1823 and 1826, such as John Taylor of Caroline's *New Views of the Constitution of the United States* (1823) and Thomas Cooper's *On the Constitution of the United States, and the Questions that Have Arisen Under It* (1826), a polemical pamphlet. Predictably, perhaps, these were written as a result of Court decisions that aroused considerable contention. Predictably also, considering that John Marshall and his nationalist interpretation rode high in the saddle during the early 1820s, these reactive publications stressed the rights of sovereign states and called for strict construction of the Constitution.

At about the same time, texts for college and law students started to emerge, an interesting phenomenon for several reasons. First, because constitutional history had been neglected by Oxford and Cambridge during the eighteenth century;[26] consequently Americans inherited a tradition of legal education, but not of constitutional history per se. Second, as colleges of arts and sciences began to be founded in the early republic, many people shared a sentiment expressed by Benjamin Rush at the birth of Dickinson College: namely, that the students should be "taught to love and admire our present excellent Constitution, and to believe [that] with its destruction will perish the remains of all the liberty in the world."[27]

Unhappily, almost twenty-five years passed before the necessary textbooks began to be prepared. When at last it happened, Philadelphia served as the focal point. In 1822, Thomas Sergeant of that city compiled the first collection of purely constitutional cases. A second edition was called for eight years later. In 1825, William Rawle, a Philadelphia Federalist who revered the Union yet recognized the right of states to secede, published the first book devoted exclusively to the Constitution in which historical background, political philosophy, and the actual articles of the document were systematically discussed. It achieved broad and lasting appeal throughout the country; a second edition appeared in 1829 and a third in 1832. Two years later Peter Stephen Duponceau, a nationalist who identified himself as a Jeffersonian Republican, delivered an address to the Law Academy of Philadelphia. Designed to clarify some of the problems faced by students, it was printed by subscription as a 106-page booklet. Duponceau conveyed its copyright to the Law Academy through a deed of trust, expressed the belief that it would bring some profits, and requested that a copy be sent to the Secretary of State, Louis McLane.[28]

Another important figure in this period, William A. Duer, was born in Rhinebeck, New York, moved to New York City as a child and later studied at law offices there, at Philadelphia, and subsequently learned Spanish and French civil law in New Orleans. After that he maintained homes as well as law offices in both Rhinebeck and New York, became a friend of Washington Irving, and from 1822 until 1829 served as a judge on the Supreme Court of New York. In 1829 he assumed the presidency of Columbia College, was well liked there, and emerged as a prominent citizen in the city. A series of lectures that he presented to seniors at Columbia on the constitutional jurisprudence of the United States was printed in outline form in 1833, was reprinted thereafter, and eventually appeared as a proper book in 1843. The American Lyceum, which Duer served as president, asked him in 1833 to prepare a book on constitutional law that could serve as a text in academies and common schools. He complied, both of his textbooks enjoyed commercial success, and they remained in print for almost half a century. Duer retired from Columbia in 1842 and spent the rest of his life quite comfortably in Morristown, New Jersey.[29]

Two other trends developed simultaneously, especially during the decade following 1829: extensive commentaries on the Constitution by legal scholars, and manuals or handbooks designed for popular use among the general public. In 1829, for instance, Professor Nathan Dane of Harvard devoted most of volume IX in his *General Abridgment and Digest of American Law* to an analysis of the Constitution. He took a strident nationalist position, insisting that the states had always been subordinate to the general government. Quite clearly, the flurry of constitutional publications that began to appear in 1829—though comprehensive in jurisprudential coverage—was particularly stimulated by South Carolina's Nullification Crisis. However unpleasant, unreasonable, and divisive such episodes have been in American history, they are notable (and valuable) as provocations for public instruction on constitutional matters.

In 1829, Joseph Story offered his *Inaugural Discourse* as Professor of Law at Harvard. (Unlike Felix Frankfurter's situation in 1939, the relaxed rules in Story's era permitted him to sit on the Supreme Court and teach law *pari passu.*) Story declared his goal quite simply: "to fix in the minds of American youth a more devout enthusiasm for the constitution of their country." Early in 1833 all three volumes of his *Commentaries on the Constitution* appeared, followed late in the spring by a 650-page abridgment that Story prepared as a textbook for "the use of colleges and high schools." The complete version became an American classic and went through many editions—the sixth in 1905, sixty years after Story's death. The abridgment, which omitted all footnotes and technical references, also appeared in revised editions; and in 1843 Story produced a third, still more simplified version entitled *The Constitutional Class Book: being a brief exposition of the Constitution of the United States. Designed for the use of the higher classes in common schools.*

Six years later the indefatigable Story put together a fourth rendition, this time a one-volume compendium aimed primarily at a lay audience. He called it *A Familiar Exposition of the Constitution of the United States: Containing a Brief Commentary on Every Clause. . . . Designed for the Use of School Libraries and General Readers.* While the original, comprehensive work was being printed back in 1832, Story told Chancellor Kent of New York that his *Commentaries* "are written with a sincere desire to commend, and to recommend the Constitution upon true, old, and elevated principles."[30] That meant the nationalist principles of John Marshall, but also the scientific ideals of this remarkable jurist who had been elected to Congress in 1808 as a Jeffersonian, yet increasingly took Federalist and Whig positions. More than any other American of the antebellum period, Story helped codify American constitutional law into a coherent and accessible system.

The initiative and success of Story, Duer, and the Philadelphia group sparked a series of commentaries meant to be popular, semischolarly, or in some instances both simultaneously. None sold nearly so well as those already mentioned. (One by Henry Baldwin, who had been appointed to the Supreme Court by Andrew Jackson in 1830, was intended as a riposte to Story's dissent in the famous Charles River Bridge case [1837]. The issue before the Court was whether rights not explicitly granted by a "contract" could be constitutionally inferred from the language of a state-granted charter. Story had disagreed with the Jacksonian majority view that contracts affecting the public interest must be interpreted flexibly.) Some of these works were planned as multivolume studies; yet no more than the first volume ever appeared. And none received more than its initial printing.[31]

The most popular among all the manuals produced during the middle third of the nineteenth century seems to have been William Hickey's *The Constitution of the United States of America, With an Alphabetical Analysis,* which was first published in Washington, D.C., in 1846. Subsequent editions emerged from Philadelphia in 1847, 1848, and every year between 1851 and 1854. After Hickey's death, Alexander Cummings's enlarged edition was printed at Baltimore in 1878 and 1879. Hickey stated his purpose explicitly: to democratize public access to the Constitution. He called attention to "the obligation incumbent on every intelligent citizen to make himself acquainted with its provisions, restrictions, and limitations, and of imparting . . . a knowledge of this paramount law of our country to the minds of the rising generation." Hickey observed that in Great Britain copies of Magna Carta "are ordered to be sent to all cathedral churches, and read twice a year to the people." He hoped to build upon that pattern but surpass it in disseminating constitutional knowledge throughout the United States.[32]

On February 18, 1847, the U.S. Senate obtained 2,000 copies of Hickey's manual at a cost of $1.25 per copy for the use of its members. Soon after that the Senate took 10,000 additional copies at $1.00 per copy; then another 2,000 in 1848; and 10,000 more in 1850. This must have been the first official attempt to disseminate constitutional information, to filter it down on a broad scale. The front matter in the manual included endorsements from all sorts of public figures. The words of Polk's Vice President, George M. Dallas, typified the populist purpose that Hickey hoped to achieve. The text of the Constitution "should be found wherever there is a capacity to read: not alone in legislative halls, judicial councils, libraries, and colleges, but also in the cabins and steerages of our mariners, at every common-school, log-hut, factory, or fireside." John B. Gibson, Chief Justice of the Supreme Court of Pennsylvania, told Hickey that his book ought to be "in the hands of the masses." And Lewis Cass, U.S. Senator from Michigan, wrote Hickey to praise his "reference to the practice of Rome and to that of the mediaeval ages in England, where the diffusion of the knowledge of their respective Constitutions, especially among the youth, was one of the cares of the government, [and] furnishes an important lesson."[33]

The wide distribution achieved by Hickey's *Constitution,* especially between 1847 and 1854, must have done some good. We do not know whether Hickey felt that his objective had been fully achieved; we do not even know whether he noticed the errors his book contained, some of them rather basic. His frontispiece as well as a second illustration placed 1789 above "The Constitution," while an encomium from J. K. Kane, federal judge for the Eastern District of Pennsylvania, referred to the Constitution's formation in 1786 (p. xiii).

There were occasional attempts to include the Constitution in what we now call adult or continuing education. In 1831, Edward Everett delivered an address entitled "Advantage of Knowledge to Workingmen," an introduction to the Franklin lecture series in Boston. He enumerated some of the special topics to be included in this program for promoting useful knowledge, and listed as number five: "A general and intelligible view of the constitution and laws of the country." The Franklin Lyceum in Providence, Rhode Island, sponsored a lecture course in 1848 that included Daniel Webster speaking on "The Early History of the American Constitution." During 1848–49 Webster gave a course of lectures at the Salem Lyceum on the "History of the Constitution of the United States."[34]

What about elementary education, which is all that most Americans formally received during the decades between the nation's founding and the Civil War? From 1789 until 1860 only one state, California, required that the Constitution be taught. Constitutional instruction, when it did occur, usually meant a shamefully short consideration of what had happened at the Philadelphia Convention. The growth and adaptation of the Constitution since 1787 received little to no attention. Catechisms or clause-by-clause glosses were the norm; judicial interpretation, even the texts of famous Supreme Court decisions, were not. Indeed, they were largely ignored.[35]

One of the most popular textbooks of that period had been prepared by the Reverend Charles A. Goodrich, *A History of the United States of America on a Plan Adapted to the Capacity of Youth*. The fifth edition, printed at Bellows Falls, Vermont, in 1825 contains 296 pages of text, in very small type, with an additional 20 pages of questions at the end. Chapter six, covering the years 1783 to 1789, is ten pages long. It explains that life under the Articles of Confederation was disappointing because "something, not yet possessed, was necessary to realize the private and publick prosperity that had been anticipated." Goodrich did note a significant point that we shall say more about in a moment, the fact that the Convention proceeded "with closed doors." The substance of the Constitution is then summarized in two and a half pages. Among the eight sets of questions offered in order to supply this chapter with pedagogical punch, the last two range from hopelessly vague and complicated to typically simplistic:

VII. What is said of the adoption of the constitution by the states?

VIII.   On the adoption of the constitution, who was chosen the first
        President? Who Vice President?

I would be hard-pressed to explain Reverend Goodrich's understanding of
"the capacity of youth."

In 1832 Noah Webster prepared a *History of the United States; To
Which is Prefixed a Brief Historical Account of Our* [English] *Ancestors.* The
1837 edition, printed in New Haven, has 293 pages of text, once again in
small type, followed by a didactic 20-page chapter called "Advice to the
Young," then Washington's Farewell Address, and finally an appendix
that covers the years 1789 to 1815 in 33 pages. Webster's chapter on the
Constitution is seventeen pages long. Its opening sentence is a dilly: "In
Asia the governments are all despotic." Then European absolutism gets
slammed. The second paragraph defines republican government, and the
next its distribution of governmental powers. After that the Constitution is
epitomized in five and a half pages. Three paragraphs follow which sum-
marize the relative advantages and disadvantages of monarchy, aristocracy, and a republican polity. Next comes a paragraph entitled "Success of
the Constitution." Most of it narrates what the new government did in
1789, and then concludes: "From that time commenced the prosperity of
the United States, which, with little interruption, has continued to this
day." That is the equivalent, in American constitutionalism, of affirming
that they all lived happily ever after. No causal link is really needed. It's a
given.

    Then, with no attempt whatever at transition, paragraphs follow
concerning the origin of civil liberty, the character of the Puritans, the institutions of the Puritans, the effects of Puritan principles and institutions,
a general description of North American geography, climate in the United
States, temperature in several regions, the frequency of severe winters,
extremes of summer heat, spring and autumn, weather westward of the
mountains, climate in regard to health, diseases of the United States, and
finally, chronic diseases. Such is Noah Webster's chapter on the Constitution: thin on substance and utterly lacking in intellectual cohesion. On
page 265 Webster declares that "by the laws of nature, reason, and religion, all men are born with equal rights." Six pages later he asserts that
"slaves escaping from their masters into another state are to be delivered
upon demand of their masters." His next two chapters, concerning "Vege-
table Productions" and "Animals of the United States," receive more
space than his chapter on the Constitution. Republicanism is marvelous.
Webster's reasoning is wonderful. His sense of proportion . . .

That's how most American children learned about the "great instrument." (The phrase is from Vice President Dallas.) Needless to say, they all lived happily ever after.

III

Professor Harold M. Hyman, one of the leading authorities on American constitutional history, has argued that the great public issues in American life during the decades preceding the Civil War "provided a generation with unprecedented expertness in the theory of the Constitution. . . ." I am skeptical because I have found too much material to the contrary. Professor Hyman makes a reasonable case that political issues frequently tended to be discussed in constitutional terms. He is also persuasive in suggesting that the popular nature and extent of public debates tended to democratize constitutional concepts and make them a part of ordinary political dialogue.[36] Even so, I must question the assertion that laymen acquired constitutional expertise.

In fact, there seems to be abundant evidence that highly placed public officials did not know their Constitution very well. As Silas Wright, formerly a member of Congress and governor of New York, wrote in 1847: "No one familiar with the affairs of our government, can have failed to notice how large a proportion of our statesmen appear never to have read the Constitution of the United States with a careful reference to its precise language and exact provisions, but rather, as occasion presents, seem to exercise their ingenuity . . . to stretch both to the line of what they, at the moment, consider expedient."[37] One month earlier Senator Sidney Breese, a Democrat from Illinois, had made the condemnation even more sweeping: "It is a lamentable fact, that the Constitution of the United States . . . has not yet had a general circulation. I hope it may be introduced into our schools, academies, and all our seminaries of learning, and studied to be understood.[38]

This lament also colors the letters of James Fenimore Cooper through the last two decades of his life. In 1834, after returning from Europe, he wrote: "I have not met a single man, since my return, who appears to me to have thoroughly examined the Constitution." He archly berated both Webster and Calhoun for being wide of the mark. A year later he complained in a public letter to the New York *Evening Post* that congressmen did not take the trouble to read the Constitution carefully. It annoyed Cooper that U.S. senators seemed to feel especially proprietary about the Constitution. Why? Because they were so often confused on constitutional issues.[39]

Cooper could be ever so self-righteous; but on constitutional matters he was also right more often than not. His journal entry for January 20, 1848, reads: "Congress making a fool of itself by betraying its utter ignorance of the Constitution." Six days later he asked (answer implicit in the question): "Does Mr. Clay understand the Constitution, or is it ignorance?" Later that year, in discussing Zachary Taylor's use of the presidential veto, he made the same point, but this time as an accusation rather than an innuendo or a question.[40] Cooper did not suffer constitutional fools gladly. What matters for our frame of reference is that he found them everywhere, and did not hesitate for a moment to name names.

Just why this ignorance should have been so widespread is not easy to explain, in part because the problem does have elusive aspects; but in part also because the answer is complex rather than monocausal. Cooper admired the Constitution as much as he did because its clarity impressed him. "It is impossible to conceive language clearer than the constitution," he remarked in 1835, a sentiment that Daniel Webster echoed in 1850: "Almost every man in the country is capable of reading it."[41] Well, yes, but reading is not the same as comprehending; and one's comprehension may or may not be correct.

During the early years of the republic, few persons owned many books and precise knowledge of the Constitution simply was not common. Four members of Congress mentioned the problem during a heated debate in 1798: "it had been conceded by all that the circulation of the Constitution as amended had been very limited, and that the amendments are unknown in some parts of the Union." Participants in the Philadelphia Convention did sit as members of Congress after 1789, to be sure, and occasionally they commented retrospectively upon the framers' intent. They thereby provided a valuable form of constitutional annotation; but we must remember that congressional debates were only reported in a few newspapers. The *Register of Debates* did not begin to appear until 1825 and the *Annals of Congress* not until 1834. Consequently much of this gratuitous commentary was either lost entirely or else lost upon the larger American public.[42]

It is not widely appreciated, moreover, that in several key respects the Supreme Court remained a remote and almost shadowy institution for the first half century of its history. Newspaper items provided the scant amount that was known about the Court's activities; and this sort of reporting was thin and imprecise. The lay public knew little about Court decisions. Nor was the bar well informed. Reviewing the third volume of Wheaton's *Reports* in 1818, Daniel Webster observed that "the sale is not very rapid. The number of law libraries which contain a complete set is comparatively small." So late as the 1830s *Supreme Court Reports* did not enjoy extensive circulation, even among lawyers. The famous Dartmouth College case (1819) did not attract much interest at the time, nor was its importance fully appreciated. Not until March 14, 1834, did it become mandatory that all opinions of the Court be filed with the clerk. An incomplete printed record of the Court's deliberations did not begin until December 1857.[43]

In the mid-1820s, more than a generation after the national government had been established, the Supreme Court's chamber in the Capitol was difficult to find and inadequate in almost every respect. An extraordinary description appeared in the *New York Statesman* on February 7 and 24, 1824:

> The apartment is not in a style which comports with the dignity of that body, or which wears a comparison with the other Halls of the Capitol. In the first place, it is like going down cellar to reach it. The room is on the basement story in an obscure part of the north wing. In arriving at it, you pass a labyrinth, and almost need the clue of Ariadne to guide you to the sanctuary of the blind goddess. A stranger might traverse the dark avenues of the Capitol for a week, without finding the remote corner in which Justice is administered to the American Republic . . . a room which is hardly capacious enough for a ward justice. The apartment is well finished; but the experience of this day has shown that in size it is wholly insufficient for the accommodation of the Bar, and the spectators who wish to attend. Many of the members were obliged to leave their seats to make room for the ladies, some of whom were *sworn in,* and with much difficulty found places within the Bar. It is a triangular, semi-circular, odd-shaped apartment, with three windows, and a profusion of arches in the ceiling, diverging like the radii of a circle from a point over the bench to the circumference. . . . Owing to the smallness of the room, the Judges are compelled to put on their robes in the presence of the spectators, which is an awkward ceremony, and destroys the effect intended to be produced by assuming the gown.

It is all the more difficult to assess the problem of public ignorance because knowledge versus ignorance was not an objective matter susceptible in retrospect of even impressionistic measurement. The question of what the American people know or are capable of knowing about the Constitution is ideologically charged. Those with populistic tendencies are most likely to give an affirmative answer. Doing so reflects their egalitarian faith. Those with a more conservative bent have been inclined to give a skeptical response. Thus we find the following polemic in Boston's *Independent Chronicle* on February 10, 1806: "The doctrine now attempted to be promulgated, to render the jury incompetent to law, is to depreciate the character of every other man in society but practitioners of it [lawyers]. It is similar to the declaration, that the people are their own 'worst enemies'—that they are ignorant as to every particular on which is founded either the political or legal principles of the constitution and of the laws."[44]

To some degree, then, the apparent issue of public comprehension of the Constitution resulted from partisan assertions rather than palpable realities. We must also recognize that comparatively little had been written for laymen about the Constitution between the debates over ratification in 1787–88 and the approach of the Civil War in 1860. The quality of what did appear left much to be desired, was belated or else fragmentary; which brings us to one of the most important events in the cultural history of the U.S. Constitution from 1788 until the present: the publication in 1840 of James Madison's *Notes,* the fullest account we possess of what transpired during the Convention.

Delegates to the Convention made a gentlemen's agreement that their discussions would be private, and that no disclosure of what had transpired should take place for half a century. This arrangement infuriated Thomas Jefferson. "I am sorry they began their deliberations," he wrote from Paris, "by so abominable a precedent as that of tying up the tongues of their members. Nothing can justify this example but the innocence of their intentions, and ignorance of the value of public discussions." Actually, the delegates' decision was neither unusual nor conspiratorial. The proceedings of the Hartford Convention of 1814, for instance, were also kept confidential. The effect, however, was that rumors about conflicts and compromises in 1787 grew steadily, causing (in the words of George Ticknor Curtis) "a great excitement in the public mind in many localities."[45]

For thirty-four years participants kept the faith and maintained their silence, with the result that what had transpired in Philadelphia, ranging from bargains struck to the motivations underlying particular clauses, all remained a public mystery. In 1819 John Quincy Adams, then Secretary of State, printed the Convention's official journal. Doing so was not an ethical breach because the journal was essentially a record of results rather than how they had been reached. In 1821, however, the notes taken by Robert Yates, a delegate from New York and later Chief Justice of that state, were published. Yates died in 1801; but John Lansing had made a copy, and it was this copy that appeared in 1821. James Madison read it and felt doubly distressed: because the fifty-year pact had been violated, and because the Yates diary contained so many inaccuracies. Madison also had personal reasons for feeling anger. Yates had become an Anti-Federalist, and along with Lansing and Citizen Genêt, who was partially responsible for the 1821 publication, shared animosity toward Madison. We now know that Yates's notes are even less reliable than Madison indicated to contemporaries, and that Genêt bowdlerized them in order to embarrass Madison wherever possible.[46]

But the vow of silence had been broken; and that resulted in Madison receiving pressure from intimate friends to publish his own journal in order to set the record straight. We know that Jefferson read the journal some time before 1815, when he told John Adams that "the whole of everything said and done there was taken down by Mr. Madison, with a labor and exactness beyond comprehension." In 1831, when Jared Sparks began writing a biography of Gouverneur Morris, he sought from Madison information about Morris's role at Philadelphia in 1787, complaining that "the published account of that convention is so meagre, such a very skeleton of dry bones."[47]

In 1821, Madison provided the fullest explanation of his ambivalent feelings about the coveted account for which he was responsible.

It is true as the public has been led to understand, that I possess materials for a pretty ample view of what passed in that Assembly. It is true also that it has not been my intention that they should for ever remain under the veil of secresy. Of the time when it might be not improper for them to see the light, I had formed no particular determination. In general it had appeared to me that it might be best to let the work be a posthumous one; or at least that its publication should be delayed till the Constitution should be well settled by practice, & till a knowledge of the controversial part of the proceedings of its framers could be turned to no improper account. Delicacy also seemed to require some respect to the rule by which the Convention "prohibited a promulgation without leave of what was spoken in it"; so long as the policy of that rule could be regarded as in any degree unexpired. As a guide in expounding and applying the provisions of the Constitution, the debates and incidental decisions of the Convention can have no authoritative character. However desirable it be that they should be preserved as a gratification to the laudable curiosity felt by every people to trace the origin and progress of their political Institutions, & as a source perhaps of some lights on the Science of Govt. the legitimate meaning of the Instrument must be derived from the text itself; or if a key is to be sought elsewhere, it must be not in the opinions or intentions of the Body which planned & proposed the Constitution, but in the sense attached to it by the people in their respective State Conventions where it recd. all the authority which it possesses.

Such being the course of my reflections I have suffered a concurrence & continuance of particular inconveniences for the time past, to prevent me from giving to my notes the fair & full preparation due to the subject of them. Of late, being aware of the growing hazards of postponement, I have taken the incipient steps for executing the task. . . .

It is my purpose now to devote a portion of my time to an exact digest of the voluminous material in my hands. How long a time it will require, under the interruptions & avocations which are probable I can not easily conjecture. Not a little will be necessary for the mere labour of making fair transcripts. By the time I get the whole into a due form for preservation, I shall be better able to decide on the question of publication.[48]

The next major development occurred on April 19, 1835, when Madison included the following in his will: "It is not an unreasonable inference that a careful and extended report of the proceedings and discussions of that body, which were with closed doors, by a member who was constant in his attendance, will be particularly gratifying to the people of the United States. . . . It is my desire that the report as made by me should be published under [Mrs. Madison's] authority and direction."[49] During the period between 1832 and 1835, Madison made revisions in his original Notes by inserting extracts from the official journal published in 1819 as well as some interlinings derived from the Yates diary published in 1821. He died on June 28, 1836. Nine months later Dolley Madison delivered her husband's papers, including the Notes, to the Library of Congress. The Notes were published in 1840.[50]

The fact that Madison scrupulously adhered to the fifty-year agreement concerning disclosure had major ramifications that are, nonetheless, difficult to measure. The argument has been made that his doing so contributed to the distortion of American constitutional history for a full half century.[51] Such a claim may be excessive; but this much, I believe, can be said. First, that between 1787 and 1840 lay Americans as well as jurists did not know as much as they might have known, and perhaps should have known, about the activities and intentions of the framers.[52] Second, that throughout much of the dispute over slavery and territorial expansion, especially in 1819–20, Madison kept his opinions private when no one else could have spoken more authoritatively than he about Congress's power to restrict slavery on the basis of the importation clause in Article I, Section 9, of the Constitution.[53] Third, that Madison's patience and silence had important implications for the constitutional positions taken by various segments of the abolitionist movement, as we shall see in the next chapter. And fourth, that when the Golden Jubilee of 1837–39 took place, it directly followed a dozen years of constitutional acrimony and misrepresentation—based in part upon self-interest, in part upon deeply felt ideological commitments, and in part upon sheer ignorance of the Constitution.

All of which may help to explain why the fiftieth anniversary of the Constitution in 1837, or of its implementation in 1839, received much less ballyhoo than one might expect for a document that William Hickey called "the fireside companion of the American citizen." Much less ballyhoo, certainly, than the fiftieth anniversary of Independence in 1826. Chief Justice Earl Warren once observed in a centennial address honoring Charles Evans Hughes that "the public recognition of anniversaries is not empty ceremonial. . . . An anniversary celebration is an invitation for introspection which our busy day-to-day tasks otherwise make impossible." In 1837 Americans must have been exceedingly pre-occupied with day-to-day tasks, because not many of them did much to commemorate the Constitution, a neglect that was duly noted when the Centennial rolled around in 1887.[54]

The Golden Jubilee of the "adoption" of the Constitution, meaning establishment of the new government, fared only slightly better. On March 4, 1839, Daniel Webster, various congressmen, and other dignitaries were present at a banquet in Washington arranged in honor of the event. The guests consumed a lot of alcohol, and toasts continued past midnight; but nothing notable seems to have been said.[55] On April 30, 1839, the New-York Historical Society sponsored a gala celebration of George Washington's inauguration, an event which is the best remembered moment of the Golden Jubilee years. It is difficult to say why. William Cullen Bryant reluctantly accepted a commission to write an ode in four stanzas, to be sung by a choir, but the piece was so mediocre that he refused to incorporate it into subsequent editions of his poetry. John Quincy Adams then delivered a two-hour discourse. Except for Adams's description of the warm reception that Washington had received from the women of Trenton—which caused the audience to weep, and Adams himself to fight back tears—he was monumentally dull. The press could not comprehend why a statesman who was so "sublime" when presenting abolitionist petitions in the House should be so tedious in reading most of an oration that required 115 pages in print.[56]

Adams's *Discourse,* a detailed narrative of what had happened from 1776 until 1787 and why, emphasized the inadequacies of Confederation government, denounced the doctrines of state sovereignty and Nullification, and insisted repeatedly that the Constitution provided a polity that was democratic as well as republican.[57] His recurrent theme, however—and in this his view was representative of his era—asserted that the Constitution of 1787 "was the complement to the Declaration of Independence; founded upon the same principles." Under Adams's close scrutiny, the two great documents "are part of one consistent whole."[58]

Despite this widely shared emphasis upon continuity and cohesion, a constitutional consensus was lacking as the first half century under national government drew to a close. A decade of volatile public disputes had made that clear, as had the constitutional commentaries, textbooks, glosses, and manuals that appeared after 1829. Partisans of state sovereignty could feel no enthusiasm for a Golden Jubilee celebrated on northern, New England, or nationalistic terms.

IV

We should return to the problem of Professor Corwin's distinction between the Constitution as instrument and as symbol; and I must repeat my contention that it emerged as a symbol both slowly and inconclusively. The U.S.S. *Constitution,* commissioned in 1797, did become the most famous warship in American history, immortalized in 1830 as "Old Ironsides" by Oliver Wendell Holmes, and once again more than a century later in a Paramount Pictures film starring Wallace Beery. A spot called Constitution Hill, in Princeton, New Jersey, was originally part of a very large tract of land belonging to Richard Stockton, a signer of the Declaration. And in 1861 locomotives named "Union" and "Constitution" could be found in Poughkeepsie, New York.[59]

On the other hand, a careful count of the names of minor civil divisions (towns and villages) and counties in the United States has turned up 324 places named Union, 182 places named Liberty, 39 named Independence, but just one named Constitution. What about the street names found in 1,280 principal American cities as of 1908? There were 603 named Union; 321 named Liberty; 128 named Congress; 85 named Federal; even 83 named Eagle; 40 named Independence; 32 named National; 20 named Enterprise; but a pathetic 9 named Constitution.[60] Newspapers fared little better. I have discovered only five established between 1799 and 1837 with names like *The Constitutional Diary* (Philadelphia) and *The Constitutionalist* (Bath, New York).

If we turn to material culture and the decorative arts in American life, we will be similarly underwhelmed, especially by comparison with the rich lode of iconography inspired by Independence and the American Revolution.[61] Iconography, as defined by Erwin Panofsky, "is that branch of the history of art which concerns itself with the subject matter or meaning of works of art, as opposed to their form." Symbolic significance rather than aesthetic form concerns the cultural historian working as iconographer. Did Supreme Court Justice William Johnson speak for most Americans in 1823 when he called the Constitution "the most wonderful instrument ever drawn by the hand of man"?[62] If we answered on the basis of iconographic evidence, the reply would have to be no, because the evidence is remarkably thin.

Much of what has survived—more than a representative sample—appears in the portfolio of illustrations. The objects, paintings, engravings, and lithographs are engaging and attractive. But why have there been so few, especially from the nineteenth century when the Constitution was supposedly venerated? To the best of my knowledge, for example, between 1787 and 1934 only a handful of artists attempted to paint any sort of tableau of the Constitutional Convention: Junius Brutus Stearns in 1856 (figure 9) and Thomas P. Rossiter sometime during the 1860s (figure 10) are the best known. It is inadequate to say that a relatively small room crowded with between thirty-nine and fifty-five men would have presented an uninteresting challenge to a painter. Many artists, after all, depicted the signing of the Declaration of Independence. Nor is it sufficient to say that purely aesthetic problems of composition made the task formidable. A British artist, Henry Singleton (1766–1839), had shown the way with a widely admired oil painting called *The Royal Academicians in General Assembly* (1795), in which forty figures are arranged, including painters, sculptors, architects, and engravers. This work, now displayed in London at the Royal Academy, proved to be so popular that in 1802 a printed key identifying each figure had to be prepared.

Would American artists have been familiar with that work? Quite likely; but it would not have been necessary. In 1822 Samuel F. B. Morse painted *The Old House of Representatives*, a large oil owned by the Corcoran Gallery of Art in Washington, D.C. Here is an early example of an American artist depicting a large group of politicians in a legislative chamber. As it happens, John Marshall and other members of the Supreme Court are even standing on a raised platform in the middle distance to the left. Curiously enough, they stand beneath a representation of the Declaration of Independence rather than the Constitution! Morse's painting failed to attract the public, was not a financial success, and had to be sold to an English gentleman for $1,000. In 1830, George Catlin painted *The Virginia Constitutional Convention of 1829–30*, a scene (now belonging to the Virginia Historical Society) that included more than a hundred men. George P. A. Healy's panoramic painting *Webster Replying to Hayne* (1851) hangs to this day in Boston's Faneuil Hall; and several other artists (including Robert Whitechurch and Thomas Doney) undertook versions of a crowded U.S. Senate chamber at midcentury.[63]

The point, therefore, is that it might not have been easy to paint a lot of people, mostly inert, seated in a smallish chamber; nor would it have been an attractive project from purely an artistic point of view. But it was possible, it had been done, and the Philadelphia Convention of 1787 surely ought to have had sufficient patriotic interest to attract more than a few painters in 150 years.

The British, by contrast, have had a stronger tradition of constitutional iconography, and it has been closely linked to the meaning of liberty in English culture. Some examples are fairly predictable, such as John Wilkes with "Magna Charta" engraved beneath his picture; or paintings of King John and the barons at Runnymede that are roughly comparable to our paintings by Stearns and Rossiter. On the other hand there is nothing in the history of American art that is comparable to the famous painting of *Arthur Beardmore Teaching His Son Magna Charta* (1764); or Sir William Allan's *Lord Lindsay Compelling Mary to Abdicate* (1824); or Charles West Cope's *Speaker Lenthall Asserting the Privileges of the Commons Against Charles I* (1866).[64]

V

The United States fares better when we make other sorts of comparisons with various cultures. After Alexander I became Czar of Russia in 1801, and throughout his twenty-five-year reign, he spoke of providing a constitution for his people. He invited friends and ministers to submit proposals, and established various commissions to draft constitutional reforms. He even asked Thomas Jefferson and Joseph Priestley to prepare a "short analytical view of our constitution"; and later he solicited suggestions for Russia from Jefferson, Jeremy Bentham, Baron Rosenkampf, and Freiherr vom Stein of Germany. Alexander never implemented any of these, however, and they remained for him little more than a cerebral exercise, a curious residue of the Enlightenment. It is clear, in fact, that the redefinition of Western constitutionalism that developed from written constitutions in the United States and France as a result of their revolutions never took hold in the Czar's mind. To him, a constitution meant "fundamental principles of administrative organization." Such issues as popular sovereignty or the separation and balance of powers were utterly beyond his ken.[65]

When the Latin American states achieved independence during the first quarter of the nineteenth century, they prepared genuine constitutions, and not just speculative theories that could be shelved one after another to suit the whims of an absolute ruler. These Latin American instruments drew heavily upon political ideas borrowed from Spain, France, and the United States—ideas that too often were ill-suited to the exigencies and realities of Latin American political culture. As the foremost authority on Latin American constitutionalism explained: "It has long been customary for commentators to point out the divergence between constitutional prescription and governmental practice in Latin America. Another way of putting it is to say that the basic laws have often served as symbols rather than as instruments. . . . It seems in order to suggest, however . . . that to the extent that those characterizations are true it is because for so many decades Latin American constitutions failed to be the creatures of their own environment; they were simply alien adoptions and adaptations."[66]

Somehow, even when major adjustments were made, the same old gap between rhetoric and reality persisted. The new Mexican constitution of 1857, for example, really did reflect contemporary revolutionary thought. Although modelled on the 1824 constitution, it represented far more of a liberal triumph. Mexico received its first bill of rights in 1857. The Roman Catholic Church lost its privileged position as the state church; and all sorts of reform legislation accompanied these renovations. Theoretical guarantees provided by the new constitution were constantly violated nonetheless. Elections at all levels became farcical. Then, in the 1860s, that strange interlude of control by Archduke Maximilian occurred, "and the long grip of porforismo effectively prevented any honest attempt to apply the spirit of that Constitution—it was consistently honored in the breach rather than the observance."[67]

By contrast, the U.S. Constitution had been a genuine outgrowth of indigenous political experience during the long phase of colonial apprenticeship and the swifter transformation of Revolutionary adolescence. The framers were fully aware of European constitutional ideas, but had drawn upon them selectively and modified them wherever it seemed appropriate. Fenimore Cooper combined chauvinism with realistic self-recognition when he wrote from Dresden in 1830 that "we are unique as a government, and we must look for our maxims in the natural corollaries of the Constitution." Twenty years later Secretary of State Daniel Webster wrote less thoughtfully but with typical panache that the U.S. Constitution "is all that gives us a NATIONAL character."[68] That was an outrageous overstatement—a half-truth at best. What matters, however, is that by 1850 a great many Americans shared his assumption. The instrument was finally becoming a symbol, one that the society regarded as culturally determinative.

CHAPTER 4

The Constitution Threatens to Be a Subject of Infinite Sects

THE CIVIL WAR HAS BEEN STUDIED AS A constitutional crisis, and the Reconstruction era has received even more attention on account of its constitutional conflicts and their consequences. We have understood for quite some time that this phase of U.S. history led to fundamental changes in our apportionment of sovereignty and civil liberties, as well as in the attendant judicial system.[1]

What we perceive so clearly with the benefit of hindsight, however, seemed clouded with uncertainty in the eyes of contemporaries; and what looks to us like a conclusive victory for nationalism, and at least a partial triumph for Negro citizenship by the 1870s, only serves to shroud the ambiguous legacy of this nation's most divisive crisis. It is too easily forgotten that with respect to issues involving race and civil rights the society was almost as torn in 1883 as it had been, say, in 1843—despite (or perhaps even because of) the passage of three major constitutional amendments and several civil rights laws.[2]

It is too easily forgotten that states' rights sentiment remained strong, in the North as well as the South, for several decades after the surrender at Appomatox Courthouse. On the other hand, it is also too easily forgotten that the years of Civil War and Reconstruction resulted in a gradual yet permanent expansion in the role of federal courts, accompanied by a diminution in the importance of state courts. A remarkable instance of quiet constitutional change occurred on March 3, 1875, when Congress empowered the national judiciary to assume complete jurisdiction over all cases arising under the Constitution and laws of the United

States. Passage of that bill received little attention at the time, even though it gave the federal courts a broad range of authority that had been dormant ever since 1789, and soon resulted in a considerable increase in the amount of litigation that came before those courts.[3]

If we acknowledge the historical significance of such trends, it is essential to regard the four decades from the early 1840s to the early 1880s as a coherent epoch (rather than seeing 1861 or 1865 as arbitrary points of ante- versus postdiluvianism). We need to do so not only because racial issues had a profound effect upon American constitutional discourse throughout this period, but because the judicial trends described in the preceding paragraph had their modest beginnings in 1842, when the Supreme Court issued two landmark decisions. *Swift* v. *Tyson* declared that federal courts were unaffected by state court decisions when resolving disputes (not involving the federal Constitution or laws) between citizens of different states. In the case of *Prigg* v. *Pennsylvania,* which concerned a conflict between the federal Fugitive Slave Law and Pennsylvania's Personal Liberty Law, passed in 1826, Justice Story, a staunch opponent of slavery, found the Pennsylvania law to be in conflict with federal law, and hence unconstitutional.[4]

Taken together, these 1842 decisions indicated that national law—statutes as well as federal common law—would be distinct from and superior to state law. Uncertain jurisdictional boundaries had begun to be clarified, a process that would continue in complicated ways throughout the century ahead. Needless to say, proponents of states' rights did not protest Story's nationalistic ruling in 1842 because it gave them the substance of what they sought: the right to recover runaway slaves in so-called free states. Nonetheless, this famous case only intensified the conflict over slavery as a constitutional issue. Why? Because the justices produced no fewer than seven different opinions! They could not agree on whether a state must, or merely could, or actually could not enact legislation that supplemented the enforcement of federal law.[5] Legislators, lawyers, and the public remained confused as to what the Court's ruling had really meant, not to mention its larger implications. Slavery as a source of constitutional ambiguity now became an explosive matter.

I

From 1787 until 1840 the Constitution, and the founders' wishes with respect to slavery, remained murky. In 1819, for example, James Madison responded *in confidence* to a query from a Philadelphia abolitionist that the Convention had not intended to prohibit the interstate movement of slaves because doing so would have made ratification impossible to achieve. Once the American Anti-Slavery Society was formed in 1833, however, abolition emerged as an overtly constitutional issue. In 1834, for example, an essay appeared in *The Emancipator,* edited by William Goodell, entitled "The Constitution of the United States versus Slavery." It attacked the Fugitive Slave Law of 1793 as improper on grounds that the Constitution did not grant Congress the power to legislate upon the subject of slavery at all, and because the despised law denied the right of trial by jury which is guaranteed by the Seventh Amendment. Acknowledging southern insistence that Congress had no right to "meddle" with slavery, the essay responded that Congress had no power to enforce the slaveowners' claims either.[6]

The appearance of Madison's *Notes* in 1840 sparked an extended debate among abolitionists and others about the founders' true intentions regarding slavery. The cultural impact of Madison's *Notes* cannot be emphasized strongly enough. To the most radical abolitionists this detailed journal provided more than adequate documentation that the founders had compromised expediently at Philadelphia and had silently built safeguards for slavery into the Constitution. Moderate abolitionists did not agree; so the movement became permanently fragmented into groups incapable of co-operation. Publication of Madison's *Notes* also contributed to prolonged vacillation over slavery cases in the courts; undermined sectional compromises that had helped to keep the Union intact; and generally added to constitutional uncertainties during the 1840s and '50s.[7]

The press burgeoned with discussions concerning the problem of fugitive slaves. By 1845 it is possible to identify gradations of abolitionist constitutional theory, ranging along a spectrum from moderate to extremely radical. After 1842 the Garrisonians insisted that both the Constitution and the Union ought to be overthrown if they sustained an immoral institution. In 1843 those societies under Garrisonian control began to pass resolutions asserting that "no abolitionist can consistently swear to support the Constitution." Then, on May 31, 1844, Garrison spoke out in favor of northern secession. As an editorial in the *Liberator* explained: "The Constitution which subjects [Negroes] to hopeless bondage, is one that we cannot swear to support."[8]

During 1844–45 Wendell Phillips, the prominent reformer, orator, and ally of Garrison, prepared a volatile pamphlet that went through three editions by 1856. Incorporating quotations from Madison's *Notes,* from debates in the Confederation Congress, from the state ratifying conventions, *The Federalist Papers*, and other documents, it argued that for half a century the correct interpretation of the Constitution with respect to slavery had been elusive. "How and where can such a question ever be settled?" Phillips responded that the courts could not supply satisfactory answers. Therefore, "what the Constitution may become a century hence, we know not; we speak of it *as it is*, and repudiate it *as it is*."[9]

Although Phillips actually cursed the Constitution from a lyceum platform, the most dramatic outburst of that sort came from William Lloyd Garrison, whose *Liberator* labelled the U.S. Constitution "A Covenant with Death and an Agreement with Hell." Subsequently, on May 24, 1854, Anthony Burns, a free Negro, was seized on his way home from work in Boston, accused of being an escaped slave, and arrested on a phony charge of robbery. Six weeks later, at an open air gathering held on the Fourth of July in Framingham, Garrison proclaimed the demise of the Union. He first set fire to a copy of the Fugitive Slave Law, and then did the same to the Constitution. As it curled into flames, he solemnly intoned: "So perish all compromises with tyranny!"[10]

What Garrison said and did at Framingham Grove is far better known than the response he received. The vast majority of his audience had come expecting to hear slavery and the Fugitive Slave Law denounced. When he burned the Constitution, a few people said "Amen"; but many others in this antislavery audience hissed and expressed disapproval.[11] Garrison's melodramatic act may have been memorable, but it was not widely acceptable. His following had shrunk by 1854, and most men and women who opposed slavery hoped it would be possible to exterminate the evil by working within the existing constitutional system. It is essential, therefore, that we recognize not only diversity within the antislavery movement, but the fact that some leaders as well as many followers shifted their positions as well.

The case of Frederick Douglass is instructive. He began as a Garrisonian. On March 16, 1849, Douglass published in *The North Star*, his Rochester-based newspaper, an essay entitled "The Constitution and Slavery." In it he conceded that the Constitution, "standing alone, and construed *only* in the light of its letter, without reference to the opinions of the men who framed and adopted it," appeared neutral. He insisted, however, that the instrument had to be understood in its historical context of racial prejudice and political concessions.

It is in such a [contextual] light that we propose to examine the Constitution; and in this light we hold it to be a most cunningly-devised and wicked compact, demanding the most constant and earnest efforts . . . for its complete overthrow. . . . Congress enacted the atrocious "law of '93," making it penal in a high degree to harbor or shelter the flying fugitive. The whole nation that adopted it, consented to become kidnappers, and the whole land converted into slave-hunting ground. . . . Thus has the North, under the Constitution, not only consented to form bulwarks around the system of slavery . . . but has planted its uncounted feet and tremendous weight on the heaving hearts of American bondmen. . . . The parties that made the Constitution, aimed to cheat and defraud the slave, who was not himself a party to the compact or agreement.[12]

By the mid-1850s, however, Douglass had repudiated Garrison, the American Anti-Slavery Society, the American and Foreign Anti-Slavery Society, and the Free Soil Party. He shifted his support instead to the Liberty Party, which he labelled the Gerrit Smith School of Abolitionists. He explained why in a lecture delivered to the Rochester Ladies' Anti-Slavery Society during January 1855. The Liberty Party, despite its modest membership, deserved adherence because it "denies that slavery is, or *can* be legalized. It denies that the Constitution of the United States is a pro-slavery instrument, and asserts the power and duty of the Federal Government to abolish slavery in every State of the Union. Strictly speaking, I say this is the only party in the country which is an abolition party."[13]

Yet even the Liberty Party offered an idiosyncratic interpretation of the Constitution. More than ten years earlier, in 1844, it had boldly declared the fugitive slave clause to be null and void. Where any component of the Constitution came into conflict with natural law or right, the latter must take priority. A similar judgment would be applied to the Fugitive Slave Act of 1850.[14]

Negative reactions to the unpatriotic or anticonstitutional positions of Garrison, Phillips, as well as some northern "doughfaces," appeared well before Garrison ever put a match to the Constitution. In 1850, James Fenimore Cooper responded sharply to the pro-slavery advocates: "They say that the Constitution requires slavery. I should like to see in what clause." Charles Francis Adams and his friends opposed slavery, were pro-Union, pro-Constitution, and felt scandalized by Garrison's exhortations. Moncure D. Conway, a radical Methodist preacher turned Unitarian and an ardent antislavery man, could not join Garrison either. As he explained in his autobiography: "I did not care about the Constitution, and my peace principles inclined me to a separation between sections that hated each other. Yet I knew good people on both sides. I also believed that slavery was to be abolished by the union of all hearts and minds opposed to it,— those who believed emancipation potential in the Constitution, as well as the Constitution burners."[15]

As early as 1836 one of Garrison's rivals, James G. Birney, had of-fered an antislavery reading of the Constitution. Following the publication of Madison's *Notes,* however, a more extended argument was needed that would carry broad appeal. Salmon P. Chase of Ohio developed an inter-pretation of American history, persuasive to thousands of northerners, that the founders had been opposed to slavery and hoped for its early demise (an interpretation excessively dependent upon Jefferson's views). Chase stated the essence of his position in December 1841: "The Constitution found slavery and left it a State institution—the creature and dependent of State law—wholly local in its existence and character. It did not make it a national institution." Moderate abolitionists, like Chase, regarded slavery as a violation of natural right and common law. The Fugitive Slave laws of 1793 and 1850 were labelled unconstitutional because Congress lacked the power to legislate on such matters. Therefore, whenever a slave entered an area under federal jurisdiction, such as a territory, he or she automati-cally became free. As Chase wrote to Joshua Giddings in 1842: "The Constitution must be vindicated from the reproach of sanctioning the doc-trine of property in men."[16]

Although no federal court accepted Chase's position before the Civil War, increasing numbers in the antislavery movement adopted it during and after the 1840s. Despite blind spots in his constitutional logic and sup-porting historical evidence, his views steadily gained adherents in the North; and the Republican Party platforms of 1856 and 1860 endorsed Chase's insistence that Congress lacked the authority to recognize or cre-ate slavery anywhere within its jurisdiction. Chase and the Republicans made a careful distinction between the founders' intentions in 1787 and a series of unconstitutional aberrations that started with passage of the Fu-gitive Slave Law in 1793, followed by congressional acceptance of a terri-torial cession from North Carolina which stipulated that slavery be permitted to exist in the ceded area, and then a pattern of similar land ces-sions from other southern states during the early nineteenth century. Eventually these all became part of the Republican recitation of stages by which the so-called Slave Power had conspired to violate the constitutional constraints upon slavery that had been intended in 1787.[17]

Looking back from the perspective of the postwar era, Congressman Jonathan Bingham observed that "everything was reduced to a Constitutional question in those days." In 1845 a Massachusetts lawyer named Lysander Spooner developed an argument for *The Unconstitutionality of Slavery* in which he criticized "cowardly" abolitionists like Garrison and Phillips: "if they have the constitution in their hands, why, in heaven's name do they not out with it, and use it?" Members of the Liberty League and most of those in the Liberty Party who refused to join the Free Soil coalition regarded the Constitution as an antislavery document and believed that it entitled Congress to abolish slavery in the states. As Aileen Kraditor has commented, however, various assertions "that the Constitution did not guarantee slavery or that it outlawed slavery did not reflect systematic analysis of that document. They represent a more or less automatic use of a ready-made weapon wielded by people who wanted to convert the public and who intuitively knew that it was to their advantage to have as many revered institutions on their side as possible."[18]

The most widely held notions in the North and West reluctantly acknowledged the Constitution's fundamental ambiguity concerning slavery and its possible extension. One variant, adopted as a plank at the Free Soil convention in 1848, declared that slavery depended entirely upon state law. Hence it could be quarantined. A more common version, and one that steadily attracted adherents, was Abraham Lincoln's candid constitutionalist stance, epitomized in a debate with Senator Stephen A. Douglas on September 11, 1858. Asserting that the Republicans regarded slavery as an evil, he promised nonetheless that "they will not overlook the constitutional guards which our forefathers have placed around it . . . but they will use every constitutional method to prevent the evil from becoming larger. . . ."[19]

Historians have argued at length about Lincoln's views pertaining to race, the status of slavery in the territories, and what the federal government might or might not do about the problem. He has been praised for his altruism and realism yet abused as a hypocrite. If we examine the larger perspective—his understanding of the U.S. Constitution—Lincoln looks impressive: sensible and sincere though not entirely consistent. He towers above so many of his contemporaries because he showed a remarkable familiarity with American constitutional history,[20] recognized uncertainties inherent in the Constitution,[21] and above all, repeated time and again his determination to contain slavery by lawful means while tolerating the Fugitive Slave Law and not tampering with the peculiar institution in those states where it had earlier received the sanction of law. The accuracy of Lincoln's historical knowledge determined the integrity of his constitutional stance. As he explained in a long speech at Peoria, Illinois, in 1854: "the fathers of the republic eschewed and rejected" slavery.

> Before the constitution, they prohibited its introduction into the north-western Territory—the only country we owned, then free from it. At the framing and adoption of the constitution, they forebore to so much as mention the word "slave" or "slavery" in the whole instrument. . . . Thus, the thing is hid away, in the constitution, just as an afflicted man hides away a wen or a cancer, which he dares not cut out at once, lest he bleed to death; with the promise, nevertheless, that the cutting may begin at the end of a given time. . . . The earliest Congress, under the constitution, took the same view of slavery. They hedged and hemmed it in to the narrowest limits of necessity.[22]

Having known and said that much, why did Lincoln temporize at all with an evil practice? Did he not mean what he wrote in a private letter to a slaveowner in 1855: "I hate to see the poor creatures hunted down, and caught, and carried back to their stripes, and unrewarded toils"?[23] I believe that he did, and that the reason for his apparent inconsistency resulted from his unswerving commitment "to the support of the Constitution and Laws." As he declared as early as 1838: "Let it become the political religion of the nation." He accepted the infamous three-fifths clause because it was embedded in the Constitution. In a speech given at Kalamazoo, Michigan, in 1856, he pleaded with Democrats as well as Republicans: "Don't interfere with anything in the Constitution. That must be maintained, for it is the only safeguard of our liberties."[24]

Because Lincoln found the Dred Scott decision of 1857 contemptible, his hostility to slavery and disdain for the Supreme Court were reflected in the debates with Douglas during 1858. He attacked Chief Justice Taney almost as often as he attacked Senator Douglas, and with equal vehemence. At the fifth debate, held at Galesburg, Lincoln mocked Douglas for supporting the Dred Scott verdict, adding: "I believe that the right of property in a slave is *not* distinctly and expressly affirmed in the Constitution, and Judge Douglas thinks it *is.*"[25]

During 1859 and 1860 Lincoln the ambitious politician confronted a tension between his ethical convictions and his historical understanding of the Constitution. He advised Salmon P. Chase that the Republican Convention should not propose to repeal the Fugitive Slave Law because doing so would "explode the convention." On September 17, 1859, in a major address at Dayton, Ohio, Lincoln stated concisely the position he had been taking and would continue to hold until southern secession altered the situation by threatening the Union's existence: "I say that we must not interfere with the institution of slavery in the states where it exists, because the constitution forbids it, and the general welfare does not require us to do so. We must not withhold an efficient fugitive slave law because the constitution requires us, as I understand it, not to withhold such a law. But we must prevent the outspreading of the institution, because neither the Constitution nor general welfare requires us to extend it. We must prevent the revival of the African slave trade and the enacting by Congress of a territorial slave code."[26] After Lincoln's election late in 1860, when he added the role of sagacious statesman to that of shrewd politician, his emphases would alter somewhat, though not the substantive views that he had articulated on numerous occasions prior to winning the Republican nomination. We will return momentarily to Lincoln's constitutional outlook as President.

Before doing so, however, it is important to acknowledge that constitutional confusion was everywhere evident after 1855, verging upon chaos once the Dred Scott decision had been announced. One newspaper editor summed up the situation succinctly in 1856: "The Constitution threatens to be a subject of infinite sects, like the Bible." The fact that almost everyone except the Garrisonians proclaimed their devotion to the Constitution only heightened the illusion that a framework for resolution (if not reconciliation) existed. The bitter upheaval caused by Kansas in 1854–55, for example, left President Pierce naïvely sanguine. "The storm of frenzy and faction must inevitably dash itself in vain against the unshaken rock of the Constitution," he exclaimed in his third annual message to Congress. Unlike Lincoln, Pierce felt a constitutional obligation to protect slavery in the territories as well as in the states where it had been shielded by law. Pierce found it inconceivable that some fanatics might wish to exclude a territory "whose Constitution clearly embraces a republican form of government" merely because "its domestic institutions may not in all respects comport with the ideas of what is wise and expedient entertained in some other State."[27]

The Dred Scott decision shattered any remaining illusion that a consensus about slavery in the territories ought to exist among rational

Americans. Republican leaders repudiated the Court and henceforth distinguished carefully between it and the cherished Constitution.[28] Democratic newspapers, by contrast, largely conservative, followed Taney's dictum with this sort of announcement: "Whoever now seeks to revive sectionalism arrays himself against the Constitution, and consequently against the Union." Still others adopted a third position, represented by the *New York Tribune*. Until the Supreme Court chose to reverse the Dred Scott decision, it insisted, "the Constitution of the United States is nothing better than the bulwark of inhumanity and oppression." Two trends became clear during the four years following 1856. First, as one editorial lamented, "our judicial decisions upon constitutional questions touching the subject of slavery are rapidly coming to be the enunciation of mere party dogmas; [and] that the country is dividing geographically upon questions of constitutional law." Second, and closely connected, during the period between the Dred Scott decision and Lincoln's inauguration, the American public maintained an unusually high degree of interest in political issues requiring constitutional resolution.[29]

The presidential election of 1860 involved, as no other election before it in U.S. history, a national constitutional debate. What made it especially quixotic, however, was that four parties (or party fragments) offered as many different constitutional doctrines, all the while professing their unswerving fealty to the fundamental law. Speaking in the Senate during January 1860, Jefferson Davis defended southerners as "a body of intelligent men, and most of them men true to our constitutional rights . . . men as true to the Constitution as if they lived in any other portion of the country. . . ."[30] John Bell, a Tennessee Whig who became the standard-bearer of the Constitutional Union Party, ran on a singular platform: "The Constitution of the Country, the Union of the States, and the Enforcement of the Laws."

John C. Breckinridge of Kentucky, who won the nomination of the most pro-slavery wing of the Democratic Party, declared that "fidelity to the Constitution of the United States, in all its parts, and in all its obligations, is the condition of the American Union, and of its perpetuation." To Breckinridge and his supporters that meant equal treatment for all states and an obligation on the part of the national government to protect citizens and their property, including chattel slaves. The Republican platform, by contrast, declared that slavery could not constitutionally exist in any territory because of the due process clause in the Fifth Amendment. On September 11, 1860, the best known Republican nationally, Senator William H. Seward, delivered a speech entitled "The Constitution Interpreted" in which he staked a position too radical for many in his own party: namely, that it would violate the Constitution if any person of any class or race should be repressed in his efforts to achieve a higher degree of liberty and happiness.[31]

Amidst all of this constitutional rhetoric and consternation, the public received virtually no assistance from educators, journalists, and scholars. Late in 1860, for example, Nathaniel C. Towle published *A History and Analysis of the Constitution of the United States.* The author explained that his purpose was "to familiarize the people with the original principles of the government under which they now live." Towle's emphasis fell almost exclusively upon the history of colonial confederations, the origins of the 1787 Convention, the cession of western territories, the addition of new states, and the administrative organization of executive departments. The book would have been utterly useless to anyone seeking illumination on the emerging crisis.

It is ironic, perhaps, that one of the most astute and sensible discussions of the impending crisis came in the form of a long address by the much-maligned Andrew Johnson, published in the *Congressional Globe* and as a separate pamphlet just when Towle's banal book appeared. Speaking to the Senate on December 18 and 19, 1860, Johnson insisted that "this battle ought to be fought not outside, but inside of the Union, and upon the battlements of the Constitution itself." He declared the act of secession to be an unconstitutional one; and quoting James Madison, he offered the premise that "the Constitution was formed for perpetuity; that it never was intended to be broken up." Johnson rambled through Revolutionary history, through the story of territorial acquisitions, through classical allusions, and spoke bitterly against Lincoln, even calling for his "overthrow" in 1864. At the end, however, Johnson expressed his love for the Constitution and the Union. "If the States have the right to secede at will and pleasure, for real or imaginary evils or oppressions . . . this Government is at an end; it is not stronger than a rope of sand."[32]

II

Despite Johnson's distress over the election of Lincoln, his speech anticipated—even coincided with—the central theme of Lincoln's remarkable public trip from Springfield to Washington during February 1861: namely, that the Union and liberty could only be saved by observing the letter of the Constitution. As Lincoln exhorted an audience at Indianapolis on February 11: "It is your business to rise up and preserve the Union and liberty. . . . I desire they shall be constitutionally preserved." He spread the same message in a dozen different ways during his pre-inaugural journey. Three days later, at Steubenville, Ohio, he acknowledged the nation's dilemma: although everyone expressed devotion to the Constitution, common ground did not exist for determining its proper application to the great issues of the day.[33] Consequently he initiated a shift in emphasis that would persist throughout the remainder of his career: the Union must not be sacrificed because of differences in constitutional interpretation or by silences in the document itself.

When Lincoln spoke at Independence Hall in Philadelphia on February 22, 1861, he stressed his ideological commitment to "the sentiments embodied in the Declaration of Independence."[34] Although his inaugural address, presented twelve days later, mentioned the Declaration, it developed primarily as a conciliatory gloss upon the Constitution. Lincoln reiterated his belief that "the Union of these States is perpetual," yet reassured southerners that he did not intend to "interfere with the institution of slavery in the States where it exists." Although that inaugural address is quoted most often because of its peroration and plea that "the mystic chords of memory" sustain the Union by touching "the better angels of our nature," its importance does not lie so much in Lincoln's eloquence, however moving, as it does in the firmness of his resolve to preserve the Union while pledging to accept certain constitutional obligations that were repugnant to him and his party. Twenty-three years earlier, in Lincoln's first great public address, he had insisted upon the belief that national survival depended upon *"a reverence for the constitution and laws"* (his emphasis). As he assumed the nation's highest office, and faced its most traumatic moment, his message remained essentially the same.[35]

If we survey newspaper responses to Lincoln's inaugural, we find a predictable range of partisan praise, hostility, and deepening constitutional confusion. The conservative *National Intelligencer,* published in Washington, D.C., lauded Lincoln for being conciliatory rather than impetuous. It assumed that he would seek to resolve the crisis by constitutional adjustment rather than by force; and offered the judgment—only half correct, as it turned out—that "the Union cannot be preserved by war, nor maintained by blood; it can only be done by peaceful means, and future difficulties can only be prevented by constitutional amendments." A similar stance, with varied nuances, appeared in *The New York Times, The Goshen* (New York) *Democrat, The Hartford Courant, Pittsburgh Gazette, Chicago Tribune,* and *Daily Alta California* (San Francisco). Most of these editorials embodied a triumph of hope over realism; found in Lincoln a desirable mix of flexibility with firmness; and assumed, with *The Emporia* (Kansas) *News,* that "the Constitution as it was made shall be his sole guide, until the people shall change it. . . . The Union, at whatever cost, will remain the Union, and the Constitution will be the supreme law of the land."[36]

Though that may have been a widely shared view in the West and North, nothing close to a consensus emerged. While the *Albany Evening Journal* found it "clear, compact, and impressive," the *Albany Argus* called it a "rambling, discursive, questioning, loose-jointed stump speech." Whereas the *New York Herald* viewed it as "a paraphrase of the vague generalities contained in his pilgrimage speeches," the *Chicago Tribune* praised it particularly for its "freedom from diplomatic vagueness and hackneyed political phrases."[37] Others made a special effort to rebuke the southern impulse toward secession, or to indicate that war would be a justifiable response to rebellion, or even to express doubt that the Union could be preserved "without bloodshed." Still others, mostly in the Middle West, either found Lincoln's response to southern disunion too weak, or else dubbed the address "a mountain of ambiguity."[38]

It will come as no surprise that the southern press considered Lincoln's inaugural "a medley of ignorance, sanctimonious cant and tenderfooted bullyism." Even so, the most striking feature of Confederate editorials is their personal vituperation against Lincoln—calling him an abolitionist, or referring to his "Yankee cunning"—and their drift away from constitutional debate. The South ignored Lincoln's conciliatory tone and his insistence that slavery would be protected where the sanction of law required it. The crisis had rapidly reached a point where such reassurance seemed irrelevant. Coercion suddenly became the key question. Consequently one of the few responses couched in constitutional terms took this form: "Does he know that force or coercion was expressly denied by the Convention which framed the Constitution, against States resisting? And hence is he not aware that this talk about coercion of States by military force, is palpable and treasonable usurpation of power, denied by the compatriots who formed the Constitution, MADISON and HAMILTON declaring that such an effort would inevitably and finally dissolve the Union, setting the seal of blood on the fatal act?"[39]

The reaction of Raleigh's *Weekly Standard* was atypical: "When he pleads for the Union we will point to the Constitution." That sharp dichotomy may seem a curious answer, at first glance, because Lincoln had made such an effort to join the two symbols by asserting "that in contemplation of universal law, and of the Constitution, the Union of these States is perpetual."[40] Like so many Americans outside the Confederacy, Lincoln regarded the Constitution and the Union as interdependent and mutually supportive. Nonetheless, the Raleigh editorialist may have sensed that one tendency during 1861, at least in some quarters, would be to elevate the sanctity of Union, if need be, above the inviolability of the Constitution. For the first time significant numbers of people, northern as well as British (such as Walter Bagehot), began to question whether the U.S. Constitution provided sufficient legitimacy for the Union or an adequate framework for its defense under crisis conditions.[41]

It is certainly true that preservation of the Union became a paramount concern in 1861. But as a popular engraving entitled *Union* demonstrates (see figure 11, which is based on a painting by T. S. Matteson, ca. 1861), Lincoln and Webster jointly display a scroll, "Constitution of the United States of America" that is the focal point for the entire scene. Calhoun and Clay, John Tyler and James Buchanan, Stephen A. Douglas and Thomas Hart Benton are also present, despite the fact that some of these men had been dead for a decade. The artist wanted to make the point that all of them were genuine patriots, fully devoted to a Union made possible by the Constitution of 1787.

The same sort of compound symbolism will be found in the thirteen silver trays designed to commemorate the seventy-fifth anniversary of the signing of the Constitution (see figure 6, made by S. H. Black of Black, Star & Gorham to be given to the governors of the thirteen original states); and is equally applicable to the mass rally held at Independence Square in Philadelphia on September 17, 1861, to celebrate the signing of the Constitution. On the cover of the souvenir program, a copy of the Constitution is supported by a firm handshake in front and firmly bound fasces behind. The legend above these symbols says: "The Union Must and Shall Be Preserved." A committee of prominent Philadelphians presented five resolutions at that mass rally. The briefest and most prominent one read: "*Resolved,* That the Union established by the adoption of the Constitution, is and was intended to be perpetual."[42]

Public recognition of that resolution, and of its implications, was reinforced during 1861–62 by the appearance of various works written by nonpoliticians. Theophilus Parsons, the Dane Professor of Law at Harvard, printed an important lecture in which he denied that secession was constitutional and affirmed the capacity of the U.S. Constitution to withstand the most severe stress. Later in 1861 a new textbook circulated for secondary school students, a "catechism of the Constitution" that made explicit the dominant northern view of the genesis and nature of the Union:

What does the Preamble make evident?
The parties who formed the Constitution and the government of the
United States.
Who are the parties that formed them?
The people of the United States, composed of the people of each of
the then existing States.
How is this made more certain?
By the language of the Preamble, which is, "We, the people of the
United States," and not we the people of the States of Massachusetts,
Connecticut, New Hampshire, &c. . . .
*For what had the Declaration of Independence and the Articles of Con-
federation prepared the people?*
For a National Constitution and a National Government of the peo-
ple, adequate to the increasing wants of the whole country.
How may we regard the Constitution?
The Constitution, as a system of supreme fundamental law is the act
of the people of the United States and not the act of the people of the
several States in their separate sovereign capacities.
What may be remarked of the objects named in the Preamble?
They are eminently national, and designed to make the people of the
United States one country, with one Constitution, and a common
destiny.[43]

By January 1862 one reviewer could claim that "the apparatus for
studying our Constitution has improved more rapidly since the integrity of
the Union was threatened than at any preceding period." The same issue
of the *North American Review* contained an essay-review (by James Russell Lowell) of eight constitutional publications. That very month, in a different journal, Judge Timothy Farrar (the respected former law partner of
Daniel Webster) published an influential essay in which he argued that the
Constitution was "adequate to all the purposes for which it was made. Our
fathers made it and put it into successful operation, under circumstances
vastly more discouraging than those in which we are now called upon to
defend it."[44]

That perspective steadily gained adherents. Daniel Agnew, a federal
judge in Pennsylvania, produced a pamphlet in 1863 that went through
several printings, shaped Unionist assumptions about the Constitution's
adaptability during a period of domestic insurrection, and also helped to
defend Lincoln's expansive interpretation of his legitimate war powers.
Agnew insisted that the South committed treason because secession had

the "avowed purpose of overthrowing the Constitution and authority of the Federal Government in the seceding states." He then contended that Americans had been "unconscious of the sleeping powers of the Constitution," and that a state of war justified the use of force to defend the nation's governmental system. Agnew argued that the President had a duty to repress insurrection, and that the source of his war powers could clearly be found in the Constitution. Lincoln's critics "overlook the fact that the injunctions of the Constitution, and the Acts of Congress in pursuance, are a grant of *express, unlimited,* and *unconditional* authority to use the whole physical force of the nation, according to his own judgment, in quelling traitors." Agnew concluded by legitimizing on constitutional grounds the President's power to declare martial law, even in localities loyal to the Union; the military emancipation of slaves; the right of military arrest; and suspension of the writ of habeas corpus under emergency circumstances. Above all, he declared that "the *duty,* the *power,* and the *means* provided by the Constitution and laws to suppress the insurrection by force of arms were plenary."[45]

By 1863 increasing numbers of northerners became persuaded that the Constitution was indeed adequate to sustain Lincoln's policies in quelling the Confederacy. Precisely because an unprecedented crisis did exist, more commentaries upon the Constitution, in one form or another, appeared between 1861 and 1864 than between 1865 and 1875, when most Americans—at least on the federal side—felt that their governmental system had been vindicated. One observer summed up the situation in 1864: "Oh, how the rebellion has interpreted for us and commented upon the Constitution."[46]

Needless to say, this proliferation of literature did not produce constitutional agreement. Some critics insisted that the federal government lacked authority to make war upon a member state, conquer and reduce it to territorial status. George Ticknor Curtis, a conservative Massachusetts Whig who married the daughter of Justice Story and wrote the most authoritative history of the Constitution published prior to the 1880s, criticized the abolitionists in 1862 for making "open and undisguised war upon the Constitution." He then added that northerners must "religiously and honestly respect the constitutional right of every state to maintain just such domestic institutions as it pleases to have, and protect that right from every species of direct and indirect interference."[47]

No wonder Joel Parker, a professor of law at Harvard, felt so troubled in 1863 by the diversity of views among Unionists, and complained of "loose Constitutional notions in the community." No wonder some observers lamented that "constitutional and unconstitutional propositions press upon us with such rapidity at the present day, that, before we have time to dispose of one set of them another claims our attention."[48] So much diversity and so many propositions resulted from at least four different stimuli.

First, the status of slaves once secession had occurred and the war began shifted gradually from being a matter of military expediency to a problem requiring constitutional clarification and, eventually, amendment. When Lincoln issued the Emancipation Proclamation on January 1, 1863, he called it "an act of justice warranted by the Constitution upon military necessity." Others invoked a combination of Christian theology, the Declaration of Independence, and, to a lesser degree, the Constitution. Still others subsequently cited the Constitution in a formulaic way, but essentially relied upon assertions of a national value system: republicanism, justice, and the utter incompatibility between freedom and slavery. As a congressman from Iowa put it: "Throughout all the dominions of slavery, republican government, constitutional liberty, the blessings of our free institutions were mere fables. . . . Let slavery die. Let its death be written in our Constitution."[49]

A second stimulus to diversity (and to constitutional dissent) came from the comments of highly intelligent foreigners whose interesting views, although unrepresentative, have received a disproportionate amount of attention from students of the era. Nevertheless, because they were well informed, thoughtful, and articulate men, their views elicited responses. I have already mentioned Walter Bagehot, an English political writer who proclaimed in 1861 that the northern and southern states could not "hope to continue united under the present Constitution, or to form parts of the same federal republic under any Constitution whatever," and then argued that inadequacies in the Constitution itself bore more responsibility than the citizenry. In Bagehot's mind, the "carefully considered provisions of the American Constitution have, in fact, deprived the American people of the guidance and government of great statesmen, just when these were most required."[50]

The German-born political scientist Francis Lieber, who taught at South Carolina College until 1856 and at Columbia University from 1857 until his death in 1872, wrote extensively on the U.S. Constitution, particularly during the Civil War years. His nationalistic view of the Constitution was unexceptionable from a northern perspective: "It is a national fundamental law, establishing a complete national government,—an organism of national life. It is not a mere league of independent states or nations." Yet his sense of the Constitution's inadequacy under crisis conditions persisted well beyond 1861, when most northerners abandoned that view. "The whole rebellion is beyond the Constitution," Lieber declared in 1864. "The Constitution was not made for such a state of things."[51]

E. L. Godkin, the Anglo-Irish journalist, emigrated to the United States in 1856, studied law, worked as a correspondent for the London *Daily News* during the Civil War, founded *The Nation* in 1865, and served as its influential editor until 1899. In 1864 he published an essay, "The Constitution and Its Defects," that was widely noticed. Like Lieber's efforts, however, it was neither persuasive nor representative. Godkin conceded at the outset that "no political arrangement has been the object of more admiration than the American Constitution." He acknowledged that recently it had become emblematic of the Union, mocked this tendency toward "Constitution-worship," and insisted that "the spell has been broken by the war. . . . To anybody who undertakes to show us that the Constitution ought to have held the Free and Slave States together, we reply, that the experiment has been fully tried, and that it did not succeed." Godkin's undiluted idealism did much to make his analysis unacceptable to many contemporaries. He explained, for example, that the mere abolition of slavery by constitutional amendment would be inadequate. It is not sufficient, Godkin argued, to acknowledge that men are born with equal abilities. A sensible system must provide them with equal opportunities to maximize those abilities. "Any democratic Constitution," he concluded, "in which this truth is not solemnly recognized furnishes . . . one of those satires on popular consistency and popular justice in which cynics and tyrants delight."[52] Too few Americans were ready to go that far with Godkin.

A third stimulus to diversity and conflict came from the Democratic Party, which clung to the same narrow constitutionalism that had characterized the party ever since the Jacksonian era a generation earlier. Democrats charged the Republicans, generally, with disregarding the Constitution rather than seeking to preserve it, and more particularly with trampling upon civil liberties. In 1862 Democratic leaders announced that their party was prepared to unite with all patriotic citizens "for the purpose of restoring the Union as it was and maintaining the Constitution as it is." That remained their slogan throughout the war, and enraged such Republican spokesmen as Edward Everett. Speaking at Faneuil Hall in Boston on October 19, 1864, for example, Everett contended that the Democratic creed was meaningless because prior to 1861 "every principle with respect to slavery on which the Union was established and the Constitution framed has been violated, and every compromise disregarded, set at naught, defeated, reversed. . . ."[53]

Democrats believed that the Constitution protected slavery as a local institution. They criticized Lincoln's administration for its antislavery policies; and eventually, quite bitterly, they opposed the Thirteenth Amendment. Many Democrats tended to equate Republicanism with abolitionism and New England fanaticism. Hence in 1863 Congressman Samuel Cox of Ohio castigated "the Constitution-breaking, law-defying, negro-loving, Pariseeism [sic] of New England." Most Democrats reiterated that the Constitution must not be manipulated, suspended, or ignored during wartime. In the presidential campaign of 1864 the Democratic platform stressed the degradation of the Constitution by sanctimonious Republicans who sought "to do in the name of God, what could not be done in the name of the Constitution."[54]

Although in retrospect the Democrats appear to have been politically motivated, racially prejudiced, unpatriotic, and petty, this much must be conceded: dispassionate modern scholars have questioned aspects of Lincoln's constitutional behavior and challenged his justifications. Even Carl Sandburg, a warm admirer, could write that Lincoln had said

> *Yes to the constitution when a help*
> *no to the constitution when a hindrance.*

Samuel J. Tilden, a prominent Democratic leader from New York, summed up his party's dilemma very well in 1863: "I am quite aware how difficult is the conduct of a constitutional opposition during the period of war; how necessary it is to guard against its degenerating into faction, and to keep its measures directed to attaining the utmost practical good for the country at every varying stage of public affairs."[55]

A fourth stimulus to constitutional conflict came from the Confederacy, whose ideological spokesmen scarcely remained quiet. Northerners could not resist answering certain southern claims because many northerners, however strong their commitment to the Union, continued to believe that states' rights ought to have a respectable role in the federal system and that government had an obligation to uphold laws and protect private property. Edward Everett devoted several pages of his long-winded speech at Gettysburg to a discussion of the Tenth Amendment, the problem of rights reserved to the states, and to southern claims for the integrity of sovereign states. Everett's solution took this form: "I do not deny that the separate States are clothed with sovereign powers for the administration of local affairs. . . . But it is equally true, that, in adopting the Federal Constitution, the States abdicated, by express renunciation, all the most important functions of national sovereignty."[56]

III

Although southern constitutionalism did not lapse into silence during the war, neither did it develop many notable new twists. Memories of the Nullification Crisis remained vivid and the legacy of John C. Calhoun persisted, disseminated by such disciples as James H. Hammond, Robert Barnwell Rhett, William Lowndes Yancey, Francis W. Pickens, and R. M. T. Hunter. Starting in 1845, Calhoun worked simultaneously on his *Disquisition on Government* and *A Discourse on the Constitution and Government of the United States.* Neither one had been completed when he died in 1850, but both were published in 1853. The central problem addressed by Calhoun in each essay concerned how best to protect the interests and customs of a minority that felt menaced by a dominant majority. In the *Disquisition* he referred far more to "minorities" and "interests" than he did to states. Calhoun took care to differentiate between the constitution of a country and its government—a distinction particularly important in the American context, yet one that has been too often neglected. His attempt at comparative constitutionalism is also impressive, and led him into discussions of the Roman, British, Polish, and Iroquois constitutions, among others.

In the last analysis, however, the feature of Calhoun's thought that remains most famous and distinctive, his theory of the concurrent majority, is also its most idiosyncratic, rendering Calhoun's scheme interesting at best yet ultimately irrelevant. "It is this negative power," he claimed, "the power of preventing or arresting the action of the government, be it called by what term it may, veto, interposition, nullification, check, or balance of power—which in fact forms the constitution."[57] Calhoun's understandable obsession with "negative power" would soon seem quaint in a society moving toward enhanced national power and tacit acceptance of the dominant role of public opinion.

Although the Confederate Constitution has not been neglected by students, misperceptions of it persist. After the Provisional Constitution was adopted on February 8, 1861, Vice President Alexander H. Stephens wrote that "it is the constitution of the United States with such changes and modifications as are necessary to meet the exigencies of the times." In Jefferson Davis's inaugural address, on February 18, he announced that "We have changed the constituent parts, but not the system of government. The constitution formed by our fathers is that of these Confederate States."[58] The obvious factor validating Davis's claim is that southern leaders felt satisfied with the U.S. Constitution as they understood it. They simply did not accept what seemed to them loose and radical lines of interpretation. The less obvious explanation is that those delegates who met in secret session at Montgomery, Alabama, represented just seven states. By making only those alterations that seemed essential, they hoped to attract states still uncommitted to the Confederacy.[59]

Clearly, they were determined to constitutionalize their commitment to Negro slavery. The document that they produced equated Negroes with slaves and included ironclad guarantees that slavery would be perpetuated. The Confederate Constitution prohibited its Congress from passing any law that might deny or jeopardize slaves as property; required Congress to protect slavery in the territories; and guaranteed to slaveowners an absolute right to take into the territories a slave lawfully possessed in any state.[60]

What is less obvious, and has not received adequate attention, is that in key respects the Confederate Constitution was more akin to the Articles of Confederation than it was to the U.S. Constitution of 1787. Despite the Dred Scott decision, for example, southerners felt a strong antipathy toward the nationalistic Supreme Court. Consequently the Confederate government never effectively implemented the vague provision for one. From 1862 until 1865 every Congress considered a bill to establish a Supreme Court, but none could pass both houses. Passions ran so high on this question that on February 4, 1863, debate was interrupted when Senator Benjamin H. Hill of Georgia hurled an inkstand at William Lowndes Yancey of Alabama.[61]

An argument appeared, many years ago, that throughout the Civil War the highest state courts tended to sustain acts passed by the Confederate Congress (rather than pursue a state sovereignty position on constitutional matters). Consequently, the implication followed, momentum to establish a confederate Supreme Court did not need to be maintained.[62] The fact of the matter remains that states' rights did impede the Confederacy politically and made its Constitution less of a clone of the parent document than many have presumed. Southern state courts enjoyed political power and legal status unknown under the United States Constitution; and the Confederate Constitution received its only significant judicial interpretation from the higher courts of the respective states.[63]

The composition of the Confederate Constitution was inevitably influenced by that of 1787; and the presence of numerous similarities cannot be denied. Nevertheless, one need only read the first sixteen words of the preamble to perceive that Confederate constitutionalism was significantly deviant—in spirit, and, as it turned out, in practice as well: "We, the people of the Confederate States, each State acting in its sovereign and independent character . . ."

IV

What enduring impact did the Civil War have upon the U.S. Constitution? It is difficult to answer with assurance. Felix Frankfurter, for example, took a minimalist view, arguing that only the amendments terminating slavery and subjecting the states to national oversight (by means of the High Court's augmented power to negate state legislation) significantly modified the earlier distribution of authority within the federal system. Well-informed scholars have recently argued for a more pervasive influence, citing the precedent of emergency powers used by the executive, expansion of the scope of congressional authority, and the populace coming to expect more from its national government.[64]

For a third and quite different perspective we may look to young Henry Adams, who lived through the era as a participant and close observer. "The essential and fatal changes in our Constitution," he wrote in 1869, "were not the results of the war, but of deeper social causes, which each need a volume to discuss." Members of the Adams family had customarily presumed complexity in matters requiring historical explanation, most especially the long-term causes of change. Hence it is no surprise that Adams seems more interested in the Civil War as a product of cultural shifts long under way. Yet by 1876, when Adams and Henry Cabot Lodge co-authored an essay on "American History and the Constitution," they acknowledged changes in the role that it performed in American society and conceded that "the Constitution has done its work. It has made a nation."[65]

Not only had Adams and Lodge arrived at a perception that remains valid, but Adams also expressed attitudes representative of relieved northerners in the aftermath of Union victory. He wrote from London in 1867 that the American people were not "disposed to abrogate or alter the

Constitution, or that they can do so." In 1876 he indicated pride that the Constitution had been able to surmount the crisis of the Union; argued that it had been remarkably successful in functional terms; and expressed the belief that it deserved veneration.[66] In so doing he joined the chorus of those who felt that Judge Timothy Farrar had been vindicated in declaring, at a dark hour during the winter of 1861–62, that the Constitution would prove adequate to overcome internal convulsions, and that American perceptions of the Constitution "must enlarge with the growth of the nation and its altering circumstances."[67]

Those perceptions would indeed change and expand in critical ways during the final third of the nineteenth century, as we shall see in chapter 6. On at least one major issue, however, historians of the Civil War era now seem to be agreed: that politics continued to work within a constitutional framework both during and after the war. Politicization of the Constitution occurred, to be sure; but by and large the commitment to constitutional restraint among legislators and jurists was so strong that it even contributed to a dilution of the commitment that many had made to achieve civil liberties for the Negro. Illinois Senator Lyman Trumbull, a staunch Republican, epitomized this attitude in 1862: "I want no other authority for putting down even this gigantic rebellion than such as may be derived from the Constitution properly interpreted. It is equal even to this great emergency; and the more we study its provisions, the more it is tried in troublous times, the greater will be our admiration of the instrument and our veneration for the wisdom of its authors."[68]

A persuasive case has been made that due regard for constitutional restraint caused the Republicans to cope with problems of Reconstruction less generously than we, in retrospect, would wish. Republican legislators were most likely to approve proposals that had been narrowly construed. The Fourteenth and Fifteenth amendments are framed in negative terms: what may *not* be done, rather than what must be done on behalf of the freedmen.[69] Throughout 1866 and '67, of course, Democrats tried to demonstrate quite the opposite—that the Republicans had ignored constitutional restraints—and this accusation was incorporated into the Democratic Party platform of 1868: "[The Republican Party] has stripped the President of his constitutional power of appointment, even of his own Cabinet. Under its repeated assaults the pillars of the government are rocking on their base, and should it succeed in November next and inaugurate its President, we will meet, as a subjected and conquered people, amid the ruins of liberty and the scattered fragments of the Constitution."[70] Although the election of 1868 and the Grant administration that took office as a result may not stand as testimonials to American statesmanship or good government, they do provide persuasive evidence that the constitutional system, gradually being altered, remained a reliable compass for the national ship of state.

The saga of Andrew Johnson's struggle with the Republicans has been written many times before and requires no retelling here. It is noteworthy, however, that Johnson defended his programs and his vetoes of Republican legislation primarily in terms of a genuine commitment to preserve the integrity of the Constitution and to conduct himself in accord with his oath of office. This objective provided the leitmotif, for example, of his third annual message to Congress: "The Union and the Constitution are inseparable. As long as one is obeyed by all parties, the other will be preserved. . . . Without the Constitution we are nothing; by, through, and under the Constitution we are what it makes us. . . . If we can not support the Constitution with the cheerful alacrity of those who love and believe in it, we must give to it at least the fidelity of public servants who act under solemn obligations and commands which they dare not disregard."[71]

Even more pertinent, Johnson's well-known battle to resist impeachment has obscured a protracted struggle, perhaps equally significant, between the executive and Congress, on the one hand, and the Supreme Court on the other. In every single year from 1850 until 1873 (except for the war years 1861–65), some form of legislation was proposed that would have diminished the Court's powers significantly. One of the few pervasive complaints registered by the northern press against Lincoln's first inaugural address referred to his paragraph critical of the Taney Court. "It is a co-ordinate branch of the government," noted a paper in Buffalo, New York, "and as such, should not be attacked by the Executive. While its decisions are not above criticism, the President is not the man to undertake this work."[72]

In 1867 *Harper's Weekly* proposed a reorganization of the Supreme Court. The *New York Herald* concurred, and added the recommendation that more justices be added—a scheme that would become notorious as "Court-packing" in 1937.[73] That proposal failed to win congressional support; but one year later the Radical Republicans discussed a plan to "change the character of the Supreme Court" because it had frustrated some of their programs by narrow five to four splits. Fearing that several key Reconstruction Acts might be declared unconstitutional, Radicals urged that such decisions require a margin of at least six to three (an unsuccessful notion that would be revived by Senator William E. Borah in 1923–24). During the winter of 1869–70, following the controversial de-

cision in *Ex parte Yerger* in which the Court refused to surrender its jurisdiction over habeas corpus cases resulting from military commissions, Republican congressmen attacked the Republican-dominated Court by
seeking to limit its jurisdiction over certain types of cases. The *New York
World* condemned this as "a bill to abolish the Constitution"; and it
failed.[74]

The essential point to keep in mind is that the Court remained politicized during the quarter century between the Dred Scott decision of 1857
and the Court's reversal in 1883 of the Reconstruction-inspired Civil
Rights Acts. One significant consequence can best be described as constitutional deterioration in the eyes of the American public. As a critic observed in 1882, the government of the United States depended upon a
Constitution, and every official swore an oath to uphold it. Nevertheless,
ambiguities in the document aggravated by differences of political opinion
created conditions of extreme uncertainty.

> One president says one measure is constitutional, and he has a large
> constituency behind him to back him; and another president says it is
> unconstitutional, and he has a large following behind him to back
> him; and the Supreme Court, the supreme arbiters, are called upon to
> decide, and four of them against three say one day that legal tenders
> are unconstitutional, and a few months afterward five of them against
> four say that legal tenders are entirely constitutional. And yet does
> anybody suppose that there is any one of the judges, or the presi-
> dents, or anybody else who is throwing the Constitution overboard?
> Who would be outside Bedlam and contend for that?[75]

We are beginning to realize that the Republican program was neither
so radical nor so single-minded as historians assumed a generation ago.
Republican sentiment on behalf of civil rights for freedmen was counterbalanced by a continuing commitment to federalism. Most Republicans
accepted the notion that a protected sphere of state jurisdiction remained
beyond the reach of national authority, and their acceptance required difficult decisions in response to perplexing alternatives. President Rutherford
B. Hayes conveyed this attitude in a message to the Senate during 1880:
"The true interests of the people of this country require that both the National and State Governments should be allowed, without jealous interference on either side, to exercise all the powers which respectively belong to
them according to a fair and practical construction of the Constitution.
State rights and the rights of the United States should be equally re-

spected. Both are essential to the preservation of our liberties and the perpetuity of our institutions."[76]

An important phenomenon that helped to sustain this balanced view
has not received the attention it deserves: the ongoing process of writing
state constitutions and reshaping old ones. Between 1863 and 1866 every
state that had seceded replaced its Confederate constitution with a new
one. Numerous referenda were held; and from 1864 until 1879, thirty-
seven new state constitutions were written and ratified. During the decade
following 1877, twenty-eight constitutional conventions took place in seventeen states. Between 1874 and 1902 the ten Confederate states replaced
their Republican-imposed charters from the early years of Reconstruction.
The six northwestern states admitted in 1889–90, plus Utah in 1896 and
Oklahoma in 1907, all entered with new constitutions. One should add to
all of that activity the need for almost every state to give frequent consideration to numerous constitutional amendments, and that a manifest trend
existed to systematize or codify state laws.[77]

Constitutionalism pertaining to problems other than race became more
prominent in American culture during the final quarter of the nineteenth
century. New sorts of issues began to be discussed in journals of opinion:
whether a commercial treaty would violate the Constitution; the problem
of presidential disability, raised by Garfield's lingering between life and
death following Guiteau's assassination effort; civil service reform and the
need to alter the Constitution more easily; what candidates for naturalization ought to know about the Constitution; and the possibility of an
amendment permitting women to vote in national elections.[78]

Churchmen as well as jurists seemed more inclined than ever before
to explore the relationship between Christianity and the Constitution. Despite the conventional wisdom that cultural secularization accelerated during the 1870s, prominent authorities stressed "the Christianity of our
Constitution" and the moral responsibility of every citizen to understand
both the Constitution and its biblical basis. The same writers were also
likely to perpetuate the customary assumption that American prosperity
derived directly from the Constitution.[79]

As the post–Reconstruction era drew to a close, two disquieting
trends emerged as harbingers of the generation that would follow. First,
national organization of the American Bar Association (ABA) in 1878 revealed a penchant for professionalization of the law and a predilection for
mystification of the Constitution. Leaders of the bar had little interest in
disseminating constitutionalism as a prominent feature of public under-

standing and discourse. Unfortunately, declared the second president of the ABA in 1879, "it is too true that [the Constitution] has become more and more a subject to be hawked about the country, debated in the newspapers, [and] discussed from the stump."[80]

Symptomatic of a second trend was the Supreme Court's decision, early in 1883, declaring unconstitutional a cluster of civil rights laws passed during Reconstruction. Most of them had been designed to elaborate upon and enforce provisions of the Fourteenth Amendment; and Negro leaders along with a minority of sympathetic whites felt deeply embittered. Nevertheless even moderate journals of opinion condoned the Court's action by declaring that however odious racial discrimination might be, "this abhorrence does not change the Constitution of the United States." The Civil Rights Act of 1875 had declared that all persons under U.S. jurisdiction were entitled to use places of public accommodation, and that violators would be penalized. The Court decided that Congress had extended its authority beyond its proper sphere because such places were local and therefore operated within state boundaries. States' rights lived whereas civil rights were dying. Late in 1884 the Court announced that native Americans were not protected by the Fourteenth Amendment because they were not born "subject to the jurisdiction" of the United States. A series of narrow, ungenerous rulings thereby reversed some of the most significant achievements of Reconstruction. As the Centennial approached, only white males (and perhaps corporations) seemed to be eligible as full beneficiaries of the U.S. Constitution.[81]

Alfred H. Kelly, a distinguished constitutional historian, once observed that almost every important commentator on the Constitution in nineteenth-century America assumed that the meaning of the document did not, and should not, change with the ebb and flow of events.[82] We could, I suppose, get bogged down in a definitional dispute over who does or does not qualify as an "important commentator." Realistically, however, all sorts of jurists, politicians, and journalists who commented upon the Constitution did so in ways that suggest that constitutional assumptions seem to have been anything but static in the period under consideration. Oliver P. Morton, for example, a prominent Republican from Indiana, admired the founders and the Constitution, yet he did not regard it as perfect and argued in 1877 that it ought to be considered flexible. A great many Americans, irrespective of their ideological or political allegiances, shared that point of view. Nevertheless, in a campaign speech that Morton had given back in 1860, he categorically declared: "We want no new views of the Constitution," meaning deviant, state sovereignty interpretations.[83] Morton's own shift was altogether characteristic of nine-teenth-century American constitutionalism. Change and perceptions of change may have been more common than consistency; and for many observers, situational expediency tells us far more than fixed adherence to the abstract notion of a document whose meaning remained constant.

V

It would be ever so easy to regard the spokesmen of this era as cynical. In 1866 Joel Parker, a Harvard law professor, warned against expedient practices: "Attempting to shield ... unauthorized measures under the pretense of constitutional authority [could] destroy the vitality of the Constitution, making it an instrument to serve the purpose of any party in power, by forced or sophistical construction."[84] I do not claim that everyone heeded Parker's admonition. Thaddeus Stevens was fully prepared to ignore the Constitution in order to "reconstruct" the South along lines that he deemed appropriate. But Stevens was no more typical of Republicans, even of Radical Republicans, than William Lloyd Garrison was typical of abolitionists. When Andrew Johnson wrote his first annual message to Congress, in December 1865, he included a long sentence that has the sound of authenticity—not merely because he genuinely meant it, but because it contains more than a kernel of essential truth: "Other nations were wasted by civil wars for ages before they could establish for themselves the necessary degree of unity; the latent conviction that our form of government is the best ever known to the world has enabled us to emerge from civil war within four years with a complete vindication of the constitutional authority of the General Government and with our local liberties and State institutions unimpaired."[85]

Despite some memorable quips, Lincoln sought to preserve the Union without violating the spirit of the U.S. Constitution. The same can be said of Johnson during Reconstruction. Listen, by contrast, to Oliver Cromwell's response when he was accused of imprisoning a man "without any lawful authority," ignoring his writ of habeas corpus, and committing the man's attorney to the Tower "for presuming to question or make doubt of his authority." Cromwell confronted the judges in the Court of King's Bench (renamed the upper bench during Cromwell's Interregnum): "When they, with all humility, mentioned the law and magna charta, Cromwell told them, with terms of contempt and derision, that 'their magna farta should not control his actions; which he knew were for the safety of the commonwealth.' "[86] That episode occurred in 1658, shortly before the Great Protector's death, and a decade after the English Civil War had been won. Although Abraham Lincoln enjoyed earthy expressions as well as any man of his time, it is impossible to imagine him impugning the Constitution with such flagrant contempt.

The cynicism with which the Frankfort constitution of 1848 and the Weimar constitution of 1919 were flouted has been depressingly documented.[87] American leaders, to be sure, have not always been paragons of restraint. George Fitzhugh scorned the U.S. Constitution. In 1912 the racist governor of South Carolina, Cole L. Blease, told reporters: "To hell with the Constitution!"[88] But they are not representative. Blease failed to be re-elected when his term expired, and for most of his remaining thirty years in public life he was an unsuccessful candidate for public office. Americans have bitterly disagreed with one another on matters of constitutional interpretation, but respect for the Constitution and the system of government it created has restrained the behavior of most citizens, especially those who have held public office. That certainly seems to have been the case during the Civil War and Reconstruction.[89] In times of crisis we do not always like the constraints that constitutionalism imposes. Yet we accept them for the most part, even while seeking to make alterations by amendment.

The great exception occurred in 1861, of course, when leading southerners refused to abide by traditional constraints. Although their political theory may have been precarious, southerners could make a strong case in historical terms. Perhaps that explains why they were subsequently more eager than northerners to rehash the constitutional history of the "War between the States," and continued to do so for a generation after Alexander H. Stephens published his *Constitutional View of the Late War* in 1868. Stephens reiterated, ad infinitum, that the United States had "a Government of States, and for States." That part, his political theory, was vulnerable to challenge. But when he insisted that "we are . . . by the assent of all, brought to the conclusion, that the Constitution . . . was formed by separate, distinct, and Sovereign States," his historical argument stood on firmer ground. The precarious nature of his polemic became clear when he shifted back to theory by means of a rhetorical device: "The great question, therefore, in this investigation was, is the Constitution a Compact between Sovereignties? If so, the Government established by it is purely, entirely, and thoroughly Federal in its nature, and no more National in any sense than all former Federal Republics."[90]

Although the passage of time did not bring detachment, it did cast southern constitutional ambiguities into clearer relief. A long editorial that appeared in *The Confederate Veteran* in 1897 conceded that "the Southern people desire to retain from the wreck in which their Constitutional views, their domestic institutions, the mass of their property . . . were lost, the knowledge that their conduct was honorable." Three years later, however, when Jabez Lamar Monroe Curry published his *Civil History of the Government of the Confederate States,* he continued to insist that the South had remained faithful to the Constitution, and that states' rights "contain the only principles or policy truly conservative of the Constitution."[91]

Northern constitutionalism did not tend as much toward self-justification, nostalgia, and what-might-have been. It veered in new directions, as we shall see in chapters 6 and 7. Republicans continued to believe that there had been a "slave power conspiracy" that aimed to seize control of the federal government and subvert the Constitution to suit its own interests. The best known example of that view would be Henry Wilson's *History of the Rise and Fall of the Slave Power in America* (1872), a work that reduced southern thought, motives, and behavior to a phrase: "rebellion against the Constitution." That phrase served as a common denominator for northerners with very different values. Wilson, on the one hand, detested slavery. General William Tecumseh Sherman was indifferent to the peculiar institution; yet looking back, years after the war, he could remark that "if the people of the South had stood by the Constitution," he would have supported their claim to keep Negroes as property.[92] Wilson and Sherman differed on many matters, but they are equally representative of the retrospective northern consensus concerning responsibility for the tragic Civil War: southern secession had flouted the Union and the U.S. Constitution—an act of treason.

PART TWO

A MACHINE THAT
WOULD GO OF ITSELF

"After our Constitution got fairly into working order it really seemed as if we had invented a machine that would go of itself, and this begot a faith in our luck which even the civil war itself but momentarily disturbed. Circumstances continued favorable, and our prosperity went on increasing. I admire the splendid complacency of my countrymen, and find something exhilarating and inspiring in it. We are a nation which has struck ile, *but we are also a nation that is sure the well will never run dry. And this confidence in our luck with the absorption in material interests, generated by unparalleled opportunity, has in some respects made us neglectful of our political duties."*

JAMES RUSSELL LOWELL (1888)

"Great constitutional provisions must be administered with caution. Some play must be allowed for the joints of the machine, and it must be remembered that legislatures are the ultimate guardians of the liberties and welfare of the people in quite as great a degree as the court."

JUSTICE OLIVER WENDELL HOLMES, JR. (1904)

CHAPTER 5

On This Day, One Hundred Years Ago

IN 1882 A YOUNG SCHOLAR NAMED J. FRANKLIN JAMESON made his initial visit to the library of the State Department in Washington, D.C., to undertake research in American constitutional history. Three years later, in the introduction to his first published monograph, Jameson explained that he had noticed a curious phenomenon: "The Constitution of the United States was kept folded up in a little tin box in the lower part of a closet, while the Declaration of Independence, mounted with all elegance, was exposed to the view of all in the central room of the library. It was evident that the former document was an object of interest to very few of the visitors of Washington. But when I was last in the library, I learned that the Constitution also was being mounted in order to be similarly placed upon exhibition, because, as I understood it, there was a more general desire to see it." Two years after that a prominent physician from Springvale, Pennsylvania, proudly accepted an invitation to attend the Centennial of the Constitution at a grand celebration in Philadelphia. Such an event, he wrote, "is a duty far paramount to that of our Declaration of Independence—for this was the giving to our nation a tangible government whose stability has been proven through those baptisms of blood during the century about to close."[1]

Although every American did not share that sentiment, it was symptomatic of a shift in popular interest. George Bancroft, the nation's best known historian, finally completed his massive *History of the United States* by publishing in 1882 a two-volume *History of the Formation of the Constitution of the United States;* and throughout the eighties other books about the Constitution, aimed at a general audience, appeared at an accelerating pace. The most famous of these, John Fiske's *The Critical Period of American History, 1783–1789*, published in 1888 midway through the two-year Centennial, is undoubtedly the most influential work ever written about the U.S. Constitution.[2] It remained in print until 1970; and its basic line of argument continues to provide a framework for much that is written about the historical context in which the Constitution was established.

I

At a dinner held in Philadelphia on December 2, 1886, to honor the newly formed Constitutional Centennial Commission, its president, Congressman John A. Kasson, proposed a toast to "Centennial Anniversaries and National Celebrations,—their Uses and Influence." He surely had in mind the six-month Exposition of 1876, when millions of Americans flocked to Philadelphia to mark a century of progress since Independence. His toast contained a touch of irony, however—both historical and prophetic—because the Golden Jubilee of the Constitution back in 1837 had not attracted much attention; and the Centennial for which Kasson assumed responsibility would turn out to be an uphill struggle of unanticipated proportions. After it concluded, or at least when the Philadelphia phase had, the Commission gave a dinner for Kasson on October 13, 1887. Looking back to the situation when they began to organize, Kasson observed that the Constitution "had become a sort of dead letter, an ancient document . . . and principally used as an incentive to and an occasion for much political wrangling. Like a text of Scripture, it had become overloaded with commentaries and burdened with speeches by partisans of theories of all sorts. The people of the country had lost sight of the Constitution itself and its practical living forces as applied to our institutions in the presence of these disputatious theories."[3]

Throughout 1887 a basic tension persisted between all of the hopeful hyperbole and, in the words of the chief marshal for civic and industrial events, "the entire absence of any interest or general sentiment in favor of the proposed celebration on the part of the public at large."[4] Typical responses to thousands of invitations assured the Commission that "the Celebration is appropriate to the great Event—the greatest in Constitutional History" (from a Virginia congressman). A lawyer in Portland, Maine, expressed the hope that the presence of thousands of distinguished Americans "will prove the strong attachment of our people to the Constitution, the great Charter of our American Liberty, and their love and reverence for the Fathers who were instrumental in its adoption."[5]

Speaking at the dinner honoring Congressman Kasson, however, Hampton L. Carson, the Commission's secretary and workhorse, reported that their task had been very tough. "Every one knew of the Fourth of July, and in a general way understood its significance. But few knew of the 17th of September, or cared to consider its claims to national recognition."[6] The chairman of the civic and industrial committee complained that "there was no public spirit or sympathy manifested for the celebration." He partially blamed problems of preparedness on the summer season, when "a large portion of our most enterprising and public-spirited citizens were enjoying an absence from the heat of the city." Above all, though, he pointed to the absence of anything "in the object of the celebration that especially awakened the interest of the people. The proposed demonstration was purely intellectual in its purpose, and appealed neither to passion nor prejudice."[7]

The explanations offered by Carson and Snowden were correct—as far as they went. But factors that they failed to mention also contributed. Some newspapers noted that a tradition of honoring the Constitution's anniversary had never really developed. One reason was the plethora of potential dates from which to choose. In the beginning, June 21, 1788, had induced the greatest jubilation because that is when New Hampshire became the ninth state to ratify, thereby legitimizing the Constitution. Benson J. Lossing, a popular historian, continued to advocate that view as late as February 1887: "The most important event in the history of our Republic was the ratification of the National Constitution. . . . Then our mere league of states, bound by a 'rope of sand', first became a *nation.*" Lossing argued against having a huge gathering in a single location because so many people would be unable to participate. Instead he proposed simultaneous celebrations to be held on June 21, 1888, in the capitals of the first nine states to ratify.[8]

That would have excluded New York, however, the eleventh state to ratify; and the nation's busiest commercial metropolis, New York City, did not intend to miss its golden opportunity. As *The New York Times* editorialized late in 1886, plans for a Philadelphia celebration on September 17, 1887, seemed fair enough; but the inauguration of George Washington on April 30, 1789, in New York City surely must have been even more momentous. "This celebration of 1889 will undoubtedly be the great one, since only then will the first century of our existence as a nation under the present form of government be completed." A few months earlier the

Times had acknowledged a whole calendar of noteworthy occasions: the opening of the Convention in Philadelphia on May 14, 1787; signing the Constitution on September 17; ratification by the first state, Delaware, on December 7, 1787; by the ninth state, New Hampshire, on June 21, 1788; the convening of the first Congress on March 4, 1789; but above all, of course, George Washington's inauguration.[9] Small wonder that a publisher preparing a notice for the 1887 *World Almanac* complained of "some confusion in the news paper accounts," especially when rumors started to circulate that Senator George F. Hoar of Massachusetts intended to sponsor a big celebration in Washington, D.C., during 1889.[10]

Considering the intensity of New York's rivalry with Philadelphia, it should come as no surprise that the governor of New York did his best to minimize events planned for Philadelphia in 1887; that Lieutenant-Governor Edward F. Jones of New York resigned from the Commission's executive committee after serving for less than three months; and that Alexander Hamilton, grandson of the author of many of *The Federalist Papers,* declined to attend the celebration in Philadelphia on the grounds that New York had done its best to defeat ratification. On the eve of Philadelphia's festivity, September 15–17, 1887, a *New York Times* editorial referred to "the celebration of the last great national event associated with its [Philadelphia's] history."[11]

Interstate rivalries and multiple anniversaries only begin to explain the Commission's problems. The *Connecticut Courant* expressed a partial truth in this statement that damned with faint praise: "It took Philadelphia a long time to get started to celebrate the Constitution's Centennial, but when she did at last wake up she was very much in earnest." It is a partial truth because in the end Philadelphians did most of the work and received either scant co-operation or outright resistance from outsiders. Even the governor of Pennsylvania accompanied his offer "to render any assistance" with the confession that he was "not desirous of taking any part in seeing legislation put through the Legislature."[12]

Although it is true that Philadelphia got a late start, so did the nation as a whole. On September 17, 1886, governors of the thirteen original states were supposed to meet in Philadelphia to initiate the planning. One year could not possibly have provided enough time for adequate preparations and the necessary financial appropriations by state legislatures; and as it turned out, only seven governors actually showed up, plus representatives from three other states. Colonel J. E. Peyton of Virginia, an early proponent of the Centennial, urged that all states and territories be asked to participate, that each one be represented by a militia regiment, and that the President and Congress provide support.

December 2 was designated as the day when every state and territory would send a high-ranking official to Philadelphia, and that this entire body would serve as a permanent organizing group. Twenty-seven delegates actually showed up (twenty-two of them governors). They resolved the following: that the President and other high federal officials should participate; that a major oration should be read and a commemorative poem be commissioned; that there ought to be military and industrial displays of some sort; and that a permanent memorial to the Constitution should be erected in Philadelphia.[13] The first of these occurred, but rather halfheartedly. Only part of the second actually developed (so many poets refused that the ode had to be abandoned); the third took place in the form of parades on September 15 and 16. The fourth never materialized at all.[14]

On December 3 a scaled-down Commission of twenty-eight members was selected: Kasson of Iowa serving as president, Congressman Henry Cabot Lodge of Massachusetts and Colonel James A. Hoyt of South Carolina as vice-presidents. Sectional equilibrium. Members of the Commission corresponded with one another from time to time, but didn't do much else. Operational responsibility was delegated to an executive committee headed by Amos R. Little along with several other Philadelphians. Too few members with too little in the way of resources and staff.

As president of the commission, Congressman Kasson had barely nine months to work with his executive committee, and he certainly did not make the most of it. Kasson had a peculiar aptitude for missing important meetings. When Hampton L. Carson, a little known Philadelphia lawyer, came to Washington to see President Cleveland and needed an influential guide, Kasson happened to be in St. Augustine, Florida, soaking up sun. In April, when Amos Little went to Washington, he did not even bother to contact Kasson. Co-ordination was not their strong suit. During June and July, the most critical phase for planning, Kasson was unavailable to the executive committee. As he explained in a letter from Spirit Lake, Iowa, if the entire committee was active in Philadelphia, "I do not think there can be great need of me." He offered to come East "if there is a cool place to stay near Phil? I must have cool nights for sleep." By the end of July Kasson still had made no arrangements for tableaux and musical staff at the Philadelphia Academy of Music, one of his prime responsibilities.[15]

Meanwhile the executive committee felt overwhelmed. Signs of confusion and failures of co-ordination abounded. A lawyer from Mississippi wrote that he was "somewhat at a loss to know precisely the display contemplated." A complaint came from a zealot in Connecticut that nothing seemed to be happening. A member of the Commission from Indiana was vexed that meetings were called on such short notice that he could never attend. "What has been done to date?" he wrote on May 21, "& what is contemplated—if you have time to inform me? I have had a hard winter, & think I shall resign my position as a member. . . . Did any of the States take action?" The states did not take very much action, partially because they could not discover what was expected of them. As late as June Governor Hill of New York said that he did not know that troops had been expected from his state. The governor of Colorado wrote angrily to Carson that he (Carson) received no responses from Colorado because he persisted in addressing his letters to "a gentleman who is not and never has been Governor of Colorado. . . . A little better knowledge of modern political American history on the part of your Commission would not interfear [sic] with the proper celebration of those glorious days which we all cherish with so much respect and veneration."[16]

Achieving full participation by all of the states, one of the Commission's paramount goals, posed an immense problem. Full participation meant, at the very least, sending a military unit and the presence of the state's governor. As a member of the executive committee observed when the governor of Illinois wrote that he probably would not attend: "The national feature of the grand parade will be seriously marred unless every State is in line." The formal invitation that went to the governors, however, explained that each state would have to bear the cost of transporting its troops "and equipage" to and from Philadelphia.[17] Moreover, the letters were sent on June 15, 1887 (rather late), and required a response by July 1 stating the number of equipped troops being sent "and whether you have sufficient tents for them." Many states responded tartly that the invitation had arrived too late for the legislature to pass a bill providing adequate funds; or else that the state's appropriation would be insufficient to cover such a large expense. The Commission's concession that it would pay a per diem allowance of fifty cents per man for a maximum duration of three days in Philadelphia did little to mollify anyone. The reply from Governor Foraker of Ohio to Congressman Kasson was typical:

> Your communications concerning the Constitutional Centennial Celebration have remained unanswered until now, because of inability

on my part to know how to answer them. Before we were invited to take any part in the Celebration, our General Assembly had adjourned. We are, consequently, without any legislation, or appropriation to enable us to do anything in the name, or on behalf of the State. It is difficult, months in advance of such an occasion to induce private citizens to make contributions, and become interested for so distant a matter. We are not, however, without appreciation for the importance of the event, and the propriety of having our State represented in connection with it; at least in some degree, and I now have the pleasure of informing you that I have succeeded in making all the necessary arrangements to enable us to send one of the regiments of our State National Guard, the Fourteenth. This is probably all we can do, as I find it impossible to arouse enough interest in the matter.

What Foraker omitted from his blunt letter emerged explicitly in a statement by the adjutant general of Ohio: the state legislature had decided not to pass an appropriation to send even a token unit of the state's national guard.[18]

The lateness of the invitation was compounded by vagueness on crucial matters of detail. Various requests for clarification, as well as delayed responses owing to midsummer, obliged the committee to send a supplementary supplication in July to all of the dilatory states and territories.[19] Despite a pervasive mood of sectional reconciliation in 1886–87, the invitation came at an awkward time for many southerners. Between 1885 and 1890 the "lost cause" theme flourished in popular journals, northern as well as southern; and numerous polite but negative replies from Dixie suggest something less than enthusiasm for a nationalistic celebration of the perdurable Union.[20] As one northern school superintendent wrote to Hampton L. Carson: "The American Eagle *today* screams over an undivided and much grown *Union*."[21]

Governors of the territories tended to be less courteous. The governor of Idaho declined because "territorial governors have no discretion about leaving their post of duty." He could not attend without the President's approval, and did not seem inclined to seek it. The governor of Alaska sent an embarrassing and categorical no. "Alaska being denied all the rights guaranteed to the other states and territories by the Constitution . . . feels that she would be entirely out of place were she to be represented. . . . Her people are patriotic and law-abiding, but the with-holding from them by Congress of the right of local self-government renders it impossible for them to provide the ways and means with which to defray the cost of sending either a Commissioner, or any portion of its militia."[22] The Constitution did not yet follow the flag completely, and that made some folks mad.

An amazing absence of congressional interest or generosity frustrated the Centennial Commission as well. On January 17, 1887, Representative Samuel J. Randall presented a bill that would have provided financial support, the appointment of federal commissioners to co-operate in planning the program, the encampment and participation of U.S. military forces at Philadelphia, and the collection as well as publication of pertinent historical documents. Senator Simon Cameron of Pennsylvania introduced it in the Senate. After being referred to the Committee on the Judiciary, the bill simply languished despite modest efforts by Randall and Representative Charles O'Neill of Pennsylvania urging swift action. One reason seems to have been a congressional preference for some sort of observance to be held in Washington during 1889 rather than in Philadelphia. On January 24, John A. Kasson wrote to Hampton Carson (from Winter Park, Florida; why wasn't he lobbying in the Capitol?): "Today I write to the chairmen of the two committees in House & Senate, calling their attention to the fact that we now ask only an inexpensive participation by the natl. govt.—their acceptance of the invitation of the states, & the furnishing of tents & rations for the volunteers for 3 days. And that our simple & appropriate celebrations need in no way interfere with plans for a later commemoration of other events."[23]

Despite this severely scaled down request, by February 8 prospects for success appeared bleak. Randall seems to have been hopelessly dilatory. On March 9 one member of the Commission from Baltimore who had been trying to stir up interest in the bill wrote to the executive committee that "our non-success with Congress proves we are not successful lobbyists. What had we best do?" The bill got nowhere, and in May a commissioner from Connecticut conveyed to Carson the "fear that the foolishness of local jealousy may prevent the country from doing what most clearly ought to be done."[24]

Congressional inaction may be explained to some degree by disinterest in the Constitution itself, and by urban chauvinism. Equally important was a strong feeling, widely shared, that celebrations of this sort should be funded by the private sector, inspired by motives of purest patriotism, or else by the incentive of commercial profit. None of these factors explains Grover Cleveland's detachment, however. Representatives of the Centennial Commission called upon the President in January to seek his support and participation. On the 18th Cleveland sent Congress a cautiously neutral message:

> I am aware that as each State acted independently in giving its adhesion to the new Constitution, the dates and anniversaries of their several ratifications are not coincident. Some actions looking to a national expression in relation to the celebration of the close of the first century of popular government under a written Constitution have already been suggested, and while stating the great interest I share in the renewed examination by the American people of the historical foundations of their Government, I do not feel warranted in discriminating in favor of or against the propositions to select one day or place in preference to all others, and therefore content myself with conveying to Congress these expressions of popular feeling and interest upon the subject, hoping that in a spirit of patriotic co-operation, rather than of local competition, fitting measures may be erected by Congress. . . .

Representative O'Neill understated the case in a letter to Carson the next day: Cleveland's cool directive "will do good but it is not as direct for Philad.ᵃ as I could have wished."[25]

Months passed without any sign of possible support from the President, even when it became clear that Philadelphia's celebration would be the major if not the only anniversary event of the Centennial year. In April a story began to circulate that Cleveland might be abroad during September. Discouraged by so little indication of federal interest, Kasson delayed the mailing of invitations to members of the cabinet, Supreme Court justices, ranking officers in the Army, Navy, and other dignitaries. When the executive committee finally asked General Philip H. Sheridan to lead the military parade on September 16, he chided them for initiating the matter at the last minute. Although he had a prior engagement to attend a reunion of the Society of the Army of Tennessee on September 14 and 15, Sheridan eventually managed to be in Philadelphia and command the columns of U.S. troops, state militia, and national guard units. Late in July the announcement came that Cleveland and some of his cabinet could attend, and that Associate Justice Samuel Miller would deliver the major oration. On the eve of the celebration one newspaper praised Philadelphia and Pennsylvania "for putting through a national event of this character without the assistance which should have been given by the federal government."[26]

II

The Centennial Committee achieved minimal success in its efforts to appoint an official poet and orator. Miller was selected as the orator only because more prominent figures who had been proposed either declined or seemed too controversial: Chief Justice Morrison R. Waite, Senators Roscoe Conkling of New York and George F. Edmunds of Vermont, General William T. Sherman, President Andrew Dickson White of Cornell, and Judge Thomas M. Cooley of Michigan, the most influential legal theorist of the day. George Bancroft initially accepted, reconsidered, and then "definitively declined." Proposals for the poet included Walt Whitman, Oliver Wendell Holmes, Sr., James Russell Lowell, Thomas Bailey Aldrich, and George H. Boker. Whitman, it was decided, "would not be safe." The same commissioner who made that judgment felt "it is also desirable that the two principal literary productions should come from different latitudes." Too bad, he said, that Paul Hayne of South Carolina (an unreconstructed Negrophobe) had died. Lowell "positively declined," as did everyone else invited. Kasson had hoped "to make this the occasion for a new & fitting nat! Hymn—new in music & new in words." John Greenleaf Whittier, the beloved New England pastoralist, refused. The final outcome? No poet at all; and the last-minute composition of an unsatisfactory, eminently forgettable hymn. The Centennial's literary, imaginative, and artistic impact would be nil.[27]

Many distinguished Americans who received invitations (see figure 13) to attend the celebration and appear on the Independence Square reviewing stand sent their regrets accompanied by diverse explanations: ill health, prohibitive expense, distance, conflicting engagements, and a Quaker who pointed out, on behalf of the Society of Friends, that "pre-arranged prayers to the Almighty" were unpalatable. Hence a Philadelphia-based committee that had not organized very much very well lost the participation of Philadelphia Friends who objected to the only aspect of the entire program whose organization seemed assured—unified prayer.[28] Large numbers of prominent churchmen, mostly bishops, though unable to attend, accompanied their courteous responses with the most fulsome and conservative expressions of devotion to "the 'Magna Charta' of American Liberty, which is just as far removed from license, as Law is from disorder."[29]

One of these bishops, Episcopalian A. Cleveland Coxe, conveyed a sentiment commonly expressed at the time by Americans of older "stock." Coxe praised those who "keep alive the National & the hereditary spirit of attachment to the Constitution, at a time when the influx of ignorant classes from abroad threatens to reverse the conditions which have, hitherto, justified the liberal spirit of that instrument."[30] The Commission itself seems to have been pulled between an elitist impulse and a rather patronizing attempt to get the participation of the two most disadvantaged groups of Americans: blacks and Indians. On the one hand, members of the executive committee repeatedly expressed their desire to invite "the living descendants of men prominent in Revolutionary history: Judges, lawyers, physicians, historians, poets, newspaper editors, inventors, explorers, [and] bishops. . . ."[31]

On the other, Carson believed that he had made a good faith effort to represent Negro progress since 1787, felt angry that the "Colored People's Display" was thrown together at the final hour, and blamed the "leading men of color" for not getting involved earlier and more fully. By contrast the press had special praise for the "fine appearance" in the opening day parade of Indian students from Carlisle, Pennsylvania. On the eve of the celebration President Kasson was asked "whether any provision is made for ladies who attend the governors and commissioners?" "None on the reviewing stand," Kasson responded. "That is because ladies prefer to look at the parades from windows on such occasions. There are also some private stands, very handsomely gotten up, where ladies will go."[32]

A desire to include ordinary Americans, or to be sensitive to class differences and perceptions of class consciousness, rarely appears in the voluminous correspondence of the executive committee. In one letter Brewster, the corresponding secretary, sought the names and addresses of civic associations, "such as the Knights of Labor, Odd Fellows, Masons, [and] Temperance Associations"; and in another the librarian of the American Baptist Historical Society declared his hope that the program "may also quicken and deepen in the hearts of all classes a reverence for and a loyalty to this Charter of our American freedom and the principles upon which it was adopted."[33]

During the summer of 1887 the committee began to realize that municipal co-ordination within Philadelphia, and even among committee members, left much to be desired. Accommodations and hospitality for visiting dignitaries had not been adequately attended to; and (as late as August 6) no arrangements had yet been made for fireworks.[34] Worst of all, it suddenly occurred to the members late in June that far too little had been done about publicity, local as well as national. Consequently, on

July 9 a mass mailing went out to all the commissioners, pleading for their help in distributing information to the press. Ten days later Brewster sent to individuals in various parts of the country "some printed matter relative to the celebration, the publication of which will serve to keep the matter alive before the public." As one apprehensive member of the Commission from Dakota Territory noted, "it will be absolutely necessary to stir up the people through the press, as during this hot term people are more inclined to rest than to consider pleasure trips, or even patriotic reunions."[35]

After so many setbacks, delays, and problems of co-ordination, three late developments occurred that helped to salvage the Centennial and make it, if not the event it might have been, at least a respectable (though superficial) success. First, on June 3 the Pennsylvania Legislature appropriated $75,000, enough to sustain the Commission's activities.[36] Second, citizens of the Philadelphia area pitched in with contributions of money and time, the most energetic and enterprising being Colonel A. Loudon Snowden, who gradually got the massive Civic and Industrial Procession into shape for opening day, September 15. It would include everything from agricultural and mill machinery products to a large float supplied by Strawbridge & Clothier, drawn by eight horses, displaying on canvas 27 feet long and 14 feet high "a store of the period of 1787" and the 1887 Strawbridge building.[37]

Third, the commercial and manufacturing interests of Philadelphia responded to Snowden's widespread appeal, dated July 16, to "make speedy arrangements for active and intelligent participation." The Pennsylvania Railroad mobilized to provide logistical support; hotels were canvassed and rates agreed upon to obviate gouging. Snowden even arranged for additional detectives to be supplied by other municipalities because Philadelphia's local force "are not acquainted with the professional thieves from other cities." Snowden put virtually everything into shape, from the procurement of old Conestoga wagons to crime control.[38]

Given the surprising success of the Civic and Industrial demonstration, it should come as no shock that organizers, participants, and spectators were duly impressed, in Snowden's words, "as to the paramount importance of upholding and guarding the Constitution as the sheet anchor of our liberties and the bulwark of our prosperity." During the course of Justice Miller's oration on September 17, he referred no fewer than five times to the link between American prosperity and the Constitution.[39]

During the month preceding the celebration, signs of public interest, even enthusiasm, finally began to appear. The executive committee received officious suggestions, and press coverage perked up. On September 13 *The New York Times* conceded that the observance might attract larger crowds than anyone had anticipated.[40] By the 15th Philadelphia had been adorned with red, white, and blue bunting. American flags flew everywhere. Hotels overflowed and large crowds made some of the principal streets impassable. The Philadelphia *Public Ledger* published an ominous caution: "If you are in a temporary stand and an alarm of any kind is sounded—sit still. There is little danger that any of the stands will give way under the mere weight of persons on them, but the strongest may collapse under a concerted movement of a great mass of people. Avoid anything like a panic. There is more safety in sitting still than in a mad rush to get off of even a falling structure."[41]

Fortunately, no major catastrophes occurred; and most of the minor mishaps went unreported. John Philip Sousa and members of the Marine Band became "very indignant" when they discovered that Sousa's name and the selections they performed were not mentioned in the official program. The press did catch one tactless gaffe and explained it "as springing from Mr. Cleveland's comparative inexperience in the matrimonial relation." (He married Frances Folsom in 1886.) The President had had a dispute with the Grand Army of the Republic veterans; but it had been patched up. He forgot to tell Mrs. Cleveland, however, and while the GAR passed the reviewing stand she reversed her chair and sat with her back to the parade. Editorials seemed to be less concerned about the First Lady's rudeness than about the lack of communication between the Clevelands.[42]

On the 15th, Snowden's huge "civic & industrial pageant" pleased a throng of visitors that the *Public Ledger* estimated at half a million, *The New York Times* at 200,000. The London *Telegraph* acknowledged that the celebration seemed "grand" and conceded that the United States was not the "grim" place that Charles Dickens had described more than four decades earlier. Better grand than grim, surely (see figure 14). On the 16th, popular Phil Sheridan led the mammoth military parade consisting of some 30,000 men. The *Times* acknowledged that 500,000 visitors were now present, along with at least a million local spectators. That morning President Cleveland attended a reception at the Commercial Club, acknowledged that "the aim and purpose of good government tend after all to the advancement of the material interests of the people," yet urged the businessmen to place patriotism above "pecuniary advantage." Following the parade Cleveland attended a Clover Club dinner at the Bellevue Hotel, an exclusive affair; and after that he spent the evening at a reception for 10,000 people held at the Academy of Music.[43]

On Saturday the 17th, which Carson's official history called "the moral and intellectual harvest," Cleveland met in the morning with thousands of dignitaries at City Hall. At eleven-thirty the featured event began at Independence Square. The vast platform displayed a photographic replica of the Constitution in front, and farther back the very chair on which George Washington had sat in 1787 while presiding at the Convention. Sousa's Marine Band did play, and patriotic songs were sung. Kasson gave a vapid introduction; Cleveland delivered an uninspired but brief address; and then came Justice Miller's historical and descriptive treatment of the remarkable men who framed the Constitution "on this day, one hundred years ago."[44]

Following these solemn ceremonies the President attended a luncheon provided by the Hibernian Society in St. George's Hall, while Mrs. Cleveland went to a reception given in her honor at an exclusive estate in Bryn Mawr. His gathering fed from a *pot-au-feu* of patriotism and politics; hers was blessed by Philadelphia's social elite. For the final festivity the University of Pennsylvania, the American Philosophical Society, the Historical Society of Pennsylvania, and the Franklin Institute joined hands to host a banquet at the Academy of Music. The President offered some complimentary platitudes about Philadelphia. Afterwards he and his party took the train back to Washington.[45]

His hosts expected him to carry away every possible souvenir: the 52-page "Official Programme," which included advertisements for the Germania Brewing Company, featuring Munich (dark) and Vienna (light) Beer; and a printed copy of the Constitution 5⅜" wide and and 3¼" high in which the revered text appeared on 14 pages of very small type followed by 24 pages of ads in very bold type, notably for First Brigade Cigars, Jacob Reed's Sons, Leading and Oldest Clothiers, John Byrd, Architectural Sheet-Metal Work, and others.[46]

Immediate assessments followed no clear pattern. Some newspapers declared that everything had been wonderful, and that Philadelphians deserved lots of credit. Others were equally generous to the host city, and lauded a century of material progress, but wondered whether the quality of American statesmanship had not seriously declined since 1787. E. L. Godkin's editorial in *The Nation* took quite a different point of view, characteristically thoughtful though atypical of the popular mood or of the press in general. Godkin's perspective is so provocative that a lengthy extract is worth noting.

It is rather curious that amid the numerous comments which the celebration of the Centennial of the Constitution has called forth, so little mention has been made of the failure of the instrument to overcome the main difficulties in the way of its original framers. Their two great difficulties were the union of slave and free States under a common government, and the merging of State allegiance in national allegiance in the mind of the citizens of the several States. Everything else was comparatively easy. But on these two points the Constitution was only partially successful. . . .

When these things are taken into account, we think it will be generally admitted that the Constitution may be fairly considered as having existed in what may be called a provisional or experimental stage down to 1861, and that a very large share of whatever glory is due to its framers belongs of right to the men of the generation now passing away. They twenty-five years ago resolved that they would cure its defects at whatever cost, and put it into an undeniably permanent shape, and did so amid difficulties compared to which those of the Convention of 1787 were a mere trifle. They took hold resolutely of all the seriously obscure or ambiguous passages in the instrument, and of all compromises which had proved difficult or incapable of execution, and eliminated them. . . .

The men who revised the Constitution in 1863–5, and who have given it to us in a shape which will probably undergo no great change as long as the social organization continues what it is at present, did not hesitate to ask the people to say whether the Federal Government had that final sanction without which no government, however deftly framed on paper, can properly be considered a government at all.

In view of all this, it seems to us as if a very large part of whatever fame the construction of the Federal Government reflects on the American people is due to those who gave the organic law its final revision; and we think it by no means unlikely that those who celebrate the next centennial of the constitution will be disposed to put the date in 1865, rather than in 1787, or will at all events hesitate between the two years.[47]

Godkin essentially was reviving and updating the "inadequate Constitution" argument that he had presented during the Civil War. He made no more converts in 1887 than in 1864; but he must have given some readers pause. As a historian he is reasonably accurate; as a logician he is insightful though idiosyncratic; and as a prophet he will prove to be wrong about the American memory in 1987.

The Centennial itself did not generate any fresh contributions to American constitutionalism, even though significant shifts took place, for other reasons, during the 1880s and '90s (to be discussed in the following chapter). A few observers did share Godkin's view that perfection had not been achieved in 1787, that a developmental angle of vision was needed, and that after a century the major problems had been resolved (at last). As a Treasury official wrote to the Commission, "the deeper meanings of the Constitution could be wrought into practical rules of government only by time, discussion, and, unhappily, even by conflict; but all seriously disputed questions are now at rest." When the governor of Virginia spoke at the Hibernian Society's luncheon on September 17, he explained that the Confederates "had fought for what they thought was a proper construction of the Constitution," but promptly added that "they were defeated. They acknowledged their defeat. They came back to their father's house, and there they are going to stay."[48]

Two tendencies seem especially apparent in popular constitutionalism by 1887. First, the feeling that major problems had been solved and crises surmounted. So long as everyone accepted the necessity for Union while maintaining a minimal respect for states' rights, the ship of state would sail smoothly on course. A second and related tendency took the form of resistance to any hasty constitutional changes. Appeals for caution were commonly phrased in religious rhetoric: the Constitution as "the Ark of the Covenant," Independence Hall as "the holiest spot of American earth," visitors as "pilgrims" in "the spirit of worshippers before a shrine," and the constant incantation of words like "reverence," "sacredness," and "hallowed ground of its birthplace."[49]

Nay-sayers or doubters were scarce in 1887. Moncure D. Conway, the old abolitionist clergyman, offered one dissenting view: "The investment in the Constitution was large enough to evolve a generation of believers that it came down from heaven. Since the overthrow of slavery the silver image has shown some signs of turning to clay." Such voices did not get much of a hearing in 1887; and the Centennial failed to elicit what Conway called for, "a thorough inquest of the Nation into its organic system."[50]

In the weeks and months that followed September 17, the group that had managed to bring it off experienced mixed emotions. Hampton Carson lauded his colleagues on the executive committee for their vision and perseverance, "not withstanding the indifference of the public, and the still greater indifference of individuals." John Kasson claimed at the concluding banquet on October 13 that their greatest success could be "found in the revival of interest in the history of the Constitution. . . . The study of the Constitution itself has been stimulated." Well, yes, to some degree, as we shall see; but there is also irony in Carson's poignant lament, written in 1888, that "few of the commissioners responded to the request for reports of the share taken by their States and Territories." The customary indifference made a predictably swift reappearance.[51]

So did interurban rivalry and the schemes of other city fathers who had been biding their time. On the eve of the celebration, Baltimore's *Daily News,* representing a community with no vested interest, praised Philadelphia's foresight and enterprise. "Other cities waited for Congress or some outside contributors to do these things for them. Even New York is guilty of such meanness." On September 19 the *Washington Post* pointed ahead to the gala events that it hoped would take place at the national capital in 1889. An editorial insisted that April 30, 1789, when George Washington took the oath of office, "is the true beginning of our Constitutional history."[52]

Philadelphians, meanwhile, felt rather smug about their good fortune and skill in arranging commemorative occasions. As the presiding officer quipped at a self-congratulatory banquet in October: "when New York undertakes to celebrate the inauguration of George Washington, whom we kindly loaned to Wall Street . . . and when Boston attempts again to celebrate Bunker Hill, if they will only come to us we will take great pleasure in showing them how."[53]

New York City would have to overcome an inferiority complex in order to get geared up for 1889. On September 18, 1887, *The New York Times* lavished praise upon the disinterested patriotism of Philadelphians, whereas "here it can scarcely be said to exist at all. . . . A Philadelphia schoolboy knows all the monuments of his city and what they commemorate, whereas a New-York schoolboy is in dense ignorance of the history of the city." By November 10, however, the New York City Chamber of Commerce, the New-York Historical Society, and a committee of civic-minded citizens headed by Mayor Abram Hewitt had begun to plan an extravaganza for April 30, 1889. During the winter of 1887–88 New Yorkers watched nervously to see whether Congress really meant to hold a conflicting celebration in Washington, D.C. *The New York Times* condemned the introduction of a bill that would have appropriated $300,000 ("wasteful and ridiculous excess") for a rival event, pointed out that New York's would be properly national in scope, and added for good measure that Washington, D.C., did not even exist in 1789.[54]

III

Considering all of the uncertainty and competitiveness that had existed prior to 1887 about the most appropriate anniversary for the major celebration—uncertainty that persisted right through 1889—the states did surprisingly little to note the centennials of their ratification. Pennsylvania even expressed concern that its observance of ratification, or of the great parade that had taken place in Philadelphia on July 4, 1788, should not "exceed in any manner our commemoration of its centennial anniversary." Not much chance of that. Connecticut did more in January 1889 to honor the 250th anniversary of its 1639 constitution, and North Carolina (a renegade Anti-Federalist holdout in 1788–89) did far more to mark the centennial of its belated ratification than any of the necessary first nine states to join the Union.[55]

On June 21, 1888, the New Hampshire Historical Society did sponsor a simple ceremony in Concord at which an oration and a poem were read, followed by a banquet.[56] Meanwhile, throughout June and July a pseudo-scholarly controversy raged in the pages of New York's newspapers concerning which centennial was most meaningful. A writer for the *Evening Post* identified as "Historicus" insisted that New York State's ratification on July 26, 1788, had really been far more momentous than Washington's inauguration. "G.H.M." disagreed and applied a scalpel to Historicus's historical logic. Then Benson J. Lossing, the best known participant in this antiquarian fray, wrote to correct factual errors made by Historicus and to refute the erroneous emphases of G.H.M. and the New-York Historical Society. Lossing regarded Washington's inauguration as little more than a formality, and felt that New York's ratification had been much less consequential than New Hampshire's. "Juvenis" then complained that so much conflict among experts left the public utterly confused about matters of historical fact: couldn't the *Times* clarify this mess? The *Times* responded blandly that no date was more meaningful than any other. Apparently, political pluralism mandated historical tolerance. Fair enough; but "R.S.G." still had to explain that the big procession that took place in New York City on July 23, 1788, had nothing to do with New York's ratification, which occurred three days later. Instead, it was a celebration to honor the fact that because nine states had ratified, the Constitution would be legitimized no matter what the other four decided to do. "Verax" then submitted a long letter attacking Historicus for glorifying Alexander Hamilton, castigating George Clinton, and minimizing the role of John Jay. Finally, G.H.M. wrote several more times to accuse both Historicus and Verax of distortion for stating that New York's approval had been conditional upon the passage of a bill of rights.[57]

Although it is impossible to measure how many readers followed this game of constitutional "Can you top this?", we do know that more than 30,000 people showed up on July 26 in Poughkeepsie, where New York had ratified a century earlier, to watch a procession of West Point cadets and a band, GAR veterans, militiamen, civic organizations, and firemen. At four o'clock ceremonies took place in the local opera house to observe the centennial of New York's reluctant ratification. A *New York Times* editorial defensively explained that what obviously seemed a stable and balanced form of government in 1888 looked suspiciously like an "untried experiment" one hundred years before.[58]

That same theme of economic immaturity and political inexperience a century earlier appeared in President Benjamin Harrison's inaugural address on March 4, 1889, a date also observed as the one hundredth anniversary of the first Congress. Washington, D.C., briefly became the focal point. Thereafter attention turned to preparations being made in New York City for two days of hoopla designed to eclipse Philadelphia's three and Washington's one. As a local chauvinist wrote: "There is no commemoration in history that can stand in comparison to this centennial."[59]

During the six weeks prior to April 30, numerous difficulties arose; and few of them could have been anticipated on the basis of Philadelphia's experience in 1887. New York's problems seem to have been peculiarly her own. Fundamentally they fall into two categories, neither of which had much to do with constitutionalism: commercial prospects and social status. As for the former, the issues may seem banal to us, but they raised a good many tempers in 1889: whether or not New York's Chamber of Commerce would have exclusive control over planning; whether or not the events would occupy more than two days as official holidays, because bankers and merchants believed that prolonged suspension of commercial transactions would be highly undesirable; what to do about the huge parades happening to fall on April 30 and May 1, the days when annual leases traditionally expired and many people moved. So many wagons and trucks were needed for the parades that most people would be unable to move their furniture—would landlords bring suit? Whether "country" merchants who customarily came to the city at this time to make purchases would be allowed to take advantage of the railroads' special Centennial excursion rates (businessmen demanded that the lower rates be extended to May 10). With almost all of the reviewing seats sold out, was it ethical to offer space in a Fifth Avenue doorway or window sill for $100, or to rent apartments overlooking Fifth Avenue between 13th and 29th Streets for as much as $1,000? And should private citizens be permitted to erect stands in front of their homes and businesses?[60]

The social problems, predictably, involved special privilege, elitism, and rebellious undercurrents of egalitarianism. Disputes did not simply arise between the privileged and the less advantaged, however. Tensions ran high, for example, between those with political clout (such as the 160 New York State legislators) and those with social status (Ward McAllister's so-called 400). As a *Times* editorial put it, "the grimy and horny-handed men of action in Albany naturally suspect the intentions of the washed and leisured clubmen of the metropolis." Accusations arose that the Centennial Committee sought to make the celebration an "exclusive" affair for patricians who wished to "seize the occasion for a mild orgy of ancestor worship, and to put themselves in evidence as the great and good descendants of the great and good men of 1789." Consequently those New York City aldermen lacking aristocratic genealogies demanded equally good seats in the reviewing stands as well as tickets to the grand ball. That was too much for the socially orthodox *Times:* "A ball at which the whole Board of Aldermen [heavily Irish] is present necessarily carries the promise and potency of a wake. The projectors of a truly refined, decorous, and exclusive celebration of the centennial are to be condoled with on this melancholy issue." The aldermen threatened that if they did not receive reserved seats, gratis, they would prohibit the erection of any stands at all because New York City streets were entirely under their jurisdiction. The aldermen got choice seats, tickets for the ball, and special VIP badges. They then asked for free banquet tickets. Eventually the legislature even passed an appropriation for the aldermen to use as they pleased; the aldermen chose to illuminate City Hall.[61]

Ward McAllister, the social czar of New York, had seemed the logical choice to serve as secretary of the committee on entertainment. He might have been fine with the "400," but he and Stuyvesant Fish alienated thousands by their arrogance in determining just who would dance in the opening quadrille, or by failing to allocate special boxes at the Metropolitan Opera House to Mrs. Alexander Hamilton, widow of the grandson of the first Secretary of the Treasury, and General Louis Fitzgerald, treasurer of the Centennial Committee. Out-of-town bluebloods named Adams, Cadwalader, Rittenhouse, Biddle, Fairfax, Lee, Pinckney, and Rutledge accused McAllister of partiality to the New York City elite, especially because this was supposed to be a national celebration.

By early April McAllister had been "eased out"; but that did not eliminate social tensions. The press demanded to know why no descendant of George Washington had been invited to take part in the opening quadrille. The army committee announced that applicants for tickets would have to supply suitable references. Stuyvesant Fish, running the entertainment committee, complained that the Centennial required him to be away from his business for too long. "I have had all the centennial celebrations I want," he said, "and you will never see me caught in another boat like this again." Gradually the realization dawned that some sort of *via media* would have to be found between elitism and modified egalitarianism if the celebration was to avoid catastrophe. A *New York Times* editorial declared that "the tentative effort made to give [the Centennial] a specially historical character, and to make conspicuous in it those whose claims to take part in it were ancestral, was quite natural and in a sense commendable." Nevertheless the committee would have to recognize that most of the people who helped to make New York a great metropolis "were not citizens of it 100 years ago." The celebration would, alas, have to be for all the people.[62]

Ambivalent attitudes and reluctant concessions persisted right up to the actual event, and were reflected in retrospective assessments. The procession on May 1, comprising a vast array of public and private organizations, ethnic societies, commercial groups, and tradesmen (in contrast to the elegant and orderly military parade on the 30th), was dubbed "the people's parade." On May 5 the *Times* praised those public-spirited men who had planned the affair, acknowledged that they had made some errors of judgment, and happily recognized "the universal interest taken in it and the uniting of all classes of people in the prevailing sentiment of the occasion." As a result it would become easier in the future to enlist "the great mass of the people." As an afterthought, and perhaps a patronizing reward, the *Times* urged that the two museums under construction in Central Park should be completed "and brought closer to the people by being accessible to them on their day of rest and leisure."[63]

During the final weeks of preparation one more major source of social conflict arose: the parade route through Manhattan. The state legislature wanted the military parade to march along "more cosmopolitan streets than Waverly-place and Fifth-avenue," and put through a resolution urging the parade to pass the monuments to Washington, Lafayette, and Lincoln in Union Square. Two days later the press complained that the original route had been selected so that residents of Washington Square and lower Fifth Avenue would be able to watch from their homes. The *Times* suggested that the army committee voluntarily democratize the itinerary, without waiting for legislative coercion. On April 16 the executive committee, the committee for plan and scope, and the army committee consented to the change; stands to accommodate 50,000 spectators began to be built around Union Square.[64]

The ultimate crisis arose from national chauvinism, and precipitated international ill-will. A military outfit from Canada declared that it would like to join in the homage to George Washington by marching in the military parade. The army committee rejected the offer, explaining that it would be inappropriate to permit foreign troops to participate in this parade. Schuyler Hamilton of the Major General Volunteers, a superpatriot with impeccably American credentials, wrote to the *Times* deploring this narrow, "No foreigners need apply" attitude. Then, on April 19, the diplomatic corps in Washington announced its anger at the Centennial Committee because the foreign emissaries felt they had not been sent an adequate number of tickets for the ball. Consequently they all declined to attend—until Stuyvesant Fish made a pilgrimage to Washington and persuaded them to relent![65]

On Sunday, April 28, churches throughout the city featured sermons concerning George Washington and the Constitution. At the Collegiate Dutch Reformed Church, the congregation heard that "the Constitution of the United States was an inspiration from God." At the Sunday School of B'nai Jeshurin Synagogue, children learned that Washington's strong belief in freedom of religion had made America a great land for Jews to live in. On the 28th President Harrison and his entourage took a night train from Washington to Elizabeth, New Jersey; they arrived at 7:30 a.m. on the 29th and ate breakfast with the governor and other state dignitaries. Then, following Washington's triumphal path one hundred years before, Harrison boarded a ship, crossed to Manhattan while hundreds of vessels whistled their salutes, and was accompanied to a reception at the Lawyers' Club by federal troops, the Loyal Legion, the Sons of the Revolution, veterans of the Seventh Regiment, and others. At three o'clock Harrison dined with an exclusive group at the Café Savarin in the Equitable Building. From there to a public reception at City Hall, then to Vice President Morton's Fifth Avenue mansion for a rest, followed by supper at the home of Stuyvesant Fish before going to the ball.[66]

Despite all the planning and negotiation, the ball turned out to be poorly organized. Because it was too crowded to dance, people jammed the supper room, made a greedy rush for the buffet tables, and scrambled for the limited number of seats. Half the guests, including most of the box-holders, never got into the room. Those who did spilled food all over the floor, drank excessive amounts of wine, became intoxicated, struggled back to the ballroom, and tore down most of the decorations. President Harrison and his party remained at their specially elevated and roped-off table for only a few minutes, then fled. At four in the morning New York's finest arrived and had to use force in order to eject some of New York's most elegant.[67]

The 30th began, for those who were sober at least, with nine o'clock services at St. Paul's Episcopal Church, where Washington had prayed a hundred years earlier before his inauguration. All of the ushers were descendants of prominent heroes of the Revolutionary War. When Bishop Potter's sermon pressed the point that the leaders of 1889 were less virtuous (in terms of patronage abuse) and less statesmanlike than those of 1789, President Harrison simply stared at the bishop. (Many felt that Potter's remarks, which continued to be discussed for days, had been in poor taste. The *Times,* however, said that Potter had only spoken the truth.) At the literary exercises held a few blocks away at the old Sub-Treasury Building on Wall Street, a poem composed by Whittier was read (Whittier had declined to write in 1887), and Chauncey Depew, president of the New York Central Railroad, delivered a tedious oration that reviewed all of American history from colonization to the present. He did at least stress the events that led to adoption of the Constitution, Washington's inauguration and presidency. Harrison concluded these exercises with brief remarks in which he commended Depew and Washington about equally.[68]

The military parade was watched by huge crowds that caused traffic jams and railroad delays. James Murray, proprietor of the posh Fifth Avenue Hotel, intended as a patriotic gesture to release an eagle from the roof of his hotel just as Harrison took his position on the reviewing stand. Instead of "soaring into the eye of the sun," however, the misguided eagle "fluttered its wings as though it were suffering from ennui and most ingloriously sank from view beneath the edge of the hotel roof." The day concluded with a big banquet at the Metropolitan Opera House—as poorly run as the ball had been the previous night. Most of the innumerable speeches emphasized the superiority of the American system of government. After remarks by Mayor Grant, Governor Hill, George William

Curtis, and ex-President Cleveland, eighty-nine-year-old George Bancroft (who also would not participate in 1887) delivered an address on "The Federal Constitution." It was unexceptional and unexceptionable, except for its conservatism and the highly symptomatic use of a metaphor that James Russell Lowell would question less than a year later: "Thus keeping pace with the onward sweep of the empire which it rendered possible, this matchless instrument vindicates its title to immortality. The conservative evolution that characterizes it has enabled it to pass the century since its birth, with its machinery, no cog or wheel displaced, still noiselessly and easily working." Still more speeches followed: "Our Literature" by Lowell (who had been unavailable in 1887); "The Senate" by former Vice President Hannibal Hamlin; "The Presidency" by ex-President Hayes; "The Judiciary" by Senator William Maxwell Evarts; "The Army and Navy" by General William Tecumseh Sherman; and finally "The United States of America" by President Harrison. All were patriotic. Only Lowell's contained a memorable thought.[69]

On May Day the civic and industrial parade "embraced almost every subject relating to the geographical and political history of this country and its educational, industrial, and commercial development." Highlights were provided by a display of fire-fighting equipment from different eras, and 2,500 Tammany "braves," who snubbed the Republican Harrison by refusing to tip their hats when they passed the President's reviewing stand.

General Abram Daly, ninety-three-year-old leader of the few surviving veterans of the War of 1812, approached President Harrison to complain that his group had not been allowed to ride in a carriage. (Harrison immediately requested one for them and the veterans proudly joined the procession.) The police and crowds clashed, resulting in numerous injuries to civilians. Complaints of police brutality continued for days. On the other hand, two brothers from Buffalo, estranged ever since a quarrel in 1862, met accidentally on the Brooklyn Bridge where one was directing traffic, and enjoyed a cordial reconciliation. One of the most popular floats, entered by the Kinney Tobacco Company, depicted a plantation scene in which Negroes (presumably slaves) stripped tobacco and gladly sang spirituals. Some stereotypes die harder than others.[70]

On the evening of May 1 various organizations sponsored festivities all over town. The National Provident Union, a patriotic society, provided music and more speeches. Senator Daniel of Virginia talked about Washington and the Constitution, stressing that Madison and Jay were just theorists, whereas Washington had been a practical man. The Loyal Legion held a supper and meeting at Delmonico's. Although 600 meals had been prepared, only 250 men showed up. A lot of Legionnaires had left, hoping to beat the crush getting out of town. The next day Ward McAllister told the press how glad he was that the grand ball had been a fiasco. He criticized Stuyvesant Fish and the entertainment committee, insisting that the ball would have been a stunning success if he had not been dismissed. Bittersweet revenge for the ne plus ultra among snobs.[71]

Although New York City had the feature attraction on April 30, and participants attended from across the country, lesser observances occurred nationwide. Banks, schools, and businesses closed for the day; Centennial church services were held. More than 30,000 people came to Portland, Oregon, to watch a parade, the largest celebration that had ever occurred in the Pacific Northwest. Major parades and fireworks displays took place in Pittsburgh, St. Louis, Denver, and San Francisco. The most elaborate program (after New York's) took place in Chicago, however, which had rebuilt after the catastrophic fire of 1871 and hoped to demonstrate its worthiness to be the site of the World's Columbian Exposition of 1892 (or 1893). There were special Centennial exercises held in the public schools, and a banquet at the Union League Club with speeches devoted to Madison, Hamilton, Jefferson, Franklin, Clay, Webster, Lincoln, and Grant.

Associate Justice John Marshall Harlan gave the principal address, on "Washington and the Constitution." He traced the history of the 1780s and called attention to the woeful inadequacies of Confederation government in order to demonstrate Washington's primacy in recognizing those inadequacies. Without his "efforts to bring about a more perfect Union of the people the existing Constitution . . . would not have been accepted by the requisite number of States." Harlan's knowledge of history may have been superior to his sense of the present, for he concluded with the assertion that Washington's hopes had been realized, that the federal system of dual sovereignty had achieved exquisite equilibrium, and that "the humblest person in our midst has a feeling of safety and repose" concerning his liberty and welfare. Perhaps there weren't too many humble people present at the Union League, or possibly Harlan had not been in touch with too many humble people in 1889. Perhaps he simply produced the hyperbole that he knew his audience had come to hear.[72]

Elsewhere that night in Chicago, at a fireworks display along Lake Front Park, fifty people were injured, some of them fatally, when an uncontrollable crowd stampeded. The newspapers did not say which were humble, patriotic persons, and which had feelings of safety and repose.[73]

IV

Although significant new developments were occurring in American constitutionalism, few of them seem to have been reflected in publications specifically generated by the Centennial. *The Century* (the most popular middle-class magazine of that era) devoted a special issue to bland pap: essays on "The Inauguration of Washington," "Washington at Mount Vernon after the Revolution," "Washington in New York in 1789," and "Original Portraits of Washington." The one exception, tucked away at the end of the issue, was John Bach McMaster's judicious and well-informed review of "A Century of Constitutional Interpretation," into which he packed a remarkable amount of information about loose constructionists and strict constructionists, "the men who believed in implied powers and the men who believed in reserved powers." McMaster also conveyed a sense that the American Constitution had not been static, exemplified by the numerous attempts that had been made to amend it just since 1870.[74]

McMaster's perspective did not predominate in 1889, however. A more popular view underpinned the belief that "this great instrument has stood the test of time." Therefore it must be fundamentally unchanged. The amendments had improved but had not altered the Constitution's fundamental principles. An editorial boasted that "the import of the instrument has been settled by a large body of judicial decisions," and concluded—without clear logic or causal relationships—that "when the second centennial shall have come, those then living will simply have a larger and grander spectacle in the past to contemplate."[75]

A sampling of what widely circulated newspapers and magazines had to say following the April 30 celebration is less remarkable for predictable platitudes than for curious (though perhaps equally predictable) distortions. Quite a number called attention to the "profound interest . . . produced in the public mind." Others went even farther, proposing that an "uprising of public sentiment has created the celebration." That claim was built upon the misleading contention that "in any other country the Government would have taken the initiative and would have directed the details. But this grand National demonstration was born in the hearts of loyal citizens"—partially true because government officials were apathetic and refused to take either initiative or responsibility. Perhaps the most arresting insight appeared in the *Atlanta Constitution* on April 30: "At the

North they are making a great deal of fuss over a Southern gentleman and slave holder. His name is George Washington."[76]

The flavor of it all lingered on because of a series of inevitable anti-climaxes. On December 11, 1889, Congress put on its own belated little celebration of Washington's inauguration. Members of the House and Senate, Harrison and his cabinet, the Supreme Court and diplomatic corps gathered in the House Chamber to listen to a seventy-five-minute oration by Chief Justice Melville Fuller. He emphasized the achievements of Washington's administration, the evolution of the Constitution, and the system somehow managing to survive the Civil War. *The New York Times* quite properly called this nonevent an "anti-climax."[77] The occasion was neither necessary nor memorable.

On February 4, 1890, ex-President Cleveland presided over the centennial of the establishment of the Supreme Court, once again in New York City. The press took little note of the event, in part because the public seemed disinterested—perhaps centennial cynicism had set in—and in part because the whole affair seemed tragically mistimed. On the preceding day the home of Secretary of the Navy Tracy had caught fire, and his wife, daughter, and housekeeper died in the blaze; another daughter and her child suffered severe injuries. Many people felt that the festivities ought to be postponed. As it was, they simply had very little impact. Some newspapers even took this opportunity to criticize the Court for its vacillation on important matters of national policy. Others merely noted that the current Court suffered from an excessive workload.[78]

What then might we expect during the quarter century after 1890? Ennui in American constitutionalism perhaps? Pure boredom, based upon the indifference so visible during the winter of 1889–90? Oddly enough, the answer is neither. Instead, the most curious phase in the entire history of American constitutionalism unfolded: a mixture of uncritical reverence by the majority and irreverent criticism by a small but highly vocal minority. During the 1890s a patriotic "cult of the Constitution" developed that surpassed anything of the kind during the preceding century. In 1895 the Constitution was removed from its steel vault in the State Department library and photographed so that a facsimile could be sent to the Cotton States Exposition in Atlanta, Georgia. The promoters had requested the original, actually; but unlike the Declaration of Independence, of which the State Department owned two copies, there was only one of the Constitution, now deemed more sacred than the Declaration anyway. So back into the steel vault it went, vouchsafed for posterity.[79]

The year 1895 would also be one when harsh attacks on the Supreme

Court could be heard, which fostered indirect criticisms of the Constitution itself—both tendencies intensifying steadily over the next two decades. In 1911, Senator Henry Cabot Lodge delivered a wistful address
entitled "The Constitution and Its Makers." Looking back to the Centennial observances of 1887 and 1889 through a haze of nostalgia, he recalled
more spontaneity and enthusiasm than the evidence could possibly warrant. Lodge had served, after all, as a vice-president of the Centennial
Commission in 1887. Once upon a time, surely, he had been aware of the
agonies that group went through to achieve any sort of respectable festivity. But perhaps not. "Through all the rejoicings of those days, in every
spoken and in every written word, ran one unbroken strain of praise for
the great instrument and of gratitude to the men who, in the exercise of
the highest wisdom, had framed it and brought it forth." Now, late in
1911, all that had changed, and Lodge's poignant lament spoke for many
patriotic Americans who could not comprehend why.

> Those celebrations of the framing of the Constitution and of the
> inauguration of the government have been almost forgotten. More
> than twenty years have come and gone since the cheers of the crowds
> which then filled the streets of New York and Philadelphia—since
> the reverberations of the cannon and the eloquent voices of the ora-
> tors died away into silence. And with those years, not very many
> after all, a change seems to have come in the spirit which at that time
> pervaded the American people from the President down to the
> humblest citizen in the land. Instead of the universal chorus of praise
> and gratitude to the framers of the Constitution the air is now rent
> with harsh voices of criticism and attack; while the vast mass of the
> American people, still believing in their Constitution and their gov-
> ernment, look on and listen, bewildered and confused, dumb thus far
> from mere surprise, and deafened by the discordant outcry so sud-
> denly raised against that which they have always revered and held
> in honor. . . . But it is also true that every one who is in distress, or in
> debt, or discontented, now assails the Constitution, merely because
> such is the present passion. Every reformer of other people's mis-
> deeds—all of that numerous class which is ever seeking to promote
> virtue at somebody else's expense—pause in their labors to point out
> the supposed shortcomings of our national charter. . . .
>   All this is quite new in our history. We have as a people deeply
> reverenced our Constitution. We have realized what it has accom-
> plished and what protection it has given to ordered freedom and indi-

vidual liberty. Even the Abolitionists, when they denounced the Constitution for the shelter which it afforded to slavery, did not deny its success in other directions, and their hostility to the Constitution was one of the most deadly weapons used against them. . . .[80]

A very peculiar coda indeed to the fêtes of 1887 and 1889. We will need to examine several different phenomena in order to comprehend both the constitutional cult that flourished in the 1890s and the emotional criticisms that emerged *pari passu*. Although they had independent causes, once each movement caught hold, it managed to energize the other in strange but significant ways. Howard Jay Graham's adage that "all centennials tend to be confessionals and carillons commingled" has much to be said for it.[81]

CHAPTER 6

The American and the British Constitution Are Two Entirely Different Things

BETWEEN THE MID-EIGHTEENTH CENTURY, when colonists customarily declared their enthusiasm for the British constitution, and the mid-twentieth century, when legal anglophiles like Felix Frankfurter, Robert H. Jackson, and Philip Kurland described their admiration for the administration of justice in Britain,[1] American feelings about the British constitution underwent several major shifts—transformations that tell us a great deal about changing perceptions of the U.S. Constitution.

The half century spanning 1885 to 1935 began and ended with such shifts. What transpired is all the more fascinating because of complicated cross-currents running simultaneously and the activity of political groups working at odds with one another. Theodore Roosevelt conveyed the most basic tension in a letter to an English friend: "I am always amused at the queer mistake that Macaulay made when fifty-odd years ago [1857] he said that the American Constitution was all sail and no ballast or anchor. Our trouble has been that we have tended to permit one set of people to hoist sails for their own amusement, and another set of people to put down anchors for their own purposes; and the result from the standpoint of progress has not been happy."[2]

What happened during the half century under scrutiny in this chapter? Americans became more self-conscious about the special virtue of having a written constitution (which made their system seem distinctive), but simultaneously more inclined to emphasize the historical evolution of their constitution (which caused it to look far more comparable to Great Britain's than it ever had before). National chauvinism and Anglo-Saxonism co-existed uneasily, not merely among divergent groups but within some of the same individuals. (A prime example can be found in the Centennial oration given by Justice Samuel F. Miller in 1887.)

If we want to situate this trend in a longer historical perspective, it is possible to discern a series of transitions in American constitutionalism that unfolded roughly as follows: first, we are different (1790s until the 1860s); second, some variations do exist but we share common constitutional roots dating back to Magna Carta and beyond (1870s until the 1920s); and third, although both systems evolved historically within a discernible Anglo-American framework, their most fundamental attributes make them profoundly dissimilar (1920s and 1930s).

In 1908, Woodrow Wilson, then the president of Princeton, summarized one explanation in a single sentence: "The Constitution of the United States as framed by the constitutional convention of 1787, was intended to be a copy of the government of England, with such changes as seemed to our statesmen necessary to safeguard the people of America against the particular sorts of prerogative and power that had worked them harm in their dealings with the government of the mother country over sea."[3] Well, yes and no. That is a reasonable approximation—succinct yet simplistic—of what happened in 1787. The cultural adjustments in Anglo-American constitutionalism between 1787 and 1908, however, require considerably more explanation. What transpired during the quarter century following 1908 is even more complicated and involves some rather unexpected twists.

I

How much did constitutionalism in the United States owe to British origins and precedents? Curiously enough, the question did not arise very often during the first century of our national existence; but when it did, the answers given stretched across such a broad range that they anticipated a fair number of responses that would appear in the age of Theodore Roosevelt and Woodrow Wilson. Many of the authors of state constitutions in 1776 and subsequently, as well as those who gathered at Philadelphia in 1787, believed that they had contributed to a new, peculiarly American concept of what a constitution meant: namely, a fundamental law, superior to statutory as well as common law, and promulgated by a specially chosen "supreme legislature."[4]

Everyone did not take quite that point of view, however. James

Duane of New York, for example, argued for "grounding our rights on the laws and constitution of the country from whence we sprung." Writing in 1787, John Adams still regarded the English constitution as "the most stupendous fabric of human invention." Nothing in the history of civilization "does more honor to the human understanding than this system of government." Throughout the Philadelphia Convention, one delegate after another praised the English prototype as the best ever devised by man.[5] In 1799, Chief Justice Oliver Ellsworth ruled that English common law was binding upon U.S. courts, thereby provoking Jeffersonians to find the "Constitution profaned by your decision" (but see figure 3); and in the famous Charles River Bridge case (1837), Chief Justice Taney insisted that "we adopt and adhere to the rules of construction known to the English common law . . . without exception."[6]

Accepting the applicability of English common law in American jurisprudence did not mean that our Constitution had simply been grafted from theirs. Senator James Hillhouse, a Connecticut Federalist, observed in 1808 that "some of the important features of our constitution were borrowed from a model which did not very well suit our condition. I mean the constitution and government of England." That elicited from John Adams a reply that many Americans would echo later in the nineteenth century: "Would it not have been more conformable to the fact to have said, that those important features of our constitution were borrowed from our colonial constitutions?"[7]

James Madison went even farther, thereby widening the spectrum of possible positions by arguing in *Federalist* Number 14 for the U.S. Constitution as a "novelty in the political world." He continued to maintain that attitude in a private letter written more than seven years after his retirement from the presidency: "I view our political system . . . as a combination and modification of powers without a model; as emphatically sui generis." In that same year, 1824, Jedidiah Morse presented a more categorical explanation, one that epitomized the conventional wisdom throughout the antebellum era: the American and English constitutions were fundamentally different, in their historical origins as well as their guiding principles. For a devoted republican the essential explanation seemed simple: "Ours is the act of the people."[8]

During the onset of the Civil War, which eventually served as a stimulus to constitutional exegesis, the range of respectable opinions broadened. Theophilus Parsons, who was Joseph Story's successor as Dane Professor of Law at Harvard, perpetuated the Madison-Morse position. No existing constitution was comparable to theirs. "A Constitution is, in

fact, an American invention. It was prepared for by a long course of antecedents, all of which pointed towards this result, and made it possible."
Britain lacked a true constitution because "real" constitutions are "inviola-
ble" in the sense that they cannot be altered by means of ordinary legislation. Sidney George Fisher, on the other hand, candidly acknowledged the
debt of constitutional influence that America owed to Britain.[9]

Each of these views would attract numerous adherents during the
final third of the nineteenth century: Parsons's position that the colonial
experience fundamentally determined the U.S. Constitution, and Fisher's
stress upon the British heritage. A third stance, symptomatic of a major
shift in American constitutionalism, is represented by Thomas M. Cooley's *Treatise on the Constitutional Limitations which Rest Upon the Legislative Power of the States of the American Union.* First published in 1868, it
underwent numerous editions and had a greater impact upon the development of constitutional law in the United States than any other work, with
the possible exception of *The Federalist Papers.* Although primarily a
jurist's commentary on state (rather than federal) law, it came to be used
extensively by lawyers, judges, and the Supreme Court in construing the
elusive due process clause of the Fourteenth Amendment. Cooley's compendium was cited more frequently in U.S. courts during the sixty years
following 1870 than any other treatise on constitutional law. Its significance in our context, therefore, is that it broadened the operative meaning
of constitutionalism to something more nearly comparable to the functional definition of that phenomenon in Great Britain: namely, a diverse
yet interacting corpus of state constitutions, plus the common law, statutes, and precedents, in addition to the federal Constitution.[10] By the
1880s and '90s, when Cooley's *General Principles of Constitutional Law in
the United States of America* (1880) had also become available, his immense
prestige enhanced the feeling of Anglo-American constitutional convergence that was already strong among certain groups for other reasons.

II

Although some response to the U.S. Constitution appeared in Britain from
the very outset in 1788–89, the raspy observations that caused real reverberations in America came from Thomas Babington Macaulay in 1857
and Walter Bagehot in 1861. Macaulay, to whom Teddy Roosevelt and
others reacted so vehemently, had written a letter (subsequently published)
to Thomas Jefferson's first serious biographer in which the famous histo-

rian quipped: "Your Constitution is all sail and no anchor," a criticism of Jeffersonian naïveté, excessive democracy, and the dangers inherent in ill-informed opinions held by a fickle populace.[11]

Bagehot's criticisms, as we have already seen, followed somewhat different lines. Although he admired federalism as an innovative solution to the dilemmas faced in 1787, he expressed scorn for American devotion to a written constitution and contrasted the rigidity of ours unfavorably with the flexibility that he claimed for Great Britain's. He shared this common ground with Macaulay: a belief that democracy needed to be carefully controlled, that the founders had recognized that fact at the Convention but had failed to produce a system capable of minimizing democratic disorder.[12]

Because Macaulay and Bagehot both enjoyed considerable prestige and were widely read, their barbs stung and stimulated vigorous reactions in the United States. Within a decade American writers began to insist, ad infinitum, that our Constitution was, in fact, flexible rather than rigid;[13] that a written constitution was superior in several respects;[14] and above all, as Henry Cabot Lodge declared in 1911, "our ancestors sought to make it as impossible as human ingenuity could devise to drag democracy down by the pretense of giving it a larger scope."[15]

British perceptions of their own constitution, particularly during the later nineteenth century, require an extended inquiry independent of this one. Nevertheless, it is necessary to indicate at least a few basic notions in order to understand British comments upon the U.S. Constitution (and, even more germane, the replies those comments evoked). By American standards, British constitutionalism seems unusually historical, inclusive, and somewhat ethereal. The historical (or evolutionary) dimension is most familiar and easiest to specify. As Lord Lyndhurst said to the Peers in 1856, "long-considered usage is the basis and principle of our laws and our constitution." The inclusive aspect, reaching from the seventeenth-century common lawyers to the nineteenth-century Burkean Whigs, was essentially undemocratic yet wide-ranging in scope: the constitution consists of all the ongoing, self-defining public activities of the nation. The ethereal element may be exemplified by Henry Hallam's well-read *Constitutional History of England from the Accession of Henry VII to the Death of George II*. Writing in 1827, Hallam made participation in the fellowship of the constitution virtually a sacrament: "We do not argue from the creed of the English constitution to those who have abandoned its communion."[16]

Two closely linked features of British constitutionalism in the Victorian era have long been clear: a remarkably unhistorical emphasis upon continuity, and the belief that gradual constitutional change was infinitely preferable to revolution or artificially contrived reform. Beginning with Bagehot's *English Constitution* in 1867, however, new issues cracked the Whig consensus that had dominated for more than a generation. Although Bagehot praised the virtue of slow, evolutionary growth, he also acknowledged the existence of phases and changes in English constitutional history. From the 1870s onward there would be intermittent discussions concerning the desirability of democracy—or more precisely, how much democracy was either desirable or acceptable. Hence that quaint Victorian fascination with the constitution of Athens. Conservative historians and political theorists exploited the ambiguous materials from ancient Greece in order to defend or discredit democracy. It cannot be said that either side "won" this circuitous debate; but British constitutionalism did acquire a new feature during the final quarter of the nineteenth century: how to dovetail a more populistic version of English constitutional origins with the orthodox account that emphasized continuity, property, and stability.[17]

One subsequent development is critical to an understanding of the Anglo-American "dialogue" over constitutionalism at the turn of the century. A major governmental crisis took place in Britain between 1906 and 1911 because the House of Lords rejected His Majesty's budget for 1909—a serious challenge to the system and a potential source of trouble that had been in the works for some while. Each side to the dispute insisted that the other had violated the constitution. Neither side would consider compromise. Both realized that, in functional terms, the British constitution had come to mean different things to different groups. By 1910 everyone involved in public affairs spent extraordinary amounts of time inspecting printed works concerning the constitution. The cabinet even considered publishing extracts from these historical sources in order to assist public understanding of the episode. Needless to say, when King George V consulted diverse authorities about the Crown's prerogatives, he got diverse answers.[18]

The well-known outcome: a diminution in the Lords' authority. The pertinent outcome for our context? First, the lesson once again that a constitutional crisis can provide a valuable means of piquing public interest in constitutional issues. And second, heightened American awareness that the distribution of power within a constitutional system, be it monarchical or republican, does not remain static. The battle of Britain involving the House of Lords had reverberations in the United States.[19]

Meanwhile, the pendulum of British perception had begun to swing away from the negativism expressed by Macaulay and Bagehot. After visiting the United States during the 1860s, Goldwin Smith and Leslie Stephen both voiced admiration for the American Constitution. In 1871 J. R. Seeley, Professor of Modern History at Cambridge University, urged consideration of the U.S. Constitution as a potential model for the "Greater Britain" that he envisioned. During the 1880s Alfred Lord Tennyson confessed conservative envy because the U.S. Constitution seemed so difficult to change; and A. V. Dicey as well as Lord Acton commended its compactness. As Acton noted, it "resembled no other constitution, for it was contained in half a dozen intelligible articles."[20]

In 1878, William E. Gladstone wrote a single sentence one half of which swiftly became the most commonly quoted observation about the U.S. Constitution. A Member of Parliament and leader of the Opposition at the time, Gladstone wanted to win friends and strengthen Anglo-American bonds. In an essay entitled "Kin Beyond Sea," he shifted to a comparative mood. After paying his respects to the American Revolution for being "a conservative revolution," he offered this contrast: "The two constitutions of the two countries express indeed rather the differences than the resemblances of the nations. The one is a thing grown, the other is a thing made. . . . But, as the British Constitution is the most subtle organism which had proceeded from the womb and the long gestation of progressive history, so the American Constitution is, so far as I can see, the most wonderful work ever struck off at a given time by the brain and purpose of man."[21] Predictably, perhaps, the last twenty-eight words of that extract came to be quoted, out of context and with a tone of validation from the Almighty, over and over again, most especially at the time of the Centennial; but also in civics texts for schoolchildren throughout the next sixty years, and especially when the observance of Constitution Day and Constitution Week became formulaic rituals during the 1920s.[22]

The impact of the last part of Gladstone's commendation really should occasion no surprise. He not only told the American people what many of them wanted to hear, but reiterated what they had actually heard before, though not from an illustrious English statesman. Back in 1823 Supreme Court Justice William Johnson had referred to the Constitution as "the most wonderful instrument ever drawn by the hand of man." (The phrasing is so incredibly close; perhaps Gladstone had read that remark somewhere.) Even Walter Bagehot, who regarded federalism as the great achievement of 1787, conceded that "nothing so remarkable was perhaps ever struck out on the impulse of the moment by persons actually charged with the practical duty of making a constitution." Once Gladstone published "Kin Beyond Sea" in 1878, famous as well as obscure Americans often paraphrased it without troubling to cite the great Liberal leader.[23]

Given the passage of time, it became possible for people naïvely to quote Gladstone out of context because they might very well have drawn from some second-hand version, already ripped from context, rather than from the original. Two factors limit the utility of that explanation, however. First, had there been any misunderstanding of Gladstone's qualified praise in 1878, it should have been clarified in 1887 when he apologized for being unable to attend the Centennial celebration in Philadelphia and repeated his earlier encomium. Second, occasional writers of newspaper editorials and other essays did quote the complete extract and thereby transmit the comparative sense of it properly.[24]

But if Gladstone (bowdlerized) fulfilled the needs of American superpatriots, Gladstone (complete) served as a stimulus—mostly to scholars initially, who not only wanted to correct the misleading impression he gave, but for the first time added a serious historical dimension to American constitutionalism. Alexander Johnston, Professor of Jurisprudence and Political Economy at Princeton, wrote several essays designed to refute Gladstone, essays that in expanded form became the widely read entry on U.S. constitutional history for the *Encyclopaedia Britannica;* and then, posthumously, a separate book. Johnston's central point? In 1787 the founders had drawn deeply upon the colonists' experience, and subsequently upon the state constitutions. "Gladstone's notion of the Constitution as a creation is altogether erroneous," he asserted; "it was a growth, or, rather, a selection from a great number of growths then before the Convention." The irony, of course, is that the nature of Johnston's argument could not have been more conservative, more Burkean, indeed, more British: "If the brilliant success of the American Constitution proves anything, it does not prove that a viable constitution can ever be 'struck off at a given time by the brain and purpose of man.' . . . On the contrary, the first century of the Constitution seems to show conclusively that natural growth alone gives the promise as well as the potency of permanence."[25]

Johnston's aggressive stance was accepted and applied in various ways by J. Franklin Jameson, James Schouler, James Harvey Robinson, and Brooks Adams. In 1900 a New England newspaperman and historical popularizer, Amos Kidder Fiske, castigated Gladstone's "oft-quoted statement" as a "rank fallacy." The U.S. Constitution, like that of Great Britain, "is a development, a growth, and it will continue to grow and to adapt itself to the needs of an expanding Nation as long as our Government endures." While many of Fiske's contemporaries merely wanted to demonstrate similarities between our Constitution and the British—both resulting from slow, steady growth—Fiske went even farther in a rather outrageous effort to invert the customary stereotypes: "The British Constitution is the creation of the British Parliament. The American Constitution is the creation of the Supreme Court, operating upon the work of the Convention of 1787 and the acts of Congress ever since that date. The process is as truly normal, it is quite as conservative, and it is more harmonious in its results, than that which has been going on at Westminster Hall. And the work of 1787 was not 'struck off at a given time,' but was the product of a hundred and fifty years of Colonial experience."[26]

Twentieth-century jurists, journalists, historians, and political theorists have not, ordinarily, gone that far in reversing conventional images. The repudiation of Gladstone seems to remain imperative nonetheless, so that Chief Justice Earl Warren, writing in *Fortune* for a general audience, would continue to proclaim, with Fiske, that "our legal system has been an organic growth, and not the overnight creation of any individual genius."[27] He wrote those words in 1955: four years after the bicentennial of James Madison's birth, the very year of John Marshall's bicentennial, and one year before Alexander Hamilton's. So much for inspired genius. Our Constitution sprang from collected wisdom of the ages, both before and since 1787.

Although William E. Gladstone does not need modern apologists, the point might be made that his controversial statement in 1878 is not necessarily incompatible with the experiential emphasis of his critics. It is, after all, possible to write a constitution in a "moment" of inspiration, even a four-month moment of inspiration, especially if that "moment" is the product or culmination of lessons learned during a century or more of practical experience. On the other hand, if Gladstone had not provoked such outrage, and if constitutionalism did not stimulate protagonists, our story would be considerably less interesting. Moncure D. Conway made a wise observation in 1887: "People have little more difficulty in reading their prepossessions into a constitution than sects have in finding their several creeds in the Bible."[28]

A younger contemporary of Gladstone, raised in Scotland, enjoyed a more favorable reception, in part because his opinions happened to coincide so well with what Americans wanted to hear in 1889, and in part because his perspective came from Great Britain at just the time when cultural anglophilia was on the rise generally and certain Americans particularly wanted to believe that their Constitution was rather like the British.

Near the outset of his *American Commonwealth,* James Bryce (then a Member of Parliament for Aberdeen), accorded this carefully phrased compliment:

> The Constitution of 1789 [sic] deserves the veneration with which the Americans have been accustomed to regard it. It is true that many criticisms have been passed upon its arrangement, upon its omissions, upon the artificial character of some of the institutions it creates. . . . And whatever success it has attained must be in large measure ascribed to the political genius, ripened by long experience, of the Anglo-American race, by whom it has been worked, and who might have managed to work even a worse drawn instrument. Yet, after all deductions, it ranks above every other written constitution for the intrinsic excellence of its scheme, its adaptation to the circumstances of the people, the simplicity, brevity, and precision of its language, its judicious mixture of definiteness in principle with elasticity in details.[29]

Lengthy reviews in journals of opinion appeared every month throughout 1889. Although the authors touched upon many aspects of Bryce's work, they delighted in using *The American Commonwealth* as a gallows from which to hang Gladstone. Hence this typical statement which appeared in *The Dial.* "Mr. Bryce's knowledge of American history has shown him that the Constitution was a growth,—not simply an emanation from the minds of the Fathers at Philadelphia, not the result of a few weeks of discussion, not a fabric reared on *a priori* principles aided by the teachings of Montesquieu and Blackstone. . . . As the author sees that our Constitution can not be said literally to have been struck off in a given time by the hand of man . . . so he recognizes that it is capable of growth and development."[30]

Bryce soon achieved accolades as Tocqueville's worthy successor, even preferable perhaps because his savvy was Anglo-Saxon rather than Gallic. For more than three decades his assessment of the U.S. Constitution would be cited as authoritative; and on occasion he updated his benediction. In 1912, for example, several thousand members of the Pennsylvania Society attended a dinner at the Waldorf-Astoria to honor the 125th anniversary of the adoption of the Constitution. Bryce, retiring as British ambassador, gave the principal address. After discussing how well the Constitution had endured the Civil War, and describing how many countries had taken the Constitution as a model, he concluded with a slightly patronizing yet candid point of view (damning with faint praise, perhaps): "With you, where class counts for so much less than it does in Europe and where traditions have not had so much power, there have been many moments when things would have gone badly had it not been for the respect you have all formed for the Constitution."[31]

III

For a full generation following 1885, fascination with Anglo-American constitutional comparisons ran high. In part this resulted from a rising concern about the relative merits of such features as ministerial responsibility in Britain and what seemed to be "monarchical" tendencies inherent in the U.S. Constitution. Professor A. Lawrence Lowell of Harvard, a political scientist who would serve as president of the university from 1909 until 1933, was particularly engaged by such matters and issued a series of pronouncements during the later 1880s: viz, "a responsible ministry cannot be grafted into our institutions without entirely changing their nature, and destroying those features of our government which we have been in the habit of contemplating with the most pride"; or, "the Constitution has been to us what a king has often been to other nationalities."[32]

Several trends figured prominently in the development of analyses along these lines. First, there were extended visits by Americans in Britain and vice versa, one result of which can best be called high-level journalism that examined the comparative condition of the two systems, highlighting paradoxical ways in which they had become more nearly alike despite the existence of fundamental differences in structure, nature (written versus unwritten), and principles of operation.[33] In 1887 the executive committee of the Constitutional Centennial Commission sent a remarkable letter to all the commissioners that included this passage:

> We would suggest that two such events as the Jubilee of Queen Victoria [also in 1887] and this great celebration of the American people, occurring so close together, naturally afford food for much reflection, and can well be made the subject of many historical comparisons and dissertations. The spontaneous manifestations of the subjects of the British Sovereign which have just raised a shout of joy around the earth, are after all but the personal congratulations extended by the millions, on the fiftieth anniversary of her coronation, to a monarch whose character has been pre-eminently pure and spot-

less, and whose reign has been wise, just and prosperous. No great principle of government, however, was held forth as matter for public approbation. The personal nature of that jubilee was marked. The American Jubilee, on the contrary, will call our people together to celebrate and applaud, not the character of an individual, but the foundation of a great Nation and the principles contained in the charter upon which its existence is based.[34]

Foreign observers, regardless of whether they were British, French, or German, seemed more inclined to acknowledge similarities, or the steady pace of constitutional convergence, than Americans were.[35] By contrast, A. Lawrence Lowell investigated the British and American forms of government "for the purpose of showing that their natures are radically different." The principal reason, Lowell declared, obvious to any American, is "the natural result of a written constitution," which created clear limitations upon government. That would become a normative judgment among many American authorities for several decades after 1888. As George Ticknor Curtis put it:

> the terms Constitutional History and Constitutional Law have in this country a signification peculiar to ourselves. In other countries, as, for example, in England, where there is no written Constitution, and where everything depends upon the will of the legislative power, Constitutional History is the history of the legislation or public action which has given form and fixture to the powers of the government and the rights of individuals. . . . With us, the bearing of Constitutional history upon any doctrine or proposition of Constitutional Law consists in the influence which public events or public action ought to have on the interpretation of a written test.[36]

The explanatory part of this argument pointed persistently to the colonists' long experience of living under charters, which "furnished our fathers with the idea and importance of written constitutions as the basis of their state governments." That interpretation had been made by the founders themselves (most of the time implicitly), by orators like Edward Everett (explicitly), and then by many different sorts of persons for half a century after 1875.[37]

Had this been the only arc of American constitutionalism during that era, or at least its predominant trajectory, our story would be relatively uncomplicated. But a symptomatic essay that appeared in 1907, entitled

"The Constitution and the People's Liberties," belittled the entire controversy concerning the virtues of written versus unwritten constitutions.
"The historic importance of our Constitution is not that it is written, but
that it embodies the first attempt of a people to control their own Government. . . . The whole of it is nothing but a code of the people's liberties,
political and civil; a code of many centuries' growth. . . ."[38] The contention that we possessed both a written and an unwritten constitution can be
found (in somewhat mystical form) at least as early as 1865 in *The American Republic* by Orestes A. Brownson. During the 1870s Henry Adams
expressed empathy for the English constitution ("that partnership of nobility and commonalty"); and early in the eighties his brother, Brooks
Adams, presented a working definition that was indisputably British:
"Properly speaking the constitutional law of our country is a collection of
customs by which the country is regulated."[39]

The leading constitutional theorists, jurists, and commentators of the
later nineteenth century tended to be anglophiles: Thomas M. Cooley admired Anglo-Saxon governmental traditions in general and the English
common law in particular; Oliver Wendell Holmes, Jr., published his best
known book, *The Common Law,* in 1881, and twenty-three years later incorporated into a decision one of his cosmic pronouncements: "the provisions of the Constitution are not mathematical formulas . . . they are
organic living institutions transplanted from English soil."[40]

Although less familiar, the most influential statement along these
lines occurred in a compact book written for laymen and students, called
The Unwritten Constitution of the United States. The author, Christopher
G. Tiedeman, a professor of law at the University of Missouri, emphasized
"the lineal descent of the American constitutional law from the British,"
and provided a very conservative justification for having a written constitution at all. Such an instrument enabled the social and political elite
(Tiedeman described them as "independent, right-minded men"), in accordance with the highest law, "to plant themselves upon the provisions of
the written Constitution, and deny to popular legislation the binding force
of law, whenever such legislation infringes a constitutional provision. This
is the real value of the written Constitution. It legalizes, and therefore
makes possible and successful, the opposition to the popular will."[41] Judicial review as an instrument of social control!

Is it any wonder that editorial writers who did not share this enthusiasm would refer to the "Anglo-maniacs . . . among us"? During the next
three decades, influential statements of constitutional anglophilia were
presented by Woodrow Wilson as well as by widely read publicists like

Alfred P. Dennis, Hannis Taylor (a lawyer, diplomat, and prolific popularizer),[42] Senator William Cabell Bruce of Maryland, and Nicholas Murray Butler, the haughty president of Columbia. What attracted them particularly was the apparent responsiveness of the British system to changing circumstances. "The true character of the British Constitution," Dennis wrote, "is to be found, not so much in the positive rules which courts will enforce, as in the spontaneous, institutional growths which have supplemented, or have superseded, the rule of law. In like manner the true genius and character of our institutions, in much greater degree than we commonly suspect, are to be found in forms of political life unknown to the written Constitution, and unenforced by the Courts."[43]

Woodrow Wilson's contribution to American constitutionalism is important for three reasons: it persisted for more than a quarter of a century; it reached a steadily expanding audience; and it is filled with the dualistic utterances of a nationalistic anglophile, a conservative liberal, and a constitutional revisionist who revered tradition. As he announced in 1885, using the royal "We" rather generously: "We of the present generation are in the first season of free outspoken, unrestrained constitutional criticism. We are the first Americans to hear our countrymen ask whether the Constitution is still adapted to serve the purpose for which it was intended." He even criticized what seemed to him "an undiscriminating and almost blind worship" of the Constitution. In a speech delivered in 1910, however, he reiterated a lifelong theme: "I have been brought up with an inveterate reverence for the text and the meaning of the Constitution of the United States."[44]

Wilson believed in broad construction and interpretive flexibility—he referred to the Constitution endlessly as "a vehicle of life"—yet he could also declare that "its prescriptions are clear and we know what they are; a written document makes lawyers of us all, and our duty as citizens should make us conscientious lawyers, reading the text of the Constitution without subtlety or sophistication." Sometimes he regretted that changes by amendment were so difficult to achieve, while at others he accepted that obstacle as a sign of the founders' sagacity. He hoped the courts would not "seek to find in the phrases of the Constitution remedies for evils which the federal government was never intended to deal with." Wilson felt that our system of separation of powers had gone too far toward isolating the branches of government, and admired the more integrated British system of ministerial intimacy with Parliament. He nevertheless regretted the growing failure to distinguish adequately "between constitutional and ordinary law" (a tendency in line with British practice), and praised the U.S.

Constitution, "which is strong and flexible chiefly because of its great, its admirable simplicity and its strictly *constitutional* scope."[45] Almost a non sequitur, but not quite.

Finally, Wilson's penchant for praising the Constitution, matter of factly, on account of its conceptual vacuum—"The Constitution contains no theories. It is as practical a document as Magna Carta"—serves to remind us that for a century Magna Carta has been invoked rather casually in American political culture, sometimes as the progenitor of our Constitution, sometimes as its counterpart, occasionally as the object of iconoclastic historical realism (de-emphasizing its importance), but more commonly cited on ceremonial occasions as "one of the cornerstones of our democratic ideology and way of life" (1950). The most poignant illustration occurred in 1965, when the United States joined with some enthusiasm in celebrating the 750th anniversary of Magna Carta. In May of that year, in a touching ceremony at Runnymede, "a little corner of the English meadow where the idea of constitutional government first stirred" was dedicated to the memory of John F. Kennedy, a different King John (more nearly a King Arthur) who evoked a latter-day Camelot.[46]

IV

The emphasis upon Anglo-American constitutionalism that reached its apogee during the quarter century after 1890 has not yet disappeared, and serves as a useful corrective to the more excessive impulses of American parochialism and chauvinism.[47] The most valuable legacy of that cultural phase, however, may well have been the inception of a serious, realistic Anglo-American dialogue about constitutional issues. Initially, and for a decade following the turn of the century, that dialogue took two principal forms: thoughtful American responses to British essays critical of the U.S. Constitution, even ones calling for its revision; and the republication in American newspapers of British press commentary upon major Supreme Court decisions, such as the controversial "insular cases."[48]

Those tendencies fostered two others: first, visits to Britain by distinguished American jurists, and vice versa, often in order to present well-reported lectures explicating the constitutions of their respective countries; and second, correspondence involving a candid (and often critical) exchange of views pertaining to Anglo-American constitutionalism. In 1911, for example, Associate Justice Horace Lurton, serving on a committee whose mission it was to revise the rules of procedure used in U.S. courts, travelled to Britain to learn about reforms that had been made in equity procedures there, and held lengthy conferences with the Lord Chancellor and Lord Chief Justice. In 1918, when Lord Charnwood made a lecture tour of the United States, one of his most popular topics was "The Modern British Constitution." In 1922 James M. Beck, Solicitor General of the United States, appeared in London before the highest court of the empire in a case involving war contracts. A poem about him promptly appeared in the press, written by "G.S.C."

> *The tale is told of James M. Beck*
> *That once, in England, he did deck*
> *His temples with a snowy wig*
> *In which his act went over—big.*
>
> *Then to his native shore he turned*
> *But do not think the wig was burned.*
> *Ah, no! He overlooks no chances*
> *But wears it still—at fancy dances.*

While there Beck delivered two lectures at Gray's Inn concerning the history and nature of the U.S. Supreme Court. These were published in a slender volume that achieved wide readership, and ten years later he returned at the invitation of the University of London to present six lectures on the Watson Foundation. His overall theme: "The United States Constitution as an Experiment in Democracy."[49]

Meanwhile in 1923 Lord Birkenhead (Frederick Edwin Smith), Lord Chancellor of Britain from 1919 until 1922, visited the United States and spoke to several organizations, most notably the American Bar Association for whom he compared the safeguards provided to Americans by their Constitution with the omnipotence of Parliament. Three years later, on George Washington's birthday, Sir Henry Lunn, a distinguished English scholar and churchman, addressed the Sulgrave Institution (an Anglophile organization) on "The Philadelphia Convention of 1787." Lunn offered harsh criticisms of Charles Beard's *Economic Interpretation of the Constitution* and, in an obvious boost for the League of Nations, praised the founders for envisioning the concept of a "super-state": varied polities united under a single "super-national authority."[50]

The constitutional consequences of World War I stimulated several frank transatlantic exchanges of letters, most notably between Lord Bryce and Henry Cabot Lodge in 1918, and between Harold Laski and Oliver

Wendell Holmes in 1923. "Our Constitutional position is singular," Bryce explained.

> We were under a Quinennial Act, passed by the present Parliament. The five years have more than run out, the length of Parliament having been extended. Previously, as you know, we were under a Septennial Act. That period will also soon have run out, and we shall have to prolong Parliament to a period not reached since 1688. There is, however, no doubt legally as to the power of Parliament to do this, and herein we have an advantage over your astronomical system. It is a curious fact that by far the greatest change ever made in our Parliamentary Franchise should have been made by a Parliament which has lost altogether what is called its "mandate," and has also lost a good deal of its moral weight. The Act recently passed has added more voters than ever were added before. . . . None of us contemplated when the war began, anything approaching the immense domestic changes which it has brought about. I gather that in the U.S. also constitutional government is almost suspended, but then, you will return to the status quo ante without difficulty, automatically, as you did after the Civil War. That may not be the case with us.

Lodge responded with a modicum of distortion and an excess of gloom: "The situation in England, as I observe it and as you describe it, seems to be extremely grave. Our own Constitution has for the time being been set aside and although the various laws which we have passed giving extraordinary powers are limited to the prosecution of the war, no one can tell how far we shall be able to return to our old constitutional limitations. I hope we shall get back to them but a great many measures have been adopted which temporarily at least lead to State socialism. . . ."[51]

During the winter of 1922–23, Harold Laski taunted Justice Holmes with such undeveloped, un-Gladstonian remarks as: "the U.S. Constitution is the worst instrument of government that the mind of man has so far conceived." When Holmes replied ("I don't lie awake nights wondering at the inspiration of those who made the Constitution but your condemnation needs to be justified"), Laski suggested that a strict separation of the executive and the judiciary seemed "one long mistake," but broke off by tantalizing Holmes once again: "if I began to state my feelings about the American Constitution I should exhaust both your patience and the vocabulary of vituperation." Holmes—an anglophile in terms of legal history, remember—could not resist: "I wish you would develop more at length your grounds for disliking our constitution. Of course it has the 18th century emphasis and Bagehot criticised forcibly the division of powers—but I suspect that you don't like the bill of rights . . . —whereas I have been rather led to the belief that we have grown so accustomed to the enjoyment of those rights that we forget that they had to be fought for and may have to be fought for again. As I have no plan for reconstructing society at all costs I am inclined to stand by them."

At last Holmes succeeded in lifting Laski's gorge sky high. The justice's brilliant young admirer laid it all out.

The American constitution. My difficulties with it are easily listable. 1. I am all for Bagehot's criticism of the non-parliamentary form of government. I think the Congressional system impairs legislative and executive responsibility, lowers the tone of the press, and keeps the best of America out of politics by making all save the Presidency an unattractive career. 2. I dislike the judicial review of congressional legislation. 3. I dislike the inaccessibility of the Constitution to amendment. 4. I dislike passionately the way in which the 14th Amendment has simply become (Holmes, J. dissenting) a cloak for the protection of obsolete property interests. 5. I dislike the senatorial power to confirm appointments, especially diplomatic appointments. 6. I dislike intensely the equal fiscal power of both chambers. It is, I think, constitutionally vital to have unequal powers in either part of a legislative assembly in financial matters. Fiscal compromises are always fiscal improprieties. 7. I think that the whole geographical basis of the Senate is now obsolete. The fiction of equality between the states really means the vicious weighting of legislation in favour of the reactionary South. 8. I dislike the legislative control of finance. It is axiomatic that the spending authority must stand or fall by its own financial policy.[52]

Holmes did not answer that explosive (but well-informed) bill of particulars. Five years later, when his dear friend Sir Frederick Pollock remarked that "I have my own private history of your Constitution," Holmes did not attempt to draw him out. Once around with Laski, apparently, had been enough.[53]

The significance of all this cerebral backing and forthing is that by the mid-1920s both sides had begun to recognize explicitly that, despite common historical roots, the British and U.S. constitutions were quite different, a major reversal of one pervasive orthodoxy just half a generation earlier. On the British side, statements came from Lord Bryce in 1921 (he found the American system so much less flexible), and from Lord Birkenhead, who reached the same conclusion but placed it in a different light: "Your Constitution is expressed and defined in documents which can be pronounced upon by the Supreme Court. In this sense your judges are the masters of your executive. Your Constitution is a cast-iron document. . . . This circumstance provides a breakwater of enormous value against ill-considered and revolutionary change."

Birkenhead was apprehensive about the uncontrolled transition to full democracy in his country, and felt that the American system was equipped with superior brakes (namely, judicial review) to the British. Ultimately, however, he acknowledged that it was too soon to know whether the United States had followed the wiser course "in trying to control the free will of a free people by judicial authority, or whether we have been right in trusting the free will and a free people to work out their own salvation." In 1926 *The New York Times* took pleasure in citing an editorial from *The Observer* conceding that the U.S. Constitution has supplanted the British as a basic model for other nations. "The Constitution of the United States is totally different from ours, and other countries look more to it for lessons. It provides for strength of the executive and stability of government and institutions."[54]

On the American side an explicit recognition of constitutional differences, accompanied by strong endorsements for our own system, came from Alton B. Parker (Chief Justice of the New York Court of Appeals) and James M. Beck in 1922; from Henry Cabot Lodge in 1923; from Charles Warren in a popularized version (1925) of his massive trilogy on the Supreme Court; from David Jayne Hill, who quoted Gladstone out of context in order to use him as a foil (1926); from Howard Lee McBain, the Ruggles Professor of Constitutional Law at Columbia, who repudiated both Bagehot and Gladstone in a book written for laymen as part of "The World Today Bookshelf" (1927); from George W. Wickersham, chairman of the widely published Wickersham Commission on the administration of justice (1931);[55] and finally from Newton D. Baker, Secretary of War under Wilson and subsequently an active member of a Cleveland law firm, who was virtually unique in taking the trouble to quote Gladstone in full and in context. Then he struck what by 1934 had become the dominant note: "The American and the British Constitution are two entirely different things. One is a series of great principles sometimes embodied in documents, beginning perhaps with the Magna Carta, and including parliamentary acts, like the Act of Settlement, evolved in revolutionary and dynastic crises in the life of England, but also involving traditional attitudes of mind. . . ." The U.S. Constitution of 1787, by contrast, was a home-grown product, deeply rooted in the colonial experience.[56]

An articulate minority, led by prominent political scientists, acknowledged the reality of Anglo-American differences but endorsed the American system with less enthusiasm. The sticking point? How much did it really matter that the United States had a written constitution? Charles A. Beard, for example, conceded that it made a big difference; yet he would not reduce his admiration for the British notion of a constitution that was cumulative and adaptive in response to socio-economic changes. In 1930, Beard continued to cite with approval Thomas M. Cooley's anglophile reading of constitutional law. To William Bennett Munro of Harvard, it seemed unrealistic to think about the complex totality of American government without recognizing all the important yet unanticipated consequences of the framers' work. Charles E. Merriam of Chicago also de-emphasized the "written" aspect of the U.S. Constitution, asserting that "each generation has produced a new constitution of government with fundamental changes in spirit and form."[57]

As the Great Depression deepened, no consensus emerged about the most desirable or legitimate programmatic solutions. Nevertheless, the need for flexibility came to be widely accepted. An Anglo-American mode of thinking about constitutionalism in terms of making the entire system of government more responsive emerged alongside a judicious recognition that in 1787 the founders had drawn upon British as well as indigenous political traditions. Writing in 1941, Alfred North Whitehead epitomized the resolution of this ongoing dialogue. He called the framing of the U.S. Constitution one of the "two occasions in history when the people in power did what needed to be done about as well as you can imagine its being possible." As for the so-called founding fathers, "they were able statesmen, they had access to a body of good ideas; they incorporated these general principles into the instrument without trying to particularize too explicitly how they should be put into effect; and they were men of immense practical experience themselves."[58]

The convolutions of Anglo-American constitutionalism abound with ironies, not the least of which is James Madison's apprehension that by 1930 excessive population growth might make a constitution like Britain's more appropriate to American needs. In several respects his prophecy was sound; and in 1933 George Bernard Shaw, addressing an audience of 3,500 people at the Metropolitan Opera House in New York City, made the half-serious recommendation: "Smash the Constitution" altogether and prepare a new one "based on purely American needs." Although Shaw created quite a stir, few people took heed. A concerted effort to write a new American constitution would not occur until the 1960s; and even then the highly serious participants knew that they were engaging in a heuristic exercise.[59] In the later 1970s a predictable inversion took place: the criticism raised by conservative British theorists that their own constitution had increasingly become a written one, thereby enhancing the power of bureaucratic state authority and minimizing the people's property and rights. Lord Hailsham appealed for "a new constitution for Britain," more like the American model.[60]

V

A parallel development during the half century following 1880 involved the emergence of constitutional history as a major field of scholarship in the United States. Most of that story should be told as part of the genesis of professional historiography, a related yet discrete phenomenon. Insofar as nationalism and Anglo-Saxon racism relate the preceding discussion to the subdiscipline of constitutional history, however, we ought to examine some connections between the two as well as their consequences.

Between 1874–78, when Bishop William Stubbs published his three-volume *Constitutional History of England,* and 1903, when A. F. Pollard was appointed to a chair in constitutional history at University College, London, the field can be said to have come of age in Great Britain.[61] Although it matured several decades earlier than in the United States, and had considerable impact upon developments there, what happened in America enjoyed a certain autonomy, nonetheless, in both professional and personal terms. As far back as 1864, for example, twenty-five-year-old James Schouler recorded in his diary: "I shall now betake myself in earnest to my historical studies, with a view of writing in time some book on our constitutional history." The book eventually expanded into seven volumes that appeared between 1880 and 1913 (five of them by 1891). In that year Schouler became a lecturer in constitutional history at The Johns Hopkins University, a position he held for seventeen years.[62]

Schouler maintained a lucrative law practice, too, specializing in war claims. He also happens to have internalized many of the ambivalent feelings discussed earlier: although a strong Unionist, he admired the states and respected their sovereignty; a staunch constitutionalist, and conservative in many ways, he nonetheless believed that revision of the U.S. Constitution had been "constantly wanting" ever since 1787. His presidential address to the American Historical Association in 1897 called for a new Convention to consider essential amendments, abolition of the electoral college, and direct election of the President. Schouler admired "the spirit of organic change and improvement," but found that spirit far more in evidence at the state level than at the federal.[63]

By 1890, Francis N. Thorpe had begun to teach American constitutional history at the University of Pennsylvania; Herbert Baxter Adams lectured on the subject at Hopkins, at Amherst College, and at Chautauqua. By the turn of the century Max Farrand introduced such a course at Stanford, and J. Franklin Jameson had done so for graduate students at Brown. In 1900 young Andrew C. McLaughlin wrote to Jameson from Ann Arbor that "I have drifted into constitutional history, which is on the very brink of political science and political philosophy. At the same time it is constitutional history, I am sure, nothing more nor less, namely, the proper interpretation of constitutional documents and speeches bearing upon the most significant constitutional questions."[64] Charles H. Hull of Cornell felt less self-assured, and confessed to Farrand (in 1901) that "the General Course is not going so badly as the course in Constitutional History. I had a faint suspicion at the outset that I did not know what Constitutional History was about, and now I am sure I don't know. . . . How the whole thing will come out I don't know, but I fear it will come out badly." By 1917, however, Hull was considerably more sanguine about the course; Farrand as well as Allen Johnson taught comparable ones at Yale, Albert Bushnell Hart did so at Harvard, and Edward S. Corwin at Princeton.[65]

Most of the growing pains that ordinarily accompany professionalization occurred: the organization of special sessions devoted to constitutional history at the annual meeting of the American Historical Association; one university or college raiding the faculty of another in quest of eminent specialists; ideological tensions when the appearance of divergent publications made it clear that interpretations of constitutional history differed significantly in the North and in the South; but, above all, personal jealousy and professional rivalry.[66] Thorpe fought with everyone. Although he controlled his impulse "to expostulate against the inaccuracy" of Schouler's writings, he accused Hart of "libel," pleaded with him to be "fair and honest" as a critic, and begged Hart not to include him in any more bibliographies: "Now, my dear Professor, if you ever make another bibliography, cut it short rather than make a fool of yourself." McLaughlin (1861–1947) and Farrand (1869–1945) feuded through the conduit of their individual correspondence with the gentle Jameson.[67]

Apart from predictable factors, such as egotism and the desire for professional primacy, these feuds also resulted from difficulties involved in doing research, in gaining access to unique documents or rare printed materials. The National Archives did not yet exist; clerks at the State Department library declared any materials they could not locate to be "lost," probably confiscated by the British during the Revolutionary War. Obtaining precise texts of crucial documents was highly problematic; and criteria for "authentic" reprinting and editing simply did not yet exist. In 1911, when workmen moved Supreme Court records from the Capitol to the new Senate Office Building, the working papers for *McCulloch* v. *Maryland* (1819) were "found in a very bad state of decomposition" along with original records for such landmarks as the Dartmouth College case, *Chisholm* v. *Georgia,* and the Dred Scott decision. Previously, according to one newspaper account, "the records were first bound and then carried to a dusty little room near the staircase leading to the dome, placed upon shelves, and allowed to remain there and accumulate dust. Some of the records are almost unintelligible, though those filed in later years are readable, but are yellow with age. . . . These records are of naturally great importance to this nation, and the work of taking care of them is one that should have commenced several years ago."[68]

Despite all of these difficulties, an unprecedented burst of publications in the field of constitutional history began to emerge in 1888. Some, like those of John Fiske, Judson S. Landon, and Sydney George Fisher, required numerous reprintings. Others appeared only once and were swiftly forgotten. Some were scholarly, some were manuals or textbooks.[69] George Ticknor Curtis seems to have been justified in 1889 when he wrote "that in our higher schools of learning there is an awakened interest in American Constitutional history; that the young men of the present day are seeking for information on this subject much more than those who immediately preceded them." In fact, it does not seem to have been a single-sex phenomenon, at least not in Boston. Alice James recorded that her friend Margaret Storer was being courted by a young lawyer named Joseph B. Warner: "they read Constitutional History and meet once a week to discuss it!"[70]

On August 9, 1893, Professor James B. Thayer of the Harvard Law School presented a paper to the Congress on Jurisprudence and Law Reform meeting at the World's Columbian Exposition in Chicago. Entitled

"The Origin and Scope of the American Doctrine of Constitutional Law," promptly published in the *Harvard Law Review* and as a pamphlet by Little, Brown, it enjoyed a broad readership among attorneys, historians, jurists, professors of law and political science, not only in the United States but in western Europe as well. To judge by the spontaneous and enthusiastic letters Thayer received, his paper may have been the counterpart in constitutional theory to the more famous address delivered by Frederick Jackson Turner at the same exposition. Why? Because Thayer sought to explain the genesis of judicial review—that distinctively American contribution to constitutionalism—and found it "mainly as a natural result of our political experience before the War of Independence,—as being colonists, governed under written charters of government proceeding from the English Crown."[71]

Thayer had judiciously managed to locate the roots of American constitutionalism in the colonists' indigenous experience without denying the debt that that experience owed to older, hard-won English traditions. His historical argument pleased both nationalists and anglophiles, many of whom wanted to be able to reconcile the two emphases while giving primacy to what had happened on American soil. He satisfied those who wanted a more inclusive view of American constitutionalism than one simply rooted in the 1787 instrument and its amendments. As Henry Baldwin (self-styled "the Custodian of American History") wrote to a friend at the Smithsonian in 1891: "American history is but little known. The Schools learn something of English History and the English Constitution, but practically, American History and American Constitutional Laws are known by few who have made these studies a specialty."[72]

The impact of Thayer's hybridized thesis lingered on for almost two generations, perpetuated particularly by Andrew C. McLaughlin's career-long insistence that federalism had not sprung from the head of Zeus or the brain of James Madison in 1787. Rather, it too had sources in the experience of colonies and states learning to work together and being forced to think about sovereignty as a divided entity rather than as a singular and unified attribute. McLaughlin defined federalism loosely as "a division of powers between governments"; and liked to suggest, therefore, that prior to 1776 the British Empire possessed many aspects of a federal system. When McLaughlin lectured at the University of London in 1918, he called attention to "the fact of Anglo-Saxon inheritance and traditions."[73]

In order to appreciate the multiplicity—as well as the untidiness—of American notions concerning the origin of their Constitution, it is necessary to note that four theories were prevalent during this period, not just

three: (1) those opposed to Gladstone who insisted upon the seminal nature of what had occurred in the colonies prior to 1776; (2) those critical
of Gladstone (though somewhat less hostile) who acknowledged the
English origins of American constitutional traditions; (3) those like
McLaughlin and Farrand who felt most comfortable with a compound of
the first two; and (4) those who believed, as Nicholas Murray Butler did,
that the U.S. Constitution was truly venerable in its longevity: "Back
through the long centuries it traces its history to the instincts and habits
and purposes of free men in the forests of Germany and on the friendly soil
of the British Isles."[74]

Curiously enough, that view had particular appeal for New
England–bred scholars like Herbert Baxter Adams, John W. Burgess
(who taught American history and institutions at three German universities in 1906–07), and Archibald Cary Coolidge of Harvard who wrote
his Ph.D. dissertation at Freiburg (1892) on "Theoretical and Foreign
Elements in the Constitution of the United States"; but it had less appeal
for the pioneering authority in Europe on the U.S. Constitution, Hermann
Eduard von Holst, with whom Coolidge studied and boarded in Freiburg.[75] Despite his German nationality and political conservatism, von
Holst insisted that "he who writes the constitutional history of the United
States must seek out the course of development of the American democ-
racy," because "the sole source of all power [there] is the people." On particular constitutional issues von Holst tended to follow the views of Justice
Story and Richard Hildreth, the Whig historian.[76]

Although more ironic twists are not really needed, it is noteworthy
that the study of German constitutional history flourished during the later
nineteenth century; and that some writers in eighteenth-century Britain,
especially Scots, called attention to the historical liberties enjoyed by the
German people and claimed that the English constitution had become the
modern embodiment of an ancient Germanic polity.[77]

Because the work of Charles A. Beard has intrigued historians, there
has been a tendency to assume that once Beard published his famous monograph, *An Economic Interpretation of the Constitution,* in 1913, perceptions of the Constitution must have shifted from the grounds we have been
discussing to the socio-economic context of what was done in 1787.
Though Beard's influence was truly significant, the fact remains that his
book was ignored by many laymen and repudiated by numerous scholars.[78]

Max Farrand's far more conventional volume, *The Framing of the
Constitution of the United States,* also appeared in 1913, created much less
controversy than Beard's study, received its twenty-eighth printing in

1976, and continues to be required reading at respectable American colleges and universities. Professor Evarts B. Greene of Columbia, for example, observed that in terms of "the mechanics of constitution making *in the convention,* it is excellent"; and added that "the suggestive but one-sided presentation of these subjects in Mr. Beard's recent book surely leaves room for a more judicial [sic] treatment, and for such work the editor of the convention records [Farrand] has had peculiar advantages." Three years later Robert Livingston Schuyler, yet another of Beard's colleagues at Columbia, argued that class conflict and economic issues had been unimportant at the Convention in 1787. Farrand perpetuated far more successfully than we have realized the point of view so prominent during the generation prior to 1913: namely, that the Constitution resembled the Articles of Confederation in basic ways and that the work of 1787 was not remarkably innovative when examined in historical perspective.[79] Farrand admired the framers very much and believed they had acted in the public interest. Subsequent work by Farrand, such as *The Fathers of the Constitution: A Chronicle of the Establishment of the Union* (1921), continued to minimize economic motives as an explanatory factor in 1787–88.

For several decades following 1887, then, much of the discussion of American constitutionalism took place in the dual context of Anglo-American comparisons and, more particularly, the historical nature of the colonial experience with charters followed by the need to write state constitutions starting in 1776. Those emphases were partially incorporated into textbooks on history written for secondary school students and civics manuals directed at adults preparing for naturalization and U.S. citizenship. Such works were especially important and widely used because of a marked increase after 1862 in the number of states that legally required some sort of instruction concerning the Constitution—a requirement that spread rapidly after 1900.[80]

The fundamental problem remaining unresolved, however, even so late as the turn of the century, involved the very nature of the Union created in 1787 and subsequently defined by political experience. A glance at two of the most widely used texts reveals a startling degree of historical uncertainty; the fragility of sectional reconciliation; the commercial imperatives of textbook publishing; and, above all, a candid concession that confusion existed about the most basic issue. "The system of the United States," Alexander Johnston noted in 1888 for the *Encyclopaedia Britannica,* "is almost the only national system, in active and successful operation, as to which the exact location of the sovereignty is still a mooted question." Writing as though he wished readers to share his perplexity, Johnston juxtaposed what he believed the historical facts had been with the powerful reality of psychological perception. "Events have shown that it was the people of the whole United States that established the Constitution, but the people of 1787 seem to have inclined to the belief that it was the people of each State for itself. This belief was never changed in the South." Johnston observed that the Civil War might have resolved the right-of-secession question, but "did not decide the location of the sovereignty." Making a conscious effort to achieve balance, to be acceptable in the North as well as the South, in Great Britain as well as the United States, he ruminated:

> The prevalent opinion is still that first formulated by Madison: that the States were sovereign before 1789; that they then gave up a part of their sovereignty to the Federal Government; that the Union and the Constitution were the work of the States, not of the whole people; and that reserved powers are reserved to the people of the States, not to the whole people. The use of this bald phrase "reserved to the people," not to the people of the several States, in the 10th amendment, seems to argue an underlying consciousness, even in 1789, that the whole people of the United States was already a political power quite distinct from the States, or the people of the States; and the tendency of later opinion is in this direction. It must be admitted that the whole people has never acted in a single capacity; but the restriction to State lines seems to be a self-imposed limitation by the national people, which it might remove, as in 1789, if an emergency should make it necessary.[81]

Andrew C. McLaughlin's high school textbook, widely used for more than twenty-five years after it first appeared in 1899, seems to have been less judicious because the author was more nationalistic. In a chapter entitled "The Confederation and the Constitution, 1781–1789," he devoted a paragraph to the instrument's "essential character."

> The new Government was not to be the agent of the States and dependent on State generosity for funds, or on State humor for obedience. It was to spring from the people and to have power over the people. The preamble of the Constitution states that "we, the people, . . . do ordain and establish this Constitution." The laws of the Government were to be direct commands to persons. . . . All power was

not bestowed on the National Government, but only certain enumerated powers; the rest belonged to the States or to the people, unless the Constitution forbade their use by any governmental authority. There were thus created *immediately* over every citizen two governments, occupying each a different sphere of political action, and each having power to order and compel obedience. The distinguishing feature of this new republic was this *distribution* of political authority between the Central Government on the one hand and the commonwealths that composed the Union on the other.

Nothing wishy-washy about "Andy Mac," right? Perhaps. But he reserved a set of options for a strategic spot, the teacher's manual. There, in the "guide" to this same chapter, we find a wonderfully expedient gambit.

We all now hold that the United States is now an indissoluble Union, and that the States are not altogether sovereign and do not have the right of secession. There are three different opinions among writers as to whether, as an historical fact, the Constitution, when adopted, established one indissoluble republic: (1) That it did so establish one republic, indissoluble and composed of indestructible States. (2) That the States retained their sovereignty, the Constitution was a compact, and the national interpretation was established by civil war, 1861–1865. (3) That the matter was left in doubt and the national interpretation was established by civil war.[82]

End of guidelines to chapter ten. We all agree that the Union cannot be dissolved. We just don't agree about the reasons why, so you can take your pick.

Thus three related tendencies may be discerned in American constitutionalism at the turn of the century. First, its historical and legal underpinnings remained precarious, a fact which only bothered a fastidious few who knew and cared about such matters.[83]

Second, the quality of books and other educational materials pertaining to the U.S. Constitution generally ranged from poor to mediocre. Strangely enough in view of the ardent nationalism that characterized this period, the emphasis in civics teaching shifted during the 1890s to state and local government. "Civil government" and "problems of democracy" became contemporary clichés, and the presumption gained currency that a child's immediate locale was more meaningful and comprehensible than the nation as a whole. As Albert Bushnell Hart wrote in 1903: "the text of constitutions and of statutes is only the enveloping husk; the real kernel is that personal interest and personal action which vitalizes government."[84]

Third, a curious phenomenon of long standing continued: the incapacity of certain well-qualified individuals to write a history of the U.S. Constitution. Edward Everett had intended to do so during the 1830s, and sent James Madison an inquiry concerning the use of his papers; but the best that Everett could produce was an oration, originally a response to a toast, that ran 113 pages in print. In 1847 Salmon P. Chase started a comprehensive work on slavery and the Constitution; that, too, was never completed. Late in the 1880s, when young Lincoln Steffens took a course in constitutional history at the University of California, he discovered to his dismay that the founders had not wanted a democratic government. As a consequence, he later explained, "I promised myself to write a true history of the making of the American Constitution."[85]

Steffens never did; but if he had, it would have been more critical than Chase's and far less fulsome than Everett's. The concern Steffens felt that an ugly chasm gaped between ideal and reality in American constitutionalism served as an accurate harbinger of new social and political tensions that would surface between the 1890s and World War I.

CHAPTER 7

The Crisis in Constitutionalism

IT HAS BEEN THE CONVENTIONAL WISDOM for more than a generation that "the 19th century did achieve a comparatively well-accepted consensus about the Constitution and the Supreme Court"—what Robert G. McCloskey called a "kind of synthesis in American constitutionalism" that only began to fall apart in the twentieth century. I am skeptical of this generalization for three reasons: first, as we have seen, the controversies of 1814–15, 1829–33, 1857–65, 1870–73 (the Legal Tender cases), and 1882–83 (the Civil Rights cases) undermine any meaningful notion of a nineteenth-century consensus; second, the sharp constitutional issues that piqued tempers in 1895 nearly shattered the durable pattern of conflict within consensus; and third, all or even most Americans at any given time simply did not hold similar feelings about the Constitution and the Supreme Court.[1]

An argument can be made for conflict within consensus so far as the Constitution alone is concerned; but it would be very difficult to make a comparable case for the Court. If a synthesis ever existed, moreover, it did not remain the same synthesis in 1789, 1840, 1870, and 1900. It shifted. Between 1895 and 1920 a cluster of major changes took place—so major that alarmed observers believed a "crisis in constitutionalism" was occurring.

I

Even as the Centennial moved toward its culmination in 1888–89, prominent politicians as well as scholars continued to grope for an acceptable definition of the very nature of the U.S. Constitution. Perhaps the most to be said for "consensus" is that people of diverse persuasions shared a commitment that might be described as elitist, resistant to change, and exceedingly anxious about unusual concentrations of governmental authority in any single branch or level of the constitutional system. Here are two sentences from Grover Cleveland's fourth annual message to Congress: "The preservation of the partitions between proper subjects of Federal and local care and regulation is of such importance under the Constitution, which is the law of our very existence, that no consideration of expediency or sentiment should tempt us to enter upon doubtful ground. We have undertaken to discover and proclaim the richest blessings of a free government, with the Constitution as our guide." And then a statement from A. Lawrence Lowell's widely read essay on "Democracy and the Constitution": "The utmost that a constitution can be expected to do is to protect directly a small number of vested rights, and to discourage and check indirectly the growth of a demand for radical measures."[2]

So much for reductive foundations of consensus. The grounds for conflict within that framework remained numerous, as we have seen. The persistence of states' rights sentiment and a desire for delicately balanced federalism were articulated in contrapuntal relation to a growing partiality for national power. One of James Bryce's admiring reviewers in 1889, for example, felt that the Scottish outsider may have presumed the existence of too exquisite an equilibrium. "The constitution presupposes the State governments," this reviewer noted, "but with equal force the State governments presuppose some authority in which they find their completion." In 1893, on the other hand, Woodrow Wilson insisted upon "those arrangements of our Constitution which are really our own, and to which our national pride properly attaches, namely, the distinct division of powers between the state and federal governments [and] the slow and solemn formalities of constitutional change. . . ."[3]

In 1895 one exhaustive constitutional *Commentary* scorned the historical precedents of states' rights; yet four years later an equally learned two-volume exegesis proclaimed the blessings of such rights.[4] Various sorts of contentions (many weak and unpersuasive) surfaced during the decade that followed, a fair number of them provoked by President Roosevelt's nationalism. The breadth of opinion is striking. Here is the strongest case for "national tendencies":

> It is not too much to assume that, in the present temper of our people, they are prepared, in all truthfulness, and within the constitutional limitations which they have themselves prescribed, and which they may enlarge at their pleasure from time to time, to surrender to the Nation, as far as practicable, substantially all such "powers" as have been deemed to be reserved to the States and the "people" by the Tenth Amendment to the Constitution, so far, at least, as such surrender may be necessary to carry us forward to a perfect and effective union as one Nation. . . . In short, the States are, in these days, treated by the people only as so many uninteresting and cumbersome, but necessary local governmental agencies for home rule and the administration of purely local affairs.[5]

A good example of the balanced approach (the least common, actually) comes from a speech made by Justice John Marshall Harlan at a dinner in his honor arranged by the Kentuckians of New York City: "Let us not give our approval to any interpretation of the Constitution that will either cripple the Nation's authority or prostrate the Nation at the feet of the States, or that will deprive the States of their just powers. Let us hold fast to the broad and liberal, and yet safe, rule of constitutional construction approved by the fathers and established by judicial decisions. In so doing we will sustain our dual system. . . ."[6]

For one of the more temperate assertions of the view that nationalizing tendencies had gone too far, listen to Henry Wade Rogers, dean of the Yale Law School (1908): "Once the question was whether the States would destroy the National Government. Now the question seems to be whether the National Government shall be permitted to destroy the States. . . . There is an increasing tendency to regard a State as a mere geographical expression, rather than as a political division of the country. . . . There is a constitutional and wholesome doctrine of State rights the maintenance of which is of the utmost importance to the continued welfare of the Republic."[7] During the twenty years that followed, increasingly strident versions of the states' rights position would be offered: by Progressives like Senator William E. Borah of Idaho; by conservative John W. Davis, Democratic nominee for President in 1924; and by many others. Their cause, which reached a vocal crescendo in the mid-1920s, is one of the most neglected chapters in the history of American political culture.[8]

States' rights received far more attention than civil rights in general or the Bill of Rights in particular. Only on occasion did discussions of such matters as unconstitutional imprisonment (without a presentment or indictment by a grand jury) or stricter separation of church and state (because numerous legislatures had passed appropriations for sectarian purposes) occur. An organization called the National League for the Protection of American Institutions promoted a new amendment designed to clarify ambiguities pertaining to religion in the First Amendment; but it met with little success.[9]

A more volatile issue that engaged public opinion intermittently for several decades following 1889 concerned how easy or difficult it ought to be to amend the U.S. Constitution. The question arose because so many amendments were proposed during the later nineteenth century: for example, a six-year nonrenewable term for the President; abolition of legal-tender notes; citizens being permitted to bring suit against states; even amendments pertaining to marriage and divorce, or government control of transportation, telegraph, and telephone systems. A majority of American citizens believed that the Constitution should not be amended too casually; but a vocal minority insisted that the founders had been "aware that experience and development would require changes."[10]

That issue was not new, and it persists; but it became particularly controversial during the decade 1906–16 for a peculiar mix of reasons: a deep feeling of frustration among Progressive reformers about the slow pace of change; racist resentment of the Fifteenth Amendment (enfranchising Negroes), which in turn aroused strong reactions from more enlightened folk; and the belief held by many that it seemed appropriate to the nature of our system for constitutional change to proceed more cautiously at the national level, a favorite argument of states' rights advocates. "The people of the United States cannot possibly act with the same promptness and directness as are possible to the people of a single State. . . . The ease with which a State Constitution may be amended and the difficulty which has been found to exist in amending the Constitution of the United States afford instructive illustration. . . . The smaller the unit of government, the more prompt, direct and intelligent its action is likely to be."[11]

It is improbable that agreement will ever be achieved on this matter. Back in 1851, its first year of publication, *The New York Times* had argued that the Constitution ought to be a flexible document; therefore "we" should amend it whenever it seemed necessary. The counterargument, especially popular among turn-of-the-century observers, asserted that barriers to amendment kept our Constitution distinctive, truly a higher law, unlike the British situation where ordinary statutes became part of (and thereby altered) the constitution. When George Bernard Shaw made his celebrated visit in 1933, he quipped that Americans were always amending their Constitution (actually a half-truth: many tried but very few succeeded), "which looks as if it were not such a fine and infallible thing as you seem to suppose."[12]

Analogies between the U.S. Constitution and a piece of machinery had appeared ever since 1787, but became more common after the middle of the nineteenth century, perhaps in part because technology began to pervade the public consciousness. The amending process, in turn, was referred to as a "mechanism," as were the Supreme Court's procedures.[13] During the late nineteenth century, precisely because machines were made and operated by human beings, those who favored slow and evolutionary change tended to abandon the mechanistic metaphor in favor of the organismic one. An organism has an adaptive life of its own, responds gradually to altered conditions in order to survive, and is best left alone. One other consideration reinforced this shift, however: the concern voiced by some critics who wondered whether the American people had begun to take their Constitution and good government for granted. It is worth recalling the observation made by James Russell Lowell in 1888:

> After our Constitution got fairly into working order it really seemed as if we had invented a machine that would go of itself, and this begot a faith in our luck which even the civil war itself but momentarily disturbed. . . . I admire the splendid complacency of my countrymen, and find something exhilarating and inspiring in it. We are a nation which has *struck ile,* but we are also a nation that is sure the well will never run dry. And this confidence in our luck with the absorption in material interests, generated by unparalleled opportunity, has in some respects made us neglectful of our political duties.[14]

II

However apathetic the American people may have been about the need for public involvement in order to keep their Constitution fully functional, the Supreme Court did not act as though the founders "had invented a machine that would go of itself." By 1890 the justices began moving into one of the most activist phases in the Court's history. As John E. Semonche and other scholars have shown, the so-called age of laissez-faire was, in truth, a pivotal period of "substantial activism." What did that mean in applied terms? It meant employing the power of judicial review to an extent unprecedented in American constitutional history: in order to reverse federal legislation; to reverse state legislation; and even to regulate railroads, the nation's most important utility.[15]

One stereotype of the Court in the 1890s that properly remains unchanged, however, is that it was a conservative body more concerned about protecting property rights than human rights. A cluster of narrowly decided verdicts in 1895—which included declaring the income tax unconstitutional and declining to find the notorious Sugar Trust unconstitutional—elicited the greatest outpouring of popular criticism and ridicule since the Dred Scott ruling in 1857. Sylvester Pennoyer, a lawyer, lumberman, and populist who served as Democratic governor of Oregon from 1886 until 1894, expressed the views of many concerned Americans: "The Supreme Court . . . has usurped the legislative prerogative of declaring what the laws shall not be. Our government has been supplanted by a judicial oligarchy. The time has now arrived when the government should be restored to its constitutional basis. . . . Congress has been thwarted in the exercise of its express constitutional power to lay and collect taxes. In plain parlance, this is nullification, pure and simple, and the grave question confronts the people of the United States, Are we now living under our constitutional government?"[16]

On the light-hearted side, one producer of patent medicine took a newspaper ad (strategically placed adjacent to coverage of the Supreme Court's decision) that began:

THE INCOME TAX
Didn't yield half so easily as the most
stubborn COUGH or COLD will if
tackled at once with
RIKER'S EXPECTORANT

More seriously, an editorial acknowledged that "the Constitution was made for a period when there were no railroads, no giant monopolies, no billionaires, no nineteenth century civilization." Although that concession was not exactly unprecedented, the dominant assumption for more than a century had been that the founders anticipated, at least implicitly, most contingencies. Even more ominous, many contemporaries felt that "the two sides divided upon two irreconcilable views of the Constitution." So much for consensus and the so-called nineteenth-century synthesis. The opposing attorneys who argued the income tax cases (*Pollock* v. *Farmer's Loan and Trust Co.*) before the Supreme Court both felt apprehensive about "the destruction of the Constitution itself."[17]

The Court's divisive rulings in 1895 had remarkable consequences for both political and popular culture. In the latter category, fiction that ridiculed the Supreme Court began to appear alongside utopian novels about a society in which the popular will could not be overruled by any judicial body. These themes comprised a new subgenre in American literature. Then, in 1896, both the Democrats and the Populists campaigned against the Supreme Court's rulings. When the Democratic Convention met at Chicago in July, an astonished press (as well as equally astonished delegates) noted the introduction of a plank calling upon Congress to reconstruct the Supreme Court. Republican newspapers, such as the Leavenworth, Kansas, *Times,* saw in the Chicago platform "the old spirit of secession and rebellion against the Constitution." In September *Harper's Weekly* ran a front-page cartoon with the caption: "A Forecast of the Consequence of a Popocratic Victory to the Supreme Court of the United States." Seven potential justices were shown, including Sylvester Pennoyer, Coxey's Army, "King" (Eugene V.) Debs, "Pitchfork Ben" Tillman, a diabolical depiction of Illinois Governor John Peter Altgeld, and "Gold Clause Mortgage" Stewart. Above and behind the evil justices, cartoonist W. A. Rogers placed the smoking skull and daggers symbolic of Anarchy; a large, devalued "50 cent Bunco Dollar"; and in the foreground, below the bench-rail, a torn and falling Constitution.[18] If radicalism prevailed, the Constitution would surely be discarded and a reign of anarchy begin.

Early in 1897 Andrew Dickson White, former president of Cornell and then a prominent diplomat and public figure, delivered an address in Wisconsin that was published as a pamphlet. He lavished praise upon the Supreme Court, the "greatest jewel" of the nation: "it seems to have been created by our fathers in a moment of Divine inspiration. When that court shall be gone or discredited, this republic will be really ended."[19] It is essential to bear in mind, despite sharp criticisms that emerged after 1895, that the Court would continue to have many staunch apologists and true believers like White.

Be that as it may, the two decades that followed 1895 were unusual, not only because the Court ceased to be sacred—that had been the situation on several prior occasions—but because criticism occurred relentlessly, came from various sectors of American society, and led eventually to questions, challenges, and ultimately accusations being made against the U.S. Constitution and its authors.[20] Only in the wake of Dred Scott had politicization of the Court been more severe, and polarization over constitutional issues more sharp. An editorial in *Collier's* summed up the situation in 1906: "The Constitution is treated with more flippancy than it ever was before the war. . . . Now the radical members of both parties are beginning to say that the Constitution was made for man, not man for the Constitution, and to chafe under its restraints. . . . What the founders of this country feared, riotous experiment, has proved the least of our temptations. Any talk therefore, about getting away from the safeguards of the Constitution, from its checks and balances, is lightly taken."[21]

Two different sorts of issues intensified these tendencies during the early years of the twentieth century. First, following Senate ratification of the peace treaty with Spain in 1899, the constitutional status of new American possessions overseas (the Philippine Islands, Guam, Hawaii, and Puerto Rico) came to be fiercely contested. In a series of cases that lingered on for almost a decade, the bitterly divided Court refused to extend the Bill of Rights in its entirety to these unincorporated territories. To judge by a wide sampling of newspaper editorials, public opinion was equally divided, as were jurists and constitutional scholars. Cartoons, rather more solemn than amusing, appeared with such captions as "The Constitution and the Flag." In 1901 Peter Finley Dunne's droll Mr. Dooley quipped that "no matter whether the Constitution follows th' flag or not, th' Supreme Coort follows th' iliction returns."[22]

Union veterans who had fought to keep slavery out of the territories believed the principle had been settled by the Civil War: the Constitution did *not* follow the flag. Those who regarded the new acquisitions as possessions, and their inhabitants as "un-American," agreed. Critics said of judges who thought otherwise that their view "reveals again the death's head at the Republican banquet." Writing in 1901, however, George S. Boutwell (a lawyer, active anti-imperialist, and former senator from Massachusetts) offered quite another perspective.

> Seven of the Justices of the Supreme Court were of opinion that the Constitution became applicable to the territory whenever such Territory was duly organized, and four of the seven expressed the opinion that the Constitution applied to the possessions whenever acquired agreeably to the law of nations. . . . In this condition of opinion, it

must happen that seven justices, and perhaps eight justices, will unite in the conclusion that the Territories of the United States, as they may from time to time be created by act of Congress and duly organized, are brought within the scope of the Constitution. . . . It follows, therefore, that, very soon, every dependency which has come into the possession of the United States through the treaty with Spain, will be organized in a Territorial government, and therefore, that, within the same period of time, the Constitution of the United States will be made applicable to each of them. . . . The practical conclusion must be that which has been demanded by the Anti-imperialists of the Country, namely: that the entire possessions of the United States that have been acquired in conformity to the law of nations will be under the jurisdiction of the Constitution. . . . Thus the demand of the Anti-imperialists will have been satisfied, though only through a process of delay.

Boutwell and others were deeply troubled by the range of differences among members of the Court—even though that range simply reflected divergence within American society as a whole. Still other critics expressed contempt for those justices, most notably Henry Billings Brown, who took what appeared to be inconsistent positions on the insular cases. The *Chicago Chronicle* called Brown a "judicial flopper," and concluded that "a judge who holds that the Constitution follows the flag in one case and in another case lays down the proposition that only a part of the Constitution follows the flag is likely in a third case to declare that no part of the Constitution follows the flag."[23]

The other controversial issue involved the right of a legislative body (state or federal) to regulate the hours of workers—men, women, and children—in order to protect individuals against exploitative employers in particular and to enhance the welfare of society in general. In 1904 the Democratic Party even included this anti-Progressive, laissez-faire plank in its campaign platform: "Constitutional guarantees are violated whenever any citizen is denied the right to labor, acquire and enjoy property. . . ." In *Lochner* v. *New York* (1905) the Supreme Court ruled that the New York State Legislature could not restrict the hours of labor in a bakery to a maximum of sixty hours per week or ten hours per day. That decision aroused more popular protest than any since 1895, and elicited Oliver Wendell Holmes's famous dissent: "The Fourteenth Amendment [protecting persons against infringements of their liberty without due process] does not enact Mr. Herbert Spencer's Social Statics. . . . A constitution is not intended to embody a particular economic theory. . . . It is made for people of fundamentally differing views, and the accident of finding certain opinions natural and familiar, or novel, and even shocking, ought not to conclude our judgement upon the question whether statutes embodying them conflict with the Constitution of the United States."[24]

Three years later, however, the Court upheld Oregon's right to restrict the number of hours that women might work. Writing for the Court, Justice David J. Brewer explained that a woman differed from a man both physiologically and owing to "the performance of maternal functions" that obviously "placed her at a disadvantage in the struggle for subsistence." Herbert Spencer's *Social Statics* had apparently not been erased entirely. Recognizing that some people might view *Muller* v. *Oregon* as a reversal of *Lochner* v. *New York,* Brewer ended by saying explicitly that it was not a reversal. Women and society required legislative protection; men did not. What about children? Congress passed a Child Labor Act in 1916, justifying it on the basis of the commerce power, a power that the Court had customarily used to sustain federal authority concerning matters of social welfare. In *Hammer* v. *Dagenhart, et al.* (1918), the Court said no (by a five to four vote) and the majority invoked states' rights. "The grant of authority over a purely federal matter [the regulation of interstate commerce] was not intended to destroy the local power always existing and carefully reserved to the States in the Tenth Amendment. . . ." Justice Holmes again dissented. Angry critics of the Court howled once again, and began to promote a constitutional amendment to regulate child labor. Although the Court had spoken, its voice sounded neither unanimous nor clear.[25]

That had been apparent ever since the late 1890s; and one consequence was a gradual increase in public interest, even curiosity, about members of the Court. In a speech given on May 3, 1907, to the Elmira, New York, Chamber of Commerce, then Governor Charles Evans Hughes observed that "we are under a Constitution, but the Constitution is what the judges say it is," a remark that immediately became, and remains, frequently quoted.[26] The good news is that the public now wanted to know who, in particular, the justices were; and the media gradually began to oblige them.[27]

The bad news is that the public mostly wanted trivia, and that is just what it got: human interest stories usually entitled something like "An Intimate View of the Supreme Court." In one the author explained that justices "are not unlike other men when once they have thrown aside their robes and have said good-by for the day to the great judges' chairs." When Chief Justice Melville W. Fuller (who died on July 4, 1910) worked in his immense library in his handsome mansion, his constant companion was Laura, a large green parrot who sat in a big cage in an alcove, speaking occasionally in Spanish. Another article appeared under this headline: "Sidelights on the Members of the Supreme Bench Show Them Delightfully Human, Yet None Dare Show Humor in Grim Presence of Body in Session."[28]

Sad to say, the most frequent and popular essays dealt in one way or another with the justices' dignity:

- Whether or not they ought to wear whiskers: Justice Stephen J. Field (on the bench 1863–97) had the first full beard ever to appear on the Court. According to one newspaper, "it made a great sensation and caused much criticism." When David J. Brewer came to the Court from Kansas in 1890, he sported "an untrimmed mustache and chin whiskers in the true far Western style." By 1891 he was clean shaven, like Justices Miller, Harlan, and Bradley, who disapproved of beards. On the eve of the great Columbian Exposition held at Chicago in 1893, national sentiment wanted Melville W. Fuller without facial hair, but Chicagoans felt it would be entirely appropriate for the Chief Justice to be "decorated with mustachios that look like the widespread wings of the bird of freedom. Once shaved, the Chief Justice would cease to be of much account as a spectacular attraction."[29]

- In 1886 the Supreme Court prohibited cameras because someone had taken a snapshot of Horace Gray dozing on the bench. "Unfortunately for Mr. Justice Gray," ran one account, "he is more given to 'nodding on the bench' than any of his associates, and when he takes a nap his head falls low upon his breast, his mouth hangs open, and he could not truthfully be called a 'sleeping beauty.' It was during one of his naps that the kodak fiend got in his work." Someone even immortalized Gray's snoozes in a poem.

> *There was an old Justice named Gray*
> *Who slept & who snored every day—*
> *His lunch he would eat*
> *Then nap on his seat*
> *And wake up with: "what did you say?"*[30]

- Did the justices truly have a private bar, "so hidden away from the public that very little is known of it"? According to one journal: "It has a genial open grate, over which hangs an old-fashioned, black iron teakettle, with a nozzle huge, black and thick. This is the kettle which has been used for heating the water employed in mixing hot punches since the days of John Marshall. There is a smart yellow man in attendance in this room who has a fine cabinet of assorted liquors, and who is an expert in making all kinds of fancy drinks." The account was accompanied by a drawing of the nine justices, arranged in two clusters, imbibing generously. Late in the 1890s the *Police Gazette* published a scandalous cartoon of the Supreme Court gathered in its sanctum sanctorum, the conference room, at a stag soirée—table littered with bottles, pipes, and cigars; dense pall of tobacco smoke above it; Justice Brewer, champagne glass in hand, giving a maudlin toast; and Justice Harlan sprawled on a divan.[31]

- Brewer received criticism from his colleagues because he readily accepted invitations to speak before lay audiences about issues of current interest. A fine orator and a moderate conservative, he regarded fair criticism of the judiciary as wholesome. When he visited Vassar in 1905, he supported women's rights. The Court has long had a tradition, particularly strong during this period, that its members might compromise themselves and the Court by speaking out on issues that could very well come before the Court for litigation. Besides, it seemed frightfully undignified.[32]

- In 1913 the Court's official "crier," Frank Green, suffered a lapse in concentration when he went to make the traditional opening admonition that people "draw nigh and give their attention for the Court is now sitting. God save the United States and this honorable court." Things went smoothly until Green reached "nigh." Then his tongue got twisted and he invited all persons to draw nigh and "attend to business." Becoming fuddled, he added: "God save, God save the Supreme Court. God save the United States. No, God save the United States and this honorable court." Chief Justice Edward D. White laughed audibly. Mr. Green turned scarlet. Associate Justice Pitney, a golfer, quipped that Green had simply "foozled his drives."[33]

From time to time newspapers noted the Court's physical obscurity and the justices' disinterest in public relations (in the sense of augmenting society's understanding of constitutionalism). A Washington paper complained in 1910 that when the Court assembled at noon each Monday, "routine announcements are made by the chief justice in a voice no one can understand. Decisions of great moment are rendered by other justices in mumbled words which are not heard." Washington journalists also pointed out that the Court was easily overlooked, its chamber difficult to find, and its proceedings uninteresting to visitors: "The stranger passing from the tumult of the House to the careless ease and quiet of the Senate, through the central corridor of the building, will encounter a guard sitting by a plain and unobtrusive door in the north end of the old freestone structure. . . . Around this door there is no waiting crowd of politicians or sight-seers. . . . There are few seats for spectators, but the number is sufficient. The proceedings are not interesting to those who have no business to transact with the court, and strangers who look in soon go out in search of more attractive scenes."[34]

The most disappointing aspect of this press coverage is that it emphasized almost everything but the Court's relationship to and impact upon the Constitution. Cases chosen for in-depth discussion seem to have been selected because of human interest or bizarre aspects rather than constitutional significance. In 1895, for instance, a case that arose from a customs inspector's decision at the Port of New York received media attention because the proper decision depended upon whether or not an imported item should be classified as a sauce, and taxed accordingly. The justice assigned to write the opinion explained the case to his wife and indicated the basis for his intended opinion. She informed him that the item in question could not possibly be a sauce, that the justices did not know what they were talking about, and, according to the press, she "openly ridiculed the Court." The justice then pleaded with his Brethren to consult their own wives, all of whom reported: not a sauce. The justices had been reversed by their spouses.[35]

Sometimes the Constitution got mentioned by way of obituary notices. On January 27, 1893, after Justice Lucius Quintus Cincinnatus Lamar was buried on a hillcrest near the "turbid" Ocmulgee River in Macon, Georgia, the local newspaper added a poignant touch. "Justice Lamar had for many years carried in his inside vest pocket a small copy of the constitution of the United States. Next to the Bible, it was the book he loved the best, and he referred to it often. In life he was never without it, and yesterday the little book was buried with him. It lies close to the heart that loved its teachings and upheld its rights at all times."[36]

One other aspect of the Court's existence seems to have attracted a modicum of public interest during these years: its workload and the sluggish pace at which it handled cases. In 1885 the American *Puck* published a two-page drawing with the caption "Our Overworked Supreme Court" (see figure 27). Nine harried justices are shown; a delivery man pours in additional cases being appealed from lower courts; and signs on the wall read: "cases unadjudicated 1880–1882" and "1883– ." A prominent editorial that accompanied the cartoon turned out not to be prophetic in the short term,[37] yet more so in the long run. The issue seems rather quaint, however, in contrast to both the rationale for FDR's "Court-packing" plan in 1937 and Warren Burger's controversial scheme to create an auxiliary Supreme Court that would serve as a sorting device and reduce the High Court's workload. According to *Puck*: "The mills of the Supreme Court may grind exceedingly fine; but they grind too slowly for this mortal world. . . . In the course of another century things will have got to such a pass that when the Supreme Court makes an award, it will be paid to the grandson of the man who brought the suit. There is no room for doubt that Congress should lose no time in adding to the number of judges. The size of the bench has not increased in proportion to the growth of the country's business."[38]

III

Human interest and sentimentalism undeniably enliven Supreme Court history. In December 1862, for example, twenty-nine-year-old John Marshall Harlan, a colonel in the 10th Kentucky Infantry (Federal), commanded a cannon situated on a bluff half a mile from the banks of the Cumberland River. He trained it upon a wagon crossing the Cumberland. In the water, on horseback just behind the wagon, rode eighteen-year-old Horace H. Lurton, a private in the 3rd Kentucky Cavalry (Confederate). Harlan tried to hit Lurton with the cannon, but did not succeed. Late in 1909 President Taft nominated Lurton to the Court; and when the Senate confirmed him, Harlan and Lurton became colleagues on the bench.[39]

Less coincidental yet more important is the protest that organized labor lodged against Lurton's nomination. Samuel Gompers and the American Federation of Labor insisted that Lurton favored corporations and regarded the Employers' Liability Act as unconstitutional. Moreover, he happened to be one of Taft's closest personal friends. The significance of these facts lies in their illustrative quality. By no means all, but many appointments to the Supreme Court have been highly political in nature.[40]

Similarly, not all but many of the policy decisions made by the Court have also been political in nature. To make such an assertion might seem roughly comparable to "discovering" that the earth is round. We all knew that, didn't we? Well, apparently not.

In 1957 Robert A. Dahl, a distinguished political scientist at Yale, published a stimulating essay (using quantitative analysis) asserting that the Supreme Court has been a political as well as a juridical institution, that is, an agency "for arriving at decisions on controversial questions of national policy." Dahl added an observation that helps to explain the essay's impact, and certainly makes it congruent with the central theme of this book. "As a political institution, the Court is highly unusual, not least because Americans are not quite willing to accept the fact that it *is* a political institution and not quite capable of denying it; so that frequently we take both positions at once." Dahl then developed a series of insights that are noteworthy in the context of this chapter. "Since much of the legitimacy of the Court's decisions rests upon the fiction that it is not a political institution but exclusively a legal one, to accept the Court as a political institution would solve one set of problems at the price of creating another. . . . Except for short-lived transitional periods when the old alliance is disintegrating and the new one is struggling to take control of political institutions, the Supreme Court is inevitably a part of the dominant national alliance."[41]

Dahl's thesis did serve as a valuable corrective to the illusion that began with Chief Justice John Marshall (quoted in note 26 above), and was perpetuated by the likes of A. Lawrence Lowell ("the interpretation of the Constitution has been taken out of politics, as far as possible").[42] On the other hand, the orthodoxies of Marshall and pieties of his nineteenth-century followers had been heavily eroded by political scientists, constitutional historians, and Supreme Court justices during the two decades prior to 1957.[43] In the period under consideration, morever, public as well as private statements suggest a significant shift away from the Marshall-Lowell outlook to one pretty much in line with Dahl's. All that is lacking among early twentieth-century analysts is agreement as to whether or not politicization of the Court was good, bad, or merely inevitable. In 1902, when Theodore Roosevelt was considering Oliver Wendell Holmes, Jr., for appointment to the Supreme Court, he asked their mutual friend, Henry Cabot Lodge, for an evaluation of Holmes. In doing so, TR ruminated along surprising lines. "In the ordinary and low sense which we attach to the words 'partisan' and 'politician,' a judge of the Supreme Court should be neither. But in the higher sense, in the proper sense, he is not in my judgment fitted for the position unless he is a party man, a constructive statesman, constantly keeping in mind his adherence to the principles and policies under which this nation has been built up and in accordance with which it must go on."[44] That perspective is quite compatible with Dahl's thesis.

Brooks Adams, writing in 1913, also anticipated Dahl; but unlike TR, Adams heartily disapproved. He regarded the administration of justice in the United States as inadequate, and blamed that failure on "the operation of the written Constitution." Under the American system, he went on, "the Constitution, or fundamental law, is expounded by judges, and this function, which, in essence, is political, has brought precisely that quality of pressure on the bench which it has been the labor of a hundred generations of our ancestors to remove. On the whole the result has been not to elevate politics, but to lower the courts toward the political level. . . ."[45]

I find echoes of Adams's position in Max Lerner's influential essays of the 1930s on constitutionalism in American political culture; reverberations in the thought of that brilliant lawyer, judge, and writer, Jerome N. Frank; and the perpetuation of TR's view in a rather unlikely person, Hugo L. Black. When Eric Sevareid and Martin Agronsky interviewed Justice Black in 1968 for a one-hour special program on CBS TV, the following dialogue took place.

SEVAREID: Justice Black, the President, of course, appoints the members of the Supreme Court, and they tend to appoint men who share their general philosophy of public affairs. A President in power a long time may appoint several Justices. Does this in any way infringe on the whole principle of separation of powers?

BLACK: I do not think so. I think that it's perfectly natural that a President would first look to the people he knew best. And he happens to know the people best in his party. Presidents have always appointed people who believed a great deal in the same things that the President who appoints them believes in.[46]

Over the *longue durée* of American politics (admittedly not so very *longue*), Dahl seems to be absolutely right in saying that most Americans "are not quite willing to accept the fact that it *is* a political institution." Two Americans who ought to know better, however, have recently addressed this issue and declared that the Court is remarkably unaffected by political influence (Justice William H. Rehnquist) and that political or ideological issues can and ought to be kept out of the Court (Judge Irving R. Kaufman).[47]

Returning to the period under consideration, we find a situation in 1911–12 when the Court became heavily politicized and, as a consequence, caused many to feel that their constitutional system had gone seriously awry. Although divergent issues fed the crisis of 1911–12, they did share a common denominator: a feeling that the judiciary had grown too powerful. The symptomatic keyword became "usurpation"; and the most egregious flaw seemed to be unbridled judicial review. A marked expansion of federal power, in general, was apparent by the 1880s. During the nineties, as we have seen, when the Court grew both activist and more conservative, its critics felt that the process of judicial review had somehow given way to an uncontrolled situation of judicial supremacy. In 1898 J. R. MacDonald, a Fabian member of the Independent Labor Party, published an essay in an American magazine, *The Independent*. "If I were to select any one feature of difference between American and British democracy," he wrote, "for the purpose of showing that, in the realities of democratic power, we are richer than the American citizen, I could not do better than to refer to the function of the American judiciary under the Constitution." Whereas Parliament enjoyed dominance in Great Britain, the Supreme Court had become overbearing in relation to policies developed by elected representatives. "A method of government which in ten years declares that 114 labor bills alone are unconstitutional suggests not merely that there is something wrong with the machinery of the American government, but casts doubt upon the claims of America to be democratically governed."[48]

Charles A. Beard, who agonized over the Court's *de facto* "usurpation" of power, had been a student in Britain at the end of the 1890s, just when the Fabians were fulminating against judicial supremacy. In May 1898, two months after the Fabian critique appeared, an editorial by young Beard asserted that "this crowned Constitution with its halo has been the bulwark of every great national sin—from slavery to monopoly."[49] Beard found allies with diverse political persuasions, ranging from Gustavus Myers, whose highly critical *History of the Supreme Court of the United States* appeared in 1912, to Brooks Adams, who argued a year later that "constant judicial interference [has] dislocated scientific legislation" and that "casting the judiciary into the vortex of civil faction has degraded it in the popular esteem." Adams moved from that perspective to a more general complaint about the Court's role in American constitutionalism.

The Supreme Court, "having once declared the meaning of a clause of the Constitution, that meaning remains fixed forever, unless the court either reverses itself, which is a disaster, or the Constitution can be amended by the states, which is not only difficult, but which, even if it be possible, entails years of delay."[50]

The noisiest critic of all, relentlessly shrill during the presidential campaign of 1912, was Theodore Roosevelt. He condemned "every strained construction of the Constitution which declares that the nation is powerless to remedy industrial conditions which cry for law"; criticized the state courts especially; and sounded more like a Populist than a Progressive by reiterating that "the people themselves must be the ultimate makers of their own Constitution, and where their agents differ in their interpretations of the Constitution, the people themselves should be given the chance after full and deliberate judgment, authoritatively to settle what interpretation it is that their representatives shall thereafter adopt as binding."[51]

Any political drama in which Roosevelt played a part was likely to abound with ironies and inconsistencies. His biography of Gouverneur Morris (1888) had lavished praise upon that framer of the Constitution because "he upheld the power of the judges, and maintained that they should have absolute decision as to the constitutionality of any law." During the presidential campaign of 1904, when TR ran for re-election, a group of conservative Democrats contended that Roosevelt governed by personal fiat. They even formed the Constitution Club, an organization with the stated purpose of re-establishing a government of law. (The club remained active in 1908.) When TR's race for the presidency got into high gear in 1911, he remained a nationalist and a broad constructionist ("I stand for the construction of the Constitution in the manner of Abraham Lincoln"); yet this man who had so often been accused of executive usurpation of authority now denounced judicial usurpation, made recall of judges by the electorate a major issue, and ran on a platform that advocated easier means of amending the Constitution.[52]

Consequently a national forum took place in 1911–12 on three related constitutional issues: first, whether passage of two amendments providing for a federal income tax and the direct election of senators would subvert the Constitution; second, whether the recall of judges would jeopardize an independent judiciary; and third, whether "the people" should be considered a higher authority than even the Constitution. *The New York Times*, for example, vehemently opposed both amendments, whereas Senator Borah of Idaho, a prominent Progressive, predicted that if the income tax amendment was not approved, "the greatest war in history will be fought around the wreck of the Supreme Court."[53]

William Howard Taft scoffed at the notion that some mystical "popular will" stood above the Constitution, and he mocked a western governor who had said that "whatever is right is constitutional." Apprehensive about "the fitful impulse of a temporary majority of an electorate," Taft opposed the recall of judges and recommended instead the traditional device of impeachment. He also asserted that criticism of the Supreme Court verged upon Communist propaganda. Andrew Dickson White, who served as a Taft delegate to the Republican Convention, declared that "the people" were not competent to consider constitutional questions. "Reversal of decisions of our courts by popular vote," he snorted, "is the most monstrous proposal ever presented to the American people, or any other people."[54]

Essentially, the incumbent Taft and his supporters permitted Roosevelt, a third-party candidate, to dominate and define a cluster of major issues in the 1912 election. Taft upheld the status quo, labelled TR's proposal for popular review of judicial decisions "grotesque," and declared that the Republican Party stood "for the Constitution as it is, with such amendments adopted according to its provisions as new conditions thoroughly understood may require."[55] TR and his supporters reiterated their arguments at every opportunity and thereby alerted a national audience to this question. Addressing the Ohio Constitutional Convention in February 1912, Roosevelt outlined his overall message.

I am emphatically a believer in constitutionalism, and because of this fact I no less emphatically protest against any theory that would make of the Constitution a means of thwarting instead of securing the absoute right of the people to rule themselves and to provide for their own social and industrial well-being. All Constitutions, those of the States no less than that of the Nation, are designed, and must be interpreted and administered, so as to fit human rights. Lincoln so interpreted and administered the National Constitution. Buchanan attempted the reverse, attempted to fit human rights to, and limit them by, the Constitution. It was Buchanan who treated the courts as a fetish, who protested against and condemned all criticism of the judges for unjust and unrighteous decisions, and upheld the Constitution as an instrument for the protection of privilege and of vested wrong. It was Lincoln who appealed to the people against the judges when the judges went wrong, who advocated and secured what was practically the recall of the Dred Scott decision, and who treated the Constitution as a living force for righteousness. We stand for applying the Constitution to the issues of to-day as Lincoln applied it to the issues of his day.

This became the most widely noticed speech of TR's campaign, and its candor cost him a fair number of supporters. During the months ahead he and others elaborated the details. In July a cartoon that appeared in the hostile *New York Times* showed TR himself presiding over the "Court of the United States."[56] He had run the gamut of constitutional criticism, from usurpation of executive authority in 1904 to fulmination against the judiciary in 1912.

Although Woodrow Wilson won the election, reverberations of these issues continued to be felt for several years. Roosevelt kept pleading with Progressives in Congress "to overthrow those who perverted the Constitution." The defeated Taft decided to form an organization, a "Constitutional League" within the Republican Party, devoted to the "preservation" of the Constitution in its "present form." And one of TR's critics, a lawyer who did not agree that "the courts have directly usurped the power to declare void a statute in conflict with the Constitution," borrowed a phrase from the nineteenth-century British historian, George Grote, that would become all the vogue a decade later: "constitutional morality." Just what it meant in 1912 is not exactly clear; but anyone impatient with traditional restraints upon governmental change was clearly guilty of "disregarding constitutional morality."[57] James M. Beck, Pierre S. DuPont, and the American Bar Association would take this up as a battle-cry during the mid-1920s.

IV

Between 1912 and about 1915 a balance existed between the forces of orthodox constitutionalism and the advocates of change. One even finds this equipoise within such individuals as William E. Borah. In one Senate speech Borah praised Hamilton because he would have given the central government too much power, and Jefferson who would have given it too little. Borah concluded that these opposing views had resulted in a healthy distribution of authority between the nation and the states. He acknowledged that the United States had two divergent constitutional traditions, neither of which could stand alone; yet together they formed an ideal system.[58]

Because the 125th anniversary of the Constitution occurred in 1912, the Convention of 1787 received more attention than usual from the press that year. In May *The New York Times* heaped scorn upon those who considered the Constitution obsolete, and praised the historical pageant planned for Fairmount Park in Philadelphia. The editorial warned that dozens of muckrakers might try to persuade Americans "that our code of organic law is worthless and should be thrown into the waste basket." On December 14 the Pennsylvania Society held a grand banquet at the Waldorf-Astoria in New York City. Attorney General George Wickersham mocked "a modern school of political thought which finds little in the Constitution to praise, much to criticize, and a great deal to alter." He warned his audience against the perils of "Constitution tinkering." Retiring Ambassador Bryce then tactfully avoided any mention of the year's hottest political issue. Senator Borah followed Bryce, thereby providing the program with perfect balance. Borah cautioned against constitutional "fetishism" and argued on behalf of sensible changes.[59]

These were peculiar years because the cycles of change caused conservatives and liberals to take positions we do not ordinarily ascribe to them. It will come as no surprise that a racist and conservative Alabama lawyer wanted to repeal the Fourteenth Amendment. But listen to the argument he mounted on behalf of flexibility. "There is a feeling abroad in America that when a given measure becomes a part of the constitution of the United States its virtue must never henceforth be questioned. There is here a tendency towards a paper worship which involves a fundamental misconception of the true nature of constitutional law." After condemning "the prevalence of this abnormal reverence for the letter of the constitution," the author pointed out how readily state constitutions were changed in order to "meet the growing needs of each succeeding generation." The same logic ought to apply to the federal Constitution because "it behooves each generation to examine for itself the political and constitutional ideals which form the basis of the federal government."[60] Not the customary line for a conservative!

A year later, in 1913, Brooks Adams played to perfection the role of conservative reformer, advocating modest changes in order to forestall more radical ones. He predicted that the Supreme Court, by refusing to give any concessions to propulsive social forces, would jeopardize property and undermine the judiciary by making revolution inevitable. "The capitalist, as I infer, regards the constitutional form of government which exists in the United States, as a convenient method of obtaining his own way against a majority, but the lawyer has learned to worship it as a fetich. Nor is this astonishing, for, were written constitutions suppressed, he would lose most of his importance and much of his income."[61]

The "fetich" was indeed on its way, and it developed in response to two decades of constitutional criticism by radical journalists; by Socialists who felt that the Constitution should be "scrapped" because it had been written at a time when the economic system was so different from what it had since become; by labor lawyers who argued that the Constitution must be outmoded because it had been prepared by "men who never saw a railroad" and could not anticipate the economic problems that would accompany industrialization; by professional historians who had absorbed Beard's cynicism and presumption of economic gain as a basic human motive; and by newspapermen, also influenced by Beard, who wrote books with titles like *The Dishonest Constitution* in which they argued that the Constitution "was not made to do what we believe it was made to do, nor was it made by the kind of men whom we believe made it."[62]

Some Americans reacted negatively to Beard without, as a consequence, participating in the new "fetich."[63] Others, such as Henry Cabot Lodge, James Ford Rhodes, and especially David Jayne Hill, felt that Beard had exceeded the bounds of propriety and typified a tendency so virulent that it required counterattack. Hill, formerly ambassador to Germany and president of the University of Rochester, published an essay called "The Crisis in Constitutionalism" that attracted wide notice and provided, more than any other statement, the slogan for a new cult. Senator Frank B. Brandegee of Connecticut read the essay into the *Congressional Record* and sent 8,000 copies to constituents. Another 10,000 were distributed in New York State. Hill had emerged as the spokesman of a cause.[64]

For most of our history, he asserted, the American people had believed in the "approximate perfection" of their constitutional system. Cherishing its stability, they sought few changes. Suddenly alterations were being proposed promiscuously, and in too many instances were passively accepted. "For the first time since it was adopted the Constitution has within very recent years been treated with open disrespect. What is the reason for this opposition? It is that the Constitution presents an obvious barrier to the designs of those who oppose it." Hill believed that the country faced a stark choice between constitutional government and political anarchy. Consequently he advocated the formation of citizens' clubs in order to achieve "the preservation of ConstitutionalGovernment." What did he fear most? An excess of new amendments; "impulsive and ill-considered action"; but above all, those democratic demagogues (like Teddy Roosevelt) who would substitute the "will of the people" for the Constitution.[65]

By 1917, Hill and many others who shared his values felt profoundly threatened by Wilson's presidency and the domestic achievements of Progressive legislation. Hill published a sequel, this time called "A Defense of the Constitution," in which he warned against the growth of "direct popular action," executive authority strong enough to "sweep away the system of checks and balances," naïve aspirations for "progress" and "social justice," and simplification of the amending process. Proponents of such foolishness would "destroy constitutionalism altogether by effacing the difference between a fundamental law and any ordinary statute." Hill asserted that "from places of the highest authority at Washington utterances are publicly made which . . . disparage the Constitution of the United States as an archaic document. . . ." Some Socialists did, indeed, hold that view, but no one in a position of authority in Wilson's administration.[66]

Hill presented two rather startling declarations. In the first he presumed to know better than the average man what was best for him: "Underlying this movement of destructive criticism is a popular ignorance of what the Constitution really means for the common man. It is not realized by the average man that all he holds most dear is wrapped up in the doctrines of the Constitution." In the second he presumed to know better than the most serious constitutional experts what the founders had really intended in 1787. After dismissing the creative achievements customarily ascribed to the Convention, Hill came up with an argument that was historically peculiar in its emphases yet swiftly attracted supporters: "The one really original idea in the American Constitution was the conception of liberty as a strictly personal prerogative to be secured by a fundamental public law. I say as a *personal* prerogative, because liberty had previously been regarded as something belonging to the people in the mass, as a trophy extorted from royalty; but the American conception was that liberty is something inherent in each individual as a moral personality; and not a concession made to the people by a government."[67]

The lines of conflict that had been drawn ideologically in 1912–13 were formalized in organizational terms within a few years. In 1915 a Committee on the Federal Constitution, led by Charles A. Beard and other Progressives, was organized in Brooklyn. Its general purpose, stated in the by-laws, would be "to study the Constitution of the United States and to suggest and further measures for bringing the Constitution under a more democratic control." Because so many members were writers, the leaders envisioned a series of well-distributed publications, beginning with one on the amending process. In May 1916 the National Association for Constitutional Government was formed in Washington, D.C., in order to promote a campaign against the movement for initiative, referendum, and recall, particularly, but more generally "to propagate a more accurate knowledge of constitutional government as conceived by the founders of the Republic, and to secure a popular realization of the vital necessity of preserving the nation's basic law unimpaired." David Jayne Hill served as the Association's first president.[68] By 1918 an American Constitutional League had also come into existence. The "fetich" was well under way.

V

A cult of the Constitution would indeed flourish for two decades following 1918, as we shall see in the next chapter. Nevertheless, anticipatory signals during the second decade of the century were ambiguous. On the positive side, one might point to the 1915 Panama-Pacific Exposition, held at San Francisco, where photographic reproductions of the engrossed sheets of the Constitution were prominently displayed; or to the desire by such organizations as the Lowell Institute of Boston to sponsor in 1915–16 a public lecture series on those responsible for "the formation or adoption of the Constitution."[69]

On the negative side, however, there is abundant evidence that constitutionalism continued to be neglected in the curricula of many schools; and that where instruction did occur, the quality was not high. As the authors of one report put it in 1916, "studying many books about a Constitution which is not read is a common practice, but one that cannot be defended." In that same year *The Chicago Tribune* called Henry Ford an "ignorant idealist." When Ford's libel suit finally came to trial in 1919, the *Tribune*'s attorney asked him what he knew about "the fundamental principles of government?" Ford's lame response could have come from many an American: "Do you mean the Constitution?" Political abstractions puzzled Ford. He didn't know much about the Constitution; but he did at least understand that it was somehow basic to the entire governmental system.[70]

One of the most poignant and revealing assessments came in 1918 from Albert J. Beveridge, a lawyer and former Progressive senator from Indiana (1899–1911), while he was struggling to complete his massive four-volume biography of John Marshall. Beveridge explained to Charles Beard his difficulty in keeping the work from growing too long: "It is made practically insoluble by the astounding ignorance of our people— even of the so-called 'well read' among them. Everything has got to be explained . . . in order to make them understand what the thing is all about." Allowing for a degree of overstatement—though evidence indicates that Beveridge's lament remained valid all through the 1920s and 1930s[71]—it is highly symptomatic because the Beveridge biography (1916–19) dramatized the complexity of the apotheosis of John Marshall (in particular) and renewed reverence for the Supreme Court (in general).

Unlike his successor, Roger B. Taney, who had been widely discredited by the Dred Scott decision and whose reputation underwent a remarkable rehabilitation after 1911,[72] Marshall's prestige remained high despite the periodic pulsations of American constitutionalism. Even so, he was not a cynosure of attention during the half century following his death in 1835. On May 10, 1884, a statue of Marshall by the sculptor William Wetmore Story, a son of Marshall's esteemed colleague, was unveiled in Washington, D.C. It had been sponsored by Congress and the American Bar Association for presentation to the Supreme Court. A *Washington Post* editorial, prepared in response to the occasion, provides an intriguing preview of James Russell Lowell's lament in 1888. "The difference between John Marshall and those who follow him is just that between him who, with a fixed object to accomplish, perfects the necessary machinery and the others who, coming after him, see that the engine is kept in motion to do its work."[73] In an optimistic atmosphere, at least some people acknowledged that the machine might not always "go of itself."

During 1885 a new biography of Marshall appeared. Late in 1900 a long-forgotten portrait of Marshall, completed in 1833, was discovered at a residence in Waukegan, Illinois. Marshall's home in Richmond, threatened with demolition in 1906, was given to the Association for the Preservation of Virginia Antiquities in 1911. Two years later that organization opened it to the public (on a selective basis) as "a shrine of American constitutionalism." One visitor to the house in 1917 wrote carefully in the guest book: "Proud to worship at the shrine of the Greatest Chief Justice."[74]

The real genesis of John Marshall's apotheosis occurred in 1901, however, when the American Bar Association chose February 4, one hundred years since the Chief Justice took his seat on the Supreme Court, as

John Marshall Day. Judge William Wirt Howe of New Orleans served as chairman of the planning committee. What is somewhat surprising—given the Golden Jubilee fiasco of 1837, the seat-of-the-pants "success" in 1887, and the ho-hum response four years later to the Centennial of the Court itself—is the nationwide nature of the celebration and the remarkable degree of support that it received. Ceremonies in Washington took place in the House of Representatives. Members of the Senate, Supreme Court, the diplomatic corps, and many others were present to hear speeches by Chief Justice Melville W. Fuller and Isaac Wayne MacVeagh, a diplomat, political reformer, Attorney General under President Garfield, and member of a prominent Washington law firm.

The Pennsylvania Bar Association sponsored an exhibition of portraits of all the chief justices and organized a parade ending at Musical Fund Hall, where a justice of the State Supreme Court spoke. Oliver Wendell Holmes, then Chief Justice of the Supreme Judicial Court of Massachusetts, gave an address in Boston; and Professor James B. Thayer, who published his highly favorable *John Marshall* in 1901, presented the oration at Harvard. Exercises were held at Albany in the assembly chamber, where John Forrest Dillon (formerly Chief Justice of the Iowa Supreme Court, then a federal judge, and subsequently Professor of Law at Columbia) virtually ignored the dominant trends of the previous fifteen years and declaimed: "The Constitution, as it exists to-day, with the exception of the late amendments, is in form and principle the Constitution as it was fashioned by Marshall and existed at his death. He is, therefore . . . more than any other man, entitled to be called the creator of our Federal Constitutional law and jurisprudence."[75]

At Chicago Senator Henry Cabot Lodge served as the principal speaker; and similar festivities took place throughout the West and South. All in all, this event was commemorated in thirty-eight states and territories (plus Washington, D.C.) with more than fifty orations that were remembered as "warm and enthusiastic." The only sour note seems to have been struck in the South, where an occasional wail reminded celebrants that John Marshall had been, above all, a nationalist. Therefore, "if Marshalism [sic] is right, then Lee should have been hanged, Jefferson Davis legally deserved the scaffold, and every Confederate soldier, from Manassas to Appomattox, was in law a rebel deserving death."[76]

In 1908 Senator Beveridge first considered writing a one-volume interpretive biography of Marshall that could be serialized. He did not start serious work on the project until 1913, however, after he had been defeated for re-election to the Senate. An ardent nationalist, Hamiltonian, and imperialist, Beveridge despised Thomas Jefferson and made him the villain of the saga, a hypocrite who would have thwarted the selfless Marshall at every critical moment. Despite the fact that Beveridge asked many experts to read his work in manuscript, and despite their warning that he came across as flagrantly partisan, Beveridge could not control his prejudices. Nor could he control his pen. Taking the four volumes together, 14 percent of the material is devoted to John Marshall himself, 34 percent to constitutional history, 32 percent to general political history, and the remaining 20 percent to miscellaneous topics. Charles Beard wrote to Beveridge in 1918: "My main criticism is that you are travelling out of the line and writing a history of the Times of J. Marshall; but you are entitled to this privilege! My second criticism is that you are too hard on the Democratic futilities and too easy on the sham and rhetoric of the other political crowd [Federalists and proto-Whigs] which was just as bigoted and foolish. Marshall could talk rot just as clotted and dishonest as Jefferson. If you are going to mete out damnation, spread it evenly, for the sake of truth and the cause."[77]

Others who read the manuscript warned that when Jefferson entered the story, Beveridge's attitude "is not wholly that of the historian." Another sort of admonition also surfaced—one highly symptomatic of the resurgence of states' rights feeling among Americans every bit as patriotic as Beveridge. Clarence W. Alvord, a prominent Illinois historian, responded: "Formerly I was myself a defender of national government against states rights, but there is something dangerous in too great an emphasis on the national spirit, a danger that might be escaped through the increased power of the individual states within the union. . . . If you wish your book to stand the test of time you must be careful to avoid being carried away by the time spirit. The growth of nationalism must be traced as one of the great events of your period and it need not be made a fetish."[78]

Despite such caveats and criticisms, the publication of volumes III and IV in 1919 brought Beveridge bountiful praise plus many awards. Congressman R. Walton Moore of Virginia cited it in a speech before the House of Representatives. Oliver Wendell Holmes called it a "noble work," but explained apologetically to Beveridge that since it had arrived in a plain brown wrapper from an Indianapolis bookstore, the package sat unopened for almost two weeks because Mrs. Holmes believed it might contain an anarchist's bomb![79] An attorney in Green Bay, Wisconsin, wrote to say that he "was never so interested in a biography or an historical work as I have been in this." His only reservation involved a matter of emphasis: Marshall's self-assumed role as constitutional tutor to a nation.

He occupied the only position in the three departments of government, or elsewhere in the nation, from which an authoritative interpretation of the constitution could come, and receive recognition. He
had to overcome deeply intrenched prejudices, being constantly augmented and intensified by the press and politicians; and that could be
done only by decisions of the court, over which he presided, created
and written by himself. Those decisions must be clothed in language
and argument so plain as to meet the understanding of the masses as
well as men of learning. You so frequently refer to his tiresome repetition and the length of his opinions. This was evidently Marshall's
idea of what was required to accomplish their purpose.

The general manager of a West Virginia coal company found the biography "so fascinating and reads so easily, I found it difficult to put it down
for either sleeping or eating."[80]

The appearance of Beveridge's magnum opus bolstered general interest in American constitutional history. Given the author's emphasis
upon warring factions led by Marshall and Jefferson, readers could not
help being reminded, at least implicitly, that they had inherited a tradition
of conflict within constitutional consensus. In 1919, Edward S. Corwin
published a briefer, more analytical biography of Marshall. Although he
differed with Beveridge on certain critical issues, notably the "correct" interpretation of Marshall's decision in *Marbury* v. *Madison* (Corwin believed that Marshall had been unsound in declaring section 13 of the
Judiciary Act unconstitutional), Corwin seemed equally smitten by Marshall's personality. Because of their two publications in 1919, Marshall was
virtually canonized. As Beveridge observed wryly to Corwin: "It does appear as though the two of us have put across something after all, doesn't
it?"[81]

Robert E. Cushman, then a professor of political science at the University of Minnesota, wrote an essay-review of the two works and followed
with a worshipful letter to Beveridge: "I felt that it would do the lawyers
here in the Twin Cities no harm to know something more about these
books than they might otherwise learn. I have a feeling that the more people who can be led to read them the better off we shall all be. . . . Mrs.
Cushman (who is not a political scientist) and I read aloud together all four
volumes with an enjoyment and avidity of interest which we seldom derive
from our various excursions into the realm of fiction."[82]

If Beveridge could make Marshall's life more compelling than fiction,
and if the scholarly Corwin could concede that his "interest in Constitu-

tional Theory gave me the impulse [to write a biography], but I soon fell quite in love with Marshall himself," then the equilibrium between cynicism and affirmation that had prevailed in American constitutionalism from the start of the century until about 1916 had been decisively tipped.[83] Some cynicism remained, but it was waning. A true cult of the Constitution was under way by 1920.

VI

Because of Beveridge's strident nationalism, he advocated close scrutiny of the Canadian constitution. It *seemed* to supply an adequate central government without selfish provincial interests pleading for the punctilios of states' rights. Beveridge believed that comparative constitutionalism would vindicate his commitment to federalism as (he understood) the Federalists had intended it back in 1787–88.[84] Few Americans were interested in comparative constitutional analysis, however, except for those comparisons with Great Britain discussed earlier in chapter 6. A more cosmopolitan perspective might have reassured Progressive critics of the Constitution, who sought greater flexibility, but also those like David Jayne Hill who felt so apprehensive about the "crisis in constitutionalism" that they were ready to ward off the worst blows that its enemies would surely inflict.

A worldly outlook could have been comforting indeed; for Britain's constitutional crisis of 1909–11, serious as it seemed, achieved a successful resolution. Elsewhere, however, the decade following 1905 brought severe constitutional strains, governmental instability, and in some instances disintegration. In czarist Russia the 1905 revolution led to a new constitution that was promulgated on April 23, 1906. The so-called Duma Monarchy contained fatal flaws, however, and the short-lived system collapsed early in 1917.[85] A constitutional crisis that occurred in Hungary during 1905–06 resulted in consequences so far-reaching that the Austro-Hungarian Empire could only limp along for a few more years within the structure that had been created in 1867. The unresolved Hungarian crisis thereby had profound implications for all of Europe.[86]

In the years after 1898, when Chinese leaders began to contemplate constitutionalism, an unfamiliar phenomenon, they did so because they regarded constitutions as a source of national unity and strength. The Ch'ing Dynasty was losing its grip and desperately needed bolstering in order to forestall radical reform or worse, revolution. In 1905 Empress Tzu-hsi decreed that a commission be sent abroad to visit various countries, examine diverse constitutional systems, and determine what form of government would best suit the needs of imperial China. The commissioners returned to Peking in August 1906. They most admired the British, German, and Japanese models because these combined monarchy with some sort of viable parliamentary government. Two months later Duke Tsai-tse, one of the commissioners, defended constitutionalism against its radical opponents. It would perpetuate the power of the dynasty, he pointed out, while shifting responsibility to ministers who would be answerable to the people (though the throne remained beyond criticism). By strengthening the internal administration of China, it would also help to prevent or minimize domestic disturbances.[87]

During the next two years a sequence of developments took place that offered more shadow than substance. Although Empress Tzu-hsi proclaimed the throne's adherence to principles of constitutionalism, she postponed the proclamation of specific constitutional institutions until China was "ready" for them. An edict dated September 28, 1907, declared that "China cannot establish such houses of representatives in a moment. We should immediately, however, establish a 'constitutional assembly' [so] that a foundation may be laid for a parliament." Eleven months later the government promulgated the so-called Principles of the Constitution. Because of their antidemocratic tone, however, accusations arose that the imperial leadership was insincere and merely sought to deceive the people. The stated purpose of the Principles was "To conserve the power of the sovereign and protect the officials and people." The Principles acknowledged two types of constitutions: those granted from above and those extracted by pressure from below. China's would be the former. "The parliament must grow out of the constitution, not the constitution out of the parliament."[88]

Although the first Chinese provincial assemblies, meeting in 1909–1910, were supposedly limited to debate, they turned out to be surprisingly independent, sometimes even truculent. During 1910 delegates who began to gather in Shanghai and Peking were prohibited from discussing the adoption of a national constitution. On December 25 the government, perhaps with a foreboding sense of imminent disaster, ordered that preparations for constitutional government be hastened. Late in 1911 the National Assembly submitted for approval a new set of "Principles of the Constitution." On November 26 the regent, in the name of the young emperor, swore before the imperial ancestral tablets to uphold the nineteen constitutional articles and obey the advice of the National Assembly. Within a week, however, rebellious provinces controlled by the advocates of republicanism (rather than constitutional monarchy) indicated their opposition to this whole scheme. The National Assembly faded into oblivion; and on February 12, 1912, the Ch'ing Dynasty fell. After a decade of protracted discussion, and five years of grudging concessions, constitutional reform patterned on Western models was moribund.[89]

Whereas constitutionalism and republicanism seemed compatible in the United States, in China they appeared to be absolutely antithetical. For much of the period from 1914 until 1922 China was governed, at least nominally, according to the provisional constitution of 1912. Cynicism about constitutional government remained commonplace. Bitter critics insisted that it offered the new elite of bureaucrats and professionals a legitimate political role without opening access to public affairs to those below them. Between 1916 and 1928 China tried no fewer than seven constitutions (not counting those developed by Sun Yat-sen and others for Canton alone). It is clear, in retrospect, that constitutionalism in China during the first quarter of the twentieth century only served to exacerbate factionalism and political disorder.[90]

The situation in Mexico between 1906 and 1916 followed a similar pattern of intermittent constitutional factionalism: the drift into anarchy (1913–15), and then Venustiano Carranza's quest for constitutional government. Yet it culminated in quite a different outcome than China's: the convention of 1916–17 and, finally, the enduring, reformist constitution of 1917 that legitimized the revolution of that year.[91] Predictably, perhaps, when President Wilson intervened in Mexico in 1913–14, he declared that the United States had a right to inquire whether a new government was in compliance with its own constitution. Wilson used constitutionalism as a test of legitimacy against the government of Victoriano Huerta, and eventually succeeded in supplanting Huerta's regime with a more acceptable one by American standards.[92]

Many Americans joined David Jayne Hill in the belief that the United States was undergoing a constitutional crisis in 1912–13. Although it may well have been a crisis by American standards, a glance around the world reveals numerous constitutional crises, all of them more severe, protracted, and unsettling. The American pattern of conflict within consensus could not *prevent* crises, but it minimized their worst effects and provided means for their resolution. The Supreme Court and judicial review served as one such mechanism; a flexible yet finite range of constitutional interpretation provided another. In 1907 Justice John Marshall Harlan, a moderate, summed up the sentiments of many: "Early in the history of the Nation some insisted upon a narrow, literal interpretation of the Constitution which, had it been approved, would have made the General Government a rope of sand, wholly inadequate to the great purposes for which it was established. But long ago that view was rejected by the Supreme Court of the United States, and its rejection has been universally approved."[93] Harlan exaggerated in using "universally," especially at that time; but the core of his assertion is largely valid. That formulation helps us to view the early twentieth-century "crisis" of American constitutionalism in clearer perspective.

PART THREE

AMERICA IS ALWAYS
TALKING ABOUT
ITS CONSTITUTION

"It may be questioned whether a majority of the voters would accept anew the Constitution from any exact knowledge of its provisions. Even among the educated classes, can one man in ten pass an intelligent examination as to its contents or give any accurate definition as to its fundamental political philosophy?"

SOLICITOR GENERAL JAMES M. BECK (1922)

"The people of the United States probably know less about the Constitution and the Supreme Court than any other important subject. Furthermore, many of them have for the Court and its members a blind adoration that makes impossible a commonsense examination."

CONGRESSMAN MAURY MAVERICK (1939)

CHAPTER 8

God Knows How Dearly We Need
a Constitutional Revival

DURING THE TWO DECADES THAT FOLLOWED 1919, constitutionalism became more controversial and assumed a more central role in American culture than it ever had before. Some of the consequences seem quite positive: a reduction in the customary level of public indifference toward the Constitution; a "filtering-down" process that stimulated popular interest in certain aspects of American government, past and present; and the construction of a permanent home for the Supreme Court.

Other consequences look less desirable: insufficient improvement in the quality of constitutional education; the efflorescence of intensely partisan organizations that promoted patriotic constitutionalism as an antidote to two dreaded nemeses, governmental centralization and socialism; and, closely linked to these phenomena, uninformed worship of the document itself. In 1920 one F. W. Phelps of Seattle issued a pamphlet in which he insisted that "we should have a kind of constitutional revival in this country." Four years later Senator William E. Borah wrote: "God knows how dearly we need a constitutional revival."[1] By 1924 the revival was well under way. The form that it took, and its impact, comprise one of the most intriguing chapters in the history of American culture.

I

In 1916 David L. Pierson, Historian General of the National Society of the Sons of the American Revolution, suggested observing September 17 (the day the Convention adjourned in 1787) as Constitution Day. Over the next two years this proposal gained support from the National Security League and the National Association for Constitutional Government. Advocates pointed out that we observed the Fourth of July, Flag Day, Labor Day, Columbus Day, the birthdays of Washington and Lincoln as well as Thanksgiving. The absence of a Constitution Day after more than 130 years seemed very odd indeed. As the educational director of the National Security League explained, "there are still myriads, even of our own people, ignorant of the real meaning of our federal Constitution, and the safety of our nation is menaced by that ignorance." Why was our safety menaced? Several explanations are plausible; but Pierson and those who picked up his suggestion emphasized their fear of ideological contagion, a theme that would be sounded throughout the 1920s: "There would be no Fourth of July celebration but for September 17th, 1787, because during the intervening years between the adoption of the Declaration of Independence and the signing of the Constitution, chaos and bolshevism reigned supreme in this country."[2]

The most ardent advocates of Constitution Day, at least at the outset, were elitists who feared a drift away from representative government toward uncontrolled democracy. Democracy seemed dangerous for many reasons, but particularly because the "average man" did not understand the American system of government. "Popular ignorance of the meaning of the Constitution is appalling," a leader of the New York Bar Association noted. "Enshrined in that document is all that the average man holds most dear—although he is little aware of it." Therefore the American Rights League, the American Defense Society, and the Boy Scouts of America joined the organizations already mentioned in planning "a preliminary campaign of popular instruction, to bring to the mass of our people a vital realization of what the Constitution really is, how it came to be, and what it has done for us." Their ultimate objective was the inculcation of "true Americanism, the best and only effective antidote against bolshevism and the other alien cults which are attacking the foundations of our institutions."[3]

Programs and exercises were held in some public schools on September 17, 1918; but the idea of a special day first gained national attention in 1919, when the National Security League announced a campaign to have the Constitution's anniversary designated as a national holiday. The governors of various states and such prominent citizens as James M. Beck, General Leonard Wood, Alton B. Parker, George Wharton Pepper, Nicholas Murray Butler, and John H. Finley agreed to give speeches on Constitution Day. David Jayne Hill now headed a National Constitutional Celebration Organization Committee; and in forty-one states the superintendents of education agreed that appropriate observances would be held in the schools.[4]

When the anticipated day arrived, Hampton L. Carson, that venerable survivor of 1887 (and now president of the American Bar Association), spoke at the First Presbyterian Church of Newark, New Jersey, while the National Security League distributed copies of the Constitution with explanatory essays to all of the children in Newark's public schools. When James M. Beck gave a talk in Philadelphia, he cited socialism and bolshevism as threats to the U.S. Constitution and proclaimed it to be "the highest assertion . . . of the morality of government that the science of politics has yet given to the world." Elihu Root presented the main address at Carnegie Hall in New York City; he used the occasion to denounce the Boston police strike as a threat to our constitutional system. The House of Representatives observed Constitution Day two days late, perhaps because federal officials felt that a "surfeit of holidays" already existed, which was bad for business. Congressman Towner of Iowa droned on about the dangers of bolshevism and the elasticity of the Constitution.[5]

On the eve of Constitution Day in 1920 a bomb exploded in Manhattan, killing more than thirty people quite close to the spot where George Washington had been inaugurated in 1789. Republican presidential candidate Warren G. Harding issued a wordy statement to the press: "To assail or belittle the flag is to invite and incur the just and passionate resentment of all country-loving men, but the Constitution may be attacked or disparaged with impunity, and all too often with approval, and yet the one is but a symbol—though a very precious symbol—while the other is the very warp and woof of our national existence."[6]

Popular participation increased each year; and in 1923 a group formed the Constitution Anniversary Association, with headquarters in Chicago. Its founders affirmed that completion of the Constitution on September 17, 1787, "was the greatest event in our national history." Therefore they intended to enlist the help of college and secondary school teachers, chambers of commerce and other businessmen's associations, women's clubs, youth groups, industrial associations of employers and employees, patriotic societies, military organizations, fraternal orders, bar associations, and writers' leagues in order to stimulate widespread study of the "writing, adoption, interpretation, and administration" of the Constitution. In 1923 Constitution Day, with all of its solemn rituals, became part of an expanded observance designated as Constitution Week by the

American Bar Association and the National Education Association, during which schools were supposed to set aside time each day for constitutional instruction and study. Also in 1923 the War Department, for the first time ever, ordered that all stations and camps conduct suitable exercises in honor of the Constitution's anniversary.[7]

Predictable themes pervaded the orations that became formulaic by the mid-1920s: the reverent homage due to Washington, Franklin, Madison, and Hamilton; the privileges of citizenship, particularly the right to vote; the protection of personal liberty and human rights; but above all the lamentable national ignorance of the Constitution. As one speaker declaimed in 1925: "It is a sharp commentary on the intelligence of the people of the United States that they know so little about their Government, for few of the people of this country understand the constitution and what it has done for them since its adoption 138 years ago today. Even the leaders in Government do not understand it." Hence *The American Standard*, an anti-Catholic, Ku Klux Klan bi-weekly, blazoned its issue for mid-September 1925 with this lead to a lengthy editorial within.

CONSTITUTION DAY

September 17, 1787

Nation Paying Tribute to Inspired Work of Immortal Founders—
Recognition of God in Our Fundamental Documents—
Thirty-five States Require Schools to Teach Constitution

In 1927 the Constitution Anniversary Association changed its name to the Constitution Educational Association and expanded the scope of its activities. In 1926 and 1927 the national slogan for Constitution Week was: "Cherish the Constitution lest we perish."[8]

By the close of the 1920s crowds at Constitution Day observances had grown somewhat smaller; but the message continued to reach ever larger numbers of people by means of the airwaves. Radio now became a vital supplement to the classroom in reminding Americans of all ages that the country was moving dangerously away from constitutional individualism toward unconstitutional centralization (Congressman James M. Beck on CBS Radio, September 17, 1930). Other officials, like Governor Franklin D. Roosevelt of New York, wrote proclamations for Constitution Day urging that laymen as well as lawyers should study "the meaning and purposes of that immortal document." Because apathy remained common, however, speakers began to reiterate James Russell Lowell's "machine-that-would-go-of-itself" admonition. One orator warned on September 17, 1931: "The Constitution was not intended to run itself, and if people fail to use their rights which are inherent in this document they can only blame themselves."[9]

As the Great Depression deepened, and as New Deal measures began to appear, Constitution Day orations continued to be conservative in tone, praising the U.S. Constitution as "a bulwark against communism and fascism." By September 17, 1934, critics of the New Deal started to use Constitution Day as a rostrum to attack Roosevelt's programs. Bainbridge Colby, Secretary of State under Woodrow Wilson, called it "political charlatanism" to tell the American people that "higher liberties" not mentioned in the Constitution—such as the liberty to live, work, or eat —are guaranteed by the Constitution. Moreover, "the unemployed of the moment and other victims of the depression are not victims of the Constitution."[10]

II

The swift appeal of Constitution Day was accompanied by other manifestations of the "fetich." On September 17, 1920, for example, a pageant called "We, the People," based upon Madison's *Notes,* was performed at Carnegie Hall by prominent Broadway actors. Scenes from the 1787 Convention alternated with fabulations of political allegory; the pageant was filmed for nationwide distribution. Copies of the Constitution along with information about it were handed to each person who entered the hall. Early in 1921 the National Security League announced that prizes would be offered in all the states for "original charades, dramatizations, or pageants designed to show how the Constitution guarantees the liberties of all the peoples."[11]

In 1920 the Constitution and the Declaration of Independence were removed from their steel vault at the State Department—for the first time since 1902—and placed on display there in order to bolster American morale in resisting bolshevism. Secretary of State Lansing invited moviemakers to film the two documents so that an estimated fifty million Americans could look at them in theaters across the country. In September 1921 President Harding signed an executive order that transferred custody of the two documents from the State Department to the Library of Congress. He did so at Secretary Colby's request because Congress refused to appropriate funds to construct special steel, fireproof cases for the two "muniments" (an old word now applied for the first time to the Declaration and the Constitution). In 1922 Congress voted $12,000 for proper storage and exhibition of the muniments at the Library of Congress: framing them in bronze and illuminating them with soft incandescent lamps. Two years later President and Mrs. Coolidge dedicated the "Shrine of the Constitution and the Declaration of Independence" (see figure 17), located on a second-floor display hall at the Library of Congress, where they would remain until December 26, 1941, when they were placed in a hermetically sealed container and stored in the vault of the U.S. Bullion Depository at Fort Knox, Kentucky.[12]

In 1926, Sol Bloom of New York introduced a bill to appropriate money for a film about the Constitution that could be shown in schools, churches, and to various civic groups. The congressman pleaded with Calvin Coolidge for his endorsement: "There is plenty of dramatic material in the Constitution for the most enthralling picture of the screen. As a motion picture it will be readily understood and enjoyed by all. The spectator will learn the lesson of the Constitution presented through motion pictures better than by any other means. He will carry away its essence as a human and living creation." When the five-million-dollar request seemed doomed to failure, Bloom's rhetoric escalated: "The Constitution is not the dry, forbidding thing that it is represented to be in most study courses. It can and should be made one of the most exciting studies. It should be made a thing of flesh and blood. Its content can be made as vivid as some of the most thrilling events of our history, which it reflects."[13] Despite the hyperbole, he received no money and no movie.

Sometimes it is difficult to tell whether men like Bloom truly believed all that they said, or felt that if they said it often enough it might gain credibility. In 1926, while the National Oratorical Contest on the Constitution was under way, James M. Beck provided a feature article for *The New York Times* in which he explained that the Constitution only seemed to be a dull, legal document. "To illustrate the great interest of the subject, if the student has a little imagination he need only take the Preamble. There is a noble dignity about it, and, as with the 'purple passages' of Shakespeare, or the lofty truths of Scripture, the more one reads it, the more one is impressed with its majesty."[14]

Beck meant what he said, as did a great many like-minded men and women who by 1927 had been designated as "Constitution Worshippers" and "Professional Patriots." Because of their passion to persuade others, they established an extraordinary network of organizations whose shared goal was to promote constitutionalism as a means of thwarting various isms that ranged in hue from pale pink (centralization) to flaming red (bolshevism). The National Association for Constitutional Government, founded in 1917, announced that its principles were "conservative, but not illiberal." From its inception until 1929 the Association published *The Constitutional Review*. The Constitutional League was launched in January 1920 to combat radicalism by educating Americans about constitutional principles. The National Security League hoped to popularize the Constitution, and remained extremely active throughout the 1920s.[15]

In 1922 a number of these organizations, including the National Association for Constitutional Government, the Public Interest League, the League for Preservation of American Independence, the Constitutional Liberty League, the Anti-Centralization Club, the Sons of the Revolution, the American Legion, the Society of the Cincinnati, the American Rights League, and the American Defense Society united under a co-operative arrangement called the Sentinels of the Republic. Its organizers hoped to persuade one million people "to pledge themselves to guard the Constitution and wage war on socialism." Their battle-cry became: "Every citizen a sentinel, every home a sentry box." By the mid-1920s these groups promoted so many activities, contests, and programs that occasional conflicts or duplication of effort occurred. On balance, however, the editors of *The Constitutional Review* seemed pleased with what had been achieved by 1927: "A better understanding of the meaning, value and importance of the Constitution of the United States is being brought about by meetings for discussion of the Constitution held throughout the country under the auspices of Chambers of Commerce and Lions, Rotary, Kiwanis and Exchange Clubs, the American and State Bar Associations, Sons and Daughters of the American Revolution, the American Legion, and other public-spirited organizations."[16]

Two noteworthy consequences ensued. First, a constitutional cult emerged that manifested strong religious overtones. When Louis Marshall spoke on NBC Radio in 1928, he referred to the Constitution as "our holy of holies, an instrument of sacred import." Many individuals believed that the composition of the Constitution had been divinely inspired.[17]

Second, an acrimonious dialogue developed which lingered intermittently from 1923 until 1937 over whether or not a "fetich of the Constitution" existed at all. Critics contended that "to most Americans a Constitution is merely a fetich. They don't know what is in it, and to them it is as the Ark of the Covenant was to the Jews, the Bible to the uneducated Catholic, or the Sacred stone to the Mohammedans." Defenders replied that "the recent frequency of amendments, the proposal of so many more, the restless identification of 'change' with 'progress,' seem to show that the 'fetish' has lost some of its power. It is to be hoped that the majority of the people will continue to be 'stagnant,' to 'venerate' a Constitution that has worked so well. Fetish or no fetish, the Constitution is preferable to the vagaries and mysteries of 'pure democracy.' "[18]

A few scholars tended to offer more judicious perspectives. Howard Lee McBain, Professor of Constitutional Law at Columbia University, phrased it this way in a compact volume prepared for the Workers Bookshelf: the Constitution "is not to be worshipped. But it is certainly to be respected." Equally predictable, most scholars did not reach a wide audience, no matter how straightforward and wise their words. Charles E. Merriam of Chicago cautioned against constitutional fetishism: "Those who worship the text, worship in reality their own attitudes which they fondly hope the interpretation of the text may produce."[19]

III

The substance of that strongly felt dialogue included new issues along with some that had become quite familiar. The most recurrent struggle pitted those who would alter or adapt the Constitution against opponents of "Constitution tinkering." A *New York Times* editorial in 1919 denounced the tinkerers, observing that the U.S. Constitution "was made up of hard and practical declarations, and we have lived by them ever since." The polemics are more perplexing than predictable because their partisans lacked consistency. In 1922, for example, another *New York Times* editorial praised *Our Changing Constitution*, "an admirable little book" by Charles W. Pierson which refuted the notion that the Constitution is rigid or "opposed to progress." Rather, it insisted that the Constitution had changed fundamentally over the years. In 1924, when Secretary of State Charles Evans Hughes traced "Our Constitutional Heritage" and advocated some modest changes, the *Times* lauded his speech and urged that his proposals receive serious consideration.[20] Was the *Times* for or against adjusting the Constitution? The answer is not clear.

It is tempting to conclude that a moderately progressive stance must have been the dominant one. Newton D. Baker epitomized that position in 1925: "In the main the Constitution has continued little changed from its original form, but it has been enriched in its content by interpretations which have adapted it to new institutional demands." Such a statement would seem to achieve equilibrium all by itself; yet it is subtly counterbalanced by Baker's assertion that the Constitution had not only been adaptable to changing conditions, "but has grown in adequacy as each demand has been made upon it." Seven years later Baker's emphasis sounded even more progressive. In a nationally broadcast speech delivered in Cleveland on Constitution Day, Baker urged that the Constitution be amended in order to require greater accountability by the political parties and to make the handling of foreign affairs less cumbersome. He added that there were two official and two unofficial ways to amend the Constitution. By "unofficial ways," he meant Supreme Court interpretation and simple "disregard" of a provision (such as ignoring prohibition). Baker designated the Supreme Court as an "adjourned session of the constitutional convention."[21]

Conservatives, however, were less likely to welcome amendments or changes, be they official or unofficial. As Chauncey M. Depew charged on the Fourth of July, 1925: "Every crank wants to throw a crank into [the Constitution]. Let us preserve it as we have had it for 140 years." Others argued that the document was not sacrosanct, and that changes were essential. Some even quoted George Washington and his fellow founders to sustain the contention that Americans would need to alter the Constitution subsequent to its adoption. Charles E. Merriam found it noteworthy "not that amendment was made difficult, but that any provision was made for orderly change."[22]

By 1931–32 some social critics declared that the Constitution was "as obsolete as the stage coach," and called for the elimination of lame duck congresses and the electoral college along with the introduction of proportional representation and measures that would make elected officials more dependent upon public opinoin. A few radicals even called for outright abolition of the Constitution. As a philosophy professor at Swarthmore asserted late in 1931: "I don't believe in one generation deciding what the others shall do. Our forefathers didn't know anything about a country of 120,000,000 people, with automobiles, trains, and radios."[23]

Conservatives defended the Constitution by denying that it lacked flexibility. Many, in fact, like Nicholas Murray Butler of Columbia, wanted to abolish whichever amendments displeased them. In Butler's mind that meant the Seventeenth, which mandated direct election of U.S. senators. Others rejected the Eighteenth, contending that only the states should exercise control over liquor consumption, not the federal government. Still others continued to complain about the Fourteenth and Fifteenth amendments.[24] We must keep in mind that those who admired the Constitution most vocally did not speak with one voice. Senator Borah took issue with Charles Warren in 1923, and Warren with James M. Beck in 1924. That pattern applies equally to those who disapproved of "Constitution worship." Charles E. Merriam's 1931 book, *The Written Constitution*, aimed its revisionist barbs at Charles A. Beard and J. Allen Smith.

Smith is representative of Progressive critics who regarded the U.S. Constitution as fundamentally undemocratic, both in the manner of its composition and in its substantive provisions. Beard, Vernon L. Parrington, and Carl L. Becker all agreed, though each one formulated his critique in a different way. Becker was the most temperate, observing that constitutions are "the imperfect and temporary products of time and place. Whatever the intention of their framers may have been, their meaning is determined by the ingenuity of judges, God helping them, to luff and fill before the shifting winds of social opinion." Beard's assault was more harsh: too many passages in the Constitution were vague and indefinite; the amending procedures proved to be too difficult; and the charter itself was insufficiently responsive to the imperatives of social change. "The most important phases of the nation's growth are not reflected," he wrote, "in the letter of its fundamental law."[25]

Like Beard, who with the passage of time became less critical of the founders and the Constitution, J. Allen Smith also changed his tone. In an influential book, *The Spirit of American Government* (1907), Smith devoted extensive discussion to undemocratic developments during the 1780s, entitled chapter 3 "The Constitution a Reactionary Document," and explained that "the immediate aim of democracy is . . . [to] make the will of the people supreme." But in his final work, published in 1930, Smith doubted the "wisdom of the people" as an abstract entity, opposed the centralization of power (even to achieve benign social ends), defended local self-government, and opposed U.S. participation in the League of Nations.[26]

What may seem most startling from a contemporary perspective is the unconcealed criticism of democracy that permeated the political culture of the 1920s. In our own time, democratic ideals usually command lip service even from conservatives. (Watch what they do, not what they say. Political rhetoric has been homogenized by expediency.) Sixty years ago a refreshing candor prevailed, like it or not. Edith Wharton proudly asserted: "There is nothing like a Revolution for making people conservative; that is one of the reasons why, for instance, our Constitution, the child of Revolution, is the most conservative in history." In an editorial published on Constitution Day in 1921, *The New York Times* suggested: "If it is true, as there is much evidence to prove, that Americans are showing themselves the most conservative nation in a turbulent world, the largest cause of it lies in our Federal Constitution."[27]

James M. Beck's widely read homily on the Constitution, published in 1924 with a foreword by President Coolidge, denounced "an individualistic democracy" (the Jeffersonian variety); found comfort in the belief that "more than any other Constitution, that of America imposes powerful restraints on democracy"; and proceeded to define democracy as "an institution which is tempered by wise and noble leadership, and in the case of America by constitutional limitations upon the powers of the masses." Beck even accepted Charles Beard's controversial thesis but lauded it by looking at it from an elitist's perspective. Delegates to the 1787 Convention were men of property "whose main purpose was to defend their property rights from the excesses of democracy." Many readers of Beck's book sent him effusive praise. These lines from a Chicago attorney are typical: "I have come to the conclusion that democracy in government is a case of too many cooks (bad cooks) spoiling the broth." Nothing agitated David Jayne Hill so much as "the restraint of unregulated democracy," a central theme of his Cutler Foundation Lecture in 1926.[28]

The conservative refrain that became commonplace after 1923, "constitutional morality," may be more comprehensible in this context. Following Coolidge's victory in 1924, Beck conceded to a correspondent that the final chapters of his book had perhaps been unduly pessimistic: "If I were rewriting these chapters now, I would modify this pessimism; for the recent election convinced me that there is still a real sense of constitutional morality in the American people; for the immensity of the result is, I think, largely attributable to Senator LaFollette's attack upon our form of Government. Evidently the people are not as indifferent to their Constitution as I had believed when I wrote the last chapters of my book."[29]

Prolonged use of such terms as "elasticity" and "constitutional morality," to the point where they seemed weary clichés to neo-Progressives and liberals, elicited this withering retort from Thurman Arnold:

> The language of the Constitution is immaterial since it represents current myths and folklore rather than rules. Out of it are spun the contradictory ideals of governmental morality. For example, in 1937 we find the *American Bar Association Journal* editorially recommending that the letter of the Constitution be disregarded in a time of crisis. Referring to the President's Supreme Court proposal, the editor says: "If the proposed act violates the spirit of the Constitution and threatens the breakdown of an essential part of it, 'constitutional

morality' certainly forbids it. To act under such circumstances is simply to exercise a brute power. And the spirit is more important than the letter. As long as the spirit of the Constitution is followed, there will be small trouble about the letter, and the great instrument and guarantee of our liberties is safe. But when the letter is followed in disregard of the spirit, catastrophe may be near." The beauty of this kind of argument is that it makes the Constitution very elastic indeed, so that it can be used on both sides of any moral question without the user being bothered with what the Constitution actually says. It is essential to constitutionalism as a vital creed that it be capable of being used in this way on both sides of any question, because it must be the creed of all groups in order to function as a unifying symbol.[30]

Later in the same lively book, Arnold asserted that most Americans were sadly ignorant of their Constitution. Although this lament was hardly new, it is notable as the single point on which liberals and conservatives could agree. Nicholas Murray Butler found the Constitution comparable in one respect to the Bible, works by Shakespeare, and *Paradise Lost*: "while everybody knows about it and speaks well of it, very few people read it." Broadcasting on nationwide radio under the sponsorship of the ABA, John W. Davis declared that those who wanted to discard the Constitution did not worry him. "The Constitution has but two enemies, whether foreign or domestic, who are in the least to be feared. The first of these is ignorance—ignorance of its contents, ignorance of its meaning, ignorance of the great truths on which it is founded and of the great things that have been done in its name. And the second is indifference which leads many people . . . to ignore both the rights and duties of citizenship."[31]

One month later the ABA's Committee on American Citizenship released a report lauding the national revival of interest while lamenting "that a very high percentage of American citizens are woefully ignorant of our form of government and the theories underlying it." In 1927 the chairman of that committee carried the condemnation one step farther: "The law schools are turning out thousands of lawyers every year who know nothing of the Constitution, and the boards of examiners require little, if any, examination on the subject, with the result that when civic organizations, like chambers of commerce, Rotary clubs, etc., seek among lawyers for speakers on the Constitution, it is very difficult to find a lawyer qualified to talk about it."[32] James M. Beck would recapitulate this theme relentlessly during the last decade of his life. As he wrote in 1926, at the peak of the revival: "The people are, at heart, not interested in their Constitution and the spirit of pragmatism dominates the consideration of every constitutional problem, if and when they consider it at all."[33]

IV

In 1919 the National Association for Constitutional Government published a *Pocket Edition of the Constitution of the United States*. By October 1920, some 50,000 copies had been distributed to schools, clubs, factories, major employers of workers, and various civic organizations. Within a few years the National Security League, Sentinels of the Republic, and the American Bar Association joined in a vigorous educational campaign. They pressured governors and state legislators to pass laws requiring that the Constitution be taught in all private and public schools. The Security League submitted a sample law for distribution to legislators. Bibliographies of books about the Constitution were compiled and circulated by the Sentinels. In 1924 Etta V. Leighton, civic secretary to the National Security League, prepared a 32-page pamphlet—really a catechism—containing a series of 115 questions and answers concerning the Constitution, followed by suggestions for reading, discussion, and debate. It was intended for schoolchildren aged twelve or thirteen to eighteen.[34]

Advocates of this campaign acknowledged that at least 50 percent of American children never went beyond elementary school (the eighth grade); so they made a survey in order to determine the earliest age at which youngsters "can begin the study of the Constitution and understand the fundamental principles of government." They agreed that "simple instruction" could effectively begin in the sixth grade. An editorial in *The New York Commercial* of May 25, 1923, observed that "a generation ago, in many of the schools, the children were required to learn to recite the entire Constitution, with the exception of those passages which had been changed by amendment." Although the editor supported the revival of that requirement, he ended with a commendably thoughtful rumination: "Perhaps the task of memorizing the entire Constitution need not be laid upon the children. Perhaps the accomplishment of such a feat would be of no service to them whatever unless it were accompanied by competent explanations of the origin, history, meaning, value, and philosophy of the Constitution."[35]

The stimuli for this vigorous campaign were varied but closely related to one another: anxiety about the impact of anarchism, socialism, and bolshevism; a strain of patriotism spawned by isolationism; and apprehension about the need to Americanize large numbers of aliens. As Gertrude Atherton, the author of popular, fictionalized biographies, wrote for Constitution Day in 1922: "If the spirit of the Constitution prevailed, trouble between capital and labor would be minimized, and were its meaning understood by immigrants, our immigration problem would disappear." Civics became a buzz-word if not a by-word; but the objectives were respect for law and loyalty to the government rather than the sort of understanding that might enable a citizen either to appreciate or criticize the government, as circumstances warranted.[36]

At first glance, the campaign seems to have been exceedingly successful. By 1923, legislation requiring constitutional instruction had been passed in twenty-three states; by 1931, forty-three states required it. Some private universities even ruled that no student would be awarded a degree who had not completed at least a one-year course on the U.S. Constitution "with specific reference to the spirit of the founders of the republic and the interpretations of the Constitution by the highest courts of the land."[37] During the mid-1920s annual lectureships devoted to the Constitution were endowed at various colleges and universities, including William and Mary, Virginia, Rochester, and Boston University.[38]

Closer scrutiny reveals some resistance to the campaign. State boards of education complained that the public had not been adequately consulted, and that "legislative additions to the curriculum" were so cumbersome that insufficient time remained to teach the basics. A gentleman from Alabama who identified himself as "an old-fashioned man and conservative" argued in 1925 that the Constitution did not require special attention. "There are many subjects of great importance with which the young mind should concern itself," he wrote. "Least pressing of all is that the time and attention of the child should be consumed in study of the vehicle which for the time being serves merely to transport our governmental institutions." Educational administrators did not like to be told that their districts were obliged to cover certain topics. And according to the ABA's Committee on American Citizenship, "the teaching profession, generally, is loath to engage in a new subject with which they are not familiar." A nationwide survey conducted early in the 1930s asked what effect the Constitution-instruction statutes were having. "None" was the response from ten major cities; "slight" from thirteen other central urban schools; and "nil" from five state supervisors.[39]

One measure of disinterest by educators may be found in the contents of journals published to serve the needs of those who taught history, social studies, and civics: *The History Teacher's Magazine, The Historical Outlook,* and *The Social Studies.* Fewer than a dozen essays appeared between 1925 and 1937—not exactly a sign of enthusiasm. Moreover, H. Arnold Bennett, the foremost authority at that time on constitutional education in the public schools, asked in 1932: "Are we not a bit too prone to teach the Constitution as a finished document—as the last word in government, as embodying certain principles which under no conditions should be modified?"[40]

Given the paucity of pedagogical guidance, it will come as no surprise that civics books and treatment of the Constitution in history and political science texts were weak. They tended to be strong on patriotism but otherwise vapid. One author found it "wonderful" that only nine amendments had been approved since the Bill of Rights in 1791, "and all of these of minor importance." He cherished the status quo and declared that the original provisions of the Constitution "cover every phase of human government. Should it not now have become sacred to our people? Why change it for something untried?"[41]

The word "dry" recurs frequently in constitutional apologetics of this era. "The study of the Constitution sounds as dry as a basket of chips," one high school teacher wrote in 1924, "but it is really the most interesting part of a course in United States history or in civics." Five years later a speaker at the annual meeting of the National Association for Constitutional Government suggested that the National Oratorical Contest, then in its sixth year, "has demonstrated what can be done in dramatizing before the youthful mind what has heretofore been a *dry, academic* and *much neglected* phase of our national education."[42]

The National Oratorical Contest may very well have been the most visible and successful aspect of the entire 1920s "revival." Supported by public as well as private high schools, and vigorously promoted by thirty major newspapers, the contest attracted more than a million participants in 1924. On June 6 the seven finalists spoke for twelve minutes each at the DAR auditorium in Washington before an audience that included Calvin Coolidge and the president of the American Bar Association. Secretary of State Charles Evans Hughes and four associate justices of the Supreme Court served as judges. The first prize of $3,500 went to a lad from Los Angeles; second prize to a girl from the District of Columbia. The following year 1,400,000 students participated. Once again Coolidge presided at the final round, and the judging was done by Chief Justice Taft, three associate justices, and the Attorney General. First prize dropped to $2,000; but all seven finalists received a cash award. In 1926 the seven finalists (the national competition was organized in seven regions) also received cash awards along with a trip to Europe—ironic, perhaps, because Europe was the source of all those dreaded left-wing isms. Presumably the finalists had acquired a strong immunity to such contagions.[43]

The most attractive side of these contests is that they did engage a great many teenagers, usually between the ages of fifteen and seventeen. By 1927 more than six million youngsters had participated in four annual competitions. Obviously their parents, teachers, and classmates must have helped and listened, too, so that a nationwide discussion of the American system of government occurred: vigorously between 1924 and 1929, with somewhat less intensity between 1930 and 1936, and then at fever pitch once again during the Sesquicentennial years, 1937–39. As Randolph Leigh, the director, put it: "the National Oratorical Contest is an agency for taking the Constitution to the people through the children of the people."[44]

Yet another positive effect resulted from the proliferation of feature stories about the Constitution that appeared in the press in conjunction with the contest. In 1926, for example, *The New York Times* devoted a full page to a symposium called "Best Thoughts on the Constitution of the United States," consisting of extracts from comments made about the Constitution ever since 1787. Informative essays assessed the eight men most responsible for writing the Constitution; the major issues that arose at the Convention and the compromises that resulted; the political philosophy that underpins the Constitution; and the evolution of the President's relationship with Congress.[45] In addition, the set topics for essay contests that also took place during these years were often sensibly chosen: the meaning of the preamble; the rationale for habeas corpus; the role of the Supreme Court; and the nature of the amending process are illustrative.[46]

On the minus side, the range of set topics for the oratorical contest could be ponderously unimaginative. In 1926, for example, a student could choose between "The Constitution," "Washington and the Constitution," "Hamilton and the Constitution," "Franklin and the Constitution," "Jefferson and the Constitution," "Marshall and the Constitution," "Madison and the Constitution," "Webster and the Constitution," "Lincoln and the Constitution," or, a real change of pace, "America's Contribution to Constitutional Government." Even worse, the ground rules established in 1924 announced that "it was a fundamental condition that all contestants must treat the Constitution in a spirit of reverent appreciation." The contests certainly did not encourage intellectual freedom or the honing of critical minds.[47]

Moreover, the few individuals who looked seriously at the substantive impact and legacy of these contests were not impressed. New constitutional materials appeared for educational purposes; but they were not usually prepared by competent people. In addition to being bland and uncritical, the new texts contained a fair number of errors or misleading statements—some of them very peculiar. "These [first ten] amendments are in the nature of a 'Bill of Rights' giving to the States authority that was not granted in the original Constitution" is a choice example.[48]

One high school principal complained that teachers concentrated upon the specifics of the Constitution rather than its spirit: "A knowledge of how old a man or woman must be for eligibility to election as a member of Congress is of little significance when compared with a grasp by the student of the rights he derives directly or indirectly from that document and the obligations that follow closely upon the enjoyment of these rights." A statement offered in 1930 by a concerned citizen praised the varied efforts that had been made to improve constitutional education, but issued a warning that echoed James Russell Lowell's 1888 admonition that the Constitution could not function as a perpetual motion machine: "The new conception of the Constitution should take into account the probability that the only foundation for a stable democracy is the sense of personal responsibility which, unless human nature changes . . . can only be realized by a system of local answerability for the community."[49]

V

Adult education pertaining to the Constitution was also available at various times and places: the National Security League offered free correspondence courses during the summer, and deposited pertinent supporting materials in local public libraries. In 1932 the Women's National Republican Club sponsored a question-and-answer "Constitution Bee."[50]

The most fascinating aspect of adult education in this period, however, pertained to the preparation of aliens for naturalization and citizenship. Feelings of hostility toward immigrants, and the fear that they could not be Americanized, supplied an extra boost to Constitution worship and an added incentive to strengthen constitutional programs in the schools. Judge Alton B. Parker expressed the views of many Americans of older stock when he spoke in 1922 at the opening of the Marshall-Wythe School of Government and Citizenship at William and Mary: "Never in the history of this country were there here so many descendants of non-

English-speaking peoples, brought up to hate the governments of which they were subjects, and who are wholly without knowledge of the principles upon which our government was so wisely builded."[51]

A cluster of closely related questions arose with mounting frequency between 1909 and 1939: How could immigrants best be prepared for citizenship? What questions should they be required to answer about the U.S. Constitution and system of government? How high should examination standards be set? What is the primary purpose of naturalization tests, anyway? Is it a thorough grounding in political science or proof of undeviating devotion to Americanism? And what should be done about major inconsistencies in the administration of citizenship tests from one region to another?

Responses to these issues vacillated with the nation's mood: self-assured at first, albeit simplistic; then with some anxiety during and after World War I; then intimately tied to Constitution worship from the early 1920s until the mid-1930s; and finally a period of almost frenetic re-assessment during the mid- to later 1930s. A transformation occurred along the way: from vague standards, inadequate procedures, and insufficient "literature" designed to assist candidates for citizenship, to capricious standards, the heterogeneous night school movement, and the development of printed materials; then to increasing uniformity, more clearly defined guidelines, and a proliferation of books and pamphlets after 1936.[52]

As early as 1907–09 the Americanization Section of the Immigration and Naturalization Service, an agency under the Department of Labor, began devoting some attention to the preparation of candidates for admission to U.S. citizenship. The administrative history of that agency, and its overall mission, remains to be written—a worthwhile project indeed. What concerns us here is simply one fragment of the story: what were applicants expected to know about the U.S. Constitution? A form prepared in 1909 for distribution to applicants provides a basic sense of the assumptions then current. A petition could not be heard until ninety days after it had been filed.

> During that time you should read carefully the Constitution of the United States and also the Constitution of your own State. If you cannot, in a general way, grasp their meaning you should have someone explain them to you. . . . You should learn about the origin of our country, the Declaration of Independence, the wars in which the United States have been engaged, and other important National matters. Unless you have a fair knowledge of the matters referred to

above you cannot intelligently take the oath of allegiance or say that you believe in the principles of the Constitution of the United States or of your own State, or be considered sufficiently intelligent to assume the duties of American citizenship. As a rule no court will admit you to citizenship unless you have a fair knowledge of these matters. . . . You should bear in mind that what is said above is only by way of suggestion. Some Judges may not require so much while other Judges may insist upon more.[53]

Despite numerous changes in the national mood and administrative regulations, that description (or prescription) remains essentially applicable three quarters of a century later.

The description is misleading in at least one respect, however. Although a "fair knowledge" allows for considerable discretion, the knowledge of history and government actually required of unsuspected petitioners has never been very rigorous. At times it has been superficial or simplistic in the extreme—unless an examiner or judge had reason to doubt the loyalty, desirability, or ideological "correctness" of an applicant. In those instances the examination might become not merely rigorous, but bewildering and unfair. The Naturalization Act of 1906 merely required that a petitioner be "attached to the principles of the Constitution of the United States." Ideally that meant understanding those principles; but in most instances it was sufficient for an applicant to answer a few predictable questions and affirm that he or she was attached to the principles of the Constitution.

In the early years there wasn't much of a system. The government offered minimal guidance to candidates. Private individuals published pamphlets or lists of typical questions for profit and offered personal counsel to applicants. That made officials at the Naturalization Service uneasy, but no one could be sure that such activities were improper, even when entrepreneurial types "placed" their booklets with court clerks, "requesting them to sell them and giving such clerks one-half of the purchase price." Standards of procedure were inchoate in 1911.[54]

By 1914 and 1915, as the number of aliens seeking to be naturalized grew and the Great War began, individuals ranging from judges and civil servants to private citizens informed the Department of Labor that standards seemed lax. As one judge wrote from Chicago: "I have presided now in over 5,000 Naturalization cases, and in my belief only a small part of those admitted to citizenship have any real knowledge of the processes of government or of the duties they are required to perform, although they are required to and do answer the long list of questions covering the administration of Government."[55] This judge, and many others, urged that the federal government take a more active role in preparing immigrants for citizenship by means of slide shows, films, and lucid publications. Such appeals recurred for more than a decade.[56] Not until the later 1920s and 1930s did the Bureau begin to do much;[57] but ever since the 1940s this material has proliferated.[58]

The Bureau's basic response in 1915–16 was to buck the whole matter to state governments, state boards of education, and local superintendents of schools—urging them to work co-operatively with federal judges in order to make sure that the instruction given to prospective citizens corresponded to the expectations of examiners. Three major developments occurred. First, a poorly co-ordinated proliferation of agencies, public and private, that attempted in various ways, with inconsistent success, to prepare aliens for naturalization. As one civil servant put it in 1915: "These efforts . . . constitute a groping in the dark for an object that may or may not be reached."[59]

Second, an emphasis upon allegiance rather than understanding, especially during the war years. Here is the core of a sixty-five-question catechism printed in 1915 by the North American Civic League for Immigrants, based in Providence, Rhode Island.

6. *Q.* Do you believe in our form of government?
   A. Yes.
7. *Q.* Will you support the constitution?
   A. Yes.
8. *Q.* What do you mean or understand by supporting the constitution?
   A. By living according to its laws, and seeing that all others do the same, and if necessary fight for its defence.
9. *Q.* What color is the American Flag?
   A. Red, White and Blue.

In 1916 New York State published a forty-five-page *Citizenship Syllabus* that concluded with a similar catechism, yet contained a fair amount of substantive information as well. It stressed at the outset that "civic training does not include so much a knowledge of the machinery of government as a knowledge of its social and reciprocal relationships to its citizens." The *Syllabus* moralized that "to be naturalized, one must believe in the principles of the Constitution of the United States." The questions and answers for a possible naturalization hearing included these two: "What is the fundamental law of this country?" and "Who made the Constitution?" The ultimate message, reiterated in many forms, was summed up by a single sentence: "Every man living in America, working in America, and having a family in America should have instilled in him the ideals of America and the desire to be a part of America." The "Elementary Course for Immigrants" prepared by New York contained no information about the Constitution at all. The "Advanced Course" did contain some, including how the Constitution came to be established, as well as a brief explanation of its major provisions.[60]

The third trend, one that continued for decades despite regional inconsistencies and inadequacies, involved the development of evening classes held at schools and settlement houses for aliens. By 1914, night school programs in Minnesota, North and South Dakota, Wisconsin, and Michigan were flourishing. The chief examiner for that district concluded a comprehensive report with the observation that "the courts throughout the entire St. Paul naturalization district have through persistent efforts on our part come to exact of the alien applicants for naturalization, particularly of those who have come to this country in more recent years, a fair knowledge of the form and principles of our Government." The region that ranged from Texas to Florida, by contrast, offered many fewer active programs. Mississippi and Georgia legislation, for example, prohibited the use of public funds for the education of adults, "which greatly handicapped any attempt to conduct night schools for foreigners."[61]

Following the war, citizenship training declined as a priority for the Department of Labor. Appropriations to support such efforts diminished; and in 1925 a "drastic curtailment" went into effect. For ten years thereafter the Americanization Section of the Immigration and Naturalization Service reduced its citizenship training work, and no innovations appeared. Some private organizations tried to take up the slack by developing educational programs and preparing new texts. Many of these, unfortunately, contained little information about the Constitution; and commendable efforts by individuals usually received a bureaucratic brush-off. In 1925, for instance, a Syrian-American in Texas proposed "the preparation of a pamphlet in the Syrian language of lessons on the Constitution of the United States[,] the same to contain a few editorials encouraging aliens of that race to take steps towards naturalization, and outlining the duties of citizenship." When U.S. Senator Earle Mayfield of Texas attempted to intervene on behalf of the project, he received a dreary response: "The Bureau of Naturalization is in no position to either use or recommend a pamphlet such as the one which Mr. Milkie suggests. . . . The Department, of course, can take no steps to encourage the filing of naturalization papers, its duty being confined to the administration of the naturalization laws. . . . It is suggested that Mr. Milkie can aid his fellow countrymen by encouraging them to take advantage of the citizenship training work in the public schools."[62]

From 1934 until 1936 the Immigration and Naturalization Service underwent extensive reassessment. District directors and regional examiners were required to survey their procedures, evaluate their effectiveness, and re-appraise their objectives. The proliferation of materials mailed to Washington provides a clear picture of the role played by constitutionalism in the naturalization process during the 1920s and 1930s. A tabulation taken in mid-1934, for example, showed these questions to have been most commonly asked of applicants (in descending order of frequency).

> What form (kind) of government have we in this country? Explain.
> Who is the governor of your state?
> Who is the President of the United States?
> What is the term of office of the President? (How long does he serve?)
> How many senators are elected from each state?
> What is the term of a senator?
> What is the highest court in the United States?
> How many houses of Congress are there?
> How does the President get his position?
> Name the U.S. Senators from this state.
> Who makes the laws for the United States?
> What is the Constitution of the United States?
> How many amendments are there to the Constitution?
> How is the Constitution amended? Describe the procedure.
> How do members of the Supreme Court get their positions?
> Have you read the Constitution of the United States (or had it read to you)?[63]

Except for the priority of some sorts of questions over others, the list seems fairly unexceptionable. Queries submitted from particular localities are more revealing: they indicate that in 1934–35, loyalty to the American government and way of life was a matter of paramount concern to examiners.

Do you believe in our country?

Do you know what anarchy is?

Do you believe in organized government?

Do you believe in a republic? What is a republic?

Do you think that it would be a good idea to divide everything up?

Do you expect to support this government?

What are the rights guaranteed by the Constitution?

Has a person accused of a crime any rights?

Are women allowed to vote in this country?

Have they always been allowed to vote?

What gave them the privilege to vote?

Did you ever hear anything about a writ of habeas corpus?[64]

The voluminous pages of sample questions and answers sent to Washington suggest that most tests must have been sensible and straightforward. The collected data do reveal, however, that many examiners envisioned a particular, almost formulaic answer to each query. Such as:

Q. Who rules in a Republic or Democracy?

A. The people, through their chosen representatives.

Q. Why is the form of Government of the United States considered a desirable form of Government?

A. The form of Government of the United States is considered a desirable form of government because the officers who exercise political authority obtain their positions by the consent of the governed.

Q. May a citizen of the United States believe in anarchy, communism or any form of rebellion against the government of the United States and at the same time be a law-abiding and loyal citizen thereof?

A. No. The Constitution provides for a government of law and order for the people thereunder and under good government respect for the law is demanded.

Q. A person who seeks citizenship must swear that he is attached to the principles of the Constitution of the United States. Tell briefly what this means to you.

A. I understand this to mean that I must believe in the Constitution of the United States and be willing to whole-heartedly abide by it; that I should know and understand at least major principles;

that I should conduct myself as an honest and honorable citizen worthy of its protection and demonstrate in my daily life that I am attached to it.[65]

Small wonder that constitutional catechisms were widely used in night school classes to prepare aliens for naturalization. Reading through the thousands of questions gathered from all over the country, as well as the covering letters written by examiners and divisional directors, it becomes clear that a great many native-born citizens, even well-educated ones, might not have been able to pass a stringently administered exam. We find, however, that many officials kept and used three sets of questions: one for well-educated applicants, one for those with an average or minimal educational background, and a third for uneducated persons. The district director in Honolulu explained that he had fifteen complex questions plus fifteen "simpler" ones, designed for applicants nearly illiterate in English, and based upon "a conception of the minimum knowledge which should authorize admissions."

> What is the highest or fundamental law of the United States?
> Have you made a study of the Constitution of the United States?
> What is the Constitution of the United States?

Many examiners admitted that they asked "trick" questions in order to fail undesirable candidates. For instance: "Which grocery stores have a right to have false scales?" The correct answer, obviously, is "None"; but the question is confusing because it implies that some category of stores was, in fact, entitled to use false scales. And there were so-called double questions, to which a yes or no answer might be acceptable depending upon the part of the question to which it was directed. Here is an example from Buffalo, New York:

> Does each State have the same number of Senators or does it depend on the population?
> Does each State have the same number of Representatives or does it depend on the population?

Many officials kept a record of their most memorable responses. In several instances the answers tell us something about the applicants' attitude toward the questions, and even toward the process itself. The following exchanges occurred in Gloucester City, New Jersey:

Q. What powers does the Federal Government have over the various States?

A. Red, Blue & White.

Q. Can you be President?

A. No.

Q. Why not?

A. They only want man.

Q. Name the three branches of the U.S. Government.

A. Deduction, Reduction—I don't know third.

Q. Ever hear of the Constitution?

A. Yes.

Q. What is it?

A. Name of ship or boat?

Q. Who was 1st Pres. of U.S.?

A. Columbus.

Q. What great written document created the Union known as the United States of America?

A. George Washington.

The following took place in Los Angeles:

Q. May the Congress of the United States make a law denying the people the right to worship the religion of their choice?

A. No.

Q. Why cannot Congress make such a law?

A. I think the Monroe Doctrine took care of that.

Q. What is your idea of what the Monroe Doctrine is?

A. It was a kind of an arrangement that no one could be forced to take any religion. I don't know about that very much—I have to guess. I think I will go to school and learn something about the government.

Q. What else have you learned about this government?

A. The executive branch, the sentimental and the judicial.

Q. Do you know the meaning of the word "sentimental"?

A. Yes, that is the branch that explain the laws.

Q. What do you think about congress making a law compelling everyone to worship the same faith—have one religion for everybody. Do you think congress has the right to make such a law?

A. The Congress builds post office buildings and makes money, and I suppose they could make everybody go to the same religion.

Q. Supposing a United States Senator should die, would his son inherit that position?

A. Yes.

Q. Can you explain why the son would inherit that position?

A. Because he is the next guy to take that place.

Q. What else have you learned about the government?

A. The laws are made in the White House.

Q. Have you read the Constitution of the United States?

A. I know some of the questions.

Q. What is the Constitution of the United States?

A. I never see that question.

Q. What is the form of government of the United States?

A. Twenty-one.

Q. Twenty-one what?

A. Twenty-one something. I don't remember.

Q. Have you ever voted?

A. Yes.

Q. Where?

A. I want to vote for everything.

From Salt Lake City:

Q. What are the duties of the Vice-President of the United States?

A. I think he don't do much.

Q. What does he do?

A. The most he does is to sit around and smoke cigars.

From Detroit:

Q. In case the President dies during his term of office, who becomes President?

A. George Washington.

From Galveston:

Q. Name some of the important duties of a citizen.

A. Love your neighbor.

From Buffalo:

Q. What is the advantage of having local government such as city and state?

A. The President can't watch everything.

Q. What are some of the principal duties and powers of the President?

A. He uses his head—he watches the United States.

And from Chicago, a sentiment that so many petitioners must have shared. At the end of her examination, Goldie Sokoloff pleaded:

Please Mister don't ask me any more questions as I want to be a citizen and I don't know any answers.[66]

As a result of extensive surveys and data gathering, the Immigration and Naturalization Service undertook throughout 1936 a major effort to achieve more uniform national standards for naturalization; a reduction in the number of capricious questions, or such questions as "Can you name five kinds of domestic enemies?"; improved co-ordination between those who taught adult education and the judges and examiners who determined how successful the preparation had been; but above all, a shift from emphasizing merely factual knowledge of the Constitution to "an understanding of the principles of the Constitution." Word went out that memorizing details and phrases would henceforth be much less important than "good moral character." According to the new guidelines distributed by Commissioner D. W. MacCormack: "Some courts have held that attachment to the principles of the Constitution may be indicated by the conduct of the applicant as shown by his daily walk in life. The general rule, however, is that attachment to the principles of the Constitution should be evidenced by a knowledge, understanding, and manifest acceptance of its major principles."[67]

The process of follow-through and fine-tuning, which continued throughout 1936–37, was impressive. Excessively legal, technical, or ambiguous questions were eliminated; and instructions sent from the Los Angeles office to all examiners in district number 20 reflected a more enlightened and compassionate outlook: "It is hoped that the schooling will be more in the nature of a course preparatory to good citizenship, than a tutelage for the sole purpose of passing an examination in naturalization proceedings. . . . On the question of knowledge of the Constitution the

applicant need be questioned only to such an extent as will serve to reasonably convince the examiner. The examination must be such as will
bring out the understanding of the applicant in his own words, rather than
a mere recitation of the exact vocabulary used in a book or by a teacher."
Other inspectors stressed the importance of flexibility, particularly in
rephrasing questions that were not immediately comprehensible. A memorandum to the Commissioner in Washington called attention to the need
for absolute clarity on the part of examiners and enumerated various ways
in which officials were not yet in full compliance with the main directive of
July 28, 1936. Looking back a year later, one officer reminded the district
director in Chicago that "it was the intention to simplify the educational
examination, not to make it more difficult."[68]

One of the most important consequences of the re-assessment, which
took nearly two years, resulted from this directive:

> That the closest possible cooperative relationship should be estab-
> lished with the State and Municipal educational authorities, and with
> other local agencies interested in the educational preparation of the
> alien for citizenship, with a view to securing the organization of
> classes for applicants for citizenship wherever the need exists. The
> instructions further provide that such relationship should be estab-
> lished only with agencies which are non-political, non-partisan, and
> non-profit making, and that every effort must be made to guard ap-
> plicants for citizenship against political, financial, or other exploita-
> tion.[69]

Complete compliance did not occur everywhere or in equal measure;
but a marked improvement in co-operation did take place, particularly in
New England because of energetic leadership provided by Robert C.
Deming, Supervisor of Adult Education for the state of Connecticut.
Owing to Deming's initiative, inconsistencies in the examining process
were reduced (particularly favoritism to English-speakers who knew little
about the Constitution over non-English-speakers who had studied assiduously but could not express themselves well); thoughtful new educational materials were prepared ("Experimental Lessons on the Principles
of the Constitution"); and a sensitive set of four new preparatory examinations winnowed down by a Committee on Educational Standards from 450
potential questions submitted by a committee of seven.[70] Such diverse organizations as the YMCA in Shoshone County, Idaho, and the DAR

headquarters in Washington, D.C., expressed enthusiasm for Commissioner MacCormack's "encyclical" of January 1, 1936, and their desire to help improve as well as implement it.[71]

Nevertheless, imperfections in the system remained. Fallible people administered the program, and complaints continued to be heard, especially that judges were often startlingly lax: "Several of the directors have been quite 'shocked' lately to find that even though examiners have failed to recommend candidates because of their lack of knowledge of government, the judges of the courts have all too often passed such people, particularly those represented by lawyers and that the judges themselves seem to fail to grasp the new attitude towards education requirements."[72]

Perhaps their honors had cause to be lax. In 1937 the House Committee on Immigration complained to the Department of Labor that it had "gone over some of the questions in executive session and [came] to the conclusion that many a college professor would not be able to answer them correctly." Frances Perkins, the Secretary of Labor, and James L. Houghteling, the new Commissioner of Immigration and Naturalization, reviewed the fifty sample questions and conceded to Congressman Samuel Dickstein that they had to agree with him. Houghteling confessed that he found several questions on the list that he could not answer "offhand." He then offered these thoughts by way of explanation:

> The Naturalization branch of my office, however, assures me that, while the fifty questions included in the "Committee Print" have all at one time or another been asked of candidates for naturalization, there has never been a case when all fifty have been asked of the same candidate. The whole tendency of the Naturalization Service of recent years has been to simplify the process of examination, to limit the number of questions and to make as many as possible susceptible to the answer "Yes" or "No." Our main object is to determine whether the applicant understands what he or she is undertaking in the oath to support and defend the Constitution of the United States. . . . We are somewhat hampered by the prejudices and predilections of some Judges who administer the oath. In some cases the Judges require that twenty-five questions be asked; in other cases Judges insist on asking the questions themselves, selecting from lists supplied them by the Naturalization Service; some Judges make up complicated questions of their own to ask the petitioners for citizenship.

There the apologetics ended, and the commissioner concluded by asserting that his Bureau was doing the best it could under the circumstances.[73]

In 1939, a report prepared at the President's request by the departments of State, Labor, and Justice presented the following conclusion to the House of Representatives' Committee on Immigration and Naturalization: "While the Constitution requires a 'uniform' rule of naturalization, the fact that more than 2,000 Federal and State courts have naturalization jurisdiction, and the lack of any statutory provision by which the Immigration and Naturalization Service might prescribe the scope and nature of the examination to be accorded petitioners for naturalization, have resulted in much inconsistency, confusion, and contrariety of opinion and decision in this field."[74] Actually, the situation was neither so grim as the report asserted nor so salutary as Commissioner Houghteling believed. It is clear that considerable progress had been made since passage of the Naturalization Act of 1906. It is also fair to say that constitutionalism in the education of immigrants made halting yet substantial strides between 1914 and 1939.

VI

Scholars had relatively little to do with the "fetich." Many of them looked askance and quietly went about their business, exchanging information, insights, and major effusions over minor triumphs. When Max Farrand sent Edward S. Corwin a laudatory letter on the publication of *Court Over Constitution* (1938), Corwin replied that he "was much struck by your way of putting things in your statement that the Framers of the Constitution 'were struggling to express an idea and their experience was as yet insufficient.' "[75] Important publications did appear during these years; some were written by informed partisans like James M. Beck, others by lawyers who doubled as gentleman scholars, like Charles Warren, still others by prominent academicians who wrote primarily for their peers and students, like Andrew C. McLaughlin.[76]

Thomas Reed Powell, Professor of Constitutional Law at Harvard, was a partial exception. This Yankee iconoclast devoted his career primarily to long and penetrating essays for law reviews rather than writing books; but because of his wit and withering criticism, public journals pleaded with him for book reviews, and every so often he obliged them. When he did, the result was a provocative event. In 1923, for example, *The New Republic* got him to unleash his wrath on three devotees of the emergent cult. Powell's opening sentences warned that a wrecking ball would follow.

> One of the periodic phenomena of American history is the mystical adulation of the Constitution in the pious faith that it contains in itself the saving grace that will shield the interests of the worshippers from the ambitions of those whose interests are adverse. Self-styled patriotic societies have spent themselves lavishly in expounding the gospel according to Mammon and identifying it with the parchment that came from Philadelphia. On such occasions we seldom hear that our first national government was the offspring of force and violence and that our present Constitution is in a legal sense the offspring of a revolution against its predecessor.[77]

Powell's most famous assault of this sort appeared in 1925, when he reviewed *The Constitution of the United States* by James M. Beck. Privately, to Irita Van Doren of the *Herald Tribune*, Powell referred to Beck as "the idiot." Publicly, his prose a parody of Beck's simplistic style, Powell mocked Beck's mixed metaphors, and suggested that here was a new kind of book about the Constitution: "You can read it without thinking." Six years later Justice Harlan Fiske Stone asked Powell to remind him where the review had appeared so that Stone could have the pleasure of rereading it. More than eleven years later, Fred Rodell of Yale, no slouch as a cutting wit himself, called it "my favorite review of all time."[78]

Powell's verbal slaughter of the Solicitor General typified an amusing yet significant set of tensions: between professors of constitutional law and conservative lawyers, and between scholars and those "publicists" who wrote for a general audience. Beck more than reciprocated the scorn of Powell and others: "As [so] often," he remarked to Chief Justice Taft in 1929, "the College Professors attempt to reverse the Supreme Court." Or, as Professor Karl N. Llewellyn of Columbia wrote to Corwin in 1936, "One amusing thing to me is the way in which a tradition-ridden discipline, amid writing and training and schooling, [sic] a tradition can grow up fresh, in less than fifty years, that the Constitution always has been what conservative lawyers conceived it to be about 1901."[79]

Although few serious scholars were active participants in the cult of the Constitution, a small number nonetheless influenced the course of constitutional history. Of no one was this more true than Charles Warren, whose *History of the American Bar* (1912) and three volumes on *The Supreme Court in United States History* (1922) had a powerful impact upon

Chief Justice Taft and Senator Henry Cabot Lodge. Taft derived from Warren's work a hymn of praise to "the sound conservatism of the people." Lodge informed Warren that he had

> brought out, as I have never seen it brought out before, the most interesting fact that at the outset there was no apparent objection to the Court passing on the constitutionality of an Act of Congress; it seems to have been generally accepted. The great contests arose over the constitutionality of State laws. Now I should say there was no question at all about the power of the Court to pass on the constitutionality of State laws, but the objection to the Court, and we have some at this time, is directed to their power to pass on the constitutionality of the laws of Congress. I do not, of course, suggest that this is a new situation, but it is certainly a very recent one which has grown.[80]

Warren also enjoys the distinction that a scholarly article written by him in 1923 became the underpinning for a major Supreme Court decision fifteen years later—an unusual instance of intellectual "filter up" that supplies an object lesson in the far-reaching potential of scholarly endeavor. Justice Brandeis, writing for the majority, declared in 1938 that the Court's decision in *Swift* v. *Tyson* (1842) had been unconstitutional—the only occasion in its entire history when the Court explicitly ruled one of its own earlier decisions to have been unconstitutional.[81]

If scholars failed to perform much of a public educational function during these years, the Supreme Court did even less. Adhering rigidly to its time-honored modes of procedure meant that press coverage of its work was bound to be slow and, even worse, unwittingly inaccurate at times. The Court provided working space for the three major press associations. Representatives of those organizations sat close enough to hear what the justices said. Other members of the press "are compelled to occupy seats on the left hand side, back among the sightseeing visitors. Trouble is often experienced in hearing in this part of the court chamber. The voice of the speaking justice reaches them in mumblings." Printed decisions were not available until 1:30 or 2:00 p.m.; and journalists simply could not wait that long because "modern newspaper methods compel them to get their stories on the wire as early as possible, in order to catch the afternoon newspaper editions throughout the country. The result is that they must follow the decisions as they are read." Serious mistakes and misinterpretations occurred. Moreover, as one editorial complained in 1920, "unless a man is familiar with the history of a case and knows exactly what the decision of the lower court was, it is almost impossible for him to tell in language that the layman can understand just exactly the nature of the decision."[82]

So the Supreme Court continued to maintain the veil of constitutional mystification—a process that enhances cults but countermands public understanding of the U.S. Constitution. Further, constitutional knowledge and insight were more difficult to come by than they had been a century earlier. David Dudley Field succinctly explained why in 1879: "The Constitution of the United States is a great code in a small compass; the decisions and the commentaries to which it has given rise have swollen to hundreds if not thousands of volumes."[83] How could laymen possibly hope to cope with so much material when most of them were unfamiliar with the "small compass" itself?

VII

The constitutional "fetich" that flourished during the 1920s and '30s had several positive consequences, however. The combination of broader popular interest and technological innovations resulted in a "filter down" process that unquestionably affected a larger proportion of the population than had ever before been reached. In 1920, when Albert J. Beveridge completed his four-volume biography of *Marshall*, the author was deluged with fan mail and suggestions such as this one: "A few days ago the Brooklyn *Daily Eagle* asked for suggestions for a series of articles and I have taken the liberty of suggesting that they prepare a series from your 'John Marshall'. . . . An effort should certainly be made to put the contents of this book before the large mass of people who could not be induced to read a book of this character, yet they would read it if it appeared in a daily paper or periodical."[84]

A similar phenomenon occurred in 1922 when Charles Warren published his magisterial volumes on *The Supreme Court in United States History*; and in this instance the phenomenon persisted for almost a decade. William B. Munro, a political scientist at Harvard, wrote to Warren immediately: "I wish it were possible for you to write a little book of two or three hundred pages giving in broad review the high spots in your monumental work. Such a book would be of very great value in connection with our classroom study of American Government. The difficulty about using the large work is that no library can afford to own more than one set or at best two sets, and this is insufficient for use by a large class."[85] In 1924 an attorney in LaCrosse, Wisconsin, made a similar suggestion, as did John W. Davis (the Democratic presidential candidate in 1924) a year later. Warren eventually obliged his admirers in 1928 with *The Making of the Constitution*, a one-volume version of his trilogy, prepared with a wide readership in mind. In 1924, meanwhile, at the request of the National Security League, Warren worked up for national distribution a pamphlet on the Supreme Court. The League sent out 15,000 copies immediately and couldn't reprint rapidly enough to keep pace with demand.[86]

A similar pattern appears in the publishing career of James M. Beck, widely regarded during the 1920s as "Mr. Constitution" (though not by Thomas Reed Powell and his friends). As early as 1919, in fact, when Beck gave an inspirational address on Constitution Day, Senator Borah read it into the *Congressional Record* and distributed thousands of reprints. Three years later, when Beck published a little volume of lectures called *The Constitution of the United States*, it enjoyed the most extraordinary ripple effect: Secretary of the Treasury Andrew W. Mellon personally paid for the distribution of 2,000 copies to libraries throughout the United States; Eldridge R. Johnson, founder and president of the Victor Talking Machine Company, sent a special reprint to 10,000 schools and libraries; the National Security League began free distribution of soft-cover copies in 1923; and four years later an abridged version appeared for use in elementary schools. In 1924, when Beck brought out a much longer volume with a similar title, *The Constitution of the United States: Yesterday, Today—and Tomorrow?*, Secretary Mellon once again paid for the distribution of copies, and Eldridge R. Johnson picked up the bill for reprints sent to schools. Beck's enterprise had begun in 1922 as a three-part serial in *The Saturday Evening Post*, after he explained to the editor that "one of the great needs of the hour is to familiarize the masses with the history and essential principles of the Constitution." By 1928, 50,000 copies had been sold, and editions were also available in French and German.[87]

Meanwhile, special broadcasts about the Constitution began to be heard on the radio as early as Washington's Birthday in 1926 and Constitution Day in 1927. By the early 1930s such programs were commonplace, often reaching an audience of millions. When the broadcasts became overtly political (rather than purely patriotic or educational), as in 1936–37, those who offered constitutional exegesis on the radio were inundated with correspondence and telegrams.[88]

During the 1930s the role of constitutionalism in American popular culture also received a boost from occasional chatty essays that appeared in mass circulation magazines like *The Reader's Digest* and *The Literary Digest* (the latter printed more than one million copies each week). Both publications offered what the elite might call "pap": heavy on human interest, light on human minds. In April 1934 *The Literary Digest* featured an essay entitled "The Supreme Court—Nine Mortal Men." The subtitle (or leader) ran: "Misty, Omniscient, Living in an Intellectual Super-World, the Slow, Awe-Inspiring, Black-Robed Procession Proves to Be Made Up of Warm, Vital Human Beings." The most prominent photograph showed Chief Justice Hughes striding paunchily across a golf course, driving iron in hand, a determined set to his white-whiskered jaw. Not the stuff of law journals; not grist for the history of ideas; but just the sort of thing to keep ordinary folks interested in the Court, its personnel, and even a few of the vital issues on their agenda.[89]

By the mid-1930s, in fact, popular interest in the Court and the Constitution seemed to be rising once again, partially because of controversies over New Deal legislation; partially because some groups and individuals anticipated the forthcoming Sesquicentennial of 1937; partially because of new publications concerning the Convention of 1787; partially because those student essay contests enjoyed a fresh surge of popularity; and partially because the Constitution received attention from the Federal Theatre Project.[90]

This revival really mattered precisely because the U.S. Constitution is not "a machine that would go of itself." No one recognized that fact more clearly than the superpatriots. James M. Beck put it this way in an address to the annual meeting of the American Bankers' Association (1924):

> We attribute a magical effect to the Constitution of the United States. We think that the document by its own inherent power has controlled the destinies of the American people. The fact is that the charter, no matter how wise its provisions were in theory, would have been a failure if there had not been a people with a sufficient genius for free government to maintain its principles. Other nations have had nobly conceived constitutions, but they became mere scraps of paper because the people for whom they were intended did not have a sufficient sense of constitutional morality to make them effective.[91]

Ten years later Newton D. Baker reminded American readers that Jefferson retained his faith in democracy despite the fact that he kept at

Monticello, "in the drawer of a desk, a hundred written constitutions of democracies, all of which had failed." That sounds apocryphal, even though Baker had a commendable purpose: to short-circuit cynicism about constitutionalism. He observed that in the wake of World War I, many older governments collapsed and subject peoples discovered that they were at last free. "They called [for] constitutional conventions imitating our model. They made bills of rights, distributions of powers," and felt assured that governmental nirvana was drawing near. "One after another, these new governments failed," Baker noted, "and they failed, of course, because the constitutions they had adopted were not the product of their progressive history. They were not the crystallizations of their own experience." Baker's position represented one side of the spectrum: that the U.S. Constitution really could not be copied or exported; that it was destined to succeed because it had developed from our own historical experience.[92]

The other end of the spectrum is represented by a 1937 newspaper editorial. It noticed that Eamon de Valera's new Irish constitution had been approved by the electorate there. "History knows more than one Constitution or statute that just managed to scrape through and lived to be enormously popular and successful." The U.S. Constitution provided a prime example: it was barely ratified by the requisite number of states, and in three of the largest (Massachusetts, Virginia, and New York) the vote had been extremely close.[93]

Thus the point of view that we had 'been fortunate, that success in constitutionalism was a chancy affair, and that other societies might enjoy good fortune as well also had proponents during the 1930s. The two sides often collided over a series of political, economic, and social issues. Most of those issues would be resolved, one way or another, by the Supreme Court. Consequently the Court became a subject of deepening controversy during the 1920s, and increasingly so in the thirties. As Constitution Day approached in 1936, Congressman Sol Bloom asked his staff to prepare a fifteen-minute radio talk for Bloom to read on NBC. "And please," he asked, "include in the talk references to Providence and to the Almighty."[94] A wise directive. Few Americans were angry at the Almighty in 1936. As for the Supreme Court justices . . . that was another matter entirely.

CHAPTER 9

Decisions Are Politics
When Constitutional Questions
Are Up for Decision

IT IS ESSENTIAL TO BEAR IN MIND THAT constitutional conflict over policy issues persisted throughout the years when the cult of Constitution worship reached its peak. As Jerome N. Frank observed so aptly: "Our peculiar constitutional system makes it clear that decisions are politics when constitutional questions are up for decision."[1] Many of the contentious positions that people took during the twenties and thirties, however, seem to have been formulated as negative responses: to the League of Nations, for example, or to the dangers of socialism and centralization, or to the New Deal.

In addition the Supreme Court became intermittently controversial during these years, especially because it exercised the prerogative of judicial review more frequently than ever before. As Chief Justice Taft wrote in 1922: "The function of the Court to ignore [i.e., reject] as invalid in its decisions, acts of Congress in conflict with the Constitution, and presumably at the time supported by a majority of the people, has made the Court a stormy petrel in the politics of the country, and has promoted serious attempts to change and minimize the constitutional function and power of the Court."[2] Remarkable as it may seem, the Supreme Court's public image underwent a series of swift shifts during these two decades: from pejorative in the early and mid-1920s to rather positive during the transition from Taft to Hughes (later twenties and early thirties), to a notorious nadir during the mid-1930s followed by recovery and renewed esteem after 1937.

One reason for these rapid vacillations was stated very well in a letter that Charles Warren wrote in 1931: "I think most foreigners, as well as Americans, are ignorant of the many differences between the Constitution as it was expected to operate and the Constitution as it actually does operate." Recognition of this gap grew steadily between 1931 and 1936, leading to an unprecedented degree of discussion about the Constitution's adequacy for a civilization so radically altered since 1787. When George Bernard Shaw proclaimed at the Metropolitan Opera House in 1933 that "America is always talking about its Constitution," he meant to be provocative; but, in fact, he was doing no more than describing the situation at that time.[3]

Then, in 1937, when the Sesquicentennial of the Constitution happened to coincide with Franklin D. Roosevelt's controversial plan to "pack" the Supreme Court, Americans talked about their Constitution more than ever. Once the fuss had finished, the outcome seemed to be beneficial. The overall trajectory from 1920 until 1938, however, traced a path of constitutional concern, tension, political agitation, and eventual resolution.

I

When Chief Justice Edward Douglass White died in 1921, the eulogy prepared by a committee of the bar and officers of the Supreme Court— presented by the soon-to-be-disgraced Attorney General, Harry M. Daugherty—praised White for a quality that rather shortly would wane: "He [White] saw the dangers resulting from an abuse of the Constitution by those who seek to invoke it through the agency of our judiciary for their own purposes and against the legitimate rights of all the people."[4]

The most flagrant illustrations of this decline involved civil liberties during the Big Red Scare, and such famous Court decisions as *Schenck* v. *United States* (1919) and *Abrams* v. *United States* (1919). The fact that Justice Holmes handled the opinion for a unanimous Court in the Schenck case yet wrote a ringing dissent in Abrams means that an element of ambiguity must be allowed for in public perception of these cases. The war seemed to have created a twilight zone for proper application of the First Amendment. Between the arrest of Communist Benjamin Gitlow in 1919 and the Supreme Court's decision in 1925 to uphold his conviction, justice in the United States clearly became politicized to an unusual degree, and with it the meaning of constitutionalism.[5]

The contradictory positions that people took on problems of international relations caused them to invoke the Constitution in all sorts of curious ways. Late in 1918, for example, George Sutherland (former U.S. senator from Utah and ex-president of the ABA) delivered a series of eight lectures at Columbia University entitled "Constitutional Power and World Affairs." Sutherland offered "an entirely new theory of the Constitution," namely, that it should be strictly interpreted at home but very loosely "in connection with world politics." Essentially, Sutherland wished to legitimize the exercise of American hegemony wherever doing so served our self-interest, including imperialistic behavior. Therefore, he argued, "the Constitution is not a petrifaction, nor the charter of a petrifaction." A progressive nation functioning in an unpredictable world required a flexible Constitution. We lacked a clause that specified the right to acquire and govern territory beyond our borders. "Without this capacity for indefinite extension the written Constitution long since would have become a tradition, and the Union itself, perhaps, have fallen apart from its own weakness." Hence the need for broad construction on behalf of colonialism. Someone was bound to say so; but Sutherland suited it up as a full-dress rationale for international power plays.[6]

The League of Nations Covenant and the volatile issue of U.S. membership has been described many times before. The germane point here is that protagonists invoked the Constitution on both sides of the polemic. Proponents of U.S. membership quoted George Washington and other founders who had conceded in 1787–88 that the Constitution was an imperfect cluster of compromises—merely the best that could be achieved under difficult circumstances, and certainly not "written on tables of stone handed down from Sinai." That is why George Washington and his colleagues had provided an amending process. Some advocates of U.S. membership in the League enjoyed citing this point explicitly from Henry Cabot Lodge's biography of Washington (1889). Another favorite ploy was to compare opponents of the League with the Anti-Federalists, labelling both groups as prophets of gloom.[7]

Although those opponents liked to use Washington's Farewell Address as ammunition, David Jayne Hill posed their most persistent query in March 1920: "Shall our conduct as a nation be controlled by our own Constitution or by an unnecessary international agreement that overrules it?" Hill and his followers warned that as a member of the League the United States might be forced into a war against its own will, and Hill could not resist a slap at Woodrow Wilson: "Undoubtedly the Constitution of the United States as seen from Paris appeared a matter of little consequence."[8]

Even though Lodge and Hill hoped to curb the executive's control over foreign relations, presidential candidate Warren G. Harding supported them wholeheartedly. Speaking on Constitution Day from the front porch of his home in Marion, Ohio, Harding viewed the issue very clearly: "The Constitution or the Covenant. . . . The two are irreconcilable." Other critics trotted through the same arguments, tacked on scholarly justifications, and joined their cause to the cult: "The Constitution of the United States is sacred. At least it ought to be."[9]

Another question that elicited constitutional casuistry was not exactly new in 1919—how difficult or easy should it be to amend the Constitution, and how often?—but the prohibition amendment meant that that issue remained volatile throughout the 1920s. As early as 1912 Progressives had offered a plan to simplify the amending process.[10] Conservative constitutionalists replied that "new amendments tend to impair the dignity of a constitution," and then drew a revealing distinction: "The Constitution would soon be reduced to practically the level of the constitutions of the states if a very easy mode of amendment were adopted."[11]

True enough as a descriptive statement; but the issue that would split conservatives on this score was the Eighteenth Amendment. James M. Beck opposed it, explaining in 1919 that the framers never intended the Constitution to legislate morality. *The New York Times* observed that "the great importance of the prohibition amendment lies in its demonstration that you can do anything with or through the Constitution," a caution against constitutional cynicism; and *The Constitutional Review* editorialized that easy passage of prohibition "has called forth, from all parts of the country, a perfect flood of jocose and derisive proposals for the alteration of the fundamental law of the land." Others, however, like the well-organized Citizens Committee of One Thousand, a dry organization, printed such pamphlets as *Uphold the Constitution*, which contained Senator Borah's speech in support of the Eighteenth Amendment.[12]

Those who were hostile to amendments regardless of their moral content argued that social reform, if truly needed, should be achieved by ordinary legislation; that so many amendments had been passed or proposed that the public felt constitutionally confused; that the post–Civil War amendments merely "raised the mischief"; but, most frightening of all, that "there has been a good deal of talk, and it is increasing, of calling a convention to revise the Constitution in its entirety or to frame a wholly new Constitution."[13]

Ironically, when that apprehension was voiced in 1919, there seems to have been scant justification for it; nor would there be throughout the 1920s. Between 1932 and 1938, however, while economic conditions remained grim, experimental calls became more frequent and took many forms. In May 1932, Mrs. Jessie Wilson Sayre (Woodrow Wilson's daughter) told the annual convention of the Massachusetts League of Women Voters that the Constitution needed to be revised. She urged that a convention be held in order to prepare the requisite modifications. A few months later the Socialist Party adopted a platform that called for seven major items of constitutional change, ranging from proportional representation and passage of a workers' rights amendment to abolition of judicial review of congressional legislation. *Commonweal* even proposed that the President have power to dissolve the Congress, form an interim government, resolve crises, and then call for new elections the following November.[14]

In Franklin D. Roosevelt's first inaugural address, he pursued a line at once less alarming yet politically expedient: "Our Constitution is so simple and practical that it is possible always to meet extraordinary needs by changes in emphasis and arrangement without loss of essential form."[15] Although variants of that theme would serve as the anthem of his administration, more radical sentiments came from liberals sympathetic to the New Deal who hoped to accelerate the pace of socio-economic change. Three weeks after FDR's inaugural, for example, one scholar called for a new constitution based upon "social guarantees" rather than "individual rights," with the forty-eight states combined into nine administrative units and Congress replaced by a board of directors. From 1934 until 1938, William Y. Elliott of Harvard issued a series of calls for reform. The Constitution of 1787, he explained, "was never intended to govern the conditions of today. In the form in which it emerged from the compromises dictated by the small states it was a travesty, but a *workable* travesty." According to Elliott, the altered conditions of a new era required a managed economy run by a strong executive. "What is wanted today," he remarked, "is not a destruction of the great work of the Constitutional Convention, but rather its logical completion and revision in the light of modern needs."[16]

Elliott eventually revealed the real villain of the system, "The Supreme Court as Censor"; and the most drastic revisions of the U.S. Constitution that he envisioned were designed "to remove social policy from the control of judges."[17] That sort of strong dissatisfaction with the judiciary in general, and especially with the High Court, had been building ever since the early 1920s. It did not emerge suddenly during the thirties.

II

The Court confronted two difficulties: abrasive internal conflict, combined with strong external resentment from both public opinion and the other branches of government. The 1919–20 term turned out to be the most divisive in the Court's history until that time. Dissenting opinions were registered in 58 of the 180 cases handled. During 1921 the acrimony over one case became so divisive that the minority accused the majority not merely of bad legal judgment but of subverting the Constitution. Between 1898 and 1921 only six bills were introduced in Congress seeking to curb the power of the Court. Between 1922 and 1924, however, no fewer than eleven such bills appeared.[18]

To complicate matters, not all Progressives emphasized the same grievances concerning the Court; and the solutions these critics proposed were as varied as their complaints. Some opposed judicial review entirely, and condemned the undemocratic nature of "judicial usurpation." Others acknowledged historical justification for the legitimacy of review, but pleaded for greater restraint in its application. Still others found the practice entirely valid, yet complained bitterly about the capriciousness of five to four decisions in which one fallible man exercised the power to negate the will of the people's elected representatives in Congress. Thus in 1920, to cite just one example, a report prepared for the American Federation of Labor offered these proposals: first, that the Supreme Court *not* be permitted to ascertain the constitutionality of congressional acts; second, that it *could* declare state laws to be in violation of the U.S. Constitution; but third, to do so would require a margin of at least seven to two.[19]

Between 1922 and 1924 proposals offered by two different sorts of Progressives stimulated immense controversy and left a residue of discontent that lasted for years. When the Supreme Court declared the second Child Labor Law unconstitutional in 1922, Senator Robert M. LaFollette of Wisconsin chose the AF of L's annual convention as the launching ground for a major reform campaign. "We cannot live under a system of government where we are forced to amend the Constitution every time we want to pass a progressive law," he lamented. Therefore LaFollette asked the AF of L to promote a constitutional amendment that would permit Congress to override the Court by repassing laws with a two-thirds majority. Much discussed in 1923–24, that proposal became the most notable plank in LaFollette's presidential campaign of 1924.[20]

Critics pulled out all the stops: praised the Court as a restraint upon abuses of legislative power, refused "to believe that the Constitution is obsolete," and warned that LaFollette's proposition "vests temporary majorities with unlimited power and absolves them from all constitutional obedience." Those people satisfied with the status quo who felt the need for a national civics lesson welcomed LaFollette's assault upon the Court. "If a collision with false constitutional propagandism can awaken this generation to a knowledge of the Constitution as a vital living principle, something not only inherited but also to be preserved and fought for, the present onslaught may yield good fruit to the nation. For our generation has faced no intensive and widespread campaign on the fundamentals of the Constitution. In fifty-two years we have had no proposed amendment that compelled us to study fundamentals." This counterattack on LaFollette, an address presented in 1923 before the California State Bar Association, expressed contempt for the judgment of "transient congresses," and warned that a "proposition to shackle the Supreme Court as the arbiter of constitutionalism and as the balance wheel which co-ordinates the work of the government is tantamount to scrapping the Constitution." During the 1924 campaign the American Legion passed a resolution "despising" LaFollette's scheme; and all members were urged to take an active part on November 1, Constitutional Safety Day. David Jayne Hill continued to ridicule LaFollette after he suffered overwhelming defeat at the polls.[21]

The other proposal offered by a senatorial Progressive appeared during the same period and was frequently paired with LaFollette's in hostile discussions. Senator Borah had long been troubled by the growing number of five to four decisions. On February 5, 1923, he introduced a bill that would have required at least a seven to two majority before the Supreme Court could declare an Act of Congress unconstitutional. Although *The New York Times*, the *Wall Street Journal*, and other newspapers endorsed the idea, several members of the House offered co-sponsorship, and private individuals and civic organizations expressed enthusiastic support, Borah's bill did not even win Senate approval.[22]

Borah commanded such wide respect, however, that most of those who disagreed with him tended to be unusually polite in expressing their dissent. A common concern, for example, came from a Philadelphian writing from a ranch in Wyoming: "Is it not obvious that your proposal involves the transfer from judges in the Supreme Court to statesmen and politicians in Congress of a portion of the power now exercised (and in the main so well exercised for many generations) by the Supreme Court? And is it not clear that the power is *judicial power* and that to that extent Senators and Congressmen will be political judges?" A harsher critique emerged when the Sentinels of the Republic held their first national convention on December 10, 1923, in Washington, D.C., and issued a formal "challenge" to all "radical senators," demanding that they "prove or publicly withdraw repeated charges that the Supreme Court has 'usurped' its power to declare unconstitutional legislation invalid."[23]

Borah reintroduced the plan in 1924 and tried to persuade jurists, but especially journalists, that he did not regard his proposal as an attack upon the Court. "If these five to four decisions could be avoided, it would add much to the respect, both of the profession and of the layman, to the decisions of the Court. . . . After a bill has passed the House of Representatives and the Senate, met with the approval of the Attorney General and received the signature of the President, upon the theory that it is constitutional, it seems to me unwise to have it set aside while there are four members of the Supreme Court who agree with the legislative and Executive departments of the government."[24] Nevertheless he enjoyed no more success in 1924 than the previous year, and drew fire from men whose support he craved and whose views respecting the Constitution were in most fundamentals similar to his own.

Late in 1923, for example, *The Saturday Evening Post* (which printed two and a quarter million copies each week) published essays by Charles Warren and Albert J. Beveridge—both of whom took dead aim at the Borah-LaFollette proposals. Warren warned that these "disappointed reformers" became "particularly savage" in discussing five to four decisions, and that this complaint "is largely insincere, or rather a mere camouflage of the real complaint." As for LaFollette's plan, it would destroy the judicial branch and deserved scorn because, in Warren's words, "a statute enacted once may be held unconstitutional by the court; but if enacted twice it shall thereafter be held constitutional. A bad statute shall become good by repetition."

Beveridge defended the Supreme Court more generally against critics of judicial review. He insisted that the Court had been tougher on capital than upon labor, that it had been "far more liberal than state supreme courts," and that "the public is never told of Supreme Court decisions repelling attacks upon state and national legislation; whereas the public always is clamorously informed of exceptional rulings nullifying laws, most of which decisions were plainly right, only a few being doubtful, and none wrong beyond question."[25]

1. WOODEN FIRE BUCKET PAINTED OCHRE WITH A DARK GREEN BANNER AND YELLOW LETTERING HIGHLIGHTED IN RED (DATED 1802 ON THE BOTTOM). (*Courtesy of the Historical Society of Pennsylvania, Philadelphia*)

2. JAMES MADISON, BY CHARLES WILLSON PEALE (PHILADELPHIA, CA. 1792). (*Courtesy of the Thomas Gilcrease Institute of American History and Art, Tulsa, Oklahoma*)

3. MR. AND MRS. OLIVER ELLSWORTH OF CONNECTICUT, BY RALPH EARL (1792). ELLSWORTH, WHO HOLDS A COPY OF THE CONSTITUTION, SUCCEEDED JOHN JAY AS CHIEF JUSTICE AND SERVED FROM 1796 UNTIL 1799. HE WAS A MEMBER OF THE U.S. SENATE, 1789–96, AND CHAIRMAN OF THE COMMITTEE THAT DRAFTED THE JUDICIARY ACT OF 1789. HE WAS CALLED THE FOUNDER "OF THE WHOLE SYSTEM OF FEDERAL COURTS." (*Courtesy of the Wadsworth Atheneum, Hartford*)

4. ANDREW JACKSON, BY DAVID RENT ETTER (CA. 1832–33). THE OPEN VOLUME ABOVE SAYS "CONSTITUTION," AND BENEATH IT "AN ADDRESS TO THE PEOPLE OF SOUTH CAROLINA, DECEMBER 10, 1832." (*Courtesy of the Independence National Historical Park Collection, Philadelphia*)

BORN TO COMMAND.

OF VETO MEMORY.

HAD I BEEN CONSULTED.

KING ANDREW THE FIRST.

5. BORN TO COMMAND. KING ANDREW THE FIRST, ANONYMOUS
LITHOGRAPH (CA. 1832). THIS PRO-WHIG CARICATURE CONDEMNS
JACKSON'S VETO OF THE RECHARTER OF THE SECOND BANK OF THE
UNITED STATES. (*Courtesy of the Prints and Photographs
Division, Library of Congress*)

6. OVAL SILVER TRAY COMMEMORATING THE SEVENTY-FIFTH ANNI-
VERSARY OF THE SIGNING OF THE CONSTITUTION (MADE BY S. H.
BLACK OF BLACK, STAR & GORHAM, CA. 1862). THIS IS ONE OF THIR-
TEEN MADE FOR THE GOVERNORS OF THE THIRTEEN ORIGINAL
STATES. THERE IS AS MUCH EMPHASIS ON 1776 IN THE SYMBOLIC DE-
TAILS AS THERE IS ON 1787. (*Courtesy of the CIGNA
Corporation, Philadelphia*)

7. PLATE TO COMMEMORATE THE DEATH OF ELIJAH LOVEJOY,
KILLED BY AN ANTI-ABOLITIONIST MOB IN ALTON, ILLINOIS (MADE
IN ENGLAND, CA. 1837). THE INSCRIPTION ON THE PLATE EMPHA-
SIZES FREEDOM OF SPEECH AND THE RIGHT TO ASSEMBLE PEACE-
ABLY, RIGHTS PROTECTED BY THE FIRST AMENDMENT. THESE PLATES
WERE SOLD IN ORDER TO RAISE MONEY FOR THE ABOLITIONIST
CAUSE. (*Courtesy of the Margaret Woodbury Strong Museum, Rochester,
New York*)

8. INTERIOR VIEW OF INDEPENDENCE HALL, PHILADELPHIA, A CHROMOLITHOGRAPH DRAWN BY MAX ROSENTHAL AND PRINTED BY L. N. ROSENTHAL (CA. 1856). THE ROOM HAD BEEN REDECORATED IN 1831 BY AN ARCHITECT NAMED JOHN HAVILAND, WHO MADE THE FIRST ATTEMPT TO RESTORE ITS APPEARANCE TO WHAT IT HAD BEEN DURING THE REVOLUTIONARY ERA. (*Courtesy of the Independence National Historical Park Collection, Philadelphia*)

9. WASHINGTON ADDRESSING THE CONSTITUTIONAL CONVENTION, BY JUNIUS BRUTUS STEARNS (1856). ALSO ENTITLED ADOPTION OF THE CONSTITUTION, IT WAS REPRODUCED ON THE THREE-CENT STAMP ISSUED IN 1937 IN HONOR OF THE SESQUICENTENNIAL. (*Courtesy of the Virginia Museum of Fine Arts, Richmond*)

10. SIGNING OF THE CONSTITUTION OF THE UNITED STATES, BY THOMAS P. ROSSITER (CA. 1860–70). THIS STUDY SKETCH, WHICH HANGS IN INDEPENDENCE HALL, WAS THE PRELIMINARY VERSION OF A MUCH LARGER PAINTING THAT HAS DISAPPEARED. (*Courtesy of the Independence National Historical Park Collection, Philadelphia*)

11. UNION, ENGRAVED BY H. S. SADD AFTER A PAINTING BY T. S. MATTESON (CA. 1861). THE CONSTITUTION IS HELD BY LINCOLN AND WEBSTER. OTHER FIGURES IN THIS STRAINED ATTEMPT AT CONSTITUTIONAL CONSENSUS INCLUDE HENRY CLAY, JOHN C. CALHOUN, STEPHEN A. DOUGLAS, JAMES BUCHANAN, THOMAS HART BENTON, AND BEN BUTLER. (*Courtesy of the New York State Historical Association, Cooperstown*)

DECLARATION OF INDEPENDENCE,
Issued July 4th, 1776.

12. CONSTITUTION & LAWS, FROM THE *Ithaca Democrat* (JULY 4, 1882), EXEMPLIFIES THE DOMINANT NINE-TEENTH-CENTURY VIEW THAT THE CONSTITUTION FULFILLED THE DECLARA-TION OF INDEPENDENCE.

13. OFFICIAL INVI-TATION TO THE CONSTITUTION CEN-TENNIAL CELEBRA-TION, SEPTEMBER 15–17, 1887, IN PHILADELPHIA. (*Courtesy of the Historical Society of Pennsyl-vania*)

14. A FLOAT IN THE CIVIC AND INDUS-TRIAL PAGEANT, CONSTITUTION CEN-TENNIAL CELEBRA-TION (SEPTEMBER 15, 1887). (*Courtesy of the Free Library of Philadelphia*)

15. CHIEF JUSTICE JOHN MARSHALL, BY WILLIAM WETMORE STORY (1884). THIS SCULPTURE WAS FIRST UNVEILED ON THE GROUNDS OF THE U.S. CAPITOL IN 1884. THE ORIGINAL IS NOW LOCATED ON THE LOWER LEVEL OF THE SUPREME COURT BUILDING. THIS CASTING, A GIFT TO THE CITY OF PHILADELPHIA IN 1930 BY JAMES M. BECK, RESTS ON THE FAIRMOUNT PARK SIDE OF THE PHILADELPHIA MUSEUM OF ART. (*Courtesy of the Fairmount Park Commission, Philadelphia*)

16. THE CONSTITUTIONAL CONVENTION—PHILADELPHIA IN 1787—THE CREATION OF A STRONG AND TRUE UNION, BY VIOLET OAKLEY (1917), A MURAL LOCATED IN THE SENATE CHAMBER OF THE PENNSYLVANIA STATE CAPITOL IN HARRISBURG.

17. PRESIDENT AND MRS. CALVIN COOLIDGE, SPEAKER OF
THE HOUSE FREDERICK H. GILLETT, LIBRARIAN OF CON-
GRESS HERBERT PUTNAM, AND OTHERS AT THE DEDICA-
TION OF THE SHRINE OF THE CONSTITUTION AND THE
DECLARATION OF INDEPENDENCE (LIBRARY OF CONGRESS,
FEBRUARY 28, 1924). (*Courtesy of the National Archives*)

18. CASS GILBERT IN 1931, ARCHITECT OF THE U.S. SUPREME COURT
BUILDING, WASHINGTON, D.C. (CONSTRUCTED 1929–35). (*Courtesy of
the Prints and Photographs Division, Library of Congress*)

19. CONGRESSMAN SOL BLOOM, DIRECTOR GEN-
ERAL OF THE UNITED STATES CONSTITUTION SES-
QUICENTENNIAL COMMISSION (1935–39).
(*Courtesy of the National Archives*)

20. REPLICA OF THE SHRINE OF THE CONSTITUTION AND THE DECLARATION OF INDEPENDENCE (1937). THESE SHRINES WERE AVAILABLE FROM THE SESQUICENTENNIAL COMMISSION IN TWO SIZES: LARGE ONES FOR PUBLIC DISPLAYS OR DEPARTMENT STORES, AND SMALLER, LESS EXPENSIVE ONES FOR PRIVATE HOMES. (*Courtesy of the National Archives*)

21. SALES DESK AT THE LIBRARY OF CONGRESS EXHIBITION FOR THE SESQUICENTENNIAL OF THE CONSTITUTION (1937). THE WOMAN WEARING A COLONIAL COSTUME IS SELLING COPIES OF *The Story of the Constitution*, BY SOL BLOOM, FOR TEN CENTS. (*Courtesy of the National Archives*)

22. WINDOW DISPLAY AT THE HECHT COMPANY DE-
PARTMENT STORE, WASHINGTON, D.C. (1937). SIM-
ILAR EXHIBITS APPEARED AT OTHER DEPARTMENT
STORES IN MAJOR CITIES. THE OFFICIAL POSTER BY
HOWARD CHANDLER CHRISTY IS FEATURED. (*Cour-
tesy of the National Archives*)

23. THE FIRST OF FIVE DISPLAY ROOMS AT THE SESQUICENTENNIAL
LOAN EXHIBITION OF PORTRAITS OF THE SIGNERS AND DELEGATES
TO THE CONVENTION OF 1787 (HELD AT THE CORCORAN GALLERY
OF ART, WASHINGTON, D.C., NOVEMBER 1937 TO MARCH 1938).
(*Courtesy of the National Archives*)

24. MRS. RALPH E. DOHERTY, A GIRL SCOUT OFFICIAL, AND IRMA
BEVERLY SIEBEL OF TROOP 114 (TOURING THE SESQUICENTENNIAL
LOAN EXHIBITION AT THE CORCORAN GALLERY ON DECEMBER 18,
1937). (*Courtesy of the National Archives*)

25. WE, THE PEOPLE, BY HOWARD CHANDLER CHRISTY (1937). THIS PAINTING BECAME THE BASIS FOR THE SESQUI-CENTENNIAL COMMISSION'S OFFICIAL POSTER. (*Courtesy of the Thomas Gilcrease Institute of American History and Art, Tulsa, Oklahoma*)

26. THE OFFICIAL SESQUICENTENNIAL MEDAL-
LION, DESIGNED BY HOWARD CHANDLER
CHRISTY (1937). (*Courtesy of the National Ar-
chives*)

27. "OUR OVERWORKED SUPREME COURT," BY
J. KEPPLER (*Puck*, December 9, 1885).

For Beveridge, as for Warren, genuine abuses of judicial review were just about inconceivable, and attempts to "curb" the Court were worse than unjustified—they threatened the very equilibrium of our entire constitutional system. Throughout 1923 and 1924 Warren waged a campaign against critics like LaFollette and Borah. He won the applause of many in public life by pointing out that attacks upon the Court in general, and judicial review in particular, dated back to the days of Jefferson and Marshall—a fact that seems to have surprised and impressed a good many senators, cabinet members, jurists, attorneys, and even some historians.[26]

In 1925 Warren brought out a 300-page polemic entitled *Congress, the Constitution, and the Supreme Court* in which he repudiated LaFollette, Borah, and Beard by stockpiling evidence, organized thematically for a lay audience, in order to demonstrate that the founders had meant to establish the judiciary as a counterweight against improper uses of authority by the other two branches of government, and that accusations against the judiciary on grounds of "usurpation of power" were utterly groundless. The book continued to be widely read and remained authoritative, especially among politicians and judges, long after the immediate provocations of 1923–24 had been forgotten.[27]

The political controversies of those years created some curious coalitions and surprising animosities. Warren, a lifelong Democrat, wrote a pamphlet for the National Security League (heavily Republican) entitled *Borah and LaFollette and the Supreme Court of the United States* (1923), a critical analysis that served an important role in the propaganda campaign of the League's Committee on Constitutional Instruction. (I use the word "propaganda" advisedly. The committee's chairman sought pamphlets that would "appeal to the emotions of the reader.")[28] Thomas Reed Powell, who did not like the LaFollette and Borah proposals any more than Charles Warren did, nevertheless wrote a cutting review of *Congress, the Constitution, and the Supreme Court*, calling it "a high-grade propaganda tract," and irritating Warren immensely.[29]

Even James M. Beck and Hampton L. Carson, Philadelphia's two pillars of patriotic constitutionalism, came to blows between 1924 and 1926. In part they did so because of a conflict that was quite characteristic among conservative constitutionalists: Beck became somewhat disenchanted with the Court, considered it "subject, as all human institutions, to change," and carped at Carson's "philiopietistic attitude toward the Supreme Court." Beck suggested late in 1924, while serving as Solicitor General, that the Court ought to co-operate more closely with Congress—even to the extent of handing down preliminary opinions on the constitutionality of proposed statutes.* Carson criticized that suggestion in two open letters, as did many members of the bar; and even Chief Justice Taft was appalled at Beck's momentary blindness to the traditional concept of an independent judiciary. In 1926, however, when Beck ran for Congress with the backing of the Republican machine, Carson opposed him on behalf of a poorly organized reform group in Philadelphia. Beck received 60,000 votes to just 2,000 for poor Carson.[30]

William Howard Taft became Chief Justice in 1921, served for nine years, and exerted a profound influence upon the Court's policies, composition, and administrative procedures. He had yearned for nomination to the "sacred shrine" for years, and held very strong views about the character of those qualified to serve on the Court.[31] He regarded Wilson's nomination of Brandeis in 1916, for example, as "one of the deepest wounds that I have had as an American and a lover of the Constitution." Taft worked assiduously and unabashedly to influence not merely the appointment of federal judges, but even the selection of members to the Judiciary Committee of the U.S. Senate.[32] In 1922 he supported Harding's choice of Associate Justice George Sutherland, just the sort of man who would help to set the Court's tone over the next sixteen years. A disciple of Herbert Spencer, Sutherland regarded the U.S. Constitution as a "divinely inspired instrument." He served as president of the ABA in 1917–18, opposed the League of Nations, and usually voted against federal as well as state regulatory legislation. He would be a staunch foe of New Deal legislation.[33]

The conservatism of Taft's Court coincided with a strong wave of sentiment against governmental centralization that emerged in 1918 and persisted throughout the twenties. To many outspoken critics, the trend toward centralization exposed a serious constitutional problem. As Henry Cabot Lodge explained to Lord Bryce, complaining about Wilson's aggrandizement of national power: "Our own Constitution has for the time being been set aside and although the various laws which we have passed giving extraordinary powers are limited to the prosecution of the war, no one can tell how far we shall be able to return to our old constitutional limitations."[34]

In 1927, when James M. Beck delivered the first Cutler Foundation Lecture at William and Mary, he articulated the apprehensions of many Americans at that time.

---

* Beck suggested that when Congress felt uncertain about the constitutionality of a proposed law, it could, "by a joint resolution passed by a two-thirds vote, and signed by the President, request the advice of the Supreme Court in advance of legislative enactment."

Nothing more strikingly illustrates the profound changes in our constitutional ideas, due to the ethos of the people than this question of centralization. When the Constitution was adopted, the states had a very real consciousness of their own sovereignty. The consciousness of national unity was a very slow growth. The reluctance with which the states granted any measure of power to the central government and the fact that the Constitution was literally wrung from the states by the sheer necessity of social conditions, illustrate this fact. The success of the national government and the immense moral influence of George Washington slowly developed the idea of a powerful union. These causes, however, were insignificant as compared with the changes which were brought about through the influences of mechanical invention. The Union is held together today, not so much by the Constitution, as by the shining pathways of steel, over which our railroads run, and the innumerable wires, which, like antennae, co-ordinate the energies of the American people.[35]

Throughout the thirties opponents of the New Deal would shift the primary blame for centralization from technological advances to excessive meddling in peoples' lives by Washington officials and their pet programs.

Meanwhile a closely related concern for states' rights surfaced as one of the major constitutional issues during the 1920s and '30s. On Memorial Day, 1925, Calvin Coolidge urged a revival of strong state and local government. Beck attracted considerable attention in 1926 when he published *The Vanishing Rights of the States*; and others explicitly targeted the Supreme Court's growing tendency, ever since the early 1890s, to strike down state laws and thereby undermine their regulatory powers. As a Boston attorney complained to Henry Cabot Lodge: "The Supreme Court shows considerable ingenuity in finding loopholes when it wants to, but I hope it will not adopt any such insidious doctrine, which, through the power of the purse, would eventually bring all the States into subjection." Ever an astute historical observer, Lodge responded that "when States desire the help of the United States Government, I notice that they are not over particular about constitutional limitations, which is a great misfortune."[36]

The Supreme Court's activism ever since the 1890s seemed excessive to many critics and elicited such epithets as "legislative intervention" and "policy-making." Woodrow Wilson's comparison of the Court to "a constitutional convention in continuous session" seemed sufficiently apt that various public figures would reiterate the phrase throughout the twenties, thirties, and forties. It became a hackneyed theme in discussions of the Court by devotees as well as detractors.[37]

When Charles Evans Hughes succeeded Taft as Chief Justice in 1930, considerable speculation occurred as to whether continuity or discontinuity would be the dominant mode. By 1931 the signals seemed clearly indicated by a swell of essays with titles like "Our Supreme Court Goes Liberal," "The Supreme Court in a New Phase," and "The Supreme Court's Shift to Liberalism." Hughes had predominantly aligned himself with Holmes, Brandeis, and Stone (once the perpetual minority); and by persuading Justice Roberts to join them, he managed to compile a remarkably liberal record on cases involving civil rights, Minnesota's "press gag" law, and a reduction in the broad application of the Fourteenth Amendment on behalf of corporations and in restraint of state regulatory power exercised for the public welfare.[38] As one journalist concluded: "Far from being a threat to our institutions, the 'liberalism' of the Supreme Court may well prove to be a safety valve against a destructive radicalism, assuring the country that its institutions will be developed along the lines of a normal Constitutional evolution."[39]

Those trends would continue for several years, and the addition of Benjamin Cardozo in 1932 gave the "liberal" quartet an apparently reliable stability. One predictable result, however, was that conservatives like Sutherland and McReynolds, who had considered retirement, now resolved to hang on; and as several observers noted, Owen Roberts could not be depended upon to vote in any consistent manner. New issues and new economic legislation might cause yet another realignment. As one prescient author put it: "Never before have the people been more interested in the personnel of the Supreme Court and if this Court continues to hold in its hands the fate of all social and economic legislation, its membership will continue to be an issue in American politics."[40]

III

Yet another development accompanied the transition from Taft to Hughes. Between 1926, when H. K. Bush-Brown proposed the construction of "A Temple to Liberty," and 1935, when the so-called Temple of Justice opened, the Supreme Court finally acquired a permanent home.[41] It had been a long time coming. Back in John Marshall's day the Court convened in a geometrically improbable chamber, at once semitriangular and semicircular, located in the basement of the U.S. Capitol. The justices faced Franzoni's bas-relief of Justice, holding her scales, while Fame (crowned by the rising sun) sat on a pedestal and held the Constitution.

When the Senate acquired its new and enlarged chamber in 1860, the Court moved to the old Senate Chamber, a crescent-shaped room near the Rotunda, and remained there comfortably despite pressure from the Senate fifty years later when it once again coveted the space. Throughout the 1880s Senator Justin Morrill urged Congress to appropriate funds so that the Court could have a permanent home. Congress was not about to spend the Treasury surplus in such a frivolous manner, however, and the whole scheme had to wait until 1929, a ten-million-dollar appropriation, and approval by the Commission of Fine Arts for Cass Gilbert's neoclassical design.[42]

Although the construction of Gilbert's Parthenon has been narrated elsewhere, ideological aspects of the story which cast a curious light upon the history of American constitutionalism remain obscure. Gilbert's preeminence as an American architect (he designed the Woolworth Building in Manhattan, served as president of the AIA, and as director of the American Academy of Arts and Letters), his partiality for traditional rather than modern forms, and his familiarity with men like Taft and Beck made his selection inevitable.[43] The cornerstone ceremonies took place on October 13, 1932; early the next year Gilbert informed a British friend that the temple was "coming on splendidly . . . and it is as pure in style as I can make it. I hope it will cause some reaction against the silly modernistic movement that has had such a hold here for the last few years."[44]

It is not Gilbert's architectural conservatism that should give us pause, however, but rather his naïveté about international politics (see figure 18). During the later 1920s, like some other Americans, Gilbert felt strong admiration for Benito Mussolini. In May 1927, Gilbert enjoyed an interview with Mussolini in Rome. Afterwards the architect and his party went out to dinner and drank to "Il Duce's health, prosperity and long continued success. My impression of Mussolini is that he is not only a very great man, but that he is a very charming and fascinating man."[45]

In August 1932 Gilbert sent Mussolini some photographs of his designs for the temple of justice, accompanied by this explanation: "I have felt that I could find no more fitting architectural style in which to express this dignity and importance than the beautiful classic architecture of Italy." He closed by extending "most cordial wishes for your health and the prosperity of your great regime and the glory of Italy."[46] Mussolini responded with an inscribed photograph of himself, a keepsake that Gilbert cherished.

Ten months later Gilbert travelled to the famous quarries near Siena in order to select personally the marble that would be used in the columns of the new Supreme Court building. But first he went to Rome, and on June 5, 1933, had another, more memorable interview with Mussolini. The next day he wrote a fifteen-page memoir of their vis-à-vis, apparently for his family and closest friends. No portion of it has been published.

> I said I had chosen Italian marble of a light buff color from Montarrenti near Siena because of the beauty of the color and its especial fitness for the place. I described the Court as the highest judicial tribunal in the United States with power to interpret the Constitution, and as the final court of appeal. . . .
>
> I had the greatest admiration for him and for what he had done and is doing for Italy, and moved to withdraw. He put out his hand across the table and said very simply, "Good-bye, Good-bye!" We shook hands and I turned and walked rapidly to the door, reaching which I turned sharply around and raised my hand in the Roman salute—as he did the same—and I shall always think of him as standing in the somewhat dim light of that great room *alone*, with his hand up above his head in that most impressive of gestures, the Roman salute, which is so characteristic of the great organization he has created— the Fascisti—and which he has led so successfully for nearly eleven years. . . .
>
> He is making Italy proud of itself. He is restoring her ancient glory. He is not doing it by war or conquest, but by wise administration and firm foreign policy abroad, and wise and firm domestic policy at home. . . . Patriotism is taught to the children and to grown people alike, and when a whole people is convinced of the greatness of their country and the wisdom and greatness of their leader that country is to be respected. Mussolini is doing all this. He is the greatest man of his time. His place in history is secure. He is a benefactor to his country and to the world. May his regime long endure in continued success and beneficence.[47]

There is a certain irony to the response of Henry W. Taft, the former Chief Justice's brother, when he received Gilbert's design for the interior of the principal chamber: "The room will be very beautiful, and the selection of the Roman feeling particularly appropriate, as the Romans were the first of the ancients who developed a system of law which has lasted down through the centuries."[48] Or at least, until Mussolini's period of personal rule.

On May 27, 1935, Chief Justice Hughes presented the Court's opinion that the National Recovery Act (NRA) was unconstitutional—a massive blow to FDR's New Deal program and a major provocation between the Court and the White House. One week later the Supreme Court met for the last time in its old chambers. Charles Warren and William E. Borah attended for sentimental reasons; but it was a quiet session by contrast to the high drama a week earlier. On October 7, 1935, the justices opened a new term in their elegant quarters. But as Willis Van Devanter wrote to his sister: "There will be no ceremony. The opening will be just as if it were in the old quarters."[49] *The New York Herald Tribune* explained that "the very manner of the assembly will exemplify the American ideal of judicial detachment from the passions of politics. The Court will sit for the first time in the relatively small, stately marble chamber in the new Corinthian temple."[50]

Van Devanter was correct about the Corinthian temple of justice, but dead wrong regarding detachment from the passions of politics. Those passions had already begun to surge, and would increase their intensity during the next two years.

IV

In July 1934, at a celebration marking the eightieth anniversary of the Republican Party, two of the party's leaders accused the Roosevelt administration of "emasculating" the Constitution. They announced that one of the Republican slogans in the forthcoming congressional campaign would be "Back to the Constitution."[51] On many grounds and in numerous ways, opponents of the New Deal would call it unconstitutional. Congress, for example, had improperly transmitted legislative power to the President. Beyond that the laments, though lacking specificity, did not lack indignation. Several antagonists pointed out that the Constitution had been designed "to guard us against hysterical procedures during so-called emergencies," and that an emergency did not provide valid cause to disregard the Constitution.[52]

Others bemoaned the demise of American individualism. A critic denounced FDR for ignoring Constitution Day in 1934, but offered an explanation: "The President knows his New Deal has violated the Constitution in a score of particulars. The President knows the Constitution is emphatically a charter of individualism. How then, having pronounced the end of individualism, could he have been expected to celebrate the birth of the Constitution?"[53] The nemesis of individualism, of course, was collectivism; and "collectivistic state" swiftly became an epithet heard interchangeably with "centralization." It should come as no surprise that many critics of the New Deal rediscovered Thomas Jefferson and turned to his writings for inspiration. The incantation of Jefferson's name became a sort of shorthand for states' rights, low taxes, economy in government, and the perpetuation of laissez-faire principles of political economy.[54]

Amidst a lot of unctuous talk about unconstitutional "dictators" and "unseen foes in the background," the opposition organized its efforts to stop Roosevelt's juggernaut. The League of War Veteran Guardsmen stood for "national economic, political and social independence and individual freedom," and was activated immediately in 1933. Its leaders intended to "overthrow those who have undermined our Constitution of the United States and who have sought to overthrow our form of Government." During the autumn of 1934 the Constitutional Protective League, Inc., mobilized in order to "uphold and defend the Constitution of the United States and the Constitutions of the forty-eight States of the United States, and to expose and resist internal and external socialism and communism." One woman donated $5,000 to the Women's National Republican Club to initiate a Fund for the Defense of the Constitution. In the fall of 1935 a coalition of Republicans and conservative Democrats created the Southern Committee to Uphold the Constitution.[55]

The Liberty League depended heavily upon the services of lawyers from large corporations and prepared widely distributed legal opinions contending that the National Labor Relations Act was unconstitutional. *The New Republic* responded with contempt that the League's corps of legal experts could be "expected to be advocates of unconstitutionality, for they will contribute their 'services in test cases involving fundamental constitutional questions'—presumably only to private clients and not as dollar-a-year men in the Department of Justice."[56] The League also commissioned and distributed in 1935–36 a number of fourteen- to twenty-one-page pamphlets that explained the vast array of reasons why the New Deal was unconstitutional.[57]

On a Saturday evening in April 1934 a notable confrontation occurred—simultaneously satirical yet deadly serious—at the Gridiron Club's spring dinner, an off-the-record affair sponsored by the Washington press corps. Associate Justice Willis Van Devanter was present and enjoyed the occasion so much that he recorded it privately in elaborate detail. Most of the skits and songs were aimed at Roosevelt's policies, especially the NRA. No wonder Van Devanter found the evening "an intellectual feast." Halfway through the dinner Republican Senator David A. Reed of Pennsylvania, introduced as "a leading defender of the Constitution," was called upon to speak. He mocked the progenitors of New Deal legislation, sparked a good many laughs, praised the Constitution, discussed "the departures which we are now making," and implied that much of FDR's program was unconstitutional.

Roosevelt responded with wit and a well-informed sense of Washington history. Referring to opponents who feared that the Constitution would be violated, he observed: "They do not know what the Constitution is. They think it means today as applied to present conditions what it meant in the beginning, as applied to the conditions of that period. They do not know or realize that the Constitution has changed with the times. . . . We revere it and have an affection for it because of the principles which it reflects, but in its material applications it of necessity has changed in keeping with the changing times and conditions."[58] Van Devanter felt vexed that when he encountered people who had attended the dinner, they did not mention the constitutional confrontation. Perhaps, he speculated,

> this is to be explained by the fact that Moley, Tugwell and various other adherents of the Administration have been saying in various magazine and newspaper articles much the same thing about the Constitution that the President said. The President said nothing about the provision in the Constitution permitting changes by way of amendment and none of these other people refer to that provision. They seem to overlook the fact that the Constitution declares that it shall be the supreme law of the land and provides for its own amendment. . . . The purpose undoubtedly was that the Constitution should be a continuing charter just as written, save as the people make changes in it under the reserved power of amendment. If the President's position be correct, there is no need for any amendment and the several amendments which have been adopted up until now represent a needless waste of effort and time.

Van Devanter judged correctly that Roosevelt had not said anything off the record that he and his supporters had not said already on numerous public occasions. FDR enjoyed quoting the conservative former Chief

Justice, Edward Douglass White, that a grave danger arose "from the constant habit which prevails where anything is opposed or objected to of referring without rhyme or reason to the Constitution as a means of preventing its accomplishment, thus creating the general impression that the Constitution is but a barrier to progress instead of being the broad highway through which alone true progress may be enjoyed."[59]

Secretary of State Cordell Hull insisted that Thomas Jefferson would support FDR's broad constructionism because Jefferson had purchased the Louisiana Territory without congressional authorization. Attorney General Homer Cummings quoted Woodrow Wilson's belief that "the Constitution is no mere lawyer's document, but the whole of the nation's life." Postmaster General James Farley hammered the Republicans for the discrepancy between their rhetoric and their voting behavior in Congress. Assistant Secretary of State R. Walton Moore mocked "what seems to be a very silly attempt by Republicans to try to persuade the country that our constitutional system is threatened."[60]

Throughout 1934 and 1935, when the big issue troubling the nation was the New Deal's constitutionality, Roosevelt received considerable support from persons outside of his administration: from the Solicitor General of New York ("The American Constitution has become, whether so intended or not, an institution of changing economic and social forces"); from Republican Senator Hiram Johnson of California, who condemned "the timid and ultra-conservative who have . . . resurrected at each forward step the bogeyman of unconstitutionality"; from *The Cleveland Plain Dealer*, which reminded its readers that "in every crisis the party of the outs has charged the ins with misusing the precious heritage of 1787"; and from the writers of letters to the editor who loved to correct historical misreadings by state and federal officials.[61]

Professors of law, government, and constitutional history did not respond as a monolithic bloc. Andrew C. McLaughlin, for example, who had interpreted the history of American constitutionalism for forty years, conveyed to colleagues his ambivalent feelings about New Deal legislation.[62] Most academicians seemed to support FDR, however, and a number of prominent ones went public in various ways. Dean Roscoe Pound of Harvard's Law School pointed out that "an American Constitution is both a political and a legal document," and concluded that "it is not the Constitution which is lapsing but a superconstitution erected in its name on the basis of ideals which have ceased to give an adequate picture of our social or economic order."[63]

Thomas Reed Powell, Zechariah Chafee, Jr., Felix Frankfurter, and their former students at Harvard transmitted advice, memoranda, and ruminations on the legitimacy of pending legislation back and forth between Cambridge and Washington.[64] Thurman Arnold of Yale's Law School began to assist the Attorney General even before joining the Justice Department (1938–43), and persuaded his Princeton mentor, Edward S. Corwin, to help prepare historical briefs designed to fend off attacks against the Social Security Act. Between 1934 and 1937 Corwin went all out on behalf of the administration: radio broadcasts and magazine articles in support of New Deal programs; books attacking the Court; speeches elucidating the subtle relationship between symbol and reality in American constitutionalism; and testimony before a Senate committee on behalf of FDR's "Court-packing" plan in March 1937.[65]

As the Court struck down one major New Deal program after another during 1935–36, it provoked blistering attacks from the administration, the news media, the professoriate, and private individuals. Most of that story has been told before. What is especially pertinent to the history of American constitutionalism, however, is that the critical response caused many people, at last, to draw a clear distinction between the Constitution and the Court. As a priest from Wisconsin put it to Justice Cardozo: "The Constitution is not a cog in the wheel, it is the wheel and woe be [sic] anybody who tampers with the even running of that wheel, even though it be the Supreme Court of the United States."[66]

Two major opinions announced in 1935 indicated that the Court might lean either way in any given case, and thereby heightened public interest whenever an important decision seemed imminent. The opinions also produced quips that were much quoted at the time and have remained memorable ever since. On February 18, 1935, when the conservative justices lost the Gold Clause cases by five to four, a deeply depressed Justice McReynolds did not read his dissent but offered a few remarks instead. Because only formal opinions are recorded, we have divergent accounts of McReynolds's outburst. According to one, he sat upright and spoke as a prophet of doom: "The Constitution, it is hardly too much to say, is gone."[67] As the *Wall Street Journal* reported it on February 23, 1935: "The constitution as many of us have understood it, the Constitution that has meant so much to us, has gone. The guarantees which men and women heretofore have supposed protected them against arbitrary action, have been swept away."

McReynolds must have been an avid reader of U.S. constitutional history because his cri de coeur had a familiar ring. John Marshall made a similar remark during his last years; and when Taney replaced Marshall,

Daniel Webster wrote that Justice Story "thinks the Supreme Court is *gone*, & I think so too."[68]

The administration's narrow victory in the Gold Clause cases caused Heywood Broun to hope that "from now on the Constitution shall cease to be a strait-jacket but [instead] a more roomy garment, allowing full play to present and pressing human needs."[69] Instead, the Court declared the NRA unconstitutional late in May 1935. On the 31st FDR held a press conference in order to appeal beyond the Court to public opinion. He spoke for almost two hours to about two hundred correspondents, and in his most solemn manner turned a phrase that would reverberate constantly during the next two years: "When the Constitution was written, this country was in the horse-and-buggy stage . . . [now] the country is right back in the horse-and-buggy stage where it started."[70]

Rumors began to circulate swiftly that Congress might pass a constitutional amendment to limit the High Court's jurisdiction, an idea that would be endorsed in 1936 by the Democratic Party platform. In October 1935 a Gallup Poll asked the question: "As a general principle, would you favor limiting the power of the Supreme Court to declare acts of Congress unconstitutional?" Thirty-one percent said yes; 53 percent said no; and 16 percent had no opinion. Roosevelt, meanwhile, believing that the Court would make itself increasingly unpopular, held his tongue and bided his time.[71]

He did not need to attack the "nine old men" directly, of course, because in 1936 that became a favorite pastime for journalists and academics with acid-dipped pens. Heywood Broun asserted to his nationwide audience early in 1936 that "if the Constitution is to be conserved from the wild and reckless attacks made upon it by the sabotaging six [justices] it will probably be necessary to pass an amendment. . . . The people of America are rather tardy in realizing the fact that the structure of the basic document has been very radically altered by the ruling majority of the Court." Broun loved tough talk, and saved some of his toughest for the finale: nothing "can serve to explain the cavalier way in which Mr. Justice Roberts and his mob removed the general welfare clause from the Constitution."[72]

During the first half of 1936 hostility toward the Court seemed to be tempered by perplexity. As Thomas Reed Powell wrote to Carl Becker, "the way the nine boys are behaving these days is enough to make one despair of having any assurance as to what they will do next." The appearance of apologetics for the Court—what Powell called "constitutional drool"[73]—elicited a wide range of acerbic charges as well as more reflective analyses. In the latter category Corwin published *The Commerce Power versus State Rights,* subtitled *"Back to the Constitution,"* a critical response to the Court's negation of the Agricultural Adjustment Act, the Railway Retirement Act, and the Guffey Coal Act. Corwin supported the dissenters who in those cases had declared that the majority opinions rested upon "a tortured construction of the Constitution." He argued that the conservative justices were using judicial review improperly as "an institution of popular government," and explained that New Deal legislation could be sustained by the commerce power (Article One, Section VIII of the U.S. Constitution), used as it had been for much of the nineteenth century. A debate entitled "Horse and Buggy Days" between a Republican congressman and a New York attorney ended with the latter asserting: "Now, everybody talks the Constitution. All are 'Constitution Conscious,' " which was true enough by September 1936.[74]

In the arena of partisan journalism, three books seem to have been especially noteworthy. First, *Whose Constitution: An Inquiry into the General Welfare* (1936), by Secretary of Agriculture Henry A. Wallace, who argued that the Constitution was meant to be adaptable rather than "a sacred and changeless authority."[75] Second, *Storm Over the Constitution* (1936), by journalist Irving Brant, who called attention to the absurdity of appealing "to the composite mind of the framers of the Constitution" when there had been so much conflict at Philadelphia in 1787.[76] And third, *The Nine Old Men* (1936), by Drew Pearson and Robert S. Allen, which remained on the best-seller list from October 1936 through April 1937.

There was also spritely journalism from men like Charles A. Beard, who noticed that neither party took a categorical stand at its quadrennial convention during the summer of 1936. "Purists may be angry that neither party has spoken more positively, in tones of dogmatic thunder. They may demand that the sacred ark shall not be touched, or that harsh things shall be done to the Constitution and the Court. They may call the Supreme Court the rock of our ages, or denounce it as the arcanum of tyranny."[77]

One of the most valuable dividends of the constitutional crisis that became so apparent in 1936–37 was the amount of thoughtful exegesis on American constitutionalism that appeared in print. *The Annals of the American Academy of Political and Social Science* devoted its entire issue in May 1936 to "The Constitution in the Twentieth Century," something it had never done in its fifty-one-year history, and explained that it aimed at an audience of "thoughtful business and professional people" rather than scholars alone. All of the contributors summarized their essays on radio broadcasts that were aired over NBC Radio between February 4 and June 9, 1936. The participants included conservative politicians and journalists as well as liberal academics and officials of the Roosevelt administration— not to mention persons somewhat beyond the political mainstream, like Norman Thomas.[78]

The predominant theme of these publications was that the Constitution as written in 1787 could not be adequately responsive to the needs of the 1930s, that the states could not supply a suitable amount of economic regulation, and that the nation would have to choose between federal control and chaos. As Thurman Arnold put it: "Hopeful people today wave the flag of national power. Timid people wave the Constitution. Neither group is quite coherent as to specific objectives, but both feel better because of these respective ceremonies. . . . The only bulwark against change is the Constitution. But with the disappearence of the economic certainties, the actual words of the Constitution no longer appear like a bulwark. There is no settled faith in our form of government as the only workable type. Therefore the unified drive which accompanies settled faith is lacking. When belief in current symbols wavers, social unrest grows."[79]

There is abundant evidence that the messages in these books and essays did filter down to reach a wide audience. They did not persuade everyone, needless to say, but they resulted in such organizations as the National Popular Government League publishing a "layman's bulletin" in order to disseminate "in simple language" the most complicated constitutional issues of the day. In addition, an annotated edition of the Constitution, published by the U.S. Senate, began to achieve wide circulation.[80] National recognition of the importance of constitutional literacy was once again at hand.

V

Although Franklin D. Roosevelt waited warily until February 5, 1937, to unveil his plan to add a Supreme Court justice for each one who reached the age of seventy but refused to retire, his bombshell could not have been quite the surprise that many students have claimed. Late in 1936, for example, George Creel wrote in *Collier's* that "nobody doubts the authority of Congress to change the number of justices. . . . The possession of power, however, does not compel its exercise. . . . We can't have a Court which holds public respect because of its freedom if the judges are suspected of being bound to any organization."[81] Remarkably prophetic and widely read words.

Although the genesis and politics of Roosevelt's "Court-packing" plan have been exhaustively discussed,[82] a few items pertaining to the implications of this episode for constitutionalism in American culture can be added. First, the impassioned correspondence that congressmen (and justices) received from ordinary constituents reveals that a great many people *still* conflated the Supreme Court with the U.S. Constitution.

- "To grant the President his requirement of a Subservient Supreme Court which will rubber stamp whatever legislative enactment he deems best for the country would destroy our constitutional system of government."

- A telegram: "This is direct attack upon American system of constitutional government."

- "In all my life, I have never been so stirred about any thing as I am about this matter, because I firmly believe that, if Roosevelt gets his way in this matter, it will result in the beginning of the end of the form of Government under our Constitution."[83]

Second, the *cause célèbre* brought to the fore once again public consideration of the LaFollette-Borah proposals of 1923–24: namely, that to declare an act of Congress unconstitutional should require more than a bare majority, and that Congress might re-enact by a two-thirds vote a law that the Supreme Court had set aside.[84]

Third, it forced Senator Borah himself into a less ambiguous stance (than he had taken during the 1920s) as a staunch defender of the Supreme Court and judicial review. Borah had decided to make strict support for the Constitution a major issue in the 1928 presidential election. Hence his wholehearted statements on behalf of prohibition, his opposition to a federal antilynch law, and his acquiescence in white supremacy where it enjoyed the support of state law. In January 1936 Borah published in *Redbook Magazine* a categorical defense of judicial review. As he explained: "We are not living under a usurped judicial power. The power of the Court to void an act of Congress on the ground that it is unconstitutional is plainly and unmistakably conferred by the terms of the Constitution." (That was not true, in fact, but Borah's essay was reprinted in *Reader's Digest* and read into the *Congressional Record* by Senator Vandenberg of Michigan, from which it enjoyed wide distribution.) Speaking at Constitution Hall on September 16, 1937, Borah revived yet again the delusionary metaphor to which James Russell Lowell had objected half a century earlier: "The strongest assurance of its [the Constitution's] perpetuity is the fact that it affords perfect machinery for gathering up, as it were, and formulating into laws and policies the reserve common sense of a great people." The Constitution perceived once more as a perfect machine for making the popular will operational.[85]

Speaking in Detroit on Constitution Day, 1937, Senator Vandenberg praised the framers for conceiving a system of checks and balances, warned against destroying that system, and attacked Roosevelt: "When the recent Senate turned back the effort to chain the Court to executive and legislative control, it not only saved this constitutional anniversary from becoming a hollow mockery but also it saved the soul of the republic." He concluded with that everlasting confusion: "When the Supreme Court speaks it is the Constitution—it is the people—speaking."[86]

If Constitution Day provided the occasion for numerous attacks on FDR, it also supplied the administration and its allies with an opportunity to remind the nation that the Constitution "is a living organism which must adjust itself, through amendment, to an ever-changing social order." Roosevelt himself addressed a huge throng on the Washington Monument grounds as well as the nation by means of live radio. Meanwhile his cabinet and many Democratic governors fanned out across the nation to convey similar messages to regional audiences.[87]

One tack that Roosevelt and his supporters liked to take de-emphasized the importance of judges and lawyers with their arcane knowledge. As Ferdinand Pecora, a justice of the New York State Supreme Court, pointed out: "Neither the Constitution nor common law was designed to shackle the present to legal rules and principles of the dead past." In his Constitution Day address, FDR declared that the Constitution was a "layman's document, not a lawyer's contract," an assertion that elicited a blistering counterattack from the ABA. That, in turn, led to a vigorous tiff during 1937–38 over whether or not it was proper to consider James Madison a lawyer; and then in 1938 to more important discussions, sparked by the appointment of Hugo L. Black, concerning how learned a lawyer needed to be in order to serve on the Supreme Court.[88]

Three related points have become clear with the advantage of hindsight. First, that a fair number of liberals and many Democrats had grave misgivings about the President's plan to enlarge the Court—some on constitutional grounds, others for reasons of political expediency.[89] Second, soon after the Senate defeated FDR's proposal and he began to utilize vacancies created by the retirement of Van Devanter and others to reshape the Court's ideological inclination, the Court's reputation rebounded and it swiftly achieved higher public esteem than it had enjoyed since 1931–32.[90] And third, we scarcely appreciate just how sensitive those olympian justices were (and are) to public opinion—the extent to which they read what is written about them and worry about their reputations.[91]

VI

In other respects the political consequences of constitutionalism during the New Deal are less clear-cut and sometimes just plain surprising. Despite the steady ascent of Thomas Jefferson's reputation during the 1930s, for example, the basic thrust of these years was Hamiltonian: toward increased centralization, nationalism, and broad construction of the U.S. Constitution as an enabling document. Although Roosevelt and his speechwriters took every opportunity to claim continuity with Jefferson, the fact remains that his values gave considerably more comfort to laissez-faire conservatives.[92] Moreover, although Madison and Hamilton have traditionally symbolized divergent strands of the American constitutional tradition, writers on the right as well as on the left increasingly tended to lump the two together like Tweedledum and Tweedledee.[93]

James M. Beck, however, admired Madison and disliked Hamilton; so did many other devotees of the states' rights tradition. Irving Brant, on the other hand, who would do more than any other writer to rehabilitate Madison's reputation *after* World War II, was exceedingly critical of Madison in 1936. Brant contended that "not one statement made by Madison after 1790 can be relied upon. In the Constitutional Convention he was the clearest expositor of a nationalism based on political and economic realism; in later partisanship he denied his own work and that of his fellows."[94]

As for the rest of our political pantheon, George Washington was commonly quoted on both sides of every constitutional issue. Abraham Lincoln, who had been accused so often of flagrantly unconstitutional behavior, was idealized in 1938 as potentially a model member of the 1787 Convention: "his would have been one of the most powerful voices for the system of checks and compromises which was actually adopted." And in 1938 the Communist Party of the United States adopted a new constitution that for the first time supported the U.S. Constitution. The preamble stated that the party would perpetuate "the traditions of Jefferson, Paine,

Jackson and Lincoln and of the Declaration of Independence," and that it "defends the United States Constitution against its reactionary enemies who would destroy democracy."[95]

By 1937–38 constitutionalism in the United States had begun to be affected, as never before, by political events in Europe. In 1936, for example, Stalin promulgated a new constitution for the Soviet Union. American liberals and radicals responded generously at first. The *New Republic* and *The Nation* proclaimed the arrival of Russian democracy. Other observers were more restrained; yet even the *Chicago Tribune* approved because the new document seemed to repudiate Communist dogma and contained the "essentials of real democratic government." As the purge trials began and continued through 1937, however, the *Washington Post* mocked Moscow's "dreams of liberating humanity," and observed that "its new and 'democratic' constitution is something to stir ironic smiles." By the early months of 1938 it had become clear, even to favorably disposed journals of opinion, that Stalin's constitution was a farce. Hence one American speaker at the Sesquicentennial in 1937 noted that despite Roosevelt's unpleasant controversy over the Court, none of the three branches of government had been able to dominate the others. "Under party-dominated constitutions, as in Russia and Germany, such conditions would have led to at least two purges."[96]

The Weimar constitution provided an even sadder spectacle of political cynicism. Its demise also helped apprehensive Americans to appreciate that their conflicts did, after all, take place within a genuine context of consensus. The Weimar constitution had been adopted by a large majority of the German National Assembly meeting at Weimar late in July 1919. Implementation of it was problematic from the outset, however, and the state of emergency declared in 1923–24 made a travesty of the new system. Dissolution of the Reichstag in June 1932 led to domination by National Socialists, who used the constitution's emergency provisions as a means of abrogating it. Hitler phrased it brutally in 1930: "The Constitution only maps out the arena of battle, not the goal." By 1933 a good many constitutional lawyers in Germany busied themselves by trying to legitimize a one-party authoritarian state within the Weimar framework. The presidential dictatorial powers contained in Article 48 of that constitution gave Hitler all the leverage he needed. After the bloodbath of June 30, 1934, constitutional government had been fully supplanted by an authoritarian state.[97]

Those who accused Franklin D. Roosevelt of "constitutional dictatorship" may have been sincere; but they must have been oblivious to the real and frightening trend taking place across the Atlantic. The failure of constitutionalism between the wars in Germany and Japan made the American experience look very good indeed.[98]

That experience had demonstrated the restorative power of its self-correcting features, despite the fulminations of those who would resist change ("why should the Court be made the whipping boy for all the ills that flesh is heir to?") and the impatience of those who sought swift solutions ("a healthy state of civil society, and not the Court, is the ultimate safeguard of all civil liberty").[99]

Unfortunately the American experience had not yet driven home one lesson definitively: that the Court as an institution was distinct and separable from the Constitution. A great many citizens, agitated by the passion of Court politics in 1937, continued to ask of Roosevelt's supporters: "Are you for the destruction of our Constitutional system?" They accused liberal academicians of being "engaged in helping the politicians, socialists, and communists in an effort to wreck the Constitution." The charge was untrue as well as unfair; and yet even the academicians seem to have lost their capacity to illuminate with clarity. For a generation after 1937, popular textbooks would continue to proclaim, taking their cue from Felix Frankfurter, that "the Court is the Constitution."[100] How any intelligent American could continue to believe that in the wake of the crisis of 1935–37, I do not know. Tired clichés do not die; they become the epigrams of textbooks.

CHAPTER 10

My God! Making a Racket out of the Constitution

ALTHOUGH THE UNITED STATES CONSTITUTION Sesquicentennial Commission did not muster its initial meeting until August 26, 1935, Congressman Sol Bloom of New York City first introduced a resolution on February 8, 1934, calling for such a commemoration. Unlike the near-fiasco of 1887, a few farsighted individuals at least ensured that advance planning would occur. In addition, the other two sources of Centennial tension, interurban rivalry and the failure of federal financial support to materialize, were not so problematic in 1937–39. (Congress authorized a total of $485,000, though only $360,000 was ultimately appropriated.)

Despite the solution of major problems that had vexed Congressman Kasson's committee in 1887, the Sesquicentennial succeeded by the seat of its pants. Once again the sponsors confronted a problem of which date or dates to celebrate—thereby provoking an unpleasant dispute between Director General Bloom and the Sons of the American Revolution—as well as difficulties inherent in dramatizing a document, albeit a very important document. Bloom and his well-meaning staff, moreover, seem to have been far more fascinated by matters of factual accuracy (their own, that of speechifying politicians, and the authors of various school texts) than they were by the nature of the governmental system that had effectively endured for a century and a half. The Washington-based staff mostly consisted of pedantic fuddy-duddies rather than political philosophers.

In Philadelphia a gala water carnival and a Solemn Pontifical Mass got almost as much attention as the Constitution's actual anniversary. In

New York the inauguration of George Washington's government in 1789 became the pretext for a festive World's Fair at which the wonderful Trylon and Perisphere overshadowed the presidency and our tripartite pattern of republican institutions.

Insofar as the nation received a civics lesson in 1937, it did so not because of the Sesquicentennial per se, but because Franklin Roosevelt's "Court-packing" plan kept a lot of people highly agitated about constitutionalism for much of the year. When the DAR gathered in Washington during April for its forty-sixth annual Continental Congress, the president of the Sons of the American Revolution, Messmore Kendall, addressed the Daughters at Constitutional Hall. "The drafting of six unneeded members of the Supreme Court won't make us walk better," he declared, "and may instead cause us to lose our balance. We must watch for political streptococci which will pollute our red, white and blue blood, and for foreign surgeons who would operate on our checks and balances and amputate our rights."[1]

Roosevelt's Court crisis probably saved the Sesquicentennial from the doldrums of dull ritual. As it turned out, a lot of folks cared, put on patriotic pageants, distributed publications of dubious distinction, mounted unimaginative exhibitions, delivered interminable speeches, and worshipped at the "Shrine of the Constitution." But they needed a cause, an antagonist, and some reason to remember what 1787 had been all about. Franklin D. Roosevelt supplied all three. When the Women's National Republican Club decided to convene a conference on Constitution Day, September 17, 1937, the organization's president explained that "this year, when the Supreme Court issue has made Americans more 'Constitution-conscious' than they have been in the 150 years since the birth of the Constitution, it is particularly fitting that we should celebrate the occasion."[2] So it was.

I

Because Sol Bloom had previously served as director of the highly successful Bicentennial of George Washington's birth (1932), he had an experienced staff ready to set its mind to the nation's next major observance. Patriotic and historical organizations willingly turned their attention to such a celebration, and Bloom's crew responded with enthusiasm. As early as 1933 the New York State Historical Association passed a resolution calling upon Congress to make funds available for a Sesquicentennial four years later: "In a world distraught by desperate experiments of arbitrary rule the sagacity and public spirit of those who framed this instrument, now oldest among written national constitutions, are especially entitled to our careful study and reverent gratitude."[3]

Considering the federal government's lamented failure to provide a penny for support in 1887–89, one might have expected a swifter and more suitable response the next time around. John C. Fitzpatrick of the Library of Congress, who served Bloom throughout the planning as a historical consultant, found it altogether fitting "that the celebration of the framing and ratification of the Constitution of the United States should be aided and directed by that Government itself, which the Constitution established."[4] Although his rationale seems perfectly sound, Congress responded slowly, failed (because of a Senate filibuster) to pass the first bill that Bloom introduced in 1934, and finally gave its authorization on August 23, 1935. Senator Henry F. Ashurst of Arizona served as co-sponsor; President Roosevelt was named titular chairman of the Commission; Ashurst as vice chairman; plus four other senators (including Borah of Idaho and Joseph T. Robinson of Arkansas); five members of the House, with Bloom as Director General; and five presidential commissioners to complete the roster. Once the Commission had formally met at Vice President Garner's office on August 26, almost all of the planning was handled by Bloom's staff.

Most of the activities they envisioned are described in a detailed forty-page document printed by the 74th Congress in 1936. Under the rubric "advance activities," it noted that Bloom had contacted the mayors of larger cities and the presidents of patriotic and historical societies in order to learn what they had been doing to observe Constitution Day in recent years and to solicit their "ideas and suggestions" for the Sesquicentennial. The Commission intended the scope of the celebration to be comprehensive—reaching to the grass roots. As Senator Ashurst had declared on February 14, 1935, the supervisory board would be authorized "to cooperate with the several States and their political units including cities, villages, towns, and hamlets in suitable commemoration of the event. The Commission shall request all churches to hold appropriate services in honor of the event. The Commission shall invite the schools, both public and private, societies, the press, the radio, and the screen to assist."

The Commission urged the appointment of a comparable planning group in each state, territory, "and insular possession as soon as practicable." Similarly, the mayors of every city and town were exhorted to form local Constitution committees that would cooperate with state and national commissions. The latter pledged to "furnish the city and town committees with plans, literature, and other assistance." Finally, "organizations and institutions of whatever character—civic, business, labor, educational, religious, fraternal, literary, social, and others—will be urged to appoint their Constitution committees to plan for the celebration within their respective organizations." All of which was summarized and structured in a most elaborate "Organization Chart" that indicated not merely who would do what, but the vast array of activities contemplated.[5]

The Commission envisioned a remarkable range of subunits: a historical division "to make available the fundamental materials upon the formation and ratification of the Constitution"; a library division to service libraries throughout the country, and to distribute "Shrines of the Constitution" (see figure 20) and prepare "an outline of appropriate ceremonies to be observed in unveiling the shrine"*; a legal division to co-operate with that profession through various channels (the ABA, law libraries, and law schools); a women's division that would "bring to every woman in any organization a deeper understanding of the past, the inspiration and power radiating from this period of history, and a knowledge of the principles of the Constitution"; and above all, an education division, whose primary responsibilities would be co-ordination with school administrators and educational agencies, as well as the preparation of an "appreciation course" whose objectives would be "to develop in the American mind a consciousness of the Sesquicentennial Celebration of the Formation of the Constitution, focalizing the interest upon the historical and educational character of this memorable observance." The education division was also supposed to stimulate a constitutional handbook for the schools, a variety of writing contests (essays, theatricals, pageants, and poems), oratorical contests, and even a "journalistic achievement series" to foster the inclusion of materials on the Constitution in high school magazines.[6]

The Commission also projected a music division, special publications, a film about the Constitution, a major art exhibition, planting millions of "Constitution trees," the distribution of posters, banners, buttons, medals,

---

*"It is planned to prepare a suitable case or shrine, to contain an exact facsimile of the Declaration of Independence and the Constitution, for the purpose of providing libraries throughout the Nation with authentic reproductions of the documents for exhibition purposes.

"Through this medium, school children, and adults as well, throughout the country, may see these great documents encased in permanent and dignified form. Each city and town may have a permanent shrine commemorating the history and tradition of America.

"The shrines, when ready at the various libraries will be installed or unveiled with appropriate ceremonies, as a permanent possession.

"It is also the plan of the Commission to have Constitution shrines made by manual-training classes of the schools throughout the United States, for use in public schools and libraries, and the Commission proposes to issue a certificate of merit to all students throughout the country contributing their services in the construction of shrines for the display of the Constitution and the Declaration of Independence."

and the promotion of "pilgrimages" to Washington, D.C., and Philadelphia. A pilgrimage certificate would be awarded as a "souvenir and keepsake" to show that the owner had visited either of the cities but especially "the Shrine of the Constitution," the case in which the document was displayed at the Library of Congress (see figure 21). Facsimiles of the Shrine were available in two sizes: a larger reproduction for department stores and civic organizations, and a smaller one suitable for reverence at home. The Commission's *Report* acknowledged quite candidly the importance of public relations. Under that category it announced the intention "to use every possible avenue for conveying information to the American people. For this purpose the newspapers, magazines, radio, motion pictures, posters, and the lecture platform will be throroughly utilized."[7]

Throughout 1935–36, Sol Bloom recognized that he faced a much more difficult challenge than the Washington Bicentennial of 1932. "First, I had a document to work with instead of a man. Second, I had not a single anniversary to commemorate, but a number, stretching over almost two years." That challenge prompted Bloom to contemplate connecting the "dry document" as much as possible to the immortal man. Hence his hope for a book to be called *Washington and the Constitution in Fact and Fable,* a scheme from which his assistants dissuaded him.[8]

Although Bloom believed that all dates significant to America's constitutional genesis ought to be observed, the purist's predilection that he shared with his staff for June 21, 1788, when New Hampshire ratified, placed him on a collision course with superpatriotic organizations. In 1936, when the Commission contemplated a shift of Constitution Day from September 17 to June 21, the Sons of the American Revolution had conniptions. John C. Fitzpatrick, a stickler for historical authenticity, provided his boss with ammunition, though to no avail. "It is our patriotic duty to conform to the plan and purpose of the Convention. That plan and purpose was that the Constitution should come into existence and become a living, vital force in the life of the nation, *the instant the ninth state ratified.* . . . June 21 was the day the Constitution became alive and no amount of patriotic custom, or disinclination to face facts, can alter the constitutional provision which brought about that date. It is unfortunate that mistaken custom has developed the wrong date of September 17 as the principle anniversary of the Constitution; but are we going to continue a mistake which is plainly proven by the text of the constitution itself?"[9] September 17 remained unchanged as Constitution Day.

Bloom, who was born in Pekin, Illinois, in 1870, had been successfully engaged in the real estate business, construction, publishing, and theatricals before entering Congress in 1923 (see figure 19). As Director General of the Commission he depended heavily upon a staff of half a dozen: Owen Kane, who dealt with the press and headed the art department (he helped to arrange for the extensive exhibition at the Corcoran Gallery of Art); Harry E. Wilhelm, who could recite from memory the Constitution (including all the amendments), the names of the signers, and the Declaration of Independence; Dr. Clarence R. Williams, once a student of Dixon Ryan Fox at Columbia and an expert on the history of ratification; and an aide named E. L. Fuegel who served as a funnel to the two fact-finding and ghost-writing gophers for the Commission: John C. Fitzpatrick and David L. Matteson.[10]

Matteson grew up in Nevada City, California, studied at Berkeley, and then (American history and government with A. B. Hart) at Harvard. He possessed a good sense of humor, could be quite irreverent about the Commission's activities, and loved to twit Bloom and others about historical inaccuracies. Whenever a historical drama or a politician's speech about the Constitution reached Bloom's desk, the congressman bucked it to Matteson for his assessment. Matteson always obliged with crisp analysis. An illustration from February 1937 concerned Joseph Lister Hill of Alabama: "This is an excellent example of what a speech by a national representative should not be. . . . He is so intent on excoriating the Supreme Court for its New Deal decisions that he gets all tangled up in his own verbosity. . . . His statement that the Constitutional Convention of 1787 four times refused to grant the Court the right it now exercises, is all wrong." Or this memorandum concerning one of Bloom's pet projects for popularization, a little "Constitution Book."

I must confess to considerable amazement when Mr. Rodgers handed me the Queries and Answers that are to go in the Constitution "Ten Cent" Book to find that there were also a bunch of anecdotes and similar little essays utterly foreign to the purpose of the book. As I understand your project, it is to give as far as possible in small compass a clear and correct understanding of the origin and meaning of the Constitution. Surely this is not promoted by sticking into the middle of the work some eleven stories or essays, none of which have any connection whatever with the subject in hand, except those that are a list of the dates and votes of ratification, which are clearly admissible; and the story of Franklin's speech for prayers in the Convention, and even the last does not tell the story with complete accuracy, but leaves at the end a quite different impression from what really happened. As to the rest, they are almost without exception not only completely lacking in relevance but apocryphal and incapable of verification.

Bloom capitulated promptly and completely, "because I want to try and make this ten-cent book full of good information, and want it to have the largest circulation of any book, or of all the other books together. There should be millions of these gotten out if we can get the right kind of book and the right material, and, thanks to you, authentic information."[11]

Matteson's obsession with historical accuracy was matched by that of Fitzpatrick, an archivist and historian who worked at the Library of Congress from 1897 until 1928, when he became the editor of a massive edition of George Washington's correspondence. In April 1936, E. L. Fuegel sent Fitzpatrick a copy of Rand McNally's most recent reader concerning the Constitution. Slips pasted at the bottom of each page noted errors that Matteson had already spotted. Bloom wanted a second opinion. Fitzpatrick agreed with Matteson that "the article on the making of the Const. is so full of errors that it is not worth while to point them out. The best correction would be to rewrite the article entire. The very first paragraph is completely wrong. . . . The entire booklet is open to so many proper criticisms that one is justified in saying it should never have been issued."[12] Obviously, Bloom was being assisted by a keen couple of watchdogs. Equally clearly, commercial publishers were not serving the public well, at least not so far as the Constitution went.

Fitzpatrick had a passel of pet peeves, such as sloppy writers who used the word "federal" when they really meant "national." An editorial in *The New York Times* guilty of that mistake prompted Fitzpatrick to observe that it demonstrated the "need of the educational campaign which the Constitutional Commission proposes to carry through." It also infuriated Fitzpatrick when authors declared that the Constitution had been "adopted" rather than the proper usage, "established," as in "We the People . . . establish . . . "[13]

An editorial that appeared in *Collier's* early in 1936 supported the Supreme Court and explained to laymen why that body had to serve "as the final interpreter of the Constitution" even though "the Court has no more power than the authority of its expressed judgment." Fitzpatrick clipped the piece because its historical underpinnings were so unsound, and sent it to Bloom "on the possibility that sometime in the future you may need to allude to it, as an example of the need of the Sesquicentennial's campaign of education. When editors of popular periodicals are so ill informed as to facts, what can be expected of the man on the street, and how little reliance he can place upon the individuals on whom he has to depend for the truth."[14]

Fitzpatrick and Matteson were not merely pedantic scholars, however, who loved to trip an editor attempting to explain complicated constitutional issues to the lay public. They served Bloom and members of Congress as ghost writers and as a data bank for the endless speeches and broadcasts that were churned out between 1936 and 1939. Bloom might decide that a radio talk should be entitled "Constitutional Misconceptions"; Fitzpatrick would then supply three pages of examples, including these: "That the Supreme Court is a superior, and not a co-ordinate branch of the Government. That Congress is in some strange way inferior to the President and the Supreme Court. That if, as Chief Justice Hughes remarks, 'The Constitution is what the Judges say it is,' the Constitution is dependent upon the Court's pronouncements. (This makes the Court greater than the Constitution which created the Court which is palpably absurdity [sic]. The created can never be greater than the creator.)"[15]

Yet the Commission's biggest challenge lay not in correcting misinformation but in generating popular interest. During the summer of 1936 Bloom asked Matteson to find out what had been done in 1837 and 1887. Matteson's report was historically accurate but hardly encouraging:

> The fiftieth anniversary of the signing of the Constitution, September 17, 1837, was entirely ignored. The country was then in the throes of a great panic, and more concerned with present mere bread and butter than in [sic] the deeper matters of its development and general welfare. Though Congress was in session, there is nothing in the reports to indicate that they were even aware of the day. . . . The Declaration and the event it symbolized were spectacular, appealing to the imagination. The Constitution was a sober document whose appeal was primarily to the mind. . . . The centenary of the Constitution was not honored by an Exposition, as was that of the Declaration. . . . The celebration of 1887–89 showed an increasing popular consciousness of the Constitution as a whole; something to exult over and realize as a thing of glory, but not requiring, on the part of the sovereigns who made it and obeyed it, any special knowledge.

Bloom also asked Matteson for an evaluation of the discourse that John Quincy Adams had delivered in April 1839 on "The Jubilee of the Constitution,"[16] presumably in order to extract caveats (and tips) for all the speeches that Bloom himself would be making. How impressive it would be to report that Bloom didn't have time to read Adams's address because he was too busy writing his own; but Matteson and Fitzpatrick did most of that. Bloom just reaped the glory and momentarily became better known than James Madison, more commonly quoted than John Marshall, and perhaps more frequently heard than Charles Evans Hughes now that the Court appeared to many as an enemy of progress.

Bloom decided rather early in the Commission's planning that "there would be speeches too, but we wanted a minimum of oratory and a maximum of participation."[17] It is difficult to judge just how broad the participation turned out to be; but Bloom surely supplied an effluent of oratory. For thirty-six months, beginning with Constitution Day in 1936, he delivered dozens of speeches on the radio, to bar association meetings, to patriotic and religious groups, at George Washington's tomb, at Fort Necessity near Pittsburgh, on the Washington Memorial Parkway (along the Potomac), at the Library of Congress in the House of Representatives, and at ceremonies honoring ratification by the states. That is how the Director General became, for a while, Mr. Constitution, U.S.A.[18]

Sol Boom did talk; but if we ask to what purpose, and with what results, the verdict has to be mixed. The Commission's top priority was educational, and Bloom disseminated information; yet he tended to swing between two expository extremes. There were, predictably, oracular platitudes: "Time does not wear down nor eat away the eternal truths of the Constitution. War cannot overturn the temple of our liberty so long as American sons are worthy of their forefathers. Instead of fading with age, the glory of the Constitution takes on new splendor with the passing of the centuries." There was also a lot of trivia. As Bloom told Matteson in a typical request: "I want to have as much detail as possible of what happened on September 17, 1787, at the Convention in Philadelphia. The idea is that I want to have the people celebrate the different things that happened—what time they met, what they had for breakfast—what time they signed and anything and everything they did on that date."[19]

Bloom and his staff believed that radio programs, films, and schoolbooks that were not produced under their supervision tended to commit a more serious sin than trivialization: they were likely to mislead the public, and above all the youth of America, with inaccuracies.[20] Consequently Fitzpatrick and Matteson were asked to prepare materials for a film about the development of the Constitution. Fitzpatrick replied that "the effect of the Constitution upon the common man . . . seems to be about the only line of approach. . . . The main idea is to picture the Constitution as it affected the American citizen of that period; the analogy being that the citizen of today will thereby be made to think about his relation to the Constitution." Late in 1937 Bloom's enthusiasm for one of the Commission's pet projects, a widely distributed booklet entitled *The Story of the Constitution,* caused him to contemplate a movie based upon the booklet. Fitzpatrick answered that "the writing of the scenario would be peculiarly difficult." That film, like the one contemplated in 1936, was never made.[21]

The Commission's preparation for Sesquicentennial programs and events was problematic despite the fact that more public interest in the Constitution existed on the eve of 1937 than had been the case a century or half a century earlier. What surely saved the Sesquicentennial, and made 1937 the year of the public civics lesson par excellence, was Roosevelt's "Court-packing" plan and the intense feelings that it generated. FDR's timing could not have been better for Bloom's purposes. Politicians promptly began to focus many of their speeches on the Constitution, as did bishops, bankers, and community leaders. Popular demand for constitutional information rose dramatically, and that's just what the Commission had stockpiled, particularly Bloom's pamphlet called *Constitutional Misconceptions* (1936); a manual entitled *From Many to One: A Pageant Service to Be Used in Churches or by Congregations or Communities* (1936); and *The Story of the Constitution* (1937), a blend of narrative about the formation of the Union plus documentary texts prepared for Bloom by Matteson and Fitzpatrick, of which 700,000 copies were eventually shipped across the land.

The Court crisis did create an awkward dilemma for Bloom. A lot of people promptly assumed that the Commission existed as some sort of propaganda unit in Roosevelt's battle with the Supreme Court. As Bloom complained less than three weeks after FDR announced his scheme, the impression existed that "this is a political commission and that we are taking sides with either the 'yes' or 'no' of the Constitution debate." Matteson drafted a form letter that could be mailed to persons who sent inquiries to their office.

> Your letter of the   indicates that you are laboring under the decidedly mistaken impression that the United States Constitution Sesquicentennial Commission has a political purpose or is doing its work under political bias. Permit me to assure you most earnestly that this is not the case in any respect whatsoever. The Commission was authorized by a practically unanimous vote of Congress and without the least political division in that vote. Morever, this authori-

zation took place on August 23, 1935, many months before the present question of interpretation of the Constitution became acute.[22]

Given the sensitivity of the situation, and the potential for misunderstanding, one might have expected Bloom to be exceedingly circumspect. In March 1937, however, he circulated a pamphlet entitled *High Courts of the World and Their Powers,* demonstrating that judicial review was not a common phenomenon in other political cultures. Some angry journalists criticized Bloom because "the data collected and promulgated" seemed "wholly irrelevant to the purpose for which the commission was created," and second, because distributing such an essay "after the President's court proposal was submitted is a clear effort to create sentiment against the Court and further the movement to nullify it." The Commission did not want to be politicized. Even the perception of politicization was unfortunate. Ironically, in fact, most of Bloom's staff did not espouse Roosevelt's cause. Matteson's in-house critique of the President's speech on Constitution Day, 1937, included the following among its twelve points. "It is bad faith to convey the idea that because the Framers refused to give the Supreme Court the veto power that thereby they intended to deny it the power to interpret laws in the light of the Constitution. I have in various reports proven, I think, conclusively that what the Convention did by this was merely to refuse to include the Judiciary in the power of the President to pass upon the advisability of laws, without reference, however, to its power to interpret them."[23]

Bloom and the Commission undoubtedly made a number of misjudgments; but they did remain largely nonpartisan amidst the constitutional fracas of 1937. Conservative politicians and journalists found enemies lurking where none but ordinary scholars sought to set the historical record straight. Combustible situations sometimes ignite on unwitting but well-intentioned civil servants.

II

On the Fourth of July, 1937, Franklin D. Roosevelt proclaimed that the nation would officially celebrate the Sesquicentennial from September 17, 1937, until April 30, 1939. "We shall recognize," he declared, "that the Constitution is an enduring instrument fit for the governing of a far-flung population of more than 130,000,000 people engaged in diverse and varied pursuits, even as it was fit for the governing of a small agrarian nation of less than 4,000,000." Roosevelt had settled into a commemorative groove. In 1935 he endorsed a proposal for celebrating the adoption of the Northwest Ordinance of 1787. In doing so he reflected upon the linkages between two seminal charters: "As the Constitution provided the Federal frame, so the 'Great Ordinance' provided for the states to be born of your region."[24]

Many business organizations as well as entrepreneurial individuals promptly spotted commercial prospects and contacted the Commission about various proposals ranging from special techniques for attractive printing to promotional work in and by newspapers.[25] The Commission responded with a "Message to Merchants" which sounded like a sermon on the benefits that business had long received from operating under the auspices of a document that provided freedom of trade and enforced contractual obligations. We can imagine the joy and enlightenment with which merchants must have received Sol Bloom's message.

> The greeting which I send to Genung's Department Stores and to the merchants throughout our country is one of appreciation of their efforts to promote the great celebration of the formation of the Union which we are now inaugurating. Their efforts are, however, merely the recognition of a duty; for the business class owes much to the Constitution. The vast mercantile development of the last 150 years would not have been possible but for the liberty of movement and action which the Constitution guarantees, for the interstate recognition of commercial obligations which it enforces, and for the freedom of trade throughout the United States which it requires. . . . Through the promotion of free interchange of commodities and the development of transportation which makes easy such interchange, the merchants of today in the smallest hamlets as well as in the greatest cities place before their customers the agricultural growth of the whole country and the productions of an industry which gathers its materials from every corner of the world and sends its manufactures into all parts of the nation. Truly, both dealers and their customers have reason to pay homage to the Constitution which has so promoted their general welfare.[26]

Well, fair enough; the Constitution even appeared to protect purveyors of sick chickens, at least if they kept to small hamlets or great cities but did not spread their sickness across state lines.

The city fathers of Philadelphia felt just as enthusiastic about the Sesquicentennial as businessmen around the country—so much so that Philadelphia thumbed its nose at the official dates in order to enjoy what amounted to a triple opportunity: a festival in May and June meant to observe the initial gathering of the Constitutional Convention in 1787; lots of hullabaloo, mostly unrelated to the Constitution, during the middle weeks of September; and then an exhibition planned for December in honor of the state's ratification. All three elicited ill-will from the Commission. When the Philadelphia planners decided to inaugurate their program on May 14, they received a starchy note from Sol Bloom. "I regret that it does not seem advisable for the National Commission to consider this preliminary observance as a part of the national program, or to advise the President to participate in it. The Commemoration which Congress has authorized and which we are planning is one on the Formation of the Union, not one on the meeting of the Convention of 1787 only, or even primarily."[27]

Bloom felt especially aggrieved because several institutions in the Philadelphia area, such as the Pennsylvania Academy of Fine Arts, refused to lend portraits that the Commission coveted for its exhibition (held at the Corcoran Gallery in Washington) of all who signed the Constitution along with members of their families. The Philadelphia Museum of Art mounted a competing display of signers, and Mayor S. Davis Wilson, a feisty character, seemed to delight in antagonizing both Roosevelt and the Commission. When FDR declined to speak at a gathering designed to recognize the 150th anniversary of the Convention, Davis ascribed it to retaliation for his own refusal to lend the Liberty Bell for the forthcoming World's Fair in New York City. "As long as I'm mayor," Wilson growled, "the Liberty Bell stays in Philadelphia." In 1938, when Wilson announced his plan for a memorial honoring the 150th anniversary of Benjamin Franklin's death (April 17, 1940), John C. Fitzpatrick vented his spleen to Sol Bloom: "I know of no city which is more clannish and self-sufficient in its attitude toward everything local than Philadelphia and the Philadelphians."[28]

During the spring of 1937, A. Atwater Kent, who had recently paid for "restoration" of the Betsy Ross House, purchased Philadelphia's old Franklin Institute building and gave it to the city as a historical museum where such "relics" as the first draft of the Constitution could be displayed. Early in May the Board of Education put on public view George Washington's copy of the Constitution, with corrections in his own hand, a rare item loaned by A. S. W. Rosenbach, the prominent Philadelphia antiquarian. On May 14 the city's opening festivities took place amid torrential rains (an omen of many soakings still to come). Mayor Wilson sounded thirteen strokes on the Liberty Bell, using a gavel cut from one of the famous old dogwood trees at Valley Forge. Chief Justice John W. Kephart of Pennsylvania's Supreme Court urged every citizen present "to take the same oath as that sworn to by public officials, to guard, protect and defend the Constitution."[29]

Other rituals followed in rapid succession. On May 16 the University of Pennsylvania opened a special exhibit of autographs, portraits, and newspapers because nine signers of the Constitution had been affiliated with the university. On May 23 a nondenominational meeting took place at Independence Square to contemplate spiritual aspects of the Constitution. On June 3 the Philadelphia Bar Association sponsored a dramatization of the Constitutional Convention, and Justice George W. Maxey of the State Supreme Court delivered an address about James Madison. On June 20 the rector of historic Gloria Dei (or Old Swedes) Church delivered a Constitution Sermon in which he praised Daniel Webster for making the nation "Constitution-conscious" a century earlier, and suggested that the nation needed another Webster "to 'sell' the Constitution again to the people."[30]

Come September, Philadelphians participated in a second series of programs that continued throughout Constitution Week, though this time there seemed to be less attention to the Constitution itself and more to pomp, play, and massive display: a huge military parade; religious exercises at most churches; a Pontifical Mass held in Municipal Stadium for 100,000 Roman Catholics; an extremely popular water carnival and regatta held on the Schuylkill River, watched by 250,000 spectators; an unprecedented out-of-season parade by the Mummers; receptions at the colonial mansions in Fairmount Park; public dancing in the streets; and finally, on the 17th, exercises at Independence Hall.[31]

Mother Nature made an all-out effort to be obstructionist. In the parade preceding the Pontifical Mass on September 12, 350 people suffered from heat prostration, exhaustion, or minor injuries. The Parade of the Nations, scheduled for the 13th, had to be postponed for one week because of heavy rain and slippery streets. On Constitution Day it rained so hard that a military parade and other outdoor activities had to be cancelled. The concluding ceremony (dedicating Marconi Square), intended for the 19th, was postponed until the 26th because of dreadful weather. All in all, Philadelphia's climate could hardly have been less co-operative to constitutional enthusiasts.[32]

By 1937 the rivalry between Philadelphia and New York had become a good-natured tradition. On May 16 and 17 a mounted policeman dressed in Revolutionary garb rode on horseback from Philadelphia in order to deliver to New York's mayor a personal invitation to participate in Philadelphia's events on Constitution Day. Scale models of Independence Hall, built by WPA workers, were sent to the President, Vice President, and governors of the other twelve original states. Because Mayor LaGuardia needed to be in New York City on September 17, Philadelphia designated the 18th as "New York Day." LaGuardia came to the City of Brotherly Love, reviewed a parade of "historic military commands" from across the United States, read a speech over nationwide radio while sitting in George Washington's chair, and visited the Franklin Institute where he used a press from Franklin's own shop to print the first six sections of Article One of the Constitution.[33]

A predictable array of activities took place elsewhere in the nation. The bipartisan Good Neighbor League sponsored three hundred dinners in thirty-three states, held at churches and synagogues. All of the guests at these dinners listened to the radio broadcast of Franklin Roosevelt's Constitution Day address. The Jewish War Veterans of Asbury Park, New Jersey, planted an avenue of 130 trees, ten for each of the thirteen original states. The granite head of Abraham Lincoln was unveiled at Mount Rushmore in the Black Hills of South Dakota. Bloom explained that the Commission had arranged for celebrations to take place in more than 50,000 communities, and that this would be the most decentralized and populistic anniversary in the nation's history: "We have adopted a new policy for observances of this kind. Instead of a few huge celebrations to which people would flock from wide areas, we have arranged to take the celebrations directly into thousands of communities."[34]

The general chairman of the Delaware County Committee, based in Muncie, Indiana, printed an announcement so that residents of the county would be very clear about their relationship to the nationwide event.

Every individual in his home and elsewhere in the nation—will be given an opportunity to participate in some exercise and to pay tribute to the Constitution of his country. The signing of the Constitution will be celebrated at Ball State Teachers College on Sept. 17th, of this year. Please bear this in mind: The Constitution Sesquicentennial Celebration is to be a nation wide commemmoration, and will not be confined to the City of Muncie or Delaware County. Every group throughout the land is free to arrange its program and carry out its own observance of this historic event with the aid and co-operation of the national and State organization and their affiliates.

Owen Kane, Jr., the member of Bloom's staff responsible for "Special Events," seems to have alerted newspapers throughout the United States to the appropriateness of publishing a special edition on September 17. He even sent each editor "a portfolio of text and photographs which could be used for your special edition."[35] Kane's ubiquitous reach helps to explain much of the uniformity and repetition that we find in this ostensibly "decentralized" Sesquicentennial.

Many educational, cultural, and historical institutions did prepare programs and exhibitions based upon their special holdings. In Washington, D.C., the Library of Congress displayed a rare fourteenth-century manuscript version of Magna Carta; Jefferson's copy of *The Spirit of the Laws* by Montesquieu; various colonial charters; and the Albany Plan of Union, among others. The Historical Society of Pennsylvania discovered, just in time for an exhibit, that it owned the earliest printed copy of the U.S. Constitution (actually the first proof sheet, with corrections by Edmund Randolph of Virginia), made from James Wilson's manuscript. The Free Library of Philadelphia opened a special show that included the most important privately owned collection of constitutional papers in the country (that of A. S. W. Rosenbach).* And the Library Company of Philadelphia, which had served throughout the Constitutional Convention as a reference collection for the delegates, mounted an exhibition of works pertaining to the origins and history of American government.[36]

The New York Public Library laid out a comparable display in 1937. Columbia University offered a special course on the U.S. Constitution. The City College of New York organized a distinguished lecture series. *The New York Times* sponsored a series of essay contests for high school students in New York, New Jersey, and Connecticut. A group of trade unions asked the New York superintendent of schools for permission to promote a contest in the schools pertaining to "Labor and the Constitution." Bloomingdale's Department Store took ads to announce that it had quantities of *The Story of the Constitution* for sale, that a replica of the Shrine of the Constitution would be dedicated on June 3, 1937, and that portraits of all the signers would be on view. All three items—the booklet, the replica, and the set of portraits—were available from the Commission;

---

* It included the only known official copy of the Articles of Confederation, dated February 14, 1777; the original record of the Annapolis Convention of 1786; the engrossed vellum manuscript of the first twelve amendments (two of which did not pass); Richard Henry Lee's "Letters from the Federal Farmer"; Charles Carroll's speech supporting the Constitution; and many other treasures.

consequently similar displays occurred at major department stores throughout the United States (see figure 22).[37]

Predictably, various publications aimed at a popular level appeared in 1936–38. Some were sponsored by the Commission and widely distributed; others were brought out by commercial publishers and enjoyed different degrees of success. Essays and series of essays were specially requested by newspapers; fifty drawings of the founders by Dwight C. Sturges were commissioned by the *Christian Science Monitor;* and scholarly editions appeared of little known texts that tended to be ignored by all but a few academics.[38]

For reasons that are unclear, historical pageants about the Constitution (usually set in 1787) began to be performed as early as 1935. Some of the sponsoring organizations sought the Commission's approval. Whenever that happened, Bloom would ask Fitzpatrick to review the text. Fitzpatrick invariably found himself disappointed, in part by the dramatic shortcomings, but above all, as he wrote in assessing one, "it is a pity that this pageant could not have been brought a little more closely into relation with the exact facts."[39]

Marie Moore Forrest, director of the Commission's Pageantry and Drama Division, worked with the Music and History divisions to prepare a "canned" pageant that could be sent to those community groups requesting one. Their collaboration resulted in a "pageant service," called *From Many to One,* which emphasized the importance of pluralism in American culture. Part One provided music and processions for Norsemen, Columbus, Cavaliers at Jamestown, Henry Hudson and the Dutch, Pilgrims, Swedes on the Delaware, Quakers, Huguenots, Germans, and Scots-Irish. Part Two, entitled "Franklin and the Rising Sun," concentrated upon the delegates signing on September 17, 1787; while Part Three described "Our Glorious Country Today."[40]

The Commission made a concerted effort, however, to encourage local groups to write their own pageants and to stimulate playwriting contests. It mailed a basic bibliography of sources and books about the Constitution to anyone who wished to write a play; and offered as first prize in the National Pageant Contest none other than a full-size replica of the Shrine of the Constitution.[41] In New York City a group from the Federal Theatre Project performed a pageant at Madison Square Garden depicting scenes from the Constitutional Convention. This theatrical, sponsored by the American Legion and the Mayor's Citizens Committee, took place on the morning of the 17th. Yet another pageant called "American Mosaic" was performed at Town Hall on the evening of the 17th. In Philadelphia a group of lawyers acted out (in four scenes) the framing of the Constitution—a widely used format.[42]

A typical high school play, sponsored by the DAR chapter in Webster City, Iowa, was entitled *The Preamble Speaks* and had the following characters: Benjamin Brown (a student who found learning about the Constitution very boring), Columbia, King John, Magna Charta, two pages, four girls to carry flags, and two girls to carry the Constitution. A more ambitious (two-act) play, *The Making of the Constitution*, was written by Miss Waive B. Ripple of West LaFayette, Ohio. Act One depicted the making, and Act Two the signing. The author's instructions noted that "bright shoe buckles will add much to the general effect of the scenes," and that "the roll call [of delegates] be given in full in order that the group [audience] may become familiar with the names of historical characters."[43]

Bloom and his staff hoped, most of all, that the Sesquicentennial would have solid educational value, both directly from the Commission's own activities and from the indirect stimulus provided to educators at the college level but especially in secondary schools throughout the United States. They did not start with high expectations because, as Fitzpatrick observed to Bloom, "Civics are taught but the teaching has always been slurred over and interest therein has never been actively aroused." Bloom had particularly ambitious plans for *The Story of the Constitution*. In July 1937 he told both Matteson and Fitzpatrick that he wanted to publish a "youth's edition," and asked them to determine what should be eliminated "so as to bring it closer to the youth of the country so that when he picks up the book to read it he will feel it is a book written for him." When the book received a hostile reception in *School Review* (published in Chicago)—criticized particularly for omissions and oversimplification—Bloom got mad. His letter to the editor of *School Review* referred with disdain to "the highbrowishness" that "some college professors might consider alone worth while."[44]

Although *The Story of the Constitution* had not in fact been treated unfairly, the educational journals certainly failed to distinguish themselves during the Sesquicentennial. They published a few essay reviews about recent works on the Constitution, but not much more than that.[45] One author offered a valid observation that "the celebration will be made more interesting and likewise more difficult for teachers to discuss, coming as it does at a time of bitter controversy over the scope and meaning of the Constitution." Needless to say, the obverse was equally true. There is no better time to interest anyone in the Constitution than when the document becomes politicized and makes the news on a daily basis. A great many social studies teachers wasted a wonderful opportunity. As the same rather timid soul wrote: "Political celebrations, like political campaigns, tend to deteriorate as they are prolonged. Education succumbs to propaganda; knowledge and learning to rhetoric and oratory."[46]

The author had a point with respect to what lay ahead between October 1937 and May 1939; but a cautious regard for the Sesquicentennial as an educational challenge meant, very simply, that it became a challenge largely lost.

III

Unlike the Centennial, when so little happened between September 1887 and April 1889, the Sesquicentennial did sustain public visibility to a much greater degree during the eighteen months following Constitution Day in 1937. It made a considerable difference that in August 1937 Congress increased the Commission's appropriation by several hundred thousand dollars. It also mattered that the loan exhibition of portraits of the signers of the Constitution and the Declaration of Independence—one of the Commission's most complicated undertakings—did not open at the Corcoran Gallery of Art in Washington until November 27, 1937, and continued until March 1938. Patterned after the popular loan exhibitions held at the Metropolitan Opera House in New York in 1889 and the George Washington Bicentennial show mounted at the Corcoran in 1932, the Sesquicentennial display owed much of its success to the astuteness and social connections of its chief organizer, Mrs. Katherine M'Cook Knox of New York and Washington, a serious student of Americana who once became so absorbed while browsing in the Library of Congress stacks that she found herself locked in for the night.[47]

Even with the diligent Mrs. Knox promoting this project, it presented enough problems to raise the blood pressure of everyone involved. As late as October 1936 the Corcoran's board of directors indicated disdain for the show. Through the gallery's director, C. Powell Minnigerode, they expressed "their disapproval of any further purely Governmental exhibitions." In June 1937 the Acting Controller General of the United States (who had to authorize payment of the Commission's bills) voiced serious doubt whether Congress had intended that federal money should be spent "for borrowing portraits of the men who made the Constitution what it is." Throughout 1936–37, moreover, the organizers received negative responses from Yale concerning its unique Trumbull Collection, from several indispensable institutions in Philadelphia, from the New York Chamber of Commerce (which owned Trumbull's portrait of Alexander Hamilton), and from Cazenove G. Lee, Jr., secretary of the Lee Society of Virginia, who wrote a vituperative, antinorthern letter in response to Mrs. Knox's request for portraits of Richard Henry Lee and Francis Lightfoot Lee.[48]

Despite so much aggravation, the show received favorable reviews and enjoyed sufficient popularity that it could be held over for an extra month (see figures 23 and 24). The Washington *Star* called it the most important collection of its kind ever assembled. Edward Alden Jewell observed that "a great deal of latitude has been permitted, so that what we get in the final throw is a miscellaneous picture of an era in American life and manners." True enough when work by the accomplished Tory Benjamin West hung alongside a portrait by Ralph Earl that seemed "homespun to the core," and portraits of John Marshall's mother, Jefferson's granddaughter, and many other kin of the signers surrounded them. The show seemed less a pantheon of politicians than a profile of post-Revolutionary, elite America: multigenerational, male and female, northern and southern, elegant and plain, masterpieces cheek by jowl with mediocre works of art.[49]

The Sesquicentennial turned out to be more of a stimulus for constitutional iconography than any other occasion in the nation's history—although that really is not saying very much. Some of what resulted, moreover, was either rebuked at the time or has been largely forgotten ever since. Most reviled was the small magenta postage stamp on which the painting by Junius Brutus Stearns entitled *Adoption of the Constitution* (see figure 9) had been engraved. An editorial in the *Philadelphia Inquirer* cast withering scorn on the three-cent commemorative:

> If it were in the ten- or twenty-cent denomination the Government might be able to afford to throw in a magnifying glass with each sale of a dozen or more, so that the purchaser could read the microscopic inscription just below the heading. This runs: "Signing of the Constitution in the Philadelphia Convention, Sept. 17, 1787, Independence Hall." Such explanation is highly necessary, since the 39 masculine figures whom the artist has seen fit to crowd into a space

less than an inch and a half wide and seven eighths of an inch deep might be doing anything, from signing the Constitution to singing the Star Spangled Banner in chorus.

Another critic noticed that the dreary stamp included some "rare symbolism": on the right side, a torch, the "emblem of enlightenment"; but on the left side, the Roman fasces, a "symbol of power" then displayed on the postage stamps of Mussolini's Italy.[50]

In November 1936 the National Archives unveiled in its rotunda two massive murals by an artist named Barry Faulkner. They represented *The Declaration of Independence* and *The Constitution,* and remain virtually unknown to this day. After Sol Bloom read a review noting that Faulkner had spent more than a year gathering historical data for the paintings, he remarked to Matteson that Faulkner "must have been reading Roman history and not American history."[51] The *Constitution* mural presents twenty-five of the thirty-nine delegates—unlike the Sesquicentennial stamp, crowding is not a problem—and the depictions, although solemn and well drawn, verge upon caricature. Alexander Hamilton looks like a militant warrior, a blend of Caesar and Napoleon. The bookish Madison is carrying papers—too many and too large. He looks like an obsequious clerk.

Matteson inspected the murals at Bloom's request and prepared an evaluation early in 1937. "These more or less Maxfield Parrish backgrounds have no significance whatever in connection with the themes of the murals; even the porticos have no resemblance to the front of Independence Hall. . . ." He complained that the groupings and relationships in the *Constitution* mural were meaningless; that men were costumed in order to indicate their principal occupations; that three men who refused to sign were included along with three others (Luther Martin, Oliver Ellsworth, and William R. Davie) who left before the Convention adjourned; that Elbridge Gerry was present in *The Constitution,* which he did not sign, but absent from *The Declaration,* which he did sign. "If the group immediately around Washington is supposed to represent the strongest minds of the Convention, it is not the selection I should have made. On the other hand, taking the mural as a whole, Wilson, Ellsworth, Madison, Washington, King, Paterson, and G. Morris stand out, with Franklin well centered but in the background, and this is a good selection. . . . [Nevertheless] the Constitution one is not very happy as a historical production."[52]

Faulkner's autobiography concedes that his "knowledge of history was inadequate to select the statesmen to be represented in murals of this importance"; informs us that the final versions of the canvasses were painted in a large space high above the north concourse of Grand Central Station in Manhattan; and that when he had finished, he gave a large cocktail party. "As the crowd of guests moved between the life-sized figures of the murals, there was a slight alcoholic confusion in my mind as to which was which."[53]

Howard Chandler Christy would be the only artist to emerge from the Sesquicentennial with added visibility and moderately enthusiastic accolades. The Commission authorized him to prepare its official poster, entitled "We, the People," which enjoyed wide circulation in 1937–38. That poster, in turn, was based upon an allegorical painting of the same name on which Christy worked during 1936–37 (see figure 25). It depicts all thirty-nine signers, with Benjamin Franklin leering up at Miss Liberty (wearing a halo). She, in turn, looks like a slightly more dignified Christy Girl, the alluring pin-ups that had made the artist famous twenty years before. The painting was exhibited at Independence Hall, and then for years at the Freedom Foundation. It travelled about the country on the Freedom Train in 1947.[54]

Although Christy painted *We, the People* on his own time, so to speak, it was reproduced on magazine covers and circulated to schools, libraries, and other public places throughout the United States. In October 1937 Bloom sent glossy prints of it, along with a key, to people who requested a copy. Christy also designed the official Sesquicentennial medallion (see figure 26) in 1937, as well as *Boy Scout Sesquicentennial Tribute,* a painting commissioned by the BSA to allegorize the Boy Scouts and good government. Its theme was clear enough. After reading the U.S. Constitution a Boy Scout has a vision of those who framed it: Franklin, Washington, Madison, and Hamilton. Reproductions were distributed to 49,000 post offices in the United States, and added lustre to Christy's renown as the Sesquicentennial artist.[55]

In consequence Congress commissioned him in 1939 to paint a huge (20 by 30 foot) mural depicting the signing of the Constitution. The National Society of Mural Painters protested because no competition had been held. Christy, sixty-seven years old, worked on it for six hours each day between September 1939 and the end of April 1940. On May 29, 1940, it was unveiled at the east stairway of the House wing in the Capitol. *Newsweek* called it "1,700 pounds of history," and *Time* referred to it as a "historical whopper." Christy took this $30,000 plum seriously, and did considerable research on the clothing, accessories, and facial details of the signers. *Newsweek* found it "no better and no worse than most of the paintings which adorn the national Capitol. . . . The redheaded George Washington at 55 was more active than conventional paunchy portraits would suggest, so the artist omitted the usual bay window."[56]

The hypercritical David Matteson gave it a mixed review.

> In general I was much pleased with the design and the evident care to make the portraits authentic, as well as to give the spirit of the occasion. I do not like the Washington figure, it is too stiff, the buttoned coat is unnatural even if allowable, and the holding of a watch on the members entirely contrary to Washington's well-known courtesy, even though intended, as I suppose it is, to register the importance of the event or hour. . . . Especially do I object to the figure of Secretary Jackson. It is much too prominent in the painting, and his own hand up with four fingers extended is like the gesture of a headwaiter for a table for four.

Back in 1935, when Sol Bloom discovered that not a single government building in Washington contained a picture commemorating the signing of the Constitution, he had hoped for "buoyancy and joyousness" when the embarrassing omission was finally remedied.[57] He certainly did not find those qualities in Faulkner's solemn neoclassical rendition. Christy offered chatty intimacy in his various versions; and despite the size of his Capitol mural, the historical figures seem very human, unlike the more precise but grimly symbolic portraits by Faulkner. Neither man's work is memorable as historical art, however, which may explain why millions of tourists who have viewed *The Constitution* and *Declaration* at the National Archives carry away no memory whatever of Faulkner's mural, which is now deteriorating. Christy's in the Capitol is only slightly better known, largely because of occasional reproductions.

On June 21, 1938, the Post Office issued a stamp to commemorate ratification of the Constitution by the states. Although the date of issue coincided with New Hampshire's clinching affirmation, the stamp was first sold at Independence Hall in Philadelphia and then made available at Convention Hall, where the Associated Stamp Clubs of southeastern Pennsylvania and Delaware were holding a philatelic show. Apparently Pennsylvania's congressional delegation had more clout than New Hampshire's. At least the stamp did not suffer from the crowded clutter that had caused the Stearns engraving to be criticized so strongly nine months earlier. This one simply showed couriers departing from a colonial-style courthouse to spread the good news, plus a motto: "the States ratify."[58]

Unlike 1887–88, most of the original states did observe the sesquicentennial of their ratification in some manner, and many of them continued to maintain constitutional committees or commissions. Delaware, the first state to ratify, unveiled a tablet on December 7, 1937, in the old State House at Dover, and dedicated memorial elms around the Dover town green as a tribute to Delaware's delegates to the Convention.[59]

Pennsylvania, the second state to ratify, held a four-day celebration from December 10 to 13. Two million schoolchildren listened to the narrative of ratification and participated in costume pageants. A pilgrimage to Brandywine Battlefield and nearby historic sites took place on the 11th. Church services with sermons emphasizing historical and political subjects were the order of the day on the 12th (to stress the constitutional guarantees of religious liberty); and at four o'clock Pennsylvania's Sons of the American Revolution commemorated the beginning of Washington's encampment at Valley Forge in 1777. On the 13th Philadelphia's Ballet Company presented three dances designed to give "colorful glimpses of America in the pre-Revolutionary period." One of the three was entitled "The Rising Sun," an allusion to Franklin's famous remark when the Convention adjourned in 1787.[60]

Bloom's staff had anticipated the importance and need for public attention to ratification. Late in 1935 Fitzpatrick proposed the following for Bloom's consideration: "On the date of a State ratification, the State or capitol city, might publish or see that the important State newspapers publish, an entertaining story of that State's struggle to ratify the Constitution; clearly describing the forces and arguments against the ratification as well as those for it. In each State this struggle surely contained some dramatic qualities and these should be emphasized." Nothing quite so sensible or balanced as that was done in 1938, however: mostly tree planting, pilgrimages, speeches, and above all, pageants. Fitzpatrick and Matteson helped as best they could to provide guidance for state ratification pageants. Although they found it "easy to visualize what a pageant should be on the subject," no pageant of any distinction emerged.[61]

On June 21, Bloom's strong commitment to the significance of New Hampshire's ratification was at last fulfilled. Governor Francis P. Murphy, Senator George H. Moses, and a student who had won the statewide oratorical contest all gave speeches at the State House. A "pageant parade" depicting New Hampshire's history followed. The New Hampshire Historical Society exhibited records and documents relating to the state's contribution in making the Constitution a practical reality; and transportation exhibits appeared at the Concord railroad station and airport. An awareness of History had to be balanced by equal time for Progress; after all, History wouldn't amount to much if it didn't contribute to Progress. On the evening of the 21st Arthur T. Vanderbilt, president of the ABA, addressed the New Hampshire Bar Association and the nation over NBC Radio. Drafting the Constitution, he declared, had been more difficult than any challenge the nation had faced since 1787, including the prosecution of five wars.[62]

Vanderbilt also made a point of praising Sam Adams and Patrick Henry for insisting throughout the ratification struggle that a Bill of Rights be added to the Constitution. The problematic absence of such a Bill was frequently noted in the course of ratification celebrations throughout 1938. The Year Book of the American Communist Party asserted that the "masses" had extracted a Bill of Rights from the elite. The press finally began to provide coverage of the Bill's historical development; and the American Civil Liberties Union organized a Sesquicentennial Celebration of the Bill of Rights for October 13, 1939, in New York City. William Allen White, the respected journalist and publisher, served as chairman of the Committee of Sponsors. "The object of the Celebration," he said, "is to arouse a greater national interest in the practical aspects of the Bill of Rights today." Comparable events were planned for other major cities.[63]

On March 4, 1939, yet another Sesquicentennial celebration took place, this time in Washington, D.C., to mark the convening of the first Congress. President Roosevelt's speech on this occasion supplied a major boost for the "re-discovery" of the Bill of Rights. "We celebrate today the completion of the building of the constitutional house. But one essential was lacking—for the house had to be made habitable. And even in the period of the building, those who put stone upon stone, those who voted to accept it from the hands of the builders knew that life within the house needed other things for its inhabitants. Without those things, indeed, they could never be secure in their tenure, happy in their toil or in their rest. Not for freedom of religion alone does this nation contend by every peaceful means. We believe in the other freedoms of the Bill of Rights."[64]

April 30, the anniversary of George Washington's first inauguration in New York City, was designated as opening day for a future-oriented World's Fair. The historical pretext for that Fair could not be entirely obscured, however. So Governor Lehman unveiled a 65-foot statue of Washington on Constitution Mall (at the fairgrounds). A re-enactment of Washington's inauguration then took place at the foot of the statue. Washington Hall housed colonial "relics," most notably objects that had belonged to the first President: his surveying instruments, his shoe buckles, his shaving kit, and so forth.[65]

Exercises were also held at the steps of the Sub-Treasury Building on Wall Street, where Washington had been inaugurated in 1789. The coalition of sponsoring organizations was wonderfully appropriate: New York City's Chamber of Commerce, the Sons of the American Revolution, the Military Society of the War of 1812, the Aztec Club of 1847 (Mexican War), the St. Nicholas Society, and the Society of the Cincinnati. Attendance was extremely poor, however, because the 30th was a Sunday and people had other if not better things to do. Downtown remained largely deserted, its customary condition on a Sunday morning. Besides, those who wanted to combine patriotism with public exuberance went to Flushing Meadows, where cartoonist Denys Wortman was dressed as Washington in the Fair's re-enactment of his inauguration.[66]

Make-believe history must have been more attractive than the real thing, which required an active mixture of memory, knowledge, and imagination. The World's Fair even had its own version of Independence Hall, in which Pennsylvania's exhibit was displayed.[67] The old rivalry between Philadelphia and New York had not been put entirely to rest; but it had been obviated by transplanting Brotherly Love to Gotham. Quirkier things may have happened in American history, but not too many.

IV

"The worship of the Constitution is at an end," Corwin wrote in 1938, "or what amounts to much the same thing, has been formalized. That spontaneous reverence for the very document . . . strikes us today as somewhat quaint." Yes and no. In support of Corwin's assertion we may cite those who preferred Flushing Meadows to the Sub-Treasury on Sunday, April 30. We may list Charles Beard and Max Farrand, distinguished scholars of divergent ideological persuasions, both of whom declined to serve on the Sesquicentennial Commission. As Beard observed to Farrand in 1936, Sol Bloom "had called together a few of the congressional members of the Commission and had got himself elected Director. . . . Then he had gone ahead merrily with his projects. Owing to the shortness of time I saw no way of getting anything done that seemed worth while or worthy of the occasion."[68]

In contradiction of Corwin's statement, however, we must recognize that groups all along the ideological spectrum, ranging from the American Legion and the Sons of the American Revolution to the Workers Defense League, participated in the Sesquicentennial with genuine enthusiasm albeit contradictory assumptions and motives. On September 16 and 17, 1937, the two most widely noticed speeches were given by President Roosevelt and Senator Borah in Washington, D.C. Although they disagreed vigorously about the Supreme Court issue, both men shared a sincere devotion to the Constitution. No better example exists of conflict within a broader framework of consensus. As *The Christian Science Monitor* put it: "These two dramatic actors; the tawny-maned lion of Idaho, and the reinvigorated Squire of Hyde Park, are worthy protagonists for the 150th observation of adoption of the American constitution, since they typify the varying views on its current role. And how appropriate that the American people should have so much education about the Constitution just at this time of internal turmoil and foreign strife!"[69]

Borah's position revealed an important shift that many traditional constitutionalists had made during the interwar years. Most of them insisted throughout the 1920s that the Constitution should only be amended cautiously and infrequently. When the Supreme Court came under attack in 1935–37, however, their tune changed dramatically. As an editorial in Washington's *Evening Star* noted: "Fundamentally, Senator Borah maintains, the Constitution as it stands at any given time is sacred. Not sacred from amendment by the people if and when they desire change, but sacred from any change made through the usurpation of power by any President and any Congress without the consent of the people." Borah's speech explicitly placed the story of the 1787 Convention in "the realm of sacred history"; and he expressed the inchoate sentiments of millions of Americans when he said, "we cherish and value it [the Constitution] . . . because of what it has done for us as a people."[70]

The use of such phrases as "sacred" and "sacred history" must be taken seriously because they recur persistently, along with "pilgrimage" and "shrine of the Constitution," throughout the rhetoric of these Sesquicentennial years. When Sol Bloom addressed the annual convention of the DAR in April 1938, he opened with this sentence: "Worship is at the core of all things."[71]

Moreover, it cannot be said that WASPs dominated the Sesquicentennial. More significant than Bloom being Jewish is the fact that Catholic, Jewish, and various ethnic organizations participated in the commemorative events with considerable conviction. On the one hand, they wanted to demonstrate their red-blooded Americanism; on the other, they also wanted to express their gratitude for the gift of religious liberty made possible by the Constitution.[72]

If anything, the evidence would seem to run counter to Professor Corwin's generalization. But the final assessment has to be at once simpler yet more paradoxical than Corwin's. It was succinctly summed up in 1939 by Representative Maury Maverick of Texas: "The people of the United States probably know less about the Constitution and the Supreme Court than any other important subject. Furthermore, many of them have for the Court and its members a blind adoration that makes impossible a commonsense examination."[73] Maverick's indictment may seem exaggerated; but it was essentially correct.

High visibility is invariably accompanied by high vulnerability, and Sol Bloom supplies a prime example. By July 1937 it became clear that a good many of his colleagues in the House, especially Republicans, regarded him as self-promoting. They defeated his bill to provide a free copy of *The Story of the Constitution* to every person about to be naturalized. The cost to the federal Treasury would have been ten cents per person. Clearly, Mr. Constitution had aroused some ill-will in the House. The minority leader snidely inquired whether Bloom's autographed picture would appear on page one. "Books of this character always have something like that." Bloom reddened. "Sol Bloom is not looking for advertising," he exploded. "There's no glory in this for me. It's all for the Constitution."[74]

In January 1938, Representative Charles Tobey of New Hampshire called for an investigation of the Sesquicentennial Commission. According to Tobey, "the Constitution had been used to cloak a racket." He accused Bloom's affiliates, including two Tammany bosses, of profiteering from the sale of Constitution-linked merchandise. Tobey's public queries were based upon criticisms that had appeared in several articles and editorials in Scripps-Howard newspapers. Fitzpatrick supplied Bloom with materials for a rebuttal; and on February 3 the indignant congressman rose on the floor of the House to deny wrongdoing and refute all charges. He had not engaged in profiteering from sales of the replica of the Shrine of the Constitution, or the Christy poster called "We, the People." And the Commission had not commercialized the Sesquicentennial; at least, not as much as it might have.

They say that we commercialized this celebration. I hold in my hand a catalog of the coronation of the King and Queen of England. This is a catalog of merchandising issued by the Army and Navy stores of Great Britain. They had every kind of merchandising, not only our kind of merchandising, selling it through England and throughout the world, cups, china plates, mugs, jewelry, flags, tree markers, garden seats, even toothbrush holders, and so forth, as high as $25 apiece, and yet we are criticized for what we did. Mr. Chairman, no celebration was ever held that they did not sell souvenirs and coins and things of that kind which had been gotten out to commemorate it, and these are all things that were gotten out in England for the coronation.

We are not doing anything different in this celebration from what we did during the bicentennial celebration. We got out a catalog. Nobody said anything about it then. Nobody would have said anything about it now if the Scripps-Howard newpapers did not want to "dump Roosevelt and get BLOOM." That is all there is to it. Here are suggestions from merchants and department-store owners in the celebration of the two hundredth anniversary of the birth of George Washington, and they were issued by the Bicentennial Commission, and millions and millions of dollars worth of material were sold by our suggestions for the celebration and no one criticized it and no one could criticize it.[75]

Representative Tobey received fifteen minutes for rebuttal. He invoked a vision of the framers gathered together in "the Elysian fields," observing "what has been going on" and wailing: "My God! Making a racket out of the Constitution." The chairman of the House Rules Committee, another Democrat from New York, defended Bloom, implied that Tobey was motivated by anti-Semitism, and refused to undertake an investigation. One day later, however, the House of Representatives decided not to appropriate an additional $50,000 for the Commission's use (recommended on February 2 by the Appropriations Committee) and determined that its activities should terminate on the last day of 1938, one year earlier than had been planned.[76]

Bloom may or may not have vindicated himself on the 3rd. Although he eluded investigation, he certainly must have felt paddled. He did not sulk, fold up, or fade away, however. He not only remained active (and much in demand as a speaker) throughout 1938; but as late as August 1939 continued to promote public awareness of the Constitution by requesting his staff to concoct some sort of creed or pledge. "The pledges now in use are all based on the Flag," he wrote, "and there are others on just about every subject but the Constitution, which is what they should be on." Bloom may have liked publicity and glory, but the sincerity of his desire to raise "Constitution consciousness" cannot be doubted.[77]

The shadow of partisan squabbling that darkened the Commission in 1938 has an ironic aspect. Although the Sesquicentennial itself did not contribute very much to the advancement of political or historical knowledge in the United States, Bloom and his staff, from the outset, promoted two themes that had been neglected yet deserved dispassionate appreciation by anyone who hoped to understand the origins and nature of American constitutionalism. The first of these called for wider recognition that conflicting views had been abundantly present at the 1787 Convention and had required a spirit of compromise and concession. As Bloom remarked in a speech at Georgia's ratification observance: "This celebrated compromise was one of the many that has caused the Constitution to be termed a document born of concession and adjustments." Fair enough: a lesson worth bearing in mind.[78]

The Commission's other theme deserved emphasis because of the extraordinary shift in governmental power that had occurred since the end of the Civil War, and especially during the 1930s. Fundamentally the second theme involved a re-affirmation of the original meaning of federalism, with special attention to the role of the states in creating the Union and the need for continued vitality in governmental agencies below the national level. As Bloom observed in a talk over CBS Radio in June 1937: "The people have ordained in the Constitution that the national government shall depend for its existence upon the perpetuity of the States. . . . The people who ordained the Constitution were passionately attached to their State and local governments."[79]

Bloom and his staff tried to be careful not to use the words "national" and "federal" interchangeably. Bloom observed in a 1936 memo to Matteson that "we have for many decades accepted our dual system of government without much thought or consideration." He stressed the point in many of his speeches, and asked for source materials that would shed new light on the establishment of that system. Remarks that he made in October 1937 are illustrative. Had they been widely heeded and discussed, the Sesquicentennial would have served a more valuable function in both educational and civic terms. "Let us give thanks for the federal as well as the national elements in our government, and remember that the local self-government of the States has removed a burden from the nation. . . .

Though there has always been and must continue to be a shifting of responsibility between the States and the Nation . . . nothing has as yet occurred or is likely to occur, to make our federalism any less necessary than is our nationalism."[80]

Similar notes were sounded on occasion, though not usually in such a balanced way, by public speakers and by the press. An editorial that appeared on Constitution Day, 1937, typifies the unrealistic and unhistorical hyperbole that abounded: "Throughout one hundred and fifty years the system of checks and balances and the division of powers between Federal Government and State Governments have succeeded beyond all dreams of the Founders."[81]

James T. Berryman drew an extended series of Sesquicentennial cartoons for the Washington *Evening Star* in 1937. Several of them stressed the national split over "Court-packing" and the need for conciliation. Others emphasized the issue of executive or national power versus local autonomy. And one gave graphic expression to the Constitution Day editorial quoted above. A DAR lady is reading the U.S. Constitution with enthusiasm. Behind her a banner proclaims: "After one hundred and fifty years it looks better than ever!"[82]

Yes, to most Americans it did; and with good reason, especially if they paid attention to what was happening in Europe and East Asia. Nevertheless, taking the Sesquicentennial all in all, the most penetrating assessment appeared in the *Chicago Tribune:* "The American people after the great attempt to overthrow the Union have generally taken their constitutional order for granted. As we confidently push a button to flood a room with light without thinking of the skilled men and elaborate machinery which make the miracle possible, so have we enjoyed the blessings of liberty under our Constitution, taking them for granted as we take the air we breathe."[83] A remarkably clear echo of James Russell Lowell in 1888. Most Americans took great pride in their Constitution, but still hadn't learned that it was not, and is not, a machine that would go of itself.

PART FOUR

THE PENDULUM OF
PUBLIC OPINION

"While the pendulum of public opinion has swung with much force away from the extreme point of State-Rights doctrine, there may be danger of its reaching an extreme point on the other side."

JUSTICE SAMUEL F. MILLER (1887)

"Constitutional questions, it is true, are not settled by even a consensus of present public opinion. . . ."

JUSTICE DAVID J. BREWER (1908)

"The very purpose of having a written Constitution is to provide safeguards for certain rights that cannot *yield to public opinion. That is why our Constitution created an independent judiciary and why judges remain apart from contemporary politics."*

CHIEF JUSTICE WARREN E. BURGER (1973)

CHAPTER 11

Illegal Defiance of Constitutional Authority

THOMAS REED POWELL OF HARVARD, the pre-eminent teacher of his generation in constitutional law, quipped during the Sesquicentennial that "in relating the conditions today to the framing of the Constitution 150 years ago, there is the danger that some will visit upon the fathers the sins of their sons." Powell believed that the Federalist founders shared a positive attitude toward change and would have been shocked by those Americans of the 1930s who regarded proposals or constitutional innovation as "impious."[1] Powell's assertion was correct as far as it went. The founders did believe that governmental improvements were urgently needed in 1787, and deliberately exceeded their authority in order to propose some unanticipated adjustments.

Nevertheless, I suspect that the men who framed our fundamental law would find it difficult to recognize (never mind approve) some of the sweeping developments that have taken place in American constitutionalism since the 1940s. Saying so disparages neither the founders nor the developments. The conditions of modern life have altered dramatically, and we must expect major changes in constitutionalism to accompany new conditions. Even so, the passing of dual federalism has shifted power to the national government far beyond the boundaries envisioned by most Federalists in 1787–88. (On that score, the Anti-Federalist prophecy of "consolidation" really has been fulfilled, whether we like it or not.) Moreover, the extensive modifications that have been required in our system of separation of powers, the relentless criticism of the Supreme Court (particularly during the Warren years), the expanded role of the Court in public affairs,[2] and the proposals by Rexford Tugwell and others for an entirely new Constitution would, in my view, disturb James Madison and others who participated in the Convention.

At least two developments might please the founders if they could look ahead and observe us through the powerful lens of a future-historical projector. They would be delighted, and perhaps surprised, that the governmental blueprint they drafted has largely survived in its original form. And they would be glad that one outcome of sustained constitutional controversy during the past generation has finally caused so many Americans to stop conflating the Constitution and the Supreme Court, which is, after all, only one among several governmental bodies delineated by the Constitution.

In 1963, a poll indicated that 70 percent of the Americans queried opposed the Supreme Court's restrictive ruling on prayer in the public schools. Desegregation and the expanded protection of civil liberties provoked comparable hostility toward the Court by people who had no complaint with the Constitution itself. They argued instead that the Court had usurped authority and acted unconstitutionally. The Court's critics may often have been wrong, and may have been motivated by racial, class, or religious preferences; but the society as a whole surely expanded its consciousness in terms of constitutional perception.

In 1943 a national poll asked this question: "Do you think the Constitution of the United States should ever be changed in any way?" Among 2,560 respondents, 34 percent answered yes, 54 percent answered no, and the remainder didn't know. In 1967 a Gallup Poll asked: "In general, what kind of rating would you give the Supreme Court?" Among 3,783 respondents, 15 percent said excellent, 30 percent said good, 29 percent said fair, 17 percent said poor, and 10 percent didn't know. To the follow-up question, "Has your opinion of the Supreme Court changed in recent years?," 45 percent replied yes, 43 percent replied no, and 11 percent had no opinion. When the very same query had been put to 3,071 Americans twenty-one years earlier, only 30 percent answered yes, 45 percent no, and 25 percent had no opinion.[3] The role of constitutionalism in American culture intensified during the decades that followed World War II.

I

One might not have anticipated such a shift in 1939, when Roosevelt's Solicitor General, Robert H. Jackson, insisted that the spirit in which the

Constitution had been applied since 1937 "is more truly the spirit of the Framers than was that which prevailed during the period of judicial negation from about 1890 down to an all-too-recent time." From the perspective of the government's legal counsel, Americans were "having something of a Constitutional Renaissance at the present time—a rediscovery of the Constitution."[4]

What that meant in Jackson's mind was a return to fundamentals, a return that cut through cumulative generations of judicial opinion and glosses. Jackson believed that unless the Constitution said the federal government could not do something, like regulate wages and prices, the government could do it. He may or may not have been constitutionally correct—strict constructionists believe the national government may only exercise those powers explicitly delegated to it—but he surely had the drift of recent history on his side. Beginning in the 1920s, but especially since the mid-1930s, government officials, attorneys, and scholars had noted the demise of federalism. The centralization of power in Washington meant that the states steadily surrendered more and more of their authority. Those who regretted this trend agreed with a lawyer in Patchogue, New York, who observed: "The Framers were profound students of governments and it was apparent that they well knew that the most enduring of all governments was the local form and that a central government was inclined to power, oppression, corruption and consequent short life, so distasteful to them."[5]

Men and women sympathetic to the New Deal, who believed that only a centralized government could really solve national problems, did not share that pessimistic perspective; and the future belonged to them. In 1941 the Supreme Court upheld the Fair Labor Standards Act of 1938, which established national minimum wage standards as well as regulations for working conditions and overtime pay.[6] This important legislation also incorporated the 1916 Child Labor Law, which prohibited the shipment in interstate commerce of any goods produced by child labor (a law declared unconstitutional by the Supreme Court in 1918).

Public officials and jurists recognized that decisions of this sort permanently diminished the viability of states' rights. Edward S. Corwin stressed the implications of undercutting state police power and the value of federal equilibrium in his influential essay called "The Passing of Dual Federalism." Even Corwin, who had been an ardent supporter of FDR and the New Deal, wondered by 1950 whether the pendulum had not swung too far. "Today the question faces us whether the constituent States of the System can be saved for any useful purpose, and thereby saved as the vital cells that they have been heretofore of democratic sentiment, impulse, and action."[7]

Cherished ideals die hard, however, and tend to survive as semifictions in the hearts of true believers, schoolchildren, and immigrants. A textbook designed by the government in 1940 for people seeking citizenship schematized "The Federal System" as though nothing had altered since 1787—a graphic that was perpetuated in one edition after another well into the 1950s (see below).[8]

Judges and scholars committed to federalism as a workable ideal spoke up with sufficient frequency during the postwar era to keep the concept credible;[9] and a strong revival of states' rights sentiment from 1955 until the mid-sixties kept federalism viable as a governmental vision, particularly for Americans who resisted racial integration. A Gallup Poll taken in 1959 asked people how they felt about a proposed amendment that would "permit each state to decide for itself what it wants to do about

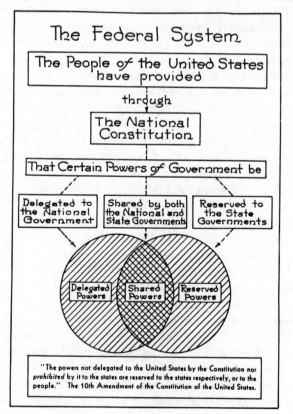

The Federal System

The People of the United States have provided

through

The National Constitution

That Certain Powers of Government be

Delegated to the National Government

Shared by both the National and State Governments

Reserved to the State Governments

Delegated Powers

Shared Powers

Reserved Powers

"The powers not delegated to the United States by the Constitution nor *prohibited* by it to the states are reserved to the states respectively, or to the people." The 10th Amendment of the Constitution of the United States.

integration of white and colored students in the schools." The responses were 51 percent in favor, 43 percent opposed, and 6 percent with no opinion.[10]

Richard M. Nixon's plan for a New Federalism and Ronald Reagan's penchant for fiscal decentralization have also kept those possibilities under consideration and partial implementation, thereby reinforcing the maxim that few trends are definitive in American constitutionalism, and that not many issues remain permanently resolved. The pliancy of our system is surely one of its most attractive features; but it does result in confusion from time to time, not merely for citizens, but for thousands of judges in the state and federal networks who look to the Supreme Court for clear guidelines.

On February 19, 1985, the Court overruled a decision it had made in 1976 and significantly enhanced the national government's power to regulate state activities that previously had been considered off-limits to federal control. The majority opinion in this revisionist five to four decision declared that federal minimum wage and hour standards applied to the employees of municipally owned mass transit systems. The rationale of the decision (*Garcia* v. *San Antonio Metropolitan Transit Authority*) also restored most other state employees to protected status under the Fair Labor Standards Act. The 1976 decision had held that the Constitution did not permit Congress to extend wage and hour coverage to state employees because doing so would "directly displace the states' freedom to structure integral operations in areas of traditional governmental functions." A *New York Times* editorial greeted the 1985 reversal as "a welcome return to a sensible federalism, even though the 5-to-4 margin is precarious and leaves disturbing uncertainties."[11]

When is federalism really nationalization, and not federalism at all? Perhaps when it is a "sensible federalism." And what did Justice Blackmun really mean when he wrote for the majority that "the Framers chose to rely on a Federal system in which special restraints on Federal power over the states inhered principally in the workings of the national Government itself, rather than in discrete limitations on the objects of Federal authority"? My purpose is not to be a partisan of either the 1976 ruling or its 1985 reversal. The point is simply that "federalism" has all but ceased to be a meaningful word-concept in the vocabulary of American jurisprudence. In 1787–88 the Federalists, who were really nationalists, appropriated their label in order to put the Anti-Federalists on the defensive. Everyone understood the ploy, however, and knew who stood for what. By contrast, the criteria of federalism and state sovereignty had become exceedingly clouded by 1985. Two centuries of increasingly vague and careless usage had obscured the original understanding of these concepts. If we set aside the substance and merits of the case, Justice O'Connor (dissenting) surely was correct in saying that "federalism cannot be reduced to the weak 'essence' distilled by the majority today."

II

We can see a comparable set of issues and adjustments in the shifting relationship between Congress, the President, and the Court. Citizens and guidebooks for aspiring citizens continued to proclaim the reassuring verities about checks and balances: "three branches zealously watching each other to the end that neither division of the Government usurp the rights not authorized by the Constitution."[12] Informed observers howled, however, at Roosevelt's unchecked expansion of executive authority when he sent destroyers to Great Britain in 1940. Why hadn't he sought congressional consent? Similar questions arose about the President's use of executive power during World War II. Roosevelt's response combined pragmatism and common sense with more than a touch of self-righteousness: "The President has the power, under the Constitution and under Congressional acts, to take measures necessary to avert a disaster which would interfere with the winning of the war. . . . I cannot tell what powers may have to be exercised in order to win this war. When the war is won, the powers under which I act automatically revert to the people—to whom they belong."[13]

When Presidents Truman and Eisenhower continued Roosevelt's penchant for implementing foreign policy by executive agreement, Senator John W. Bricker of Ohio proposed a constitutional amendment designed to give Congress additional control over the treaty-making process and strike especially hard at the trend toward unapproved executive agreements. In March 1951, Bricker charged that Truman's intention of committing American troops to a NATO defense force had precipitated a governmental crisis: "The constitutional power of Congress to determine American foreign policy is at stake. It is our duty to preserve that power against presidential encroachment." Bricker introduced his amendment in four successive congresses between 1951 and 1958.[14]

Ultimately, Eisenhower's image as a canny leader in the Cold War helped him cope with congressional challenges to executive authority. Even Bricker acknowledged the force of the administration's counterargument: namely, that the President should be unhampered in conducting the struggle against international communism. Although his proposal never passed, Bricker gained a good many supporters and alerted the nation to a new and genuine problem. One contemporary observer called it "the most radical constitutional change to gain serious attention in forty years. The issue is fundamental: which is to lead in the formulation of American foreign policy, the President or Congress?"[15]

Failure to pass the Bricker Amendment did not simply result from Eisenhower's image as a leader who could stand firm against the Eastern bloc if given sufficient discretionary authority. A thorough study of Congress's feelings about its constitutional role has found, from Franklin Roosevelt's presidency until Lyndon Johnson's, "a continuing discord in Congress over the concurrent [constitutional] responsibility and capability of judges and members of Congress." When asked in 1959 whether Congress should "pass constitutional questions along to the courts rather than form its own considered judgment on them," the 535 members could not agree (though a majority did say no). When the Jenner-Butler bill came before the Senate in 1958, aimed at curtailing the Supreme Court's appellate jurisdiction over certain issues, such as internal security, it provoked a significant debate over the Senate's power "to tell the Court what is constitutional." The senators split on this question also. Henry Jackson and Jacob Javits were just as loyal to the U.S. Constitution as Jenner and Butler; but they understood the document and its development differently— yet another illustration of conflict within consensus, and of Congress's growing incapacity to define co-ordinated constitutional responsibilities in relation to the executive and judicial branches.[16]

Despite the plausible notion of an "imperial presidency," so persuasive during the Johnson and Nixon years, the executive is harassed from time to time by conscientious members of Congress who regard themselves as constitutional watchdogs. Senator Sam Ervin of North Carolina, for example, constantly reiterated that Congress's power to legislate took priority over executive orders that made policy and served as ersatz legislation.[17]

The complexity of Congress's relationship to the presidency was underscored in 1983, when the Supreme Court issued an unanticipated decision declaring the so-called legislative veto unconstitutional. This practice began in 1932 when Congress worked out an arrangement with Herbert Hoover. Congress approved a law giving Hoover the authority he wanted to reorganize the executive branch but retained the right to override him if it did not like the way he did it. As administrative problems became more complex during the next half century, similar provisions appeared in other laws (more than 350 legislative veto stipulations contained in some 200 laws). This kind of collusion proved to be efficient and convenient for both branches. Unfortunately, it also violated the principle of separation of powers because it circumvented the prescribed manner by which each branch was supposed to proceed in approving or rejecting legislation. No shortcuts, please, became the essence of Chief Justice Burger's opinion (for a seven to two majority), a firm civics lesson to the other two branches. Congress would have to re-assume its full constitutional responsibility to govern; the President would have to stop poaching on legislative prerogatives. The Supreme Court had spoken, and no one seems to have resented the decision.[18] That is not typical of the Court's position in public life during the past three decades.

III

The Roosevelt Court of the 1940s, and its successors, have been analyzed extensively; hence only selected developments need to be touched upon here. A number of the appointments made by FDR, Truman, and Eisenhower seemed undistinguished to contemporaries. Sherman Minton, for example (1949–56), disappointed civil libertarians and found it a painful experience when several of his opinions were sharply denounced. Hugo Black, on the other hand, was mocked by journalists, legal scholars, colleagues on the Court, and northern liberals for years after his appointment in 1937, yet he grew in stature, overcame his educational limitations and the Ku Klux Klan stigma, and emerged after a decade as the acknowledged leader of an important school of judicial interpretation.[19] His disciples increased and his impact upon the process by which the Bill of Rights came to be applied to the states (as well as in federal courts) was immense.

"Liberal" and "conservative" ceased to be very meaningful as categories for the justices. All of them had supported the New Deal; but many would take unanticipated positions on sensitive cases involving civil liberties, government regulation of the economy, and the very nature of the Court's own authority. A number of them, moreover, underwent judicial journeys during their years on the Court—some becoming more traditional or cautious, others more populistic. Although most of them shared Rooseveltian assumptions about the government's responsibility for the general welfare, the justices tended to differ over issues involving judicial activism versus restraint. Even that dichotomy is misleading, however, because an important figure like Harlan Fiske Stone might be found in either camp, depending upon the case. Sharp differences there were, however, and by 1943 Court-watchers liked to say that it suffered from "dissentia praecox." Personality conflicts also abounded, in part because two of the justices, Jackson and Douglas, appeared to have presidential aspirations.[20]

Early in 1944 Charles Beard asked his old friend Thomas Reed Powell a confidential question that re-opens for us the enduring issue of the Court's role as a creative expositor of American constitutionalism. From Beard's perspective, "in the statements of facts and law, in the opinions, and in the animadversions of the Justices, the documents of the Court show increasing confusion and imprecision—in thinking and writing." Powell, replying with a comprehensive four-page letter, basically agreed. Extracts from that letter are revealing because they help to clarify why the public received so little illumination from the justices.

> One trouble is that they suffer somewhat from intellectualism. Felix [Frankfurter] in dissent and in concurring opinions has devoted himself to a considerable extent to slamming inadequacies in the intellectual methods of his opponents and to that extent neglecting to deal with the issues of the case. . . . The reason for confusion and imprecision is that the judges are making a lot of new law without confessing it. Black is still the legislator wanting each case to go the way he wants it to go, irrespective of how it fits into the established system or of what it does to that system. . . . I think that the boys behave pretty badly in seizing upon insignificant points of difference and in slamming each other.[21]

Although Frankfurter disliked Black and Douglas, and Jackson engaged in nasty public name-calling with Black in 1946, the Court as a whole swung generally left of center—not without significant resistance—and the differences between Frankfurter and Black owed almost as much to temperamental qualities as they did to substantive differences in judicial philosophy. It is possible to cite quotations from each one that sound exactly like what one would anticipate from the other.[22]

Despite the much-publicized tension between Frankfurter and Black over the proper scope of judicial activism, the Stone and Vinson Courts exercised their power of review and rejection much more cautiously between 1937 and 1953 than during the previous sixteen years. Why? There are several reasons, among them a collective desire to reduce the Court's long-standing reputation as a barrier to progress. The Tenth Amendment ceased to be regarded as much of a constraint upon federal action. The anomalous use of substantive due process as a protective shield for business enterprises against governmental regulation largely ended. The presumption that congressional legislation was likely to be constitutional became very strong (except for civil liberties guaranteed by the first eight amendments and incorporated into the Fourteenth). After that long and difficult period with the "nine old men," William Y. Elliott summed up the new mood very well: "Our Constitutional system is not only what the judges say it is, but what the amending power can make it, and what usage will make it."[23]

Starting in 1954, however, and continuing for another sixteen-year stretch, the Court began to exercise a range of authority that seemed to many without precedent in American judicial history. The Court did so, moreover, despite steadily mounting criticism and intermittent attempts to reduce its reach. Between 1957 and 1960 hostile members of Congress not only hoped to reverse particular decisions but sought to restrain the exercise of judicial review in general. The reasons why this conservative counterattack failed had little to do with the legitimacy of judicial review as an established constitutional principle. Rather, the counterattack narrowly failed because Senators Jenner and Butler and their allies made a cluster of political miscalculations; because Lyndon B. Johnson, Senate Majority Leader at the time, had strong presidential ambitions and needed to attract northern and western support; because many liberals sincerely supported the desegregation decisions and fought to prevent their reversal; and because of a genuine humanitarian concern to protect civil liberties when anticommunism and anxiety about internal security became excessively virulent.[24]

The uproar over desegregation that started in 1954 precipitated a series of notable developments in American constitutionalism: notable, first of all, because so many segregationists took care to differentiate between the Constitution and the despised Court. Many claimed that in order to obey the former they were obliged to disregard the latter. Second, because a number of federal judges in the South courageously challenged the doctrinal absurdity of Interposition. As one of them declared: "Interposition is not a constitutional doctrine. If taken seriously, it is illegal defiance of constitutional authority." Third, because the Supreme Court strangely refused to hear a whole series of follow-up suits relating to desegregation, thereby conveying the impression that it did not intend to pursue the landmark case of *Brown* v. *Board of Education* and encouraging southern defiance.[25]

Once again, however, a tension-filled crisis situation at least had the redeeming virtue that political stress made people Constitution-conscious. The document needed to be read and reflected upon in order to develop rationalizations in its name. The Constitution may have been deliberately misconstrued, but at least it appeared in the forefront of public discourse. In 1956, for example, ninety-six members of the South's congressional delegation issued a Southern Manifesto that they called a Declaration of Constitutional Principles. A Georgian produced a pamphlet entitled *The Supreme Court, the Broken Constitution, and the Shattered Bill of Rights* that got reprinted in the *Congressional Record.* An Arkansas congressman produced a short book that epitomized a great deal of southern distress at the time. *The Constitutional Crisis* referred constantly to the Warren Court's "usurpation of power" and asked whether "administrative centralism" should be permitted to subvert "constitutional liberty."[26]

If we look at these familiar developments in the light of forgotten public opinion polls, we are obliged to conclude that public sensitivity to constitutionalism in current events tends to respond somewhat sluggishly. On the issue of judicial review, for instance, let us look at two polls taken twenty years apart. The results in each case are rather surprising. In 1936, right after Roosevelt's landslide victory, the Gallup Organization asked 2,720 Americans this question: "As a general policy, are you in favor of limiting the power of the Supreme Court to declare acts of Congress unconstitutional?" Only 34 percent answered yes, 49 percent no, and 17 percent had no opinion. In 1956, two years after the desegregation decision, Gallup asked: "Do you think that the U.S. Supreme Court is taking on more authority than the Constitution intended it to have, or not?" This time only 27 percent said yes, 47 percent no, and fully 25 percent had no opinion (or else "mispunched"). One year later Gallup put this query to 1,534 Americans: "Some people say that the Supreme Court has too much power these days. Do you agree or disagree with this?" Twenty-six percent agreed, 53 percent did not, and 20 percent had no opinion.[27]

Looking at these responses leaves us unprepared for the varied and harsh attacks upon the Court that persisted for more than a decade following 1957. "Curb the Court" became a popular catch phrase in 1958. Senator Strom Thurmond and others introduced legislation designed to reduce the scope of the Court's appellate jurisdiction. Several bills stipulated that the Court should only be able to invalidate a provision of a state constitution, or statute passed by a state legislature, by unanimous decision. Organizations like the Defenders of the American Constitution became very active. They believed that the Court, by protecting the civil rights of Communists in 1956, was bent on destroying the nation's barriers against internal subversion. Consequently they took radical steps "out of a deep concern for the preservation of the Constitution of the United States as it was meant to be." The American Bar Association and many state chief justices joined in this attack. The national debate topic for students throughout the United States in 1959–60 essentially read: Resolved, that Congress be given the right to reverse Supreme Court decisions. When Senator Paul Douglas of Illinois introduced a legislative amendment expressing congressional support for "the recent, historic decisions of the Supreme Court," pandemonium broke loose in the Senate because feelings ran so high.[28]

During the early and mid-1960s, three sorts of decisions stirred up still more controversy over the Warren Court's constitutional activism: first, the reapportionment cases that mandated a new distribution of voting power (from rural to urban districts) within the states; second, strict application of the First Amendment with the effect of excluding prayer from public schools; and third, the extension of much greater protection to persons accused of crimes or unable to pay for their own legal defense.[29]

In 1964 *Life* magazine labelled the Court a storm center of justice. The widely respected federal Judge Learned Hand, as well as lawyers who practiced before the Court, were quoted in support of the view that the justices had overreached their authority. *Life* did not look at the Court very often; so when it did, we can be sure that millions of Americans must have shared some interest or concern. A *Life* editorial about the Court in 1958 had taken a middle of the road position—hoping that the Jenner-Butler bill would fail but complaining that decisions in the field of civil liberties had created a situation where "the layman can scarcely discern what basic principles of justice are at work."[30] The problem lay partially in the justices' assumption that their opinions were self-explanatory, which was decidedly not true; partially in their unwillingness to hear numerous cases that followed in the wake of *Brown* v. *Board;* and partially in the proliferation of separate opinions, both concurring and dissenting (a phenomenon that *Life* ascribed to excessive egotism on the bench).

These tendencies and caveats conveyed to the broadest possible audience what insiders and sympathetic critics had acknowledged for years. Chief Justice Stone once told Justice James F. Byrnes that experience had demonstrated "the unwisdom of departing from the sound judicial policy of not deciding constitutional questions unnecessarily, or placing decision on novel constitutional doctrine when it may rest as well on long accepted constitutional principles," advice that Stone repeated to William O. Douglas in 1946. The title of a widely read essay by Philip B. Kurland summed up the feelings of many Americans: "The Court Should Decide Less and Explain More." Kurland called in particular for more carefully reasoned opinions, greater respect for the proper role of state legislatures and lower federal courts, and clearer explanations of why judicial precedents needed to be amended or rejected.[31]

In terms of American constitutionalism and its dynamics, three consequences are especially noteworthy: the willingness of governmental agencies, lower courts, and state legislatures to flout Supreme Court decisions they do not like; the proclivity of disaffected politicians and organizations to attack the Court quite savagely; and the tendency for public esteem regarding the Court to plummet rather swiftly.

Despite the oath taken by public officials to uphold the Constitution of the United States, persons in all three branches of the federal government have been known to ignore, misunderstand, or willfully misinterpret an unwanted Supreme Court decision. Even where good faith is not a problem, studies have shown that Court rulings can be read and implemented in divergent ways by different parts of the country. *McCollum* v. *Board of Education* (1948), for example, invalidated a so-called released time system of religious education in the public schools of Champaign, Illinois. Classes involving religious instruction had been held in the public schools during regular hours, and teachers acted under supervision from the local superintendent. In numerous situations the McCollum decision led to the termination or extensive modification of weekday programs held during school hours. In many other locations, however, community leaders decided that because of some minor variation *McCollum* simply did not apply to them. In some instances no changes whatever were made in weekday programs, regardless of their dependence upon public school time and buildings. In parts of the country compliance began the day after *McCollum* was issued. Elsewhere the ruling was flagrantly disregarded.[32]

The most outrageous cases of constitutional disobedience occurred in response to the school desegregation decisions. State legislatures passed laws prohibiting desegregation. The Louisiana legislature alone enacted more than forty unconstitutional laws. Some federal judges in the South proclaimed that *Brown* v. *Board* was unconstitutional; therefore, to enforce it would involve a knowing violation of their oath sworn to sustain the Constitution. Every member of an American school board also takes an oath to uphold the U.S. Constitution—any provision in the laws or constitution of his or her own state to the contrary notwithstanding. Needless to say, for many years a large number of school board members petulantly violated their oaths.[33]

In 1957, Representative Clare E. Hoffman of Michigan proposed the impeachment of all nine Supreme Court justices "on the theory that the Court is attempting to overthrow the Government through fallacious reasoning, rendering decisions which make constitutional provisions void." Although Hoffman's initiative may have been extreme, it anticipated recurrent campaigns throughout the 1960s to impeach individuals, notably Chief Justice Warren and Justice William O. Douglas. Between 1961 and 1968 the John Birch Society covered the country with billboards that urged Warren's impeachment. What appeared most alarming to Robert Welch, Jr., and the Birchites, even more than desegregation, were opinions that Warren had written constraining the freedom of congressional committees to investigate suspected Communists. Warren believed that the First Amendment and a "right to privacy" protected persons from unlimited inquiries and from the compulsion to identify other persons who might have been Party members. Warren's removal from office became the Birchites' top priority during the sixties. As Welch explained, "I personally do not think we can save our country unless we can ultimately impeach Warren, nor that the Communist conspiracy can survive if we do." Despite an extensive petition drive designed to mobilize public opinion, and letter-writing campaigns to put pressure on Congress, the John Birch Society was unable to gain support from the *National Review* and other conservative journals.[34]

In 1964, however, when Barry Goldwater's attack upon the Supreme Court became a central feature of his presidential campaign, he received considerable sympathy from conservative journalists and from Americans of both parties who felt that in "coddling" criminals and banishing religion from public schools the Court had gone too far and threatened traditional values as well as national security. Even before Goldwater proclaimed that the Supreme Court "needs to be curbed by constitutional amendment and by legislation where possible," and that it needed to be reconstituted as well, editorials written by the likes of David Lawrence lamented FBI reports that crime rates had increased, and called for a "War Against Crime."[35]

Goldwater launched his candidacy at the Republican Convention in 1964 by pleading that "we revitalize our constitutional principles in all branches of government." Although the Court's directives pertaining to legislative reapportionment (1962–64) troubled him deeply, liberal reforms in the administration of criminal justice angered him most of all: the new emphasis upon an accused person's right to counsel, restraints upon the manner of obtaining confessions, and upon prolonged interrogation of an unrepresented defendant by the police. During the earlier stages of his campaign, the thrust of Goldwater's message was very pointed: "Today's Supreme Court is the least faithful to the constitutional tradition of limited government." He subsequently warned that "when vacancies occur . . . we want men appointed to the Court who will support the Constitution and not scoff at it." As the election approached, his argument became more of a generalized jeremiad: "Either we continue the suicidal drift of the last generation away from constitutional government, away from moral order, away from freedom and away from peace and order in the world community. Or we chart a new course of peace, freedom, morality, and constitutional order based on the wisdom of our history."[36]

Not since LaFollette's campaign in 1924 had a presidential candidate criticized the Supreme Court so harshly; and not since Teddy Roosevelt's assault in 1912 had the judiciary in general been such a national issue. Although Goldwater lost to Lyndon Johnson by a substantial margin, his assault—supported by journals of opinion that ran editorials with captions like "Our Vanishing Constitution"—contributed significantly to a steady slide in the Court's reputation.[37] Several Gallup polls help to demonstrate the decline. In 1963 and again in 1969 Americans were asked, "In general, what kind of a rating would you give the Supreme Court?" The responses ran as follows:[38]

	1963	1969
Excellent	10%	8%
Good	33%	25%
Fair	27%	31%
Poor	15%	23%
Don't Know	15%	13%

In 1965 a series of 405 interviews were conducted in which diverse residents of Seattle, Washington, responded to questions in much greater depth than a conventional public opinion poll permits. To cite just two representative responses, an insurance adjuster regarded the Court unfavorably because "the outcome as to what is constitutional or unconstitutional depends too much on one individual." An employee of the telephone company felt that "the Supreme Court has usurped power and bypassed the Constitution."[39]

A Gallup Poll conducted in 1967 asked almost 3,800 Americans how their perception of the Supreme Court had changed in recent years. The responses varied greatly and ranged across an ideological spectrum. The four leading replies, however, give us a clear sense of public opinion at the time.

30%   registered general disapproval, indicated a decline in respect, and believed that the Court was "going downhill."

12%   felt the justices had stifled the police, "made it too easy for the criminal" and "protects the guilty."

9%   complained that the Court had become too liberal, and saw a "lean to the left."

8%   disapproved of the rulings that had eliminated prayers from the public schools.[40]

At about the same time a Louis Harris Poll revealed that 52 percent of the American people viewed the Court's performance as "only fair" or "poor." Six years later, after Warren Burger had replaced Earl Warren, but had not significantly altered the justices' inclinations, a Gallup Poll asked whether the Court seemed "too liberal or too conservative in its decisions?" Too liberal was the dominant response (35 percent); too conservative received 26 percent; "about right" was the reaction of 17 percent; and the rest had no opinion.[41]

Although the Court became less controversial under Burger than it had been under Warren, too few people realize how much residual hostility remains during the 1980s, and how politically advantageous it can be to attack the justices. In 1982 there were no fewer than thirty proposals pending in Congress to restrict the Court's powers to interpret constitutional matters—proposals explicitly designed to by-pass the cumbersome and slow process of amending the Constitution. Busing to achieve school desegregation, legalizing abortion, and expanding the rights of criminal defendants were just a few of the provocations that aroused animosity. President Reagan and his Attorney General, William French Smith, condemned individual Supreme Court decisions as well as "judicial activism" in general.[42]

Major differences of opinion may be inevitable as part of the ongoing pattern of conflict within consensus. But in the forms just described they are neither edifying nor especially educational for the general public. The quality and role of constitutionalism in American culture are not enhanced when three branches of government sharply disagree about the scope of

A P P E N D I X C

"A Constitution for the New Deal,"
by H. L. Mencken

THIS SATIRICAL PIECE FIRST APPEARED IN *The American Mercury,* 41 (June 1937), 129–36, and was reprinted in condensed form by *The Reader's Digest,* 31 (July 1937), 27–29. In order to indicate what reached the widest audience, the condensed version appears here.

The principal cause of the uproar in Washington is a conflict between the swift-moving idealism of the New Deal and the unyielding hunkerousness of the Constitution of 1788. What is needed, obviously, is a wholly new Constitution, drawn up with enough boldness and imagination to cover the whole program of the More Abundant Life, now and hereafter.

That is what I presume to offer here. The Constitution that follows is not my invention, and in more than one detail I have unhappy doubts of its wisdom. But I believe that it sets forth with reasonable accuracy the plan of government that the More Abundant Life wizards have sought to substitute for the plan of the Fathers. They have themselves argued at one time or another, by word or deed, for everything contained herein:

PREAMBLE

We, the people of the United States, in order to form a more
perfect union, establish social justice, draw the fangs of privilege,
effect the redistribution of property, remove the burden of liberty
from ourselves and our posterity, and insure the continuance
of the New Deal, do ordain and establish this Constitution.

ARTICLE I

The Executive

All governmental power of whatever sort shall be vested in a President of the United States. He shall hold office during a series of terms of four years each, and shall take the following oath: "I do solemnly swear that I will (in so far as I deem it feasible and convenient) faithfully execute the office of President of the United States, and will (to the best of my recollection and in the light of experiment and second thought) carry out the pledges made by me during my campaign for election (or such of them as I may select)."

The President shall be commander-in-chief of the Army and Navy, and of the militia, Boy Scouts, C.I.O., People's Front, and other armed forces of the nation.

The President shall have the power:

To lay and collect taxes, and to expend the income of the United States in such manner as he may deem to be to their or his advantage;

To borrow money on the credit of the United States, and to provide for its repayment on such terms as he may fix;

To regulate all commerce with foreign nations, and among the several states, and within them; to license all persons engaged or proposing to engage in business; to regulate their affairs; to limit their profits by proclamation from time to time; and to fix wages, prices and hours of work;

To coin money, regulate the content and value thereof, and of foreign coin, and to amend or repudiate any contract requiring the payment by the United States, or by any private person, of coin of a given weight or fineness;

To repeal or amend, in his discretion, any so-called natural law, including Gresham's law, the law of diminishing returns, and the law of gravitation.

The President shall be assisted by a Cabinet of eight or more persons, whose duties shall be to make speeches whenever so instructed and to expend the public funds in such manner as to guarantee the President's continuance in office.

The President may establish such executive agencies as he deems necessary, and clothe them with such powers as he sees fit. No person shall be a member to any such bureau who has had any practical experience of the matters he is appointed to deal with.

One of the members of the Cabinet shall be an Attorney General. It shall be his duty to provide legal opinions certifying to the constitutionality of all measures undertaken by the President, and to gather evidence of the senility of judges.

ARTICLE II

The Legislature

The legislature of the United States shall consist of a Senate and a House of Representatives. Every bill shall be prepared under the direction of the President, and transmitted to the two Houses at his order by their presiding officers. No member shall propose any amendment to a bill without permission in writing from the President or one of his authorized agents. In case any member shall doubt the wisdom of a bill he may apply to the President for light upon it, and thereafter he shall be counted as voting aye. In all cases a majority of members shall be counted as voting aye.

Both Houses may appoint special committees to investigate the business practices, political views, and private lives of any persons known to be inimical to the President; and such committees shall publish at public cost any evidence discovered that appears to be damaging to the persons investigated.

Members of both Houses shall be agents of the President in the distribution of public offices, federal appropriations, and other gratuities in their several states, and shall be rewarded in ratio to their fidelity to his ideals and commands.

ARTICLE III

The Judiciary

The judges of the Supreme Court and of all inferior courts shall be appointed by the President, and shall hold their offices until he determines by proclamation that they have become senile. The number of judges appointed to the Supreme Court shall be prescribed by the President, and may be changed at his discretion. All decisions of the Supreme Court shall be unanimous.

The jurisdiction and powers of all courts shall be determined by the President. No act that he has approved shall be declared unconstitutional by any court.

ARTICLE IV

Bill of Rights

There shall be complete freedom of speech and of the press—subject to such regulations as the President or his agents may from time to time promulgate.

The freedom of communication by radio shall not be abridged; but the President and such persons as he may designate shall have the first call on the time of all stations.

In disputes between capital and labor, all the arbitrators shall be representatives of labor.

Every person whose annual income falls below a minimum to be fixed by the President shall receive from the public funds an amount sufficient to bring it up to that minimum.

No labor union shall be incorporated and no officer or member thereof shall be accountable for loss of life or damage to person or property during a strike.

All powers not delegated herein to the President are reserved to him, to be used at his discretion.

The Constitution of the United States of America

WE THE PEOPLE OF THE UNITED STATES, in Order to form a more perfect Union, establish Justice, insure domestic Tranquility, provide for the common defence, promote the general Welfare, and secure the Blessings of Liberty to ourselves and our Posterity, do ordain and establish this CONSTITUTION for the United States of America.

ARTICLE I

Section 1.

All legislative Powers herein granted shall be vested in a Congress of the United States, which shall consist of a Senate and House of Representatives.

Section 2.

The House of Representatives shall be composed of Members chosen every second Year by the People of the several States, and the Electors in each State shall have the Qualifications requisite for Electors of the most numerous Branch of the State Legislature.

No Person shall be a Representative who shall not have attained to the Age of twenty-five Years, and been seven Years a Citizen of the United States, and who shall not, when elected, be an Inhabitant of that State in which he shall be chosen.

[Representatives and direct Taxes shall be apportioned among the several States which may be included within this Union, according to their respective Numbers, which shall be determined by adding to the whole Number of free Persons, including those bound to Service for a Term of Years, and excluding Indians not taxed, three fifths of all other Persons.] The actual Enumeration shall be made within three Years after the first Meeting of the Congress of the United States, and within every subsequent Term of ten Years, in such Manner as they shall by Law direct. The Number of Representatives shall not exceed one for every thirty Thousand, but each State shall have at Least one Representative; and until such enumeration shall be made, the

State of New Hampshire shall be entitled to chuse three, Massachusetts eight, Rhode-Island and Providence Plantations one, Connecticut five, New York six, New Jersey four, Pennsylvania eight, Delaware one, Maryland six, Virginia ten, North Carolina five, South Carolina five, and Georgia three.

When vacancies happen in the Representation from any State, the Executive Authority thereof shall issue Writs of Election to fill such Vacancies.

The House of Representatives shall chuse their Speaker and other Officers; and shall have the sole Power of Impeachment.

Section 3.

The Senate of the United States shall be composed of two Senators from each State, chosen by the Legislature thereof, for six Years; and each Senator shall have one Vote.

Immediately after they shall be assembled in Consequence of the first Election, they shall be divided as equally as may be into three Classes. The Seats of the Senators of the first Class shall be vacated at the Expiration of the second Year, of the second Class at the Expiration of the fourth Year, and of the third Class at the Expiration of the sixth Year, so that one-third may be chosen every second Year; and if Vacancies happen by Resignation, or otherwise, during the Recess of the Legislature of any State, the Executive thereof may make temporary Appointments until the next Meeting of the Legislature, which shall then fill such Vacancies.

No Person shall be a Senator who shall not have attained to the Age of thirty Years, and been nine Years a Citizen of the United States, and who shall not, when elected, be an Inhabitant of that State for which he shall be chosen.

The Vice President of the United States shall be President of the Senate, but shall have no vote, unless they be equally divided.

The Senate shall chuse their other Officers, and also a President pro tempore, in the absence of the Vice President, or when he shall exercise the Office of President of the United States.

The Senate shall have the sole Power to try all Impeachments. When sitting for that purpose they shall be on Oath or Affirmation. When the President of the United States is tried, the Chief Justice shall preside: And no person shall be convicted without the Concurrence of two thirds of the Members present.

Judgment in Cases of Impeachment shall not extend further than to removal from Office, and disqualification to hold and enjoy any Office of honor, Trust, or Profit under the United States: but the Party convicted shall nevertheless be liable and subject to Indictment, Trial, Judgment, and Punishment, according to Law.

Section 4.

The Times, Places and Manner of holding Elections for Senators and Representatives, shall be prescribed in each State by the Legislature thereof; but the Congress may at any time by Law make or alter such Regulations, except as to the Places of Chusing Senators.

The Congress shall assemble at least once in every Year, and such Meeting shall be on the first Monday in December, unless they shall by Law appoint a different Day.

Section 5.

Each House shall be the Judge of the Elections, Returns and Qualifications of its own Members, and a Majority of each shall constitute a Quorum to do Business; but a smaller number may adjourn from day to day, and may be authorized to compel the Attendance of absent Members, in such Manner, and under such Penalties, as each House may provide.

Each House may determine the Rules of its Proceedings, punish its Members for disorderly Behaviour, and, with the Concurrence of two thirds, expel a Member.

Each House shall keep a Journal of its Proceedings, and from time to time publish the same, excepting such Parts as may in their Judgment require Secrecy; and the Yeas and Nays of the Members of either House on any question shall, at the Desire of one fifth of those Present, be entered on the Journal.

Neither House, during the Session of Congress, shall, without the Consent of the other, adjourn for more than three days, nor to any other Place than that in which the two Houses shall be sitting.

Section 6.

The Senators and Representatives shall receive a Compensation for their Services, to be ascertained by Law, and paid out of the Treasury of the United States. They shall in all Cases, except Treason, Felony, and Breach of the Peace, be privileged from Arrest during their Attendance at the Session of their respective Houses, and in going to and returning from the same; and for any Speech or Debate in either House, they shall not be questioned in any other Place.

No Senator or Representative shall, during the Time for which he was elected, be appointed to any civil Office under the Authority of the United States, which shall have been created, or the Emoluments whereof shall have been increased, during such time; and no Person holding any Office under the United States shall be a Member of either house during his continuance in Office.

Section 7.

All Bills for raising Revenue shall originate in the House of Representatives; but the Senate may propose or concur with Amendments as on other bills.

Every Bill which shall have passed the House of Representatives and the Senate, shall, before it become a Law, be presented to the President of the United States; If he approve he shall sign it, but if not he shall return it, with his Objections, to that House in which it shall have originated, who shall enter the Objections at large on their Journal, and proceed to reconsider it. If after such Reconsideration two thirds of that House shall agree to pass the bill, it shall be sent, together with the objections, to the other House, by which it shall likewise be reconsidered, and if approved by two thirds of that House, it shall become a Law. But in all such Cases the Votes of both Houses shall be determined by Yeas and Nays, and the Names of the Persons voting for and against the Bill shall be entered on the Journal of each House respectively. If any Bill shall not be returned by the President within ten Days (Sundays excepted) after it shall have been presented to him, the Same shall be a Law, in like Manner as if he had signed it, unless the Congress by their Adjournment prevent its Return, in which Case it shall not be a Law.

Every Order, Resolution, or Vote to which the Concurrence of the Senate and House of Representatives may be necessary (except on a question of Adjournment) shall be presented to the President of the United States; and before the Same shall take Effect, shall be approved by him, or being disapproved by him, shall be repassed by two thirds of the Senate and House of Representatives, according to the Rules and Limitations prescribed in the Case of a Bill.

Section 8.

The Congress shall have Power To lay and collect Taxes, Duties, Imposts and Excises, to pay the Debts and provide for the common Defence and general Welfare of the United States; but all Duties, Imposts and Excises shall be uniform throughout the United States;

To borrow money on the credit of the United States;

To regulate Commerce with foreign Nations, and among the several States, and with the Indian Tribes;

To establish an uniform rule of Naturalization, and uniform Laws on the subject of Bankruptcies throughout the United States;

To coin Money, regulate the Value thereof, and of foreign Coin, and fix the Standard of Weights and Measures;

To provide for the Punishment of counterfeiting the Securities and current Coin of the United States;

To establish Post Offices and post Roads;

To promote the Progress of Science and useful Arts, by securing for limited Times to Authors and Inventors the exclusive Right to their respective Writings and Discoveries;

To constitute Tribunals inferior to the Supreme Court;

To define and punish Piracies and Felonies committed on the high Seas, and Offenses against the Law of Nations;

To declare War, grant Letters of Marque and Reprisal, and make Rules concerning Captures on Land and Water;

To raise and support Armies, but no Appropriation of Money to that Use shall be for a longer Term than two Years;

To provide and maintain a Navy;

To make Rules for the Government and Regulation of the land and naval forces;

To provide for calling forth the Militia to execute the Laws of the Union, suppress Insurrections and repel Invasions;

To provide for organizing, arming, and disciplining the Militia, and for governing such Part of them as may be employed in the Service of the United States, reserving to the States respectively, the Appointment of the Officers, and the Authority of training the Militia according to the discipline prescribed by Congress;

To exercise exclusive Legislation in all Cases whatsoever, over such District (not exceeding ten Miles square) as may, by Cession of particular States, and the acceptance of Congress, become the Seat of the Government of the United States, and to exercise like Authority over all Places purchased by the Consent of the Legislature of the State in which the Same shall be, for the Erection of Forts, Magazines, Arsenals, Dock-yards, and other needful Buildings;—And

To make all Laws which shall be necessary and proper for carrying into Execution the foregoing Powers, and all other Powers vested by this Constitution in the Government of the United States, or in any Department or Officer thereof.

Section 9.

The Migration or Importation of such Persons as any of the States now existing shall think proper to admit, shall not be prohibited by the Congress prior to the Year one thousand eight hundred and eight, but a tax or duty may be imposed on such Importation, not exceeding ten dollars for each Person.

The privilege of the Writ of Habeas Corpus shall not be suspended, unless when in Cases of Rebellion or Invasion the public Safety may require it.

No bill of Attainder or ex post facto Law shall be passed.

No capitation, or other direct, Tax shall be laid unless in Proportion to the Census or Enumeration herein before directed to be taken.

No Tax or Duty shall be laid on Articles exported from any State.

No Preference shall be given by any Regulation of Commerce or Revenue to the Ports of one State over those of another: nor shall Vessels bound to, or from, one State, be obliged to enter, clear, or pay Duties in another.

No Money shall be drawn from the Treasury, but in Consequence of Appropriations made by Law; and a regular Statement and Account of the Receipts and Expenditures of all public Money shall be published from time to time.

No Title of Nobility shall be granted by the United States: And no Person holding any Office of Profit or Trust under them, shall, without the Consent of the Congress, accept of any present, Emolument, Office, or Title, of any kind whatever, from any King, Prince, or foreign State.

Section 10.

No State shall enter into any Treaty, Alliance, or Confederation; grant Letters of Marque and Reprisal; coin Money; emit Bills of Credit; make any Thing but gold and silver Coin a Tender in Payment of Debts; pass any Bill of Attainder, ex post facto Law, or Law impairing the Obligation of Contracts, or grant any Title of Nobility.

No State shall, without the Consent of the Congress, lay any Imposts or Duties on Imports or Exports, except what may be absolutely necessary for executing its inspection Laws; and the net Produce of all Duties and Imposts, laid by any State on Imports or Exports, shall be for the Use of the Treasury of the United States; and all such Laws shall be subject to the Revision and Control of the Congress.

No state shall, without the Consent of Congress, lay any duty of Tonnage, keep Troops, or Ships of War in time of Peace, enter into any Agreement or Compact with another State, or with a foreign Power, or engage in War, unless actually invaded, or in such imminent Danger as will not admit of delay.

ARTICLE II

Section 1.

The executive Power shall be vested in a President of the United States of America. He shall hold his Office during the Term of four years, and, together with the Vice President, chosen for the same Term, be elected, as follows:

Each State shall appoint, in such Manner as the Legislature thereof may direct, a Number of Electors, equal to the whole Number of Senators and Representatives to which the State may be entitled in the Congress: but no Senator or Representative, or Person holding an Office of Trust or Profit under the United States, shall be appointed an Elector.

[The Electors shall meet in their respective States, and vote by Ballot for two persons, of whom one at least shall not be an Inhabitant of the same State with themselves. And they shall make a List of all the Persons voted for, and of the Number of Votes for each; which List they shall sign and certify, and transmit sealed to the Seat of the Government of the United States, directed to the President of the Senate. The

President of the Senate shall, in the Presence of the Senate and House of Representatives, open all the Certificates, and the Votes shall then be counted. The Person having the greatest Number of Votes shall be the President, if such Number be a Majority of the whole Number of Electors appointed; and if there be more than one who have such Majority, and have an equal Number of Votes, then the House of Representatives shall immediately chuse by Ballot one of them for President; and if no Person have a Majority, then from the five highest on the List the said House shall in like Manner chuse the President. But in chusing the President, the Votes shall be taken by States, the Representation from each State having one Vote; a quorum for this Purpose shall consist of a Member or Members from two-thirds of the States, and a Majority of all the States shall be necessary to a Choice. In every Case, after the Choice of the President, the Person having the greatest Number of Votes of the Electors shall be the Vice President. But if there should remain two or more who have equal votes, the Senate shall chuse from them by Ballot the Vice President.]

The Congress may determine the Time of chusing the Electors, and the Day on which they shall give their Votes; which Day shall be the same throughout the United States.

No person except a natural-born Citizen, or a Citizen of the United States, at the time of the Adoption of this Constitution, shall be eligible to the Office of President; neither shall any Person be eligible to that Office who shall not have attained to the Age of thirty-five years, and been fourteen Years a Resident within the United States.

In Case of the Removal of the President from Office, or of his Death, Resignation, or Inability to discharge the Powers and Duties of the said Office, the same shall devolve on the Vice President, and the Congress may by Law provide for the Case of Removal, Death, Resignation, or Inability, both of the President and Vice President, declaring what Officer shall then act as President, and such Officer shall act accordingly, until the disability be removed, or a President shall be elected.

The President shall, at stated Times, receive for his Services a Compensation, which shall neither be increased nor diminished during the Period for which he shall have been elected, and he shall not receive within that Period any other Emolument from the United States, or any of them.

Before he enter on the execution of his Office, he shall take the following Oath or Affirmation:—"I do solemnly swear (or affirm) that I will faithfully execute the Office of President of the United States, and will, to the best of my Ability, preserve, protect, and defend the Constitution of the United States."

Section 2.

The President shall be Commander in Chief of the Army and Navy of the United States, and of the Militia of the several States, when called into the actual Service of the United States; he may require the Opinion, in writing, of the principal Officer in each of the executive Departments, upon any subject relating to the Duties of their respective Offices, and he shall have Power to Grant Reprieves and Pardons for Offenses against the United States, except in Cases of Impeachment.

He shall have Power, by and with the Advice and Consent of the Senate, to make Treaties, provided two-thirds of the Senators present concur; and he shall nominate, and by and with the Advice and Consent of the Senate, shall appoint Ambassadors, other public Ministers and Consuls, Judges of the supreme Court, and all other Officers of the United States, whose Appointments are not herein otherwise provided for, and which shall be established by Law: but the Congress may by Law vest the Appointment of such inferior Officers, as they think proper, in the President alone, in the Courts of Law, or in the Heads of Departments.

The President shall have Power to fill up all Vacancies that may happen during the recess of the Senate, by granting Commissions which shall expire at the End of their next Session.

Section 3.

He shall from time to time give to the Congress Information of the State of the Union, and recommend to their Consideration such Measures as he shall judge necessary and expedient; he may, on extraordinary occasions, convene both Houses, or either of them, and in Case of Disagreement between them, with respect to the Time of Adjournment, he may adjourn them to such Time as he shall think proper; he shall receive Ambassadors and other public Ministers; he shall take care that the Laws be faithfully executed, and shall Commission all the Officers of the United States.

Section 4.

The President, Vice President and all civil Officers of the United States, shall be removed from Office on Impeachment for, and Conviction of, Treason, Bribery, or other high Crimes and Misdemeanors.

ARTICLE III

Section 1.

The judicial Power of the United States, shall be vested in one supreme Court, and in such inferior Courts as the Congress may from time to time ordain and establish. The Judges, both of the supreme and inferior Courts, shall hold their Offices during good Behaviour, and shall, at stated Times, receive for their Services, a Compensation, which shall not be diminished during their Continuance in Office.

Section 2.

The judicial Power shall extend to all Cases, in Law and Equity, arising under this Constitution, the Laws of the United States, and Treaties made, or which shall be made, under their Authority;—to all Cases affecting ambassadors, other public ministers and consuls;—to all cases of admiralty and maritime Jurisdiction;—to Controversies to which the United States shall be a Party;—to Controversies between two or more States;—between a State and Citizens of another State;—between Citizens of different States;—between Citizens of the same State claiming Lands under Grants of different States, and between a State, or the Citizens thereof, and foreign States, Citizens or Subjects.

In all Cases affecting Ambassadors, other public Ministers and Consuls, and those in which a State shall be Party, the supreme Court shall have original Jurisdiction. In all the other Cases before mentioned, the supreme Court shall have appellate Jurisdiction, both as to Law and Fact, with such Exceptions, and under such Regulations as the Congress shall make.

The trial of all Crimes, except in Cases of Impeachment, shall be by Jury; and such Trial shall be held in the State where the said Crimes shall have been committed; but when not committed within any State, the Trial shall be at such Place or Places as the Congress may by Law have directed.

Section 3.

Treason against the United States, shall consist only in levying War against them, or in adhering to their Enemies, giving them Aid and Comfort. No Person shall be convicted of Treason unless on the Testimony of two Witnesses to the same overt Act, or on Confession in open Court.

The Congress shall have power to declare the Punishment of Treason, but no Attainder of Treason shall work Corruption of Blood, or Forfeiture except during the Life of the Person attainted.

ARTICLE IV

Section 1.

Full Faith and Credit shall be given in each State to the public Acts, Records, and judicial Proceedings of every other State. And the Congress may by general Laws prescribe the Manner in which such Acts, Records and Proceedings shall be proved, and the Effect thereof.

Section 2.

The Citizens of each State shall be entitled to all Privileges and Immunities of Citizens in the several States.

A Person charged in any State with Treason, Felony, or other Crime, who shall flee from Justice, and be found in another State, shall on demand of the executive Authority of the State from which he fled, be delivered up, to be removed to the State having Jurisdiction of the crime.

No Person held to Service or Labour in one State, under the Laws thereof, escaping into another, shall, in Consequence of any Law or Regulation therein, be discharged from such Service or Labour, but shall be delivered up on Claim of the Party to whom such Service or Labour may be due.

Section 3.

New States may be admitted by the Congress into this Union; but no new State shall be formed or erected within the Jurisdiction of any other State; nor any State be formed by the Junction of two or more States, or parts of States, without the Consent of the Legislatures of the States concerned as well as of the Congress.

The Congress shall have Power to dispose of and make all needful Rules and Regulations respecting the Territory or other Property belonging to the United States; and nothing in this Constitution shall be so construed as to Prejudice any Claims of the United States, or of any particular State.

Section 4.

The United States shall guarantee to every State in this Union a Republican Form of Government, and shall protect each of them against Invasion; and on Application of the Legislature, or of the Executive (when the Legislature cannot be convened) against domestic Violence.

ARTICLE V

The Congress, whenever two-thirds of both Houses shall deem it necessary, shall propose Amendments to this Constitution, or, on the Application of the Legislatures of two-thirds of the several States, shall call a Convention for proposing Amendments, which, in either Case, shall be valid to all Intents and Purposes, as part of this Constitution, when ratified by the Legislatures of three-fourths of the several States, or by Conventions in three-fourths thereof, as the one or the other Mode of Ratification may be proposed by the Congress; Provided that no Amendment which may be made prior to the Year One thousand eight hundred and eight shall in any manner affect the first and fourth Clauses in the Ninth Section of the first Article; and that no State, without its Consent, shall be deprived of its equal Suffrage in the Senate.

ARTICLE VI

All Debts contracted and Engagements entered into, before the Adoption of this Constitution, shall be as valid against the United States under this Constitution, as under the Confederation.

This Constitution, and the Laws of the United States which shall be made in Pursuance thereof; and all Treaties made, or which shall be made, under the Authority of the United States, shall be the supreme Law of the Land; and the Judges in every State shall be bound thereby, any Thing in the Constitution or Laws of any State to the Contrary notwithstanding.

The Senators and Representatives before mentioned, and the Members of the several State Legislatures, and all executive and judicial Officers, both of the United States and of the several States, shall be bound by Oath or Affirmation to support this Constitution; but no religious Test shall ever be required as a qualification to any Office or public Trust under the United States.

ARTICLE VII

The Ratification of the Conventions of nine States shall be sufficient for the Establishment of this Constitution between the States so ratifying the same.

Done in Convention by the Unanimous Consent of the States present the Seventeenth Day of September in the Year of our Lord one thousand seven hundred and Eighty seven, and of the Independence of the United States of America the Twelfth. In Witness whereof We have hereunto subscribed our Names.

George Washington
President and deputy from Virginia

NEW HAMPSHIRE	NEW JERSEY	DELAWARE	NORTH CAROLINA
John Langdon	William Livingston	George Read	William Blount
Nicholas Gilman	David Brearley	Gunning Bedford, Jr.	Richard Dobbs
	William Paterson	John Dickinson	Spaight
	Jonathan Dayton	Richard Bassett	Hugh Williamson
		Jacob Broom	
MASSACHUSETTS	PENNSYLVANIA	MARYLAND	SOUTH CAROLINA
Nathaniel Gorham	Benjamin Franklin	James McHenry	John Rutledge
Rufus King	Thomas Mifflin	Daniel of	Charles Cotesworth
	Robert Morris	St. Thomas Jenifer	Pinckney
CONNECTICUT	George Clymer	Daniel Carroll	Charles Pinckney
	Thomas FitzSimons		Pierce Butler
William Samuel	Jared Ingersoll		
Johnson	James Wilson		
Roger Sherman	Gouverneur Morris		

NEW YORK	VIRGINIA	GEORGIA
Alexander Hamilton	John Blair James Madison, Jr.	William Few Abraham Baldwin

Articles in Addition to, and Amendment of, the Constitution of the United States of America, Proposed by Congress, and Ratified by the Legislatures of the Several States, Pursuant to the Fifth Article of the Original Constitution

[ARTICLE I]

Congress shall make no law respecting an establishment of religion, or prohibiting the free exercise thereof; or abridging the freedom of speech, or of the press; or the right of the people peaceably to assemble, and to petition the Government for a redress of grievances.

[ARTICLE II]

A well regulated Militia, being necessary to the security of a free State, the right of the people to keep and bear Arms shall not be infringed.

[ARTICLE III]

No Soldier shall, in time of peace, be quartered in any house, without the consent of the Owner, nor in time of war, but in a manner to be prescribed by law.

[ARTICLE IV]

The right of the people to be secure in their persons, houses, papers, and effects, against unreasonable searches and seizures, shall not be violated, and no Warrants shall issue, but upon probable cause, supported by Oath or affirmation, and particularly describing the place to be searched, and the persons or things to be seized.

[ARTICLE V]

No person shall be held to answer for a capital or otherwise infamous crime, unless on a presentment or indictment of a Grand Jury, except in cases arising in the land or naval forces, or in the Militia, when in actual service in time of War or public danger; nor shall any person be subject for the same offence to be twice put in jeopardy of life or limb; nor shall be compelled in any criminal case to be a witness against himself, nor be deprived of life, liberty, or property, without due process of law; nor shall private property be taken for public use, without just compensation.

[ARTICLE VI]

In all criminal prosecutions, the accused shall enjoy the right to a speedy and public trial, by an impartial jury of the State and district wherein the crime shall have been committed, which district shall have been previously ascertained by law, and to be informed of the nature and cause of the accusation; to be confronted with the witnesses against him; to have compulsory process for obtaining witnesses in his favour, and to have the Assistance of Counsel for his defence.

[ARTICLE VII]

In suits of common law, where the value in controversy shall exceed twenty dollars, the right of trial by jury shall be preserved, and no fact tried by a jury, shall be otherwise reexamined in any Court of the United States, than according to the rules of the common law.

[ARTICLE VIII]

Excessive bail shall not be required, nor excessive fines imposed, nor cruel and unusual punishments inflicted.

[ARTICLE IX]

The enumeration of the Constitution, of certain rights, shall not be construed to deny or disparage others retained by the people.

[ARTICLE X]

The powers not delegated to the United States by the Constitution, nor prohibited by it to the States, are reserved to the States respectively, or to the people.
[Amendments I-X, in force 1791.)

[ARTICLE XI]

The Judicial power of the United States shall not be construed to extend to any suit in law or equity, commenced or prosecuted against one of the United States by Citizens of another State, or by Citizens or Subjects of any Foreign State.

[ARTICLE XII]

The Electors shall meet in their respective States and vote by ballot for President and Vice-President, one of whom, at least, shall not be an inhabitant of the same State with themselves; they shall name in their ballots the person voted for as President, and in distinct ballots the person voted for as Vice-President, and they shall make distinct lists of all persons voted for as President, and of all persons voted for as Vice-President, and of the number of votes for each, which lists they shall sign and certify, and transmit sealed to the seat of the government of the United States, directed to the President of the Senate;—The President of the Senate shall, in the presence of the Senate and House of Representatives, open all the certificates and the votes shall then be counted;—The person having the greatest number of votes for President, shall be the President, if such number be a majority of the whole number of Electors appointed; and if no person have such majority, then from the persons having the highest numbers not exceeding three on the list of those voted for as President, the House of Representatives shall choose immediately, by ballot, the President. But in choosing the President, the votes shall be taken by states, the representation from each state having one vote; a quorum for this purpose shall consist of a member or members from two-thirds of the states, and a majority of all the states shall be necessary to a choice. And if the House of Representatives shall not choose a President whenever the right of choice shall devolve upon them, before the fourth day of March next following, then the Vice-President shall act as President, as in the case of the death or other constitutional disability of the President.—The person having the greatest number of votes as Vice-President, shall be the Vice-President, if such number be a majority of the whole number of Electors appointed, and if no person have a majority, then from the two highest numbers on the list, the Senate shall choose the Vice-President, a quorum for the purpose shall consist of two-thirds of the whole number of Senators, and a majority of the whole number shall be necessary to a choice. But no person constitutionally ineligible to the office of President shall be eligible to that of Vice-President of the United States.

[ARTICLE XIII]

Section 1.

Neither slavery nor involuntary servitude, except as a punishment for crime whereof the party shall have been duly convicted, shall exist within the United States, or any place subject to their jurisdiction.

Section 2.

Congress shall have power to enforce this article by appropriate legislation.

[ARTICLE XIV]

Section 1.

All persons born or naturalized in the United States, and subject to the jurisdiction thereof, are citizens of the United States and of the State wherein they reside. No State shall abridge the privileges or immunities of citizens of the United States; nor shall any State deprive any person of life, liberty, or property, without due process of law; nor deny to any person within its jurisdiction the equal protection of the laws.

Section 2.

Representatives shall be apportioned among the several States according to their respective numbers, counting the whole number of persons in each State, excluding Indians not taxed. But when the right to vote at any election for the choice of electors for President and Vice President of the United States, Representatives in Congress, the Executive and Judicial officers of a State, or the members of the Legislature thereof, is denied to any of the male inhabitants of such State, being twenty-one years of age, and citizens of the United States, or in any way abridged, except for participation in rebellion, or other crime, the basis of representation therein shall be reduced in the proportion which the number of such male citizens shall bear to the whole number of male citizens twenty-one years of age in such State.

Section 3.

No person shall be a Senator or Representative in Congress, or elector of President and Vice-President, or hold any office, civil or military, under the United States, or under any State, who, having previously taken an oath, as a member of Congress, or as an officer of the United States, or as a member of any State legislature, or as an executive or judicial officer of any State, to support the Constitution of the United States, shall have engaged in insurrection or rebellion against the same, or given aid or comfort to the enemies thereof. But Congress may by a vote of two-thirds of each House, remove such disability.

Section 4.

The validity of the public debt of the United States, authorized by law, including debts incurred for payment of pensions and bounties for services in suppressing insurrection or rebellion, shall not be questioned. But neither the United States nor any State shall assume or pay any debts or obligation incurred in aid of insurrection or rebellion against the United States, or any claim for the loss or emancipation of any slave; but all such debts, obligations, and claims shall be held illegal and void.

Section 5.

The Congress shall have the power to enforce, by appropriate legislation, the provisions of this article.

[ARTICLE XV]

Section 1.

The right of citizens of the United States to vote shall not be denied or abridged by the United States or by any State on account of race, color, or previous condition of servitude—

Section 2.

The Congress shall have power to enforce this article by appropriate legislation.

[ARTICLE XVI]

The Congress shall have power to lay and collect taxes on incomes, from whatever source derived, without apportionment among the several States, and without regard to any census or enumeration.

[ARTICLE XVII]

The Senate of the United States shall be composed of two Senators from each State, elected by the people thereof, for six years; and each Senator shall have one vote. The electors in each State shall have the qualifications requisite for electors of the most numerous branch of the State legislatures.

When vacancies happen in the representation of any State in the Senate, the executive authority of such State shall issue writs of election to fill such vacancies: *Provided,* That the legislature of any State may empower the executive thereof to make temporary appointments until the people fill the vacancies by election as the legislature may direct.

This amendment shall not be so construed as to affect the election or term of any Senator chosen before it becomes valid as part of the Constitution.

[ARTICLE XVIII]

Section 1.

After one year from the ratification of this article the manufacture, sale, or transportation of intoxicating liquors within, the importation thereof into, or the exportation thereof from the United States and all territory subject to the jurisdiction thereof for beverage purposes is hereby prohibited.

Section 2.

The Congress and the several States shall have concurrent power to enforce this article by appropriate legislation.

Section 3.

The article shall be inoperative unless it shall have been ratified as an amendment to the Constitution by the legislatures of the several States, as provided in the Constitution, within seven years from the date of the submission hereof to the States by the Congress.

[ARTICLE XIX]

The right of citizens of the United States to vote shall not be denied or abridged by the United States or by any State on account of sex.

Congress shall have power to enforce this article by appropriate legislation.

[ARTICLE XX]

Section 1.

The terms of the President and Vice-President shall end at noon on the 20th day of January, and the terms of Senators and Representatives at noon on the 3d day of January, of the years in which such terms would have ended if this article had not been ratified; and the terms of their successors shall then begin.

Section 2.

The Congress shall assemble at least once in every year, and such meeting shall begin at noon on the 3d day of January, unless they shall by law appoint a different day.

Section 3.

If, at the time fixed for the beginning of the term of the President, the President elect shall have died, the Vice-President elect shall become President. If a President shall not have been chosen before the time fixed for the beginning of his term, or if the President elect shall have failed to qualify, then the Vice-President elect shall act as President until a President shall have qualified; and the Congress may by law provide for the case wherein neither a President elect nor a Vice-President elect shall have qualified, declaring who shall then act as President, or the manner in which one who is to act shall be selected, and such person shall act accordingly until a President or Vice-President shall have qualified.

Section 4.

The Congress may by law provide for the case of the death of any of the persons from whom the House of Representatives may choose a President whenever the right of choice shall have devolved upon them, and for the case of the death of any of the persons from whom the Senate may choose a Vice-President whenever the right of choice shall have devolved upon them.

Section 5.

Sections 1 and 2 shall take effect on the 15th day of October following the ratification of this article.

Section 6.

This article shall be inoperative unless it shall have been ratified as an amendment to the Constitution by the legislatures of three-fourths of the several States within seven years from the date of its submission.

[ARTICLE XXI]

Section 1.

The eighteenth article of amendment to the Constitution of the United States is hereby repealed.

Section 2.

The transportation or importation into any State, Territory, or possession of the United States for delivery or use therein of intoxicating liquors, in violation of the laws thereof, is hereby prohibited.

Section 3.

This article shall be inoperative unless it shall have been ratified as an amendment to the Constitution by conventions in the several States, as provided in the Constitution, within seven years from the date of the submission hereof to the States by the Congress.

[ARTICLE XXII]

No person shall be elected to the office of the President more than twice, and no person who has held the office of President, or acted as President, for more than two years of a term to which some other person was elected President shall be elected to the office of the President more than once.

But this Article shall not apply to any person holding the office of President when this Article was proposed by the Congress, and shall not prevent any person who may be holding the office of President, or acting as President, during the term within which this Article becomes operative from holding the office of President or acting as President during the remainder of such term.

This article shall be inoperative unless it shall have been ratified as an amendment to the Constitution by the legislatures of three-fourths of the several states within seven years from the date of its submission to the states by the Congress.

[ARTICLE XXIII]

Section 1.

The District constituting the Seat of Government of the United States shall appoint in such manner as the Congress may direct:

A number of electors of President and Vice-President equal to the whole number of Senators and Representatives in Congress to which the District would be entitled if it were a State, but in no event more than the least populous State; they shall be in addition to those appointed by the States, but they shall be considered, for the purposes of the election of President and Vice-President, to be electors appointed by a State; and they shall meet in the District and perform such duties as provided by the twelfth article of amendment.

Section 2.

The Congress shall have power to enforce this article by appropriate legislation.

[ARTICLE XXIV]

Section 1.

The right of citizens of the United States to vote in any primary or other election for President or Vice President, for electors for President or Vice President, or for Senator or Representative in Congress, shall not be denied or abridged by the United States or any state by reason of failure to pay any poll tax or other tax.

Section 2.

The Congress shall have the power to enforce this article by appropriate legislation.

[ARTICLE XXV]

Section 1.

In case of the removal of the President from office or of his death or resignation, the Vice President shall become President.

Section 2.

Whenever there is a vacancy in the office of the Vice President, the President shall nominate a Vice President who shall take office upon confirmation by a majority vote of both Houses of Congress.

Section 3.

Whenever the President transmits to the President Pro Tempore of the Senate and the Speaker of the House of Representatives his written declaration that he is unable to discharge the powers and duties of his office, and until he transmits to them a written declaration to the contrary, such powers and duties shall be discharged by the Vice President as Acting President.

Section 4.

Whenever the Vice President and a majority of either the principal officers of the executive departments or of such other body as Congress may by law provide, transmit to the President Pro Tempore of the Senate and the Speaker of the House of Representatives their written declaration that the President is unable to discharge the powers and duties of his office, the Vice President shall immediately assume the powers and duties of the office as Acting President.

Thereafter, when the President transmits to the President Pro Tempore of the Senate and the Speaker of the House of Representatives his written declaration that no inability exists, he shall resume the powers and duties of his office unless the Vice President and a majority of either the principal officers of the executive departments or of such other body as Congress may by law provide, transmit within four days to the President Pro Tempore of the Senate and the Speaker of the House of Representatives their written declaration that the President is unable to discharge the powers and duties of his office. Thereupon Congress shall decide the issue, assembling within forty-eight hours for that purpose if not in session. If the Congress, within twenty-one days after receipt of the latter written declaration, or, if Congress is not in session, within twenty-one days after Congress is required to assemble, determines by two-thirds vote of both Houses that the President is unable to discharge the powers and duties of his office, the Vice President shall continue to discharge the same as Acting President; otherwise, the President shall resume the powers and duties of his office.

[ARTICLE XXVI]

Section 1.

The right of citizens of the United States, who are eighteen years of age or older, to vote shall not be denied or abridged by the United States or by any State on account of age.

Section 2.

The Congress shall have power to enforce this article by appropriate legislation.

Abbreviations

AAAPSS	*Annals of the American Academy of Political and Social Science*
ABAJ	*American Bar Association Journal*
AHR	*American Historical Review*
AJLH	*American Journal of Legal History*
APSR	*American Political Science Review*
CH	*Current History*
CLR	*Columbia Law Review*
CR	*The Constitutional Review*
CREC	*The Congressional Record*
CUBL	Columbia University, Butler Library, Rare Books and Manuscripts, New York City
CUL	Cornell University, Olin Library, Department of Manuscripts and University Archives, Ithaca, N.Y.
DAB	*Dictionary of American Biography* (1927–)
HEH	Henry E. Huntington Library, San Marino, Calif.
HLR	*Harvard Law Review*
HLSL	Harvard Law School Library, Langdell Hall, Cambridge, Mass.
HSP	Historical Society of Pennsylvania, Philadelphia, Pa.
HUHL	Harvard University, Houghton Library, Cambridge, Mass.
HUPL	Harvard University, Pusey Library, Cambridge, Mass.
JAH	*Journal of American History*
JP	*Journal of Politics*
JPL	*Journal of Public Law*
LCMD	Library of Congress, Manuscript Division, Madison Building, Washington, D.C.
MHS	Massachusetts Historical Society, Boston, Mass.
MVHR	*Mississippi Valley Historical Review*
NA	National Archives
NAR	*The North American Review*

NR	*The New Republic*
NYSHA	New York State Historical Association
NYT	*The New York Times*
PSQ	*Political Science Quarterly*
PUML	Princeton University, Seeley G. Mudd Manuscript Library, Princeton, N.J.
RC	The Roper Center, Office of Archival Development, University of Connecticut, Storrs, Conn.
RD	*The Reader's Digest*
RP	*Review of Politics*
SAQ	*South Atlantic Quarterly*
SCR	*The Supreme Court Review*
UCA	University of Chicago Archives, Regenstein Library, Special Collections, Chicago, Ill.
UFYL	University of Florida, P. K. Yonge Library, Gainesville, Fla.
UMUA	University of Minnesota, University Archives, Minneapolis, Minn.
VLR	*Vanderbilt Law Review*
VSD	*Vital Speeches of the Day*
WMQ	*William and Mary Quarterly*
WMSL	College of William and Mary, Swem Library, Manuscripts and Rare Books Department, Williamsburg, Va.
YLJ	*Yale Law Journal*

250 U.S. 616 (1919) is the standard form of citation for *United States Reports: Cases Adjudged in the Supreme Court,* referring in this instance to volume 250 (1918–19 term), the case of *Abrams et al.* v. *United States,* pp. 616–31.

Notes

1   Beck, *The Constitution of the United States: Yesterday, Today—and Tomorrow?* (New York, 1924), 205. See also Beck, "The Anniversary of the Constitution," CR, 13 (1929), 187; James A. Van Osdol, "Future Organization and Defense of the Constitution," *ibid.* (1929), 124.

2   Samuel T. Williamson, *Frank Gannett: A Biography* (New York, 1940), 179–80; *The Autobiography of Sol Bloom* (New York, 1948), 222.

3   Beveridge to Corwin, Feb. 9, 1918, Beveridge Papers, box 212, LCMD: Farrand to Arthur M. Schlesinger, Mar. 11, 1924, Schlesinger Papers, HUPL.

4   *Memoirs of Halidé Edib* [Adivar] (New York, n.d.), ch. 9, "The Constitutional Revolution of 1908," esp. 252–60.

5   Richard Loss, ed., *Corwin on the Constitution,* I (Ithaca, N.Y., 1981), ch. 1, "The Worship of the Constitution" [1920], 47–55.

6   Leon Harris, *Upton Sinclair: American Rebel* (New York, 1975), 197–98.

7   Upton Sinclair, *My Lifetime in Letters* (Columbia, Mo., 1960), 55, 297; Floyd Dell, *Upton Sinclair: A Study in Social Protest* (New York, 1927), 180–81.

8   *The Autobiography of Upton Sinclair* (New York, 1962), 229–31. Sinclair's letter was printed as a leaflet and circulated widely in Los Angeles. It was also reprinted in *The Nation* on June 6, 1923, accompanied by an editorial note which included these two sentences: "The law gives a police officer the right to enter private property only in two cases: if he has a warrant of arrest, or if a felony is actually being committed. Neither of these excuses existed in Los Angeles."

9   *Ibid.,* 231–32.

10 Quoted in Harris, *Sinclair,* 198. For incidents around the turn of the century in which police officials expressed attitudes similar to those in the Sinclair

episode, see Ernest S. Bates, *This Land of Liberty* (New York, 1930), 78–79.

11 Walton H. Hamilton, "Constitutionalism," in *Encyclopedia of the Social Sciences* (New York, 1931), IV, 255–58. See also Carl J. Friedrich, "Constitutions and Constitutionalism," in *International Encyclopedia of the Social Sciences* (New York, 1968), III, 318–26. Charles A. Beard defined constitutionalism as "the proposition that the powers of all officials are restrained by fundamental rights reserved to the people." *The Republic: Conversations on Fundamentals* (New York, 1943), 37.

12 James F. Beard, ed., *The Letters and Journals of James Fenimore Cooper* (Cambridge, Mass., 1964), III, 8; Taft's opinion in *Bailey* v. *Drexel Furniture Company,* in Henry Steele Commager, ed., *Documents of American History* (7th ed.: New York, 1963), 153.

13 Farrand to Charles M. Andrews, April 14, 1910, Farrand Papers, HEH; James G. Randall, "The Interrelation of Social and Constitutional History," AHR, 35 (1929), 1–13; William T. Hutchinson, "The Significance of the Constitution of the United States in the Teaching of American History," *The Historian,* 13 (1950), 8.

14 Commager to McLaughlin, May 9, 1935, McLaughlin Papers, box 2, UCA. See also James McLaughlin to Andrew C. McLaughlin, March 21, 1935, *ibid.*

15 Elton, *The Future of the Past* (Cambridge, Eng., 1968), 24–25.

16 James D. Richardson, ed., *A Compilation of the Messages and Papers of the Presidents, 1789–1897* (Washington, D.C., 1896), I, 467–68.

17 J. W. Burrow, *A Liberal Descent: Victorian Historians and the English Past* (Cambridge, Eng., 1981), 241.

18 Roosevelt to Frederick G. Fincke, June 7, 1901, in Elting E. Morison, *et al.,* eds., *The Letters of Theodore Roosevelt* (Cambridge, Mass., 1951), III, 89.

19 Wyzanski, "Judicial Review in America: Some Reflections," in Ronald K. L. Collins, ed., *Constitutional Government in America: Essays and Proceedings from Southwestern University Law Review's First West Coast Conference on Constitutional Law* (Durham, N.C., 1980), 485.

• CHAPTER I *The Problem of Constitutionalism in American Culture*

1 Jefferson, "First Inaugural," March 4, 1801, in Merrill D. Peterson, ed., *The Portable Thomas Jefferson* (New York, 1975), 294; Roberts, *U.S.* v. *Sprague,* 282 U.S. 731.

2 [Sarah Rogers Haight], *Letters from the Old World by a Lady of New York* (New York, 1840), I, 87; Ruth Miller Elson, *Guardians of Tradition: American Schoolbooks of the Nineteenth Century* (Lincoln, Nebr., 1964), 60, 62, 292–93.

3 "Education and Civilization," Aug. 7, 1852, in Everett, *Orations and Speeches on Various Occasions* (Boston, 1879), III, 123; A. T. Southworth, *The Common Sense of the Constitution of the United States* (Boston, 1924), iii.

4 Beck, *The Constitution of the United States: Yesterday, Today—and Tomorrow?* (New York, 1924), 267–68; Beck to Mencken, Dec. 15, 1924, Beck Papers, box 2, PUML.

5   Transcript of the CBS News Special, "Justice Black and the Bill of Rights," Dec. 3, 1968, p. 3, courtesy of CBS.

6   See Roderic H. Davison, "The Post-Prandial Musings of a Historian Who Has Been Working in the Ottoman Archives," *Middle East Studies Association Bulletin,* 10 (1976), 5.

7   See Charles Warren, "Sources of Knowledge of the Constitution," CR, 11 (1927), 174–82; Kenneth M. Stampp, "The Concept of a Perpetual Union," JAH, 65 (1978), 5, 9–10; Harry V. Jaffa, *Equality and Liberty: Theory and Practice in American Politics* (New York, 1965), 174.

8   Quoted in Edward S. Corwin, *Court Over Constitution: A Study of Judicial Review as an Instrument of Popular Government* (Princeton, 1938), 182–83. See also Corwin to W. L. Carpenter, Feb. 14, 1936, Corwin Papers, box 2, PUML. "There are 8 or 10 words of the Constitution, the meaning of which has always been very uncertain and continues to be uncertain. The Supreme Court has been interpreting these words ('commerce,' 'regulate,' 'due process of law,' 'liberty,' etc.) for over 140 years now and from a great many points of view and under the influence of a great variety of interests, and today it has at its command often sharply divergent answers to questions which are put to it regarding the meaning of these terms."

9   See Harold M. Hyman, *A More Perfect Union: The Impact of the Civil War and Reconstruction on the Constitution* (New York, 1973), 96–98, 103, 445, 474–75; Samuel J. May, *Some Recollections of Our Antislavery Conflict* (Boston, 1869), 143–44. Even Joseph Story conceded in his *Commentaries* and elsewhere that the Constitution contained major ambiguities. See R. Kent Newmyer, *Supreme Court Justice Joseph Story: Statesman of the Old Republic* (Chapel Hill, N.C., 1985), 191, 371–76.

10   Alan Jones, "Thomas M. Cooley and 'Laissez-Faire Constitutionalism': A Reconsideration," JAH, 53 (1967), 759, 768, 770; Jonathan Prude, "Portrait of a Civil Libertarian: The Faith and Fear of Zechariah Chafee, Jr.," JAH, 60 (1973), 643, 645, 656. See also Martin Diamond, "Conservatives, Liberals, and the Constitution," *The Public Interest,* no. 1 (1965), 109.

11   See Perry Miller, *The Life of the Mind in America from the Revolution to the Civil War* (New York, 1965), 152; Don E. Fehrenbacher, *Slavery, Law, and Politics: The Dred Scott Case in Historical Perspective* (abr. ed., New York, 1981), 151–52, 155; William M. Wiecek, *The Sources of Antislavery Constitutionalism in America, 1760–1848* (Ithaca, N.Y., 1977), 139; and Paul Finkelman, *An Imperfect Union: Slavery, Federalism, and Comity* (Chapel Hill, N.C., 1981), 17.

12   Edward S. Corwin, *Constitutional Revolution, Ltd.* (Claremont, Calif., 1941), 26, 111–12; Corwin, *The Twilight of the Supreme Court: A History of Our Constitutional Theory* (New Haven, Conn., 1934), ch. 2; Richard C. Cortner, *The Supreme Court and the Second Bill of Rights: The Fourteenth Amendment and the Nationalization of Civil Liberties* (Madison, Wis., 1981), ix.

13   William O. Douglas, *The Court Years, 1939–1975* (New York, 1980), 387; McCloskey, *The Modern Supreme Court* (Cambridge, Mass., 1972), 330–31, as well as 60, 105–06.

14   Frankfurter, "The United States Supreme Court Molding the Constitu-

tion," CH, 32 (1930), 240; Alpheus T. Mason and William M. Beaney, *The Supreme Court in a Free Society* (Englewood Cliffs, N.J., 1959), 1, "The Court Is the Constitution."

15   Kennedy's news conference, June 27, 1962, in *Public Papers of the Presidents of the United States: John F. Kennedy; Containing the Public Messages, Speeches, and Statements of the President, 1962* (Washington, D.C., 1963), 510–11; letters to Rep. Joseph E. Hendricks (D., Fla.) from Mabel Dean, Feb. 8, 1937; Clara Krop, n.d.; A. J. Wilcomb, Feb. 20, 1937; Fred N. Burt, Feb. 26, 1937; Hendricks Papers, box 2, UFYL.

16   McCloskey, "Principles, Powers and Values: The Establishment Clause and the Supreme Court," *Religion and the Public Order* (1964), 3; McCloskey, *Modern Supreme Court,* 290–91. See Donald G. Morgan, *Congress and the Constitution: A Study of Responsibility* (Cambridge, Mass., 1966), 361: "millions of Americans, including many in high places, identify the Constitution with the Supreme Court."

17   For Jackson, see Alan H. Monroe, "The Supreme Court and the Constitution," APSR, 18 (1924), 739; for Lincoln's first inaugural address, see Roy P. Basler, ed., *The Collected Works of Abraham Lincoln* (New Brunswick, N.J., 1953), IV, esp. 268; for FDR's fireside chat of Mar. 9, 1937, see Samuel I. Rosenman, ed., *The Public Papers and Addresses of Franklin D. Roosevelt* (New York, 1941), VI, 126. See also FDR's speech on Sept. 17, 1937, when he asked the American people to "give their fealty to the Constitution *itself* and not to its misinterpreters," *ibid.,* 367.

18   See Maxwell Bloomfield, "The Supreme Court in American Popular Culture," *Journal of American Culture,* 4 (1981), 9; Edward S. Corwin, *Court Over Constitution* (1938), *passim.*

19   Monroe, "Supreme Court and the Constitution," 746–47; Walter F. Murphy, *Congress and the Court: A Case Study in the American Political Process* (Chicago, 1962), 172; Dale Alford, *The Constitutional Crisis: Its Threat to Liberty and Its Remedy* (New York, 1960), 49. For examples of southerners located at opposite ends of the political-ideological spectrum (yet equally devoted to the Constitution) who reached the same conclusion, see "Justice Black and the Bill of Rights," CBS transcript, p. 11, and Sam J. Ervin, Jr., *Humor of a Country Lawyer* (Chapel Hill, N.C., 1983), 4, 38–39, and esp. 168: "I have taken an oath to support the Constitution . . . and I shall keep it. But I've never taken an oath to support judicial aberrations. . . ."

20   Heywood Hale Broun, ed., *Collected Edition of Heywood Broun* (New York, 1941), 343; Lawrence, "Our Vanishing Constitution," *U.S. News and World Report,* July 20, 1964, 104.

21   Transcript of CBS Reports, "Mr. Justice Douglas," Sept. 6, 1972, p. 42, courtesy of CBS.

22   Howe, "Faith and Skepticism in American Constitutional Law," *Perspectives USA,* 9 (1954), 5, 16.

23   Jackson's opinion in *Youngstown Co.* v. *Sawyer,* 343 U.S. 653 (1951); Gerald W. Johnson, *America-Watching: Perspectives in the Course of an Incredible Century* (Owings Mills, Md., 1976), 101; Monroe, "Supreme Court and the Constitution," 750–51; McCloskey, *Modern Supreme Court,*

352, 357. For a popularized version of this point, see Eugene H. Methvin, "Is the Supreme Court Really Supreme?" RD, 91 (July 1967), 85.

24   See John Bach McMaster, "A Century of Constitutional Interpretation," *The Century Magazine,* 37 (1889), 866–78; Charles Warren, "Legislative and Judicial Attacks on the Supreme Court of the United States . . . ," *American Law Review,* 47 (1913), 189.

25   Walter F. Dodd to Max Farrand, Nov. 20, 1909, Farrand Papers, HEH.

26   Howard Lee McBain, *The Living Constitution: A Consideration of the Realities and Legends of Our Fundamental Law* (New York, 1927), 33; Stone to Edward S. Corwin, Dec. 1, 1939, Corwin Papers, box 1, PUML. See also August O. Spain, *The Political Theory of John C. Calhoun* (New York, 1951), 61.

27   See Irving Brant, *James Madison: Commander in Chief, 1812–1836* (Indianapolis, 1961), VI, 468–532; and for invocations of Jefferson and Madison during the 1950s by southern congressmen who opposed school desegregation, see Jack W. Peltason, *Fifty-Eight Lonely Men: Southern Federal Judges and School Desegregation* (New York, 1961), 41–42.

28   George H. Tinkham to Albert B. Hart, Apr. 5, 1923, Hart Papers, box 4, HUPL. See also George Wolfskill, *The Revolt of the Conservatives: A History of the American Liberty League, 1934–1940* (Boston, 1962), 37–43.

29   See Alan F. Westin, ed., *An Autobiography of the Supreme Court: Off-the-Bench Commentary by the Justices* (New York, 1963), 106; Bryce, *American Commonwealth* (London, 1891), I, 348; speech by Martin W. Littleton reported in NYT, Nov. 15, 1922, p. 14.

30   Sidney Ratner to Edward S. Corwin, Nov. 28, 1938, Corwin Papers, box 3, PUML, after reading Corwin's *Court Over Constitution* (1938). See also Corwin to Andrew C. McLaughlin, Mar. 27, 1935, McLaughlin Papers, box 2, UCA; Philip B. Kurland, "Magna Carta and Constitutionalism in the United States: 'The Noble Lie,' " in *The Great Charter: Four Essays on Magna Carta and the History of Our Liberty* (New York, 1965), 56–57, 70–71.

31   J. P. Mayer, ed., *Democracy in America* (Anchor Books ed.: Garden City, N.Y., 1969), 164–65.

32   For numerous and diverse instances, see Charles Warren, *The Supreme Court in United States History* (Boston, 1922), I, 3, 132, 179–81, 211, 214, 323, 488, 520, and 522; *ibid.,* III, 14, 32, 150n., 154, 163, 181, 297, 304, 315, 366, 393, 416, and 473 spanning the years 1795 to 1887; Richard E. Ellis, *The Jeffersonian Crisis: Courts and Politics in the Young Republic* (New York, 1971), 194; NAR, 99 (July 1864), 130–31; John A. Garraty, ed., *Quarrels That Have Shaped the Constitution* (New York, 1964), 28, 149, 183.

33   See John E. Semonche, *Charting the Future: The Supreme Court Responds to a Changing Society, 1890–1920* (Westport, Conn., 1978), 220; Burger, "The Chief Justice Talks about the Court," RD, 102 (February 1973), 95.

34   Tiedeman, "The Income Tax Decisions as an Object Lesson in Constitutional Construction," AAAPSS, 6 (1895), 268; Beck is quoted in an editorial, "The Constitution, a Bulwark Against Anarchy," CR, 3 (1919),

115–16; Henry Hazlitt, "Our Obsolete Constitution," RD, 18 (April 1931), 1099.

35   Max Farrand to Allen Johnson, Aug. 6, 1919, responding to Johnson's letter of Aug. 3, Farrand Papers, HEH. Johnson had just read the typescript of Farrand's *The Fathers of the Constitution: A Chronicle of the Establishment of the Union* (New Haven, Conn., 1921), and urged him to discuss "that elusive thing, public opinion, so far as it is suggested by fugitive pamphlets and popular writings of one sort and another."

36   See H. Arnold Bennett, *The Constitution in School and College* (New York, 1936), 47, 85; Beck's speech to the Bond Club in New York, reported in NYT, Dec. 19, 1929, p. 30.

37   See Garraty, ed., *Quarrels That Have Shaped the Constitution*, 192; John C. Fitzpatrick to Sol Bloom, Oct. 22, 1935, and Apr. 6, 1936, Fitzpatrick Papers, box 16, LCMD; George M. Lawton to Joe Hendricks, Feb. 24, 1937, Hendricks Papers, box 2, UFYL.

38   *The Federalist* Numbers 12 and 13; Eric Foner, *Tom Paine and Revolutionary America* (New York, 1976), 205–06; Jefferson to Benjamin Vaughan, May 11, 1791, Paul L. Ford, ed., *The Works of Thomas Jefferson* (New York, 1904), VI, 261.

39   Lee is quoted in Edward S. Corwin, *The "Higher Law" Background of American Constitutional Law* (Ithaca, N.Y., 1955), 2–3; George Ticknor Curtis, *Constitutional History of the United States from their Declaration of Independence to the Close of their Civil War* (New York, 1889), II, 8; Thomas I. Wharton, *An Oration Delivered on the Fourth of July, 1827. . . .* (Philadelphia, 1827), 3; Edward Everett, *Orations and Speeches on Various Occasions* (Boston, 1879), I, 166, and III, 362–63.

40   See Warren, *Supreme Court in U.S. History*, I, 51, 60, 211; Stanley I. Kutler, *Privilege and Creative Destruction: The Charles River Bridge Case* (New York, 1971); John P. Frank, *Marble Palace: The Supreme Court in American Life* (New York, 1958), 233. There is evidence to suggest English antecedents. In 1478, for example, Sir John Fortescue asserted that English legal institutions sustained the nation's prosperity. I have not, however, noticed signs that a link between constitutionalism and prosperity ever became a pervasive theme in British political culture.

41   Dolley Madison to Andrew Jackson, Nov. 15, 1836, in James D. Richardson, ed., *A Compilation of the Messages and Papers of the Presidents, 1789–1897* (Washington, D.C., 1897), III, 262; Fillmore, Dec. 6, 1852, *ibid.*, V, 182; Hayes, "National Aid to Education," *The Independent,* 35 (July 12, 1883), 2; Hampton L. Carson, ed., *History of the Celebration of the One Hundredth Anniversary of the Promulgation of the Constitution of the United States* (Philadelphia, 1889), I, 375–76.

42   Adams, *An Oration Addressed to the Citizens of the Town of Quincy on the Fourth of July, 1831. . . .* (Boston, 1831), 29; Adams, *The Jubilee of the Constitution. A Discourse. . . .* (New York, 1839), 48; Basler, ed., *Collected Works of Abraham Lincoln,* IV, 168–69.

43   Quoted in Martin E. Marty, *Pilgrims in Their Own Land: 500 Years of American Religion* (Boston, 1984), 282–83.

44   Archibald Hopkins, "Proposals for a Constitutional Party," CR, 7 (1923), 165; Wallace McCamant, "The Constitution Maintained Is Freedom Pre-

served," CR, 8 (1924), 21–22; Henry H. Wilson, "The Influence of the American Doctrine of Judicial Review on Modern Constitutional Development," CR, 9 (1925), 102; James M. Beck, "The Anniversary of the Constitution," CR, 13 (1929), 186.

45 Albert H. Smyth, ed., *The Writings of Benjamin Franklin* (New York, 1905–07), III, 242; Marshall's opinion in *McCulloch* v. *Maryland* (1819) in Stanley I. Kutler, ed., *The Supreme Court and the Constitution: Readings in American Constitutional History* (2nd ed.: New York, 1977), 51; Percival E. Jackson, ed., *The Wisdom of the Supreme Court* (Norman, Okla., 1962), 49; Justice Brewer's opinion in *South Carolina* v. *U.S.*, 199 U.S. 437, 448 (1905); John Marshall Harlan's opinion in *Reynolds* v. *Sims*, 377 U.S. 624–25 (1963); William Henry Harrison's inaugural address, Mar. 4, 1841, in Richardson, ed., *Messages and Papers of the Presidents*, IV, 9; Worthington C. Ford to Max Farrand, May 16, 1911, Farrand Papers, HEH; Harry F. Atwood, "The Birthday of Our Constitution," CR, 3 (1919), 20–21; John C. Fitzpatrick to Sol Bloom, Mar. 14, 1935, Fitzpatrick Papers, box 16, LCMD.

46 Peterson, ed., *Portable Jefferson*, 293; Zephaniah Swift Moore, "An Oration on the Anniversary of the Independence of the United States of America" (Worcester, Mass., 1802), in Charles S. Hyneman and Donald S. Lutz, eds., *American Political Writing during the Founding Era, 1760–1805* (Indianapolis, 1983), II, 1218.

47 "Speech on Secession," Dec. 18–19, 1860, in Leroy P. Graf, *et al.*, eds., *The Papers of Andrew Johnson*, IV (Knoxville, Tenn., 1976), 38; Richmond C. Beatty, *Lord Macaulay: Victorian Liberal* (Norman, Okla., 1938), 367; Alan F. Westin, "Out-of-Court Commentary by United States Supreme Court Justices, 1790–1962," CLR, 62 (1962), 651–52; Hugh Henry Brown, "Our Generation and the Constitution," CR, 8 (1924), 151; Charles Evans Hughes, "Justice Our Anchor," VSD, 6 (1940), 259–60.

48 Carl L. Becker, *The Heavenly City of the Eighteenth-Century Philosophers* (New Haven, Conn., 1932), 56, 161.

49 Corwin, *"Higher Law" Background of American Constitutional Law*, 81; "Novanglus" No. 7, in Charles Francis Adams, ed., *The Works of John Adams* (Boston, 1851), IV, 108; Max Farrand, ed., *The Records of the Federal Convention of 1787* (New Haven, Conn., 1937), II, 278; John P. Kaminski and Gaspare J. Saladino, eds., *Commentaries on the Constitution, Public and Private*, II (Madison, Wis., 1983), 11.

50 See Paul C. Nagel, *One Nation Indivisible: The Union in American Thought, 1776–1861* (New York, 1964), 59; Warren, *Supreme Court in U.S. History*, I, 165, 525, III, 29–30; Dagobert D. Runes, ed., *The Selected Writings of Benjamin Rush* (New York, 1947), 92; Richard K. Crallé, ed., *The Works of John C. Calhoun* (Columbia, S.C., 1851–67), I, 78–79; Ernest Samuels, *The Young Henry Adams* (Cambridge, Mass., 1967), 271. British observers often referred to the U.S. Constitution as a machine, but less frequently applied the same metaphor to their own. See Frances Wright, *Views of Society and Manners in America* (1821: Cambridge, Mass., 1963), 193; Norman St John-Stevas, ed., *The Collected Works of Walter Bagehot* (Cambridge, Mass., 1968), IV, 277, 308; William E. Gladstone, "Kin Beyond Sea," NAR, 127 (September 1878), 209; and John Buchan,

Memory-Hold-the-Door (London, 1940), 265. Harlan Fiske Stone explained to Edward S. Corwin on Nov. 5, 1942, that Blackstone was responsible because he "gave to both lawyers and judges artificial notions of the law which, when applied to constitutional interpretation made the Constitution a mechanical and inadequate instrument of government." Corwin Papers, box 1, PUML.

51   Jack Nips [John Leland], "The Yankee Spy" (1794), in Hyneman and Lutz, eds., *American Political Writing during the Founding Era, 1760–1805,* II, 977; Adams, *Jubilee of the Constitution,* 47; and see Adams, *Oration to the Citizens of the Town of Quincy, 1831,* 27–28, as well as Newmyer, *Justice Joseph Story,* 247.

52   Cooper to the *Albany Argus* [Apr. 4, 1848?], in James F. Beard, ed., *The Letters and Journals of James Fenimore Cooper* (Cambridge, Mass., 1968), V, 333–34; Lowell, "The Place of the Independent in Politics," in *Political Essays* (Boston, 1888), 312. The scientific management of production became a goal of American business during the 1880s. In 1885, Henry Metcalfe published the first book to be written in the United States on cost accounting in manufacturing enterprises. His statement of aspiration, "if I were sure that an order once given would go of itself through the works," sounds remarkably similar to the political climate that Lowell feared. See Alfred D. Chandler, *The Visible Hand: The Mangerial Revolution in American Business* (Cambridge, Mass., 1977), 272–73.

53   See Benjamin R. Twiss, *Lawyers and the Constitution. How Laissez Faire Came to the Supreme Court* (Princeton, 1942), 159; Washington *Evening Star,* Feb. 17, 1894, p. 4; Bennett, *Constitution in School and College,* 68, 180; Holmes's opinion in *Missouri, Kansas & Texas Ry. Co.* v. *May,* 194 U.S. 270 (1904); Andrew C. McLaughlin, *The Confederation and the Constitution, 1783–1789* (New York, 1905), 247; Beck, "Anniversary of the Constitution," 188; Rosenman, ed., *Public Papers and Addresses of Franklin D. Roosevelt,* II, 14–15.

54   See two editorials, "The Constitution, a Bulwark Against Anarchy," CR, 3 (1919), 115; and "Teaching the Constitution in the Schools," CR, 9 (1925), 118; Hazlitt, "Our Obsolete Constitution," 1097; and William Yandell Elliott, *The Need for Constitutional Reform: A Program for National Security* (New York, 1935), 188–89, 205, 207.

55   Jackson, ed., *Wisdom of the Supreme Court,* 47, 48, 52. See also Glendon Schubert, "The Rhetoric of Constitutional Change," JPL, 16 (1967), 16–50.

56   Lowell, *Essays on Government* (Boston, 1889), 1–4; Wilson, *The New Freedom* (Garden City, N.Y., 1913, 1921), 46–48.

57   Fiske, NYT, Dec. 16, 1900, p. 19; Curtis, *Constitutional History of the U.S.,* II, iv (Curtis died in March 1894, and this second volume did not appear until 1896); Hill, "The Covenant or the Constitution?" NAR, 211 (March 1920), 327; Newton D. Baker, *Progress and the Constitution* (New York, 1925), 8–9.

58   Tocqueville, *Democracy in America,* 114; Franklin Pierce's second annual message to Congress, Dec. 4, 1854, in Richardson, ed., *Messages and Papers of the Presidents,* V, 292; R. H. Smith, *An Address to the Citizens of Alabama on the Constitution and Laws of the Confederate States of America* (Mobile,

Ala., 1861), 14; Alexander H. Stephens, *A Constitutional View of the Late War between the States* (Philadelphia, 1868–70), I, 118; Ben Perley Poore, comp., *The Federal and State Constitutions, Colonial Charters, and Other Organic Laws of the United States* (Washington, D.C., 1877), 2 vols.; Crallé, ed., *Works of John C. Calhoun,* I, 12, 29–33.

59 See "Constitutional Patchwork," NAR, 149 (August 1889), 253–55; Twiss, *Lawyers and the Constitution,* 154; James Ford Rhodes, *Historical Essays* (New York, 1909), 216; "The National Association for Constitutional Government," CR, 1 (1917), 35, 37; Joseph R. Long, "Tinkering with the Constitution," CR, 2 (1918), 14–16; W. P. Stacy, "The Constitution of the United States, the Supreme Law," CR, 8 (1924), 41; Harry F. Atwood, "Constitution Week—What It Means," *Daughters of the American Revolution Magazine,* 58 (1924), 214; Bennett, *Constitution in School and College,* 178; James A. Van Osdol, "Future Organization and Defense of the Constitution," CR, 13 (1929), 123; and 74th Congress, 1st Session, S.J. Resolution 59, Feb. 14, 1935, in Fitzpatrick Papers, box 16, LCMD.

60 See James M. Lindgren, "The Gospel of Preservation in Virginia and New England: Historic Preservation and the Regeneration of Traditionalism" (unpubl. Ph.D. diss., College of William and Mary, 1984), 166–67; John F. Dillon, *The Laws and Jurisprudence of England and America* (New York, 1894), 15, 196; CR, 3 (1919), 173, 176; Charles Kerr, "Constitutional Conservation," *Virginia Law Review,* 9 (1923), 335; "Constitutional Patchwork," NAR, 253–54.

61 Charles A. and William Beard, *The American Leviathan: The Republic in the Machine Age* (New York, 1930), 20; Walton H. Hamilton, "Constitutionalism," *Encyclopedia of the Social Sciences* (New York, 1931), IV, 257; Elliott, *Need for Constitutional Reform,* 186; Johnson, *America-Watching,* 124 (an essay published in 1940).

62 Bennett, *Constitution in School and College,* 77–78. For an important revisionist exception, see Martin Diamond, "The Declaration and the Constitution: Liberty, Democracy, and the Founders," in Nathan Glazer and Irving Kristol, eds., *The American Commonwealth: 1976* (New York, 1976), 39–55.

63 Henry A. Hawken, ed., *Trumpets of Glory: Fourth of July Orations, 1786–1861* (Granby, Conn., 1976), 12; Carson, *Celebration of the . . . Promulgation of the Constitution,* I, 264, 409.

64 *Ibid.,* 265–66, 276; Adams, *Jubilee of the Constitution,* 40–41; Wharton, *Oration Delivered on the Fourth of July, 1827,* 3, 16; Newmyer, *Justice Joseph Story,* 189; John C. Hurd, *The Centennial of a Revolution: An Address by a Revolutionist* (New York, 1888); *Ithaca Democrat,* July 4, 1882, p. 1.

65 J. M. Ashley, "Constitution Worship," *Public Opinion,* 19 (Dec. 5, 1895), 734–35; Charles G. Haines to Max Farrand, Nov. 15, 1937, with a five-page memorandum attached "relative to the development of constitution worship," and Farrand to Haines, Nov. 24, 1937, Farrand Papers, HEH; Catherine L. Albanese, *Sons of the Fathers: The Civil Religion of the American Revolution* (Philadelphia, 1976), 208, 216.

66 Ralph H. Gabriel, *The Course of American Democratic Thought: An Intellectual History Since 1815* (New York, 1940), 398–99; von Holst, *Constitu-*

tional and Political History of the U.S. (Chicago, 1876–92), I, 65–66, 71, 78–79.

67   Lowell, "The Responsibilities of American Lawyers," in *Essays on Government,* 126–27; Ashley, "Constitution Worship," 734–35.

68   Greene reviewing Farrand's *The Framing of the Constitution* (1913) in MVHR, 1 (1914), 291; Edward S. Corwin, "The Worship of the Constitution" [1920], in Richard Loss, ed., *Corwin on the Constitution,* I (Ithaca, N.Y., 1981), 55; Frederic C. Howe, *The Confessions of a Reformer* (New York, 1925), 169, 176.

69   Sidney Howard, "Our Professional Patriots: The Constitution Worshippers," NR, 40 (Oct. 15, 1924), 171.

70   Everett, "The Birthday of Washington," a speech made in New York on Feb. 22, 1851, in response to a toast: "The Constitution of the United States," in Everett, *Orations and Speeches,* III, 67; Garraty, ed., *Quarrels That Have Shaped the Constitution,* vii. The most widely used manual or guide to the Constitution during the middle decades of the nineteenth century, W. Hickey's *The Constitution,* has as its frontispiece a lithograph of a solemn eagle sitting on a rock. On the side of the rock is carved, white and bright, 1789. H. L. Mencken called it the Constitution of 1788 (in *The American Mercury,* 1937); but Mencken liked to be perverse.

71   Poore, *Federal and State Constitutions,* I, iii.

72   William Caleb Loring to Henry Cabot Lodge, June 6, 1886, Lodge Papers, box 6, MHS; Beck to David Jayne Hill, Aug. 23, 1924, Beck Papers, box 1, PUML.

73   Jefferson to Thomas Ritchie, Dec. 25, 1820, in Andrew A. Lipscomb, ed., *The Writings of Thomas Jefferson* (Washington, D.C., 1903), XV, 298–99; Brant, *Madison,* VI, 454.

74   See Brant, *Madison,* VI, 469–71, 516; Warren, "Sources of Knowledge of the Constitution," 180.

75   Beck to Mencken, Dec. 15, 1924, Beck Papers, box 2, PUML; Benjamin Ginzburg to Edward S. Corwin, Sept. 27, 1936, Corwin Papers, box 2, PUML.

76   Jefferson to Thomas Ritchie, Dec. 25, 1820, Lipscomb, ed., *Writings of Jefferson,* XV, 297–98.

77   Westin, "Out-of-Court Commentary by Supreme Court Justices," 650–51, 654–56.

78   Harry C. Butcher to Van Devanter, May 18, 1937; K. H. Berkeley to Van Devanter, May 26, 1937; Joseph Bondy to Van Devanter, July 10, 1937, Van Devanter Papers, box 38, LCMD; Van Devanter to Bondy, July 14, 1937, *ibid.,* box 19, letterbook 54; Masters to Van Devanter, Sept. 21 and 26, 1937, *ibid.,* box 38; Van Devanter to Masters, Sept. 22, 1937, *ibid.,* box 20, letterbook 55. In his second letter, Masters admitted that the literary agent who had prodded him into approaching Van Devanter wanted "me to ask you just how opinions are arrived at in the Supreme Court. I think that amounts to nothing, and it well might be that an ex-judge would not want to get into such revelations. To such ideas do the 'pulp' and the million circulation publications run." It well might be, indeed, Mr. Masters.

79   *The Memoirs of Earl Warren* (Garden City, N.Y., 1977), 335, 342; Lewis, "Problems of a Washington Correspondent," *Connecticut Bar Journal,* 33

(1959), 366–67; Friedman in *NYT Book Review,* June 26, 1984, p. 18.

80 Warren, *Supreme Court in U.S. History,* III, 145–46, 261; Otto H. Olsen, ed., *The Thin Disguise: Turning Point in Negro History. Plessy v. Ferguson: A Documentary Presentation (1864–1896)* (New York, 1967), 123–30; Garraty, ed., *Quarrels That Have Shaped the Constitution,* 157.

81 *Saturday Evening Post,* 196 (Dec. 15, 1923), 25, 119, 121–22, 125–26, 129; Beveridge to Edward S. Corwin, Jan. 28, 1924, Corwin Papers, box 2, PUML; Louis A. Coolidge to Charles Warren, Dec. 20, 1923, Warren Papers, box 2, LCMD; Sen. Joseph C. O'Mahoney to Edward S. Corwin, Jan. 16, 1937, Corwin Papers, box 1, PUML.

82 Robert Lee Bullard to Cass Gilbert, July 15, 1931, Gilbert Papers, box 13, LCMD; W. L. Carpenter to Edward S. Corwin, Feb. 12, 1936, Corwin Papers, box 2, PUML; William L. Underwood to Corwin, Feb. 13, 1936, *ibid.;* A. J. Richard to Willis Van Devanter, Apr. 12, 1937, Van Devanter Papers, box 38, LCMD.

83 See Lance Banning, "Republican Ideology and the Triumph of the Constitution, 1789 to 1793," WMQ, 31 (1974), 167–88; Charles R. Lee, Jr., *The Confederate Constitutions* (Chapel Hill, N.C., 1963); Phillip S. Paludan, *A Covenant with Death: The Constitution, Law and Equality in the Civil War Era* (Urbana, Ill., 1975), 223; Joel H. Silbey, *A Respectable Minority: The Democratic Party in the Civil War Era, 1860–1868* (New York, 1977); and Hyman, *A More Perfect Union: The Impact of the Civil War and Reconstruction on the Constitution,* 436, 438, 448, 544.

84 McMaster, "A Century of Constitutional Interpretation," 866–67; Madison to William A. Duer, June 5, 1835, in Gaillard Hunt, ed., *The Writings of James Madison* (New York, 1910), IX, 557; Jefferson to Wilson C. Nicholas, Sept. 7, 1803, Lipscomb, ed., *Writings of Jefferson,* X, 420; Roosevelt to William H. Moody, Sept. 21, 1907, in Elting E. Morison, ed., *The Letters of Theodore Roosevelt* (Cambridge, Mass., 1954), V, 802; TR to Cecil Arthur Spring Rice, Aug. 22, 1911, *ibid.,* VII 333; TR to Charles D. Willard, Oct. 28, 1911, *ibid.,* VII, 427; J. Allen Smith, *The Spirit of American Government,* ed. by Cushing Strout (1907: Cambridge, Mass., 1965), xxix, xxxii; Pearson and Robert S. Allen, *The Nine Old Men* (Garden City, N.Y., 1936), 287–89; Bates to Edward S. Corwin, Jan. 18, 1935, Corwin Papers, box 2, PUML; William L. Underwood to Corwin, Apr. 2, 1936, *ibid.*

85 Arnold, *The Symbols of Government* (New Haven, Conn., 1935), 230–31, 268–69. For an affirmation of conflict within consensus from a very different perspective, see Diamond, "Conservatives, Liberals, and the Constitution," 96–109.

86 See Lord Birkenhead (Frederick Edwin Smith), *America Revisited* (Boston, 1924), 147–50.

87 See Charles G. Haines, *The American Doctrine of Judicial Supremacy* (2nd ed.: Berkeley, Calif., 1932), 9–10; Paludan, *Covenant with Death,* 105, 227–28; Stanley I. Kutler, *Judicial Power and Reconstruction Politics* (Chicago, 1968), 64–88; Kutler, "*Ex Parte McCardle:* Judicial Impotency? The Supreme Court and Reconstruction Reconsidered," AHR, 72 (1967), 849; Murphy, *Congress and the Court,* 169; Leonard W. Levy, ed., *Judicial Review and the Supreme Court: Selected Essays* (New York, 1967), 73; C.

Herman Pritchett, *Congress versus the Supreme Court, 1957–1960* (Minneapolis, 1961), vii, 28–31.

88 Warren, *Supreme Court in U.S. History,* III, 255; Monroe, "Supreme Court and the Constitution," 748; Corwin, *Twilight of the Supreme Court,* 181; and Alan F. Westin, "Charles Beard and American Debate Over Judicial Review, 1790–1961," the introduction to Westin's edition of Beard, *The Supreme Court and the Constitution* (New York, 1912; Englewood Cliffs, N.J., 1962), 1–34.

89 See Fehrenbacher, *Dred Scott Case in Historical Perspective,* 241; Walter Clark, "Judicial Supremacy Unwarranted by the Constitution," *The Public,* 21 (June 29, 1918), 821–22; Max Farrand to Charles G. Haines, June 6, 1935, Farrand Papers, HEH; Farrand to Edward S. Corwin, Jan. 3, 1939, Corwin Papers, box 3, PUML; Beck to Corwin, Mar. 7, 1933, *ibid.,* box 1; Henry M. Bates to Corwin, Jan. 28, 1936, *ibid.;* Corwin to J. Edward Hoffmeister, Mar. 19, 1937, *ibid.,* box 2.

90 An extensive literature has been stimulated by John Hart Ely, *Democracy and Distrust: A Theory of Judicial Review* (Cambridge, Mass., 1980), and to a lesser degree by Jesse H. Choper, *Judicial Review and the National Political Process: A Functional Reconsideration of the Role of the Supreme Court* (Chicago, 1980).

91 See Bernard Bailyn, ed., "A Dialogue between an American and a European Englishman" [1768], in *Perspectives in American History,* 9 (1975), 404–05; Willi Paul Adams, *The First American Constitutions: Republican Ideology and the Making of the State Constitutions in the Revolutionary Era* (Chapel Hill, N.C., 1980), 269–70. Cf. Raoul Berger, *Congress v. the Supreme Court* (Cambridge, Mass., 1969).

92 *Collected Edition of Heywood Broun,* 344; Stone to Corwin, Mar. 6, 1939, Corwin Papers, box 1, PUML.

93 Elizabeth Kelley Bauer, *Commentaries on the Constitution, 1790–1860* (New York, 1952), 179–80; Charles Black, *The People and the Court: Judicial Review in a Democracy* (New York, 1960); Murphy, *Congress and the Court,* 187, for Warren's majority opinion in *Trop* v. *Dulles* (1958), a vigorous reaffirmation of judicial review as a right as well as a responsibility.

94 See Warren, *Supreme Court in U.S. History,* I, 82; III, 411, 425, 465–66; Alan F. Westin, "When the Public Judges the Court," NYT *Magazine,* May 31, 1959, pp. 16, 41.

95 See J. W. Burrow, *A Liberal Descent: Victorian Historians and the English Past* (Cambridge, Eng., 1981), 155, 162, 165, 183–84, 192–94, 295. Whig historians like Macaulay and Freeman were obsessed by the notion of continuity with an ancient constitution. Their society's attraction to such a notion came, at least partially, in response to the problematic transition to democracy and industrialization.

96 Peter Odegard, "The Future of States' Rights," NAR, 240 (September 1935), 238–63; James Hart, "A Unified Economy and States' Rights," AAAPSS, 185(1936), 102–14.

97 Holmes's famous dissent in *Abrams* v. *U.S.,* 250 U.S. 630 (1919); and see Felix Frankfurter, *Mr. Justice Holmes and the Supreme Court* (Cambridge, Mass., 1961), 80; W. L. Carpenter to Edward S. Corwin, Feb. 12, 1936, Corwin Papers, box 2, PUML.

98 NYT, Oct. 16, 1851, p. 2; Simon Sterne, *Constitutional History and Political Development of the United States* (New York, 1882), viii; Howe, *Confessions of a Reformer,* 169; Brown is quoted in Westin, "Out-of-Court Commentary by Supreme Court Justices," 653; Andrew C. McLaughlin, "A Written Constitution in Some of Its Historical Aspects," *Michigan Law Review,* 5 (1907), 19; Munroe Smith, "Shall We Make Our Constitution Flexible?" NAR, 194 (November 1911), 657–73.

99 Robert Cruden, *James Ford Rhodes: The Man, the Historian, and His Work* (Cleveland, 1961), 214; Moody's opinion in *The Employers' Liability Cases,* 207 U.S. 521–22 (1908); and see Hannis Taylor, *The Origin and Growth of the American Constitution* (New York, 1911), 25.

100 Warren, "The Law and the Future," *Fortune,* 52 (November 1955), 107, 224; Pritchett, *Congress versus the Supreme Court,* 30.

101 Anne Pallister, *Magna Carta: The Heritage of Liberty* (Oxford, 1971), 32, 37–38, 73, 89.

102 *Ibid.,* 42, 51–52, 54–62, 106; William H. Dunham, Jr., "Magna Carta and British Constitutionalism," in *Four Essays on Magna Carta and the History of Our Liberty,* 20–47; Howard Nenner, "Constitutional Uncertainty and the Declaration of Rights," in Barbara C. Malament, ed., *After the Reformation: Essays in Honor of J. H. Hexter* (Philadelphia, 1980), 291–308, esp. 306.

103 Quoted in Pallister, *Magna Carta,* 62, 69.

104 Francis Mulhern's introduction to Regis Debray, *Le pouvoir intellectuel en France* (Paris, 1979), trans. as *Teachers, Writers, Celebrities: The Intellectuals of Modern France* (London, 1981), xxi.

105 See Leonard Bruni, "Panegyric to the City of Florence" (1403–04), in Benjamin Kohl and Ronald G. Witt, eds., *The Earthly Republic: Italian Humanists on Government and Society* (Philadelphia, 1978), 168–74; Eric Cochrane, *Florence in the Forgotten Centuries, 1527–1800* (Chicago, 1973), 6, 28, 57, 62, 457, 462–64.

106 The cavalier question was supposedly put to President Grover Cleveland by a Tammany congressman; but I have not been able to ascertain which congressman, or when. See James M. Beck, "Anniversary of the Constitution," CR, 13 (1929), 191; Isidore Starr, "Our Constitution: Is It Alive and Well?" *Social Education,* 37 (1973), 361; and see Johnson, *America-Watching,* 82, 236.

107 Note the contemptuous crack by A. Lawrence Lowell, in *Essays on Government,* 127–28: France "has had a dozen constitutions, each as sacred as such an instrument can be, but they have all been short-lived, and no one supposes that their frail existence could have been preserved by granting to the French courts the powers possessed by our own."

108 Arnold, *The Folklore of Capitalism* (New Haven, Conn., 1937), 79.

• CHAPTER 2 *To Make the Constitution a Practical System*

1 Washington to Lafayette, Sept. 18, 1787, in John C. Fitzpatrick, ed., *The Writings of George Washington,* XXIX (Washington, D.C., 1939), 277.

2 Aristotle, *Politics,* Bk IV, ch. 1.

3 Adams to Jefferson, Nov. 10, 1787; Jefferson to Adams, Nov. 13, 1787;

Adams to Jefferson, Dec. 6, 1787, and Mar. 1, 1789; Abigail Adams to Jefferson, Oct. 25, 1804; Jefferson to J. Adams, Oct. 28, 1813, in Lester J. Cappon, ed., *The Adams-Jefferson Letters* (Chapel Hill, N.C., 1959), 209–10, 212–14, 281–82, 391; Jefferson to David Humphreys, Mar. 18, 1789, in Julian P. Boyd, ed., *The Papers of Thomas Jefferson* (Princeton, 1950–   ), XIV, 678; David Freeman Hawke, "John Adams' Tragic Flaw—Despair," in James S. Saeger, ed., *Perspectives on Revolutionary Constitutionalism: Essays of the Lawrence Henry Gipson Institute for Eighteenth Century Studies* (Bethlehem, Pa. [1977]), 34–35.

4   Griffin to Thomas Fitzsimons, Feb. 18 and Mar. 3, 1788, Gratz Collection, case 1, box 6, HSP; John Shippen to Joseph Shippen, Jan. 3, 1788, Shippen Papers, box 1, folder 11, HSP; Tench Coxe to William Tilghman, May 14, 1788, Tilghman Papers, HSP.

5   Tenney to Gilman, Mar. 12, 1788, Gratz Collection, case 7, box 34, HSP.

6   Rush to [Elias Boudinot?], July 9, 1788, in L. H. Butterfield, ed., *The Letters of Benjamin Rush* (Princeton, 1951), I, 473, 475.

7   Thomasine Clifford to Sarah Dowell Clifford, July 9, 1788; Anna Clifford to Sarah Dowell Clifford, July 11, 1788; Thomas Clifford, Jr., to Sarah Clifford, July 11, 1788, in Pemberton Papers, Clifford correspondence, VIII, ff. 278–80, HSP.

8   Wills, *Explaining America: The Federalist* (Garden City, N.Y., 1981), 132, 159, 163; Charles G. Haines to Max Farrand, Oct. 20, 1941, Farrand Papers, HEH; Baldwin, *A General View of the Origin and Nature of the Constitution and Government of the United States* (Philadelphia, 1837), which is really an exegesis of American political history, 1774–88.

9   Hermann E. von Holst, *The Constitutional and Political History of the United States* (Chicago, 1876), I, 65, 73–74; Wilson is quoted in Edward S. Corwin, *Court Over Constitution: A Study of Judicial Review as an Instrument of Popular Government* (Princeton, 1938), 211; Banning, "Republican Ideology and the Triumph of the Constitution, 1789 to 1793," WMQ, 31 (1974), 168; Madison to J. G. Jackson, Dec. 27, 1821, in *Documentary History of the Constitution . . . 1786–1870,* Part II, in *Bulletin of the Bureau of Rolls and Library of the Department of State* (Washington, D.C., 1905), V, 315.

10   Cf. Frank I. Schechter, "The Early History of the Tradition of the Constitution," APSR, 9 (1915), 707–34; Charles G. Haines to Max Farrand, Nov. 15, 1937, and the attached memorandum, Farrand Papers, HEH.

11   John Adams to Francis Adrian Van der Kemp, Mar. 19, 1793, Adams Letters, p. 20, HSP; Sergeant to Thomas Biddle, Jan. 10, 1808, Simon Gratz Collection, case 4, box 2, HSP.

12   Crawford quoted in W. Y. Elliott, "The Constitution as the American Social Myth," in Conyers Read, ed., *The Constitution Reconsidered* (New York, 1938), 219n.; Webster quoted in Richard M. Rollins, "Words as Social Control: Noah Webster and the Creation of the American Dictionary," in Leila Zenderland, ed., *Recycling the Past: Popular Uses of American History* (Philadelphia, 1978), 55; Jefferson to Adams, June 27, 1813, in Cappon, ed., *Adams-Jefferson Letters,* 336–37; Jefferson to Samuel Kercheval, July 12, 1816, in Andrew A. Lipscomb, ed., *The Writings of Thomas Jefferson* (Washington, D.C., 1903), XV, 40.

13   See William M. Wiecek, *The Sources of Antislavery Constitutionalism in America, 1760–1848* (Ithaca, N.Y., 1977), 137–39.

14   Richard E. Ellis, *The Jeffersonian Crisis: Courts and Politics in the Young Republic* (New York, 1971), 57, 80; Charles Warren, *The Supreme Court in United States History* (Boston, 1922), I, 209–14.

15   Samuel Tenney to Benjamin Bourn, Mar. 3, 1802, Simon Gratz Collection, case 7, box 34, HSP; Ellis, *Jeffersonian Crisis,* 172; Warren, *Supreme Court in U.S. History,* I, 297.

16   Adams is quoted in Willi Paul Adams, *The First American Constitutions: Republican Ideology and the Making of the State Constitutions in the Revolutionary Era* (Chapel Hill, N.C., 1980), 3; Kenneth M. Stampp, "The Concept of a Perpetual Union," JAH, 65 (1978), 21; Jefferson to Washington, May 8, 1791, Paul L. Ford, ed., *The Works of Thomas Jefferson* (New York, 1904), VI, 256; Alfred F. Young, *The Democratic Republicans of New York: The Origins, 1763–1797* (Chapel Hill, N.C., 1967), 460–66, 580, esp. 461; Ellis, *Jeffersonian Crisis,* 46, 52, 61.

17   Alexis de Tocqueville, *Democracy in America,* ed. by J. P. Mayer (Garden City, N.Y., 1969), 149–51. See also George L. Haskins, "Law Versus Politics in the Early Years of the Marshall Court," *University of Pennsylvania Law Review,* 30 (1981), 1–27.

18   See Dwight Jessup, "Reaction and Accommodation: The United States Supreme Court and Political Conflict, 1809–1835" (unpub. Ph.D. dissertation, University of Minnesota, 1978); Robert B. Highsaw, *Edward Douglass White: Defender of the Conservative Faith* (Baton Rouge, La., 1981), 139; August O. Spain, *The Political Theory of John C. Calhoun* (New York, 1951), 62; Ellis, *Jeffersonian Crisis,* 66.

19   Charles Grove Haines, *The American Doctrine of Judicial Supremacy* (2nd ed.: Berkeley, Calif., 1932), 20, 29, 469; Warren, *Supreme Court in U.S. History,* I, 519; Bray Hammond, "The Bank Cases," in John A. Garraty, ed., *Quarrels That Have Shaped the Constitution* (New York, 1964), 39; and Perry Miller, *The Life of the Mind in America from the Revolution to the Civil War* (New York, 1965), 217–22.

20   Miller, *The Life of the Mind in America,* 107; Jefferson to Spencer Roane, Sept. 6, 1819, Ford, ed., *Works of Jefferson,* XII, 137; Jefferson to Cartwright, June 5, 1824, Lipscomb, ed., *Writings of Jefferson,* XVI, 47–48. See also Jefferson to Judge Augustus B. Woodward, May 27, 1809, *ibid.,* XII, 283.

21   W. L. Carpenter to Edward S. Corwin, Feb. 12, 1936, Corwin Papers, box 2, PUML; Warren, *Supreme Court in U.S. History,* II, 213–16, 219; John P. Frank, *Marble Palace: The Supreme Court in American Life* (New York, 1958), 39; Henry A. Hawken, ed., *Trumpets of Glory: Fourth of July Orations, 1786–1861* (Granby, Conn., 1976), 160–61. For an explanation of Jackson's apparent inconsistency regarding national power and states' rights, see Phillip S. Paludan, *A Covenant with Death: The Constitution, Law, and Equality in the Civil War Era* (Urbana, Ill., 1975), 237.

22   Story, "Progress of Jurisprudence," Sept. 4, 1821, in William W. Story, ed., *The Miscellaneous Writings of Joseph Story* (Boston, 1852), 230–31; William Fleming to Charles Thompson, Nov. 7, 1823, Ferdinand J. Dreer Collection, HSP. For an interesting though highly egotistical anticipation of

23   this view, see Alexander Hamilton to Gouverneur Morris [Feb. 29, 1802], in Harold C. Syrett, ed., *The Papers of Alexander Hamilton* (New York, 1977), XXV, 544–45.

23   Marshall to Story, Dec. 30, 1827, in John S. Adams, ed., *An Autobiographical Sketch by John Marshall* (Ann Arbor, Mich., 1937), 43; James M. Beck, "John Marshall, Jurist and Statesman," VSD, 1 (June 3, 1935), 556. Beck gave this address (at memorial exercises to commemorate the centennial of Marshall's death) under the auspices of the Richmond Bar Association, the Virginia Historical Society, and the Association for the Preservation of Virginia Antiquities. In 1935, when many Americans also harbored doubts about the future of their constitutional system, Marshall's letter to Story was widely quoted—with solace derived from the recognition that the nation had survived a major crisis early in the 1830s and probably would also survive the current one. See R. L. Duffus, "Marshall's Words Still Mold the Law," NYT, June 30, 1935, sec. 7, p. 6.

24   Story to Kent, in Adams, ed., *Autobiographical Sketch by Marshall*, 98–99; Joseph Hopkinson to Richard Peters, May 10, 1837, Peters Papers, II, 40, HSP; Hopkinson to Richard Henry Lee, April 4, 1838, Simon Gratz Collection, case 6, box 31, HSP.

25   See Charles Francis Adams to James Madison, Sept. 30, 1835, Autograph Collection, case 19, box 1, HSP; Marc Friedlander and L. H. Butterfield, eds., *The Diary of Charles Francis Adams,* Oct. 21, 1835 (Cambridge, Mass., 1974), VI, 247; Charles Francis Adams, Jr., *Charles Francis Adams* (Cambridge, Mass., 1900), 26–27. This particular episode concerned constitutionalism and the politics of patronage.

26   Although the terms "state sovereignty" and "states' rights" have been used rather loosely and interchangeably for many years, the former seems more suitable in discussing the period before 1861, and the latter more appropriate for the past century. The so-called states' rights advocates of the antebellum era actually believed that the states had retained most of their domestic sovereignty, whereas those who remained sensitive to states' rights after 1865, including many northerners, as well as states' rights devotees during the period 1918–38 acknowledged a diminution in state sovereignty but insisted that certain rights and privileges (e.g., pertaining to the police power) had never been surrendered. John Norton Pomeroy noted this distinction in 1886. Hence the heightened interest in the Tenth Amendment during the later nineteenth century. See Paludan, *Covenant with Death*, 225–26, 246.

27   James Morton Smith, *Freedom's Fetters: The Alien and Sedition Laws and American Liberties* (Ithaca, N.Y., 1956), 263, 335, 345; Warren, *Supreme Court in U.S. History*, I, 164–65; Paul C. Nagel, *This Sacred Trust: American Nationality, 1798–1898* (New York, 1971), 20.

28   Warren, *Supreme Court in U.S. History*, I, 9, 77; Stampp, "Concept of a Perpetual Union," 27; for the Court decisions see Stanley I. Kutler, ed., *The Supreme Court and the Constitution: Readings in American Constitutional History* (2nd ed.: New York, 1977), 36–40, 63–71.

29   Warren, *Supreme Court in U.S. History*, I, 365; James M. Banner, *To the Hartford Convention: The Federalists and the Origins of Party Politics in Massachusetts, 1789–1815* (New York, 1970); St. George Tucker, *Blackstone's*

Commentaries: with Notes of Reference, to the Constitution and Laws, of the Federal Government of the United States (Philadelphia, 1803), I, 140–377 ("View of the Constitution of the United States"); John Taylor, *New Views of the Constitution of the United States* (Washington, D.C., 1823); Adams, *History of the United States of America during the Second Administration of James Madison* (New York, 1891), IX, 188.

30 Paul C. Nagel, *One Nation Indivisible: The Union in American Thought, 1776–1861* (New York, 1964), 55–56; Spain, *Political Theory of Calhoun*, 155, 191–92; Richard K. Crallé, ed., *The Works of John C. Calhoun* (Columbia, S.C., 1855), VI, 63, 69. The italics are Calhoun's.

31 "The Constitution not a Compact between Sovereign States," in *The Writings and Speeches of Daniel Webster* (Boston, 1903), VI, 185–86. The entire speech spans pp. 181–238.

32 *Ibid.*, 197–99, 236. The italics are Webster's. William W. Freehling has made the significant yet neglected point that constitutional polemics comprised the least important part of Webster's famous oration against Senator Hayne in 1830. Throughout these debates Webster held to the historical interpretation that the English colonies revolted as part of a unified crusade. Hence the Union had antedated the states. John Marshall, John Quincy Adams, Andrew Jackson, and later Abraham Lincoln all followed the same line. See Freehling, *Prelude to Civil War: The Nullification Controversy in South Carolina, 1816–1836* (New York, 1966), 185–86.

33 Cooper to William B. Shubrick, Sept. 20, 1830, in James F. Beard, ed., *The Letters and Journals of James Fenimore Cooper* (Cambridge, Mass., 1960), II, 21, 24 (the italics are Cooper's); Adams, *An Oration Addressed to the Citizens of the Town of Quincy on the Fourth of July, 1831* (Boston, 1831), 23, 25–29, 34–35, 38.

34 Tocqueville, *Democracy in America*, 156–57.

35 How did Madison acquire this honorific title? There are conflicting accounts. According to Douglass Adair, it came from a eulogy given by John Quincy Adams in 1836 following Madison's death. According to Irving Brant, however, Charles J. Ingersoll, a Philadelphia lawyer, congressman, and U.S. District Attorney (1815–29), referred to Madison in 1827 as "the father and guardian of the Constitution" at a dinner of Pennsylvania manufacturers who felt particular gratitude to Madison for supporting the constitutionality of the protective tariff. See Trevor Colbourn, ed., *Fame and the Founding Fathers: Essays by Douglass Adair* (New York, 1974), 78 n.6; and Irving Brant, *James Madison: Commander in Chief, 1812–1836* (Indianapolis, 1961), VI, 471.

36 Brant, *Madison*, VI, 474–75; Webster, "The Constitution Not a Compact," 232–33.

37 Brant, *Madison*, VI, 470–71, 473, 476–80, 482–83, 488–94, 499. The italics are Madison's. For the text of Madison's letter in the NAR, see Marvin Meyers, ed., *The Mind of the Founder: Sources of the Political Thought of James Madison* (Indianapolis, 1973), 531–44.

38 Brant, *Madison*, VI, 468–69, 475.

39 *Ibid.*, 512–13, 530–31; Adrienne Koch, *Madison's "Advice to My Country"* (Princeton, 1966), ch. 3; Nagel, *One Nation Indivisible*, 53.

40 *The Federalist* Number 39; letter from Carl N. Degler, NR (June 2, 1982),

6; Madison to Nicholas P. Trist, Dec. 1831, in *Documentary History of the Constitution* (1905), V, 377. For Madison's inconsistencies regarding national authority over the domestic slave trade, see Walter Berns, "The Constitution and Migration of Slaves," YLJ, 78 (1968), 215–17, 219, 225. Cf. Lance Banning, "The Hamiltonian Madison: A Reconsideration," *Virginia Magazine of History and Biography*, 92 (1984), 3–28.

41   Max Farrand, ed., *The Records of the Federal Convention of 1787* (2nd ed.: New Haven, Conn., 1937), I, 422; *The Federalist* Number 49; Herbert J. Storing, *What the Anti-Federalists Were For* (Chicago, 1981), 74; Wills, *Explaining America*, 160. In 1932 James M. Beck gave a shrill echo of Madison, arguing that it would be dangerous to hold a new constitutional convention because "it might prove a 'witches' sabbath' of socialistic demagoguery," and that "we could no longer make any successful attempt to embody the needs of a highly complex age in a written form of government, without the possibility of infinite follies and injustices." NYT, June 28, 1932, p. 6.

42   Madison to Robert Walsh, Nov. 27, 1819, and Madison to James Monroe, Feb. 23, 1820, in Gaillard Hunt, ed., *The Writings of James Madison* (New York, 1910), IX, 1–4, 25; Madison to Monroe, Feb. 10, 1820, in *Documentary History of the Constitution* (1905), V, 307; Orestes A. Brownson, *The American Republic: Its Constitution, Tendencies, and Destiny* (New York, 1865), 244–45.

43   Brant, *Madison*, VI, 433–34; Jefferson to Garnett, Feb. 14, 1824, Lipscomb, ed., *Writings of Jefferson*, XVI, 14–15. See also Jefferson's "Notes for a Constitution" (1794), in Ford, ed., *Works of Jefferson*, VIII, 159–62; and Jefferson's "Drafts of a Constitution for Virginia" (June 1776), in Boyd, ed., *Papers of Jefferson*, I, 344–65. For Madison's concerted opposition to the Marshall Court in 1819–21, see his three long letters to Judge Spencer Roane in Meyers, ed., *Political Thought of Madison*, 456–69.

44   Jefferson to Levi Lincoln, Aug. 30, 1803, in Lipscomb, ed., *Writings of Jefferson*, X, 417; Jefferson to Wilson C. Nicholas, Sept. 7, 1803, *ibid.*, 418–20; Henry Adams, *History of the United States during the First Administration of Jefferson*, II, 86.

45   Monroe to Madison, Dec. 22, 1817, and Madison to Monroe, Dec. 27, 1817, Madison Papers, series 1, microfilm reel 18, LCMD; Madison to Henry St. George Tucker, Dec. 23, 1817, *ibid.*; Brant, *Madison*, VI, 426.

46   For Jackson's veto of the Maysville Road bill, see Henry Steele Commager, ed., *Documents of American History* (7th ed.: New York, 1963), 253–55; Madison to Monroe, Dec. 20, 1822, Madison Papers, series 1, reel 20, LCMD; Abbott Lawrence to Clay, Mar. 26, 1833, in Warren, *Supreme Court in U.S. History*, I, viii n.1.

47   Hunt, ed., *Writings of Madison*, VIII, 49; Van Buren in James D. Richardson, ed., *A Compilation of the Messages and Papers of the Presidents, 1789–1897* (Washington, D.C., 1896–99), III, 319; Pierce in *ibid.*, V, 201.

48   Jedidiah Morse, "A Concise View of the Principles of the Constitution and Government of the United States . . . ," in Morse, *Annals of the American Revolution. . . .* (Hartford, Conn., 1824), 400.

49   See Alexander Hamilton to Edward Carrington, May 26, 1792, in Syrett, ed., *Papers of Hamilton*, XI, 443; "The United States' Constitution," *The United States Magazine, and Democratic Review*, 22 (May 1848), 387–94.

50   See *The Richmond Enquirer*, Feb. 23, 1839, p. 4, an essay on Madison reprinted from the *Philadelphia Daily Advertiser;* Nagel, *This Sacred Trust*, 120; Nagel, *One Nation Indivisible*, 57–58.

51   Charles Chauncey Binney, *The Life of Horace Binney, with selections from his letters* (Philadelphia, 1903), 132–33.

52   "New Territory versus No Territory," *The U.S. Magazine, and Democratic Review*, 21 (October 1847), 285–86; Seward, *California, Union and Freedom* (Washington, D.C., 1850), 8; Nagel, *One Nation Indivisible*, 156–57, 187–88. See the important but little known essay by Arthur Bestor, "Constitutionalism and the Settlement of the West: The Attainment of Consensus, 1754–1784," in John Porter Bloom, ed., *The American Territorial System* (Athens, Ohio, 1973), 13–44, esp. 33.

53   *U.S. Magazine, and Democratic Review*, 22 (May 1848), 387–94, esp. 390–91, 392, 394.

54   Michael Meyer and W. L. Sherman, *The Course of Mexican History* (New York, 1979), 313–14, 327, 379, 483.

55   Erich Angermann, "Early German Constitutionalism and the American Model," in *Reports: XIV International Congress of the Historical Sciences* (New York, 1977), III, 1499–1516; Gordon A. Craig, *The Germans* (New York, 1982), 172–73.

56   Eric Cochrane, *Florence in the Forgotten Centuries, 1527–1800* (Chicago, 1973), 462–64; Andrew Dickson White, "The Statesmanship of Cavour," *Atlantic Monthly*, 99 (1907), 299–300, 304.

57   See Isaac Kramnick, "Republican Revisionism Revisited," AHR, 87 (1982), 647–49, 655; Herbert Butterfield, *George III, Lord North, and the People, 1779–1780* (London, 1949), 345–47, 349–51; Edward S. Corwin, *Court Over Constitution*, 218; Antoine Sérieys, *Les Révolutions en France ou La Liberté, poème national en dix chants, avec des notes qui renferment un précis historique de la Révolution et d'autres détails intéressants* (Paris, 1790); Thomas Paine to George Washington, May 1, 1790, in Philip S. Foner, ed., *The Complete Writings of Thomas Paine* (New York, 1945), II, 1302–04; Kenneth and Anna Roberts, eds., *Moreau de St. Méry's American Journey* [1793–98] (Garden City, N.Y., 1947), 202; Russell H. Fitzgibbon, ed., *The Constitutions of the Americas* (Chicago, 1948), 4.

58   Harold J. Laski, "The English Constitution and French Public Opinion, 1789–1794" (1938), in Laski, *The Danger of Being a Gentleman and Other Essays* (New York, 1940), 151–53, 158.

59   *Ibid.*, 139; Gabriel Bonnot, Abbé de Mably, *Observations sur l'histoire de France* (Kehll, Germany, 1788); Anne Pallister, *Magna Carta: The Heritage of Liberty* (Oxford, 1971), 82.

60   Jefferson to A. Coray, Oct. 31, 1823, in Lipscomb, ed., *Writings of Jefferson*, XV, 484.

61   Wright, *Views of Society and Manners in America*, ed. by Paul R. Baker (1821: Cambridge, Mass., 1963), 173–74, 192–93.

62   *Ibid.*, 192.

63   Cooper to Benjamin Silliman, June 10, 1831, in Beard, ed., *Letters and Journals of Cooper*, II, 96–97. Cooper's italics.

64 Stampp, "The Concept of a Perpetual Union," 31–32; Alfred H. Kelly, *et al., The American Constitution: Its Origins and Development* (6th ed.: New York, 1983), 211–12.

• CHAPTER 3 *All That Gives Us a National Character*

1 APSR, 30 (1936), 1071–85.

2 See Charles H. McIlwain, *Constitutionalism: Ancient and Modern* (Ithaca, N.Y., 1940); Francis D. Wormuth, *The Origins of Modern Constitutionalism* (New York, 1949), esp. part 2; Philip S. Foner, ed., *The Complete Writings of Thomas Paine* (New York, 1945), I, 29; Sol Bloom to John C. Fitzpatrick, Aug. 4, 1936, Fitzpatrick Papers, box 16, LCMD.

3 Jacob Rader Marcus, ed., *American Jewry: Documents, Eighteenth Century* (Cincinnati, 1959), 148–67. For an emphasis upon origins rather than impact, see William P. Trent, "The Period of Constitution-Making in the American Churches," in J. Franklin Jameson, ed., *Essays in the Constitutional History of the United States in the Formative Period, 1775–1789* (Boston, 1889), 186–262.

4 I am indebted for this insight to Peter J. Parker, director of the HSP.

5 Thomas I. Wharton, *An Oration Delivered on the Fourth of July, 1827.* . . . (Philadelphia, 1827), 3, 4; Everett, "The History of Liberty" (an oration at Charlestown, Mass., 1828), in Everett, *Orations and Speeches on Various Occasions* (9th ed.: Boston, 1878), I, 167.

6 "The Settlement of Dedham" (Sept. 21, 1836), Everett, *Orations and Speeches on Various Occasions,* II, 181.

7 Everett, delivered in Cambridge, Mass., in *ibid.*, I, 129; Madison's Will, Apr. 19, 1835, in Gaillard Hunt, ed., *The Writings of James Madison* (New York, 1910), IX, 549.

8 James D. Richardson, ed., *A Compilation of the Messages and Papers of the Presidents, 1789–1897* (Washington, D.C., 1896–99), I, 218; Harry Atwood, "The Constitution Week Movement," CR, 13 (1929), 181. The Farewell Address was first printed on Sept. 19, 1796, in a Philadelphia newspaper, David Claypoole's *American Daily Advertiser.* On Nov. 28, 1794, the House of Representatives had responded to Washington's sixth annual address by assuring him that "the great body of [the American people] everywhere are equally attached to the luminous and vital principle of our Constitution. . . ," Richardson, ed., *Messages and Papers,* I, 170.

9 Madison, Dec. 3, 1816, and Adams, Mar. 4, 1825, in *ibid.*, I, 579–80, II, 294.

10 Harrison's death notice in *ibid.*, IV, 22; Tyler's protest to the House, Aug. 30, 1842, in *ibid.*, IV, 193.

11 Taylor, Dec. 4, 1849, and Pierce, Dec. 2, 1856, in *ibid.*, V, 24, 397–98.

12 *Washington Post,* Sept. 13, 1936, p. B2; David C. Mearns and Verner W. Clapp, *The Constitution of the United States together with an Account of Its Travels* (Washington, D.C., 1952), 11.

13 *Ibid.*, 15–16; *Washington Post,* Sept. 13, 1936, pp. B2 and 10.

14 Cutler to Rev. Dana, Dec. 5, 1801, Society Collection, HSP; Rush to

Adams, June 13, 1808, in John A. Schutz and Douglass Adair, eds., *The Spur of Fame: Dialogues of John Adams and Benjamin Rush, 1805–1813* (San Marino, Calif., 1966), 108; Paul C. Nagel, *One Nation Indivisible: The Union in American Thought, 1776–1861* (New York, 1964), 54; "The Relative Status of the North and the South," *De Bow's Review,* 32 (February 1857), 128.

15   The earliest reference to *The Federalist* in a Supreme Court opinion came from Samuel Chase in 1798, followed by John Marshall in 1803. See Charles W. Pierson, "The Federalist in the Supreme Court," YLJ, 33 (1924), 728–35.

16   Morris to Timothy Pickering, Dec. 22, 1814, in Anne Cary Morris, ed., *The Diary and Letters of Gouverneur Morris* (New York, 1888), II, 573–74.

17   Madison to Henry St. George Tucker, Dec. 23, 1817, Madison Papers, series 1, reel 18, LCMD.

18   Cooper to Jedediah Hunt, Jr., Sept. 18, 1844, in James F. Beard, ed., *The Letters and Journals of James Fenimore Cooper* (Cambridge, Mass., 1964), IV, 478–79.

19   Quoted anonymously in Perry Miller, *The Life of the Mind in America from the Revolution to the Civil War* (New York, 1965), 119. See also William Anderson, "The Intention of the Framers: A Note on Constitutional Interpretation," APSR, 49 (1955), 340–52.

20   Adams to Joseph Hopkinson, Feb. 8, 1831, Redwood Collection (Am 12905, p. 67), HSP. See also Kermit L. Hall, *et al.,* eds., *The Constitutional Convention as an Amending Device* (Washington, D.C., 1981), 60–61.

21   Washington to Lafayette, April 28, 1788, in John C. Fitzpatrick, ed., *The Writings of George Washington,* XXIX (Washington, D.C., 1939), 478; Herbert J. Storing, *What the Anti-Federalists Were For* (Chicago, 1981), 54.

22   Quoted in H. Arnold Bennett, *The Constitution in School and College* (New York, 1935), 49 n.2.

23   See Charles Warren, *The Supreme Court in United States History* (Boston, 1922), I, 245; Warren, "Sources of Knowledge of the Constitution," CR, 11 (1927), 179, 181.

24   I am indebted to the breakdown calculated by Stuart S. Nagel, "Court-Curbing Periods in American History," VLR, 18 (1965), 925–44.

25   *Farmer's Weekly Museum,* June 17, 1799, quoted in Warren, *Supreme Court in U.S. History,* I, 59; Alan F. Westin, ed., *An Autobiography of the Supreme Court: Off-the-Bench Commentary by the Justices* (New York, 1963), 57–58.

26   See Catharine Macaulay, *The History of England, from the Accession of James I to that of the Brunswick Line* (London, 1763), I, vii, xiv.

27   Rush to John Montgomery, June 21, 1799, in L. H. Butterfield, ed., *The Letters of Benjamin Rush* (Princeton, 1951), II, 812.

28   Sergeant, *Constitutional Law: Being a view of the practice and jurisdiction of the courts of the United States, and of constitutional points decided* (Philadelphia, 1822, 1830); Rawle, *A View of the Constitution of the United States of America* (Philadelphia, 1825, 1829, 1832); Duponceau, *A Brief View of the*

Constitution of the United States (Philadelphia, 1834); Duponceau to Job R. Tyson, John Cadwalader, and Peter McCall, May 19, 1834, in the Cadwalader Collection, Law Academy correspondence, HSP.

29 Duer, *Outlines of the constitutional jurisprudence of the United States; designed as a text book for lectures, as a class book for academies and common schools, and as a manual for popular use* (New York, 1833); Duer, *A Course of Lectures on the Constitutional Jurisprudence of the United States delivered annually in Columbia College* (New York, 1843, reprinted in 1844, 1845, 1855, revised in 1856, reprinted in 1868 and 1874); Carl Bode, *The American Lyceum: Town Meeting of the Mind* (New York, 1956), 104; "Duer," DAB.

30 Elizabeth Kelley Bauer, *Commentaries on the Constitution, 1790–1860* (New York, 1952), 152, 154; William Wetmore Story, *Life and Letters of Joseph Story* (Boston, 1851), II, 109, 129–41.

31 See Edwin Williams, comp., *The Book of the Constitution. Containing the Constitution of the United States; [and] a synopsis of the several state constitutions* (New York, 1833); Benjamin E. Hale, *Familiar Conversations upon the Constitution of the United States* (Boston, 1835); Baldwin, *A General View of the Origin and Nature of the Constitution and Government of the United States. . . .* (Philadelphia, 1837): William Archer Cocke, *The Constitutional History of the United States, from the adoption of the articles of confederation to the close of Jackson's administration* (Philadelphia, 1858); only the first of two volumes ever appeared.

32 From the 1853 edition, viii, xxv. This edition is 521 pages long.

33 *Ibid.*, x, xii, xvii–xviii, xx–xxi.

34 Everett, *Orations and Speeches*, I, 308; Bode, *American Lyceum*, 137, 191.

35 Bennett, *Constitution in School and College*, 26 n.5, 63–64, 103; Alice W. Spieseke, *The First Textbooks in American History and Their Compiler John M'Culloch* (New York, 1938), 100–01; Daniel C. Knowlton, "The United States Constitution in the Schoolbooks of the Past," *The Social Studies*, 29 (1938), 7–14. Charles A. Goodrich, *The Child's History of the United States. . . .* (32nd ed.: Philadelphia, 1845), devotes a total of three brief sentences to the Constitution (thirty-four words in all).

36 Hyman, *A More Perfect Union: The Impact of the Civil War and Reconstruction on the Constitution* (New York, 1973), 4–5, 7.

37 Wright to William Hickey, April 9, 1847, in Hickey, *The Constitution* (1853 edition), xv–xvi.

38 Breese to Hickey, Mar. 6, 1847, *ibid.*, xiv.

39 Cooper to Micah Sterling, Oct. 27, 1834; to *The Evening Post,* Jan. 8, 1835, Feb. 7, 1835, and Mar. 14, 1835; and to Horatio Greenough, Aug. 9, 1836, in Beard, ed., *Letters and Journals of Cooper,* III, 58–59, 83, 98, 115, 233.

40 Cooper's Journal, Jan. 20 and 26, 1848; Cooper to Samuel L. Harris, Sept. 5, 1848, in *ibid.,* V, 260, 262, 377–79.

41 Cooper to *The Evening Post,* Jan. 9, 1835, in *ibid.,* III, 86–87; see also 117–18, 123, 126, 134; Webster to William Hickey, Dec. 11, 1850, in Hickey, *The Constitution,* xxii.

42 See Warren, "Sources of Knowledge of the Constitution," 175–77.

43 Warren, *Supreme Court in U.S. History,* I, 455, 456 n.1, 475–76, 487–88.

See Maurice G. Baxter, *Daniel Webster & the Supreme Court* ([Amherst, Mass.], 1966).

44 Quoted in Richard E. Ellis, *The Jeffersonian Crisis: Courts and Politics in the Young Republic* (New York, 1971), 202.

45 Jefferson to John Adams, Aug. 30, 1787, in Lester J. Cappon, ed., *The Adams-Jefferson Letters* (Chapel Hill, N.C., 1959), I, 196; William Manning, *The Key of Libberty* (1798), ed. by Samuel Eliot Morison (Billerica, Mass., 1922), 42; Curtis, *Constitutional History of the United States from their Declaration of Independence to the Close of their Civil War* (2nd ed.: New York, 1889), I, 623.

46 James H. Hutson, "Robert Yates's Notes on the Constitutional Convention of 1787: Citizen Genet's Edition," *Quarterly Journal of the Library of Congress,* 35 (1978), 173–82. The Yates material was published as *Secret Proceedings and Debates of the Convention Assembled at Philadelphia in the Year 1787 . . . from Notes Taken by the Late Robert Yates.* It supplies a useful record of early political alignments in the Convention; but because Yates left Philadelphia on July 10, 1787, his notes are incomplete.

47 Jefferson to Adams, Aug. 10, 1815, in Cappon, ed., *Adams-Jefferson Letters,* II, 453; Sparks to Madison, Mar. 30, 1831, in *Documentary History of the Constitution of the United States of America, 1786–1870,* in *Bulletin of the Bureau of Rolls and Library of the Department of State* (Washington, D.C., 1905), V 365. Considering that Gouverneur Morris was responsible for much of the Constitution's actual prose, Madison responded modestly when admirers called him "*the* writer of the Constitution." See Madison to William Cogswell, Mar. 10, 1834, in Hunt, ed., *Writings of Madison,* IX, 533.

48 Madison to Thomas Ritchie, Sept. 15, 1821, in *Documentary History of the Constitution,* 310–11. See also Madison to J. G. Jackson, Dec. 27, 1821, *ibid.,* 312–15; and to Nicholas P. Trist, December 1831, in *ibid.,* 375–78.

49 Hunt, ed., *Writings of Madison,* IX, 549–50.

50 Irving Brant, "The Madison Heritage," *New York University Law Review,* 35 (1960), 882–902.

51 Irving Brant, *Storm Over the Constitution* (Indianapolis, 1936), 92.

52 Authorities on the history of the Constitution liked to emphasize this point during the early decades of the twentieth century, when the Constitution and its genesis became especially controversial. See Hannis Taylor, *The Origin and Growth of the American Constitution* (New York, 1911), 9–10; NYT, June 16, 1922, p. 16, reporting a speech by James M. Beck. Taylor regretted the delay, writing: "During the half-century of mystery and suppression that followed the adjournment of the Federal Convention, the mythical history of what actually took place in the secret conclave crystallized into a series of misty and misleading impressions that became so fixed in the minds of many that it is now difficult to dislodge them even with the aid of clear and explicit documentary evidence." Beck, by contrast, concluded that "if the framers of the Constitution had met as similar conventions have within recent years met at Versailles and Genoa, with the world as their gallery and with the representatives of the press as an integral part of the conference, they would have accomplished nothing." Regrettably, in my view, both men were undoubtedly correct.

53   See William M. Wiecek, *The Sources of Antislavery Constitutionalism in America, 1760–1848* (Ithaca, N.Y., 1977), 112, 239, 263; Paul Finkelman, *An Imperfect Union: Slavery, Federalism, and Comity* (Chapel Hill, N.C., 1981), 29.

54   Hickey, *The Constitution*, vii; Warren, *Hughes and the Court* (Hamilton, N.Y., 1962), 1; NYT, Sept. 17, 1887, p. 4.

55   *Richmond Enquirer*, Mar. 14, 1839, p. 4.

56   Parke Goodwin, *A Biography of William Cullen Bryant* (New York, 1883), I, 354; New York *Morning Herald*, May 1, 1839, p. 2. Bryant's ode was printed in the *Richmond Enquirer*, May 7, 1839, p. 4.

57   Adams, *The Jubilee of the Constitution: A Discourse Delivered . . . in the City of New York, on Tuesday, the 30th of April, 1839. . . .* (New York, 1839), 22, 53, 115.

58   *Ibid.*, 11, 38–40, 44, 50–51, 54, 118. For similar expressions of this non-Beardian point of view, see Edward Everett, "The Principle of the American Constitutions" (an oration delivered at Cambridge, July 4, 1826) and "The History of Liberty" (an oration delivered at Charlestown, July 4, 1828), in Everett, *Orations and Speeches on Various Occasions*, I, 118, 122, 167; and for James G. Birney, the abolitionist, Aileen S. Kraditor, *Means and Ends in American Abolitionism: Garrison and His Critics on Strategy and Tactics, 1834–1850* (New York, 1969), 190.

59   See Tyrone G. Martin, *A Most Fortunate Ship: A Narrative History of "Old Ironsides"* (Chester, Conn., 1980); Philadelphia *Public Ledger*, Feb. 22, 1837, p. 4; Roy P. Basler, ed., *The Collected Works of Abraham Lincoln* (New Brunswick, N.J., 1953), IV, 228.

60   See Wilbur Zelinsky, "Nationalism in the American Place-Name Cover," *Names*, 31 (1983), 15–18.

61   See Michael Kammen, *A Season of Youth: The American Revolution and the Historical Imagination* (New York, 1978), ch. 3. Although the several chambers occupied over the years by the Supreme Court have contained representations of justice, we have nothing remotely comparable to the European tradition. See Samuel Y. Edgerton, Jr., "Icons of Justice," *Past & Present*, no. 89 (1980), 23–38. In the original (and now handsomely restored) Court chamber located in the basement of the U.S. Captiol, Carlo Franzoni's bas-relief adorns the rear wall faced by the justices. An allegorical figure of Fame (crowned by the rising sun) sits on a pedestal and holds the Constitution, while a larger, neoclassical figure of Justice holds her scales evenly balanced.

62   Panofsky, *Studies in Iconology: Humanistic Themes in the Art of the Renaissance* (New York, 1939), 3; Johnson is quoted in Corwin, "Constitution as Instrument and as Symbol," 1075; Hickey, *The Constitution*, xxvii.

63   See Andrew Oliver, *The Portraits of John Marshall* (Charlottesville, Va., 1977), 41, 119; and Robert A. Rutland, *et al., James Madison and the Search for Nationhood* (Washington, D.C., 1981), 82, for a small engraving, *Convention at Philadelphia 1787*, that appeared in Charles A. Goodrich, *A History of the United States of America* (1823). The engraving by Whitechurch and the mezzotint by Doney will both be found at the National Portrait Gallery in Washington, D.C.

64   Anne Pallister, *Magna Carta: The Heritage of Liberty* (Oxford, 1971) plates

1–5; Roy Strong, *And When Did You Last See Your Father? The Victorian Painter and British History* (London, 1978), 19, 29, 62, 141, 157. A portrait like *Andrew Jackson* by David Rent Etter (see figure 4), which is unusual in American iconography, has numerous counterparts in European art. See, for example, the portrait of Jean Anthony d'Averhout by Louis Leopold Boilly (ca. 1792) at the Centraal Museum of Utrecht in the Netherlands. D'Averhout played an important role in the Dutch patriotic movement during the 1780s. He fled to France in 1787, was naturalized, and in 1792 became president of the National Assembly. In Boilly's portrait, d'Averhout sits with an open volume labelled "French Constitution."

65　Marc Raeff, *Michael Speransky: Statesman of Imperial Russia, 1772–1839* (The Hague, 1957), ch. 2, esp. 38–42; Jefferson to Priestley, Nov. 29, 1802, in N. Hans, ed., "Tsar Alexander I and Jefferson: Unpublished Correspondence," *Slavonic and East European Review,* 32 (1953), 217.

66　Russell H. Fitzgibbon, ed., *The Constitutions of the Americas* (Chicago, 1948), 11. See also Glen Dealy, "Prolegomena on the Spanish American Political Tradition," *The Hispanic American Historical Review,* 48 (1968), 37–58.

67　Michael Meyer and W. L. Sherman, *The Course of Mexican History* (New York, 1979), 379, 483; Fitzgibbon, ed., *Constitutions of the Americas,* 7–8.

68　Cooper to Peter A. Jay, July 15, 1830, in Beard, ed., *Letters and Journals of Cooper,* I, 422; Webster to William Hickey, Dec. 11, 1850, in Hickey, *The Constitution,* xxii. Webster's point was anticipated at the 1787 Convention by Charles Pinckney of South Carolina. See Max Farrand, ed., *The Records of the Federal Convention of 1787* (rev. ed.: New Haven, Conn., 1937), I, 398–99.

●　CHAPTER 4 *The Constitution Threatens to Be a Subject of Infinite Sects*

1　See Arthur Bestor, "The American Civil War as a Constitutional Crisis," AHR, 69 (1964), 327–52; Bestor, "State Sovereignty and Slavery: A Reinterpretation of Proslavery Constitutional Doctrine, 1846–1860," *Journal of the Illinois State Historical Society,* 54 (1961), 117–80; Harold M. Hyman, *A More Perfect Union: The Impact of the Civil War and Reconstruction on the Constitution* (New York, 1973); Phillip S. Paludan, *A Covenant with Death: The Constitution, Law, and Equality in the Civil War Era* (Urbana, Ill., 1975).

2　For the similar perspectives of a conservative white New Englander and a reform-minded mulatto veteran, see George Ticknor Curtis, *Constitutional History of the United States from their Declaration of Independence to the Close of their Civil War* (New York, 1889), I, iii; and George W. Williams, *The Constitutional Results of the War of the Rebellion: An Oration, Memorial Day . . . 1889* (Worcester, Mass., 1889), 15, 19. Williams wondered whether the constitutional consequences of the war would be permanent or transitory. Curtis explained that after the war, "many more years elapsed before I could feel that the Constitution had come out of the turmoil with its principles in a fair state of preservation."

3　J. David Hoeveler, Jr., "Reconstruction and the Federal Courts: The Civil

Rights Act of 1875," *The Historian,* 31 (1969), 615–16; John Hope Franklin, "Enforcement of the Civil Rights Act of 1875," *Prologue,* 6 (1974), 225–35; and Patricia M. L. Lucie, "Confiscation: Constitutional Crossroads," *Civil War History,* 23 (1977), 321.

4   William R. Leslie, "The Influence of Joseph Story's Theory of the Conflict of Laws on Constitutional Nationalism," MVHR, 35 (1948), 203–20, esp. 218.

5   Harold M. Hyman and William M. Wiecek, *Equal Justice Under Law: Constitutional Development, 1835–1875* (New York, 1982), 108.

6   Madison to R. J. Evans, June 15, 1819, quoted in Irving Brant, *James Madison: Commander in Chief, 1812–1836* (Indianapolis, 1961), VI, 431; William M. Wiecek, *The Sources of Antislavery Constitutionalism in America, 1760–1848* (Ithaca, N.Y., 1977), 168–69, 171; *The Emancipator, and Journal of Public Morals,* Nov. 4, 1834, pp. 2–3.

7   See Wiecek, *Sources of Antislavery Constitutionalism,* 81, 239–40, 245, 256, 263.

8   William M. Wiecek, "Slavery and Abolition before the United States Supreme Court, 1820–1860," JAH, 65 (1978), 47, esp. notes 50 and 52; Ronald G. Walters, *The Antislavery Appeal: American Abolitionism after 1830* (Baltimore, 1976), 8, 131; *Liberator,* May 31, 1844, in George M. Fredrickson, ed., *William Lloyd Garrison* (Englewood Cliffs, N.J., 1968), 53.

9   Phillips, *The Constitution a Pro-Slavery Compact* (3rd ed.: New York, 1856), 8, emphasis in the original; Staughton Lynd, "The Abolitionist Critique of the United States Constitution," in Martin Duberman, ed., *The Antislavery Vanguard: New Essays on the Abolitionists* (Princeton, 1965), 209–39.

10   Carl Bode, *The American Lyceum: Town Meeting of the Mind* (New York, 1956), 206; John L. Thomas, *The Liberator: William Lloyd Garrison* (Boston, 1963), 384, 387.

11   Paludan, *The Constitution, Law, and Equality,* 3. Ralph Waldo Emerson and William Ellery Channing, however, supported Garrison's position. See Robert A. Ferguson, *Law and Letters in American Culture* (Cambridge, Mass., 1984), 203, 235.

12   Philip Foner, ed., *The Life and Writings of Frederick Douglass* (New York, 1855), I, 361–67.

13   *Ibid.,* II, 353. See also Douglass, *The Constitution of the United States: Is It Pro-Slavery or Anti-Slavery?* (Halifax, N.S. [1860]), esp. 19–20.

14   Bestor, "State Sovereignty and Slavery," 132–33

15   Cooper to William B. Shubrick, July 22, 1850, in James F. Beard, ed., *The Letters and Journals of James Fenimore Cooper* (Cambridge, Mass., 1968), VI, 207; Ernest Samuels, *The Young Henry Adams* (Cambridge, Mass., 1967), 79; Conway, *Autobiography: Memories and Experiences* (Boston, 1904), I, 185–86.

16   Eric Foner, *Free Soil, Free Labor, Free Men: The Ideology of the Republican Party before the Civil War* (New York, 1970), 73, 75–77, 85.

17   *Ibid.,* 82–86, 89. For a representative elaboration of Chase's position, see Charles W. Upham, *Speech in the House of Representatives of Massachusetts on the Compromises of the Constitution. . . .* (Salem, Mass., 1849).

18   Walters, *Antislavery Appeal,* 42; Aileen S. Kraditor, *Means and Ends in American Abolitionism: Garrison and His Critics on Strategy and Tactics, 1834–1850* (New York, 1969), 186–95.

19   Lincoln's speech at Edwardsville, Ill., Sept. 11, 1858, in Roy P. Basler, ed., *The Collected Works of Abraham Lincoln* (New Brunswick, N.J., 1953), III, 92. For other instances between 1852 and 1860 when Lincoln described his position regarding slavery as hostile yet historically constitutional, see *ibid.*, II, 156, 401, 454, 494; III, 311, 368, 435, 460; and IV, 50.

20   See Lincoln to William H. Herndon, Feb. 15, 1848, Lincoln's speech in the House of Representatives on Internal Improvements, June 20, 1848, and Lincoln's speech to the Springfield Scott Club, Aug. 14, 1852, in *ibid.*, I, 451–52, 485–88; II, 142–43.

21   See Lincoln's speech on the Sub-Treasury, Dec. 26, 1839, and his address at the Cooper Institute, Feb. 27, 1860, when he observed that "the question of federal control of slavery in the territories, seems not to have been directly before the Convention which framed the original Constitution." *Ibid.*, I, 170–72; III, 522–50, esp. 525.

22   Lincoln's speech at Peoria, Oct. 16, 1854, *ibid.*, II, 274.

23   Lincoln to Joshua F. Speed, Aug. 24, 1855, *ibid.*, III, 320.

24   Lincoln's Address before the Young Men's Lyceum of Springfield, Ill., Jan. 27, 1838, *ibid.*, I, 112, 115. Speech at Kalamazoo, Aug. 27, 1856, *ibid.*, II, 363, 366.

25   Lincoln's reply to Douglas, Oct. 7, 1858, at Galesburg, Ill., in their fifth debate, *ibid.*, III, 231–33. For a sequence of consistent statements by Lincoln in 1858 concerning Dred Scott, the Court, the Constitution, and slavery, see *ibid.*, II, 466–67, 492, 494, 513, 515, 520–21; III, 87, 96.

26   Lincoln to Chase, June 20, 1859, *ibid.*, 386; speech at Dayton, Sept. 17, 1859, *ibid.*, 460. See also *ibid.*, III, 78–79, 307, 439–40, 466; IV, 11, 22.

27   Don E. Fehrenbacher, *Slavery, Law, and Politics: The Dred Scott Case in Historical Perspective* (abr. ed.: New York, 1981), 94; Isaac F. Shepard, *Liberty and Its Mission: An Oration Delivered before the Citizens of West Killingley, Conn., July 4, 1856* (Boston, 1856), 19; Pierce, Third Annual Message, Dec. 31, 1855, in James D. Richardson, ed., *A Compilation of the Messages and Papers of the Presidents, 1789–1897* (Washington, D.C., 1896–99), VII, 2882–83.

28   Throughout Lincoln's career he consistently took the position that the Supreme Court alone could not define the Constitution. Following the Dred Scott decision, and especially during the 1858 debates with Douglas, Lincoln denied the Court an unqualified, final voice on constitutional matters. See Gary J. Jacobsohn, "Abraham Lincoln 'On this Question of Judicial Authority': The Theory of Constitutional Aspiration," *Western Political Quarterly,* 36 (1983), 54, 56.

29   Hyman, *A More Perfect Union,* 25, 28; Charles Warren, *The Supreme Court in United States History* (Boston, 1922), III, 11, 27–28, 33.

30   See Bestor, "Civil War as a Constitutional Crisis," 345–46, 351; Dunbar Rowland, ed., *Jefferson Davis, Constitutionalist: His Letters, Papers and Speeches* (Jackson, Miss., 1923), IV, 126; but see *ibid.*, 167, for Davis's declaration in the Senate that southern "loyalty to the Constitution" might "require them to take that last and regretful step."

31   NYT, July 25, 1860, p. 2; Foner, *Ideology of the Republican Party,* 133, 142, 224; George E. Baker, ed., *The Works of William H. Seward* (Boston, 1884), IV, 329.

32   "Speech on Secession," in Leroy P. Graf and Ralph W. Haskins, eds., *The Papers of Andrew Johnson* (Knoxville, Tenn., 1976), IV, 4–6, 9, 17.

33   Basler, ed., *Works of Lincoln,* IV, 193–97, 206–07.

34   *Ibid.,* 240, an echo of his 1838 speech at the Springfield Lyceum. See *ibid.,* I, 112.

35   *Ibid.,* IV, 262–71; I, 115.

36   *Daily National Intelligencer,* Mar. 5, 1861, p. 3, Mar. 7, 1861, p. 2; NYT, Mar. 5, 1861, p. 4; *Goshen Democrat,* Mar. 7, 1861, p. 2; *Hartford Weekly Courant,* Mar. 9, 1861, p. 2; *Pittsburgh Gazette,* Mar. 5, 1861, p. 2; *Chicago Tribune,* Mar. 5, 1861, p. 1; *Emporia News,* Mar. 9, 1861, p. 2; *Daily Alta California,* Mar. 19, 1861, p. 2; and the *Chicago Weekly Democrat,* Mar. 9, 1861, p. 3, which featured a survey of how the inaugural address had been received in all sections of the country and by newspapers of various political persuasions.

37   *Albany Evening Journal,* Mar. 5, 1861, p. 22; *Atlas of Argus,* Mar. 5, 1861, p. 2; *New York Herald,* Mar. 5, 1861, p. 4; *Chicago Tribune,* Mar. 5, 1861, p. 1.

38   *Rochester Democrat,* Mar. 5, 1861, p. 1; *Chicago Weekly Democrat,* Mar. 9, 1861, p. 2; *Nebraska City News,* Mar. 9, 1861, p. 3; *Illinois State Register,* Mar. 6, 1861, p. 2, and Mar. 7, p. 2.

39   *Southern Confederacy* [Atlanta], Mar. 5, 1861, p. 2; *Nashville Union & American,* Mar. 6, 1861, p. 2. See also *Charleston Mercury,* Mar. 5, 1861, p. 1; *Southern Banner* [Athens, Ga.], Mar. 6, 1861, p. 3, Mar. 13, 1861, p. 2; *Daily Picayune* [New Orleans], Mar. 6, 1861, p. 1; and *Weekly Raleigh Register,* Mar. 13, 1861, p. 2.

40   Mar. 13, 1861, p. 1; Basler, ed., *Works of Lincoln,* IV, 264.

41   Hyman, *A More Perfect Union,* ch. 7; Bagehot, "The Practical Operation of the American Constitution at the Present Extreme Crisis" (June 1861) and "The American Constitution at the Present Crisis" (October 1861), in Norman St John-Stevas, ed., *The Collected Works of Walter Bagehot* (Cambridge, Mass., 1968), IV, 277–313.

42   Souvenirs and other material pertaining to the Philadelphia rally will be found in the Meredith Papers (Collection #1509), correspondence and general papers, HSP.

43   Parsons, *The Constitution, Its Origin, Function, and Authority* (Boston, 1861), 20, 30; George S. Williams, *The Constitution of the United States. For the Use of Schools and Academies* (Cambridge, Mass., 1861), 42–43.

44   Anon. reviewer, NAR, 94 (January 1862), 271; Lowell, "Loyalty," *ibid.,* 153–74; Farrar, "The Adequacy of the Constitution," *The New Englander,* 21 (January 1862), 51–73.

45   Agnew, *Our National Constitution: Its Adaptation to a State of War or Insurrection* (Philadelphia, 1863), 8, 11–12, 15–16, 38. All emphases are Agnew's. For Lincoln's own defense of his actions, see his lengthy letter concerning the warmaking powers to Erastus Corning and others, [June 12] 1863, in Basler, ed., *Works of Lincoln,* VI, 261–69.

46   Henry Everett Russell, quoted in Hyman, *A More Perfect Union*, 271; see also *ibid.*, 290.

47   Anon. essay-review, "Constitutional Law," NAR, 94 (April 1862), 456; Curtis, "An Oration delivered on the 4th of July, 1862, before the Municipal Authorities of the City of Boston," in Curtis, *Constitutional History of the United States from their Declaration of Independence to the Close of their Civil War* (2nd ed.: New York, 1896), II, 558, 561.

48   Paludan, *The Constitution, Law, and Equality in the Civil War Era*, 151; anon., "Constitutional Law," 457–58. Lucie, "Confiscation: Constitutional Crossroads," shows how divided the Republicans were in 1861–63 over constitutional issues.

49   For the Emancipation Proclamation, see Henry Steele Commager, ed., *Documents of American History* (7th ed.: New York, 1963), 420–21; Edward F. Bullard, *The Nation's Trial: The* [Emancipation] *Proclamation: Dormant Powers of the Government: The Constitution a Charter of Freedom and Not "A Covenant with Hell"* (New York, 1863), 16, 19, 44, 56–57; James F. Wilson, *A Free Constitution* (Washington, D.C., 1864), 2, 7, 10–12, 16.

50   Bagehot, "The American Constitution at the Present Crisis," 296, 305, 307–08, 312–13. This essay first appeared in Britain's *National Review* (October 1861).

51   See Lieber, "Contributions to Constitutional Law," in Lieber, *Contributions to Political Science, Including Lectures on the Constitution of the United States* (Philadelphia, 1881), II, 17–136; Paludan, *The Constitution, Law, and Equality in the Civil War Era*, 89. Lieber's strong emphasis upon the Constitution as an "organism" reveals the influence of Hegel.

52   NAR, 99 (July 1864), 117–45, esp. 117–18, 123–24, 131–32. See also Hyman, *A More Perfect Union*, 102.

53   Joel H. Silbey, *A Respectable Minority: The Democratic Party in the Civil War Era, 1860–1868* (New York, 1977), 69, 72–73, 75, 77–78, 86–87, 117, 131–32; Everett, "The Duty of Supporting the Government," in Everett, *Orations and Speeches on Various Occasions* (9th ed.: Boston, 1878), IV, 721–22.

54   Silbey, *A Respectable Minority*, 80, 82, 130, 137, 182, 229; Cox, *Puritanism in Politics* (New York, 1863), 4–7, 10–12; Society for the Diffusion of Political Knowledge, *The Constitution* (New York, 1864), a collection of anti-administration speeches, letters, and editorials emphasizing Lincoln's alleged transgressions against the Constitution.

55   See Edward S. Corwin, *Court Over Constitution: A Study of Judicial Review as an Instrument of Popular Government* (Princeton, 1938), 229; Sandburg quoted in Peter Karsten, *Patriot-Heroes in England and America: Political Symbolism and Changing Values over Three Centuries* (Madison, Wis., 1978), 100; John Bigelow, *The Life of Samuel J. Tilden* (New York, 1895), I, 171. The classic assessment is James G. Randall, *Constitutional Problems under Lincoln* (Urbana, Ill., 1926; rev. ed. 1951).

56   James A. Hamilton, *The Constitution Vindicated: Nationality, Secession, Slavery* (New York, 1864), twelve-page tract; Everett, "Address at the Consecration of the National Cemetery at Gettysburg, November 19, 1863," *Orations and Speeches*, IV, 648–49.

57   C. Gordon Post, ed., Calhoun, *A Disquisition on Government and Selections from the Discourse* (New York, 1953), 28; August O. Spain, *The Political Theory of John C. Calhoun* (New York, 1951).

58   Charles Robert Lee, Jr., *The Confederate Constitutions* (Chapel Hill, N.C., 1963), 71, 80; Davis, "Inaugural Address," Feb. 18, 1861, in Rowland, ed., *Jefferson Davis, Constitutionalist,* V, 53.

59   Lee, *Confederate Constitutions,* 62–63, 87, 122, 130; William R. Leslie, "The Confederate Constitution," *Michigan Quarterly Review,* 2 (1963), 153, 155–56, 159.

60   For The Constitution of the Confederate States of America, Mar. 11, 1861, see Commager, ed., *Documents of American History,* 376–84.

61   Leslie, "Confederate Constitution," 156, 164; Lee, *Confederate Constitutions,* 108–10. Cf. James Truslow Adams to Lawrence H. Gipson, Mar. 30, 1940, Adams Papers, box 1, CUBL.

62   Sidney D. Brummer, "The Judicial Interpretation of the Confederate Constitution," in *Studies in Southern History and Politics Inscribed to William Archibald Dunning* (New York, 1914), 105–33.

63   J. G. de Roulhac Hamilton, "The State Courts and the Confederate Constitution," *Journal of Southern History,* 4 (1938), 425–48.

64   Frankfurter, *Mr. Justice Holmes and the Supreme Court* (Cambridge, Mass., 1961), 94; Hyman, *A More Perfect Union,* 232.

65   Adams to Charles Francis Adams, Jr., May 17, 1869, in Worthington C. Ford, ed., *Letters of Henry Adams, 1858–1891* (Boston, 1930), 157–58; Samuels, *Young Henry Adams,* 183, 266–75, esp. 269.

66   Adams to Charles Francis Adams, Jr., April 3, 1867, in Ford, ed., *Letters,* 125–26; Samuels, *Young Henry Adams,* 270.

67   H. T. Blake, "Judge Farrar on the Constitution," *New Englander,* 26 (1867), 725–39. For a recapitulation of the "adequate Constitution" argument at the 1887 Centennial celebration, see the speech given by Associate Justice Samuel F. Miller, in Hampton L. Carson, ed., *History of the Celebration of the One Hundredth Anniversary of the Promulgation of the Constitution of the United States* (Philadelphia, 1889), II, 282.

68   See Hyman, *A More Perfect Union,* 278–84, 291, 294, 437–38, 511; Paludan, *The Constitution, Law, and Equality in the Civil War Era,* 27, 44–45; Trumbull is quoted on p. 38.

69   Michael Les Benedict, "Preserving the Constitution: The Conservative Basis of Radical Reconstruction," JAH, 61 (1974), 69, 87, 90; David Donald, *Liberty and Union* (Boston, 1978), 175 ff; Alexander M. Bickel, "The Original Understanding and the Segregation Decision," HLR, 69 (1955), 1–65.

70   Kirk H. Porter and Donald B. Johnson, eds., *National ·Party Platforms, 1840–1976* (2nd ed.: Urbana, Ill., 1978), 38; Silbey, *Democratic Party in the Civil War Era,* 189, 192. See also *Speech of Gen. Durbin Ward at Mason, Ohio, September 18, 1869* (Library of Congress fifteen-page pamphlet).

71   Johnson's messages to Congress, Mar. 2, 1867, Dec. 3, 1867, and July 18, 1868, in Richardson, ed., *Messages and Papers of the Presidents,* VI, 500, 559, 561–62, 641. Eric L. McKitrick, *Andrew Johnson and Reconstruction* (Chicago, 1960), 118–19, supplies an excellent overview of the Constitu-

tion in American culture during the Civil War era. Chapter 5 offers a particularly fine analysis of constitutional issues during the most critical phase of Reconstruction.

72   Warren, *Supreme Court in U.S. History*, III, 285; *Buffalo Daily Courier*, Mar. 5, 1861, p. 2.

73   In February 1801 the "lame duck" Federalist Congress passed a Circuit Court Act that upon the next vacancy would have reduced the Court's membership from six to five. If Associate Justice Stephen J. Field had been successful in his presidential aspirations (1884), he intended to enlarge the Supreme Court to twenty-one members in order to "pack" it with twelve reliable conservatives and reverse several major decisions from which he had dissented. See Thomas Reed Powell, *Vagaries and Varieties in Constitutional Interpretation* (New York, 1956), 9–10; Howard Jay Graham, *Everyman's Constitution: Historical Essays on the Fourteenth Amendment, the "Conspiracy Theory," and American Constitutionalism* (Madison, Wis., 1968), 25.

74   Warren, *Supreme Court in U.S. History*, III, 168–69, 190–93, 215–16; Stanley I. Kutler, *"Ex parte McCardle:* Judicial Impotency? The Supreme Court and Reconstruction Reconsidered," AHR, 72 (1967), 835–52.

75   Charles Theodore Russell, "How They Feel at Andover," *The Independent*, 34 (July 6, 1882), 6. For similar concerns expressed in newspaper editorials during the mid-1870s, see Warren, *Supreme Court in U.S. History*, III, 328.

76   Hayes, Message to the Senate, June 15, 1880 (citing the Supreme Court's decision in *Ex parte Siebold*, 1879), in Richardson, ed., *Messages and Papers of the Presidents*, VII, 595; Michael Les Benedict, "Preserving Federalism: Reconstruction and the Waite Court," *SCR 1978* (Chicago, 1978), 39–80; Bertram Wyatt-Brown, "The Civil Rights Act of 1875," *Western Political Quarterly*, 18 (1965), 763–75; Paludan, *The Constitution, Law, and Equality in the Civil War Era*, 152, 157, 219–48; George Ticknor Curtis to Hampton L. Carson, Aug. 28, 1887, in Carson, ed., *History of the Celebration of the Promulgation of the Constitution*, I, 407–08.

77   See Kermit L. Hall, "The Judiciary on Trial: State Constitutional Reform and the Rise of an Elected Judiciary, 1846–1860," *The Historian*, 45 (1983), 337–54; Morton Keller, *Affairs of State: Public Life in Late Nineteenth Century America* (Cambridge, Mass., 1977), 111–12, 120, 200–07, 212–14, 319, 347; John Alexander Jameson, *The Constitutional Convention: Its History, Powers, and Modes of Proceeding* (New York, 1867), which went through four editions between 1867 and 1887; and Ben Perley Poore, comp., *The Federal and State Constitutions, colonial charters, and other organic laws of the United States* (Washington, D.C., 1877), 2 vols.

78   See *The Independent*, 32 (Jan. 29, 1880), 16–17; 33 (Sept. 8, 1881), 16; 35 (July 12, 1883), 1–12; *Lippincott's Monthly Magazine*, 28 (December 1881), 623–24; Porter and Johnson, *National Party Platforms*, 70.

79   John King, *A Commentary on the Law and True Construction of the Federal Constitution* (Cincinnati, 1871), esp. 337–68; Bishop A. Cleveland Coxe, "Christianity and the Constitution," *The Independent*, 32 (Apr. 15, 1880), 2.

80   Edward J. Phelps, quoted in Benjamin R. Twiss, *Lawyers and the Constitu-*

tion: *How Laissez Faire Came to the Supreme Court* (Princeton, 1942), 151; John A. Matzko, " 'The Best Men of the Bar': The Founding of the American Bar Association," in Gerard Gawalt, ed., *The New High Priests: Lawyers in Post-Civil War America* (Westport, Conn., 1984), 75–96. For a comparable condemnation in 1952, see Jonathan Prude, "Portrait of a Civil Libertarian: The Faith and Fear of Zechariah Chafee, Jr.," JAH, 60 (1973), 649.

81 *The Independent,* 35 (Feb. 1, 1883), 17; *ibid.,* (Oct. 25, 1883), 16–17; 36 (Apr. 3, 1884), 17; *ibid.* (May 22, 1884), 17; *ibid.* (Nov. 27, 1884), 17. See also Michael J. Horan, "Political Economy and Sociological Theory as Influences upon Judicial Policy-Making: The Civil Rights Cases of 1883," AJLH, 16 (1972), 71–86.

82 Kelly, "Clio and the Court: An Illicit Love Affair," SCR *1965* (Chicago, 1965), 122.

83 Compare Morton, "The American Constitution," NAR, 124 (May 1877), 341–46, with William M. French, ed., *Life, Speeches, State Papers and Public Services of Gov. Oliver P. Morton* (Cincinnati, 1866), 87–88. See also Colis P. Huntington to Hampton L. Carson, Aug. 25, 1887, in Carson, ed., *Celebration of the Promulgation of the Constitution of the United States,* I, 421.

84 Parker, *Revolution and Reconstruction: Two Lectures Delivered in the Law School of Harvard College in January 1865 and January 1866* (New York, 1866), 70–71.

85 Johnson, First Annual Message, Dec. 4, 1865, in Richardson, ed., *Messages and Papers of the Presidents,* VI, 370.

86 Edward, Earl of Clarendon, *The History of the Rebellion and Civil Wars in England.* . . . (1702–04: new ed., Oxford, 1826), VII, 295–96.

87 See Karl Dietrich Bracher, *The German Dictatorship: The Origins, Structure, and Effects of National Socialism* (New York, 1970), 205, 208, 211, 232.

88 NYT, Dec. 8, 1912, p. 13.

89 In addition to the various illustrations cited earlier in this chapter, see Paludan, *The Constitution, Law, and Equality in the Civil War Era,* 27–29, 36–38, 41, 44–48, 51–54.

90 Alexander H. Stephens, *A Constitutional View of the Late War between the States: Its Causes, Character, Conduct and Results* (Philadelphia, 1868), I, 137, 477, 485. For contemporary interest in federal systems of government, see the massive work by Edward A. Freemen, an Oxford scholar, *History of Federal Government, from the Foundation of the Achaian League to the Disruption of the United States* (London, 1863). Freeman relied heavily upon four examples: the Achaian League in ancient Greece, the Swiss Confederation, the Netherlands, and the United States (to which he gave little chance for survival). It seems likely that Alexander Stephens read Freeman's tome some time between 1864 and 1867. Freeman began his preface with these words: "I trust that no one will think that the present work owes its origin to the excitement of the War of Secession in America. It is the first instalment of a scheme formed long ago. . . . All that late events in America have done has been to increase my interest in a subject which had already long occupied my thoughts."

91 "Patriotic School Histories," *The Confederate Veteran,* 5 (1897), 450–52; J. L. M. Curry, *Civil History of the Government of the Confederate States*

with Some Personal Reminiscences (Richmond, Va., 1900), 242–43. For other expressions of southern devotion to the Constitution, with emphasis upon the ironic complexities of southern constitutionalism, see Nathaniel W. Stephenson, "The Confederacy, Fifty Years After," *Atlantic Monthly,* 123 (1919), 750–55.

92 Wilson, *History of the Rise and Fall of the Slave Power in America* (Boston, 1872), esp. chs. 4 and 33; Edmund Wilson, *Patriotic Gore: Studies in the Literature of the American Civil War* (New York, 1962), 186.

• CHAPTER 5 *On This Day, One Hundred Years Ago*

1 Jameson, *An Introduction to the Study of the Constitutional and Political History of the United States* (Baltimore, 1886), 5; William B. Bigler to Hampton L. Carson, Aug. 12, 1887, U.S. Constitutional Centennial Commission Papers, box 1, HSP. This extraordinary collection of 2,200 items provides the basis for much of sections I and II in this chapter. The collection will be cited hereafter as CCC Papers. For superlatives that exceed even Bigler's, see Noah Porter (president of Yale) to Carson, Sept. 13, 1887, *ibid.,* box 4, in which Porter calls the Constitution "the most significant and important event in the political history of man."

2 Letter from Houghton Mifflin Company to the author, Mar. 31, 1983; for the contemporary reception of Fiske's book, see NYT, Dec. 2, 1888, p. 12; and for a preview essay, Fiske, "The Adoption of the Constitution," *Atlantic Monthly,* 60 (1887), 673–91.

3 Hampton L. Carson, ed., *History of the Celebration of the One Hundredth Anniversary of the Promulgation of the Constitution of the United States* (Philadelphia, 1889), I, 277, II, 422. When the executive committee of the Commission issued an "address" (really a proclamation) to the people of the United States about the forthcoming celebration, it reviewed the nationwide commemorative activities of 1875–81. Centennials of Revolutionary events had become a part of the American way of life. They had also, apparently, become somewhat tiresome. *Ibid.,* I, 296–97.

4 Col. A. Loudon Snowden to John Kasson and others, n.d., *ibid.,* II, 6.

5 J. R. Tucker to the Commission, Aug. 8, 1887, Hampton L. Carson Papers, box 1874–1905, HSP; Joseph A. Locke to Carson, Sept. 12, 1887, CCC Papers, box 1.

6 Carson, ed., *Celebration of the Promulgation of the Constitution,* II, 423–25.

7 *Ibid.,* 6.

8 *The Detroit Free Press,* Sept. 16, 1887, p. 4; NYT, Sept. 17, 1887, p. 4; Lossing, "The Centennial of the Constitution," *The Independent,* 39 (Feb. 10, 1887), 2–3.

9 NYT, Sept. 18, 1886, p. 4; Dec. 6, 1886, p. 4; July 25, 1887, p. 4.

10 George W. Olney to Amos R. Little, Dec. 28, 1886, CCC Papers, box 7; Henry C. Robinson to Hampton L. Carson, Jan. 18, 1887, *ibid.,* box 1.

11 Edward F. Jones to Amos R. Little, Dec. 27, 1886, CCC Papers, box 7; Governor Hill's secretary to Hampton L. Carson, Jan. 6, 1887, *ibid.;* Hamilton to John A. Kasson, Aug. 25, 1887, in Carson, ed., *Celebration of the Promulgation of the Constitution,* I, 420; NYT, Sept. 13, 1887, p. 4.

12   *Connecticut Courant,* Sept. 15, 1887, p. 4; James A. Beaver to Hampton L. Carson, Jan. 28, 1887, CCC Papers, box 2.

13   NYT, Sept. 18, 1886, p. 5; NYT, Dec. 3, 1886, p. 5; *The Proceedings of the Convention of Governors of the Thirteen Colonial States, Held at Philadelphia, September 17, 1886. With the Proceedings of the Constitutional Centennial Commission, Held December 2d and 3d, 1886, at Philadelphia* (21-page pamphlet, CCC Papers); Carson, ed., *Celebration of the Promulgation of the Constitution,* I, 261–66, 269, 271, 276, 323.

14   See Carson, ed., *Celebration of the Promulgation of the Constitution,* I, 274; NYT, Feb. 15, 1890, p. 2, and Feb. 23, 1890, p. 14. At a meeting held on George Washington's Birthday, 1890, an understanding was reached that the monument would not "merely" commemorate the framing of the Constitution, but the Declaration of Independence, the establishment of a new government in 1789, and other significant events. Here is an instance of expanding the context but diluting the concept.

15   Kasson to Carson, Jan. 1, 1887, CCC Papers, box 2; Kasson to Carson, Apr. 18, 1887, *ibid.,* box 6; Kasson to Little, July 15, 1887, *ibid.,* box 3. The Commission finally created a music committee on July 26 simply because it received an attractive proposal that day from the Junger Maennerchor Singing Society of Philadelphia to perform at the Centennial Celebration. See Louis Boss to Hampton L. Carson, July 23, 1887, and Frederick C. Brewster, Jr., to Boss, July 26, 1887, *ibid.*

16   Marcellus Green to Carson, Feb. 9, 1887, *ibid.,* box 1; J. C. Kinney to John O. Nicholson, Apr. 26, 1887, *ibid.,* box 7; C. H. Reeve to Carson, May 21, 1887, *ibid.,* box 2; William Wirt Henry to Carson, May 21, 1887, *ibid.*; Frederick C. Brewster, Jr., to Charles E. Fenner, June 25, 1887, *ibid.,* box 3; Alva Adams to Carson, July 11, 1887, *ibid.*

17   Frederick C. Brewster, Jr., to R. J. Oglesby, July 21, 1887, *ibid.*; see also Brewster's pleading letter to Governor J. M. Martin of Kansas, July 15, 1887, *ibid.*

18   Rowland Hazard to Brewster, June 20, 1887, and Brewster to Hazard, June 22, 1887, *ibid.*; printed circular from Clinton P. Paine, chairman, Headquarters Committee on Military Display, July 20, 1887, *ibid.*; Foraker to Kasson, Aug. 1, 1887, *ibid.*; and H. A. Axline to A. T. Goshorn, June 24, 1887, *ibid.*

19   Henry C. Robinson to Carson, June 16, 1887, *ibid.,* box 2; copies of the follow-up letter will be found in box 8; negative replies from Arkansas, Florida, Indiana, Kansas, Kentucky, Minnesota, Wisconsin, and Nebraska will be found in box 3.

20   See Rollin G. Osterweis, *The Myth of the Lost Cause, 1865–1900* (Hamden, Conn., 1973), 54–55, 57, 103, 133–34, 140; Carson, ed., *Celebration of the Promulgation of the Constitution,* I, 264–65, 424; Brewster to J. K. Jackson (private secretary to the governor of Alabama), July 22, 1887, CCC Papers, box 3; J. B. Gordon (Atlanta) to Kasson, July 25, 1887, *ibid.*; governor of Mississippi to Amos Little, Aug. 25, 1887, *ibid.,* box 1; A. R. Winfield to Carson, Aug. 29, 1887, *ibid.,* box 7.

21   J. E. Hillard to Carson, Aug. 29, 1887, *ibid.,* box 7. For similar sentiments, see Thomas Moore (governor of Wyoming) to Kasson, June 20, 1887, *ibid.,* box 3.

22 E. A. Stevenson (Idaho) to Brewster, July 15, 1887, *ibid.*; E. G. Ross (New Mexico) to Carson, July 14, 1887, *ibid.*; Samuel A. Henszey (Arizona) to Carson, July 18, 1887, *ibid.*; A. P. Swineford (Alaska) to Carson, July 5, 1887, *ibid.*

23 The original typescript of the bill is in *ibid.*, box 7; a printed copy with handwritten emendations in box 6; O'Neill to Carson, Jan. 17, 1887, *ibid.*, box 1; Clinton P. Paine to Carson, Jan. 19, 1887, *ibid.*, box 2; O'Neill to Carson, Jan. 21 and 23, 1887, *ibid.*, box 1; James A. Hoyt to Carson, Jan. 19, 1887, *ibid.*; Kasson to Carson, Jan. 24, 1887, *ibid.*, box 2.

24 Randall to Carson, Feb. 5, 1887, *ibid.*, box 1; Clinton P. Paine to Carson, Feb. 8 and Mar. 9, 1887, *ibid.*, boxes 1 and 5; Henry C. Robinson to Carson, May 20, 1887, *ibid.*, box 1. Congressional consideration of the bill (and inertia) may be traced in the pages of CR, 49th Congress, 1st Session, XVII, 7669, 7718, 7775; XVIII, 240, 322, 478, 598, 712, 735; the Senate bill is S3133.

25 For Cleveland's message, CR, 49th Congress, 2nd Session, XVIII, 770, 785; U.S. Senate Executive Document no. 33, reported and discussed in NYT, Jan. 19, 1887, pp. 3, 4; O'Neill to Carson, Jan. 19, 1887, CCC Papers, box 2; Little to Carson, Jan. 23, 1887, *ibid.*

26 Kasson to Carson, Apr. 18, 1887, *ibid.*, box 6; Kasson to Little, June 7, 1887, *ibid.*, box 2; Sheridan to Carson, July 21, 1887, *ibid.*, box 3; NYT, July 29, 1887, p. 3; *Connecticut Courant,* Sept. 15, 1887, p. 4.

27 Kasson to Carson, Jan. 1, 1887, CCC Papers, box 2; Rowland Hazard to Carson, Jan. 26, 1887, *ibid.;* Henry C. Robinson to Carson, Jan. 28, 1887, *ibid.*, box 7; C. G. Garrison to Carson, n.d., *ibid.*, box 2; William Wirt Henry to Carson, Mar. 10, 1887, *ibid.*; Brewster to Kasson, June 30, 1887, *ibid.*, box 3; Brewster to Little, July 1, 1887, *ibid.*; Kasson to Boker, July 30, 1887, *ibid.*; Minute book of the CCC, entry for May 24, 1887, *ibid.*, box 5; Carson, ed., *Celebration of the Promulgation of the Constitution,* I, 305–06, 324–25, 330.

28 James O. Broadhead to Kasson and others, Sept. 10, 1887, CCC Papers, box 7; Josiah W. Leeds to Kasson, Sept. 10 and 13, 1887, Hampton L. Carson Papers, box 1874–1905, HSP.

29 Thomas A. Becker (bishop of Savannah) to Kasson and others, Sept. 6, 1887, CCC Papers, box 1.

30 A. Cleveland Coxe (bishop of western New York) to Kasson, Sept. 3, 1887, *ibid.*; see also Richmond Mayo Smith's essay-review, PSQ, 2 (1887), 521: "One-half of the people of Massachusetts can no longer speak of the Constitution as the work of the [founding fathers] except in an adoptive sense."

31 Brewster to Rowland Hazard, to James A. Hoyt, to Henry C. Robinson, all on Aug. 6, 1887, CCC Papers, box 3; A. Loudon Snowden to Carson, Aug. 10, 1887, *ibid.*, box 6; NYT, Aug. 19, 1887, p. 3, and Aug. 20, 1887, p. 3. One of those descendants offered to sell "the veritable suit of clothes worn by President Washington on the occasion of his first inauguration." T. A. Washington to Kasson, Aug. 6, 1887 (misdated 1886), CCC Papers, box 3.

32 Carson, ed., *Celebration of the Promulgation of the Constitution,* I, 324, II, 70–71; NYT, Sept. 21, 1887, p. 4.

33 Brewster to Snowden, Aug. 8, 1887, CCC Papers, box 3; Henry E. Lincoln to Carson, Aug. 26, 1887, *ibid.*, box 1. For the patriotic gratitude of a Jew

who was invited, see Samuel Hirsch to Kasson and others, Aug. 23, 1887, *ibid.*

34   William E. Stewart to Thomas Cochran, June 16, 1887, *ibid.*, box 2; Brewster to Little, and Little to Brewster, June 30 and July 2, 1887, *ibid.*, box 3; J. B. Townsend to Carson, Sept. 13, 1887, *ibid.*, box 7; diary of J. Granville Leach, entries for July 21, Sept. 17 and 18, 1887, Autograph Collection, HSP.

35   Little to Brewster, July 3, 1887, CCC Papers, box 3; N. G. Ordway to Carson, July 18, 1887, *ibid.*; Brewster to Ordway, July 19, 1887, *ibid.*, Brewster to James C. Tappan, July 19, 1887, *ibid.*; Frank Leslie's Publishing House to the Commission, Aug. 29, 1887, *ibid.*, box 7.

36   Brewster to the editor of the *Boston Advertiser,* June 30, 1887, *ibid.*, box 3; Carson, ed., *Celebration of the Promulgation of the Constitution,* I, 284–85, and 320–21 for a candid discussion of the Commission's financial problems.

37   *Ibid.*, I, 285, 290–91; Brewster to Kasson, July 16, 1887, CCC Papers, box 3; Thomas M. Thompson to Kasson, Aug. 5, 1887, *ibid.*; a "personal" solicitation, dated Aug. 23, 1887, was mailed by the Citizens' Committee in order to raise $60,000.

38   NYT, July 10, 1887, p. 1; Snowden's July 16 appeal is in CCC Papers, box 6; William J. Latta to Amos R. Little, July 23, 1887, *ibid.*, box 3; Snowden to Robert C. Lippincott, president of the Philadelphia Lumber Exchange, July 28, 1887, *ibid.*, box 4; Brewster to Thomas M. Thompson, Aug. 9, 1887, *ibid.*, box 3; Snowden to Carson, Aug. 29, 1887, *ibid.*

39   Snowden to the governors of all the states and territories, July 7, 1887, *ibid.*, box 4; Snowden's printed circular to all potential participants, July 29, 1887, *ibid.*, box 6; Joseph Rademacher (bishop of Nashville) to Carson, Sept. 10, 1887, *ibid.*, box 1; for the recurrent obsession with a causal connection between the Constitution and prosperity, see Carson, ed., *Celebration of the Promulgation of the Constitution,* I, 298, 421, 433, II, 255, 258, 348, 351, 370, 405. For Miller's oration, *ibid.*, 283, 286, 289. NYT editorial, Sept. 15, 1887, p. 4.

40   See R. K. Buehrle (City Superintendent, Lancaster, Pa., Public Schools) to Carson, Aug. 8, 1887, CCC Papers, box 7; S. J. Flickinger (editor, *Ohio State Journal*) to Carson, Aug. 12, 1887, *ibid.*; H. H. Byram (editor, *Pittsburgh Chronicle Telegraph*) to Carson, Aug. 30, 1887, *ibid.*; William M. Allison (editor, *The Juniata Herald*) to Carson, Sept. 1, 1887, *ibid.*; M. L. Peirce to Carson, Sept. 1, 1887, *ibid.*; NYT, Aug. 24, p. 1; Sept. 5, p. 2; Sept. 13, p. 5; Sept. 14, p. 5.

41   NYT, Sept. 15, 1887, p. 4; *Public Ledger,* Sept. 15, 1887, pp. 2, 4.

42   A. H. Rosewig to Kasson, Sept. 15, 1887, CCC Papers, box 7; *Chicago Tribune,* Sept. 19, 1887, p. 4.

43   *Public Ledger,* Sept. 16, 1887, pp. 2, 5; NYT, Sept. 16, 1887, pp. 1, 2; NYT, Sept. 17, pp. 1, 2.

44   Carson, ed., *Celebration of the Promulgation of the Constitution,* I, 324; II, 256; for Cleveland's address, *ibid.*, II, 259–62; for Miller's, II, 262–90; NYT, Sept. 18, 1887, pp. 1, 2.

45   NYT, Sept. 18, 1887, p. 2.

46   The souvenirs will be found in CCC Papers, boxes 2, 5, and 9.

47   *Washington Post,* Sept. 17, 1887, p. 2; *Connecticut Courant,* Sept. 22, 1887, p. 4; *Detroit Free Press,* Sept. 16, 1887, p. 4; Godkin, "Some Things Overlooked at the Centennial," *The Nation,* Sept. 22, 1887, p. 226.

48   W. L. Trenholm to Kasson and others, Aug. 11, 1887, in Carson, ed., *Celebration of the Promulgation of the Constitution,* I, 423; II, 348.

49   *Ibid.,* I, 261, 266, 269, 276, 282, 296, 299; II, 276–77, 283.

50   Conway, "Our King in Dress Coat," NAR, 144 (February 1887), 120.

51   Carson to Little, Sept. 21, 1887, CCC Papers, box 1; Carson, ed., *Celebration of the Promulgation of the Constitution,* I, vii; II, 422.

52   Baltimore *Daily News* reprinted in the Philadelphia *Public Ledger,* Sept. 15, 1887, p. 2; *Washington Post,* Sept. 19, 1887, p. 2.

53   Charles Emory Smith on Oct. 13, 1887, in Carson, ed., *Celebration of the Promulgation of the Constitution,* II, 418.

54   David M. Stone (editor-in-chief of *The New York Journal of Commerce*) to Hampton L. Carson, Aug. 11, 1887, CCC Papers, box 1; NYT, Sept. 18, 1887, p. 4; NYT, Nov. 11, 1887, p. 2; NYT, Feb. 13, 1888, p. 4; NYT, March 2, 1888, p. 1; NYT, Feb. 14, 1889, p. 4.

55   NYT, Jan. 13, 1889, p. 4; NYT, Nov. 21, 1889, p. 5. But see John Bach McMaster and Frederick D. Stone, eds., *Pennsylvania and the Federal Constitution, 1787–1788* (Philadelphia, 1888).

56   NYT, Nov. 13, 1887, p. 16; June 22, 1888, p. 4; June 25, 1888, p. 4.

57   NYT, May 30, 1888, p. 5; June 3, 1888, p. 11; June 5, 1888, p. 3; June 8, 1888, p. 6; June 9, 1888, p. 4; June 11, 1888, p. 2; June 24, 1888, p. 11; July 23, 1888, p. 2; July 26, 1888, p. 5; July 27, 1888, p. 8; July 29, 1888, p. 12; Aug. 19, 1888, p. 6.

58   NYT, May 24, 1888, p. 4; July 22, 1888, p. 5; July 27, 1888, p. 4.

59   James D. Richardson, ed., *A Compilation of the Messages and Papers of the Presidents, 1789–1897* (Washington, D.C., 1896–99), IX, 6; NYT, Mar. 4, 1889, p. 4; NYT, Apr. 28, 1889, p. 20; NYT, May 19, 1889, p. 16.

60   NYT, Nov. 10, 1887, p. 8; Nov. 10, 1888, p. 4; Apr. 2, 1889, p. 8; Apr. 9, 1889, p. 4; Apr. 12, 1889, p. 5; Apr. 15, 1889, p. 5; Apr. 16, 1889, p. 8; Apr. 20, 1889, p. 4; Apr. 23, 1889, p. 4; Apr. 28, 1889, pp. 4, 11; Apr. 29, 1889, p. 8.

61   NYT, Mar. 30, 1889, p. 4; Apr. 2, 1889, pp. 4, 8; Apr. 3, 1889, p. 5; Apr. 16, 1889, p. 4. In the end, Brooklyn's aldermen felt snubbed by the Centennial Commission, and erected their own stands in Union Square for the exclusive use of Brooklynites. Moreover, the borough decided to hold a separate banquet at the Academy of Music on May 1, and put on its own display of fireworks. NYT, Apr. 28, 1889, p. 16.

62   NYT, Mar. 3, 1889, p. 16; Apr. 5, 1889, p. 8; Apr. 7, 1889, p. 20; Apr. 9, 1889, p. 2; Apr. 11, 1889, p. 4; Apr. 16, 1889, p. 5; Apr. 28, 1889, p. 2; Apr. 30, 1889, p. 12. For the editorial, Apr. 3, 1889, p. 4.

63   NYT, Apr. 26, 1889, p. 2; May 2, 1889, p. 4; May 5, 1889, p. 4.

64   NYT, Apr. 10, 1889, p. 1; Apr. 12, 1889, p. 4; Apr. 13, 1889, p. 5; Apr. 16, 1889, pp. 1, 2; Apr. 18, 1889, p. 5.

65   NYT, Apr. 11, 1889, p. 5; Apr. 13, p. 5; Apr. 19, p. 5.

66   NYT, Apr. 29, 1889, p. 12; Apr. 30, pp. 1, 2, 3.

67   NYT, May 1, 1889, p. 12.

68   NYT, May 1, 1889, pp. 9, 10; May 4, 1889, p. 4; May 9, 1889, p. 4.

69   NYT, May 1, 1889, pp. 1, 2, 3, 4, 6; Edward Everett Hale, *James Russell Lowell and Friends* (Boston, 1899), 269.

70   NYT, May 2, 1889, pp. 1, 2, 3, 4, 9; May 3, p. 5; May 4, p. 8.

71   NYT, May 2, 1889, pp. 4, 5, 8; May 3, 1889, p. 5.

72   NYT, May 1, 1889, p. 1; the text of Harlan's speech is reported in full under "The Centennial Celebration" in *Chicago Legal News,* 21 (May 4, 1889), pp. 301–02.

73   NYT, May 1, 1889, p. 1; *The Nation's Birthday: Chicago's Centennial Celebration of Washington's Inauguration, April 30, 1889* (Chicago, 1889).

74   *The Century Magazine,* 37 (1889), 866–78; NYT, Apr. 5, 1889, p. 4.

75   "The Constitution for a Century," *The Independent,* 41 (Apr. 25, 1889), 23.

76   For the sampling, see *Public Opinion,* 7 (May 4, 1889), 69–74.

77   NYT, Dec. 12, 1889, pp. 1, 4.

78   *Chicago Tribune,* Feb. 4, 1890, pp. 3, 4; NYT, Feb. 5, 1890, p. 4; New Orleans *Daily Picayune,* Feb. 5, 1890, p. 4; Hampton L. Carson, *The Supreme Court of the United States: Its History and Its Centennial Celebration* (Philadelphia, 1891), 581–729.

79   Wallace E. Davies, *Patriotism on Parade: The Story of Veterans' and Hereditary Organizations in America, 1783–1900* (Cambridge, Mass., 1955), 77; NYT, July 13, 1895, p. 13.

80   Lodge, "The Constitution and Its Makers" (1911), in Lodge, *The Democracy of the Constitution* (New York, 1915), 32–37.

81   Graham, *Everyman's Constitution: Historical Essays on the Fourteenth Amendment, the "Conspiracy Theory," and American Constitutionalism* (Madison, Wis., 1968), 20.

•   CHAPTER 6 *The American and the British Constitution Are Two Entirely Different Things*

1   Frankfurter's memoranda to his eight "Brethren," Mar. 20, 1953, and Apr. 30, 1954, in Harold H. Burton Papers, boxes 86 and 92, LCMD; Robert H. Jackson, *The Supreme Court in the American System of Government* (Cambridge, Mass., 1955), 81–82; Kurland, "The Lord Chancellor of the United States," *Trial,* 7 (November 1971), 11, 28.

2   Roosevelt to Cecil Arthur Spring Rice, Aug. 22, 1911, in Elting E. Morison, ed., *The Letters of Theodore Roosevelt* (Cambridge, Mass., 1954), VII, 333.

3   Wilson, *Constitutional Government in the United States* (New York, 1908), 42. For shifts and inconsistencies in Wilson's thinking, see Christopher Wolfe, "Woodrow Wilson: Interpreting the Constitution," RP, 41 (1979), 121–42.

4   For an excellent series of illustrations, see Gordon S. Wood, *The Creation of the American Republic, 1776–1787* (Chapel Hill, N.C., 1969), 259–60, 267, 281, 337, 338.

5   Duane's Speech to the Committee on Rights (Sept. 8, 1774), in Paul H. Smith, ed., *Letters of Delegates to Congress, 1774–1789* (Washington, D.C.,

1976), I, 52–53; Douglass Adair, " 'Experience Must Be Our Only
Guide': History, Democratic Theory, and the United States Constitution,"
in Trevor Colbourn, ed., *Fame and the Founding Fathers. Essays by Douglass
Adair* (New York, 1974), 113, 119.

6   For Ellsworth, see Charles Warren, *The Supreme Court in United States
History* (Boston, 1922), I, 159–61, 163–64; for Taney, see Stanley I.
Kutler, ed., *The Supreme Court and the Constitution: Readings in American
Constitutional History* (2nd ed.: New York, 1977), 115.

7   Adams, "Review of the Propositions for Amending the Constitution submitted by Mr. Hillhouse to the Senate of the United States in 1808" (a
pamphlet), in Charles F. Adams, ed., *Works of John Adams* (Boston, 1851),
VI, 523–50, esp. 528; Adams to Jefferson, May 3, 1812, in Lester J. Cappon, ed., *The Adams-Jefferson Letters* (Chapel Hill, N.C., 1959), II, 303.
See also R. Kent Newmyer, *Supreme Court Justice Joseph Story: Statesman of
the Old Republic* (Chapel Hill, N.C., 1985), 186, 189.

8   Adair, "History, Democratic Theory, and the United States Constitution,"
120; Madison to Edward Livingston, Apr. 17, 1824, and to William Cabell
Rives, Mar. 12, 1833, in Gaillard Hunt, ed., *The Writings of James Madison*
(New York, 1910), IX, 188, 511; Morse, "A Concise View of the Princi-
ples of the Constitution and Government of the United States," in Morse,
Annals of the American Revolution; Or, A Record of Their Causes and Events
(Hartford, Conn., 1824), 386–87.

9   Parsons, *The Constitution: Its Origin, Function, and Authority* (Boston, 1861,
3, 6–7, 9; Fisher, *The Trial of the Constitution* (Philadelphia, 1863),
99–138.

10   Alan Jones, "Thomas M. Cooley and 'Laissez-Faire Constitutionalism': A
Reconsideration," JAH, 53 (1967), 751–71; Clyde E. Jacobs, *Law Writers
and the Courts: The Influence of Thomas M. Cooley, Christopher G. Tiedeman, and John F. Dillon upon American Constitutional Law* (Berkeley, Calif.,
1954), esp. 26–29, 116–19.

11   See Leon Fraser, *English Opinion of the American Constitution and Government, 1783–1798* (New York, 1915). Macaulay's much-cited letter to
Henry S. Randall, May 23, 1857, along with James M. Beck's retrospective
rejoinder, appear in Beck, *The Constitution of the United States: Yesterday,
Today—and Tomorrow?* (New York, 1924), 271, 343–46.

12   Bagehot, "The Practical Operation of the American Constitution at the
Present Extreme Crisis" (June 1861), and "The American Constitution at
the Present Crisis" (October 1861), in Norman St John-Stevas, ed., *The
Collected Works of Walter Bagehot* (Cambridge, Mass., 1968) IV, 277–313,
esp. 281, 283. See also the superb essay in Stefan Collini, Donald Winch,
and John Burrow, *That Noble Science of Politics: A Study in Nineteenth-Century Intellectual History* (Cambridge, Eng., 1983), ch. 5, "Bagehot and the
Nature of Political Understanding."

13   Woodrow Wilson asserted repeatedly that "the Constitution was not made
to fit us like a strait-jacket. In its elasticity lies its chief greatness." Arthur S.
Link, ed., *The Papers of Woodrow Wilson* (Princeton, 1973), XV, 537;
Wilson, *Constitutional Government in the United States*, 167, 192. For his repudiation of Bagehot, *ibid.*, 59. See also Thomas Francis Moran, *The Formation and Development of the Constitution* (Philadelphia, 1904), v; NYT,

May 23, 1923, p. 14; NYT, Feb. 12, 1931, p. 20; NYT, Sept. 16, 1934, sec. 6, pp. 3, 12.

14   See Edmund Morris, *The Rise of Theodore Roosevelt* (New York, 1979), 370; Hampton L. Carson, ed., *History of the Celebration of the One Hundredth Anniversary of the Promulgation of the Constitution of the United States* (Philadelphia, 1889), II, 284–85; A. Lawrence Lowell, *Essays on Government* (Boston, 1889), 40; Wilson, *Constitutional Government in the United States,* 69.

15   Lodge, "The Constitution and Its Makers," in Lodge, *The Democracy of the Constitution* (New York, 1915), 83; Woodrow Wilson, *A History of the American People* (New York, 1902), III, 183–84; Andrew C. McLaughlin, "Democracy and the Constitution," *Proceedings of the American Antiquarian Society,* n.s., 22 (1912), 317, NYT, May 23, 1923, p. 14; Beck, *Constitution of the United States,* 271.

16   For Lyndhurst and the years 1832–1914, see G. H. L. Le May, *The Victorian Constitution: Conventions, Usages and Contingencies* (New York, 1979), 14, 16, 63, 146. For a more subtle analysis that deals with major works by George Brodie (1823), Hallam (1827), Bagehot's classic *The English Constitution* (1867), E. A. Freeman (1872), Bishop William Stubbs (1873–78), and Macaulay's scattered essays pertaining to the constitution, see Burrow, *Victorian Historians and the English Past,* 31–32, 37–38, 105.

17   Burrow, *Victorian Historians and the English Past,* 125, 288, 294, 297; Frank M. Turner, *The Greek Heritage in Victorian Britain* (New Haven, Conn., 1981), ch. 5, "The Debate over the Athenian Constitution." For the next major contribution to British constitutionalism after Bagehot, see Albert Venn Dicey, *Introduction to the Study of the Law of the Constitution* (London, 1885); and Richard A. Cosgrove, *The Rule of Law: Albert Venn Dicey, Victorian Jurist* (Chapel Hill, N.C., 1980).

18   See Le May, *Victorian Constitution,* ch. 7.

19   See McLaughlin, "Democracy and the Constitution," 293–320; William L. Ransom, *Majority Rule and the Judiciary* (New York, 1912); John E. Semonche, *Charting the Future: The Supreme Court Responds to a Changing Society, 1890–1920* (Westport, Conn., 1978), esp. chs. 7–8; Robert G. McCloskey, ed., *Essays in Constitutional Law* (New York, 1957), 20–58, 85–101.

20   Edmund Ions, *James Bryce and American Democracy, 1870–1922* (London, 1968), 37; Deborah Wormell, *Sir John Seeley and the Uses of History* (Cambridge, Eng., 1980), 162; Moncure D. Conway, "An Unpublished Draft of a National Constitution by Edmund Randolph found among the papers of George Mason," *Scribner's Magazine,* 2 (September 1887), 319–20; William E. H. Lecky, *Democracy and Liberty* (1896: Indianapolis, 1981), I, 99, 116; Dicey, *Study of the Law of the Constitution,* 4; Edward S. Corwin, "The Worship of the Constitution," in Richard Loss, ed., *Corwin on the Constitution* (Ithaca, N.Y., 1981), 54.

21   Gladstone, "Kin Beyond Sea," NAR, 127 (September 1878), 185.

22   Carson, ed., *Celebration of the Promulgation of the Constitution of the United States,* I, 266, II, 288; NYT, July 27, 1888, p. 4; Smith Burnham, *The Making of Our Country* (Philadelphia, 1920), 167; Henry W. Elson, *United States: Its Past and Present* (New York, 1926), 195; Bessie Louise Pierce,

Civic Attitudes in American School Textbooks (Chicago, 1930), 104, 142; Harry F. Atwood, "Constitution Week—What It Means," *D.A.R. Magazine*, 58 (1924), 215; Samuel P. Weaver, "The Constitution in Our Public Schools," CR, 11 (1927), 109.

23 Johnson is quoted in Corwin, "The Constitution as Instrument and Symbol," APSR, 30 (1936), 1075; Bagehot, "The American Constitution at the Present Crisis" (October 1861), *Works of Bagehot*, IV, 291; D. H. Reynolds (from Lake Village, Arkansas) to Hampton L. Carson, Sept. 6, 1887, CCC Papers, box 1, HSP; James Russell Lowell, *Political Essays* (Boston, 1888), 311.

24 See Carson, ed., *Celebration of the Promulgation of the Constitution*, I, 402; Harry Atwood, "The Constitution Week Movement," CR, 13 (1929), 183; New Orleans *Daily Picayune*, Sept. 15, 1887, p. 4.

25 Johnston, "The First Century of the Constitution," *The New Princeton Review*, 4 (1887), 176, 178, 186–87; Johnston, *The United States: Its History and Constitution* (New York, 1889), esp. ch. 5.

26 Herman Belz, "The Constitution in the Gilded Age: The Beginnings of Constitutional Realism in American Scholarship," AJLH, 13 (1969), 114–15; J. Franklin Jameson, ed., *Essays in the Constitutional History of the United States in the Formative Period, 1775–1789* (Boston, 1889), viii–xi; Fiske, "The Constitution: An Organism, Not a Mechanism," NYT, Dec. 16, 1900, p. 19.

27 See Moran, *Formation and Development of the Constitution*, v; Varnum Lansing Collins to Max Farrand, Apr. 20, 1913, Farrand Papers, HEH; T. Scott Offutt, "The Growth and Trend of the Constitution," CR, 11 (1927), 212; Edward S. Corwin, *Court Over Constitution: A Study of Judicial Review as an Instrument of Popular Government* (Princeton, 1938), 216–17; Earl Warren, "The Law and the Future," *Fortune*, 52 (November 1955), 107.

28 Conway, "Unpublished Draft of a National Constitution," 319–20. In support of my more general point, see Carl L. Becker, *The Heavenly City of the Eighteenth-Century Philosophers* (New Haven, Conn., 1932), 138, for an excellent example from revolutionary France.

29 Bryce, *The American Commonwealth* (2nd ed.: London, 1891), I, 24–25.

30 Andrew C. McLaughlin, "Mr. Bryce on America," *Dial*, 9 (February 1889), 255–56. See also Edward Eggleston, "A Full-Length Portrait of the United States: James Bryce's 'The American Commonwealth,'" *The Century*, 37 (1889), 791–92; anon., "Professor James Bryce, M.P.," *The Century*, 39 (1890), 470–72. At least one reviewer believed Bryce to be repeating Gladstone's gaffe. See D. H. Chamberlain, "Bryce's 'American Commonwealth,'" *New Englander and Yale Review*, 50 (1889), 399.

31 James Bryce, *Studies in History and Jurisprudence* (New York, 1901), 2 vols.; Bryce, "America Revisited: The Changes of a Quarter Century," *The Outlook*, 79 (Mar. 25 and Apr. 1, 1905), 733–40, 846–55; NYT, Dec. 15, 1912, p. 3. See also the fascinating letter assessing Bryce's impact, written after his death in 1922 by Lord Charnwood to Henry Cabot Lodge, n.d., Lodge Papers, box 66, MHS.

32 Lowell, "Ministerial Responsibility and the Constitution," *Atlantic Monthly*, 57 (1886), 181; Lowell, *Essays on Government*, 126.

33 See W. B. Lawrence, "The Monarchical Principle in Our Constitution," NAR, 131 (November 1880), 385–410; Goldwin Smith, "Is the Constitution Outworn?" *Public Opinion*, 24 (Mar. 31, 1898), 394–95.

34 John A. Kasson and others to the commissioners, July 9, 1887, CCC Papers, box 6, HSP.

35 For the Marquis de Chambrun in 1887, see Carson, ed., *Celebration of the Promulgation of the Constitution*, II, 400; for Gladstone, NYT, Nov. 16, 1887, p. 5; Friedrich Engels to F. A. Sorge, Nov. 11, 1893, in Alexander Trachtenberg, ed., *Marx and Engels: Letters to Americans, 1848–1895* (New York, 1953), 258.

36 Lowell, *Essays on Government*, 5, 40; Curtis, *Constitutional History of the United States from their Declaration of Independence to the Close of their Civil War* (New York, 1889), I, iv–v; John King, *A Commentary on the Law and True Construction of the Federal Constitution* (Cincinnati, 1871), 368; Wilson, *Constitutional Government in the United States*, 69.

37 See Willi Paul Adams, *The First American Constitutions: Republican Ideology and the Making of the State Constitutions in the Revolutionary Era* (Chapel Hill, N.C., 1980), 18–22; Everett, "The Principle of the American Constitutions," an oration delivered at Cambridge, Mass., July 4, 1826, in Everett, *Orations and Speeches on Various Occasions* (9th ed.: Boston, 1878), I, 128; King, *Commentary on the Federal Constitution*, 24–25; William C. Morey, "The Genesis of a Written Constitution," AAAPSS, 1 (1891), 529–57; Hampton L. Carson, "The Constitution of the United States," CR, 5 (1921), 150; Robert L. Schuyler, *The Constitution of the United States: An Historical Survey of Its Formation* (New York, 1923), 5–6; Charles Warren, *Congress, the Constitution, and the Supreme Court* (Boston, 1925), 10–12, 22, 83–84.

38 F. J. Stimson, "The Constitution and the People's Liberties," NAR, 184 (Mar. 1, 1907), 508, 510, 512.

39 Brownson, *The American Republic: Its Constitution, Tendencies, and Destiny* (New York, 1865), ch. 10, esp. pp. 218, 243; Ernest Samuels, *The Young Henry Adams* (Cambridge, Mass., 1948), 257; Samuels, *Henry Adams: The Middle Years* (Cambridge, Mass., 1965), 179–80. For the similarity of Brooks Adams's views to those of William Stubbs, see Stubbs, *The Constitutional History of England*, ed. by James Cornford (Chicago, 1979), ix.

40 Jones, "Cooley and 'Laissez-Faire Constitutionalism,'" 758, 760, 763, 766, 769; Charles A. Beard, *The American Leviathan: The Republic in the Machine Age* (New York, 1930), 38–39; Holmes's opinion in *Gompers* v. *U.S.*, 233 U.S. 610 (1914). See also James K. Hosmer, *A Short History of Anglo-Saxon Freedom: The Polity of the English-Speaking Race* (New York, 1890).

41 Tiedeman, *The Unwritten Constitution of the United States: A Philosophical Inquiry into the Fundamentals of American Constitutional Law* (New York, 1890), 21–23, 155–65, esp. 163. See also John Forrest Dillon, *The Laws and Jurisprudence of England and America* (Boston, 1894), which emphasized the beneficent impact of Blackstone and Bentham in the United States, and declared obsequiously: "the bar and judges of England cordially acknowledge that the debt which we owe is being paid" (186–87). For Dillon's lavish encomium to the British constitution, see esp. 136.

42 Taylor wrote *The Origin and Growth of the English Constitution* (Boston, 1889–98), a two-volume work that had little impact. In 1911, however, he kicked up quite a fuss by publishing a 676-page book and then a 26-page address he had delivered before the Union League Club of New York, both entitled *The Origin and Growth of the American Constitution*. Taylor recognized a large debt to British constitutionalism generally, but insisted that one Pelatiah Webster (a Congregationalist clergyman from Connecticut) rather than James Madison had been the real "architect" of the U.S. Constitution, and cited a pamphlet that Webster wrote in 1783 called *Dissertation on the Political Union and Constitution of the Thirteen United States of America*. To follow this tempest, see Taylor, "The Designer of the Constitution of the United States," NAR, 185 (August 1907), 813–24; NYT, Aug. 27, 1911, sec. 6, pp. 513, 514; NYT, Dec. 15, 1911, pp. 8, 12; NYT, Dec. 27, 1911, p. 6; Gaillard Hunt to Max Farrand, Oct. 3, 1911, Farrand Papers, HEH; Farrand's critical review of Taylor's book, AHR, 17 (1911), 162–64; and Gaillard Hunt's snide investigation, "Pelatiah Webster and the Constitution," *The Nation*, Dec. 28, 1911, reprinted with Taylor's essay as *The Real Authorship of the Constitution of the United States Explained*, 62nd Congress, 2nd Session, document no. 787 (Washington, D.C., 1912), 87-page pamphlet.

43 *Public Opinion*, 7 (May 4, 1889), 74; Wilson, *An Old Master and Other Political Essays* (New York, 1893), esp. 135, 143, 164, 179; Dennis, "Our Changing Constitution," *Atlantic Monthly*, 96 (1905), 526, 531, 535; NYT, Mar. 28, 1926, sec. 8, pp. 15–16; Butler, "The Constitution One Hundred and Forty Years After," CR, 12 (1928), 127.

44 Wilson, *Congressional Government: A Study in American Politics* (Boston, 1885), 5–6, 332; Address to the Short Ballot Organization, Jan. 21, 1910, in Link, ed., *Papers of Wilson*, XX, 37.

45 Wilson to Alfred Hayes, Jr., May 23, 1910, *ibid.*, 467; Address to the National Democratic Club of New York, Apr. 16, 1906, *ibid.*, XVI, 364; Wilson, *Constitutional Government in the United States*, 69, 80, 157–58, 192, 195; Albert Fried, ed., *A Day of Dedication: The Essential Writings and Speeches of Woodrow Wilson* (New York, 1965), 71–72; Wilson, *The State: Elements of Historical and Practical Politics* (Boston, 1898), 474, 524, 542.

46 Wilson, *Constitutional Government in the United States*, 9, 60; NYT, Feb. 3, 1929, sec. 9, pp. 5, 8; NYT, Feb. 10, 1929, sec. 10 p. 6; Max Radin, "The Myth of Magna Carta," HLR, 60 (1947), 1060–91, an anglophile essay insisting that Magna Carta had just the same relation to positive law that the U.S. Constitution has to statutes; "Magna Charta . . . together with explanatory notes to the Charter," presented by Senator Hubert Humphrey on "legislative day" (June 7, 1950), 81st Congress, 2d Session, Senate doc. no. 180; William F. Swindler, *Magna Carta: Legend and Legacy* (Indianapolis, 1965); Philip B. Kurland, "Magna Carta and Constitutionalism in the United States: 'The Noble Lie,' " in Erwin N. Griswold, ed., *The Great Charter: Four Essays on Magna Carta and the History of Our Liberty* (New York, 1965), 48–74; NYT, May 15, 1965, p. 1.

47 See D. H. Chamberlain, "Bryce's 'American Commonwealth,' " *New Englander and Yale Review*, 50 (1889), 399; Felix Frankfurter to his eight "Brethren," Mar. 20, 1953, and Apr. 30, 1954, Burton Papers, boxes 86

and 92, LCMD; Robert G. McCloskey, ed., *Essays in Constitutional Law* (New York, 1957), 252.

48   See Goldwin Smith, "Is the Constitution Outworn?" *Public Opinion*, 24 (Mar. 31, 1898), 394–95; Smith, "Chief-Justice Clark on the Defects of the American Constitution [concerning a pamphlet by Chief Justice Walter Clark of North Carolina]," NAR, 183 (Nov. 2, 1906), 845–51; NYT, May 29, 1901, p. 2; NYT, May 30, 1901, p. 1; NYT, May 31, 1901, p. 5.

49   Newspaper clipping dated Aug. 19, 1911, collection of scrapbooks pertaining to the Supreme Court's history, 1880–1935, scrapbook #10, p. 16, Record Group 267, NA, Judicial, Fiscal, & Social Branch; for the poem about Beck, clipping in *ibid.*, scrapbook #11, p. 47; Beck to Viscount Burnham, Sept. 9, 1922, James M. Beck Papers, box 1, PUML; Beck to Charles Warren, Apr. 7, 1931, Warren Papers, box 2, LCMD; NYT, June 16, 1932, p. 7; NYT, June 19, 1932, sec. 8, p. 2; NYT, June 21, 1932, p. 2.

50   Birkenhead, *America Revisited* (Boston, 1924), 142–67; NYT, Feb. 23, 1926, p. 5; NYT, Mar. 14, 1926, sec. 8, p. 15.

51   Bryce to Lodge, July 5, 1918, and Lodge to Bryce, Aug. 2, 1918, Lodge Papers, box 45, MHS. See also Theodore Roosevelt to George William Russell, Aug. 6, 1917, in Morison, ed., *Letters of Roosevelt*, VIII, 1219.

52   Laski to Holmes, Jan. 21, 1923; Holmes to Laski, Feb. 5, 1923; Laski to Holmes, Aug. 10, 1923; Holmes to Laski, Aug. 25, 1923; Laski to Holmes, Sept. 7, 1923, in Mark DeWolfe Howe, ed., *Holmes-Laski Letters: The Correspondence of Mr. Justice Holmes and Harold J. Laski, 1916–1935* (Cambridge, Mass., 1953), I, 475, 478, 494, 524, 529, 535.

53   Pollock to Holmes, July 2, 1928, in Mark DeWolfe Howe, ed., *Holmes-Pollock Letters: The Correspondence of Mr. Justice Holmes and Sir Frederick Pollock, 1874–1932* (2nd ed.: Cambridge, Mass., 1961), II, 223, 224.

54   See Bryce to Max Farrand, Oct. 6 and Dec. 3, 1919, Farrand Papers, HEH; Bryce, *Modern Democracies* (New York, 1921), esp. ch. 39 and II, 10; NYT, Feb. 12, 1931, p. 20; Birkenhead, *America Revisited*, 145, 147, 149–50,167; NYT, Apr. 11, 1926, sec. 1, p. 14; *ibid.*, sec. 9, p. 12.

55   See Alton B. Parker, "American Constitutional Government," CR, 6 (1922), 79, 89; Beck, *The Constitution of the United States* (New York, 1922); Lodge to Beck, July 17, 1923, Lodge Papers, box 71, MHS; Warren, *Congress, the Constitution, and the Supreme Court* (Boston, 1925), v–vi; Hill, *Human Nature in the Constitution* (Rochester, N.Y., 1926), 55; McBain, *The Living Constitution: A Consideration of the Realities and Legends of Our Fundamental Law* (New York, 1927), 13–14, 16–17; Joseph I. Arnold, "Historic Roots of the Supremacy of the Constitution," CR, 11 (1927), 151–60; Wickersham to Charles Warren, Jan. 30, 1930, Warren Papers, box 2, LCMD. "We have this advantage," Wickersham wrote, "over the English situation, that our courts have and do exercise jurisdiction to determine whether or not the constitutional limitations have been exceeded in such delegation, and that if a case is sufficiently flagrant, they may hold the legislative delegation unconstitutional; whereas, in England, there is no such redress. . . . I am perfectly aware that barriers which our Constitution sought to erect for the protection of the citizen have been greatly weakened by the course of decision in the Supreme Court in recent years.

Nevertheless, there is something left, but in England there appears to be nothing except possibly an aroused public sentiment. . . ."

56 Baker, *The Making and Keeping of the Constitution* (Williamsburg, Va., 1935), 15, 18–19. See also William Howard Taft, *Liberty Under Law* (New Haven, Conn., 1922), 22.

57 Beard, *American Leviathan*, 20, 30, 38–39; Ellen Nore, *Charles A. Beard: An Intellectual Biography* (Carbondale, Ill., 1983), 135; Munro, *The Makers of the Unwritten Constitution* (New York, 1930); Merriam, *The Written Constitution and the Unwritten Attitude* (New York, 1931), 9, 12; NYT, June 16, 1932, p. 7. See also Karl N. Llewellyn, "The Constitution as an Institution," CLR, 34 (1934), 1–40.

58 NYT, Oct. 3, 1937, sec. 7, p. 25; Lucien Price, ed., *Dialogues of Alfred North Whitehead* (Boston, 1954), 161, 203. Whitehead made that observation on June 28, 1941. What other historical occasion did he have in mind? When Caesar Augustus saved Rome from the Romans, i.e., from the bankruptcy of Republican government!

59 Adair, " 'Experience Must Be Our Only Guide,' " in *Fame and the Founding Fathers*, 118; NYT, Apr. 12, 1933, pp. 1, 14–15; NYT, Sept. 17, 1934, p. 16. See pp. 332–34.

60 Lord Hailsham (Quentin Hogg), *The Dilemma of Democracy: Diagnosis and Prescription* (London, 1978), 133–40, 226–30.

61 See Burrow, *Victorian Historians and the English Past*, 144; Cornford's Introduction to Stubbs's *Constitutional History of England* (Chicago, 1979), xi–xxix.

62 Schouler, *The History of the United States of America, under the Constitution* (New York, 1880–1913); Lewis Ethan Ellis, "James Schouler," in William T. Hutchinson, ed., *The Marcus W. Jernegan Essays in American Historiography* (Chicago, 1937), 84–101, esp. 88–89.

63 Schouler, "A New Federal Convention," In *Ideals of the Republic* (Boston, 1908), 291–304; Schouler, *Constitutional Studies, State and Federal* (New York, 1897).

64 Adams to Jameson, July 3 and 14, 1890, Jameson Papers, box 46, LCMD; Jameson to Max Farrand, Oct. 22, 1900, Farrand Papers, HEH; McLaughlin to Jameson, Oct. 15, 1900, Jameson Papers, box 110, LCMD.

65 Hull to Farrand, Nov. 22 and Dec. 23, 1901, Feb. 1, 1917, Farrand Papers, HEH; William J. Ryland to Farrand, Dec. 14, 1924, *ibid.*; Johnson to Farrand, Dec. 14, 1917, *ibid.*; W. T. Root to Andrew C. McLaughlin, Jan. 18, 1923, McLaughlin Papers, box 2, UCA; James G. Randall to McLaughlin, May 16, 1926, *ibid.*; Robert T. McKinley to McLaughlin, Jan. 30, 1935, *ibid.*

66 McLaughlin to Albert B. Hart, Aug. 3, 1907, Hart Papers, box 1, HUPL; William R. Harper to McLaughlin, Apr. 29, 1905, McLaughlin Papers, box 1, UCA; [illegible name] to McLaughlin, Oct. 22, 1904, *ibid.*; McLaughlin to his son James, Mar. 25, 1935, *ibid.*, box 2.

67 Francis N. Thorpe to Jameson, Oct. 26, 1897, and Feb. 22 and 28, 1910, Jameson Papers, box 131, LCMD; Thorpe to Hart, June 20, 1904, Hart Papers, box 1, HUPL; McLaughlin to Jameson [Nov. 10, 1902], and Apr. 4, 1904, Jameson Papers, box 110, LCMD.

68   William F. Wharton to Henry Cabot Lodge, Feb. 27, 1890, and Sumner R. Albee to Albert B. Hart, May 15, 1890, Hart Papers, general correspondence, box 1881–1910, HUPL; William L. Post to McLaughlin, Oct. 16, 1908, McLaughlin Papers, box 1, UCA; Francis N. Thorpe to J. Franklin Jameson, Feb. 22 and 28, 1910, Jameson Papers, box 131, LCMD; Chandler P. Anderson to Max Farrand, Dec. 21, 1912, Farrand Papers, HEH; undated newspaper clipping [spring 1911?], Supreme Court scrapbook #10, p. 16, Record Group 267, NA.

69   See John Fiske, *The Critical Period of American History, 1783–1789* (Boston, 1888); Judge Judson S. Landon, *The Constitutional History and Government of the United States* (Boston, 1889); J. I. Clark Hare, *American Constitutional Law* (Boston, 1889); 2 vols.; Samuel F. Miller, *Lectures on the Constitution of the United States* (New York, 1891); Sydney George Fisher, *The Evolution of the Constitution of the United States, showing that it is a development of progressive history and not an isolated document struck off at a given time or an imitation of English or Dutch forms of Government* (Philadelphia, 1897); William G. Bullitt, *Review of the Constitution of the United States including changes by interpretation and amendment for lawyers and those not learned in the law* (Cincinnati, 1899); Hamilton P. Richardson, *The Journal of the Federal Convention of 1787 Analyzed* (San Francisco, 1899); Francis N. Thorpe, *The Constitutional History of the United States (1765–1895)* (Chicago, 1901), 3 vols.; Thorpe, *A Short Constitutional History of the United States* (Boston, 1904); Nelson Case, *Constitutional History of the United States* (New York, 1904); Roger Sherman Hoar, *Constitutional Conventions: Their Nature, Powers and Limitations* (Boston, 1917).

70   Curtis, *Constitutional History of the United States,* I, vi–vii; Jean Strouse, *Alice James: A Biography* (Boston, 1980), 163.

71   Thayer, "Origin and Scope of the American Doctrine of Constitutional Law," HLR, 7 (1893), 130. For examples of the cordial response that Thayer received, see Austin Abbott to Thayer, Nov. 4, 1893; J. M. Dickinson to Thayer, Dec. 5, 1893; and Austin Scott to Thayer, Dec. 5 and 6, 1893, Thayer Papers, V, folders 16–7 and 16–8, HLSL.

72   See Jameson, preface to *Essays in the Constitutional History of the United States in the Formative Period, 1775–1789,* ix–xi; Baldwin to G. Brown Goode, Oct. 20, 1891, in Library Americana, box #60, New York Public Library, Department of Manuscripts (Annex); James Harvey Robinson, "The Original and Derived Features of the Constitution," AAAPSS, 1 (1890), 203–43; William C. Morey, "The Genesis of a Written Constitution," *ibid.* (1891), 529–57; C. Ellis Stevens, *Sources of the Constitution of the United States Considered in Relation to Colonial and English History* (New York, 1894), Nore, *Beard: An Intellectual Biography,* 9, 14–15.

73   George B. Adams to McLaughlin, Sept. 29, 1918, and McLaughlin to Adams, Oct. 3, 1918; W. T. Root to McLaughlin, Jan. 28, 1923, McLaughlin Papers, box 2, UCA; McLaughlin, "The Background of American Federalism," APSR, 12 (1918), 215–40; a brief autobiographical sketch by McLaughlin, original in the Newberry Library, Chicago, Ill., copy with the McLaughlin Papers, UCA. For similar sentiments at that time, see George C. Fraser to Max Farrand, Dec. 28, 1918, Farrand Papers, HEH; and J. Franklin Jameson to McLaughlin, Feb. 15, 1926, Ja-

meson Papers, box 110, LCMD. "As I see it," Jameson wrote, "nearly all Americans, including especially those hundred-percenters that think it of vital importance to 'have the Constitution taught,' take a very distorted and erroneous view of their own form of government by paying very little attention to those parts of it that are not mentioned in the fundamental document but consist of law and custom, just as the whole of the English Constitution does. I hope that your Constitutional History, to whose issue I look forward as of a classical publication, is going to take due account of the history of these accretions, as well as of all that concerns the good old document itself."

74 Butler, "The Constitution One Hundred and Forty Years After," CR, 12 (1928), 127, reprinted from NYT, Mar. 4, 1928.

75 William R. Shepherd, "John W. Burgess," in Howard W. Odum, ed., *American Masters of Social Science* (New York, 1927), 23–57; Burgess, "The American Commonwealth: Changes in Its Relation to the Nation," PSQ, 1 (1886), 9–35. Von Holst was more influenced by the politics of Bismarck's Germany than he was by the history of German constitutionalism.

76 See Eric F. Goldman, "Hermann Eduard von Holst: Plumed Knight of American Historiography," MVHR, 23 (1937), 517–18, 522–26; Charles R. Wilson, "Hermann Eduard von Holst," in *Jernegan Essays in American Historiography*, 73; and for a characteristically critical response to von Holst's work, see anon., "The Close of von Holst's Work," *Atlantic Monthly*, 70 (1892), 838–41.

77 See Herbert Tuttle, *History of Prussia to the Accession of Frederic the Great, 1134–1740* (1883: Boston, 1897), esp. the preface to vol. I; Gilbert Stuart, *An Historical Dissertation Concerning the Antiquity of the English Constitution* (Edinburgh, 1768).

78 See Albert B. Hart to William E. Dodd, Apr. 17, 1917, Hart Papers, box 2, HUPL; Oliver Wendell Holmes, Jr., to Harold J. Laski, July 14, 1916, Nov. 13, 1928, in Howe, ed., *Holmes-Laski Letters*, I, 4, II, 1109; Holmes to Sir Frederick Pollock, June 20, 1928, in Howe, ed., *Holmes-Pollock Letters*, II, 222–23, 232; Beard to Farrand, May 5, 1913, Farrand Papers, HEH. Beard wrote that he "was more belligerent than was necessary and overemphasized a number of matters in order to get a hearing that might not have been accorded to a milder statement."

79 Farrand's book was reviewed by Greene in MVHR, 1 (1914), 291–92, and by W. F. Dodd in AHR, 19 (1914), 401–02; A. Lawrence Lowell to Farrand, Oct. 7, 1915, June 26, 1916; W. T. Sedgwick to Farrand, Oct. 4, 1916, Farrand Papers, HEH; Schuyler, "Agreement in the Federal Convention," PSQ, 31 (1916), 289–99.

80 See Israel Ward Andrews, *Manual of the Constitution of the United States, designed for the Instruction of American Youth in the duties, obligations, and rights of citizenship* (Cincinnati and New York, 1874, 1878, 1887; rev. ed. by Homer Morris in 1900, 1912, 1916), published in the "Eclectic Educational Series"; Simon Sterne, *Constitutional History and Political Development of the United States* (New York, 1882, 1883, 1888, 1894); Luther Henry Porter, *Outlines of the Constitutional History of the United States* (New York, 1883); *Public Opinion*, 4 (Feb. 11, 1888), 445, and VII (Sept. 28,

1889), 526; Westel Woodbury Willoughby, *The Rights and Duties of American Citizenship* (New York, 1898, 1910, 1926); Nannie McCormick Coleman, *The Constitution and Its Framers* (Chicago, 1904, 1910, 1939); H. Arnold Bennett, *The Constitution in School and College* (New York, 1935), 72, 104–05.

81   Johnston, *The United States: Its History and Constitution* (New York, 1889), 95, 109; revised editions appeared in 1890, 1891, 1892, 1896, 1900, 1902, and 1905. For an explicit echo of these ambiguities, see Charles F. Adams, Jr., to J. Franklin Jameson, Jan. 23, 1903, Jameson Papers, box 45, LCMD; Andrew C. McLaughlin to Jameson, Feb. 2, 1903, *ibid.*, box 110; and Francis Rawle to Max Farrand, Jan. 8, 1914, Farrand Papers, HEH.

82   McLaughlin, *A History of the American Nation* (revised ed.: New York, 1919), 193–94; McLaughlin, *The Teaching of American History, with selected references designed to accompany a history of the American nation* (New York, 1899), 19–20. See also James A. James, *et al.*, *The Study of History in the Elementary Schools: Report to the American Historical Association by the Committee of Eight* (New York, 1909), 72–73, 107–10.

83   When Andrew C. McLaughlin retired in 1935 and completed his magnum opus, *A Constitutional History of the United States,* a former student then teaching at Allegheny College in Meadville, Pa., expressed the hope that he would now have all the time he wanted "to put into the elucidation of the Constitution. God send it doesn't vanish before we can get an adequate legal theory on which to interpret it!" Warner F. Woodring to McLaughlin, Feb. 17, 1935, McLaughlin Papers, box 2, UCA.

84   See Bennett, *Constitution in School and College,* 32–36, 65–66, 72–74; Hart, *Actual Government* (New York, 1903), preface.

85   See Irving Brant, *James Madison: Commander in Chief, 1812–1836* (Indianapolis, 1961), VI, 515, 578 n.19; Everett, *The Constitution of the United States: Response to a Toast at the Celebration of Washington's Birth-Day, at New-York on the 22d of February, 1851* (New York, 1851); Chase to Lewis Tappan, Mar. 4, 1847, Chase Papers, Letterbook, p. 74, LCMD; *The Autobiography of Lincoln Steffens* (New York, 1931), 125.

•   CHAPTER 7 *The Crisis in Constitutionalism*

1   See Robert G. McCloskey, ed., *Essays in Constitutional Law* (New York, 1957), introduction, esp. 4–7, 10, 19. The notion of consensus in nineteenth-century constitutionalism is particularly difficult to sustain when one considers the sense of a controversial "experiment" that continued for almost one full generation after 1787; the varied threats of secession that occurred spasmodically for more than forty years after 1787; the bitter constitutional divisions within the ranks of the abolitionists; and the considerable yet too often neglected number of southern Unionists during the pre–Civil War period.

2   Cleveland's message, Dec. 3, 1888, in James D. Richardson, ed., *A Compilation of the Messages and Papers of the Presidents, 1789–1897* (Washington, D.C., 1896–99), VIII, 778; Lowell, *Essays on Government* (Boston, 1889),

106. See also Edward Stanwood, "Fretting about the Constitution," NAR, 151 (July 1890), 122–24.

3   Anon., "A Bird's-Eye View of the United States," *Atlantic Monthly,* 63 (1889), 420; Wilson, *An Old Master, and Other Political Essays* (New York, 1893), 179.

4   Roger Foster, *Commentaries on the Constitution of the United States, Historical and Juridical with Observations upon the Ordinary Provisions of State Constitutions and a Comparison with the Constitutions of Other Countries* (Boston, 1895), 204; John Randolph Tucker, *The Constitution of the United States. A Critical Discussion of Its Genesis, Development, and Interpretation* (Chicago, 1899), 2 vols. See Charles E. Larsen, "Nationalism and States' Rights in Commentaries on the Constitution after the Civil War," AJLH, 3 (1959), 366–68.

5   John R. Rogers, "The Trusts Constitutional," *The Independent,* 51 (July 13, 1899), 1861–62; review of Nelson Case, *Constitutional History of the United States,* in *Public Opinion,* 37 (July 21, 1904), 90; anon., "Power of Congress to Reduce Representation in Congress and in the Electoral College," NAR 182 (February 1906), 238; and William V. Rowe, "National Tendencies and the Constitution," NAR, 185 (May 17, 1907), 154–56, 175, from which the extract is taken.

6   *Washington Herald,* Dec. 24, 1907, in the collection of Supreme Court Scrapbooks, 1880–1935, #6, pp. 10, 37, Record Group 267, NA, Judicial, Fiscal, & Social Branch. For a similar speech by Justice David J. Brewer, see NYT, May 31, 1908, sec. 5, p. 1. Also Elihu Root, "How to Preserve the Local Self-Government of the States: A Brief Study of National Tendencies" (Dec. 12, 1906), in Root, *Addresses on Government and Citizenship* (Cambridge, Mass., 1916), 363–70; *Collier's,* June 15, 1907, p. 7, and Aug. 10, 1907, p. 5.

7   Rogers, "The Constitution and the New Federalism," NAR, 188 (September 1908), 323.

8   See Claudius O. Johnson, *Borah of Idaho* (2nd ed.: Seattle, 1967), 181–83, 187–88; John E. Briggs, "State Rights," *Iowa Law Bulletin,* 10 (1925), 297–312; anon., "Coolidge, the Jeffersonian," *Outlook,* 143 (Aug. 18, 1926), 529–30; and Michael Kammen, "La Rinascita dei Diritti degli Stati nella Cultura Americana, ca. 1918–1938," in Luigi De Rosa and Ennio Di Nolfo, eds., *Regionalismo e Centralizzazione nella Storia di Italia e Stati Uniti* (Florence, 1986), 171–202. To be published in 1987 as "The Revival of States' Rights in American Political Culture, ca. 1918–1938: Reflections on the Ambiguities of Ideological Constitutionalism."

9   "Unconstitutional Imprisonment," *The Independent,* 37 (Dec. 3, 1885), 21–22; "The New Bill of Rights," *ibid.,* 38 (Apr. 1, 1886), 20; "Separation of Church and State: Proposed Amendment to the U.S. Constitution," and "The Proposed 16th Amendment," *ibid.,* 44 (Jan. 14, 1892), 1–5, 14.

10   "Amendments to the Constitution," *The Independent,* 41 (Jan. 10, 1889), 43; Lowell, *Essays on Government,* 41–42; Walter Clark, "Inevitable Constitutional Changes," NAR, 163 (October 1896), 462–69, esp. 463. In 1884 the Greenback Party incorporated into its platform a proposed amendment in favor of women's suffrage. See Kirk H. Porter and Donald

B. Johnson, eds., *National Party Platforms, 1840–1976* (2nd ed.: Urbana, Ill., 1978), 70. For the social and political antagonisms aroused by polygamy, culminating in a proposed amendment to make polygamy unconstitutional, see *The Independent*, 35 (Feb. 15, 1883), 17; *ibid.* (Dec. 13, 1883), 17; *ibid.*, 38 (May 6, 1886), 17; *ibid.* (June 3, 1886), 21. For congressional unwillingness during the 1880s to pass a prohibition amendment, despite intense public pressure, see *The Independent*, 34 (Aug. 24, 1882), 4; *ibid.*, 35 (July 12, 1883), 8, 10; *ibid.*, 36 (Oct. 2, 1884) 6; *ibid.*, 40 (Apr. 19, 1888), 4–5; Stanwood, "Fretting about the Constitution," 124.

11 Hannis Taylor, "Elasticity of Written Constitutions," NAR, 182 (February 1906), 204–14; M. F. Morris, "The Fifteenth Amendment to the Federal Constitution," NAR, 189 (January 1909), 82–92; Albert E. Pillsbury, "The War Amendments" (a rebuttal to Morris, who regarded the Fifteenth Amendment as a "calamity"), *ibid.* (May 1909), 740–51; Rogers, "The Constitution and the New Federalism," 330, 332; Joseph H. Choate, Jr., "Constitutional Change Without Amendment," *ibid.*, 203 (January 1916), 75–80.

12 NYT, Oct. 16, 1851, p. 2; NYT, Sept. 17, 1934, p. 16; "The Poor Old Constitution," *The Nation*, 83 (Dec. 13, 1906), 500–01.

13 NYT, Oct. 16, 1851, p. 2; John King, *A Commentary on the Law and True Construction of the Federal Constitution* (Cincinnati, 1871), 9; Washington, *Evening Star*, Feb. 17, 1894, in Supreme Court Scrapbooks, #4, p. 4; Taylor, "Elasticity of Written Constitutions," 210.

14 Lowell, "The Place of the Independent in Politics," in *Political Essays* (Boston, 1888), 312. For a clear echo, see A. Lawrence Lowell, "Cabinet Responsibility and the Constitution," in *Essays on Government*, 58.

15 Semonche, *Charting the Future: The Supreme Court Responds to a Changing Society, 1890–1920* (Westport, Conn., 1978), esp. 95, 116, 430, 432. For an older yet attractively presented view, see Robert G. McCloskey, *American Conservatism in the Age of Enterprise, 1865–1910* (Cambridge, Mass., 1951); and for a recent revisionist view, see Michael Les Benedict, "Laissez-Faire and Liberty: A Re-evaluation of the Meaning and Origins of Laissez-Faire Constitutionalism," *Law and History Review*, 3 (1985), 293–331.

16 Pennoyer, "The Income Tax Decision and the Power of the Supreme Court to Nullify Acts of Congress," *American Law Review*, 29 (1895), 550, 558.

17 NYT, May 22, 1895, p. 2; *Public Opinion*, 18 (May 2, 1895), 467; Edward S. Martin, *The Life of Joseph Hodges Choate as gathered chiefly from his letters* (New York, 1920), II, 3–17.

18 Maxwell Bloomfield, "The Supreme Court in American Popular Culture," *Journal of American Culture*, 4 (1981), 4–7; Alan F. Westin, "The Supreme Court, the Populist Movement and the Campaign of 1896," JP, 15 (1953), 31–33; *Harper's Weekly*, 40 (Sept. 12, 1896), front page. The Populists, or People's Party, held their convention at St. Louis on July 24. Two sections of the Populist platform attacking the Supreme Court were virtually identical with the Democrats' position.

19 White, "Evolution vs. Revolution in Politics," biennial address given to the

State Historical Society of Wisconsin, Feb. 9, 1897 (Madison, Wis., 1897), esp. 12.

20   For illustrations from 1884–86 pertaining to the legal tender problem and not previously mentioned, see *The Nation,* 38 (Mar. 20, 1884), 248; *The Independent,* 36 (Mar. 13, 1884), 16; *ibid.* (June 12, 1884), 20; *ibid.,* 38 (Feb. 11, 1886), 20. *The Nation*'s critical editorial, entitled "A New View of the Constitution," mocked the Court's decision that the rationale for governmental borrowing differed from that of private individuals. "The Court really need not have taken the trouble to invent this curious species of argument; for the judges had before them a clause of the Constitution which would have required no such stretching to make it meet the case. . . . When we talk of our government being one of limited powers, we mean powers limited by the Constitution and defined by the courts. If the limits are to be imposed and the definitions framed by Congress, the use of the Supreme Court for keeping one branch of the Government from encroaching upon another or upon private rights is pretty nearly gone. Practically, there seems no way of avoiding this consequence of the legal-tender decision except through a new amendment, and we have got to pass such an amendment, or else adopt a view of the Constitution and Government wholly different from any hitherto held either by strict or free constitutionalists."

21   *Collier's,* 37 (June 2, 1906), 6. See also Bloomfield, "Supreme Court in American Popular Culture," 7–8.

22   *Public Opinion,* 28 (May 17, 1900), 611–12; James M. Beck to John W. Jordan, Sept. 18, 1900, Society Collection, case 19, box 11, HSP; cartoon in *Washington Times,* Jan. 12, 1901, in Supreme Court Scrapbooks, 1880–1935, #5, p. 4, NA; *Washington Post,* June 9, 1901, *ibid.;* Semonche, *Supreme Court Responds to a Changing Society,* 141; Robert B. Highsaw, *Edward Douglass White: Defender of the Conservative Faith* (Baton Rouge, La., 1981), 165.

23   Boutwell, "The Supreme Court and the Dependencies," NAR, 173 (August 1901), 156, 159; Hannis Taylor, "Conquered Territory and the Constitution," *ibid.* (November 1901), 577–93; undated clipping from *Chicago Chronicle,* Supreme Court Scrapbooks, 1880–1935, #1, NA.

24   Porter and Johnson, *National Party Platforms, 1840–1976,* 132; Semonche, *Supreme Court Responds to a Changing Society, 1890–1920,* 184; Henry Steele Commager, ed., *Documents of American History* (7th ed.: New York, 1963), II, 39–41.

25   Commager, ed., *Documents of American History,* II, 43–45, 119–22; Semonche, *Supreme Court Responds to a Changing Society,* 355–57.

26   Hughes, *Addresses and Papers* (New York, 1908), 139. In 1931, Walton Hamilton gave Hughes's statement a cynical twist: "The skilled interpreter [a Supreme Court justice] knows how to march language and meaning along the same line of argument in opposite directions. It is this rare art which transforms the ritual of constitutionalism into an institution of social control"—Hamilton, "Constitutionalism," *Encyclopedia of the Social Sciences* (New York, 1931), IV, 258. If cynicism is tantamount to candid realism, then quite a transformation had taken place since 1824, when John Marshall declared that "judicial power, as contradistinguished from the

power of the laws, has no existence. Courts are the mere instruments of the law, and can will nothing." Marshall's opinion in *Osborn et al.* v. *the Bank of the United States,* 22 U.S. 866.

27   It is important once again to differentiate between the Court and the Constitution. To cite just two examples, between 1880 and 1918 *Harper's Monthly Magazine* did not print a single article pertaining to the U.S. Constitution; and from 1887 until 1918 *Scribner's Magazine* contained just a single entry on the Constitution, in September 1887.

28   See Henry Beach Needham, "An Intimate View of the Supreme Court," *Saturday Evening Post,* Aug. 16, 1913, pp. 12, 13, 36; Augusta Prescott, *Washington Post,* May 6, 1894, in Supreme Court Scrapbooks, 1880–1935, #4, p. 8, NA; *Denver Daily News,* Feb. 1, 1903, *ibid.,* #5.

29   *New York Recorder,* Feb. 18, 1891, *ibid.,* #3, pp. 32–33; *Chicago Tribune,* n.d., *ibid.,* #2, p. 24.

30   Both items, ca. 1886, appear in *ibid.,* #1, unpaginated.

31   "The Judges' Snuggery," n.d., *ibid.,* accompanied by a letter of complaint from a clergyman, a denial by a justice, and an item saying that a reporter had been admitted to the Court's private rooms and found no "snuggery."

32   See Hampton L. Carson, *The Supreme Court of the United States: Its History* (Philadelphia, 1891), 539–40; Alan F. Westin, ed., *An Autobiography of the Supreme Court: Off-the-Bench Commentary by the Justices* (New York, 1963), 122–33, 191–93; Brewer, "Two Periods in the History of the Supreme Court," *Report of the 18th Annual Meeting of the Virginia Bar Association* (1906), 144–45; Semonche, *Supreme Court Responds to a Changing Society,* 221.

33   Clipping in Supreme Court Scrapbooks, 1880–1935, #10, NA.

34   *Washington Times,* Jan. 12, 1910, *ibid.,* p. 1; unidentified clipping, "The Supreme Court," *ibid.,* #1, no page.

35   See *New York Sun,* June 23, 1895, *ibid.,* #4, p. 18, *New York Evening Post,* Feb. 11, 1911, *ibid.,* #10, p. 39.

36   *Macon Telegraph,* Jan. 28, 1893, *ibid.,* #3, p. 46. Similar stories are associated with Justice Hugo L. Black and Senator Sam J. Ervin, Jr.

37   By 1911 the Court had only a one-year backlog rather than four years; and by 1913 it came close to catching up with its entire docket. Clipping in *ibid.,* #9, p. 46; Washington *Herald,* Nov. 19, 1913, *ibid.,* #11.

38   Drawing by J. Kepler, *Puck,* 18 (Dec. 9, 1885), 226, 232–34. On Feb. 17, 1894, the Washington *Evening Star* complained that the Court had too many cases waiting and that its procedures needed to be streamlined. "The great mechanism of procrastination has been lacking a cog-wheel." (That mechanism metaphor once again.)

39   *New York Tribune,* Jan. 8, 1911, Supreme Court Scrapbooks, 1880–1935, #9, p. 15, NA.

40   See Walter F. Murphy, "In His Own Image: Mr. Chief Justice Taft and Supreme Court Appointments," SCR *1961* (Chicago, 1961), 159–93; Henry J. Abraham, *Justices and Presidents: A Political History of Appointments to the Supreme Court* (2nd ed.: New York, 1985).

41   Dahl, "Decision-Making in a Democracy: The Supreme Court as a National Policy-Maker," JPL, 6 (1957), 279, 280–81, 293.

42   Lowell, "Democracy and the Constitution," in *Essays on Government,* 103.

43   See Robert J. Harris, "The Decline of Judicial Review," JP, 10 (1948), 1–19; Robert H. Jackson, *The Supreme Court in the American System of Government* (Cambridge, Mass., 1955), ch. 3, "The Supreme Court as a Political Institution"; Fred Rodell, *Nine Men: A Political History of the Supreme Court from 1790 to 1955* (New York, 1955).

44   Roosevelt to Lodge, July 10, 1902, in Elting E. Morison, ed., *The Letters of Theodore Roosevelt* (Cambridge, Mass., 1951), III, 289.

45   Adams, *The Theory of Social Revolutions* (New York, 1913), 45–46.

46   Max Lerner, "The Supreme Court and American Capitalism," YLJ, 42 (1933), 668–701; Lerner, "Constitution and Court as Symbols," *ibid.*, 46 (1937), 1290–1319; Frank to Thomas Reed Powell, Feb. 5, 1931, Powell Papers, box A, folder 5, HLSL; transcript of the CBS News Special, "Justice Black and the Bill of Rights," Dec. 3, 1968, p. 9.

47   "Rehnquist Asserts Most Attempts by Presidents to Pack Court Fail," NYT, Oct. 21, 1984, p. A1; Kaufman, "Keeping Politics Out of the Court," NYT *Magazine*, Dec. 10, 1984, pp. 72ff.

48   Charles Warren, *The Supreme Court in U.S. History* (Boston, 1922), III, 391; Alpheus T. Mason, "America's Political Heritage: Revolution and Free Government," in M. Judd Harmon, ed., *Essays on the Constitution of the United States* (Port Washington, N.Y., 1978), 26; J. R. MacDonald, "The Power of the Judiciary in America," *Independent*, 50 (Mar. 24, 1898), 4–5; William M. Meigs, "Some Recent Attacks on the American Doctrine of Judicial Power," *American Law Review*, 40 (1906), 641–70.

49   See Alan F. Westin's valuable edition of Beard, *The Supreme Court and the Constitution* (New York, 1912; Englewood Cliffs, N.J., 1962), esp. Westin's introduction, "Charles Beard and American Debate over Judicial Review, 1790–1961," 1–34; Ellen Nore, *Charles A. Beard: An Intellectual Biography* (Carbondale, Ill., 1983), 9.

50   Adams, *Theory of Social Revolutions*, 47–48, 83–84. Cf. Edward S. Corwin, *The Doctrine of Judicial Review, Its Legal and Historical Basis, and Other Essays* (Princeton, 1914).

51   Roosevelt to Simeon Eben Baldwin, Nov. 2, 1910, in Morison, ed., *Letters of Theodore Roosevelt*, VII, 150; TR's speech to the Progressive Party Convention at Chicago, Aug. 6, 1912, "Purposes and Policies of the Progressive Party," Senate Document no. 904, 62nd Congress, 2d Session (1911–12), 9–10.

52   Roosevelt, *Gouverneur Morris* (Boston, 1888), 115–18, 134–35; TR to Nicholas Murray Butler, Aug. 6, 1904, in Morison, ed., *Letters of Roosevelt*, IV, 884, and VI, 1229; TR to John O. Jackson, June 19, 1911, *ibid.*, VII, 288–89; TR to Edgar Aldrich, Aug. 1, 1911, *ibid.*, 319; Porter and Johnson, eds. *National Party Platforms, 1840–1976*, I, 176.

53   NYT, Apr. 27, 1911, p. 8; NYT, Apr. 28, 1911, p. 12; Johnson, *Borah*, 123–24. Borah opposed the recall of judges, however, because of his strong commitment to an independent judiciary (see *ibid.*, 130–31).

54   Taft is quoted in *The Outlook*, 100 (Mar. 23, 1912), 604–05; Michael E. Parrish, *Felix Frankfurter and His Times: The Reform Years* (New York, 1982), 53–55; NYT, Mar. 7, 1912, p. 3; NYT, Mar. 19, 1912, p. 4. See also Thomas Nelson Page, "The Virginians and Constitutional Government," NAR, 197 (March 1913), 371–91, for a pro-Wilson, anti-Roose-

velt blast that found the U.S. Constitution "complex, it is true, but so arranged that it can be reasonably, lawfully, and wisely adjusted to meet whatever situation may arise."

55   *The Outlook,* 101 (Aug. 10, 1912), 793–94.

56   Roosevelt, "A Charter of Democracy: Address before the Ohio Constitutional Convention," *The Outlook,* 100 (Feb. 24, 1912), 390–402, the extract at 390–91. See also Roosevelt, "The Recall of Judicial Decisions," address at Philadelphia, Apr. 10, 1912, *The Works of Theodore Roosevelt* (memorial edition: New York, 1925), XIX, 260–62; William L. Ransom, *Majority Rule and the Judiciary: An Examination of Current Proposals for Constitutional Change Affecting the Relation of Courts to Legislation,* introduction by Theodore Roosevelt (New York, 1912).

57   TR to George U. Crocker, Nov. 19, 1912, in Morison, ed., *Letters of Theodore Roosevelt,* VII, 652; TR to the Progressives in Congress, Apr. 2, 1913, *ibid.,* 719; for Taft, NYT, Nov. 10, 1912, p. 14; William D. Guthrie, "Constitutional Morality," NAR, 196 (Aug. 12, 1912), 154–73.

58   Speech delivered on Mar. 17, 1914, quoted in Johnson, *Borah,* 181. See Judge Robert H. Bork's speech, "Tradition and Morality in Constitutional Law," given Dec. 6, 1984, in which he praised our governmental institutions because they "embody wholesome inconsistencies." NYT, Jan. 4, 1985, p. A16.

59   NYT, May 12, 1912, sec. 6, p. 13; *ibid.,* p. 16; NYT, Dec. 15, 1912, p. 3.

60   Charles Wallace Collins, Jr., "The Failure of the Fourteenth Amendment as a Constitutional Idea," SAQ, 11 (1912), 101–15, esp. 101.

61   Adams, *Theory of Social Revolutions,* 34, 80, 214. See Alan H. Monroe, "The Supreme Court and the Constitution," APSR, 18 (1924), 737–59.

62   NYT, Apr. 24, 1911, p. 8; NYT, Dec. 27, 1911, p. 8; Charles Grove Haines, *The American Doctrine of Judicial Supremacy* (2nd ed: Berkeley, Calif., 1932), 491; Nore, *Beard: An Intellectual Biography,* 59; William E. Dodd, "History and Patriotism," SAQ, 12 (1913), 109–21; Allan L. Benson, *Our Dishonest Constitution* (New York, 1914), 1, 4.

63   Oliver Wendell Holmes to Harold J. Laski, July 14, 1916, and Nov. 13, 1928, in Mark DeWolfe Howe, ed., *Holmes-Laski Letters: The Correspondence of Mr. Justice Holmes and Harold J. Laski, 1916–1935* (Cambridge, Mass., 1953), 4, 1109; Holmes to Sir Frederick Pollock, June 20, 1928, in Mark DeWolfe Howe, ed., *Holmes-Pollock Letters: The Correspondence of Mr. Justice Holmes and Sir Frederick Pollock, 1874–1932* (2nd ed.: Cambridge, Mass., 1961), II 222–23, 232; Albert B. Hart to William E. Dodd, Apr. 17, 1917, Hart Papers, box 2, HUPL. Holmes welcomed Charles Warren's *The Making of the Constitution* (1928), prepared for laymen, because it "finally smashes the humbug talked about the economic origin of the Constitution. I thought Beard's book on that theme a stinker. . . . Warren has the sense to realize that some men have emotions not dependent on their pocketbooks. . . ."—Holmes to Laski, Nov. 13, 1928.

64   Rhodes to Lodge, Apr. 13 [1912?], quoted in Robert Cruden, *James Ford Rhodes: The Man, the Historian, and His Work* (Cleveland, 1961), 129–30; Lodge, "The Constitution and Its Makers" (1911), in Lodge, *The Democracy of the Constitution and Other Addresses and Essays* (New York, 1915), 32–87; Aubrey Parkman, *David Jayne Hill and the Problem of World Peace*

(Lewisburg, Pa., 1975), 157; Hill, "Crisis in Constitutionalism," NAR, 198 (December 1913), 769–78.

65   *Ibid.*, esp. 771, 775–76. *The North American Review* ran a supportive editorial entitled "For Constitutional Clubs" in the same issue, 763–64. Hill reprinted his essay as ch. 2 in *Americanism: What It Is* (New York, 1916).

66   Hill, "A Defense of the Constitution," NAR, 205 (March 1917), 395–96.

67   *Ibid.*, 389–91.

68   Seba Eldridge to Albert B. Hart, Apr. 21, 1915, and Hart to Eldridge, June 22, 1915, Hart Papers, box 2, HUPL; NYT, May 7, 1916, p. 8; NYT, May 9, 1916, p. 10.

69   J. Franklin Jameson to Max Farrand, Oct. 28, 1915, Farrand Papers, HEH; A. Lawrence Lowell to Farrand, Oct. 7, 1915, and June 26, 1916, *ibid.*; W. T. Sedgwick to Farrand, Oct. 4, 1916, *ibid.*; Farrand to Frank L. Polk, Feb. 12, 1916, *ibid.*

70   "Suggestions for a Course in Civics for Senior High School" (1916), quoted in H. Arnold Bennett, *The Constitution in School and College* (New York, 1935), 36; Keith Sward, *The Legend of Henry Ford* (New York, 1948), 103.

71   Beveridge to Beard, Feb. 27, 1918, Beveridge Papers, box 212, LCMD; Samuel P. Weaver, "The Constitution in Our Public Schools," CR, 11 (1927), 105; Howard Jay Graham, *Everyman's Constitution: Historical Essays on the Fourteenth Amendment, the "Conspiracy Theory," and American Constitutionalism* (Madison, Wis., 1968), 4, 66.

72   See William M. Wiecek, "Slavery and Abolition before the United States Supreme Court, 1820–1860," JAH, 65 (1978), 34–35.

73   *Washington Post*, May 10, 1884, p. 2; *ibid.*, May 11, 1884, pp. 4, 5; NYT, May 11, 1884, p. 8. In 1928 James M. Beck commissioned a replica of Story's statue as a gift to the city of Philadelphia. Ever since 1930 the replica has sat in the open air on the west side of the Philadelphia Museum of Art (see figure 15). Story's original has been moved from the grounds of the U.S. Capitol to the lower level of the Supreme Court building.

74   Allan B. Magruder, *John Marshall* (Boston, 1885); NYT, Dec. 31, 1900, p. 5; Joseph P. Cotton, Jr., *The Constitutional Decisions of John Marshall* (New York, 1905); James M. Lindgren, "The Gospel of Preservation in Virginia and New England: Historic Preservation and the Regeneration of Traditionalism" (unpub. Ph.D. dissertation, College of William and Mary, 1984), 107, 109, 391. See also Francis N. Stites, *John Marshall: Defender of the Constitution* (Boston, 1981), 169–71.

75   See NYT, May 27, 1900, p. 17, for the planning. Coverage of events in various cities appears in NYT, Feb. 5, 1901, p. 5.

76   John F. Dillon, comp., *John Marshall: Life, Character and Judicial Services as portrayed in the centenary and memorial addresses and proceedings throughout the United States on Marshall Day, 1901. . . .* (Chicago, 1903), 3 vols.; NYT, Feb. 5, 1901, p. 5. The strong protest came from John W. Aiken, a former president of the ABA, in the form of an open letter released to the press.

77   Tracy E. Strevey, "Albert J. Beveridge," in William T. Hutchinson, ed., *The Marcus W. Jernegan Essays in American Historiography* (New York, 1937), 380, 383; Beard to Beveridge, Feb. 24 [1918], and Jan. 15, 1919,

Beveridge Papers, boxes 212 and 217, LCMD; Beveridge to Beard, Feb. 4, 1919, *ibid.*, box 217. See also Beveridge to Max Farrand, Apr. 8, 1918, and Jan. 7, 1919; Farrand to Beveridge, Apr. 8, 1918, and Sept. 13, 1918, Farrand Papers, HEH.

78   Clarence W. Alvord to Beveridge, Jan. 22 and July 1, 1919, Beveridge Papers, box 217, LCMD. See also Beveridge to Henry Cabot Lodge, Dec. 9 and 28, 1918, and Lodge to Beveridge, Dec. 30, 1918, Lodge Papers, box 45, MHS.

79   See Nicholas Murray Butler to Beveridge, Feb. 19, 1918, Beveridge Papers, box 212, LCMD; Moore to Beveridge, Oct. 10, 1919, with printed speech (Sept. 19, 1919) enclosed, *ibid.*, box 222; Holmes to Beveridge, Dec. 8, 1919, *ibid.*

80   H. G. Fairchild to Beveridge, Feb. 18, 1920, *ibid.*; W. M. Wiley to Beveridge, Mar. 11, 1920, *ibid.*

81   Beveridge to Corwin, Mar. 22, 1918, Jan. 4, 1919, Corwin Papers, box 2, PUML; Corwin to J. Franklin Jameson, Oct. 7, 1919, and Jameson to Corwin, Oct. 8, 1919, Jameson Papers, box 74, LCMD; Beveridge to Corwin, Apr. 29, 1920, Corwin Papers, box 2, PUML.

82   Cushman to Beveridge, Dec. 8, 1920, Beveridge Papers, box 222, LCMD; Corwin's review of Beveridge, *Marshall,* vols. III and IV, appeared in YLJ, 29 (1920), 586–88.

83   Corwin to Jameson, Oct. 7, 1919, Jameson Papers, box 74, LCMD.

84   Strevey, "Albert J. Beveridge," *Jernegan Essays in American Historiography,* 389. Oddly enough, Beveridge seriously underestimated the parochial zealousness of the Canadian provinces. See p. 395.

85   Marc Szeftel, *The Russian Constitution of April 23, 1906: Political Institutions of the Duma Monarchy* (Brussels, 1976).

86   Peter F. Sugar, "An Underrated Event: The Hungarian Constitutional Crisis of 1905–06," *East European Quarterly,* 15 (1981), 281–306; János M. Bak and Anna Gara-Bak, "The Ideology of a 'Millennial Constitution' in Hungary," *ibid.*, 307–26.

87   Meribeth E. Cameron, *The Reform Movement in China, 1898–1912* (Stanford, Calif., 1931), esp. ch. 6, "Constitutional Reform"; E-Tu Zen Sun, "The Chinese Constitutional Missions of 1905–1906," *Journal of Modern History,* 24 (1952), 251–68.

88   Cameron, *Reform Movement in China,* 110, 113–15.

89   *Ibid.*, 121–24, 127, 131, 133–35; cf. P'eng-yüan Chang, "The Constitutionalists," in Mary C. Wright, ed., *China in Revolution: The First Phase, 1900–1913* (New Haven, Conn., 1968), 143–83, esp. 145–48, 153, 182, for a more detailed and positive account of the constitutionalists' activities and achievements.

90   Andrew J. Nathan, *Peking Politics, 1918–1923: Factionalism and the Failure of Constitutionalism* (Berkeley, Calif., 1976), 5–7, 18–19, 25–26, 176, 200, 223–24.

91   Michael Meyer and W. L. Sherman, *The Course of Mexican History* (New York, 1979), 524–27, 532–33, 542–45. See also Richard N. Adams, *The Second Sowing: Power and Secondary Development in Latin America* (San Francisco, 1967), 180–82, for a stimulating theoretical analysis.

92   Howard F. Cline, *The United States and Mexico* (Cambridge, Mass., 1953),
      117, 136, 142, 145, 151–55, 165–71.

93   Harlan, "Remarks" delivered on Dec. 23, 1907, in New York City, clip-
      ping in Supreme Court Scrapbooks, 1880–1935, #6, p. 7, NA (see note 6
      above). See also T. Roosevelt to George William Russell (the Irish poet and
      painter known as AE), Aug. 6, 1917, in Morison, ed., *Letters of Roosevelt*,
      VIII, 1219: "I am certain that if the people who framed the constitution of
      the United States, and that was a matter of compromise from first to last,
      had adjourned midway, and gone back to their respective States to explain
      the various proposals and why they were for or against this or that proposal,
      there never would have been a constitution adopted. What they did was to
      meet, debate, agree, compromise and vote for a constitution. It was a
      patchwork and it was nothing but compromise. But it has lived, and under
      it, as interpreted by our Supreme Court, this country has grown to a hun-
      dred million, and has fought three small wars, and one of the greatest wars
      in history, abolished slavery and now, thank God, is taking its part in this
      war. Even that constitution was reluctantly adopted by the necessary two
      thirds. But it was put to them either to take that or anarchy."

•   CHAPTER 8 *God Knows How Dearly We Need a Constitutional Revival*

1   Phelps's pamphlet, *The United States Constitution Simplified*, was sum-
      marized and discussed in "Popularizing the Federal Constitution," CR, 4
      (1920), 235–39; Borah to James M. Beck, Dec. 4, 1924, Beck Papers, box
      2, PUML.

2   Harry F. Atwood, "The Birthday of Our Constitution," CR, 3 (1919),
      20–24; Walter Evans Hampton, "A 'Constitution Day,'" *ibid.*, 16–19.

3   *Ibid.*, 18; editorial, "Constitution Day, September Seventeenth," CR, 3
      (July 1919), 181–84; NYT, Mar. 30, 1919, sec. 2, p. 1; NYT, Aug. 29,
      1919, p. 7.

4   NYT, Sept. 18, 1918, p. 6; NYT, June 29, 1919, sec. 2, p. 1; NYT, July
      28, 1919, p. 10; NYT, Aug. 3, 1919, sec. 2, p. 6; NYT, Aug. 25, 1919, p.
      14.

5   NYT, Sept. 18, 1919, p. 4; NYT, Sept. 20, 1919, p. 3; and see James M.
      Lindgren, "The Gospel of Preservation in Virginia and New England: His-
      toric Preservation and the Regeneration of Traditionalism" (unpub. Ph.D.
      dissertation, William and Mary, 1984), 127.

6   NYT, Sept. 17, 1920, p. 17; NYT, Sept. 18, 1920, p. 1.

7   NYT, June 5, 1921, sec. 1, p. 19; NYT, Sept. 18, 1921, sec. 1, p. 10;
      NYT, Sept. 16, 1922, p. 14; NYT, Sept. 17, 1922, sec. 1, p. 16; "The
      Constitution Anniversary Association," CR, 7 (1923), 191–93; NYT,
      Sept. 15, 1923, p. 16; NYT, Sept. 16, 1923, sec. 1, p. 5; NYT, Sept. 17,
      1923, p. 17; NYT, Sept. 11, 1924, p. 13; NYT, Sept. 17, 1934, p. 22;
      NYT, Sept. 29, 1934, p. 3.

8   NYT, Sept. 14, 1925, p. 40; NYT, Sept. 17, 1925, p. 10; NYT, Sept. 18,
      1925, p. 24 (for the lengthy quotation about American ignorance); C.
      Lewis Fowler, "Constitution Day," *The American Standard*, 2 (Sept. 15,

1925), cover and p. 420; NYT, Sept. 17, 1926, p. 12; NYT, Sept. 18, 1926, p. 19; NYT, Sept. 11, 1927, sec. 2, p. 8; NYT, Sept. 12, 1927, p. 14; NYT, Sept. 17, 1928, p. 22; NYT, Sept. 18, 1929, p. 24; Harry Atwood, "The Constitution Week Movement," CR, 13 (1929), 181–85; NYT, Sept. 16, 1927, p. 8.

9   NYT, Sept. 14, 1930, sec. 2, p. 6; NYT, Sept. 17, 1930, pp. 17, 22; NYT, Sept. 18, 1930, p. 19; NYT, Feb. 15, 1931, sec. 2, p. 6; NYT, Sept. 12, 1931, p. 14; NYT, Sept. 14, 1931, p. 19; NYT, Sept. 17, 1931, p. 27; NYT, Sept. 18, 1931, p. 3. The speaker quoted was General Louis W. Stotesbury.

10   NYT, Sept. 11, 1932, sec. 1, p. 26; NYT, Sept. 17, 1932, p. 17; NYT, Sept. 18, 1932, sec. 1, p. 9; NYT, Sept. 19, 1932, p. 19; NYT, Sept. 7, 1933, p. 12; NYT, Sept. 18, 1933, p. 18; NYT, Sept. 19, 1933, p. 23; NYT, Sept. 10, 1934, p. 19; NYT, Sept. 16, 1934, sec. 2, pp. 1, 2; NYT, Sept. 17, 1934, p. 17; NYT, Sept. 18, 1934, pp. 1, 2, NYT, Sept. 18, 1934, pp. 2, 4; NYT, Sept. 18, 1935, pp. 1, 11, 12; NYT, Sept. 18, 1936, p. 26.

11   NYT, Sept. 18, 1920, p. 9; NYT, Jan. 9, 1921, sec. 2, p. 1; NYT, May 22, 1921, sec. 1, p. 22.

12   NYT, Jan. 18, 1920, sec. 2, pp. 1, 2; NYT, Sept. 30, 1921, pp. 2, 17; NYT Feb. 13, 1922, p. 2; NYT, June 11, 1926, p. 5; David C. Mearns and Verner W. Clapp, *The Constitution of the United States together with an Account of Its Travels since September 17, 1787* (Washington, D.C., 1937), 16–18; NYT, Jan. 16, 1985, p. A16.

13   NYT, Nov. 1, 1926, p. 14; NYT, Nov. 21, 1926, sec. 9, p. 14.

14   NYT, Mar. 21, 1926, sec. 9, p. 6.

15   Sidney Howard, "Our Professional Patriots: The Constitution Worshippers," NR, 40 (Oct. 15, 1924), 171–73; Norman Hapgood, ed., *Professional Patriots: An Exposure of the Personalities, Methods and Objectives Involved in the Organized Effort to Exploit Patriotic Impulses in these United States During and After the Late War* (New York, 1927); Henry St. George Tucker to Lyon G. Tyler, Mar. 2, 1918, Tyler Family Papers, Group I, box 24, WMSL; Henry S. Carr to Albert B. Hart, Aug. 24, 1918, Hart Papers, box 11, HUPL; Louis Annin Ames to Clifford L. Hilton, July 31, 1919, Minn. Society of the Sons of the Am. Rev. Papers, box 1, Minn. Hist. Soc.; Ames to Fred A. Bill, June 2, 1921, *ibid.*; NYT, Jan. 15, 1920, p. 4; NYT, July 27, 1920, p. 11; Morton Keller, *In Defense of Yesterday: James M. Beck and the Politics of Conservatism, 1861–1936* (New York, 1958), 162.

16   NYT, Oct. 1, 1922, sec. 2, p. 1; NYT, July 5, 1925, sec. 1, p. 13; Rouget D. Jenkins to Ralph Budd, Dec. 4, 1925, Great Northern Presidential Papers, box 372, Minn. Hist. Soc.; Helene E. Jackson to Albert B. Hart [n.d., 1927 or 1928], Hart Papers, box 6, HUPL; "Public Interest in the Constitution," CR, 11 (1927), 246–47.

17   William Nelson Cromwell to James Beck, March 23, 1924, Beck Papers, box 1, PUML; NYT, Apr. 19, 1925, sec. 1, pp. 1, 22; NYT, Nov. 23, 1926, p. 13; NYT, Mar. 7, 1928, p. 27; James C. Fitzpatrick to Sol Bloom, Jan. 29, 1936, Fitzpatrick Papers, box 16, LCMD. In 1930, James Beck criticized the "sacerdotal conception of law" which equated the Constitution

with the Bible as "infallible and omnipotent." See Keller, *Beck and the Politics of Conservatism,* 221.

18   Charles Willis Thompson, "That Dark Secret—The Constitution," NYT *Magazine,* June 29, 1924, p. 9; NYT, May 23, 1923, p. 14; NYT, Dec. 24, 1923, p. 11; NYT, Feb. 23, 1926, p. 8.

19   McBain, *The Living Constitution: A Consideration of the Realities and Legends of Our Fundamental Law* (New York, 1927), 272; Merriam, *The Written Constitution and the Unwritten Attitude* (New York, 1931), 30. See also Ralph Henry Gabriel, "Constitutional Democracy: A Nineteenth-Century Faith," in Conyers Read, ed., *The Constitution Reconsidered* (New York, 1938), 252.

20   NYT, Sept. 21, 1919, sec. 3, p. 1; NYT, July 25, 1920, sec. 8, p. 8; NYT, Oct. 29, 1922, sec. 2, p. 6; NYT, Oct. 18, 1924, pp. 6, 14.

21   Baker, *Progress and the Constitution* (New York, 1925), 5, 32; NYT, Sept. 18, 1932, sec. 1, p. 33; lengthy excerpts from Baker's speech appear in NYT, Sept. 25, 1932, sec. 8, p. 4.

22   NYT, July 5, 1925, sec. 1, p. 17; NYT, May 3, 1928, p. 26; NYT, Aug. 5, 1928, sec. 2, p. 7; Merriam, *Written Constitution and the Unwritten Attitude,* 7.

23   Henry Hazlitt, "Our Obsolete Constitution," *The Nation* (Feb. 4, 1931), abridged in RD, 18 (April 1931), 1097–99; NYT, Dec. 28, 1931, p. 12; NYT, May 18, 1932, p. 11.

24   NYT, Oct. 18, 1932, p. 15; James M. Beck, *The Constitution of the United States: Yesterday, Today—and Tomorrow?* (New York, 1924), 201, where he praises "the elasticity of the instrument. Its vitality is due to the fact that, by usage, judicial interpretation, and, when necessary, formal amendment, it can be thus adapted to the ever-accelerating changes of the most progressive age in history."

25   Becker, "Afterthoughts on Constitutions," in Read, ed., *Constitution Reconsidered,* 426; Beard, *The American Leviathan: The Republic in the Machine Age* (New York, 1930), 22–23, 41–42, 51. For the context of American concern during the 1920s about legal ambiguities and conflicts in jurisprudence, see Edward A. Purcell, Jr., *The Crisis of Democratic Theory: Scientific Naturalism & the Problem of Value* (Lexington, Ky., 1973), 79–80, 85.

26   Smith, *The Spirit of American Government,* ed. Cushing Strout (Cambridge, Mass., 1965), chs. 3, 7, 13, 15, and p. 383; Smith, *The Growth and Decadence of Constitutional Government,* ed. Vernon L. Parrington (New York, 1930), 82, 97, 101, 114, 251, and ch. 9, "Centralization and Popular Control."

27   Edith Wharton, *French Ways and Their Meaning* (New York, 1919), 34–35; NYT, Sept. 17, 1921, pp. 12, 13; William Howard Taft, *Liberty Under Law* (New Haven, Conn., 1922), 20.

28   Beck, *The Constitution of the United States,* 202, 277, 288, 290–91, 303; John W. Walsh to Beck, Feb. 7, 1925, Beck Papers, box 1, PUML; Hill, *Human Nature in the Constitution* (Rochester, N.Y. 1926), 60–61.

29   Beck to F. Dumont Smith, Nov. 13, 1924, Beck Papers, box 1, PUML. See also Pierre S. DuPont to Henry Cabot Lodge, Jan. 17, 1925, Lodge Papers, box 75, MHS; Beck, "The Anniversary of the Constitution," CR,

13 (1929), 189–90. For the survival of this notion, see Willmoore Kendall and George W. Carey, *The Basic Symbols of the American Political Tradition* (Baton Rouge, La., 1970), ch. 6, "Constitutional Morality and *The Federalist.*"

30 Arnold, *The Folklore of Capitalism* (New Haven, Conn., 1937), 29.

31 *Ibid.*, 79; Butler, "The Constitution of the United States," CR, 9 (1925), 131; Davis, "What Does the Constitution Mean to You?" ABAJ, 11 (1925), 442.

32 NYT, Aug. 16, 1925, sec. 2, p. 2; NYT, Nov. 29, 1925, sec. 1, p. 28; Samuel P. Weaver, "The Constitution in Our Public Schools," CR, 11 (1927), 105.

33 Beck to Judge John M. Gest, Dec. 27, 1926, quoted in Keller, *Beck and the Politics of Conservatism,* 194; Beck to Edward S. Corwin, Nov. 22, 1930, Corwin Papers, box 1, PUML. See also Newton D. Baker, *The Making and Keeping of the Constitution* (Williamsburg, Va., 1935), 24.

34 *The Pocket Edition* is discussed in CR, 4, (1920), 63–64; NYT, Feb. 20, 1922, p. 11; Louis A. Coolidge (chairman of the Sentinels) to Charles Warren, Dec. 20 and 27, 1923, Warren Papers, box 2, LCMD; Leighton, *Our Constitution in My Town and My Life* (New York, 1924).

35 "Teaching the Constitution in the Schools," CR, 7 (1923), 255–58; NYT, Jan. 31, 1924, p. 13. See generally Bessie Louise Pierce, *Civic Attitudes in American School Textbooks* (Chicago, 1930).

36 George S. Mumford, Summary Report prepared for the National Security League [c. 1919?], Albert B. Hart Papers, box 20, HUPL; NYT, Sept. 16, 1922, p. 14; Louis A. Coolidge to Charles Warren, Dec. 20 and 27, 1923, Warren Papers, box 2, LCMD; Weaver, "Constitution in Our Public Schools" (1927), 111; Herbert Hoover's message for Constitution Week, NYT, Sept. 17, 1929, p. 3.

37 H. Arnold Bennett, *The Constitution in School and College* (New York, 1935), 38, 105–07; NYT, Mar. 13, 1924, p. 19; NYT, Mar. 31, 1924, p. 6; NYT, June 11, 1922, sec. 1, p. 9; minutes of a meeting of the Sons of the American Revolution, Boston, Dec. 2, 1932, in Hart Papers, box 24, HUPL.

38 NYT, Jan. 15, 1922, sec. 1, p. 16; see *The Bacon Lectures on the Constitution of the United States Given at Boston University, 1928–1938* (Worcester, Mass. [1939]).

39 NYT, Mar. 11, 1923, sec. 1, p. 5; "Teaching the Constitution in the Schools," CR, 9 (1925), 118; Weaver, "Constitution in Our Public Schools" (1927), 106; Bennett, *Constitution in School and College,* 39, 124, 131, 134.

40 "Legislation Relating to Teaching the Constitution," *Historical Outlook,* 16 (1925), 207–11; Bennett, "A New Approach to the Study of the Constitution," *ibid.*, 20 (1929), 337–41; Bennett, "The Constitution and the Teacher," *ibid.*, 23 (1932), 170–71; Alden L. Powell, "The Guardian of the Constitution: Article V," *ibid.*, 24 (1933), 72–76; Daniel C. Knowlton, "The United States Constitution in the Schoolbooks of the Past," *The Social Studies,* 29 (1938), 7–14.

41 Judge Daniel K. Carey to James M. Beck, Oct. 19, 1929, and Beck to Carey, Nov. 18, 1929, Beck Papers, box 8, PUML; Walter Sanders

Faulkner, *A Child's History and Interpretation of the Constitution of the United States* (n.p., 1941; Lebanon, Tenn., 1947), 2, 139; James Mussatti, *Constitutionism: The Origin of Liberty under the Constitution* (San Francisco, 1941), revised as *The Constitution of the United States: Our Charter of Liberties* (Princeton, 1960).

42   A. T. Southworth, *The Common Sense of the Constitution of the United States* (Boston, 1924), iv; James A. Van Osdol, "Future Organization and Defense of the Constitution," CR, 13 (1929), 124. Italics in the original.

43   NYT, June 7, 1924, p. 5; "The National Oratorical Contest," CR, 8 (1924), 245–48; NYT, May 9, 1925, pp. 1, 2; NYT, Jan. 24, 1926, sec. 2, pp. 1, 2; NYT, Feb. 22, 1926, p. 35; NYT, Mar. 21, 1926, sec. 2, p. 1.

44   "National Oratorical Contest," CR, 11 (1927), 187–89; NYT, May 9, 1925, p. 14; NYT, May 26, 1937, p. 24.

45   NYT, Feb. 28, 1926, sec. 9, p. 6; NYT, Mar. 7, 1926, sec. 8, p. 17; NYT, Feb. 20, 1927, sec. 8, p. 6; NYT, Feb. 27, 1927, sec. 8, p. 6; NYT, Mar. 13, 1927, sec. 8, p. 6; NYT, Mar. 18, 1928, sec. 9, p. 17; NYT, Feb. 17, 1929, sec. 10, p. 6; NYT, Apr. 20, 1930, sec. 9, p. 9.

46   NYT, Feb. 22, 1924, p. 5; NYT, Jan. 31, 1927, p. 3. It is not at all clear why, but winners of the essay contests were predominantly female. This is not true of the oratorical competitions. See NYT, June 7, 1924, p. 5; NYT, May 23, 1937, sec. 2, p. 5.

47   NYT, Jan. 24, 1926, sec. 2, pp. 1, 2; "National Oratorical Contest," CR, 8 (1924), 245. Beginning in 1924, students in the USSR were required to write laudatory essays about V. I. Lenin and the best of these essays were published. This phenomenon was part of a Lenin cult that Stalin and others actively fostered. See Nina Tumarkin, *Lenin Lives! The Lenin Cult in Soviet Russia* (Cambridge, Mass., 1983), esp. 228–29.

48   Weaver, "Constitution in Our Public Schools," CR, 11 (1927), 108; Bennett, *Constitution in School and College,* 90–91, 94; Grace R. Hebard, *Civics: State, National, and Community* (2nd ed.: San Francisco, 1928), 147.

49   NYT, Mar. 18, 1928, sec. 10, p. 6; NYT, Mar. 31, 1930, p. 20, col. 7.

50   NYT, July 13, 1927, p. 22; NYT, Mar. 1, 1932, p. 4; "What Do You Know About the Constitution?", a four-page list of questions (n.d.), suggested by 150 prominent educators, that Americans ought to be able to answer, typescript in the Douglas S. Freeman Papers, box 3, Alderman Library, University of Virginia.

51   Parker, "American Constitutional Government," CR, 6 (1922), 90–91. This sentiment was not entirely new in 1922, but was more widely shared than ever before. See William W. Morrow, "The Americanism of the Constitution of the United States," CR, 4 (1920), 35. Morrow, a federal judge, admitted what the more extreme xenophobes usually omitted: "We have in addition to the large body of aliens who are not voters a very large body of voters who do not understand or appreciate our form of government."

52   The generalizations in these two paragraphs as well as particulars in the pages that follow are based upon an extraordinary cache of primary source material that has been little used by historians. The cache will be found at the National Archives, Washington, D.C., in the Judicial, Fiscal, & Social Branch of the Civil Archives Division. That branch is the repository for two

extensive series of Immigration and Naturalization Service records. The Citizenship Training Division files document the naturalization program as administered by the Department of Labor; the Citizenship Education Program files document the program after responsibility had been transferred to the Department of Justice.

53 "Suggestions to Petitioners for Naturalization," typescript form letter dated May 7, 1909, Record Group 85, file 27671, box 1, NA.

54 John W. Caldwell to John Speed Smith, Jan. 18, 1911, with sample questions and promotional materials attached, Record Group 85, E20/10, box 13, NA; Smith to the Chief, Division of Naturalization, Washington, D.C., Jan. 19, 1911, *ibid.*; Caldwell, *Helpful Hints on How to Become a Citizen of the United States of America* (Tacoma, Wash., n.d.), 45 pages, *ibid.*; Caldwell, *Epitome of the Civil Government of the United States*, 25 pages, *ibid.*

55 Judge Clarence N. Goodwin to Louis F. Post, Dec. 16, 1914, Record Group 85, file 27671/25, box 6; Richard K. Campbell to Louis F. Post, Dec. 22, 1914, *ibid.*; Campbell to the Secretary of Labor, Jan. 21, 1915, *ibid.*

56 Early in December 1927 members of the U.S. Patriotic Society visited President Coolidge and urged him to authorize the printing of the U.S. Constitution in many foreign languages and distribution of the document to every alien who entered the country. NYT, Dec. 9, 1927, p. 8.

57 Between 1918 and 1934, with increasing frequency after 1930, Raymond F. Crist of the Bureau of Naturalization, and others subsequently, prepared a *Federal Textbook on Citizenship Training*. It was published in Washington by the Department of Labor and eventually was improved by Lillian P. Clark, a consultant on adult immigrant education. See the fascinating five-page memorandum from John Speed Smith to the Commissioner of Naturalization, Nov. 14, 1923, Record Group 85, file E-2, box 1.

58 See Catheryn Seckler-Hudson, *Our Constitution and Government: Lessons on the Constitution and Government of the United States for Use in the Public Schools by Candidates for Citizenship* (Washington, D.C., 1940; reprinted and revised in 1945, 1948, 1951, 1954); a Simplified Edition was prepared by John G. Hervey, Dean and Professor of Constitutional Law at Temple University (Washington, D.C., 1942); Frances O. Thomas, *Federal Textbook on Citizenship: Our Constitution Lives and Grows: A Citizenship Reader for Use in the Public Schools by Candidates for Naturalization* (Washington, D.C., 1944), printed in three versions using the same material at different levels of simplicity-complexity (16, 24, and 32 pp.); *Federal Textbook on Citizenship. A Home Study Course in English and Government for Candidates for Naturalization* (Washington, D.C., 1946, 1947, 1948, 1950, 1951, 1955); Carl B. Hyatt, *Gateway to Citizenship* (Washington, D.C., 1943, with many subsequent revisions through the 1970s). Most of these manuals and readers are unavailable in university libraries. A complete collection that includes each printing and revision will be found in Record Group 85, boxes 94–96, NA.

59 "Memorandum: The Matter of Obtaining Satisfactory Assurance that Applicants for Citizenship Are Attached to the Principles of the Constitution of the United States," Feb. 11, 1915, Record Group 85, E25, part 3, box 6,

p. 1, NA. For context, see Edward G. Hartmann, *The Movement to Americanize the Immigrant* (New York, 1948), esp. 153, 155–56.

60   "Questions and Answers for Citizenship," North American Civic League for Immigrants (1915), copy in Record Group 85, box 331, NA; *Citizenship Syllabus: A Course of Study and Syllabus in Civic Training and Naturalization for Adult Immigrants in Evening Schools* (Albany, N.Y., 1916), esp. 7, 11, 36–37, 43.

61   Robert S. Coleman to Commissioner of Naturalization, Oct. 24, 1914, and Commissioner to Coleman, Oct. 28, 1914, Record Group 85, Citizenship Training Files, E25, box 6, NA; Oran T. Moore to Commissioner of Naturalization, Feb. 28, 1916, *ibid.* For a remarkable ten-page report (really a short history) of Americanization efforts in Minnesota, see R. K. Doe to Raymond F. Crist, Sept. 13, 1924, *ibid.*, E20/10, box 6, NA.

62   Compare the Annual Report of the Secretary of Labor for 1915, pp. 83–84, with the Annual Report for 1923, pp. 74–75; F. A. Cleveland to Albert B. Hart, Oct. 28, 1920, Hart Papers, box 2, HUPL; Earle B. Mayfield to C. F. Tucker, Oct. 26, 1925; Tucker to Mayfield, Oct. 30, 1925; Tucker to the Commissioner of the Naturalization Service, Oct. 30, 1925; and R. Carl White to Mayfield, Nov. 6, 1925 (from which the quotations come; White was Assistant Secretary of Labor), all in Record Group 85, file E38/24, box 13, NA.

63   From a tabulation dated June 2, 1934, Record Group 85, file 152, box 8.

64   Typical questions asked in examinations for naturalization, 42 pages, Lodi, Calif., December 1934, June 1935, December 1935, *ibid.*

65   The treasure trove of Citizenship Education Program files of the Immigration and Naturalization Service will be found primarily in *ibid.*, boxes 8 and 9. Most of them are dated January 1936.

66   These illustrations, many others, and examples of trick questions are located in Record Group 85, file 152/9, box 12, NA.

67   MacCormack's widely circulated eight-page description of the Citizenship Program that went into effect in 1936, *ibid.*, box 8.

68   Memorandum, "Naturalization: Knowledge of the Constitution," May 4, 1936, *ibid.*, box 12; G. C. Wilmoth to R. A. Scott, Sept. 30, 1936, *ibid.*; three-page memorandum for the Commissioner, Oct. 15, 1936 (#152-Gen.), *ibid.*; Henry B. Hazard to Chicago district director, Aug. 31, 1937, *ibid.*

69   Charles P. Muller to "all examiners," Aug. 24, 1936, *ibid.*, box 8.

70   Robert C. Deming to D. W. MacCormack, Mar. 2, 1936, *ibid.*; I. F. Wixon to District Commissioner, Boston, Mar. 17, 1936, *ibid.*; Henry B. Hazard to Robert C. Deming, May 27, 1936, *ibid.*; Robert C. Deming, administrative letter to the Local Directors of Adult Education, Sept. 24, 1936, *ibid.*

71   Raymond D. Wilder to A. E. Burnett, Mar. 7, 1936, *ibid.* (in teaching the history of American government, Wilder wrote, "as we come down to the present year we take pains to see how the machine actually works. . . ." The metaphor died a very slow death); Mrs. Paul Scharf to Daniel MacCormack, June 23, 1936, *ibid.*; MacCormack to Mrs. Scharf, Aug. 6, 1936, *ibid.*; Summary of Conference Held by Naturalization Examiners

with Supervisors and Teachers of Naturalization, held at Boston on Oct. 16, 1936 (5 pp. of minutes), *ibid.*

72   Robert C. Deming to Henry B. Hazard, Sept. 29, 1936, *ibid.*

73   Frances Perkins to James L. Houghteling, Aug. 23, 1937, and Houghteling to Samuel Dickstein, Sept. 28, 1937, *ibid.*, box 9. See also Houghteling to Sen. Millard E. Tydings, Oct. 22, 1937, *ibid.* The purpose of the test, Houghteling explained, is to ensure "that when the alien takes the oath to support and defend the Constitution of the United States and to forswear his former allegiance, he understands what he is doing and is acting in good faith."

74   *Codification of the Nationality Laws of the United States,* 76th Congress, 1st Session (Washington, D.C., 1939), Part I, 39. See also 2–3, 19, 23.

75   Martin A. Roberts to Max Farrand, July 23 [1925?], Farrand Papers, HEH; Farrand to William Y. Elliott, Feb. 20, 1936, *ibid.*; Corwin to Farrand, Jan. 20, 1939, *ibid.*; James G. Randall to Andrew C. McLaughlin, Jan. 3, 1934, McLaughlin Papers, box 2, UCA. "I like your statement," Randall wrote his former teacher, "that the very consciousness of constitutional difficulties was in itself significant."

76   McLaughlin's major contribution was *A Constitutional History of the United States* (New York, 1935). The author attempted "to discuss those matters which in my own judgment the American citizen, not highly trained in the law, should know familiarly."

77   Powell, "Constitutional Interpretation and Misinterpretation," NR, 33 (Feb. 7, 1923), 297–98.

78   Powell, "Constitutional Metaphors," NR, 41 (Feb. 11, 1925), 314–15; Stone to Powell, Jan. 12, 1931, Powell Papers, box A, folder A13, HLSL; Rodell to Powell [June 1936?], *ibid.*, folder A12.

79   Beck to Taft, Oct. 24, 1929, Beck Papers, box 2, PUML; Llewellyn to Corwin, Aug. 11, 1936, Corwin Papers, box 2, PUML.

80   Taft to Warren, Oct. 28, 1922, Warren Papers, box 1, LCMD; Lodge to Warren, July 19, 1923, Lodge Papers, box 73; MHS; Warren to Lodge, July 30, 1923, *ibid.*

81   The influential essay is Warren, "New Light on the History of the Federal Judiciary Act of 1789," HLR, 37 (1923), 49–132. The decision is *Erie Railroad Co.* v. *Tompkins,* 304 U.S. 64 (1938); Warren's work is cited on pp. 72–73. See also Chief Justice William Howard Taft to Warren, Nov. 11, 1926, Warren Papers, box 2, LCMD.

82   *The Brooklyn Daily Eagle* [Mar. 11, 1920], clipping in scrapbooks pertaining to Supreme Court History, 1880–1935, #13, Record Group 267, NA.

83   David Dudley Field, "The Codes of New York and Codification in General," address given in Buffalo, Feb. 6, 1879, in Field, *Speeches, Arguments, and Miscellaneous Papers,* ed. by A. P. Sprague (New York, 1884), I, 379.

84   John Eben Bleekman to Beveridge, Jan. 14, 1920, Beveridge Papers, box 222, LCMD. See also James S. Beacom to Beveridge, July 12, 1920, *ibid.*; Beveridge to Robert E. O'Malley, July 21, 1920, and the enclosure attached to O'Malley's letter to Beveridge, July 16, 1920, *ibid.*; Robert W. De Forest to Beveridge, Nov. 22, 1920, *ibid.* For an anticipation of this de-

sire to popularize serious books about the U.S. Constitution, see Camillus G. Kidder to Max Farrand, Apr. 28, 1913, Farrand Papers, HEH.

85   Munro to Warren, Nov. 20, 1922, Warren Papers, box 1, LCMD. See also Rep. Harry B. Hawes to Warren, Feb. 10, 1923, *ibid.*; Alexander R. Lawton to Warren, Mar. 22, 1923, *ibid.*, box 2; Frank W. Stearns to Warren, Aug.1, 1923, *ibid.*; C. Lee Cook to Warren, Oct. 25, 1923, *ibid.*; W. R. Webb to Warren, Dec. 26, 1923, *ibid.*; F. G. Stutz to Warren, Jan. 19, 1924, *ibid.*; and John W. Davis to Warren, Sept. 28, 1932, *ibid.*

86   John E. McConnell to Warren, Oct. 28, 1924, *ibid.*; Davis to Josiah Marvel (chairman of the Committee on American Citizenship), Dec. 7, 1925, *ibid.*; E. L. Harvey to Warren, Feb. 14 and 16, 1924, *ibid.* Warren's 1928 volume, prepared for "the student, the layman, and the lawyer," was reissued in 1937 and 1947.

87   Beck to Borah, Oct. 31, 1919, Beck Papers, box 2, PUML; Beck to John A. Garver, Sept. 2, 1924, *ibid.*; Beck to Mellon, Oct. 23, 1924, and Jan. 10, 1925, *ibid.*, box 1; Beck to George H. Putnam, Sept. 11, 1928, *ibid.*, box 2; Beck to George H. Lorimer, May 15, 1922, Lorimer Papers, *Post* series, HSP; Lorimer to Beck, May 17, 1922, *ibid.*; NYT, Aug. 15, 1923, p. 12; NYT, Jan. 26, 1925, p. 5; Keller, *Beck and the Politics of Conservatism,* 157–60.

88   James M. Beck to Claude Bowers, Feb. 23, 1926, Beck Papers, box 2, PUML; NYT, Sept. 18, 1927, sec. 1, p. 21; NYT, Mar. 27, 1930, pp. 12, 26; W. L. Carpenter to Edward S. Corwin, Feb. 12, 1936, Corwin Papers, box 2, PUML; NYT, Sept. 10, 1936 and Feb. 14, 1937; telegram from Scott Howe Bowen to Corwin, Feb. 16, 1937, Corwin Papers, box 2; Edward W. Lane, Jr., to Corwin, Feb. 19, 1937, *ibid.*

89   Elizabeth Glendower Evans, "Mr. Justice Brandeis, the People's Tribune," RD, 20 (January 1932), 98; Jay Franklin, "Go Political, Young Man," *ibid.*, 25 (July 1934), 53–55; anon., "How We Got Our Constitution," *ibid.*, 29 (October 1936), 103–04; Marquis W. Childs, "The Supreme Court Today," *ibid.*, 32 (June 1938), 72–73; Theodore C. Wallen, "The Supreme Court—Nine Mortal Men," *Literary Digest,* 117 (Apr. 7, 1934), 9, 45–47.

90   Randolph G. Adams to Tracy W. McGregor, Sept. 17, 1934, McGregor Papers, Alderman Library, University of Virginia; NYT, June 16, 1935, sec. 7, p. 4; NYT, Aug. 5, 1935, p. 17; Joseph R. Strayer, ed., *The Delegate from New York* [John Lansing, Jr.]: *Proceedings of the Federal Convention of 1787* (Princeton, 1939); NYT, Sept. 13, 1936, sec. 2, p. 4; NYT, Sept. 20, 1936, sec. 2, p. 1; Barbara Melosh, "History as Drama: The Constitution in the Federal Theatre Project," *this Constitution,* 2 (Spring 1984), 9–19.

91   Beck, "A Rising or a Setting Sun?" CR, 8 (1924), 13.

92   Baker, *The Making and Keeping of the Constitution* (Williamsburg, Va., 1935), 19, 34. For a supporting view from a comparative scholarly perspective, see J. Lloyd Mecham, "Latin American Constitutions: Nominal and Real," JP, 21 (1959), 258–75.

93   NYT, July 8, 1937, p. 22.

94   E. L. Fuegel to David M. Matteson, Aug. 31, 1936, Matteson Papers, box 1, Record Group 200, NA.

•   CHAPTER 9 *Decisions Are Politics When Constitutional Questions Are Up for Decision*

1   Jerome N. Frank to Thomas Reed Powell, Feb. 5, 1931, Powell Papers, box A, folder 5, HLSL

2   William Howard Taft to Charles Warren, Oct. 28, 1922, Warren Papers, box 1, LCMD.

3   Warren to James M. Beck, Apr. 10, 1931, Beck Papers, box 2, PUML; Shaw's remarks recalled in NYT, Sept. 17, 1934, p. 16.

4   Quoted in Robert B. Highsaw, *Edward Douglass White: Defender of the Conservative Faith* (Baton Rouge, La., 1981), 164.

5   See Harold Josephson, "Political Justice During the Red Scare: The Trial of Benjamin Gitlow," in Michael R. Belknap, ed., *American Political Trials* (Westport, Conn., 1981), 153–75.

6   NYT, Dec. 10, 1918, p. 12; NYT, Dec. 12, 1918, p. 14; NYT, Dec. 14, 1918, p. 16.

7   See NYT, Mar. 11, 1919, p. 10; NYT, Mar. 12, 1919, p. 10; NYT, Apr. 2, 1919, p. 10; NYT, July 6, 1919, sec. 3, p. 2; NYT, Sept. 7, 1919, sec. 3, p. 1; NYT, Sept. 29, 1919, p. 12; NYT, Oct. 5, 1919, sec. 3, p. 2; NYT, Oct. 17, 1920, sec. 2, p. 2; NYT, June 24, 1923, sec. 2, p. 4; "The constitution weathered the storm and so will the league of nations covenant" (four-page pamphlet reprinted from the St. Louis *Post-Dispatch* and published by the League to Enforce Peace, n.d.).

8   Hill, "The Covenant or the Constitution?" NAR, 211 (March 1920), 321, 326, 328.

9   Henry Cabot Lodge to Max Farrand, May 11, 1920, Farrand Papers, HEH; Harding is quoted in NYT, Sept. 18, 1920, p. 14; C. A. Hereshoff Bartlett, "The Constitution or the League of Nations—Which?" *American Law Review*, 53 (1919), 513–34, the quotation at 513. See also Curtis P. Nettels, "The Washington Theme in American History," MHS *Proceedings*, 68 (1952), 184–85.

10 NYT, Jan. 18, 1915, p. 6; Ellen Nore, *Charles A. Beard: An Intellectual Biography* (Carbondale, Ill., 1983), 48; Charles G. Haines, *The American Doctrine of Judicial Supremacy* (2nd. ed.: Berkeley, Calif., 1932), 485–86.

11 Joseph R. Long, "Tinkering with the Constitution," CR, 2 (1918), 9, 13.

12 NYT, Feb. 23, 1919, sec. 1, p. 16; "Proposals to Change the Constitution," CR, 3 (1919), 168–69; LeRoy Ashby, *The Spearless Leader: Senator Borah and the Progressive Movement in the 1920s* (Urbana, Ill., 1972), 238–39. See also "Proposed Amendments to the Constitution," CR, 7 (1923), 123–27.

13 NYT, June 16, 1922, p. 20; NYT, June 21, 1925, sec. 9, p. 14; NYT, Jan. 29, 1933, sec. 8, p. 2; Charles G. Welch to James M. Beck, Aug. 2, 1933, Beck Papers, box 8, PUML; "Proposals to Change the Constitution," CR, 3 (1919), 175.

14 NYT, May 24, 1932, p. 11; Donald B. Johnson, ed., *National Party Platforms, 1840–1956* (Urbana, Ill., 1978), I, 353; *Commonweal*, 16 (July 13, 1932), 287.

15 FDR is quoted in William E. Leuchtenburg, "The Origins of Franklin D.

Roosevelt's 'Court-Packing' Plan," SCR (1966), 349. Donald Richberg quoted a bitter remark reported during the 1934 congressional elections: "You cannot eat the Constitution." See Richberg, "The Preservation of Constitutional Liberty under the New Deal," VSD, I (Dec. 3, 1934), 136. The point, needless to say, was that constitutional guarantees meant little without economic security and sustenance.

16 NYT, Mar. 26, 1933, sec. I, p. 9; NYT, Apr. 24, 1934, p. 25; Elliott, *The Need for Constitutional Reform: A Program for National Security* (New York, 1935), 183, 185, 206.

17 See *ibid.*, part III, esp. 204. See also Stephen B. Wood, *Constitutional Politics in the Progressive Era: Child Labor and the Law* (Chicago, 1968), esp. chs. 5 and 6.

18 John E. Semonche, *Charting the Future: The Supreme Court Responds to a Changing Society, 1890–1920* (Westport, Conn., 1978), 379, 411, 425.

19 Nore, *Beard: An Intellectual Biography*, 54; Jackson H. Ralston, "Judicial Control Over Legislatures as to Constitutional Questions," *American Law Review*, 54 (1920), 225.

20 David P. Thelen, *Robert M. LaFollette and the Insurgent Spirit* (Boston, 1976), 172–73, 180.

21 Hugh Henry Brown, "Our Generation and the Constitution," CR, 8 (1924), 140–51, esp. 140–42, 144–45; NYT, Oct. 30, 1924, p. 2; Hill, "The Assault on the Constitution and the Courts," CR, 9 (1925), 12–17.

22 Much of the pertinent material, both for and against, will be found in the Borah Papers, box 144, LCMD. See esp. Borah to W. P. Hamilton, Feb. 8, 1923; E. Ben Johnson to Borah, Feb. 28, 1923; Rose S. Young to Borah, Apr. 14, 1923; Fiorello LaGuardia to Borah, Oct. 31, 1923; Borah to La-Guardia, Nov. 1, 1923; Louis W. Cunningham to Borah, Jan. 8, 1924; H. E. Wayt to Borah, Feb. 8, 1924; and William A. Bemis to Borah, Feb. 8, 1923 (from Rochester, N.Y.): "It is high time something was done to limit the power of the Court of last resort . . . & if they are not brought up sharp, the time will come when they will practicaly rule the land. Many a good law they have throteled, in what they call, in the name of the Consti-tution. As presently constitud they are Ultra-Conservative, and no Liberal law that would benefit the people at large has a ghost of a show when brought before them. I am not a Socialist or Boshilwick, but I think it would be a mighty good thing for the common people if the Court was entirely abolished." The issue clearly aroused strong feelings among people with di-verse levels of education.

23 Ira Jewell Williams to Borah, Sept. 17, 1923, *ibid.*; Borah responded cor-dially on Sept. 24, 1923, *ibid.*; Louis A. Coolidge to the "radical senators," n.d., *ibid.*, box 168; Borah to Coolidge, Dec. 10, 1923, *ibid.*

24 Borah to J. Ward Arney, Jan. 2, 1924, *ibid.*; Ashby, *Borah and the Progressive Movement in the 1920s*, 32–33; Alan H. Monroe, "The Su-preme Court and the Constitution," APSR, 18 (1924), 737–59.

25 Warren, "Borah and LaFollette vs. the Supreme Court," *Saturday Evening Post* (Oct. 13, 1923), 31, 190, 192–94; Beveridge, "Common Sense and the Constitution," *ibid.*, Dec. 15, 1923, 25, 119, 121, 122, 125, 126, 129.

26 Warren, "The Early History of the United States in Connection with Mod-ern Attacks on the Judiciary" (an address delivered to the Massachusetts

Bar Association at Salem on Oct. 14, 1922, published in pamphlet form and mailed widely in February 1923); Sen. Bert M. Fernald to Warren, Feb. 14, 1923, Warren Papers, box 2, LCMD; John W. Davis to Warren, Feb. 23, 1923, *ibid.* ("I always hear any criticism of the Supreme Court with about as much tolerance as I do that of the Bible. I want to feel that the Court is right even if I think it wrong"); Moorfield Storey to Warren, Sept. 9, 1923, *ibid.*; Benjamin Loring Young to Warren, Oct. 23, 1923, *ibid.*; F. G. Stutz for the West Publishing Company to Warren, Jan. 19, 1924, *ibid.*; Albert Bushnell Hart to Warren, May 2, 1924, Hart Papers, box 4, HUPL.

27   Rep. Henry St. George Tucker to Warren, July 15, 1926, Warren Papers, box 2, LCMD; George W. Anderson to Warren, Sept. 17, 1928, and June 19, 1929, *ibid.*; Warren to Anderson, July 11, 1929, *ibid.*

28   Albert B. Hart to Lloyd Taylor, Apr. 4, 1924, Hart Papers, box 26, HUPL; Taylor to Hart, Apr. 17, 1924, *ibid.*; Bertha Golde to board of directors of the National Security League, Sept. 21, 1927, *ibid.*, box 20.

29   Powell, "Why Curb the Courts?" *The Nation,* 121 (Dec. 23, 1925), 736–37; Warren to Powell, Jan. 28, 1926, Powell Papers, box A, HLSL; Powell to Warren, Feb. 1, 1926, Warren Papers, box 2, LCMD.

30   Carson to Beck, Dec. 22, 1924, and Beck to Carson, Jan. 30, 1925, Beck Papers, box 7, 1925, PUML; Bayard Henry to Charles Warren, Feb. 3, 1925, Warren Papers, box 2, LCMD; Beck, *Our Changing Constitution* (Williamsburg, Va., 1927); Morton Keller, *In Defense of Yesterday: James M. Beck and the Politics of Conservatism, 1861–1936* (New York, 1958), 182, 195–96.

31   See Beveridge, "Common Sense and the Constitution," *Saturday Evening Post,* Dec. 15, 1923, 125.

32   See Walter F. Murphy, "In His Own Image: Mr. Chief Justice Taft and Supreme Court Appointments," SCR (1961), 159–93; Taft to Henry Cabot Lodge, Jan. 17, 1922, Lodge Papers, MHS; Alpheus Thomas Mason, *Brandeis: A Free Man's Life* (New York, 1956), 470.

33   "Sutherland," DAB, *Supplement* II. For thoughtful reflections on the manner of selecting Supreme Court justices at that time, see Thomas Reed Powell to Harlan Fiske Stone, Oct. 9, 1928, and Stone to Powell, Oct. 15, 1928, Powell Papers, box A, folder 2, HLSL.

34   Theodore Roosevelt to Miles Poindexter, May 22, 1918, in Elting E. Morison, ed., *The Letters of Theodore Roosevelt* (Cambridge, Mass., 1954), VIII, 1322; Lodge to Bryce, Aug. 2, 1918, Lodge Papers, box 45, MHS. Al Smith of New York is known to have quipped that in time of war, "we adjourn the Constitution." It is noteworthy, however, that he chose the word "adjourn" rather than "abolish." See Gerald W. Johnson, *America-Watching: Perspectives in the Course of an Incredible Century* (Owings Mills, Md., 1976), 303.

35   Beck, *Our Changing Constitution* (Williamsburg, Va., 1927), 23–24.

36   NYT, May 31, 1925, p. 1; Beck, *The Vanishing Rights of the States* (New York, 1926); Henry L. Shattuck to Lodge, Mar. 27, 1922, and Lodge to Shattuck, Mar. 29, 1922, Lodge Papers, box 68, MHS.

37   See Paul L. Murphy, *The Constitution in Crisis Times, 1918–1969* (New

York, 1972), 11, 148; Peter Odegard, "The Future of States' Rights," NAR, 240 (September 1935), 241; William O. Douglas, *The Court Years, 1939–1975: Autobiography* (New York, 1980), 37.

38   Anon., "The Supreme Court's Shift to Liberalism," *The Literary Digest,* 109 (June 13, 1931), 8; D. E. Wolf, "The Supreme Court in a New Phase," CH, 34 (1931), 590–93; Joseph Percival Pollard, "Our Supreme Court Goes Liberal," *Forum and Century,* 86 (1931), 193–99; Zechariah Chafee, Jr., "Liberal Trends in the Supreme Court," CH, 35 (1931), 338–44.

39   Oliver McKee, Jr., "A Liberal Supreme Court," *Outlook and Independent,* 159 (Oct. 7, 1931), 171–73. See also Paul L. Murphy, "*Near v. Minnesota* in the Context of Historical Developments," *Minnesota Law Review,* 66 (1981), 95–160.

40   Walton H. Hamilton, "The Legal Philosophy of Justices Holmes and Brandeis," CH, 33 (1931), 654–60; A.F.C., "Backstage in Washington," *Outlook and Independent,* 158 (June 10, 1931), 170; Joseph Percival Pollard, "Four New Dissenters," NR, 68 (Sept. 2, 1931), 61–64; Dudley C. Lunt, "Let X = Roberts and Y = Hughes," *The World's Work,* 60 (October 1931), 46–47; and Robert S. Rankin, "President Hoover and the Supreme Court," SAQ, 30 (1931), 438.

41   The notion of the Court's home as a "temple" predated 1935 by almost two generations. At the Centennial on Sept. 17, 1887, Cardinal Gibbons had invoked the image in his closing prayer. The superintendent of the Capitol envisioned a "Temple of Justice" in 1911, and by 1926 that idea had become widespread. See Hampton L. Carson, ed., *History of the Celebration of the One Hundredth Anniversary of the Promulgation of the Constitution of the United States* (Philadelphia, 1889), II, 298; Scrapbooks on Supreme Court History, 1880–1935; Record Group 267, NA, #11, p. 17, and #13, p. 34; *The Washington Post,* Oct. 7, 1935, p. 1.

42   *The Supreme Court Chamber, 1810–1860* (13-page pamphlet published by the U.S. Senate Commission on Art and Antiquities, 1981); Supreme Court Scrapbook #3, p. 14 (clipping from the *New York Star,* Feb. 2, 1890); Charles Moore to William Howard Taft, May 29, 1929, Cass Gilbert Papers, box 12, LCMD.

43   See Gilbert's revealing and explanatory letter to Beck, Nov. 28, 1933, *ibid.,* box 15; Beck to Gilbert, Dec. 6, 1933, *ibid.*

44   See esp. the entry in Gilbert's diary for Dec. 19, 1929, Gilbert Papers, box 1, LCMD; Gilbert to his wife, Julie, Apr. 10, 1929, and Apr. 26, 1930, *ibid.,* boxes 12 and 13; Charles Moore to Gilbert, June 12, 1929, *ibid.,* box 12; Wendell W. Mischler to Gilbert, Feb. 5, 1930, *ibid.,* box 13; William P. MacCracken, Jr., to Gilbert, Sept. 23, 1932, *ibid.;* Gilbert to Sir Reginald Bloomfield, Apr. 5, 1933, *ibid.,* box 14.

45   Gilbert's diary, May 18, 1927, *ibid.,* box 13. For context, see John P. Diggins, *Mussolini and Fascism: The View from America* (Princeton, 1972), ch. 4, "Mussolini as American Hero." Diggins's thorough study does not mention Cass Gilbert.

46   Gilbert to Mussolini, Aug. 11, 1932, from Perthshire, Scotland, Gilbert Papers, box 13, LCMD.

47   Typed memoir simply entitled "Mussolini," dated Rome, June 6, 1933,

ibid., box 17. The interview took place in the Palazzo Venezia. This extract is taken from pp. 10–15. Gilbert also had some sympathy for Hitler as an anti-Communist "stopper." See Gilbert to G. B. Rose, Oct. 4, 1933, *ibid.*, box 14.

48 Taft to Gilbert, Feb. 15, 1932, *ibid.*, box 13.

49 *The Washington Post,* June 4, 1935, p. 1; NYT, June 4, 1935, p. 8; Van Devanter to Robert H. Kelley, June 3, 1935, Van Devanter Papers, box 18, LCMD; Van Devanter to Mrs. John W. Lacey, Oct. 7, 1935, *ibid.*; Van Devanter to Sterling Myer, Oct. 23, 1935, *ibid.*

50 *Herald Tribune,* Oct. 6, 1935, sec. 2, p. 1.

51 NYT, July 8, 1934, sec. 1, pp. 1, 18. "Emasculation" became a popular codeword among traditional constitutionalists. See the remarks of Miss Sybil Holmes, Assistant Attorney General of Massachusetts, NYT, Jan. 21, 1934, sec. 2, pp. 1, 3; and F. M. Gillingham to Rep. Joe Hendricks, Mar. 1, 1937, Hendricks Papers, box 2, UFYL.

52 NYT, Jan. 28, 1934, sec. 1, p. 13; NYT, Sept. 20, 1934, p. 22.

53 NYT, Sept. 3, 1933, sec. 1, p. 15; NYT, Sept. 23, 1934, sec. 4, p. 5; George Whitefield Betts to Edward S. Corwin, Sept. 14, 1936, Corwin Papers, box 2, PUML.

54 NYT, Dec. 22, 1933, p. 4; NYT, Feb. 6, 1934, p. 20; NYT, Aug. 30, 1934, p. 9; NYT, July 5, 1935, p. 3; Nettels, "Washington Theme in American History," 191–92; Merrill D. Peterson, *The Jefferson Image in the American Mind* (New York, 1960), 363–76.

55 Frank W. Clark to James M. Beck, May 28, 1933, Beck Papers, box 3, PUML; NYT, Apr. 29, 1934, sec. 4, p. 5; NYT, May 28, 1934, p. 21; NYT, June 17, 1934, sec. 1, p. 8; NYT, Oct. 2, 1934, p. 3; Keller, *Beck and the Politics of Conservatism,* 268.

56 "Liberty League Lawyers," NR, 84 (Oct. 2, 1935), 203; "A Conspiracy by Lawyers," *The Nation,* 141 (Oct. 2, 1935), 369; George Wolfskill, *The Revolt of the Conservatives: A History of the American Liberty League, 1934–1940* (Boston, 1962).

57 A collection of these pamphlets will be found in the William E. Borah Papers, box 811, LCMD. See also Raoul E. Desvernine, *Democratic Despotism* (New York, 1936), a book-length statement of the Liberty League's understanding of American constitutionalism. Desvernine served as chairman of the League's lawyers committee.

58 Van Devanter to Mrs. John W. Lacey, April 18, 1934, Van Devanter papers, letterbook 48, box 18, LCMD.

59 NYT, Oct. 1, 1934, pp. 1, 3.

60 NYT, June 12, 1934, p. 18; NYT, July 7, 1934, p. 24; NYT, July 10, 1934, p. 2; Moore to Douglas Southall Freeman, Oct. 16, 1935, Freeman Papers, box 25, LCMD.

61 NYT, Aug. 28, 1934, p. 2; NYT, Sept. 4, 1934, p. 6; NYT, Sept. 23, 1934, sec. 4, p. 4; NYT, May 26, 1934, p. 16; clipping of a letter by S. Boyd Darling from NYT, September 1934, in the Col. John Bigelow Papers, box 70, LCMD.

62 McLaughlin to Edward S. Corwin, Jan. 14, 1936, Corwin Papers, box 2, PUML; NYT, Aug. 31, 1934, p. 6.

63 NYT, Aug. 29, 1934, p. 4; NYT, Sept. 9, 1934, sec. 8, pp. 3, 10.

64   Henry M. Hart, Jr., to Zechariah Chafee, Jr., Jan. 4, 1934, Hart Papers, box 1, folder 22, HLSL; Hart, "The Constitution Is What the Judges Say It Is," typescript [1935–36], *ibid.*, box 24, folder 3; Alanson W. Willcox to Thomas Reed Powell, Jan. 11, 1936, and Powell to Willcox, Jan. 12, 1935, Powell Papers, box A, folder 13, HLSL.

65   Corwin, *The Twilight of the Supreme Court: A History of Our Constitutional Theory* (New Haven, Conn., 1934), a book that Henry M. Hart called "the best general introduction to the constitutionality of the New Deal"; Arnold to Corwin, Oct. 5, 1936, Corwin Papers, box 1, PUML; Corwin, "The Constitution as Instrument and Symbol," APSR, 30 (1936), 1072–85.

66   Rev. Leo C. Pollack to Cardozo, May 22, 1936, copy in Corwin Papers, box 2, PUML. Some individuals got excessively carried away. One man wrote to FDR on Jan. 7, 1936, that "I'm in favor of doing away with the Constitution if it's going to interfere with the general welfare of the people." Quoted in Leuchtenburg, "Origins of Roosevelt's 'Court-Packing' Plan," SCR (1966), 366.

67   NYT, Feb. 24, 1935, sec. 4, p. 1. For McReynolds's dissent, see 294 U.S. 361–81. For a very surprising and unknown follow-up story, see NYT, June 9, 1935, sec. 1, p. 3.

68   Maurice G. Baxter, *One and Inseparable: Daniel Webster and the Union* (Cambridge, Mass., 1984), 444.

69   Broun, *It Seems to Me, 1925–1935* (New York, 1935), 320.

70   Once again there seem to have been anticipations of the phrase. Woodrow Wilson had written in 1908 that "the Constitution was not meant to hold the government back to the time of horses and wagons. . . ." *Constitutional Government in the United States* (New York, 1908), 169. For FDR's press conference, see *The Washington Post,* June 1, 1935, p. 2; Drew Pearson and Robert S. Allen, *The Nine Old Men* (New York, 1936), 271–72. For some of the echoes, see Joseph Ginsberg to Joseph Hendricks, Feb. 10, 1937, Hendricks Papers, box 2, UFYL; Bishop Freeman's remarks at the Sesquicentennial service in Washington National Cathedral, Washington *Evening Star,* Sept. 20, 1937, p. B4; Walter F. Murphy, *Congress and the Court: A Case Study in the American Political Process* (Chicago, 1962), 174.

71   See Michael E. Parrish, *Felix Frankfurter and His Times: The Reform Years* (New York, 1982), 262–63, 266–67; Leuchtenburg, "Origins of Roosevelt's 'Court-Packing' Plan," SCR (1966), 363, 373; Willis Van Devanter to Dennis T. Flynn, Dec. 5, 1935, Van Devanter Papers, box 19, LCMD; Harold L. Ickes, *The Secret Diary: The First Thousand Days, 1933–1936* (New York, 1953), I, 524.

72   "Majority Opinion," in Heywood Hale Broun, ed., *Collected Edition of Heywood Broun* (New York, 1941), 343, 345. See also p. 396 for Broun's support of FDR's "Court-packing" plan in 1937.

73   Powell to Becker, Apr. 6, 1936, Powell Papers, box A, folder 3, HLSL; Powell to Robert L. Schuyler, Sept. 21, 1936, *ibid.*, folder 12.

74   "Horse and Buggy Days," in *Both Sides,* 1 (September 1936), 45–52.

75   Wallace, *Whose Constitution? An Inquiry into the General Welfare* (New York, 1936), 323. "Under the present interpretation of the Constitution by the Supreme Court, it is not possible to devise a national program which works toward both long-time and short-time objectives" (p. 281).

76 *Storm Over the Constitution* (Indianapolis, 1936), 23. Brant wrote to Virginius Dabney on Mar. 21, 1975, that "Tom Corcoran told me that F.D.R. took the book with him on a South American cruise and that it was a prime factor in his decision to shift from a constitutional amendment to reform of the Supreme Court." Brant Papers, box 5, LCMD.

77 Beard, "Rendezvous with the Supreme Court," NR, 88 (Sept. 2, 1936), 92–94. For the conventional rhetoric of "sacred document" and "sacred history," see William E. Borah, "Constitutional Government," VSD, 4 (Oct. 15, 1937), 4–5.

78 See Thomas, "A Socialist Looks at the Constitution," and W. Y. Elliott, "Getting a New Constitution," AAAPSS, 185 (1936), 92–101, 115–22.

79 Arnold, *The Symbols of Government* (New Haven, Conn., 1935), 231. See also Walton H. Hamilton and Douglass Adair, *The Power to Govern: The Constitution—Then and Now* (New York, 1937), 184–86.

80 R. M. Pettey (on behalf of the National Association for the Calling of a United States Constitutional Convention, based in New York City) to Edward S. Corwin, Sept. 10, 1936, Corwin Papers, box 2, PUML; Judson King to Corwin, Apr. 15, 1937, *ibid.*; John C. Fitzpatrick to Sol Bloom, Mar. 17, 1936, Fitzpatrick Papers, box 16, LCMD.

81 Creel, "Roosevelt's Plans and Purposes," *Collier's*, Dec. 26, 1936, 7–9, 39–40. See also *Collier's* editorial on p. 54; and the mimeographed call for a "Meeting on the Constitution" to be held Jan. 22–24, 1937, at the Brookings Institution in Washington, D.C., Corwin Papers, box 2, PUML.

82 In addition to Leuchtenburg, "Origins of Roosevelt's 'Court-Packing' Plan," SCR (1966), 347–400, see Leuchtenburg, "Franklin D. Roosevelt's Court 'Packing' Plan," in Harold M. Hollingsworth, ed., *Essays on the New Deal* (Austin, Tex., 1969), 69–115.

83 Curtis Basch to Rep. Joe Hendricks, Feb. 9, 1937, Hendricks Papers, box 2, UFYL; Alec Baker to Hendricks, Feb. 10, 1937, *ibid.*; Paul Bakewell to Willis Van Devanter, Mar. 2, 1937, Van Devanter Papers, box 38, LCMD.

84 See Leuchtenburg, "Origins of Roosevelt's 'Court-Packing' Plan," SCR (1966), 354, 359; "Meeting on the Constitution," Jan. 22–24, 1937, Corwin Papers, box 2, PUML.

85 Claudius O. Johnson, *Borah of Idaho* (2nd ed.: Seattle, Wash., 1967), 490–93; Ashby, *Borah and the Progressive Movement in the 1920s*, 238–40; Borah, "The Supreme Court," RD, 28 (March 1936), 1–6; a reprint of the *Redbook* essay appeared in CREC on Jan. 6, 1936, copy in Borah Papers, box 809, LCMD; Borah, "Constitutional Government," VSD, 4 (Oct. 15, 1937), 7.

86 NYT, Sept. 18, 1937, pp. 1, 3. See also NYT, Sept. 17, 1937, pp. 1, 20; Hugh S. Johnson, "Why Have Any Constitution at All?—If we're not going to follow it," VSD, 4 (Oct. 15, 1937), 8–12.

87 NYT, Aug. 4, 1937, p. 11; NYT, Sept. 18, 1937, pp. 2, 3.

88 NYT, Sept. 29, 1937, p. 22; NYT, Oct. 9, 1937, p. 18; NYT, Oct. 17, 1937, sec. 4, p. 8; NYT, Apr. 24, 1938, sec. 1, p. 2; William Y. Elliott, *The Crisis of the American Constitution* (Williamsburg, Va., 1938), 13–17; and Marquis W. Childs, "The Supreme Court To-Day," *Harper's Magazine*, 176 (1938), 581–88.

89   In addition to Elliott and Childs, cited in the previous note, see Max Farrand to Benjamin M. Anderson, Jr., Mar. 1, 1937, and Anderson to Farrand, Mar. 4, 1937, Farrand Papers, HEH; Farrand to Charles G. Haines, May 29, 1937, *ibid.*; Lois C. Kimball Rosenberry to Farrand, Sept. 30 [1937], *ibid.*

90   C. Herman Pritchett, *The Roosevelt Court: A Study in Judicial Politics and Values, 1937–1947* (Chicago, 1948).

91   See Louis D. Brandeis to Harlan F. Stone, Sept. 7, 1931, Stone Papers, box 73, LCMD; Stone to Brandeis, June 23, 1936, *ibid.*; Brandeis to Stone, Aug. 5, 1936, *ibid.*; Stone to James F. Byrnes, Dec. 7, 1941, *ibid.*, box 74; Stone to E. S. Corwin, Sept. 7, 1941, Corwin Papers, box 1, PUML.

92   For an excellent discussion of this point, see Edward S. Corwin, *Constitutional Revolution, Ltd.* (Claremont, Calif., 1941), 8–9. In 1933, Rexford Tugwell called Hamilton "the father of our Constitution." See Tugwell, "Ideas Behind the New Deal," NYT *Sunday Magazine,* Aug. 20, 1933, sec. 4, p. 5.

93   Desvernine, *Democratic Despotism, 243;* Corwin, *Commerce Power versus States Rights,* ix; see also NYT, Sept. 12, 1927, p. 27.

94   Beck to Claude Bowers, Feb. 18, 1926, Beck Papers, box 2, PUML; Gaillard Hunt, "Madison, the Statesman," CR, 5 (1921), 14–18; the program for Madison Memorial Day, June 28, 1934, chaired by Sen. Harry F. Byrd of Virginia, Lyon G. Tyler Papers, Group I, box 24, WMSL; Brant, *Storm Over the Constitution,* 92.

95   William E. Borah, "Constitutional Government," VSD, 4 (Oct. 15, 1937), 4; NYT, Mar. 7, 1938, p. 16; NYT, Feb. 6, 1938, sec. 8, p. 5; and NYT, June 1, 1938, p. 6.

96   See Thomas R. Maddux, *Years of Estrangement: American Relations with the Soviet Union, 1933–1941* (Gainesville, Fla., 1980), 74–77; NYT, Oct. 7, 1937, p. 25; NYT, Oct. 12, 1937, p. 20; David Matteson to Sol Bloom, Oct. 8, 1937, Matteson Papers, box 1, NA.

97   Karl Dietrich Bracher, "Stages of Totalitarian 'Integration': The Consolidation of National Socialist Rule in 1933 and 1934," in Hajo Holborn, ed., *Republic to Reich: The Making of the Nazi Revolution* (New York, 1972), 111–12, 114; Bracher, *The German Dictatorship: The Origins, Structure, and Effects of National Socialism* (New York, 1970), 48, 69, 75, 110, 170, 175, 193–95, 208, 232.

98   Evva Skelton Tomb to Edward S. Corwin, Mar. 17, 1937, Corwin Papers, PUML; NYT, July 20, 1937, p. 2; NYT, Sept. 17, 1937, p. 24; Frank O. Miller, *Minobe Tatsukichi: Interpreter of Constitutionalism in Japan* (Berkeley, Calif., 1965), ch. 6, "Constitutional Government in Crisis."

99   These representative statements come from a debate between Henry M. Hart, Jr., (pro), and Charles C. Burlingham (con) in "The United States Supreme Court," *Harvard Alumni Bulletin,* 39 (Apr. 16, 1937), 767–73, esp. 767 and 773. See also Appendix C on pp. 407–09, H. L. Mencken's "A Constitution for the New Deal" (1937).

100   Louis O. Van Doren to Edward S. Corwin, Feb. 18 and Mar. 11, 1937, Corwin Papers, box 2, PUML; Alpheus T. Mason and William M. Beaney, *The Supreme Court in a Free Society* (Englewood Cliffs, N.J., 1959), ch. 1, esp. p. 1.

CHAPTER 10 *My God! Making a Racket out of the Constitution*

1   Washington *Evening Star,* Apr. 20, 1937, pp. 1, 4. See the interesting mixed metaphor produced by the George Washington Centennial planners in 1889: "It is the hope of the committee that this souvenir volume may obtain wide circulation. They believe that its pages contain patriotic germs which should sink deep into the minds and hearts of the young, and hereafter bear fruit that will be for the glory of the republic." *The Nation's Birthday: Chicago's Centennial Celebration of Washington's Inauguration, April 30, 1889* (Chicago, 1889), v.

2   NYT, Sept. 7, 1937, p. 8.

3   David M. Matteson to Sol Bloom, Oct. 24, 1933, Matteson Papers, box 1, Record Group 200, NA; M. E. Gilfond to Matteson, Apr. 6, 1934, *ibid.*; NYT, Sept. 16, 1933, p. 15; Dixon Ryan Fox to Julian P. Boyd, Feb. 16, 1934, Fox Papers, box 3, NYSHA.

4   John C. Fitzpatrick to Bloom, Mar. 25, 1935, Fitzpatrick Papers, box 16, LCMD.

5   Ashurst's speech, Senate Joint Resolution 59, p. 3, Feb. 14, 1935, 74th Congress, 1st Session; *Report of the U.S. Constitution Sesquicentennial Commission,* House Document no. 311, 74th Congress, 2d Session (Washington, D.C., 1936), esp. 2–3, 5–6, 8, 10.

6   *Report of the U.S. Constitution Sesquicentennial Commission,* 14–15, 22–26, 29–34.

7   *Ibid.,* 20–21, 34–35, 36–40. See also Bloom to Mrs. John Henry Hammond, Jan. 18, 1936, and Bloom to Mrs. Cass Gilbert, Mar. 20 and May 6, 1936, Cass Gilbert Papers, box 15, LCMD.

8   *The Autobiography of Sol Bloom* (New York, 1948), 222; Sol Bloom, ed., *Our Heritage: George Washington and the Establishment of the American Union* (New York, 1944), 254–356; Bloom to John C. Fitzpatrick, and Fitzpatrick to Bloom, Aug. 10 and 12, 1935, Fitzpatrick Papers, box 16, LCMD.

9   Bloom to Fitzpatrick, May 6, 1936, and Fitzpatrick to Bloom, May 1936, *ibid.*; NYT, Apr. 21, 1935, sec. 1, p. 24; NYT, Oct. 11, 1936, p. E9.

10   See Fuegel to Fitzpatrick, July 29, 1936, Fitzpatrick Papers, box 16, LCMD.

11   Matteson to Bloom Feb. 10, 1937, Matteson Papers, box 1, NA; Matteson to Bloom, Feb. 14, 1936, and Bloom to Matteson, Feb. 15, 1936, *ibid.*

12   Fuegel to Fitzpatrick, Apr. 21, 1936, and Fitzpatrick to Fuegel, Apr. 23, 1936, Fitzpatrick Papers, box 16, LCMD.

13   Fitzpatrick to Bloom, Feb. 3, 1936, referring to an editorial, NYT, Jan. 25, 1936; Fitzpatrick to Bloom, three-page memo [n.d., May 1936?]; Fuegel to Fitzpatrick, Aug. 3, 1936, *ibid.*

14   Fitzpatrick to Bloom, Feb. 10, 1936, *ibid.*; "Last Resort," *Collier's,* Feb. 15, 1936, 78.

15   Bloom to Fitzpatrick, Aug. 30, 1935, and Fitzpatrick to Bloom, Sept. 16, 1935, Fitzpatrick Papers, box 16, LCMD. See also Bloom to Fitzpatrick, May 15, 1936, and Fitzpatrick to Bloom, June 2, 1936, *ibid.*; Fitzpatrick to

Bloom, July 6, 1936, and Mar. 1, 1937, *ibid.*; John Overton to Matteson, Sept. 25, 1937, Matteson Papers, box 1. (Matteson had supplied Senator Overton of Louisiana with materials and ideas for a speech presented in New Orleans on Constitution Day before the Society of the Sons of the American Revolution.) Bloom to Matteson, Dec. 7, 1937, *ibid.* ("Please get me several good quotations by Americans in praise of the Constitution, in place of Gladstone's famous remark. They should be short enough to go on a Christmas card.")

16   See Matteson's five-page memorandum with Fuegel's cover sheet, dated July 29, 1936, attached, *ibid.*; Matteson to Bloom, Aug. 31, 1936, *ibid.* Matteson found Adams's address "a long-winded affair."

17   *Autobiography of Sol Bloom,* 222.

18   Drafts and texts of these speeches will be found in Record Group 148, Minor Congressional Commissions: Records of Exposition, Anniversary, and Memorial Commissions, box 14, NA (Legislative & Diplomatic Branch); and in Matteson Papers, box 1, NA.

19   The platitude is from "The Heart and Soul of the Constitution," Aug. 21, 1937 (Washington, D.C., 1938), 8; Bloom to Matteson, July 20, 1937, Matteson Papers, box 1, NA: Bloom to Fitzpatrick, July 20, 1937, Fitzpatrick Papers, box 16, LCMD.

20   Fitzpatrick to Bloom, Oct. 21, 1935, *ibid.* (concerning a book for teenagers called *The Story of Our Country*); a commercial film made by MGM, *Servant of the People: The Story of the Constitution of the United States,* opened in January 1937 but did not enjoy a long run; Fitzpatrick to Bloom, June 7, 1937, *ibid.* (concerning "Know Your Constitution," published in Rochester, N.Y., by the *Democrat and Chronicle* and distributed by the Council for Better Citizenship of the Rochester Chamber of Commerce); Matteson to Bloom, Sept. 24, 1937, Matteson Papers, box 1.

21   Matteson to Bloom, Apr. 21, 1936, Matteson Papers, *ibid.*; Fitzpatrick to Bloom, Apr. 6, 1936; Bloom to Fitzpatrick, Oct. 28, 1937, and Fitzpatrick to Bloom, Oct. 29, 1937, Fitzpatrick Papers, box 16, LCMD.

22   Bloom to Fitzpatrick, Feb. 24, 1937, *ibid.*; Matteson to Bloom, Feb. 27, 1937, Matteson Papers, box 1; NYT, June 12, 1937, p. 21; NYT, June 15, 1937, p. 22.

23   Frank Kent, "The Game of Politics," *Boston Evening Transcript,* Mar. 17, 1937; NYT, Sept. 18, 1937, pp. 1, 4, for the text of FDR's address; Matteson to Bloom, Sept. 23, 1937, Matteson Papers, box 1, NA.

24   NYT, July 5, 1937, p. 2; Roosevelt to George White, *et al.,* Apr. 20, 1935, Papers of the Northwest Territory Celebration Commission, Minnesota Historical Society, Manuscripts Division.

25   Edward Stern & Co. to Sol Bloom, Sept. 21, 1936, in Minor Congressional Commissions, Record Group 148, box 13, NA; Herman H. Diers to Sol Bloom, Mar. 1 and Aug. 12, 1937, *ibid.*, box 12; Owen Kane to Mr. Crawford, Aug. 16, 1937, *ibid.*; Phoenix *Republic and Gazette* to Sol Bloom, July 2, 1937, *ibid.*; Thomas W. Briggs Company to Bloom, Jan. 29, 1937, and Matteson to Bloom, Feb. 8, 1937, Matteson Papers, box 1, NA.

26   A copy of "A Message to Merchants" in *ibid.*

27   Sol Bloom to Mr. Melvin, late April 1937, *ibid.* In May 1938 Pennsylvania politicians fell to fighting among themselves for the use of Independence

Hall on favored occasions. The major antagonists were Mayor Wilson and Governor Earle. See NYT, May 27, 1938, p. 6; NYT, May 28, 1938, p. 2; NYT, May 31, 1938, p. 18.

28 Edward Hopkinson, Jr., to Mrs. K. M. Knox, Apr. 6, 1937; Pennsylvania Academy of Fine Arts to Bloom, Apr. 15, 1937, U.S. Sesquicentennial Commission Papers, box 11, Record Group 148, NA; John P. Rossi, "Philadelphia's Forgotten Mayor: S. Davis Wilson," *Pennsylvania History,* 51 (1984), 162; Fitzpatrick to Bloom, Jan. 13, 1938, Fitzpatrick Papers, box 16, LCMD.

29 NYT, May 1, 1937, p. 15; *Philadelphia Inquirer,* May 2, 1937, pp. 8, 14, May 8, p. 19, May 9, pp. 1, 10, May 14, p. 14, May 15, p. 3, May 16, p. 3, May 24, p. 3, all 1937.

30 NYT, May 16, 1937, sec. 2, p. 8; NYT, May 24, 1937, p. 22: *Philadelphia Inquirer,* May 2, 1937, p. 8; *ibid.,* May 8, p. 19; *ibid.,* June 21, 1937. p. 2; NYT, July 18, 1937, sec. 1, p. 26.

31 *Philadelphia Inquirer,* Sept. 3, p. 4; Sept. 5, p. 1; Sept. 6, p. 8; Sept. 11, pp. 1, 3; Sept. 12, pp. 1, 6, 8, 19; Sept. 13, pp. 1, 10, 17; Sept. 16, p. 1; Sept. 18, pp. 4, 8.

32 *Ibid.,* Sept. 13, p. 9; Sept. 14, p. 17; Sept. 27, p. 2; NYT, Sept. 18, 1937, p. 2.

33 NYT, May 18, p. 14; NYT, Sept. 9, p. 12; NYT, Sept. 19, sec. 1, p. 42; *Philadelphia Inquirer,* Sept. 19, 1937, p. 4.

34 NYT, Sept. 16, 1937, p. 25; Washington *Evening Star,* Sept. 9, 1937, p. 8.

35 The remarkable nine-paragraph broadside (ca. August 1937), prepared by Horace G. Murphy, appears in Record Group 148, Minor Congressional Commissions, box 12, NA; for samples of Kane's form letter, dated Aug. 20, 1937, see *ibid.,* box 10.

36 Washington *Sunday Star,* Sept. 12, 1937, B4; NYT, Sept. 12, 1937, sec. 1, p. 4; *Philadelphia Inquirer,* Sept. 7, 1937, p. 10; *ibid.,* Sept. 15, 1937, p. 19; Frank L. Polk to Max Farrand, June 23, 1937, Farrand Papers, HEH; NYT, June 20, 1937, sec. 6, p. 19; NYT, Aug. 22, 1937, sec. 7, p. 22.

37 For a catalogue of the New York Public Library show, see Minor Congressional Commissions, box 12, Record Group 148; NA: NYT, Jan. 2, 1938, sec. 2, p. 4; NYT, Jan. 26, 1936, sec. 2, p. 1; NYT, Sept. 5, 1937, sec. 2, p. 2; NYT, Sept. 18, 1937, p. 2; NYT, July 3, 1937, p. 17; NYT, June 3, 1937, p. 8; NYT, June 4, 1937, p. 26.

38 David M. Matteson to H. E. Kjorlie, Sept. 16 and Oct. 19, 1937, Matteson Papers, box 1, NA; Benjamin W. Blanchard and Russell Duane, *Your America: Its Constitution and Its Laws* (Philadelphia, 1936); George L. Knapp and Ellen L. Buell, *The Story of Our Constitution* (New York, 1936); Wilson Parkhill and Ellen L. Buell, *The Constitution Explained* (New York, 1936): Burton J. Hendrick, *Bulwark of the Republic: A Biography of the Constitution* (Boston, 1937); NYT *Magazine,* May 9, 1937, sec. 8, pp. 12–13, 24; *ibid.,* Sept. 12, 1937, sec. 8, pp. 1–2, 19; *ibid.,* pp. 3, 21; 50 essays on "The Making of the Constitution" by Tully Nettleton, *The Christian Science Monitor,* May 20–Sept. 17, 1937, published subsequently in booklet form; John C. Fitzpatrick to Sol Bloom, Mar. 12 and Dec. 19, 1935, Fitzpatrick Papers, box 16, LCMD; Washington *Evening Star,* Sept. 9, 1937, p. 8.

39   Fitzpatrick to Bloom Jan. 2 and Dec. 19, 1935, Fitzpatrick Papers, box 16, LCMD. "The costumes were affective [sic]," Fitzpatrick reported. "They could not have been better although I would have paid more attention to the knee lengths of the breeches in many cases."

40   Fitzpatrick to Bloom, May 12, 1937, *ibid.*; Sol Bloom to Mrs. Cass Gilbert, July 31, 1937, Gilbert Papers, box 15, LCMD.

41   Undated five-page press release [1936 or early 1937], "Project for Creative Writing Plays and Pageants," U.S. Constitution Sesquicentennial Commission, Archives of the National Society Daughters of the American Revolution (NSDAR), Washington, D.C.

42   NYT, Sept. 12, 1937, sec. 2, p. 8; NYT, Sept. 15, 1937, p. 25; NYT, Sept. 17, 1937, pp. 13, 20; NYT, Sept. 18, 1937, p. 3; NYT, Oct. 24, 1937, sec. 1, p. 34; Julian P. Boyd to Dixon Ryan Fox, May 23, 1937, Fox Papers, box 1, NYSHA.

43   Bessie L. Lyon, "The Preamble Speaks," four-page mimeographed play; Waive B. Ripple, "The Making of the Constitution," thirteen-page mimeographed play, both from the Archives of the NSDAR, courtesy of Miss Elva B. Crawford, Archivist.

44   Fitzpatrick to Bloom, Oct. 15, 1934, and Bloom to Fitzpatrick, July 16, 1937, Fitzpatrick Papers, box 16, LCMD; Matteson to Bloom, Oct. 2, 1936, and Dec. 6, 1937, Matteson Papers, box 1, NA; Bloom to Matteson, July 16, 1937, *ibid.*; Hazel B. Nielson to Matteson, Feb. 16, 1938, and Bloom to *School Review,* Apr. 2, 1938, *ibid.*

45   For book reviews, see *Social Education,* 1 (January 1937), 74; *ibid.* (March 1937), 213; *ibid.* (April 1937), 235–42.

46   Leonard S. Kenworthy, "Sesquicentennial of the Constitution, 1787 to 1937," *ibid.* (March 1937), 163–65.

47   Sol Bloom to Charles F. Hurley, Dec. 21, 1936, Minor Congressional Commissions, box 11, Record Group 148, NA; Katherine Knox to Owen Kane, Aug. 17, 1937, *ibid.*; NYT, May 4, 1937, clipping in *ibid.*

48   Owen Kane to Sol Bloom, Oct. 17, 1936, *ibid.*; Kane to Bloom, Mar. 27, Apr. 3, Aug. 13 and 23, Sept. 28, and Nov. 19, 1937, *ibid.*, box 10; John Hill Morgan to Sol Bloom, Apr. 29, 1936, *ibid.*, box 11; Kane to Morgan, Apr. 27, 1937, *ibid.*, clipping from the Washington *Evening Star,* ca. June 22, 1937, *ibid.*; Lee to Knox, Jan. 19, 1937, *ibid.*; and Lee to Kane, May 1, 1937, *ibid.*

49   Washington *Sunday Star,* Nov. 28, 1937, F5; NYT, Nov. 28, 1937, sec. 11, p. 9, *The Magazine Antiques,* 32 (1937), 314; *The Art Digest,* 12 (Dec. 15, 1937), 14; *The Connoisseur,* 101 (1938), 91. For Mrs. Knox's bitterness about inadequate national publicity, see her fascinating letter to Sol Bloom, Dec. 11, 1937, and Bloom's response, Dec. 13, 1937, as well as Owen Kane's memorandum to Bloom, Dec. 10, 1937, all in Records of the U.S. Constitution Sesquicentennial Commission, box 10, Record Group 148, NA.

50   *Philadelphia Inquirer,* Sept. 25, 1937, p. 6; NYT, Aug. 1 and 29, 1937, sec. 11, p. 8 in both issues.

51   Bloom to Matteson, Nov. 14, 1936, Matteson Papers, box 1, NA.

52   Matteson to Bloom, Jan. 26, 1937, *ibid.* See NYT, Nov. 15, 1936, sec. 6, p. 6.

53   Barry Faulkner, *Sketches from an Artist's Life* (Dublin, N.H., 1973), 158–61.

54   Bloom to Fitzpatrick, Dec. 12, 1935, Fitzpatrick Papers, box 16, LCMD; Owen Kane to Bloom, Oct. 31, 1936, Records of the U.S. Constitution Sesquicentennial Commission, box 11, Record Group 148, NA.

55   Bloom to Horace G. Murphy, Aug. 24, 1937, *ibid.*, box 12; NYT, Sept. 5, 1937, sec. 9, pp. 4–5.

56   *Newsweek,* June 17, 1940, p. 49; *Time,* Sept. 29, 1941, p. 49.

57   Matteson to Bloom, Jan. 29, 1940, Matteson Papers, box 1, NA; Fitzpatrick, to Bloom, Nov. 18, 1935, Fitzpatrick Papers, box 16, LCMD.

58   NYT, May 29, 1938, sec. 11, p. 8; NYT, June 19, 1938, sec. 10, p. 14; Matteson to Bloom, May 16, 1938, Matteson Papers, box 1, NA.

59   Correspondence between the states and the Commission will be found in *ibid.*; NYT, Nov. 12, 1937, p. 3; NYT, Dec. 14, 1937, p. 32; Washington *Evening Star,* Dec. 7, 1937, p. A7; Governor E. D. Rivers of Georgia to Bloom, Dec. 6, 1937, Records of the U.S. Constitution Sesquicentennial Commission, Record Group 148, box 11, NA.

60   *Philadelphia Inquirer,* Dec. 11, 1937, p. 2; Dec. 12, p. 1; Dec. 13, pp. 2, 10; Dec. 14, p. 17.

61   Fitzpatrick to Bloom, Dec. 20, 1935, and Nov. 19, 1937, Bloom to Fitzpatrick, Nov. 15, 1937, Fitzpatrick Papers, box 16, LCMD; Matteson to Bloom, Nov. 23, 1937, Matteson Papers, box 1, NA.

62   Matteson to Bloom, Dec. 10, 1937, *ibid.*; Bloom to the New Hampshire Sesquicentennial Commission, Mar. 8, 1938, *ibid.*; NYT, June 19, 1938, sec. 10, p. 1; NYT, June 22, 1938, p. 5. For the linkage between progress and the 1939 World's Fair, see NYT, Sept. 12, 1937, sec. 2, p. 1.

63   Matteson to Bloom, Feb. 24, Nov. 24, and Dec. 20, 1938, Matteson Papers, box 1, NA; Mary E. Wooley, *et al.,* to Edward S. Corwin, Jan. 18, 1939, Corwin Papers, box 3, PUML; Harry F. Ward to Corwin, Mar. 8, 1939, *ibid.*

64   NYT, Mar. 5, 1939, pp. 44–45. Chief Justice Hughes and Senator Key Pittman of Nevada also spoke on this occasion. One representative from each branch of government.

65   NYT, Apr. 2, 1939, sec. 1, p. 31; NYT, Apr. 10, 1939, pp. 1, 14; NYT, May 3, 1939, p. 17; Washington *Evening Star,* May 1, 1939, pp. A2, A8.

66   NYT, Apr. 28, 1939, p. 20; NYT, Apr. 29, 1939, p. 16; NYT, May 1, 1939, p. 8; NYT, May 2, 1939, p. 25.

67   *Philadelphia Inquirer,* Apr. 27, 1939, p. 2; *ibid.*, Apr. 30, 1939, p. 8; *ibid.*, May 1, 1939, p. 5. For an excellent analysis of the 1939 World's Fair, see Warren I. Susman, *Culture as History: The Transformation of American Society in the Twentieth Century* (New York, 1984), 211–29.

68   Edward S. Corwin, *Court Over Constitution: A Study of Judicial Review as an Instrument of Popular Government* (Princeton, 1938), 227–28; Farrand to R. Walton Moore, Jan. 11, 1936, Farrand Papers, HEH; Beard to Farrand, Jan. 19 [1936], *ibid.*; NYT, Sept. 16, 1937, p. 18.

69   *Christian Science Monitor,* Sept. 13, 1937, p. 20.

70   Washington *Evening Star,* Sept. 17, 1937, p. A10 for the editorial and B6 for the text of Borah's speech. For additional evidence of the swing to amending the Constitution rather than altering the Court, see Matteson's

71 long memorandum (concerning an amendment proposed by Republican Sen. George W. Norris of Nebraska) to Bloom, Apr. 1, 1938, Matteson Papers, box 1, NA.

71 NYT, Oct. 1, 1937, p. 10; NYT, Mar. 6, 1938, sec. 6, p. 3; Bloom's DAR speech is in Matteson Papers, box 1, NA. See also Bloom to Fitzpatrick, Aug. 31, 1936, Fitzpatrick Papers, box 16, LCMD.

72 NYT, July 3, 1937, p. 16; NYT, Sept. 19, 1937, sec. 2, p. 8; NYT, Sept. 20, 1937, p. 26; NYT, Sept. 25, 1937, p. 15; NYT, Oct. 17, 1937, p. 7, NYT, Dec. 11, 1937, p. 20; NYT, May 6, 1939, p. 14; NYT, May 9, 1939, p. 18.

73 Maverick, *In Blood and Ink: The Life and Documents of American Democracy* (New York, 1939), 124. See also John R. Turner to Dixon R. Fox, Sept. 29, 1938, Fox Papers, Schaffer Library, Union College, Schenectady, N.Y.

74 *N.Y. Herald Tribune,* July 29, 1937, clipping in Fitzpatrick Papers, box 16, LCMD.

75 NYT, Jan. 7, 1938, p. 5; CREC, 83, part 1 (75th Congress, 3rd Session), 1467–72.

76 *Ibid.,* 1471–72; NYT, Feb. 3, 1938, p. 10; NYT, Feb. 5, 1938, p. 7.

77 Bloom to Matteson, May 31, 1938, Matteson Papers, box 1, NA; Matteson to Bloom, Oct. 24, 1938, *ibid.*; Bloom to Matteson, Aug. 17, 1939, and Matteson to Bloom, Aug. 22 and Sept. 20, 1939, *ibid.*

78 Fitzpatrick to Bloom, Dec. 19, 1935, Fitzpatrick Papers, box 16, LCMD; speech by Sen. Alben W. Barkley reported in NYT, Sept. 17, 1937, p. 20; a typescript of Bloom's address in Augusta, Ga., Jan. 2, 1938, is in Records of the U.S. Constitution Sesquicentennial Commission, box 14, Record Group 148, NA.

79 A typescript of Bloom's talk, "The Constitution," June 16, 1937, in *ibid.*

80 Bloom to Matteson, Dec. 16, 1936, Matteson Papers, box 1, NA: Bloom to Joseph W. Cheyney, Apr. 24, 1937, *ibid.*; Matteson to Bloom, Apr. 24, 1937, *ibid.*; Bloom's address, "The Symbolism of the Trees," Oct. 1937, p. 3, *ibid.*

81 Bloom to Matteson, Oct. 18, 1936, concerning a speech by Glenn Frank, *ibid.*; *Philadelphia Inquirer,* Sept. 17, 1937, p. 12.

82 The Berryman cartoons on constitutional matters appeared on Jan. 8, Feb. 1, 6, and 26, Mar. 2 and 24, Apr. 30, May 3, June 1, 9, 11, 12, and Aug. 5, all on p. 1. The DAR cartoon coincided with the Daughters' annual convention in Washington (Apr. 20).

83 *Chicago Daily Tribune,* Sept. 18, 1937, p. 12.

• CHAPTER 11 *Illegal Defiance of Constitutional Authority*

1 Powell spoke at a symposium sponsored by Wellesley College in honor of the Sesquicentennial. NYT, Nov. 16, 1937, p. 12.

2 See Raoul Berger to Henry M. Hart, Jan. 24, 1968, Hart Papers, box 1, folder 7, HLSL, for Berger's conclusion, following years of research, that the founders held a "narrow view" of the Supreme Court's potential role in the polity.

3   Unless otherwise indicated, the polls cited in Part Four of this book are derived from the Roper Center's Office of Archival Development at the University of Connecticut, a repository for thirty-five polling organizations active since the later 1930s. Particular polls will be cited by their computerized identification number and by date. See RC, NORCØ217, question 21 (Nov. 1943); RC, AIPOØ747, questions 15A–B (June 22–27, 1967); RC, AIPOØ373, question 19 (June 14–19, 1946).

4   Jackson, "Back to the Constitution," ABAJ, 25 (1939), 745, 748.

5   William L. Underwood to Edward S. Corwin, Apr. 2, 1936, Corwin Papers, box 2, PUML. See also James M. Beck. *The Constitution of the United States: Yesterday, Today—and Tomorrow?* (New York, 1924), 209–12; William Y. Elliott, *The Crisis of the American Constitution* (Williamsburg, Va., 1938), 8.

6   See *U.S.* v. *Darby Lumber Company,* 312 U.S. 100.

7   *Virginia Law Review,* 36 (1950), 1–24, the quotation on p. 23. When New York University's School of Law planned its 1951 conference to celebrate the bicentennial of Madison's birth, the Dean invited Corwin to present a paper on Madison and American federalism. Corwin must have found that assignment hopelessly irrelevant because he prepared instead an essay on "James Madison: Layman, Publicist, and Exegete," reprinted in Richard Loss, ed., *Corwin on the Constitution,* I (Ithaca N.Y., 1981), 213–30. See Russell D. Niles to Corwin, July 18, 1950, Corwin Papers, box 3, PUML.

8   Catheryn Seckler-Hudson, *Our Constitution and Government: Lessons on the Constitution and Government of the United States for Use in the Public Schools by Candidates for Citizenship* (Washington, D.C., 1940), 82.

9   Edward S. Corwin to Lewis H. Kenney, Mar. 3, 1952, Corwin Papers, box 3, PUML; NYT, Sept. 24, 1955, p. 38, quoting Judge William H. Hastie of the Third Circuit Court of Appeals speaking at a conference held in Cambridge, Mass., honoring the bicentennial of John Marshall's birth; Robert G. McCloskey to Marjorie Fine, Feb. 14, 1966, McCloskey Papers, box 1966, HUPL. *Publius, The Journal of Federalism,* began to appear in 1970 as a quarterly publication of Temple University's Center for the Study of Federalism, directed by Daniel J. Elazar.

10   RC, AIPOØ610, question 30 (Feb. 4–9, 1959). See also RC, AIPOØ673, question 31 (May 23–28, 1963), and RC, MINNØ224, question 16 (June 7–11, 1963); Walter F. Murphy, *Congress and the Court: A Case Study in the American Political Process* (Chicago, 1962), 129, 253.

11   NYT, Feb. 20, 1985, p. 1; editorial on Feb. 21, 1985, A22. The 1976 case was *National League of Cities* v. *Usery.* See also NYT, Mar. 13, 1983, p. E9, for *Equal Employment Opportunity Commission* v. *Wyoming.*

12   William L. Underwood to Edward S. Corwin, Feb. 13, 1936, Corwin Papers, box 2, PUML.

13   Corwin's letter to NYT, Oct. 13, 1940, E6–7; William T. Couch to Corwin, Oct. 14, 1940, Corwin Papers, box 3, PUML; Charles A. Beard to Corwin, Oct. 20, 1941, *ibid.*; FDR is quoted in Merlo J. Pusey, *The Way We Go to War* (Boston, 1969), 77.

14   Gary W. Reichard, "Eisenhower and the Bricker Amendment," *Prologue,* 6 (1974), 88–99; Glendon A. Schubert, "Politics and the Constitution: The Bricker Amendment during 1953," JP, 16 (1954), 257–98.

15   *Ibid.*, 258; for Eisenhower's comments on the Bricker Amendment at his July 1, 1953, news conference, see *Congressional Quarterly Almanac,* 9 (1953), 236; NYT, July 2, 1953, p. 4. See also Philip A. Grant, "The Bricker Amendment Controversy," *Presidential Studies Quarterly,* 15 (1985), 572–82.

16   Donald G. Morgan, *Congress and the Constitution: A Study of Responsibility* (Cambridge, Mass., 1966), 5–8, 12. Morgan argues vigorously that constitutional history involves far more than courts and cases, or at least ought to; and he laments Congress's "abdication" of its proper role as one among several agencies required to exercise judgment on constitutional questions.

17   See *Congressional Digest,* 44 (1970), 83; *Time,* Apr. 16, 1973, 11; *Newsweek,* Aug. 6, 1973, 20.

18   NYT, June 25, 1983, p. A8; NYT, June 26, 1983, p. E1; E. Donald Elliott, "INS v. Chadha: The Administrative Constitution, the Constitution, and the Legislative Veto," SCR (1983), 125–76.

19   "Minton," DAB, *Supplement* VII; for characteristic scorn directed at Black, see Carl Becker to Max Farrand, Oct. 3, 1937, Farrand Papers, HEH; and numerous letters sent to Harlan Fiske Stone and other justices, Stone Papers, box 73, LCMD. For context generally, see Sidney Fine, *Frank Murphy: The Washington Years* (Ann Arbor, Mich., 1984), ch. 9.

20   Thomas Reed Powell to William O. Douglas, June 14, 1943, and Dec. 23, 1946, Powell Papers, box B, fol. 16, HLSL; Paul Freund to Powell, July 19, 1944, *ibid.*, fol. 25.

21   Beard to Powell, Jan. 22 [1944], and Powell to Beard, Feb. 3, 1944, *ibid.*, box A, fol. 19. See also the candid letters from Philip B. Kurland to Powell, July 16 and Nov. 7, 1945, *ibid.*, box B, fol. 47.

22   For a shrewd statement of just how far the political pendulum had swung to the left, see Harlan Fiske Stone to Powell, Nov. 8, 1945, *ibid.*, box C, fol. 32. On the matter of differentiating between Frankfurter and Black, see Alan Barth, *Prophets with Honor: Great Dissents and Great Dissenters in the Supreme Court* (New York, 1974), 190; and Mark Silverstein, *Constitutional Faiths: Felix Frankfurter, Hugo Black, and the Process of Judicial Decision Making* (Ithaca, N.Y., 1984).

23   Robert J. Harris, "The Decline of Judicial Review," JP, 10 (1948), 1–19; Robert G. McCloskey, *The Modern Supreme Court* (Cambridge, Mass., 1972), 82–83; Edward S. Corwin, *Constitutional Revolution, Ltd.* (Claremont, Calif., 1941), 108–09, 113; Elliott, *Crisis of the American Constitution,* 14.

24   McCloskey, *Modern Supreme Court,* 291, 326, 343–45; Morgan, *Congress and the Constitution,* 6; C. Herman Pritchett, *Congress Versus the Supreme Court, 1957–1960* (Minneapolis, 1961), vii, 31, 122.

25   Paul L. Murphy, *The Constitution in Crisis Times, 1918–1969* (New York, 1972), 340; Jack W. Peltason, *Fifty-Eight Lonely Men: Southern Federal Judges and School Desegregation* (New York, 1961), 28–29, 40, 53n., 68, 86, 147, 185–86, 189–90, 235, 245.

26   NYT, Mar. 12, 1956, pp. 1, 19; R. C. Pittman, "The Supreme Court, the Broken Constitution, and the Shattered Bill of Rights," CREC, 102, *84th Congress, 2nd Session* (Feb. 28, 1956), Part 16, 1858–63; Alford Dale, *The Constitutional Crisis: Its Threat to Liberty and Its Remedy* (New York, 1960).

27 RC, AIPO∅∅57, question 3 (Nov. 15–20, 1936); RC, AIPO∅565, question 16 (May 31–June 5, 1956), when the sample size was 1,974; RC, AIPO∅586, question 6 (July 18–23, 1957).

28 Pritchett, *Congress Versus the Supreme Court*, 28; Murphy, *Congress and the Court: A Case Study in the American Political Process*, 115–16, 154–59, 163, 201–02, 208–09, 235–37, 245–46; "How U.S. Judges Feel About the Supreme Court," *U.S. News and World Report*, Oct. 24, 1958, 110–18; Fred Rodell, "The Crux of the Court Hullabaloo," NYT *Magazine*, May 29, 1960, pp. 13, 29, 32.

29 For a compact summary, see G. Theodore Mitau, *Decade of Decision: The Supreme Court and the Constitutional Revolution, 1954–1964* (New York, 1967); and for public opinion on legislative re-apportionment, RC, AIPO∅694, question 6 (June 25–30, 1964).

30 Ernest Havemann, "Storm Center of Justice," *Life*, May 22, 1964, 108–24; John Osborne, "One Supreme Court," *Life*, June 16, 1958, 92–94ff.

31 Harlan Fiske Stone to Byrnes, Nov. 1, 1941, and Stone to Douglas, Jan. 24, 1946, Stone Papers, box 74, LCMD; Thomas Reed Powell to Matthew Josephson, May 13, 1941, Powell Papers, box B, fol. 43, HLSL; Kurland in NYT *Magazine*, June 9, 1968, pp. 34–35.

32 Harlan Fiske Stone to Edward S. Corwin, Mar. 6, 1939, Corwin Papers, box 1, PUML; Gordon Patric, "The Impact of a Court Decision: Aftermath of the McCollum Case," JPL, 6 (1957), 455–64. See also Kenneth M. Dolbeare and Phillip E. Hammond, *The School Prayer Decisions: From Court Policy to Local Practice* (Chicago, 1971), and David Margolick, "State Judiciaries Are Shaping Law That Goes Beyond Supreme Court," NYT, May 19, 1982, pp. A1, B8, for more recent developments.

33 Peltason, *Fifty-Eight Lonely Men*, 30, 109–13, 121–22, 157, 208–09, 230–31, 233, 236.

34 Murphy, *Congress and the Court*, 116; G. Edward White, *Earl Warren: A Public Life* (New York, 1982), 247–48; Welch, *The White Book of the John Birch Society* (January 1962), 11–12; L. Brent Bozell, "Should We Impeach Earl Warren?" *National Review*, Sept. 9, 1961, p. 155; Herbert Block, *Straight Herblock* (New York, 1964), 114 for a Birch cartoon dated Apr. 5, 1961. See also *The Autobiography of William O. Douglas: The Court Years, 1939–1975* (New York, 1980), 360–64; and James F. Simon, *Independent Journey: The Life of William O. Douglas* (New York, 1980), 401–11.

35 Walter F. Murphy and Joseph Tanenhaus, "Public Opinion and the Supreme Court: The Goldwater Campaign," *Public Opinion Quarterly*, 32 (1968), 31–50; Lawrence, "The War Against Crime," *U.S. News and World Report*, June 29, 1964, 111–12.

36 *Time*, July 17, 1964, 20; Alexander M. Bickel, "Barry Fights the Court," NR, 151 (Oct. 10, 1964), 9–11; "The Candidates Spell Out the Issues," NYT, Sept. 12, 1964, p. 10; NYT *Magazine*, Nov. 1, 1964, pp. 23, 79.

37 McCloskey, *Modern Supreme Court*, 359; "Our Vanishing Constitution," *U.S. News and World Report*, July 20, 1964, 104.

38 RC, AIPO∅675, question 6 (July 18–23, 1963); RC, AIPO 781k, question 5 (May 22–27, 1969).

39   John H. Kessel, "Public Perceptions of the Supreme Court," *Midwest Journal of Political Science,* 10 (1966), 173–74. The comments made by respondents indicated a fairly low level of informational support for their attitudes—a troublesome and ongoing aspect of the Constitution in American culture.

40   RC, AIPOØ747, question 15b (June 22–27, 1967).

41   Eugene H. Methvin, "Is the Supreme Court Really Supreme?" RD, 91 (1967), 80; RC, AIPOØ874, question 6 (July 6–9, 1973).

42   Stuart Taylor, Jr., "Attacks on Federal Courts Could Shift Historic Roles," NYT, May 16, 1982, pp. 1, 58; Richard P. Nathan and Fred C. Doolittle, "The Untold Story of Reagan's 'New Federalism,' " *The Public Interest,* no. 77 (1984), 96–105.

43   From Powell's review of Charles Beard, *The Republic* (New York, 1943), in HLR, 57 (1944), 580.

44   RC, RFORØØ13, question 1 (December 1939); RC, RFORØØ56, question 12 (September 1946).

45   Wallace, *Our Obsolete Constitution* (New York, 1932), 51, 155, 181; Hazlitt, *A New Constitution Now* (New York, 1942), 8. See also William MacDonald, *A New Constitution for a New America* (New York, 1921); Alexander Hehmyer, *Time for Change: A Proposal for a Second Constitutional Convention* (New York, 1943); and Leland D. Baldwin, *Reframing the Constitution: An Interpretation for Modern America* (Santa Barbara, Calif., 1972).

46   Pepper to Edward S. Corwin, Oct. 24, 1951, Corwin Papers, box 3, PUML. For northern proposals in 1861–62 to redesign the Constitution, see Harold M. Hyman, *A More Perfect Union: The Impact of the Civil War and Reconstruction on the Constitution* (New York, 1973), 114, 119, 443.

47   Tugwell, "The Emerging Constitution," *The Center Diary* (April 1966), 8, 12; Frank K. Kelly, *Court of Reason: Robert Hutchins and the Fund for the Republic* (New York, 1981), 415–17, 420. During the later 1960s both CORE (Congress of Racial Equality) and the Black Panthers issued calls for a new American Constitution.

48   See issues of *The Center Magazine* throughout 1970 and 1971, but especially September–October 1970; a compilation of material drawn from them called *A Model Constitution for a United Republics of America* (Palo Alto, Calif., 1970), prepared for discussion by college students; Tugwell, *The Emerging Constitution* (New York, 1974); Tugwell, *The Compromising of the Constitution* (South Bend, Ind., 1976).

49   Tugwell, *Emerging Constitution,* 34, 84.

50   *Ibid.,* 417, 432.

51   *Ibid.,* 84, 475, 487–88, 615. Collegial New Dealers who had lived through the same Supreme Court responses for a generation (1930s to 1960s) did not even share the same perception of how the Court functioned and why. Thurman Arnold wrote the following to Tugwell on Aug. 22, 1967: "I disagree with you about the Supreme Court being an inadequate instrument for social change. I think it is most useful because it never presents a controversial issue in a way that requires any immediate action. It moves along from case to case as it has in the Apportionment cases and on the racial question. You remember it changed under Roosevelt's attack." Gene M.

Gressley, ed., *Voltaire and the Cowboy: The Letters of Thurman Arnold* (Boulder, Col., 1977), 473.

52   "Tugwell's Constitution," *Newsweek*, Sept. 21, 1970, 69, 70. See also NYT, Sept. 8, 1970, pp. 1, 30; NYT, Oct. 3, 1970, p. 31; NYT, Nov. 12, 1970, p. 38. The Center did receive a fair amount of mail about the proposed Constitution, and some of the most "challenging" letters were published in the *Center Magazine* during 1971.

53   NYT, July 25, 1979, p. 22. For residual interest, however, we see Leland D. Baldwin, *Reframing the Constitution: An Imperative for Modern America* (Santa Barbara, Calif., 1972), and Wilbur Edel, *A Constitutional Convention: Threat or Challenge?* (New York, 1981).

54   Gene Roddenberry, "The Omega Glory," in James Blish, ed., *Star Trek 10* (New York, 1974), 137–64.

•   CHAPTER 12 *Our Bill of Rights Is Under Subtle and Pervasive Attack*

1   Broun, *It Seems to Me, 1925–1935* (New York, 1935), 321; Corwin, *Constitutional Revolution, Ltd.* (Claremont, Calif., 1941), 115; Jackson, *The Struggle for Judicial Supremacy* (New York, 1941), 22–24, 57–68, 71, 284–85.

2   The quotation from Einstein's letter, dated Mar. 3, 1954, was prominently printed in publications of the Civil Liberties Committee. For a thorough survey of contemporary attitudes, see Herbert McClosky and Alida Brill, *Dimensions of Tolerance: What Americans Believe about Civil Liberties* (New York, 1983).

3   Mencken to James M. Beck, Dec. 12 [1924], Beck Papers, box 2, PUML. For other scattered examples from this period, see the essay by Nicholas Murray Butler, NYT, Mar. 4, 1928, sec. 10, p. 5; Arthur N. Holcombe to Charles Warren, Feb. 17, 1932, Warren Papers, box 2, LCMD; Gerald W. Johnson, "This Terrifying Freedom," *Harper's Magazine*, 171 (1935), 754–60.

4   John Speed Smith to the Commissioner of Naturalization, Nov. 14, 1923, Record Group 85, file E-2, box 1, NA; Carl B. Hyatt, *Gateway to Citizenship* (Washington, D.C., 1943, revised 1948), 10.

5   NYT, Aug. 11, 1931, p. 12.

6   Ernest J. Hopkins, "The Lawless Arm of the Law," *Atlantic Monthly*, 148 (1931), 279–87. See Paul L. Murphy, *The Constitution in Crisis Times, 1918–1969* (New York, 1972), 427 for the later 1960s.

7   Alpheus T. Mason, *Harlan Fiske Stone: Pillar of the Law* (New York, 1956), 272.

8   See William E. Leuchtenburg, "Franklin D. Roosevelt's Supreme Court 'Packing' Plan," in Harold M. Hollingsworth, ed., *Essays on the New Deal* (Austin, Tex., 1969), 87–88, 115; John A. Garraty, ed., *Quarrels That Have Shaped the Constitution* (New York, 1975), 228.

9   NYT, June 22, 1938, p. 5. See also the Free Speech cases, decided by the Supreme Court during the 1938–39 term. *Schneider* v. *State* (*Town of Irvington*), 308 U.S. 147 (1939), in which freedom of speech and the press

were secured to all persons by the Fourteenth Amendment against abridg-ment by a state.

10   Adams, "Shield of Our Liberty: The Bill of Rights," RD, 34 (1939), 26–29, condensed from the NYT *Magazine.* See also NYT, Apr. 17, 1939, p. 34. The American Legion held a rally in the Bronx "to arouse interest in support of the Bill of Rights and United States institutions."

11   Hays, *Democracy Works* (New York, 1939), summarized in *ibid.* (1939), 111–27. See also Henry Steele Commager's historical survey of the Bill of Rights in NYT *Magazine,* Apr. 9, 1939, pp. 4, 16.

12   *The Bill of Rights Review: A Quarterly,* 1 (1940), 3; *ibid.* (Spring 1941), 181–82; NYT, Feb. 6, 1940, p. 5.

13   NYT, Feb. 16, 1941, p. 36; editorial, *ibid.,* sec. 4, p. 8; NYT, Dec. 6, 1941, p. 8; NYT, Dec. 11, 1941, p. 30; NYT, Dec. 18, 1941, p. 26; NYT, Dec. 21, 1941, p. 6; NYT, Feb. 15, 1944, p. 16; NYT, Dec. 15, 1944, p. 18; NYT, Dec. 16, 1944, p. 11.

14   See Henry Steele Commager, *Majority Rule and Minority Rights* (New York, 1943); Peter Irons, *Justice at War* (New York, 1983); Jacobus ten-Broek, *et al., Prejudice, War and the Constitution* (Berkeley, Calif., 1954).

15   RC, NORC∅217 (#4311–217), question 3 (November 1943); NYT, Apr. 18, 1944, p. 20. See also Charles A. Beard, *The Republic: Conversa-tions on Fundamentals* (New York, 1943), 125: "It has become the fashion recently to exalt the Bill of Rights ... as if no rights were proclaimed or taken into account by the original instrument itself."

16   Taken from newspaper clippings in the Robert E. Cushman Papers on Civil Liberties, CUL. See also Cushman, "Civil Liberty after the War," APSR, 38 (1944), 1–20.

17   McCloskey, *The Modern Supreme Court* (Cambridge, Mass., 1972), 332; Alan Barth, *Prophets with Honor: Great Dissents and Great Dissenters in the Supreme Court* (New York, 1974), 108–30; Henry J. Abraham, *Freedom and the Court: Civil Rights and Liberties in the United States* (4th ed.: New York, 1982).

18   *Schneiderman* v. *U.S.,* 320 U.S. 118; NYT, Mar. 13, 1943, p. 15; NYT, June 22, 1943, pp. 1, 6; *San Francisco Chronicle,* June 22, 1943, p. 12.

19   "Message to the Congress on the State of the Union," Jan. 11, 1944, in Samuel Rosenman, ed., *The Public Papers and Addresses of Franklin D. Roosevelt* (New York, 1938–50), XIII, 41.

20   Burton's "Bill of Rights" appeared in the *Cleveland News* on July 14, 1945, and was read into CREC (79th Congress, 1st Session) two days later; Knowland, "Why Not a Bill of Rights for Labor?" RD, 72 (1958), 78–79, reprinted from *The American Mercury* (March 1958).

21   Frank K. Kelly, *Court of Reason: Robert Hutchins and the Fund for the Re-public* (New York, 1981), 34, 39. For symptomatic cartoons in 1946 and 1947, see Herbert Block, *The Herblock Book* (Boston, 1952), 54–55.

22   RC, AIPO∅4∅5, form T, question 7b (Oct. 3–8, 1947).

23   RC, AIPO∅526, question 16 (Jan. 28–Feb. 2, 1954); RC, NORC∅4∅1, question 23 (December 1956).

24   RC, AIPO∅581, question 34 (Apr. 6–11, 1957). See also RC, MINN∅16∅, question 17 (Apr. 12–18, 1957). In the latter poll 612 people

were asked whether they considered the Fifth Amendment a good one or a poor one; 47% said good, 44% said poor, and 9% no opinion or "other."

25　Donald Culross Peattie, "Your Bill of Rights," RD, 50 (1947), 91–94; *TV Guide,* Aug. 17, 1957, inside cover.

26　NYT, Dec. 14, 1947, sec. 4, p. 8; NYT, Dec. 15, 1947, pp. 12, 24.

27　NYT, Dec. 16, 1947, p. 24.

28　Murrow to Thomas Reed Powell, Nov. 18, 1948, Powell Papers, box C, fol. 42, HLSL. See also Powell to Richard M. Nixon, Feb. 3, 1948, *ibid.*; Powell to Alexander Wiley, May 27, 1948, *ibid.*; Mark DeWolfe Howe to Helen Cam, Feb. 2, 1953, Howe Papers, box 1, HLSL; James W. Hook to Paul G. Hoffman, July 18, 1957, Fund for the Republic Papers, box 55, PUML.

29　Black, "Memorandum to the Conference" (Re *Feldman* v. *U.S.*), May 26, 1944, Harlan Fiske Stone Papers, box 73, LCMD. Boxes 73 to 79 of the Stone Papers, containing Stone's communications with his fellow justices, indicate the extent to which the Court became far more concerned about the Bill of Rights during the 1940s than it had been previously.

30　For Black's dissent in *Adamson,* see 332 U.S. 46 at 68–123; and for the leading critique, Fairman, "Does the Fourteenth Amendment Incorporate the Bill of Rights? The Original Understanding," *Stanford Law Review,* 2 (1949), 5–173.

31　*Dennis et al.* v. *U.S.,* 341 U.S. 494 (1951). For the dissents, see 579–81 (Black) and 581–91 (Douglas).

32　Black, "The Bill of Rights," *NYU Law Review,* 35 (1960), 865–81.

33　See Archibald MacLeish (chairman of the ad hoc committee to lift the ban on *The Nation*) to Zechariah Chafee, Jr., Oct. 9, 1948, with the attached four-page "Appeal to Reason and Conscience: In Defense of the Right of Freedom of Inquiry in the United States," Chafee Papers, box 2, fol. 10, HLSL.

34　White to the *N.Y. Herald Tribune,* Nov. 29, 1947, in Dorothy L. Guth, ed., *Letters of E. B. White* (New York, 1976), 285–86; Scott Elledge, *E. B. White: A Biography* (New York, 1984), 272. The loyalty oath issue lingered on in troublesome ways for more than a decade. See Mark DeWolfe Howe to Edmund Wilson, Apr. 28, 1959, Howe Papers, box 5, HLSL; Herbert Block, *Straight Herblock* (New York, 1964), 122, for a cartoon dated June 3, 1964; and above all the splendid work of Harold M. Hyman, *To Try Men's Souls: Loyalty Tests in American History* (Berkeley, Calif., 1959), ch. 13.

35　See Jackson, *The Supreme Court in the American System of Government* (Cambridge, Mass., 1955); Alan F. Westin, "Liberals and the Supreme Court: Making Peace with the 'Nine Old Men,' " *Commentary,* 22 (1956), 23.

36　Freund, "The Supreme Court and Fundamental Freedoms," in Leonard W. Levy, ed., *Judicial Review and the Supreme Court: Selected Essays* (New York, 1967), 124–40; Freund, *On Understanding the Supreme Court* (Boston, 1949), ch. 1; *Christian Science Monitor,* Sept. 23, 1955, p. 20.

37　See Barton J. Bernstein and Allen J. Matusow, eds., *The Truman Administration: A Documentary History* (New York, 1966), 95, 108–10; NYT,

Oct. 30, 1947, pp. 1, 14, 16; NYT, Oct. 31, 1947, pp. 20, 22; NYT, Nov. 2, 1947, sec. 3, p. 1.

38 See Barth, *Prophets with Honor,* 180; typed memo entitled "The Fifth Anniversary of the Bill of Rights Fund," Nov. 4, 1959, Mark Howe Papers, box 6, HLSL.

39 Warren, "The Law and the Future," *Fortune,* 52 (1955), 106–07, 224–30, esp. 223–24, 226; Warren, "The Bill of Rights and the Military" (1962), in Alan F. Westin, ed., *An Autobiography of the Supreme Court: Off-the-Bench Commentary by the Justices* (New York, 1963), 470.

40 *84th Congress (First Session), Senate Committee on the Judiciary, Subcommittee on Constitutional Rights,* S.R. 94, Sept. 19, 1955 (Washington, D.C., 1955), 5, 16, 20, 22, 24, 26.

41 *Ibid.,* 32, 37–38, 43.

42 NYT, Sept. 18, 1955, pp. 1, 14, 29.

43 Westin, ed., *Autobiography of the Supreme Court,* 170; RC, USAIPO-SPECPOSA959, question 57 (July 1957).

44 "Fund Uses Ads to Carry Freedom Message," *Printers' Ink,* Jan. 10, 1958, p. 50.

45 *Newsweek,* June 1, 1962, 19–22; Ervin, "Alexander Hamilton's Phantom," VSD, 22 (Oct. 15, 1955), 23–26; Ervin, "The Case for Segregation," *Look,* Apr. 3, 1956, 33.

46 Ervin, "The Case for Segregation," *Look,* Apr. 3, 1956, 32–33; Ervin, "The Power to Interpret Is Not the Power to Amend," *U.S. News and World Report,* May 11, 1959, 120; NYT, Aug. 31, 1967, p. 19.

47 *Congressional Digest,* 50 (1971), 237; *U.S. News and World Report,* Mar. 6, 1972, 42–45; Ervin, "Justice, the Constitution, and Privacy," VSD, 34 (Sept. 1, 1973), 677–81.

48 Ervin, *Humor of a Country Lawyer* (Chapel Hill, N.C., 1983), 104, 160, 193; NYT, Mar. 19, 1985, A20.

49 RC, AIPO∅747, questions 15c–d (June 22–27, 1967).

50 RC, AIPO∅72∅, question 107a (Nov. 18–23, 1965); Nathan Glazer, "Civil Liberties and the American People: Tolerance and Anti-Communism," *Commentary,* 20 (1955), 171. A Gallup Poll in 1953 had shown 67% opposed to freedom of speech for Communists. See *The Gallup Poll: Public Opinion 1935–1971* (New York, 1972), II, 1191.

51 Methvin, "Let's Have Justice for Non-Criminals, Too!" RD, 89 (1966), 53–60; C. Herman Pritchett, *Constitutional Civil Liberties* (Englewood Cliffs, N.J., 1984), 205, 214.

52 Harris Wofford, Jr., "Segregation and the Constitution," RD, 74 (1959), 183–86; Lino A. Graglia, *Disaster by Decree: The Supreme Court Decisions on Race and the Schools* (Ithaca, N.Y., 1976), esp. chs. 7–9.

53 "Free Speech on TV," *TV Guide,* Apr. 25, 1964, pp. 15–19; Martin Mayer, "Fair Trials vs. Free Press—A Clash of Rights," *ibid.,* Aug. 17, 1974, p. 2; "First Amendment Dilemma," *ibid.,* Oct. 29, 1977, pp. 4–8.

54 NYT, June 16, 1983, pp. A1, B10–11; NYT, June 17, 1983, p. A16; *Ithaca Journal,* June 16, 1983, p. 1.

55 Linda R. Hirshman, "The Constitution and Women's Liberation," *Social Education,* 37 (1973), 381–82, 385.

56   *Ibid.*, 384–85.

57   Lawrence, "14th Amendment Unlawfully Adopted," New Orleans *Times-Picayune,* Feb. 9, 1959.

58   Ashbrook, "Are Judges Abusing Our Rights?" RD, 119 (1981), 77–80.

59   NYT, Mar. 11, 1985, p. E2. *The Burger Court: The Counter-Revolution That Wasn't,* ed. by Vincent Blasi (New Haven, Conn., 1983), minimized changes in the Court's orientation, 1969–82, and argued that moderates and conservatives have so much respect for *stare decisis* that they permit many liberal decisions to stand. Opinions rendered during the 1983–84, 1984–85, and 1985–86 terms undermined the presumption of continuity between the Warren and Burger Courts. Discontinuity has begun to be apparent in areas particularly pertinent to the Bill of Rights. See Monroe H. Freedman, "Gideon II," NYT, Nov. 7, 1982, p. E17; "The Supreme Court Apologizes," NYT, June 10, 1983, p. A26; Linda Greenhouse, "The Court's Conservatives Are Making Their Mark," NYT, July 15, 1984, p. E2; and James J. Kilpatrick, "Judicial Restraint," *Baltimore Sun,* June 28, 1983, p. A7.

•   CHAPTER 13 *The Public Got Strange and Distorted Views of the Court and Its Rulings*

1   See Woodrow Wilson, *An Old Master and Other Political Essays* (New York, 1893), 151; Louis D. Brandeis to Alice Goldmark, Dec. 28, 1890, in Melvin I. Urofsky and David W. Levy, eds., *Letters of Louis D. Brandeis* (Albany, N.Y., 1971), I, 97; Spencer Miller, Jr., to Edward S. Corwin, Sept. 29, 1942, Corwin Papers, box 3, PUML. Miller served at that time as chairman of the New Jersey Constitution Foundation.

2   Jaffe is quoted in Anthony Lewis, *Gideon's Trumpet* (New York, 1964), 210; and see John P. Frank, *Marble Palace: The Supreme Court in American Life* (New York, 1958), 50–52.

3   *The Memoirs of Earl Warren* (Garden City, N.Y., 1977), 335. Warren worked on these memoirs from 1970 until his death in 1974. Chapters 9 and 10 deal with his years as Chief Justice.

4   David L. Grey, *The Supreme Court and the News Media* (Evanston, Ill., 1968), 4, 37; NYT, May 3, 1922, p. 7; G. Edward White, "The Supreme Court's Public and the Public's Supreme Court," *Virginia Quarterly Review,* 52 (1976), 370–88.

5   Clipping from an unidentified newspaper (1921) in Scrapbooks on Supreme Court History, 1880–1935, scrapbook #13, Record Group 267, NA. (For the confusing case, see *American Steel Foundries* v. *Tri-Cities Trades Council,* 257 U.S. 184).

6   Alan Barth, *Prophets with Honor: Great Dissents and Great Dissenters in the Supreme Court* (New York, 1974), 69; Hughes, "Justice Our Anchor," VSD, 6 (1940), 260; Grey, *Supreme Court and the News Media,* 105–06, 118–19, 139.

7   Grey, *Supreme Court and the News Media,* 21, 123; Anthony Lewis, "Problems of a Washington Correspondent," *Connecticut Bar Journal,* 33 (1959), 369.

8   NYT *Magazine,* May 21, 1950, p. 12; for the full opinion, see 339 U.S. 382 (1950). Jackson found "contradictions between what meets the eye and what is covertly done, which, in my view of the issues, provide a rational basis upon which Congress reasonably could have concluded that the Communist party is something different in fact from any other substantial party we have known, and hence may constitutionally be treated as something different in law."

9   D. Walter Bell to Van Devanter, Feb. 12, 1937, Van Devanter Papers, box 38, LCMD; Van Devanter to Bell, Feb. 15, 1937, *ibid.,* box 19; for Van Devanter's stubborn unwillingness to give interviews at the time of his retirement, see *ibid.,* box 44; Frankfurter to Edward S. Corwin, Nov. 20, 1945, Corwin Papers, box 1, PUML.

10   Alpheus T. Mason, *Brandeis: A Free Man's Life* (New York, 1946), 569, 620, 629. The former clerk was James Willard Hurst.

11   Marquis W. Childs, "The Supreme Court Today," *Harper's Magazine,* 176 (1938), 581–88; Washington *Daily News,* May 12, 1938, p. 6.

12   See Gerald T. Dunne, *Hugo Black and the Judicial Revolution* (New York, 1977), ch. 11. In 1944 and 1945, William O. Douglas was identified as the justice who committed indiscretions in "leaking" information about pending cases to columnist Drew Pearson. Douglas sent indignant memoranda to Chief Justice Stone denying any responsibility for "the whole affair." Douglas to Stone, Jan. 5 and 6, 1944, May 21, 1945, Stone Papers, box 74, LCMD.

13   "Justice Black and the Bill of Rights," CBS News Special, Dec. 3, 1968, p. 8, transcript courtesy of CBS.

14   "Mr. Justice Douglas," CBS Reports, Sept. 6, 1972, p. 18, transcript courtesy of CBS; G. Edward White, *Earl Warren: A Public Life* (New York, 1982), 324. See also "Constitutional Interpretation: An Interview with Justice Lewis Powell," *Kenyon College Alumni Bulletin* (Summer 1979), 14–18.

15   NYT, Aug. 5, 1984, pp. 1, 29; NYT, Sept. 22, 1984, p. B32. See also NYT, Sept. 10, 1982, p. A21; for Justice Brennan's outspoken concern, NYT, May 5, 1985, p. A42; and for Stevens most recently, NYT, July 8, 1985, p. B5.

16   NYT, Oct. 21, 1984, p. A1; John A. Jenkins, "The Partisan: A Talk with Justice Rehnquist," NYT *Magazine,* Mar. 3, 1985, 28ff.

17   See Bruce Allen Murphy, *The Brandeis/Frankfurter Connection: The Secret Political Activities of Two Supreme Court Justices* (New York, 1982). For evidence that some contemporaries were not oblivious to the phenomenon, see Thomas Reed Powell to Raymond Moley, May 3, 1934, Powell Papers, box A, fol. 11, HLSL; and *The Autobiography of William O. Douglas: The Court Years, 1939–1975* (New York, 1980), 253.

18   R. Kent Newmyer, *Supreme Court Justice Joseph Story: Statesman of the Old Republic* (Chapel Hill, N.C., 1985), 171–73; Alpheus T. Mason, *Harlan Fiske Stone: Pillar of the Law* (New York, 1956), 303.

19   NYT, Feb. 18, 1982, A22; NYT, Dec. 31, 1984, p. A7; NYT, Jan. 5, 1985, p. A20; NYT, Mar. 12, 1985, p. A30; Samuel Estreicher and John Sexton, "Streamlining the High Court," NYT, Mar. 27, 1985, p. A27.

20   "The Chief Justice Talks about the Court," RD, 102 (1973), 95–99.

21   *Ibid.*, 96; *Memoirs of Earl Warren,* 302.

22   NYT, June 28, 1962, p. 17; NYT, July 1, 1962, sec. 4, p. 10; NYT, July 4, 1962, pp. 1, 8; Herbert Block, *Straight Herblock* (New York, 1964), 150, 152–54; *Memoirs of Earl Warren,* 303.

23   For an example of "crank letters," see Harold H. Burton Papers, boxes 52, 65, 69, 75, 80, 86, 92, 96, 100, 105, 110, 117, LCMD; letter from Ms. Toni House to the author, May 8, 1984. Also Gary J. Aichele (executive director of the Supreme Court Historical Society) to the author, April 13, 1984, which reads in part: "Correspondence of a business nature, especially if pertaining to individual cases, generally finds its way to the Clerk's Office where it is filed in the case files if sufficiently pertinent. Much routine mail is sent to the Public Information Office where it is answered and generally filed, or thrown away if characterized as 'nuisance' mail. To the best of my knowledge, it would be most difficult to reconstruct the correspondence to the Court from a given period of time, or with reference to specific cases or issues."

24   *Memoirs of Earl Warren,* 342.

25   Greenhouse, "Of Meaty Tea Leaves and Other Bafflements," NYT, Mar. 12, 1985, p. A26; Greenhouse, "Mysteries of Tie Votes and Calls for Reargument," NYT, Apr. 3, 1985, p. A20.; Grey, *The Supreme Court and the News Media,* 2.

26   Wright is quoted in Grey, *The Supreme Court and the News Media,* 140; the undated column by Pearson (late May 1935?) is in Scrapbooks on Supreme Court History, 1880–1935, #14, Record Group 267, NA.

27   Grey, *The Supreme Court and the News Media,* 112–13. The famous ruling on the Miranda confession case was one of eight decisions issued a week later on June 13, 1965. See NYT, June 14, 1965, p. 38.

28   Paul F. Healy, "Backstage at the Supreme Court," *Saturday Evening Post,* Jan. 2, 1960, 54.

29   Grey, *The Supreme Court and the News Media,* 50; *Memoirs of Earl Warren,* 335.

30   Douglas, *The Court Years, 1939–1975,* 205–06, 278–79.

31   Dilliard, "A Supreme Court Majority?" *Harper's,* 173 (1936), 598–601; Dilliard to the author, June 8, 1984.

32   Lowell Mellett (1884–1960) covered the Supreme Court for the Washington *Daily News* during the 1920s, wrote a five-part series about the attempt to curb the power of the Court in 1923–24, and after a long career in journalism served as an administrative assistant to Franklin D. Roosevelt, 1940–44. Perry Arnold (1885–1946) joined the Washington staff of United Press in 1907 as a political writer with special interests in the presidency and the Supreme Court.

33   Cranberg, "What Did the Supreme Court Say?" *Saturday Review,* Apr. 8, 1967, 90–92.

34   Lewis, "Problems of a Washington Correspondent," 365; James E. Clayton, *The Making of Justice: The Supreme Court in Action* (New York, 1964), 303–04; Linda Greenhouse, "Taking the Supreme Court's Pulse," NYT, Jan. 28, 1984, p. A8; Jack Anderson, "Chief Justice Burger Takes a Stand above the Law," *Ithaca Journal,* Nov. 9, 1982, p. 8.

35   NYT, June 14, 1965, p. 38.

36   *Ibid.*; NYT, Nov. 15, 1984, p. 10.

37   Address by Justice Stevens at Dedication of Law Library Building, Florida
      State University, Tallahassee (Jan. 26, 1985), text courtesy of the Public
      Information Office, U.S. Supreme Court.

38   NYT, Nov. 15, 1984, p. A10; NYT, Jan. 22, 1984, p. E9; Douglas, *The
      Court Years, 1939–1975,* 39–40.

39   Cranberg, "What Did the Supreme Court Say?" 92; Supreme Court His-
      torical Society *Quarterly,* 5 (Spring 1983), 8; NYT, Mar. 19, 1985, p.
      A19.

40   NYT, Sept. 27, 1984, p. A16.

41   Douglas, *The Court Years, 1939–1975,* 205; Grey, *The Supreme Court and
      the News Media,* 148.

42   Grey, *The Supreme Court and the News Media,* 83, 87–91; Professor Paul
      Freund's observations at the time concur: CBS Reports, "Storm Over the
      Supreme Court," Part 2, Mar. 13, 1963, p. 22, and Part 3, June 19, 1963,
      p. 23.

43   A Hearst Report, *The American Public, the Media & The Judicial System: A
      National Survey on Public Awareness and Personal Experience* (New York,
      1983), 6–7.

44   See M. M. Chambers, "Constitutional Issues as Current Events," *Social
      Education,* 2 (1938), 395–98; P. J. Ross, Jr., "Constitutional Government
      Challenges Teachers," *ibid.,* 7 (1943), 352–54; Homer T. Knight,
      "Teaching the Constitution from Sources," *The Social Studies,* 31 (1940),
      159–60; John J. Reed, "The Economic Interpretation of the Constitution,"
      ibid., 34 (1943), 23–28; Robert E. Jewett, "A Study of the Constitu-
      tion—An Approach to Civic Education," *ibid.,* 41 (1950), 123–25.

45   Evelyn Eisenstadt to Dorothy Canfield Fisher, June 1, 1951, Fisher Papers,
      University of Vermont; Allan Nevins to Irving Brant, Apr. 22, 1954, Brant
      Papers, box 15, LCMD; *Educational Film Locator of the Consortium of Uni-
      versity Film Centers* (New York, 1980), 1197–98. For future prospects, see
      Agency for Instructional Technology, *A Video Project to Increase Under-
      standing of the United States Constitution in Junior and Senior High School*
      (Bloomington, Ind., September, 1984), a 27-page prospectus.

46   Powell to Moley, Sept. 27, 1933, Powell Papers, HLSL; McCloskey to
      Benjamin F. Wright, May 5, 1966, McCloskey Papers, box 1966, HUPL.

47   Beard, *The Republic: Conversations on Fundamentals* (New York, 1943);
      Ellen Nore, *Charles A. Beard: An Intellectual Biography* (Carbondale, Ill.,
      1983), 194–98; Schlesinger, "The Supreme Court: 1947," *Fortune,* 35
      (1947), 208.

48   Bob Woodward and Scott Armstrong, *The Brethren: Inside the Supreme
      Court* (New York, 1979).

49   See "The Supreme Court," *Time,* July 1, 1957, 11–16; "Our Vanishing
      Constitution," *U.S. News and World Report,* July 20, 1964, 104; Ernest
      Havemann, "The Warren Court: Storm Center of Justice," RD, 85
      (1964), 130–35; Eugene H. Methvin, "Is the Supreme Court Really Su-
      preme?" RD, 91 (1967), 80–85.

50   See *TV Guide* (Scranton–Wilkes Barre edition), Aug. 17, 1957, p. 2; Apr.
      11, 1964, pp. 22–25; Apr. 18, 1964, pp. 22–25; Apr. 25, 1964, pp. 15–19;
      May 22, 1971, p. 1; Aug. 14, 1971, p. 1.

51   *Ibid.*, July 10, 1965, p. 3; Mar. 3, 1973, p. 1.

52   *Ibid.*, May 22, 1971, p. 1; July 10, 1971, p. 1; Aug. 14, 1971, p. 1.

53   *Ibid.*, Oct. 19, 1963, p. 2; Apr. 11, 1964, p. 4; Oct. 12, 1968, p. 2; Harry S. Ashmore, *Fear in the Air: Broadcasting and the First Amendment—The Anatomy of a Constitutional Crisis* (New York, 1973), esp. 26–27; and Thomas L. Tedford, *Freedom of Speech in the United States* (New York, 1985), 380–410.

54   Roscoe L. Barrow, "The Fairness Doctrine: A Double Standard for Electronic and Print Media," *The Hastings Law Journal*, 26 (1975), 659–708; Fred W. Friendly, *The Good Guys, the Bad Guys, and the First Amendment: Free Speech vs. Fairness in Broadcasting* (New York, 1976).

55   Vincent Terrace, *The Complete Encyclopedia of Television Programs, 1947–1979* (2nd ed.: New York, 1979), 520, 633; Tim Brooks and Earle Marsh, *The Complete Directory to Prime Time Network TV Shows: 1946–Present* (New York, 1979), 5–6, 36, 137, 142, 152, 192, 315, 339, 343, 622, 657, 689, 702.

56   Paul L. Murphy, *The Constitution in Crisis Times, 1918–1969* (New York, 1972), 380, 472; *Time*, July 16, 1965, p. 23; Brooks and Marsh, *Complete Directory to Prime Time Network TV Shows*, 2.

57   CBS Reports, "The School Prayer Case," Mar. 13, 1963, transcript courtesy of CBS News.

58   CBS Reports, "Bible Reading in the Public Schools," June 19, 1963, transcript courtesy of CBS News; NYT, June 14, 1965, p. 38.

59   CBS Reports, "Storm Over the Supreme Court," Feb. 20, 1963, transcript courtesy of CBS News.

60   Joseph N. Welch *et al.*, *The Constitution* (Boston, 1956), xiii.

61   See Dan T. Carter, *Scottsboro: A Tragedy of the American South* (rev. ed.: Baton Rouge, La., 1979), 416–62; "60 Minutes," vol. XII, no. 12, Dec. 2, 1979, transcript courtesy of CBS News; NYT, Dec. 29, 1984, p. 42.

62   See the Chafee Papers, HUG4273.22, HUPL.

63   *TV Guide* (Pa.–N.Y. edition), June 25, 1977, p. 36.

64   NYT, Dec. 12, 1984, p. C30. Fred W. Friendly and Martha J. H. Elliott, *The Constitution: That Delicate Balance* (New York, 1984), is not the series script in book form; rather, it is a history of important Supreme Court decisions designed as a text to accompany the video series in college courses. There is also a study guide prepared by George McKenna, as well as Discussion Leader Guides "for less structured uses" of the television programs.

65   "Mr. Justice Douglas," pp. 2, 15, transcript courtesy of CBS News; "Invasion of Privacy—How Big a Threat?" [an interview with Sam Ervin], *U.S. News and World Report*, Mar. 6, 1972, 42–45; Ervin, "Justice, the Constitution, and Privacy," VSD, 34 (Sept. 1, 1973), 677–81.

•   CHAPTER 14 *It's What Holds Us All Together*

1   Maverick, *In Blood and Ink: The Life and Documents of American Democracy* (New York, 1939), 184. Italics his.

2   *Ibid.*, 4. In preparing this short book, Maverick had the assistance of

Charles Beard, Leon Henderson, and Thurman Arnold (who was responsible for the section on the Bill of Rights).

3   G. Edward White, *Earl Warren: A Public Life* (New York, 1982), 320–25; NYT, Sept. 14, 1982, p. A24; NYT, Oct. 4, 1982, p. A18; NYT, Feb. 7, 1983, p. A1; NYT, Dec. 31, 1984, p. A7; NYT, Jan. 5, 1985, p. A20; NYT, Mar. 12, 1985, p. A30; Samuel Estreicher and John Sexton, "Streamlining the High Court," NYT, Mar. 27, 1985, p. A27.

4   Hampton L. Carson, ed., *History of the Celebration of the One Hundredth Anniversary of the Promulgation of the Constitution of the United States* (Philadelphia, 1889), II, 313–14.

5   Interview with Ervin, NYT, Sept. 19, 1983, p. B8; Rusk, *In Praise of Consensus: Reflections Upon the American Constitution* (Athens, Ga., 1984), 10.

6   Herbert McClosky and Alida Brill, *Dimensions of Tolerance: What Americans Believe about Civil Liberties* (New York, 1983), 148, 433, 464. For a telling anecdote illustrative of racial prejudice as well as constitutional ignorance, see Lawrence W. Levine, *Black Culture and Black Consciousness: Afro-American Folk Thought from Slavery to Freedom* (New York, 1977), 319.

7   The American Legion National Americanism Commission, *National High School Oratorical Contest* (Indianapolis, 1957), 103-page booklet in which the winning speech from each state appeared.

8   H. Trevor Colbourn, "Madison Eulogized: The Hearst Tournament of Orators Glorifies (one year early) the Anniversary of the Birth of the Father of the Constitution," WMQ, 8 (1951), 108–19; *DAR Magazine*, 105 (October 1971), 720–23, 780; letter from Elva B. Crawford (Archivist, NSDAR), to the author, June 19, 1984, with enclosures. See also Louis Filler, "The Constitution Doesn't Say That 'All Men Are Created Equal,'" *The Social Sciences*, 55 (1964), 181–85.

9   See Howard D. Mehlinger, ed., *Teaching About the Constitution in American Secondary Schools* (Washington, D.C., 1981), based upon a conference held at Indiana University in October 1980; letter from Elsie T. Freeman (Chief, Education Branch, National Archives) to the author, Mar. 19, 1985, with enclosures.

10   Robert M. O'Neil, "The Constitution, the Supreme Court, and Youth," *Social Education*, 37 (1973), 397–99; Barbara Hall, "Close Encounters with Democracy," NYT *Education Summer Survey*, Aug. 19, 1984, sec. 12, p. 23.

11   NYT, Dec. 12, 1978, p. C6; *International Herald Tribune*, Mar. 19, 1981; NYT, July 23, 1984, p. A8; NYT, Dec. 28, 1984, p. A16.

12   For one way of exploring these dualisms, see Martin Diamond, "Conservatives, Liberals, and the Constitution," *The Public Interest*, no. 1 (1965), 96–109.

13   See Smith, *The Spirit of American Government* (New York, 1907), esp. chs. 3 and 7; Myers, *History of the Supreme Court of the United States* (Chicago, 1912).

14   See Robert A. Goldwin and William A. Schambra, eds., *How Democratic Is the Constitution?* (Washington, D.C., 1980), esp. 17, 111–12.

15   Dahl, *A Preface to Democratic Theory* (Chicago, 1956), 143. See, however,

John Hart Ely, *Democracy and Distrust. A Theory of Judicial Review* (Cambridge, Mass., 1980), esp. 120-24.

16   Compare Bork, *Tradition and Morality in Constitutional Law* (Washington, D.C., 1984), esp. p. 10, and Miller, *Social Change and Fundamental Law: America's Evolving Constitution* (Westport, Conn., 1979), esp. p. 8 and ch. 2. See also William H. Rehnquist, "The Notion of a Living Constitution," *Texas Law Review,* 54 (1976), 693-706.

17   Richard C. Cortner, *The Supreme Court and the Second Bill of Rights: The Fourteenth Amendment and the Nationalization of Civil Liberties* (Madison, Wis., 1981).

18   Eckhardt and Black, *The Tides of Power: Conversations on the American Constitution* (New Haven, Conn., 1976), 1, 3. For a critical response to this shift, see the views expressed by Justice Brennan in May 1985, NYT, May 5, 1985, p. A42.

19   McClosky and Brill, *What Americans Believe about Civil Liberties,* 417; Herbert J. Storing, "The Constitution and the Bill of Rights," in M. Judd Harmon, ed., *Essays on the Constitution of the United States* (Port Washington, N.Y., 1978), 33; Richard E. Morgan, *Disabling America: The "Rights Industry" in Our Time* (New York, 1984), 5.

20   Johnson, *America-Watching: Perspectives in the Course of an Incredible Century* (Owings Mills, Md., 1976), 313; Frank J. Sorauf, "The Political Potential of an Amending Convention," in Kermit L. Hall, *et al., The Constitutional Convention as an Amending Device* (Washington, D.C., 1981), 114.

21   Marc Leepson, "Calls for Constitutional Conventions," *Editorial Research Reports,* I (Mar. 16, 1979), 187-204; Harriet Pilpel, "Constitution Changing," NYT, Jan. 20, 1979, p. A21; Ferdinand Lundberg, *Cracks in the Constitution* (Secaucus, N.J., 1980), ch. 10, "A Renewed Call for a Second Convention"; Wilbur Edel, "To Avert a 'Runaway' Constitutional Convention," NYT, June 22, 1984, p. A26.

22   NYT, Nov. 2, 1981, p. B5; TRB, "Constitutional Questions," NR, Mar. 28, 1983, pp. 4, 37.

23   NYT, Feb. 6, 1982, p. A22; NYT, Feb. 20, 1982, p. A22; NYT, Aug. 22, 1982, p. E4; NYT, Aug. 21, 1983, p. A31.

24   Rusk, *In Praise of Consensus: Reflections Upon the American Constitution,* 4.

25   RC, AIPOØ373K & T G, question 19, form T (June 14-19, 1946).

26   NYT, May 25, 1983, pp. A1, 22.

27   NYT, Aug. 6, 1984, p. A16; NYT, Oct. 16, 1984, p. A27.

28   See Alan F. Westin, "Charles Beard and American Debate Over Judicial Review, 1790-1961," in Charles A. Beard, *The Supreme Court and the Constitution,* ed. by Alan F. Westin (Englewood Cliffs, N.J., 1960), 1-34; Raoul Berger, *Congress v. the Supreme Court* (Cambridge, Mass., 1969); and Berger, *Government by Judiciary: The Transformation of the Fourteenth Amendment* (Cambridge, Mass., 1977).

29   Tom Wicker, "Court-Strippers and U.S. Rights," NYT, Apr. 24, 1981, p. A31.

30   *Ibid.*; NYT, Mar. 12, 1982, p. A18; Max Baucus, "Proper Helmsmen: The Court," NYT, Sept. 7, 1982, p. A23. Baucus, a Democrat from Montana, serves on the Senate Judiciary Committee.

31   Anthony Lewis, "Mr. Zero Goes to Washington," NYT, Jan. 28, 1982, p. A23; NYT, Feb. 26, 1983, p. A7.

32   NYT, Jan. 28, 1982, p. A23; NYT, Sept. 7, 1982, p. A23.

33   Charles Evans Hughes, "Justice Our Anchor," VSD, 6 (1940), 260.

34   NYT, Sept. 14, 1983, p. B6; NYT, Dec. 17, 1983, p. A7. See Lawrence Ward Beer, ed., *Constitutionalism in Asia: Asian Views of the American Influence* (Berkeley, Calif., 1979).

35   Russell H. Fitzgibbon, ed., *The Constitutions of the Americas* (Chicago, 1948), 8–9. For a more critical and pessimistic perspective, see J. Lloyd Mecham, "Latin American Constitutions, Nominal and Real," JP, 21 (1959), 258–75.

36   NYT, Apr. 18, 1982, p. A1. For Australia's constitutional crises of 1932 and 1975, see W. G. McMinn, *A Constitutional History of Australia* (Melbourne, 1979), 161–68; Heather Radi and Peter Spearritt, eds., *Jack Lang* (Neutral Bay, New South Wales, 1977), 160–78; and Michael Sexton, *Illusions of Power: The Fate of a Reform Government* (Sydney, 1979), 201–69. Two similarities with the American experience are apparent in these Australian crises: first, that ambiguities or omissions in the Australian constitution provided no means of resolution for certain situations of political stalemate; and second, that social stability prevailed despite political and constitutional turmoil.

37   NYT, Feb. 19, 1985, p. A8.

38   NYT, Oct. 9, 1983, p. A1; NYT, Nov. 6, 1983, p. E3.

39   NYT, Sept. 10, 1983, p. A3.

40   NYT, Dec. 3, 1982, p. A14; NYT, Dec. 5, 1982, p. A23. See also Edward Shils, "The Fortunes of Constitutional Government in the Political Development of the New States," in Shils, *Center and Periphery* (Chicago, 1975), 456–82.

41   See J. W. Burrow, *A Liberal Descent: Victorian Historians and the English Past* (Cambridge, Eng., 1981), 43, 105–06.

42   Maverick, *In Blood and Ink*, 85.

43   See, e.g., David H. Donald, *Liberty and Union* (Boston, 1978), 175–83; Herbert Wechsler, *The Nationalization of Civil Liberties and Civil Rights* (Austin, Tex., 1970), 25; and Eckhardt and Black, *Conversations on the American Constitution, passim.*

44   Steven V. Roberts, "Gadfly Says What Others Will Not," NYT, Nov. 30, 1981, p. B8.

45   Rush, *A Plan for the Establishment of Public Schools . . . to Which Are Added, Thoughts upon the Mode of Education, Proper in a Republic* (Philadelphia, 1786), in Frederick Rudolph, ed., *Essays on Education in the Early Republic* (Cambridge, Mass., 1965), 17.

46   Lippmann, *A Preface to Politics* (New York, 1913), 17–18.

47   See Morton Keller, "The Politics of State Constitutional Revision, 1820–1930," in Hall, ed., *The Constitutional Convention as an Amending Device*, 67; Robert H. Jackson, *The Supreme Court in the American System of Government* (Cambridge, Mass., 1955), 65, 68, 74–75.

Index

abolition, as constitutional issue, 97–105
  passim
abortion, right to, 354
Abrams v. *United States* case (1919), 256,
  341
Acton, John Emerich Edward Dalberg,
  Lord, 162
Adams, Brooks, on Constitution: Anglo-
  American view of, 168; Court's role
  and, 201–2, 205; political aspect of
  interpreting, 200
Adams, Charles Francis, 99
Adams, Henry, 52, 116–17, 168
Adams, Herbert Baxter, 177, 180
Adams, James Truslow, 339
Adams, John:
  on British constitution: his admiration
    of, 158; as "machine," 17
  on Constitution: as based on colonial
    institutions, 158; his reservations
    about, 43–4
Adams, John Quincy:
  on Constitution: and Declaration of In-
    dependence, 21, 90; as machine, 18;
    as national symbol, 71; and prosper-
    ity, 16; and state sovereignty, 55
  Discourse (April 1839), 90
  publishes Constitutional Convention
    journal (1819), 86–7
Adams, Samuel, 48

Adamson v. *California* case (1947), 345,
  346
adaptability of Constitution, *see* altering
  Constitution; flexibility of Constitution
adult education, constitutional, 28–9, 77,
  78, 79–81, 235, 374–80
  for naturalization, 120, 235–48 *passim*
  by television, 376–80
Agnew, Daniel, 109–10
Alexander I, Czar of Russia, 93
Alien and Sedition Acts (1798–99),
  51–2, 56
Allen, Robert S.: *Nine Old Men, The,*
  275, 375
altering Constitution:
  by amendment, *see* amendment of
    Constitution
  dialogue on (twentieth century),
    226–7, 331–5
  ease of, 120, 169, 186
  "promiscuity" of, 206–7
  resistance to, 142, 316, 331, 382
  totally rewriting, 176, 206, 227, 258,
    316; Tugwell's effort, 316, 332–4,
    335
Alvord, Clarence W., 211
amendment of Constitution:
  v. Court's interpretation, as system of
    altering Constitution, 227

amendment of Constitution (*Continued*)
difficulty or ease of, 169, 188–9, 202, 227, 258–9
efforts to bypass, concerning Supreme Court, 330
fear of and opposition to, 20, 207, 382
number of efforts at, 11
Progressives and, 258
public view of, 152, 331
and U.S. membership in League of Nations, 257
Van Devanter on, 271
see also Constitution, U.S., Amendments

American Bar Association (ABA):
and Bill of Rights, 338, 339
on constitutional morality, 204
and Constitution Week, 222
on ignorance of Constitution, 230–1
on judicial review, 326, 393
mystification of Constitution by, 120–1
proclaims John Marshall Day (1901), 209–10

American Constitutional League, 208
American Defense Society, 220, 225
American Liberty League, 38
American Rights League, 220, 225
anarchy, threat of, 206
anchor (Constitution as), 17
anniversaries and celebrations of Constitution:
125th (1912), 205
public interest in, 385; *see also under specific anniversaries*
Warren (E.) on, 89
see also Bill of Rights Week; Centennial (1887–89); Constitution Day; Constitution Week; Golden Jubilee (1837–39); Sesquicentennial (1937–39)

Anti-Federalists:
accommodation of, with Federalists, 29
and Constitution, 44, 52; its comprehensibility by the people, 75
apathy, *see* indifference toward Constitution
Aristotle, 43
Arnold, Thurman W., 30–1, 38, 229–30, 273, 276, 495 n. 51

Articles of Confederation:
and Confederate Constitution, 115
and Constitution of 1787, 181
displayed (1937), 297 n.
Ashbrook, John, 355
Ashmore, Harry S., 368
Ashurst, Henry F., 284
Athens, constitution of, 161
Atherton, Gertrude, 232
Australian constitution, 507 n. 36

Bagehot, Walter, 34, 108, 111, 159, 160, 162
English Constitution, 161
Baker, Newton D., 174–5, 226–7, 253–4
balance of powers:
among branches of government, 71, 261, 263, 312, 320–2; attacks on, 392
state and national, *see* state sovereignty; states' rights
Baldwin, Henry, 46, 79, 179
Bancroft, George:
"Federal Constitution, The" (1889), 150
History of the United States, 127
Banning, Lance, 46
Bates, Henry M., 30
Beard, Charles A.:
on Beveridge's biography of Marshall, 211
changing ideology of, 6
and Committee on the Federal Constitution, 207
on Constitution: and British constitution, 175; his criticism of, 228; democracy of, 387; worship of, 23
on Constitutional Convention, 21
Dishonest Constitution, The, 206
Economic Interpretation of the Constitution, 180; Lunn on, 171
Merriam *v.*, 228
Republic, The, 374
and Sesquicentennial Commission, 307–8
on Supreme Court, 201, 275
Beck, James M.:
on Constitution, xii, 224, 253; and British constitution, 174; as "dead" as instrument of commerce, 14;

Beck, James M. (*Continued*)
  Eighteenth Amendment, 258; flexibility of, 471 n. 24; public ignorance of, 217; public indifference toward, 4; public opinion and, 14, 217
  on centralization of government, 264–5
  on Constitutional Convention, secrecy of, 435 n. 52
  on constitutional conventions, danger of, 430 n. 41
  as constitutional educator, 26
  on constitutional morality, 204, 229, 253
  Constitution of the United States, The, 249, 252
  criticizes "individualistic democracy," 229
  on Fiske's work, 25
  lectures in England (1922), 171
  on Madison and Hamilton, 279
  publications by, 252
  on Supreme Court, 263–4 and n.
  Vanishing Rights of the States, The, 265
  v. Warren (C.), 228
Becker, Carl L., 228
Bell, John, 104
Bennett, H. Arnold, 233
Berger, Raoul, 355
Berryman, James T., 312
Beveridge, Albert J., xiii
  biography of Marshall, 209, 210–13, 251
  "Common Sense and the Constitution," 29
  on Supreme Court, 262–3
Bill of Rights (1789–91), 336–56 *passim,* 388–9
  applicability of, to states, 7, 322, 345, 388
  commemoration of, 306
  physical location of, 73
  public interest in and support for, 188, 336–41, 344–5, 353
  public knowledge and understanding of, 340–1, 343, 350
  Sesquicentennial of (1941), 339
  Sinclair (U.) attempts to read publicly (1923), xiv–xv
  in territories, 192

Bill of Rights Institute, 348
Bill of Rights Week, 339
Bingham, Jonathan, 101
Binney, Horace, 62
Birch (John) Society, 328
Birkenhead, Lord, *see* Smith, F. E.
Birney, James G., 100
Black, Hugo L.:
  on appointment of justices, 200
  on Constitution: Bill of Rights, 345–6; public understanding of, 4
  and Frankfurter, 323
  and Jackson (R. H.), 360–1
  and publicity, 360; televised interview (1968), 4, 200, 346, 353, 361, 378
  qualifications of, to be justice, 278, 322, 360
black citizens:
  and Centennial celebration, 137
  franchise for, *see* Fifteenth Amendment
  see also civil rights; integration, racial
Blackmun, Harry Andrew, 319, 362
Blaine, James G., 21
Blake, Eugene Carson, 349
Blanshard, Paul, 346
Blaustein, Albert P., 394
Blease, Cole L., 123
Bloom, Sol, 254, 286, 308
  on Constitution, xiii, 224
  and Sesquicentennial, 282, 283–300 *passim,* 309–11
Borah, William E.:
  on Constitution: his contradictory views on, 204–5; on Eighteenth Amendment, 258; public interest in, xiii, 219; its sacredness, 308; *v.* Warren (C.) on, 227–8
  and judicial review, 31, 277–8
  on margin of Supreme Court decisions, 118, 261–2, 277
  on states' rights, 187
Bork, Robert, 388, 392
Boutwell, George S., 192–3
Brandegee, Frank B., 206
Brandeis, Louis D.:
  appointment of, to Court (1916), 264
  and Frankfurter, 362–3
  ideology of, 7
  and publicity, 360

Brandeis, Louis D. (*Continued*)
    on public opinion, 14
    on *Swift* v. *Tyson* (1842), 250
Brant, Irving, 279, 368
    Storm Over the Constitution, 275, 368
Breckinridge, John C., 104
Breese, Sidney, 41, 83
Brewer, David J.:
    on public opinion, 14
    public talks by, 27, 196
    on working women, 194
Bricker Amendment (1951), 320–1
Britain:
    constitutional dialogue and exchanges
        of visits with, 170–3
    governmental crisis in (1906–11),
        161, 213
British constitution, 35–7, 156–84,
        397–8
    British perceptions of (nineteenth cen-
        tury), 160–1
    continuity of, 33, 161
    Enlightenment admiration for, 65
    flexibility and responsiveness of, 14,
        34, 67, 161, 162, 163–4, 169, 397
    as "machine" (Adams), 17
    relation of U.S. Constitution to,
        156–76, 180, 456–7 n. 55
    shortcomings of (Cooper on), 66–7
British responses to U.S. Constitution,
        34, 36–7, 108, 111, 159–63,
        171–3, 174, 175–6
Broun, Heywood, 9, 32, 274, 336
Brown, Henry Billings, 34, 193
Brown v. *Board of Education* case
        (1954), 324, 326, 327
Bruce, William Cabell, 169
Bryant, William Cullen, 89–90
Bryce, James, Lord, 34, 164–6, 171–2,
        174, 205
    American Commonwealth, The, 13, 165
Burger, Warren:
    as chief justice, 330
    on legislative veto, 322
    plan to create auxiliary Supreme
        Court, 198, 382
    and publicity, 362, 363, 370, 371
    on public opinion, 14
Burgess, John W., 180
Burke, Edmund, 397
Burr, Aaron (trial of), 5, 49

Burton, Harold H., 342
Bush-Brown, H. K., 266
businessmen:
    and Constitution, 23
    and Sesquicentennial celebrations, 293
Butler, Nicholas Murray, 169, 227,
        230

Calhoun, John C.:
    and Constitution, 57
    *Discourse on the Constitution and Gov-
        ernment of the United States, A*, 114
    Disquisition on Government, 20, 114
    in Nullification movement, 53, 55
    South Carolina "Exposition" (1828)
        by, 55
Canadian constitution, 213, 395
Cardozo, Benjamin, 19, 266
Carson, Hampton L., 129, 137, 142–3,
        221, 263, 264
Carter, Jimmy, 358
Cartwright, John, 50
Cass, Lewis, 80
Catlin, George: *Virginia Constitutional
        Convention of 1829–30, The*, 92
celebrations, *see* anniversaries and cele-
        brations of Constitution
Centennial of Constitution (1887–89),
        127–51
    celebrations of, 137–40; in New York
        City, 129–30, 143–4, 145–51, 153;
        in Philadelphia, 129–30, 137–40,
        143; by states, 144–5, 151
    Commission for, 128–38 *passim*,
        142–3; elitism of, 137, 146; letter
        on British and American constitu-
        tions, 166–7
    funding of, 130, 134, 138, 143–4
    interstate and interurban rivalries in,
        129–30, 143
    planning of (national), 130–8
    publications generated by, 152–3
    public interest in, 128–9, 133, 138–9,
        152, 153, 289
Center for the Study of Democratic In-
        stitutions, Santa Barbara, Calif.,
        332–4
Cerutti, Joseph Antoine, 65
Chafee, Zechariah, Jr., 6, 272–3
    "Constitution and Human Rights,
        The," 379

change, constitutional, *see* altering Constitution; amendment of Constitution; flexibility of Constitution

Charles River Bridge case (1837), 15, 79, 158

Chase, Salmon P., 100, 184

Chase, Samuel, 49

checks and balances, 71, 261, 263, 312, 320–2

  attacks on, 392

Child Labor laws, 194, 260, 317

Chinese constitutions, 213–15, 396–7

Chisholm v. *Georgia* case (1793), 49, 178

Christy, Howard Chandler, 303–4

Citizens Committee of One Thousand, 258

citizenship tests, 120, 235–48

citizenship training, 239–40

civil rights:

  of Communists, 256, 325–6, 328, 336, 341, 344

  of criminals, 326, 329, 336, 352, 353, 355–6

  interest in: *v.* property rights, 336, 347; *v.* states' rights, 188

  police and, 337–8

  Supreme Court cases, 341; (1883), 28, 119, 121; 1930s, 266; 1954 and following, 33, 324–5, 345, 352–6

  of women, 354–5

  see also Bill of Rights

Civil Rights Act (1875), 121

Civil War:

  Confederate Constitution during, 114–16

  and Constitution, 116–17; attitudes toward, 29–30, 123, 158–9; as crisis for, 95, 112; survival of Constitution, 116–17, 122, 427 n. 2

  and state sovereignty, 182

Clark, Tom C., 344

Cleveland, Grover, 16, 186

  and Centennial celebrations, 134–5, 139–40, 153

Colby, Bainbridge, 223

colonial constitutions and charters, 69, 158, 164, 167, 179–80

Commager, Henry Steele, xix, 31

commerce:

  Constitution and, 14, 15, 55, 275

  Supreme Court and, 49

Committee on the Constitutional System, 390

Committee on the Federal Constitution, 207–8

communism (international), American opposition to, 321, 344

Communists in U.S.:

  anxiety about and investigation of, 328, 336–7, 352

  on Bill of Rights, 306

  civil rights of, 256, 325–6, 328, 336, 341, 344

  on Constitution, 279–80

  Jackson (R. H.) on, 359, 501 n. 8

  registration of, 348, 352

  Smith Act and, 345

"compact" *v.* constitution (Webster), 53–4

concurrent majority, 114

Confederate Constitution, 29, 114–16

conflict, constitutional:

  in Civil War era, 95–124

  consensus and, *see* conflict within consensus

  creative aspects of, 30–1; clarification of values, 37–9; interest in Constitution, 386–90

  in early years of Constitution, 46–8

  as integral to American history, xvii

  origins of, 30

  see also judicial review; state sovereignty; Supreme Court

conflict within consensus, 29–31, 35, 46, 185–6, 212, 215, 308, 330, 380, 381, 386, 399

Congress:

  and Centennial celebrations, 134–5

  debates of (publication of), 84

  knowledge of Constitution by members of, 84

  and slavery, jurisdiction over, 97, 100, 101

  see also constitutionality of legislation; judicial review

Congress and Constitution:

  conflict between, 255; *see also* judicial review

  "contempt" for Constitution, 13

  see also checks and balances

Congress and President, 320–2; *see also* checks and balances

Congress and Supreme Court:
  legislative efforts to curb Court, 76
    and *table,* 118–19, 260–3, 274, 325,
    328–9, 330, 392–3, 479 n. 22
  preliminary opinions by Court on leg-
    islation, proposed, 263–4 and n.
  see also checks and balances; constitu-
    tionality of legislation; judicial re-
    view

consensus, political, 29–30, 90
  claimed: for first era of Constitution,
    46, 48; for nineteenth-century con-
    stitutionalism, 185, 186, 191, 460
    n. 1
  conflict and, *see* conflict within con-
    sensus

conservatives, constitutional, 20, 31
  and altering Constitution, 227, 258,
    331
  and Constitutional Convention
    (1787), 21
  in early twentieth century, 205–6,
    227, 228–9
  and judicial review, 33, 392, 393
  on politicization of Court, 391
  strict constructionists, 30, 317
  writings of, and constitutional educa-
    tion, 77

constitution, early usage and develop-
    ment of term, 68–9

Constitution (U.S., 1787):
  ambiguities in, 5–6, 74–5, 119, 415 n.
    8; *see also* framers of Constitution,
    intentions of
  anniversaries of, *see* anniversaries and
    celebrations of Constitution
  applicability of, to other countries, 22,
    65–6, 254
  commentaries on, 78, 79–80; *see also*
    scholars
  continuity and discontinuity of, 33–4,
    67, 160, 399; *see also* flexibility of
    Constitution
  crises of confidence in: 1820s, 50;
    1840s–50s, 63; Civil War era, 95;
    twentieth century, 206–8, 213,
    215–6
  democratic character of, debated,
    387–8

as "dry" document, xii–xiii, 224, 233,
    286
  interpretation of, *see* conservatives,
    constitutional: strict constructionists;
    interpretation of Constitution; liber-
    als, constitutional: broad construc-
    tionists; Supreme Court
  physical location of, 72–3, 127, 153,
    223–4
  as symbol, *see* symbolic function of
    Constitution
  Washington's copy of, displayed,
    294–5

Constitution, U.S., Amendments:
  conservatives on abolishing of, 227
  physical location of, 73
  First, *see* First Amendment
  Fourth, 353
  Fifth, 338, 343, 356
  Sixth, 356
  Tenth, 113–14, 323–4, 428 n. 26
  Eleventh, 49
  Thirteenth, 113
  Fourteenth, *see* Fourteenth Amend-
    ment
  Fifteenth, 117, 188, 227
  Seventeenth, 227
  Eighteenth, 227, 258
  see also amendment of Constitution;
    Bill of Rights

Constitution, U.S., Preamble, 224

Constitution, U.S., proposed amend-
    ments:
  late nineteenth century, 188
    (1897), 177
  twentieth century, 207, 389–90
  Bricker's (1951), 320–1
  on limiting Supreme Court, 274,
    328–9
  number and periodicity of, 11
  on slavery, 11

Constitution (warship), 90

Constitutional Convention (Philadelphia,
    1787):
  compromise at, 311, 469 n. 93
  as "conservative counterrevolution,"
    21
  on English constitution, 17, 158
  graphic depictions of, 91–2
  Madison's notes on, 26, 86–9, 97, 100
  official journal of, published, 86–7

secrecy of, 86–7, 435 n. 52
social and economic issues at, 181, 229
see also framers of Constitution, intentions of
constitutional convention(s), proposed:
(1897), 177
twentieth century, 389–90
danger of, 258–9, 390, 430 n. 41
Madison on, 58
constitutional convention(s), state, 120
constitutional education, *see* education, constitutional
constitutional history (as professional discipline), xix–xx, 176–81
concentrated on Supreme Court, 9
German, 180
publications in, 178–81; *see also* textbooks on constitutionalism; *specific authors and titles*
constitutional morality, 23, 204, 229–30, 253
constitutionalism:
definition of, xvii–xviii
see also altering Constitution; amendment of Constitution; conflict, constitutional; Constitution (U.S., 1787); cult of Constitution; flexibility of Constitution; interest in Constitution; interpretation of Constitution; public opinion and Constitution; symbolic function of Constitution; understanding of Constitution; worship of Constitution
constitutionality of legislation, 10–11
1930s–1950s, 324, 325–6
1970s and 1980s, 319, 321
American v. British jurisdiction over, 456 n. 55
Borah on, 277–8
on internal domestic improvements, 60–1
New Deal programs, 15, 269, 270–3, 275, 317
Supreme Court and: efforts to reduce this power, 392–3; exclusive jurisdiction over, 7, 26–8, 76–7, 250–1; size of majority in decisions of, 260; preliminary opinions proposed (Beck), 263–4 and n.; *see also* judicial review; Supreme Court

Constitutional League, 225
Constitutional Protective League, 270
Constitutional Rights Foundation, 353
Constitutional Safety Day, 261
Constitutional Anniversary Association, *see* Constitution Education Association
Constitution Day, 162, 220–3, 278, 284, 348–9, 385
Constitution Education Association, 221, 222
"Constitution in the Twentieth Century, The" (1936), 275–6
constitutions, colonial, 69, 158, 164, 167, 179–80; *see also* constitutions, state
constitutions, national, *see* Constitution (U.S., 1787); *and under specific countries*
constitutions, state:
as "charters," 69
Constitution (U.S.) and, 11–12, 52, 163
defense of (1930s), 270
included in definition of constitutionalism (Cooley), 159
and judicial review, 32
need for, 181
uniqueness of, 157
writing and revising of (nineteenth century), 120
see also constitutions, colonial
constitutions, written:
v. British constitution, 167–8, 175
and judicial review, 179
and public opinion, 14
and reason, 75
security in, 59, 156
as unique to America, 20
Constitution Week, 162, 221–2
contests on Constitution:
essay, 253, 297, 384
oratorical, 224, 233–5, 384
pageant, 298
Continental Congress, 5, 69
controversy, constitutional, *see* conflict, constitutional
convention(s), constitutional (proposed), *see* constitutional convention(s), proposed
Conway, Moncure D., 99–100, 142, 164
Cooley, Thomas M.:
anglophilia of, 168, 175

Cooley, Thomas M. (*Continued*)
*General Principles of Constitutional Law
. . .*, 159
ideology of, 6
*Treatise on the Constitutional Limita-
tions*, 159
Coolidge, Archibald Cary, 180
Coolidge, Calvin, 224, 265
Cooper, James Fenimore:
on British constitution, 66–7
on Constitution, 94; as "great national
car," 18; ignorance of, 83–4; interpretation of, 74–5; slavery in, 99;
and state sovereignty, 54
Cooper, Thomas: *On the Constitution of
the United States*, 77
Corcoran Gallery of Art, Washington,
D.C., 299–300
Corwin, Edward S., 177
biography of Marshall (1919), 212
*Commerce Power versus State Rights,
The*, 275
Court Over Constitution, 248
"Constitution as Instrument and Symbol, The," 68
on cult of Constitution, xiv
and New Deal, 273
"Passing of Dual Federalism, The,"
317–18
on Supreme Court and civil rights,
336
"Court-packing" plan of FDR (1937),
9, 198, 273, 276–7, 278–9, 382
and interest in Constitution, 256, 283,
291
opposition to, xiii, 8–9, 15
Coxe, A. Cleveland, bishop, 136–7
Cranberg, Gilbert, 368–9
Crawford, William H., 47
Creel, George, 276–7
Crime Control Act (1968), 353
criminals, civil rights of, 326, 329, 336,
352, 353, 355–6
Cromwell, Oliver, 17, 122–3
cult of Constitution, xiv, 22–3, 153, 208,
213, 249–50
religious overtones of, 225
see also worship of Constitution
Cummings, Alexander, 80
Cummings, Homer, 272
Curry, Jabez Lamar Monroe: *Civil History of the Government of the
Confederate States*, 124
Curtis, George Ticknor, 20, 86, 110,
167, 178, 437 n. 2
Cushman, Robert E., 212
Cutler, Menasseh, 73
cynicism about Constitution, 37, 254,
463 n. 26

Dahl, Robert A., 199, 200, 387–8
Dallas, George M., 80
Dane, Nathan, 78
Dartmouth College case (1819), 85, 178
Daugherty, Harry M., 256
Davis, Jefferson, 62, 104, 115
Davis, John W., 187, 230, 252
Declaration of Constitutional Principles
(1956), 325
Declaration of Independence and Constitution:
as complementary (J. Q. Adams), 90
display and storage of, 73, 127,
223–4; for Sesquicentennial, 300
Lincoln on (1861), 106
murals by Faulkner on, 302–3
relative attention to, 21, 127
shrines of, 285 and n.
Defenders of the American Constitution,
325
Deming, Robert C., 246–7
democracy:
American *v.* British, 201
of Constitution, 387–8
excess of, as danger, 220, 226, 228–9
Jefferson and, 253–4
Madison and, 58
Democrats:
and Constitution (Civil War era),
29–30, 112–13
and Dred Scott decision, 104
platforms of: (1864), 113; (1868),
117; (1896), 191; (1904), 193;
(1936), 274, 275
Dennis, Alfred P., 169
Dennis v. *United States* case (1951), 345
Depew, Chauncey M., 227
Depression (1930s):
conservative response to, 223
and flexibility of Constitution, 175
prosperity-and-Constitution linkage in,
14
see also New Deal programs

desegregation, *see* integration, racial

Dicey, A. V., 162

Dilliard, Irving, 367–8

Dillon, John Forrest, 210

discrimination, racial, *see* civil rights; integration, racial; racial issues

discrimination, sexual, 354–5

disobedience, constitutional, 327–8

Douglas, Stephen A., 101, 102

Douglas, William O.:
    and Bill of Rights, 345
    on Court and Constitution, 10
    impeachment of, attempted, 328
    and leak of information from Court, 501 n. 12
    on press coverage of Court, 367
    television interview with (1972), 10, 361, 378, 380

Douglass, Frederick, 98–9

Dred Scott case (1854–57), 7, 31, 102, 103–4, 178, 192, 439 n. 28

Duane, James, 157–8

Duer, William A., 78

Dunne, Peter Finley, 192

Duponceau, Peter Stephen, 78

DuPont, Pierre S., 204

education, constitutional, 41, 75–83, 208, 373–80
    twentieth century, 219, 231–48, 373–4
    contests in support of, 224, 233–5, 253, 297, 298, 384
    dissemination of information to public, 28–9, 77, 78, 79–81; *see also* press
    elementary, 81–3, 231
    in higher education, 77–8, 79, 232; *see also* constitutional history (as professional discipline)
    for immigrants, 235–48
    by radio, 222, 252, 254, 374
    reluctance of public leaders to undertake, 25–6, 57
    by scholars, 176–81, 248–50, 374–5
    with Sesquicentennial, 285–88 *passim*, 299–300, 308
    Supreme Court and, 7, 26–8, 76–7, 250–1; *see also* Supreme Court: press coverage of
    by television, 374, 375–80

textbooks, *see* textbooks and constitutionalism
    see also adult education; ignorance of Constitution; understanding of Constitution

Einstein, Albert, 337

Eisenhower, Dwight David, 320

elections and campaigns, presidential:
    (1860), 104–5
    (1868), 117–18
    (1904), 202
    (1912), 202–4
    (1964), 328–9
    constitutional clarification from, 38

electoral college, 177

Elliott, William Y., 259, 324

Ellsworth, Oliver, 158

Elton, G. R., xix–xx

Emancipation Proclamation (1863), 111

Emerging Constitution, The (1974), 332

England, *see* Britain; British constitution; British responses to U.S. Constitution

Equal Rights Amendment (ERA, 1972), 354

Ervin, Sam J., 321, 350–1, 383

Europe, constitutions of, 63–5, 66; *see also* British constitution; Florence, Italy; France; German constitutions; Hungary; Irish constitution

Everett, Edward, 69–70, 167, 184
    on ignorance of Constitution, 4
    on slavery and Constitution, 112–13
    on state sovereignty, 113–14

executive branch, *see* balance of powers; President(s) (U.S.)

Ex parte Milligan case (1866), 28

Ex parte Yerger case (1869–70), 118–19

Fair Employment Practices Act, 348

Fair Labor Standards Act (1938), 317, 319

Fairman, Charles, 345

Farley, James, 272

Farrand, Max, xiii, 22, 177, 178, 248, 307
    Framing of the Constitution . . . , The, 180–1

Farrar, Timothy, 109, 117
Faulkner, Barry: murals, 302–3, 304
federalism:
  antecedents of, 179, 444 n. 90
  in Britain (eighteenth century), 179
  twentieth century, 317–20
  v. nationalism: conflated, 55, 311–12;
    Madison on, 58
  v. states' rights, *see* state sovereignty;
    states' rights
Federalist, The:
  as amplification of Constitution, 74
  prosperity and Constitution in, 15
  (Number 14), 158
  (Number 39), 45
Federalists:
  accommodation of, with Anti-Federal-
    ists, 29
  on Constitution, 47, 48
  and Jefferson's bills on judiciary, 47
  as nationalists, 319
  on state sovereignty, 52
Federal Theatre Project, 253, 298
fetish, Constitution as, 36–7, 206,
  225–6, 248, 251
Field, David Dudley, 251
Fifteenth Amendment, 117, 188, 227
Fillmore, Millard, 15–16
films of and about Constitution, 15, 223,
  224, 290–1, 374
First Amendment:
  free press in, 346
  religion in, 188, 326, 351
  and suspected Communists, 328, 336
  World War I and, 256
Fish, Stuyvesant, 146–7, 151
Fisher, Dorothy Canfield: *Our Indepen-
  dence and the Constitution,* 374
Fisher, Sydney George, 159, 178
Fiske, Amos Kidder:
  "Constitution, The: An Organism
    ...," 20
  on U.S. *v.* British constitutions,
    163–4
Fiske, John, 178
  *Critical Period of American History,
    1783–1789, The,* 25, 128
Fitzhugh, George, 123
Fitzpatrick, John C., 284, 286, 287,
  288–90, 294, 298, 305, 309
Fletcher v. *Peck* case (1810), 52

flexibility of Constitution, 34–5,
  121–2, 175, 188, 205
  v. British constitution, 14, 67, 160,
    162, 163–4, 397–8
  conservatives on (1920s), 227–8, 230
  Jefferson on, 15
  and world affairs, 257
  see also amendment of Constitution:
    difficulty or ease of; Constitution
    (U.S., 1787): continuity and discon-
    tinuity of; modern society, Constitu-
    tion and
Florence, Italy, constitution of, 37, 64
Ford, Henry, 208
foreign relations (twentieth century),
  Constitution and, 257–8
  Bricker Amendment, 320–1
  see also World War I; World War II
Forrest, Marie Moore, 298
founding fathers, *see* framers of the Constitution
Fourteenth Amendment, 121
  criticism of, 227
  "due process" clause, 7, 193, 345
  equal protection clause, 354, 355
  interpretation of, 266
  and nationalization of Bill of Rights,
    353
  negative format of, 117
Fourth of July orations:
  Constitution in, 21, 227
  prosperity in, 15
  state sovereignty in, 55
framers of Constitution, intentions of,
  398
  on Bill of Rights, 345
  on comprehensibility of Constitution, 3
  on distribution of power (state-
    national), 317, 319
  on federal control of territories, 63
  on judicial review, 32, 392
  on personal liberty, 207, 388
  relayed to Congress (after 1789), 84
  on slavery, 5, 89, 96–7, 100
  see also Constitutional Convention
    (Philadelphia, 1787)
France, constitutional instability of, 37,
  64, 65, 425 n. 107
franchise, *see* voting rights
Frank, Jerome N., 200, 255
Frankfort constitution (1848), 123

Frankfurter, Felix:
  and Black, 323
  and Brandeis, 362-3
  on Constitution: and Civil War, 116;
    as organism, 19
  and New Deal, 272-3
  on publicity, 360, 371
  on Supreme Court and Constitution, 8
Franklin, Benjamin, 17
Freedman, Max, 358
Freedom Train, 344
Freehling, William W., 429 n. 32
Freeman, Edward A.: *History of Federal
  Government . . .* , 444 n. 90
Freund, Paul, 347
Friedman, Lawrence M., 28
Fuegel, E. L., 287
Fugitive Slave Act (1850), 99, 100
Fugitive Slave Law (1793), 96, 97, 98,
  99, 100, 102, 103
Fuller, Melville W., 153, 195, 210
Fund for the Defense of the Constitu-
  tion, 270

Gannett, Frank, xii-xiii
Garcia v. *San Antonio Metropolitan Tran-
  sit Authority* case (1985), 319
Garfield, James A., 120
Garrison, William Lloyd, 47, 97, 98, 99
Genêt, Citizen, 87
German constitutions, 64, 123, 280-1
Gianni, Francesco, 64
Gibbons v. *Ogden* case (1824), 15
Gibson, John B., 80
Gilbert, Cass, 267-8
Giles, William Branch, 56
Gitlow, Benjamin, 256
Gladstone, William E., 162-3, 164
Godkin, E. L., 112, 140-1
Gold Clause cases (1935), 273, 274
Golden Jubilee of Constitution
  (1837-39), 18
  ignorance of Constitution and, 89
  public interest in, 89-90, 128, 289
Goldwater, Barry, 328-9, 392
Gompers, Samuel, 198
Goodrich, Charles A.: *History of the
  United States . . .* , *A*, 81-2
Great Britain, *see* Britain; British consti-
  tution; British responses to U.S.
  Constitution

Green, Frank, 196
Greene, Evarts B., 23, 181
Greenhouse, Linda, 365
Griffin, Cyrus, 44
Grote, George, 23, 204

Hailsham, Lord, *see* Hogg, Quentin
Hallam, Henry: *Constitutional History of
  England,* 160
Hamilton, Alexander, 45, 48
Hamilton, Walton H., xvii-xviii, 463 n.
  26
Hammer v. *Dagenhart et al.* case (1918),
  194
Hand, Learned, 31, 326, 347
happiness, Constitution and, 14
Harding, Warren G., 221, 223, 258
Harlan, John Marshall:
  Centennial address (1889), 151
  on interpretation of Constitution,
    215-16
  and Lurton, 198
  on states' rights (1907), 187
Harrison, Benjamin, 145, 148-9, 150,
  153
Harrison, William Henry, 71
Hart, Albert Bushnell, 177, 183-4
Hartford Convention (1814), 15
Hayes, Rutherford B., 16
Hayne, Robert Y., 53, 55-6
Hays, Arthur Garfield, 339
Hazlitt, Henry, 332
Healy, George P. A.: *Webster Replying
  to Hayne,* 92
Hickey, William, 89
  Constitution of the United States . . .,
    The, 80-1
Hildreth, Richard, 180
Hill, David Jayne, 20, 174, 206-7, 208,
  257-8, 261
  "Crisis in Constitutionalism, The,"
    206
  "Defense of the Constitution, A," 207
  on democracy, 229
Hillhouse, James, 158
history, constitutional, *see* constitutional
  history
Hitler, Adolf, 280
Hoar, George F., 130
Hoffman, Clare E., 328
Hofstadter, Richard, 378

Hogg, Quentin, Lord Hailsham, 176

Holmes, Oliver Wendell, Jr., 13, 90, 194
  appointment of, to Court, 199
  on Constitution, 172–3; Bill of Rights,
    337; Fourteenth Amendment,
    193–4; as living organism, 19, 168;
    as machine, 125
  on Marshall, 210; Beveridge's biogra-
    phy of, 211

Hoover, Herbert, 6, 321

Houghteling, James L., 247

Howe, Mark, 10

Hughes, Charles Evans:
  as Chief Justice, 266
  on Constitution: altering of, 226;
    Court's interpretation of, 194
  ideology of, 7, 266
  "Our Constitutional Heritage," 226
  on Supreme Court: as impartial, 394;
    and public opinion, 359

Hull, Charles H., 177

Hull, Cordell, 272

Hume, David, 17

Hungary, constitutional crisis of
  (1905–06), 213

Hutchins, Robert M., 332, 342

Hyman, Harold M., 83

iconography, constitutional, 91–2, 108,
    422 n. 70
  Sesquicentennial and, 300–4

ignorance of Constitution, xvii, 3, 4,
    83–4, 217, 222, 230, 309, 383–4,
    473 n. 51
  of Bill of Rights, 340–1, 343, 350
  and confusion about, reasons for,
    5–13; Supreme Court and, 7–11
  as danger, 220, 230–1
  and Golden Jubilee, 89
  Hill (D. J.) on, 207
  by lawyers, 230
  see also education, constitutional; indif-
    ference toward Constitution; under-
    standing of Constitution

imagery (graphic) for Constitution, see
  iconography of Constitution

imagery (verbal) for Constitution, xx,
    16–19

immigrants:
  constitutional catechisms for, 240–5;
    Bill of Rights in, 337

  hostility toward, 137, 235
  knowledge of Constitution by, 232; for
    naturalization, 120, 235–48

Immigration and Naturalization Service,
    236–40 *passim*, 245–7 *passim*

impeachment:
  of President, 5, 118
  of Supreme Court justices, 203, 328

inaccuracies about Constitution:
  by Fiske, 25
  by Hickey, 80–1
  and Sesquicentennial, 287–9, 290
  in textbooks, 4, 24

income tax, constitutionality of, 190,
    191, 202–3

Indians, *see* native Americans

indifference toward Constitution, xx, 3,
    4, 189, 380, 383–4
  Beck on, 229, 230–1
  Butler on, 230
  and Centennial celebrations, 134, 143;
    see also Centennial of Constitution
    (1887–89): public interest in
  and Constitution Day, 222–3
  by educators, 232–3
  see also ignorance of Constitution; in-
    terest in Constitution

instrument, Constitution as, 17

integration, racial:
  Ervin opposes, 350
  public opinion on, 318–19, 354
  state legislatures and school boards
    and, 327–8
  Supreme Court and, 324–5

interest in Constitution:
  (1920–40), 219, 253
  anniversaries and celebrations and,
    385–6; at Centennial, 127, 143; at
    Sesquicentennial, 289
  civil-rights Court decisions and, 325
  conflict (constitutional) and, 386–90;
    "Court-packing" plan and, 256,
    283, 291
  lack of, *see* indifference toward Consti-
    tution
  see also public opinion and Constitution

international relations (twentieth cen-
    tury), Constitution and, 257–8
  Bricker Amendment, 320–1
  see also World War I; World War II

Interposition, doctrine of, 324

interpretation of Constitution:
accumulation of, as extension of Constitution, 12
v. altering Constitution, 226–7
Court's authority in (Hughes), 194
Harlan on (1907), 215–16
McMaster on (1889), 152
political/apolitical nature of, 199–201
subtle shifts in, 10
see also conservatives, constitutional: strict constructionists; liberals, constitutional: broad constructionists; Supreme Court
Irish constitution (1937), 254
Italy, constitutions in, 64–5

Jackson, Andrew, 9, 50, 61
accused of despotism, 50, 67
Jackson, Robert H.:
and Black, 360–1
on Communists, 359, 501 n. 8
on Constitution: civil rights in, 336; interpretation of, 10, 316–17
ideology of, 7, 347
Jaffe, Louis L., 357
Jameson, J. Franklin, 127, 177, 178, 459 n. 73
Jefferson, Thomas:
cited during New Deal, 279
on Constitution, 43–4; as "anchor," 17; flexibility of, 15; as "machine," 17; reverence for, 47; strict construction of, 59–60; as "text of civil instruction," 3
on Constitutional Convention, secrecy of, 86
on constitutional education, 25–6
and democracy, 253–4
inaugural address of (first, 1801), 17
and Louisiana Territory, 37, 59–60
on state sovereignty, 58–9
on Supreme Court, 27, 49–50
Johnson, Allen, 177
Johnson, Andrew, 17, 105, 118, 122
Johnson, Eldridge R., 252
Johnson, Gerald W., 389
Johnson, Lyndon B., 321, 324
Johnson, William, 91, 162
Johnston, Alexander, 163

Encyclopaedia Britannica article (1888), 181–2
Jones, Isaac, 75
journalists, covering Supreme Court, 367–70, 372, 502 n. 32; *see also* press; Supreme Court: press coverage of
judicial review, 31–3
late nineteenth century, 190
twentieth century, 201, 260–3, 265, 275, 324
Birkenhead on, 174
Borah on, 31, 277–8
v. constitutional crises, 215
efforts to reduce Supreme Court's power in, 392–3
v. judicial supremacy, 31–2
by Marshall Court, 48, 49
Presidents and, 31, 49–50
public opinion on, 325–6
Sesquicentennial Commission and, 292
and social control, 168
Thayer (J. B.) on, 179
see also constitutionality of legislation
judiciary, Confederate, 115–16
judiciary, federal:
Congress further empowers (1875), 95–6
dissatisfaction with (twentieth century), 259
early development of, 76–7
v. power of state courts, 95
see also Supreme Court
justices of Supreme Court, *see* Supreme Court justices

Kane, Owen, Jr., 287, 297
Kasson, John A., 128, 131, 137, 143
Kaufman, Irving R., 201, 359
Kelly, Alfred H., 121
Kendall, Messmore, 283
Kennedy, John F., 8
Kentucky Resolutions (1798–99), 51–2, 58
knowledge of Constitution, *see* education, constitutional; ignorance of Constitution; understanding of Constitution
Knox, Katherine M'Cook, 300
Kraditor, Aileen, 101
Kurland, Philip B., 327

labor, *see* workers

labor unions, and Lurton, 198–9

LaFollette, Robert M.:
 and judicial review, 31
 on Supreme Court: and Constitution, 9; reform of, 260–1

Lamar, Lucius Quintus Cincinnatus, 197

Lamont, Corliss, 348

Landon, Judson S., 178

Lansing, John, 87

Laski, Harold, 171, 172–3

Latin American constitutions, 93–4, 394; *see also* Mexico, constitutions of

Lawrence, David, 9–10, 328, 355, 358–9, 375

League of Nations Covenant, U.S. ratification of, 257–8

Lee, Richard Bland, 15, 41

legislation, constitutionality of, *see* constitutionality of legislation; judicial review

Leigh, Randolph, 234

Leighton, Etta V., 231

Lenin, V. I., 473 n. 47

Lerner, Max, 200

Lewis, Anthony, 28, 369, 372
 Gideon's Trumpet, 374

liberals, constitutional:
 and alteration of Constitution, 331
 broad constructionists, 30; Brown (H. B.) on, 34; and New Deal, 272; and world affairs, 257
 and judicial review, 33
 on politicization of Court, 391
 see also Progressives and Progressive era

Liberty Bell, 294, 295

Liberty League, 68, 101, 270

Liberty Party, 99, 101

Lieber, Francis, 31, 111–12

Lincoln, Abraham:
 on Constitution, 102; and prosperity, 16; and Union, 105–8, 122–3
 Emancipation Proclamation (1863), 111
 idealized in twentieth century, 279
 inaugural address (1861) and responses to, 106–8

 on race and slavery, 101–4, 111; Democratic criticism of, 113
 on Supreme Court, 118, 439 n. 28

Lippmann, Walter: *Preface to Politics, A,* 399

Livingston, Edward, 56

Llewellyn, Karl N., 249

Lochner v. *New York* case (1905), 193, 194

Lodge, Henry Cabot, 206, 210
 on Constitution, 154–5, 264; and British constitution, 174; *v.* Bryce on, 171–2; and Civil War, 116; importance of, 21; stability of, 160
 as member of Centennial Commission, 131
 Warren (C.) and, 250

Lossing, Benson J., 129, 144

Louisiana Territory, purchase of (1803), 37, 59–60

Lovejoy, Owen, 62

Lowell, A. Lawrence:
 on Constitution, 166; apolitical interpretation of, 199; and British constitution, 167; as machine, 19; worship of, 22–3
 "Democracy and the Constitution," 186
 on French constitutionalism, 425 n. 107

Lowell, James Russell, 136
 on Constitution: as "machine that would go of itself," 18, 125, 189, 222–3, 312, 399, 420 n. 52; review of publications on, 109
 "Our Literature" (1889), 150

loyalty oaths, 38, 346

Lunn, Sir Henry, 171

Lurton, Horace H., 170–1, 198

McAllister, Ward, 146–7, 151

Macaulay, Thomas Babington, 17, 156, 159–60, 397

McBain, Howard Lee, 174, 226

McCloskey, Robert G., 7–8, 9, 185, 341, 374

McCollum v. *Board of Education* case (1948), 327

McCulloch v. *Maryland* case (1819), 49, 178

MacDonald, J. R., 201

machine, constitution as, 17–19, 62, 125, 189, 209, 278, 420 n. 50
"that would go of itself" (Lowell), 18, 125, 189, 222–3, 312, 399, 420 n. 52
McLaughlin, Andrew C., 177, 178, 179, 182–3, 272, 460 n. 83
McMaster, John Bach, 30
"Century of Constitutional Interpretation, A," 152
McReynolds, James Clark, 266, 273
MacVeagh, Isaac Wayne, 210
Madison, Dolley, 88
Madison, James:
"Advice to My Country" (1834), 57
annual message (eighth, 1816), 71
cited in New Deal era, 279
on Constitution: its adaptability to changing society, 58, 175; consensus on, 46; division of attitudes toward, 30; and internal improvements, 60–1; interpretation of, 74; and judicial review, 50; as national symbol, 71; as novelty, 158; and prosperity, 15; ratification of, 45; its role, xx; on slavery, 97; and state sovereignty, 46, 55–6, 57, 58
on Constitutional Convention, his notes, 26; his feelings about, 87–8; publication of, 26, 86–9, 97, 100
and constitutional education, 26, 57
eulogies for, 77
as "father of Constitution," 58, 429 n. 35
Federalist, The, 45, 158
ideology of: changes in, 6, 56, 57–8; contradictions and ambivalence of, 55–8
inaugural address of (first, 1809), 61
letters, 58
reputation of (in twentieth century), 345–6
Virginia Report (1800), 56
will of (1835), 15, 70, 88
Magna Carta, 35–6, 80, 170, 455 n. 46
Mallory v. *United States* case (1957), 352
Manning, William, xxiii
Marbury v. *Madison* case (1803), 212
Marshall, John, 13, 209–13
attacks on, 49

Beveridge biography of, 209, 210–13
on Constitution: as "instrument," 17; his pessimism about future of, 50–1, 273; ratification of, 45; and state sovereignty, 52
Corwin biography of, 212
on Court opinions and public, 27
eulogies for, 77
influence of, on constitutional conflicts, 30
v. Jefferson, 49
on judicial power, 199, 463–4 n. 26
misrepresented, 12
statue of, 209, 467 n. 73
Marshall, Thurgood, 350, 369
Martin v. *Hunter's Lessee* case (1816), 49, 52
Mason, Alpheus T.: *Brandeis: A Free Man's Life,* 374
Mason, George, 44
Matteson, David L., 287–90, 291–2, 302, 304
Maverick, Maury, 217, 309, 381–2, 397
Mayfield, Earle, 239
media, *see* press; radio addresses; television
Mellon, Andrew W., 252
Mencken, H. L., 337
Merriam, Charles E., 175, 226, 227
Written Constitution, The, 228
metaphors for Constitution, xx, 16–19
Methvin, Eugene H., 352
Mexico, constitutions of:
(1824), 64
(1857), 93–4
(1917), 215, 394–5
Miller, Arthur Selwyn, 388
Miller, Samuel F., 27
Centennial oration (1887), 135, 136, 138, 140, 157
minority rights, 114; *see also* civil rights
Minton, Sherman, 322
Miranda v. *Arizona* case (1966), 355, 356
modern society, Constitution and:
1940s to present, 315, 338, 495 n. 51
Madison on, 58, 175
in New Deal era, 20, 256, 259, 271, 278, 471 n. 24
during Sesquicentennial, 33–4

modern society, Constitution and
(*Continued*)
  Socialists on, 206, 259
  Supreme Court and, 190–1
Monroe, James, 60
Moody, William H., 34–5
Moore, R. Walton, 272
morality, constitutional, 23, 204, 229–30,
    253
Morris, Gouverneur, 74
Morrow, William W., 473 n. 51
Morse, Jedidiah, 158
Morse, Samuel F. B.: *Old House of Rep-
    resentatives, The,* 92
Morton, Oliver P., 121–2
motion pictures of and about Constitu-
    tion, 15, 223, 224, 290–1, 374
Mulhern, Francis, 36–7
Munroe, William Bennett, 175, 251–2
Murrow, Edward R., 345
Mussolini, Benito: Gilbert (C.) and,
    267–8
Myers, Gustavus, 23, 201, 387

Naples, Italy, constitution of, 64
National Association for Constitutional
    Government, 208, 220, 225
  Pocket Edition of the Constitution, 231
National Constitutional Celebration Or-
    ganizing Committee, 221
National Emergency Civil Liberties
    Committee, 353
National Labor Relations Act (1935),
    constitutionality of, 270
National League for the Protection of
    American Institutions, 188
National Oratorical Contest on the Con-
    stitution, 224, 233–5
National Popular Government League,
    276
National Recovery Act (NRA, 1933),
    constitutionality of, 269, 274, 366
National Security League, 29, 220, 221,
    223, 225, 231, 252
native Americans, 121, 137
Naturalization Act (1906), 237, 248
naturalization of citizens, knowledge of
    Constitution for, 120, 235–48, 337
New Deal programs:
  and adaptation of Constitution, 20,
    258, 271, 278, 471, n. 24

  constitutionality of, 15, 269, 270–3,
    275, 317
  opposition to, 223, 265, 269–73
  and public interest in Constitution, 253
New York City:
  Centennial celebrations in, 129–30,
    143–4, 145–51, 153
  125th anniversary celebrations in
    (1912), 205
  Sesquicentennial celebrations in, 283,
    297, 306–7
New York Times, editorial positions of:
  on Centennial of Constitution, 130,
    143, 144, 145, 146, 147, 148, 149,
    153
  on Constitution, 174, 188–9, 205,
    226, 228–9, 258, 288; Bill of
    Rights, 340–1; proposed amend-
    ments to, 202; Tugwell's efforts to
    revise, 334
  on Supreme Court decisions, 261, 319
Nixon, Richard M., 319, 321, 351
NRA (National Recovery Act, 1933),
    constitutionality of, 269, 274, 366
Nullification Crisis (1829–33), 50,
    52–3, 55, 64, 67, 114
  Madison and, 56, 57

O'Connor, Sandra Day, 320, 354
oratorical contests, 224, 233–5, 384
organism, Constitution as, 19–20, 164,
    168, 189
organizations:
  on Bill of Rights, 339, 348, 353
  governance of, Constitution and, 69
  partisan, for constitutional issues, 207–8,
    219, 224–5, 270; and Constitution
    Day, 220–1; on constitutional edu-
    cation, 231; on judicial review,
    325–6
overseas possessions, constitutional status
    of, 192

pageants on Constitution, 15
  for Sesquicentennial, 298–9, 305
  "We, the People" (1920), 223
Paine, Thomas, 69
Panama-Pacific Exposition (San Fran-
    cisco, 1915), 208
Parker, Alton B., 174, 235–6
Parker, Joel, 110, 122

Parrington, Vernon L., 228
Parsons, Theophilus, 108, 158–9
Pearson, Drew, 30, 366, 501 n. 12
 Nine Old Men, The, 275, 375
Pecora, Ferdinand, 278
Pennoyer, Sylvester, 190
Pepper, George Wharton, 332
Perkins, Frances, 247
Philadelphia:
 and Centennial celebrations, 129–30,
 137–40, 143; monument proposed,
 131, 446 n. 14
 Convention at (1787), *see* Constitu-
 tional Convention (Philadelphia,
 1787)
 and Sesquicentennial celebrations, 282,
 294–6, 299, 305
Phillips, Wendell, 97–8
Pierce, Franklin, 61–2, 71–2, 103
Pierson, Charles W.: *Our Changing Con-
 stitution,* 226
Pierson, David L., 219, 220
place names, constitutional, 91
Plessy v. *Ferguson* case (1896), 28
Pocket Edition of the Constitution, 231
police, and civil liberties, xiv–xvii, 337–8,
 352, 355–6
Pollard, A. F., 176
Pollock, Sir Frederick, 173
Polybius: *Histories,* 65
Pomeroy, John Norton, 428 n. 26
Poore, Ben Perley: *Federal and State
 Constitutions, The,* 24
Pound, Roscoe, 272
Powell, Thomas Reed, 248–9, 263,
 272–3, 274, 315, 323, 331, 374
Presidents (U.S.):
 accused of ignoring constitutional restraints, 37, 50, 67, 320
 and Congress, 320–2
 and Constitution as national symbol,
 70–2
 disability of, 120
 impeachment of: constitutional
 grounds for, 5; of Johnson, 118
 inaugural addresses of, Constitution in,
 61–2
 on judicial review, 31, 49–50
 powers of, in Constitution, 110, 320
 on prosperity and Constitution, 15–16

 Supreme Court and, 362; *see also*
 "Court-packing" plan of FDR
 (1937)
 see also individual presidents by name
press:
 coverage of Supreme Court by, 7, 10,
 28, 76, 84, 194–7, 250–1, 253,
 357–80; Court's view of, 366–7,
 372; misrepresentations in media,
 250–1, 358–9, 566–7, 369
 freedom of, 346, 349, 350, 354
Prigg v. *Pennsylvania* case (1842), 96
Progressives and Progressive era:
 and Committee on the Federal Constitution, 207–8
 on Constitution, 20, 188, 228; amending of, 258; democracy of, 387
 and Supreme Court, 260–3
 as threat to conservatives, 207
Prohibition, 258
property rights, defense of, 33, 190, 205,
 229, 336, 347
prosperity and Constitution, 14–16, 41,
 70, 82, 120
 English antecedents of, 418 n. 40
public opinion and Constitution:
 on amending Constitution, 152, 331
 role of, 13–14, 357
 Wilson (W.) on, xxiii
 see also Bill of Rights: public interest in
 and support for; ignorance of Constitution; interest in Constitution
public opinion and Supreme Court, 316,
 325, 329 and *table,* 330, 351–3,
 364, 391; *see also* Supreme Court:
 lack of explanation about its procedures and decisions; Supreme Court:
 press coverage of

racial issues, 347, 349, 350; *see also* civil
 rights; integration, racial
radio addresses, on constitutional issues,
 222, 252, 254, 374
Randall, Samuel J., 134
Randolph, Edmund, 52
ratification of Constitution:
 anniversary commemorations of, 304–6
 debates on (1787–88), 18, 44–5
 Federalist arguments for, 15
 Webster on, 21
Rawle, William, 77–8

Reader's Digest, 253, 277, 339, 363, 375

Reagan, Ronald, 319, 330, 351, 354, 393

Reconstruction:
and Constitution, 95, 123
Republicans and, 117–18
Supreme Court and, 121

Reed v. *Reed* case (1972), 355

Rehnquist, William H., 201, 362, 393

religion in/and Constitution, 120, 254
in cult of Constitution, 225
in First Amendment, 188, 326, 351
and schools, 327, 328

Republicans:
and civil rights, 119
and Reconstruction, 117–18
reverence of, for Constitution (Civil War era), 29–30
on slavery, 100–1, 103, 124; and Dred Scott decision, 104; in 1860 platform, 104–5
and states' rights, 119–20
and Supreme Court, 118–19, 275

reverence for Constitution, *see* worship of Constitution

Revolutionary War (American) and Constitution, 21–2

Rhodes, James Ford, 34, 206

roads and canals, constitutionality of appropriations for, 60–1

Robbins, Asher, 50

Roberts, Owen J., 3, 266

Roche, Austin J., 337–8

Rodell, Fred, 249

Rogers, Henry Wade, 187

Rogers, W. A., 191

Roosevelt, Franklin D.:
on Bill of Rights, 306; "second," 342
on Constitution: durability of, 292–3; flexibility and altering of, 259, 271; as layman's document, 278
"Court-packing" plan of (1937), 9, 198, 273, 276–7, 278–9, 382; and interest in Constitution, 256, 283, 291; opposition to, xiii, 8–9, 15
defends New Deal programs, 269–74 *passim*
executive authority expanded by, 37, 320
inaugural address of (first, 1933), 18, 259

on National Recovery Act, 274
and Sesquicentennial, 292–3, 306, 308
and Supreme Court, 274

Roosevelt, Theodore:
on Constitution, 203–4; its accessibility to layman's judgment, xx
its formation and survival, 469 n. 93
liberal and conservative views of, 30
on Macaulay's "sail" and "anchor" critique, 156
in election of 1912, 202, 203–4
on Supreme Court: his criticism of, 202; political aspects of, 199–200

Root, Elihu, 221

Rosenbach, A. S. W., 294, 297

Rossiter, Thomas P., 91

Rush, Benjamin, 45, 73–4, 77, 398

Russia:
constitutions of, 93, 213
see also Soviet Union [after 1917]

Sandburg, Carl, 113

Sayre, Jessie Wilson, 259

Schenk v. *United States* case (1919), 256, 341

Schlesinger, Arthur M., Jr., 374–5

Schneiderman v. *United States* case (1943), 341

scholars:
conflicts among, 386–9
as constitutional educators, 248–50, 374–5
in constitutional history, 176–81
and New Deal, 272–3

schools:
constitutional education in, *see* education, constitutional
racial integration in, 318–19
religion in, 327, 328

Schouler, James, 176–7

Schuyler, Robert Livingston, 181

secession:
constitutionality of, 107, 108, 183
Johnson (A.) on, 105
nationalist opposition to, 20
as treason, 109–10, 124

Seeley, J. R., 162

Semonche, John E., 190

Sentinels of the Republic, 29, 225, 262

separation of powers:
and appointment of justices, 200

and judicial review, 50
and legislative veto, 322
Wilson (W.) on, 169, 186
see also balance of powers
Sergeant, John, 46-7
Sergeant, Thomas, 77
Sesquicentennial of Constitution
(1937–39), 282–312
celebrations, 294–307; and iconography, 300–4; by institutions, 297;
loan exhibition of portraits for,
299–300; nationwide, 296; in New
York, 283, 297, 306–7; pageants in,
298–9, 305; in Philadelphia, 294–6;
postage stamps for, 301–2, 304–6;
in Washington, D.C., 300–1,
302–5, 306
commercialized aspects of, 309–10
Commission for, 282–93 *passim;* investigation of, 309–11; partisan/non-
partisan aspect of, 291–2; scholars
decline to serve on, 307–8
educational emphasis of, 285–8 *passim,*
299–300, 308
funding of, 282, 283–4, 300, 310
pageants and films for, 15, 298–9, 305
planning for, 283–93
publications generated by, 291, 297,
298
public interest in, 289
and public interest in Constitution,
253, 256, 291, 300
Seward, William H., 63, 104–5
Shaw, George Bernard, 175–6, 189, 256
Sheridan, Gen. Philip H., 135, 139
Sherman, Gen. William Tecumseh, 124
"Shrines of the Constitution," 285 and
n., 286, 297
Sinclair, Upton, xiv–xvii, 413 n. 8
Singleton, Henry, 91–2
Slaughterhouse cases (1873), 28
slavery:
in Confederate Constitution, 115
Constitution and, 47, 49, 96–105;
amendments (proposed) on, 11;
Democrats on, 113; Lincoln on,
101–4, 111; Steffens and, 184
extension of, to new territories, 62–3,
101, 103–4, 192–3
founders' intentions on, 5, 89, 96–7,
100

Smith, Frederick Edwin, Lord Birken-
head, 171, 174
Smith, Goldwin, 162
Smith, J. Allen, 21, 23, 228, 387
Spirit of American Government, The,
228
Smith, William French, 330, 393
Smith Act (1940), 344, 345
Snowden, Col. A. Loudon, 129, 138, 139
Socialists and Socialism:
on Constitution, 206, 207; amend-
ments to, 259
organizations united against, 225
as threat to Constitution, 221, 231–2
Social Security Act (1935), constitution-
ality of, 273
Society for Constitutional Information
(Britain), 65
Sons of the American Revolution, 225,
286
South Africa, constitution of, 395–6
South Carolina:
in antebellum era, 395
"Exposition" (1828), 55
and Nullification Crisis, 50, 52–3
Soviet Union:
constitution of (1936), 280
see also Russia [before 1917]
Sparks, Jared, 87
Spencer, Herbert: *Social Statics,* 193, 194
Spooner, Lysander, 101
stability of Constitution, *see* Constitution
(U.S., 1787): continuity and discontinuity of
Stalin, Joseph, 280
Stanton, Frank, 370, 376
"Star Trek" television series, "Omega
Glory" episode (1966), 334–5
state constitutions:
as "charters," 69
Constitution (U.S.) and, 11–12, 52,
163
defense of (1930s), 270
included in definition of constitutionalism (Cooley), 159
and judicial review, 32
need for, 181
uniqueness of, 157
writing and revising of (nineteenth
century), 120
see also constitutions, colonial

states:
  applicability of Bill of Rights to, 7,
    322, 345, 388
  authority of, 186
  charters of, 69
  laws of, and judicial review, *see* consti-
    tutionality of legislation; judicial re-
    view
  rights of, *see* states' rights
  secession of, *see* secession
  sovereignty of, *see* state sovereignty
  v. "whole body of the people," and
    ratification of Constitution, 45–6,
    123, 182–3
state sovereignty, 51–7, 62, 72, 77, 90,
    182–3, 265, 312, 317
  Civil War and, 182
  Confederates on, 113
  and Constitution, 45–6, 123
  Everett on, 114
  Jefferson on, 58–9
  Madison on, 46, 55–6, 57, 58
  nationalist opposition to, 20
  v. states' rights, 34, 428 n. 26
  surrender of, to central government, 5,
    54, 182, 265, 317
  see also states' rights
states' rights:
  1880s to 1920s, 186–8, 211
  1920s and 1930s, 265
  1950s to present, 317–18
  and Constitution, 124
  Madison and Jefferson misrepresented
    on, 12
  Republicans on, 119-20
  v. state sovereignty, 34, 428 n. 26
  support of, after Civil War, 95, 121
  v. Supreme Court, 49; *see also* judicial
    review
  see also state sovereignty
Stearns, Junius Brutus, 91
  Adoption of the Constitution, 301–2
Steffens, Lincoln, 184
Stephen, Leslie, 162
Stephens, Alexander H., 114–15
  Constitutional View of the Late War,
    123, 444 n. 90
Stevens, John Paul, 362, 370–1
Stevens, Thaddeus, 122
Stewart, Potter, 35, 379

Stone, Harlan Fiske, 249, 323
  on Bill of Rights, 338
  and dissemination of information from
    Supreme Court, 360, 363, 366
  on interpretation of Constitution, 12,
    326–7
  on judicial review, 32–3
"Storm Over the Supreme Court" televi-
  sion program (1963), 377–8
Story, Joseph, 78–9, 180
  Commentaries (1833), 13, 79
  on Constitution: criticism of, 50, 51;
    popular perception of, xxiii; his pes-
    simism about, 274
  Constitutional Class Book, The, 79
  *Familiar Exposition of the Constitution
    ..., The,* 79
Story, William Wetmore, 209, 467 n.
  73
Story of the Constitution, The (1937),
    291, 297, 299, 309
Stubbs, William, bishop: *Constitutional
  History of England,* 176
Supreme Court, 189–202, 255–6,
    322–31, 357–80
  activist phases of, 7, 10, 190, 201,
    265–6, 323–4, 391–2
  ambivalence and changeableness of,
    7–11, 194, 266, 322–3, 363
  appointments to, *see* Supreme Court
    justices: appointments of, and con-
    troversy over
  attacks on and criticism of: (1890),
    153; (1895), 153–4; (1896), 191;
    twentieth century, 192, 201–2,
    259–66, 274–5, 316, 324, 327,
    328–9, 331, 392–3, 479 n. 22;
    Brewer on, 196; Ervin's, 350; Gold-
    water's, 328–9; over judicial review,
    31, 33, 49, 51, 174, 190, 201, 265,
    275; "usurpation of power"
    charged, 31, 49, 53, 190, 201, 262,
    263, 316, 325, 329, 350
  and civil rights, 28, 33, 119, 121, 266,
    324–5, 341, 345, 352–6
  and constitutional education, 7, 26–8,
    76–7, 250–1; *see also* Supreme
    Court: press coverage of
  and constitutionality of legislation,
    jurisdiction of, 29, 48–50, 53, 250;
    see also judicial review

decisions by, *see* Supreme Court decisions

and economic growth of U.S., 15

efforts to curb and regulate, 76 and *table*, 118–19, 260–3, 274, 325, 328–9, 330, 392–3, 479 n. 22

justices of, *see* Supreme Court justices

lack of explanation about its procedures and decisions, 7, 26–8, 84–5, 96–7, 251, 326–7, 358–60, 361, 365, 369

mail received by, 364–5, 502 n. 23

openness of (E. Warren on), 28, 358, 365

physical location of, 85, 196, 219, 266–9, 436 n. 61, 481 n. 41

politicization of, 118–19, 192, 198–201, 255, 256, 269, 386, 391–4

and President, 362; *see also* "Court-packing" plan of FDR (1937)

press coverage of, 7, 10, 28, 76, 84, 194–7, 250–1, 253, 357–80; Court's view of, 366–7, 372; misrepresentations in media, 250–1, 358–9, 366–7, 369

public interest in and reputation of, 194, 198, 253–4, 273, 316, 325, 329 and *table*, 330, 351-3, 364, 391

sessions of: televising of, 370–2; transcripts of, 366, 369

social control by, 168, 463 n. 26

southerners and, 115

usurpation of power by, *see* Supreme Court: attacks on, "usurpation of power" charged

workload of, 198, 382, 464 n. 38

Supreme Court and Congress:

legislative efforts to curb court, 76 and *table*, 118–19, 260–3, 274, 325, 328–9, 330, 392–3, 479 n. 22

preliminary opinions by Court on legislation, proposed, 263–4 and n.

see also checks and balances; constitutionality of legislation; judicial review

Supreme Court and Constitution:

conflation of, 8–9, 10, 277, 278, 281, 316

Court defines Constitution, 391

Court "violates" Constitution, 9–10

differentiation between, 9, 10, 316, 324, 464 n. 27; after Dred Scott decision, 104; in New Deal era, 273, 281

Fiske on, 164

Goldwater on, 329

Lincoln on, 439 n. 28

press and, 197

see also interpretation of Constitution

Supreme Court decisions:

early nineteenth century, 49

late nineteenth century, 190–1

post–World War I, 256

1960s, 326, 366, 372–3

1970s and 1980s, 319

accumulation of, as extension of Constitution, 12

on civil rights, *see* civil rights

and constitutional education, 76, 77

on federal over state law, 96

flouting of, 327–8

on New Deal legislation, 15, 269, 270–3, 275, 317

political overtones of, *see* Supreme Court: politicization of

publicity on and public awareness of, 7, 28–9, 76, 84–5, 250–1, 357, 358–9, 366, 371–3

records of, 178

size of majority in, attempts to regulate, 49, 118, 260, 261–2, 277, 363

Supreme court justices:

appointments of, and controversy over, 198, 199, 200, 264, 322, 338, 350, 357–8, 362

and constitutional education of public, 7, 26–8, 76–7, 250–1

and flexibility of Constitution, 34–5

impeachment of, 203, 328

mixed ideology of, 7

number of, 118, 198, 443 n. 73; *see also* "Court-packing" plan of FDR (1937)

public interest in, 194–6, 253, 266

and publicity (individual), 360–4

on public opinion, 14, 27, 364, 365–6

visits to circuit courts, educational aspects of, 76–7

see also individual justices by name

Sutherland, George:
  "Constitutional Power and World Affairs" (1918), 257
  on Supreme Court, 264, 266
Swift v. *Tyson* case (1842), 96, 250
symbolic function of Constitution, 22–3, 67, 68, 75, 90–1, 94
  iconography of, 91–2
  physical location of document and, 72–3
  Presidents and, 70–2
  representing political maturity, 69–70
  slowed by criticism, 73–4

Taft, Henry W., 268–9
Taft, William Howard, 204
  as Chief Justice, 250, 255, 264
  as President, 198, 203
Taney, Roger Brooke, 15, 158, 273
  Lincoln and, 102
tariff laws, 56
taxes and taxation:
  direct *v.* indirect, 5
  income, constitutionality of, 190, 191, 202–3
Taylor, Hannis, 169, 455 n. 42
Taylor, John, 52, 53
  New Views of the Constitution, 77
Taylor, Zachary, 71, 84
television:
  and constitutional education, 374, 375–80
  and Supreme Court, 370–2
Tenney, Samuel, 44–5
Tennyson, Alfred, Lord, 162
territories:
  Bill of Rights and, 192
  constitutional status of, 192–3
  federal control of, 63
  slavery and, 62–3, 101, 103–4, 192–3
  see also overseas possessions
textbooks and constitutionalism:
  1796, first, 14
  nineteenth century, 3–4, 24, 79, 81–2, 108–9, 181–2
  (1900), 24
  twentieth century, 233, 281, 288, 318
  for college and law students, 77–8, 79
  inaccuracies in, 4, 24
  for secondary schools, 79, 108–9, 181–3

Thayer, James B., 178–9, 210
Thomas, Norman, 276
Thorpe, Francis N., 177–8
Tiedeman, Christopher G., 14
  Unwritten Constitution of the United States, The, 168
Tilden, Samuel J., 113
Tobey, Charles, 309–10
Tocqueville, Alexis de:
  on Constitution, 20; organic nature of, 20; and state sovereignty, 55
  on "legal fictions" at base of U.S. government, 13
  on Supreme Court, 48
Toombs, Robert, 63
To Secure These Rights (1947), 347–8
Towle, Nathaniel C.: *History and Analysis of the Constitution . . . , A,* 105
Trumbull, Lyman, 117
Tucker, St. George, 52
Tugwell, Rexford G., 316, 332–4, 335
Turkey, constitution of, xiii–xiv
TV Guide, 375–6
Tyler, John, 71
Tzu-hsi, empress, 213, 214

understanding of Constitution, 23, 225
  American Bar Association and, 120–1
  Anti-Federalists on, 75
  by candidates for naturalization, 120, 232, 235–48
  by ordinary citizens, 3, 75
  difficulty of assessing, 85–6
  intended by framers, 3
  lack of, *see* ignorance of Constitution
  media and, *see* press; radio; television
  see also education, constitutional
Union:
  and Constitution, 62–3; Johnson (A.) on, 118; Lincoln on, 105–8, 122–3
  genesis of, 5, 20, 63, 429 n. 32
unions, and Lurton's nomination, 198–9
usurpation of power:
  by President, 37, 50, 67, 320
  by Supreme Court, 31, 49, 53, 190, 201, 262, 263, 316, 325, 329, 350

Van Buren, Martin, 61
Vandenberg, Arthur H., 278
Vanderbilt, Arthur T., 306

Van Devanter, Willis, 269, 270–1
and publicity, 27–8, 360, 422 n. 78
veneration of Constitution, *see* worship of
Constitution
veto, legislative, 321–2
Virginia Resolutions (1798), 51–2, 58
Von Holst, Hermann Eduard, 180
on Constitution: rapid apotheosis of,
46; veneration of, 22
*Constitutional and Political History of
the United States, The,* 22
voting rights:
of blacks, *see* Fifteenth Amendment
of women, 120, 354

Waite, Morrison R., 17
Wallace, Henry A.: *Whose Constitution,*
275
Wallace, William Kay, 332
Warner, Joseph B., 178
Warren, Charles, 29, 174, 228, 256, 262
*Borah and LaFollette and the Supreme
Court,* 263
*Congress, the Constitution, and the Su-
preme Court,* 263
History of the American Bar, 249–50
Making of the Constitution, The, 252
*Supreme Court in United States History,
The,* 249–50, 251–2
Warren, Earl:
on Constitution: anniversary celebrations of, 89; Bill of Rights, 348;
flexibility of, 35; organic growth of,
164
as constitutional educator, 348
impeachment of, threatened, 328
Memoirs, 358, 365, 366–7
on openness of Supreme Court, 28,
358, 365
and publicity, 361, 366–7; television,
370
Washington, George:
cited in New Deal era, 279
on Constitution, 71; amendment of,
257; need for education in, 75; its
popular reception, 43
his copy of Constitution displayed
(1937), 294
Farewell Address (1796), 70–1, 257
inauguration of, anniversary celebrations of: New York City, 89–90,

129–30, 306–7; Washington, D.C.,
143, 153
Washington, D.C.:
and Centennial celebrations, 143, 145,
153
and Sesquicentennial celebrations, 306;
art and exhibitions, 300–1, 302–5
Webster, Daniel:
cites Madison, 55–6
on Constitution: as "instrument," 17;
misquotation by, 25; and national
character, 94; ratification of, 21
and constitutional education, 81
oration against Hayne (1830), 53–4,
55–6, 429 n. 32; Healy's painting
of, 92
Webster, Noah, 47
History of the United States, 82
Weicker, Lowell P., 398
Weimar constitution (1919), 123, 280
Welch, Robert, Jr., 328
Welles, Sumner, 338
Wharton, Edith, 228
White, Andrew Dickson, 191, 203
White, E. B., 346–7
White, Edward Douglass, 256, 272
White, William Allen, 306
Whitehead, Alfred North, 175
Whitman, Walt, 136
Whittier, John Greenleaf, 136
Wickersham, George W., 174, 205,
456–7 n. 55
Wickersham Commission, 337–8
Wiggins, James Russell, 349
Wilkins, Roy, 349
Wilhelm, Harry E., 287
Williams, Clarence R., 287
Wills, Garry, 46
Wilson, Henry: *History of the Rise and
Fall of the Slave Power . . . ,* 124
Wilson, James, 45
Wilson, S. Davis, 294, 295
Wilson, Woodrow:
on Constitution, 19, 169–70, 399; and
British constitution, 157, 168–9;
public opinion and, xxiii; rapid
apotheosis of Constitution, 46; sepa-
ration of powers in, 169, 186
and League of Nations, 257–8
and Mexican constitutionalism, 215

Wilson, Woodrow (*Continued*)
New Freedom, The, 19
on Supreme Court, 265
women:
civil rights of, 354-5
voting rights of, 120, 354
as workers, 194
Worcester v. *Georgia* case (1832), 50, 67
workers:
bill of rights for, 342
children as, 194
hours of, 193-4, 319
minimum wages for, 319
unemployment of, 223
women as, 194
World's Columbian Exposition (Chicago, 1893), 16, 151
World War I, constitutional consequences of, 171-2, 254, 256
World War II, and civil liberties, 340
worship of Constitution, xviii, 3, 22-3, 36-7, 112, 165, 205-6, 219, 224-6

1930s, 38, 307-9
Adams (H.) on, 117
as fetish, 36-7, 206, 225-6, 248, 251
Jefferson on, 47
and naturalization of immigrants, 236
"Star Trek" on (1966), 334-5
in textbooks, 3
Wilson (W.) on, 169
see also cult of Constitution
Wright, Frances, 66
Wright, J. Skelly, 365-6
Wright, Silas, 83
written constitutions:
v. British constitution, 167-8, 175
and judicial review, 179
and public opinion, 14
and reason, 75
security in, 59, 156
as unique to America, 20
Wyzanski, Charles E., xx

Yates, Robert, 87, 88

A Note About the Author

Michael Kammen was born in Rochester, New York, in 1936. He graduated from The George Washington University in 1958 and received his A.M. (1959) and Ph.D. (1964) from Harvard University. He has taught at Cornell University since 1965, becoming the Newton C. Farr Professor of American History and Culture in 1973. From 1977 to 1980 he was Director of Cornell's Society for the Humanities and in 1980–81 was the first holder of the chair in American History at the Ecole des Hautes Etudes en Sciences Sociales, Paris. He was a Fellow of the Humanities Center at The Johns Hopkins University, 1968–69; a Senior Fellow of the National Endowment for the Humanities, 1972–73; a Fellow at the Center for Advanced Study in the Behavioral Sciences, Stanford, 1976–77; a John Simon Guggenheim Fellow, 1980–81; and a Constitutional Fellow, National Endowment for the Humanities, 1984–85.

Professor Kammen has been elected to membership in The Society of American Historians, the American Antiquarian Society, the Society of Scholars in The Johns Hopkins University, the Massachusetts Historical Society, the Colonial Society of Massachusetts, and the American Academy of Arts and Sciences. In 1976 he was elected to the Council of the American Historical Association, in 1978 to the Council of the Institute of Early American History and Culture, and in 1981 to the Board of Trustees of the New York State Historical Association. In 1975–76 he served as host and moderator for "The States of the Union," a series of fifty one-hour programs broadcast by National Public Radio.

He is the author of *A Rope of Sand: The Colonial Agents, British Politics, and the American Revolution* (1968); *Deputyes & Libertyes: The Origins of Representative Government in Colonial America* (1969); *Empire & Interest: The American Colonies and the Politics of Mercantilism* (1970); *People of Paradox: An Inquiry Concerning the Origins of American Civilization* (1972); *Colonial New York: A History* (1975); *A Season of Youth: The American Revolution and the Historical Imagination* (1978); and *Spheres of Liberty: Changing Perceptions of Liberty in American Culture* (1986). He has edited and co-authored numerous other works and lectured throughout the world. In 1973 he was awarded the Pulitzer Prize in History for *People of Paradox*.